ANNUAL REVIEW OF ANTHROPOLOGY

BERNARD J. SIEGEL, *Editor*
Stanford University

ALAN R. BEALS, *Associate Editor*
University of California, Riverside

STEPHEN A. TYLER, *Associate Editor*
Rice University

VOLUME 6

1977

ANNUAL REVIEWS INC.   4139 EL CAMINO WAY   PALO ALTO, CALIFORNIA 94306

ANNUAL REVIEWS INC.
Palo Alto, California, USA

International Standard Book Number: 0-8243-1906-0
Library of Congress Catalog Card Number: 72-82136

Annual Reviews Inc. and the Editors of its publications assume no
responsibility for the statements expressed by the contributors to this Review.

REPRINTS

The conspicuous number aligned in the margin with the title of each article in this
volume is a key for use in ordering reprints. Available reprints are priced at the
uniform rate of $1 each postpaid. The minimum acceptable reprint order is 10
reprints and/or $10.00 prepaid. A quantity discount is available.

PRINTED AND BOUND IN THE UNITED STATES OF AMERICA

CONTENTS

ANNUAL REVIEWS INC. is a nonprofit corporation established to promote the advancement of the sciences. Beginning in 1932 with the *Annual Review of Biochemistry*, the Company has pursued as its principal function the publication of high quality, reasonably priced Annual Review volumes. The volumes are organized by Editors and Editorial Committees who invite qualified authors to contribute critical articles reviewing significant developments within each major discipline.

Annual Reviews Inc. is administered by a Board of Directors whose members serve without compensation.

Annual Reviews are published in the following sciences: Anthropology, Astronomy and Astrophysics, Biochemistry, Biophysics and Bioengineering, Earth and Planetary Sciences, Ecology and Systematics, Energy, Entomology, Fluid Mechanics, Genetics, Materials Science, Medicine, Microbiology, Nuclear Science, Pharmacology and Toxicology, Physical Chemistry, Physiology, Phytopathology, Plant Physiology, Psychology, and Sociology. The *Annual Review of Neuroscience* will begin publication in 1978. In addition, two special volumes have been published by Annual Reviews Inc.: *History of Entomology* (1973) and *The Excitement and Fascination of Science* (1965).

Ann. Rev. Anthropol. 1977. 6:1–10
Copyright © 1977 by Annual Reviews Inc. All rights reserved

OVERVIEW

❖9584

Carleton S. Coon

Bust by Walker F. Hancock

Carleton S. Coon

Ann. Rev. Anthropol. 1977. 6:1–10

OVERVIEW ❖9584

Carleton S. Coon

Professor of Anthropology (Retired), Harvard and University of Pennsylvania,
Honorary Associate in Ethnology, Peabody Museum, Harvard[1]

Following this brief essay, twenty other chapters appear in this volume. They cover
a wide range of subjects, including applied anthropology, archaeology, physical
anthropology, ethnology, linguistics, and social anthropology.

Of the total chapters, only four are devoted to specific subjects, while the others
are broad surveys and exercises in theory. This choice mirrors that of the two most
recent numbers of the *American Anthropologist,*, Volume 78, Numbers 2 and 3.
Each of them carries four main articles. Not one of those in Number 2 is of a factual
or descriptive nature. In Number 3, three articles boil down to "women's lib," and
the fourth is about "anti-languages," i.e. words which show hostility to our modern
societies: unrest comparable to the anti-male papers of Number 2.

These eight articles thus faithfully reflect two of the three major issues that beset
the American and related Western peoples at the present time: the feminist movement, which includes attacks on that illiterate misnomer, "male chauvinism," and
the general socioeconomic disturbances of the peoples concerned—presumably a
product of our own technological advances which have pierced our planet's atmospheric skin, and a haunting fear of the imminent end of the world. I trust that these
comments are not applicable to the other chapters of this volume, which I have not
seen.

For a specific comparison, let us spin time backward a half century to look at
Volume 27, Numbers 2 and 3, of the *American Anthropologist,* issued in 1925, the
first ones that I received after having joined the American Anthropological Association. Each number carries five lead articles. Seven of the ten are completely objective, factual descriptions. Two are cross-cultural surveys, also objective.

Only one is polemic. It is on the third delicate subject unmentioned in the 1976
numbers. It is "Anthropology, Race, and Culture," by J. R. Kantor. The author
denies the existence of racial differences in mental faculties on the ground that the
collective mind of a people reflects their culture. "Most carefully must we guard

[1]Mailing address: 207 Concord Street, Gloucester, Massachusetts 01930.

against the temptation to take some actual fact of a biological sort and transform it into an illegitimate process. . . . in the study of psychological phenomena the data are not involved in all the problems of nature and nurture."

"What makes a culture?" He did not say. His paper was published midway between Franz Boas's first and second editions of *The Mind of Primitive Man,* during which span the pacemaker swung from belief to disbelief.

Volume 78, Number 2 of the *American Anthropologist* contains a narrative account of Boas's early career in America, authored by Curtis M. Hinsley Jr. and Bill Holm. For those who still argue about Boas's influence on modern American anthropology, this pathetic and sympathetic article is recommended.

I have cited the *American Anthropologist* files glibly because I joined the Association in 1925. The membership then was 665. On December 6, 1976, it was ca 10,000, a growth of 150-fold in half a century. George Peter Murdock's *Ethnographic Atlas* (1975), lists 862 societies (i.e. "ethnic groups") in the world which by then had been studied to some extent. I can hardly believe that more than an equal number remain unexplored, unstudied, and unsullied by the avalanche of modern, Western civilization. In the proposed 1977 AAA meeting, only 1100 members will be allowed to read papers—one out of every nine. What can they all find to talk about?

How wonderful it was to become a fledgling professional anthropologist in 1925, at the age of 21, with the wide world to choose from, and to be able to participate in the active lives of brave and honorable people who would adopt you if you pleased them, or might kill or even eat you if you didn't please them. Beside learning the details and frameworks of their cultures, you might measure their bodies and dig up old tools and bones in their caves. Owing to the maligned institution of colonialism, travel was much safer in many countries then than it is today, when newly formed governments which crosscut tribal boundaries have tried to imitate those of their ex-masters and protectors (from other Western powers), instead of returning to their traditional forms.

The first meeting of the American Anthropological Association that I attended was held in Peabody House, Andover, Massachusetts, across the street from the dormitory I had lived in only four years previously. Aleš Hrdlička, who was no little dove, as his name implied, held the presidential chair, and the saintly Alfred V. Kidder acted as secretary. He lived in Andover; that was what brought us there.

The Harvard triumvirate of Tozzer, Dixon, and Hooton were on deck, along with Joe Spinden, probably Pliny Goddard, Robert Lowie, and Alfred Kroeber. It was all very jolly. Everyone knew everyone else. I don't think I saw Boas, but Ruth Bunzel and Hortense Powdermaker proxied for him.

Of the many heated discussions, I remember only one. Franz Weidenreich was trying to explain foetalization in man by comparing him to the King Charles Spaniel —a bulgy browed, popeyed pooch resembling a Pekinese.

Hrdlička interrupted, his eyes flashing impatiently, as he asked: "Vot haf ducks to do vit man?"

To which Weidenreich retorted with the same aplomb that had accompanied his offhand rejection, sight unseen, of Piltdown as a fake: "I vas not spiking about ducks. I vas spiking about dugs!"

Eleven years later, the crown prince of functional anthropology came to Cambridge, Massachusetts to participate in Harvard's Tercentary Ceremonies. The Yard was crawling with foreign pundits garbed in odd robes and odder hats. The latter ranged from Beefeater models to portable Leaning Towers of Pisa. It was not Malinowski's headgear that distinguished him from the rest, but his fame for his provocative book titles, *Argonauts of the Western Pacific* and *The Sexual Lives of Savages,* plus his smile, his boldness, and his wit.

As befitted the guest of honor, Malinowski was domiciled with the Honorable Leverett Saltonstall, then Speaker of the Massachusetts House of Representatives, later destined to become governor of his state and its Republican senator in Washington. Malinowski was a Polish Catholic. Harvard was surrounded by Catholic citizens, mostly Irish. Who could make a more suitable pilot orator than a distinguished foreign Catholic layman?

For some unknown reason, I was assigned to take care of Malinowski, and particularly to police his speech. In my house, he read it aloud. The words were elegant, but his strong Oxford accent a catastrophe. We had only one day. I telephoned my father, who loaned me a limousine and chauffeur. In it Malinowski and I rode about, passing by the merry-go-rounds and shoot-the-chutes at Revere Beach and the iron-fenced estates of the North Shore of Massachusetts Bay, for many hours.

First I read his speech to him, not in the phoney Harvard accent which some middlewestern-born professors learn to fake, but in my own, rustic north-of-Bostonese. Then my companion read it back to me, imitating my rendition to a T. We repeated this ploy many times, until we both had memorized his script. When he delivered it from the rostrum, silk hats were waved. The audience cheered. And Harvard, Fair Harvard, had won the game that day.

Meanwhile in Chicago Malinowski's only rival for the functional school's crown was indoctrinating his own students, including William Lloyd Warner, who soon afterward moved to Harvard, where he taught Eliot D. Chapple and Conrad M. Arensberg in offices adjacent to mine. The rival's name was variously A. R. Brown, A. R. Radcliffe-Brown, or other combinations of the same ingredients. To his friends and students, he was Rex.

Basically, the functional school was anti-historical. It ignored one leg of the cosmic tripod of space, energy, and time. It had arisen in protest against the historical school, whose adherents posed most of their weight on the supposedly immutable parameter that their new detractors had chosen to ignore.

Malinowski had succeeded in this two-dimensional framework because his lively Trobriand Islanders' culture was rolling along full blast, whereas Brown's Andaman Islanders consisted of a single relict villageful of miniature shoreline hunters and harpooners clinging to the simplified debris of their ancestors' more complicated past.

Brown did not try to study the culture of the Jarawa, the neighbors of his villagers, who bordered them to the south. They were still alive and fighting; their culture remains unknown. Had Brown tried to interview them, their arrows could have wafted him into another lens of time.

Instead he turned his attention to Arnhem Land in North Australia, and to the complexities of its Aboriginal kinship systems, which, like everyone else except the Aborigines, he had trouble unraveling. Lloyd Warner followed Rex in this mind-bending task, then came to Harvard in 1938, where and when we first met.

Harvard was then a poor place for sociology, the palliative discipline of minorities. President Lowell discouraged its pursuit, reputedly on the grounds that its name was a bastard label, half Latin and half Greek. Nothing daunted, Warner invaded that realm and applied his functional methods to a modern urban community within commuting distance—Newburyport, Massachusetts. The product was his book *Yankee City*.

Among his staff members were Eliot D. Chapple and Conrad M. Arensberg. Once the Newburyport study had been completed, they continued with a project of their own in which I joined after Arensberg had left to work elsewhere. My role was to help Chapple with ethnographic coverage derived from my teaching schedule, which had included courses on the races and cultures of the world.

Chapple's idea was that time is an intrinsic element in the structure of any culture, and so is biology. We leaped the time-lens hurdle by labeling it "the Ethnographic Present," first used in our book *The Principles of Anthropology* (1942).

The biological factor was the "interaction rate." Chapple studied it by measuring the durations of origins and responses on a moving tape. (You "originate" an event in interaction when you take the lead.) He found that these rates are constant for each person, immutable without breakdown and heritable. Regardless of the content of speech—much of which is just an excuse for interaction—each person's rate tags him almost as tightly as his fingerprints do.

People interact in pairs or *sets* (groups of three or more). Interaction of both kinds takes place in institutions: the family, political, economic, and religious institutions; and voluntary associations (sodalities, guilds, clubs). Each institution has its leaders (successful originators in set events): its formal or informal table of organization; and its own internal equilibrium which is maintained by the cosmic principle of least effort, as are those of the components of atoms, the solar system, galaxies, and the vast universe itself.

As men's (not man's) utilization of our planet's resources waxed after their discovery of fire, so did their craftsmanship, divisions of labor, and the numbers and complexities of social groups. The orderly transitions which the nineteenth century philosophers had postulated, we documented and amplified. (So did Leslie White in Ann Arbor, alone and bitter in his easily misunderstood acidulous style).

In *Principles of Anthropology* Chapple and I postulated that men convert energy into social structure. In 1948 I plotted quanta of energy against time on a double-log chart in an exhibit in the Hall of Man in the University Museum in Philadelphia, but viewers took little notice of it. It showed the line to rise at an exponentially increasing rate to a point where energy was already approaching infinity while time and space shrank close to zero. In 1954 I published this in *The Story of Man*.

After decades of neglect, proponents of space factories and the colonization of other planets have revived it, with due credit, as a working principle, leapfrogging over many of the social anthropologists who are still absorbed with the details of kinship, dual organization, and the interpretation of myths.

Equally unacclaimed by his peers had been the discoveries of Edward T. Hall of Northwestern University, whose two truly basic books, *The Silent Language* (1959) and *The Hidden Dimension* (1966) are not even mentioned in The Fifth International Directory of Anthropologists (1975), although the technical name of his subject, *Proxemics,* is.

Hall studied and analyzed cultural differences in nonverbal communication and in the social utilization of space, thus both supplementing and complementing Chapple's interaction studies which measured mostly the flow of words. City planners, appointed diplomats, global architects, and spaceship and space platform designers can use Hall's findings too.

Meanwhile social anthropology was being either fortified or diverted (reader's choice) by the ethology of Lorenz and Tinbergen and by the primate studies begun by Clarence R. Carpenter. Carpenter was followed by George Schaller and by Sherwood Washburn and his students as well as by the photogenic Jane Goodall, and Desmond Morris, the Naked Apester of the London Zoo.

A movement almost too late to conserve marginal hunting-gathering peoples from their inevitable fates led to intensive studies of the Bushmen by the Marshall family, Irven DeVore, Richard Lee, and others, and also to a most perceptive and sensitive wedding of archaeology and ethnography by Richard Gould, published in his book *Yiwara of the Australian Desert* (1969). Like several older books and films, Gould's volume contained one photograph of a human circumcision table, without the body of the boy scheduled for the operation anywhere in sight. By an unpredictable fluke of misfortune, some Aboriginal girls who were not supposed to know about the props for this rite of passage were shown this picture, and thereby were reportedly barred from matrimony. For this unpremeditated act, the wrath of the Ethics committee of the American Anthropological Association fell on the author's head.

Gould's case raises an important question. In this time of global jitters, must anthropological information be classified "top secret?" Or must we just lie down and say our prayers? Far more pertinently than to cultural anthropology does this dilemma relate to its biological counterpart, physical anthropology, including the tinderbox issue of race. For this issue we now turn back to the placid 1920s, when it was only relatively lukewarm.

Earnest Albert Hooton taught more budding physical anthropologists in his bone-filled, top-floor laboratory in Harvard's Peabody Museum than did anyone else in America at that time. His students included Harry Shapiro, Mischa Titev, Charles Snow, William W. Howells, William Laughlin, Alice Brues, H. T. L. Herzberg, Sherwood Washburn, Wesley Dupertuis, Gabriel Lasker, Carl Seltzer, Robert Ehrich, Joseph Birdsell, Stanley Garn, Loring Brace, Charles Shade, Paul Gebhard, and others whose names elude me.

William Krogman, who taught at the Universities of Chicago and then Pennsylvania, had studied in London under Sir Arthur Keith, and so had Theodore McCown of the University of California at Berkeley. T. Wingate Todd of Western Reserve taught Mildred Trotter of Washington University in St. Louis and W. Montague Cobb of Howard University. Adolf Schultz of Zurich and Johns Hopkins taught T. Dale Stewart and William L. Straus at Johns Hopkins. Most of the other physical anthropologists of America who did not slide in via the medical profession are or were the students of one or more of the men and women listed above.

Hooton taught us only osteology, but he did it very thoroughly, training us to identify small bits of whole bones by age, sex, and sometimes race. Very strict he was about our showing respect for the deceased. Once when a student had placed a cigarette between the jaws of a mounted skeleton he lectured us severely, while the miscreant quaked.

In a corner of his laboratory stood a large glass jar containing three superimposed human heads; those of an American Indian, an Indian Indian, and a Chinese. So tightly did they fit in their container that the tips of their noses were pressed against the glass, like those of children through a window near the door at Christmas time, awaiting the postman's arrival.

Once, for some unstated reason, Hooton moved the jar to the corridor outside the room, near the head of the stairs. A pregnant visitress, panting after her five-story climb, had a miscarriage, and threatened to sue Harvard. Hooton brought the jar back inside.

About that time a Polish neuroanatomist doing research at the Harvard Medical School heard of it. He was studying the effects of alcohol on the human brain. Because the heads had been in alcohol for nearly a century, he sought and obtained Hooton's permission to remove the brains and carry them to the Medical School. When the question of transportation arose, Hooton pointed to me and said: "Carl Coon has a car down at the door. He can give you and your brains a ride."

And so I did, in a topless old Cadillac, driving a little fast, while the Polish doctor held the brains uncovered in a glass tray. A siren whirred, a motorcycle officer pulled up. "Where are you going in such a hurry, young man," he asked.

"To the Harvard Medical School," I answered. "We must get these brains there on time!"

"Step on it! I'll give you an escort," he said, and did.

Hrdlička started the *American Journal of Physical Anthropology* in 1918, during wartime, with a handful of members in its eponymous association. Nineteen years later its rolls had risen to 132, most of whom were anatomists, dentists, and other specialists in disciplines peripheral to our own. In 1976 we number only 676 voting members, plus 598 student and 103 foreign members. Our increase is modest compared to that of the American Anthropological Association. We are still, more or less, a club. As club members, with a few exceptions, we are polite to one another when we disagree. Because we deal with living organisms, mostly human, and their remains, our work requires precision. Most of it can be treated mathematically. We are little swayed by women's lib, race when it does not involve intelligence, or the putatively impending Apocalypse.

At our eighth annual meeting, held at the Harvard Faculty Club in April 1937, 25 papers were read. Three were on teeth. The others covered racial analyses of both the quick and the dead, anthropometric techniques, statistical analysis, physiology, and infant mortality. Harry L. Shapiro showed slides and read a paper on his then recent study of the 202 living descendants of six mutineers of the Bounty and their 12 or 13 Tahitian female consorts, who had borne an average of 11.2 children, ". . . despite their inbreeding [they] are healthy, vigorous, and free from stigmata of degeneracy."

William C. Boyd revealed his blood group findings from the shrunken tissues of Egyptian, Peruvian, U.S. Southwestern Indian, and Aleut mummies, finding Groups A, B, and O in different populations. His paper was No. 15; mine, on "A Racial Analysis of Ethiopians and Somalis," was No. 24. Boyd's revelations did not move me much because we were classmates and old friends and because I had already published my *Tribes of the Rif* (1932). In it I had shown that the blood groups of Moroccan Berbers and Arabs bore no statistical relation to any metrical or morphological trait. Others have confirmed this since.

In 1950 Boyd published his *Genetics and the Races of Man,* in which he classified races by blood groups alone. This caused a loud splash. Now we could fold up our calipers and anthropometers and creep away. Then the hawk-eyed Alice Brues showed that the A and B substances had to be subject to selection like other genetic traits (*AJPA* 1954, NS 12, pp. 557–59).

It did not take us long to find some of the hazards they were selected by; e.g. smallpox, plague, infant diarrhea. Instead of being the only genetic criteria of race, the blood groups became useful in tracing who had inherited what specific disease resistance from whom. It turned out that urban populations need more A and B-resistant genes than did the pre-conquest Australian Aborigines or American Indians, who more sparsely occupied cleaner space than their invaders had. If their ancestors had had the genes for A and B, they had sloughed them off through the principle of relaxation of selection, first enunciated by Richard Post in reference to color blindness. Still it made peace-loving people more comfortable to classify others by a coded alphabet soup than to use old-fashioned words for well-known races.

Since 1950, field anthropometry has declined, and blood-drawing in the field has increased, while both are still done in laboratories. In 1929–30, I still wanted to take blood samples of the North Albanian mountaineers but could not, because they let it only in feuds and in pacts of blood-brotherhood. But they liked having their heads and bodies measured, because when I was calling out the numbers, they thought that I was praying for them.

Along with racially oriented anthropometry, somatotyping was also nixed by the Establishment, however constituted. Hippocrates had noticed individual differences in body build and temperament, and Herodotus had described the Scythians in these terms. During the Renaissance, master painters had depicted aristocrats as long and lean, peasants as broad-shouldered and broad-hipped, while sly, self-indulgent merchants were shown as thin-nosed, thin-fingered, and fat of paunch and jowl. Later, German anatomists had documented the existence of such types (horrid word) statistically. In America, after he had viewed the corpses of American soldiers killed by influenza in 1918, Dr. George Draper noticed that almost all of them were constitutionally alike.

A follower of Dr. Draper, William H. Sheldon, M.D., PhD, kept very busy in the office to my right in the Peabody Museum at Harvard in the 1930s, while Eliot Chapple was analyzing interaction rates in the office to my left. Sheldon realized that "pure" endomorphs, mesomorphs, and ectomorphs, (fat, solid, and lean) were virtually nonexistent, because everyone shares the three embryonic, organic layers of endoderm, mesoderm, and ectoderm—from which arise the digestive tract; bone and muscle; and skin, hair, nails, and brain. He measured each of his components on a scale of 1 to 7. Because one man might have solid legs and a skinny chest, he rated the parts of the body separately, noting 60 variables for each subject. His total estimate was expressed by a 1-to-7 score for each component, e.g. a mesomorph might be rated 3-7-2.

The Greeks, Germans, Draper, and Sheldon attributed psychological and behavioral characteristics to their somatotypes. Sheldon's own work was drawn into fine focus when he teamed with S. Smith Stevens, a most eminent Harvard psychologist, whose life work was a totally objective mathematical study of the human reception and tolerance of tones and decibels of sound. As Chapple had done with interaction rates, Sheldon and Stevens showed that temperament is hereditary. So are patterns of behavior, while external influences can work failure or success, but cannot erase the blueprints of the genes.

For almost 30 years, Sheldon's and Stevens's work has been unofficially but effectively proscribed on several flimsy grounds—the real one being that by referring clinically to individuals, they disturb the equilibrium of the present Age of Homogenization, in which ladies wear trousers, there are no left-handed can openers, etc ... etc ... etc.

In 1976, a ray of dawn has begun to break. An article in the *American Journal of Physical Anthropology* shows that the somatotypes of individuals vary during childhood and adolescence before attaining their fully adult state. Sheldon had anticipated this observation early in his work, by describing the PPJ, or Pyknic Practical Joke—a young woman with small hands and feet and a beautiful figure before marriage, but who, after childbirth, became a plump endomorph, like an Upper Paleolithic portable Venus, as of Willendorf. Like the first bluebird of spring, is Sheldon's life's work coming back?

By the same token, the tables of contents of the last years of the *American Journal of Physical Anthropology* seem healthy and hearty. Turning pages at random, we encounter "Response to Hand Cooling Among the Chinese," by Joseph K. So; "Anatomical Differences in the Femur and Tibia between Negroids and Caucasoids and their Effects on Locomotion," by M. H. Farrally and W. J. Moore; "Comparative Anatomy of the Larynx in Man and the Chimpanzee: Implications for Language in Neanderthal," by Dean Falk; a whole number (Vol. 42, No. 2, 1975) on dermatoglyphics, covering both specific populations and analysis. Number 3 contains four papers on the related functions of eye color and skin color with reference to racial differences in vitamin D irradiation by ultraviolet, and the latest news about the discovery of the oldest fossil man on the shore of Lake Turkana (Rudolf, until yesterday), by Richard Leakey and Alan Walker.

In these reports, this aging and battle-scarred viewer sees no rancor, no issues other than the origin of man and of his races, and the genetic markers, immunological and otherwise, that pull them together or push them apart. Our physical anthropologists are keeping up with the twiddlesome technology of the physicists and chemists, while sticking to their own lasts. They realize that the human body is more than its culture, which emanates from it and guides it with varying degrees of success. It is the watchtower from which all sciences derive. Their practitioners are still *Homines,* fallible if *sapientes.* If shorn of freedom, how can they free the world?

One easy jump drops us underground on the local ladder of time to Prehistoric Archaeology, which links the anatomical and neurological potentialities of our ancestors to things they made and ate. Pots and flints, seeds and the bones of animals, domesticated and wild, tell us not only about their foodgetting and kitchen styles, but help us to date their presence, and its climate, layer by layer.

In 1925 when I first dug, Carbon-14 had not been discovered, nor any of the other dating techniques since devised. The Director of Antiquities of Morocco had suggested an open-air site at Tit Mellil, the water supply of Casablanca, then a small town. There I found handaxes and rhinoceros bones and horncores in profusion, all unstratified. Later I learned that the waterworks men had been there earlier, scrambling the layers.

Fourteen years later I excavated the High Cave of Tangier, now a tourist trap, then a millstone quarry. My companions were millstone cutters and local laborers, prime workers who halted only once. We had opened a sealed inner cave in which, they said, lived a horrid jinn. To get them back to work, I crawled inside the suspicious chamber and scolded the jinn in the dark, in two voices, his and mine, until he fled. What we found was published. Because measuring people had become unfashionable, I excavated other caves, in Iraq, Iran, Afghanistan, Syria, and Sierra Leone.

Caves draw us back to the times when men first had fire. Earlier than that, most prehistoric archaeology is done in open air sites, often riverbeds. My personal objective was to combine archaeology with exploration, just as I had done earlier with anthropometry.

By specializing in caves it is possible to develop and to practice a routine that yields the maximum information per unit of space, time, and energy spent. This let me reach bedrock or sterile soil in a single season, and then move on to new frontiers and new problems, traveling light, for wherever there is limestone, caves are easy to find.

After the first round at the High Cave, all of them were excavated after World War II, which had left me restless. Everywhere I went, the men I trained became my companions, like the men in my "Special Operations" outfit during the war. Other men excavated village mounds, city sites, and temples. Such work is sedentary, may go on in one place for years, and requires a large and often ill-sorted staff whose members sometimes quarrel with each other and the boss. Logistics are a plague; so sometimes are hassles with government functionaries and antiquities thieves.

Generals of archaeology who command such grounded expeditions have included, among my own acquaintances, George A. Reisner, Alfred V. Kidder, Gordon Willey, Robert Dyson, Rodney Young, Sylvanus Morley, Joseph Spinden, Eric Schmidt, Robert Braidwood, Robert Adams, Kathleen Kenyon, and Carl Lamberg-Karlowski; theirs are names that stick in my head. Cavemen-commandos like Scotty MacNeish and Buffalo Smith can wear both hats, and Hallam Movius, the master of Abri Pataud, is simply unique.

Some archaeologsts believe in God and even go to church. The struggle between the sexes, race, and the end of the world interest them less than a football game.

Linguistics is either the fourth leg or an appendage, fore or aft, of Anthropology, or more practically it is a cognate discipline of its own, and linguists who are not anthropologists take a similar view of us. My personal experience with linguistics has been limited, and I dare not deal with it here.

Presently I hold a dubious and purely biological distinction. As far as I know, only Li Chi, of the Academia Sinica of Taiwan, and Harry Shapiro, of the American Museum of Natural History in New York, hold American doctorates in anthropology, all three from Harvard, which go back to 1928 (my date) or earlier. This places me in the role of anecdotal historian for graduate students coming from near and far. They are writing their dissertations on the lives and times of such antique stars as Hrdlička, Hooton, and Lloyd Warner, whom I see as brightly as I did so long ago. I like this trend. High time it is, that the younger generation stops sneering at its predecessors.

Some of us live on principally in anecdotes transferred through students' generations. In the early 1920s we at Harvard firmly believed that Warren K. Moorehead, the Andover archaeologist, had once been working in an Indian mound near the Merrimack River. He was sitting on the rim of a trench, excavating carefully with trowel and brush, when he struck and uncovered something shiny, curved, and brown.

"Aha! An Indian skull!" he is alleged to have cried. As he removed more earth, he found that the object in question was one of his own shoes, enclosing his own foot. About 20 years later, this tale was told of me. Whose foot is in that shoe now?

Ann. Rev. Anthropol. 1977. 6:11–32

THE LOWER PALEOLITHIC: CURRENT EVIDENCE AND INTERPRETATIONS

♦9585

Arthur J. Jelinek

Department of Anthropology, University of Arizona, Tucson, Arizona 85721

The earliest evidences of deliberate manufacture of tools by man's ancestors have been of deep interest to prehistorians since the general recognition of the significance of the collections of Boucher de Perthes in the mid-nineteenth century. Within these Lower Paleolithic collections of stone artifacts lies much of our evidence of the beginnings of the patterns of cultural behavior that distinguish man from other creatures.

The term "Lower Paleolithic" is to some degree an outmoded survival of late nineteenth century thinking based upon typological constructs drawn from a limited sample of artifacts, most of which had been found in northern and southwest France. It was first used by de Mortillet in 1872 (48) to distinguish those chipped stone industries in which bone and antler tools were then unknown from an "Upper Paleolithic" in which such tools were associated with those of chipped stone. By the early twentieth century the term had been restricted to Acheulian and pre-Acheulian hand axe (biface) industries and the subsequent Mousterian. The Mousterian was eventually distinguished from the earlier industries as the "Middle Paleolithic," although the initial justification for this division now appears weak. It was based upon an apparently greater frequency of flake tools (predominantly scrapers) in the Middle Paleolithic, as opposed to core tools (predominantly hand axes) in the Lower Paleolithic, a difference which was largely the result of the collecting techniques of the nineteenth century. At that time the earlier Paleolithic of western Europe was known primarily from collections made by unskilled laborers from terrace gravels in northern France: the specimens collected tended to be restricted to symmetrical and easily recognizable bifaces. The appeal of symmetry and regular flake patterns on these specimens for the collectors employing the workmen was probably also a factor in determining what was saved as "representative" of these industries. In contrast, while hand axes were present in the Mousterian, it was known primarily from more objective samples of chipped stone

11

implements, including a predominance of scrapers made on flakes, derived from rock shelter deposits in southwest France. Subsequent methodical excavation of earlier Paleolithic sites has shown that instances in which bifaces predominate over flake tools are rare and that in most sites where bifaces are present their ratio to flake tools is low. Thus the use of these kinds of ratios as a typological basis for distinguishing between a Lower and Middle Paleolithic is open to question. There is little doubt, however, that more refined typological studies initiated by Bordes (3) have resulted in the isolation of Mousterian assemblages in the early phases of the Würm glaciation that are distinct from earlier assemblages and warrant the transitional status of "Middle" Paleolithic. The recognition of the particular Mousterian assemblages isolated by Bordes in western Europe becomes increasingly questionable with distance as technological and typological emphases appear which are not closely paralleled in the European industries. While they may not be identical to the Mousterian of western Europe, all of these assemblages seem to be a part of the same trends toward diversity of contemporary industries and diminishing emphasis on biface manufacture throughout the western Old World. This suggests a significant change in technological patterns at the end of the Middle Pleistocene (beginning of the Last Interglacial) in most areas in which chronological placement is possible and thus favors a termination for Lower Paleolithic industries at that time.

As a result of these more recent interpretations, de Mortilliet's term "Lower Paleolithic" is now generally accepted by prehistorians to include all evidence of cultural activity from the earliest appearance of chipped stone tools in the Lower Pleistocene up to the onset of the last interglacial episode (the beginning of the Upper Pleistocene). Even this usage, however, is not without some inconsistencies since it is evident that in some areas Acheulian hand axe industries or other patterns typical of the Lower Paleolithic persist well into the last interglacial. The inconsistencies are hardly surprising since the term refers to a cultural manifestation rather than a time period and thus exhibits the differing temporal persistence of characteristic Middle Pleistocene industries in each geographical region.

One question that emerges from an initial consideration of the archaeological evidence from the Lower and Middle Pleistocene is whether these data show patterns through time sufficiently similar to justify lumping them under a single label, or whether there exist internal differences of an order comparable to the distinctions between Middle and Upper Paleolithic. If the latter situation obtains, would it be desirable, in the interests of consistent usage, to subdivide the Lower Paleolithic into two or more units? This is not a novel proposition; similar classifications were proposed near the turn of the century to incorporate questionable artifacts underlying the hand axe industries into an "Eolithic," while as recently as 1961 Grahame Clark (12) presented a quadrimodal division of Paleolithic industries in which the first two modes correspond to the Lower Paleolithic. The major basis for these proposed chronological subdivisions has been the absence of bifaces in an earlier phase as opposed to the presence of this form through the later portion of the sequence. Since the temporal priority of nonbiface industries has been well demonstrated in east and northwest Africa and seems indicated by recent discoveries in Europe (8, 21, 53), and since, in a technological sense, the process of biface manufacture seems to imply a qualitative step in the preconception of tool form and character, it would appear that there is some real justification for proposing a "Basal Paleolithic" phase to precede the traditional Lower Paleolithic. Several complicating factors emerge, however, when such a division is proposed. Chief among them is the presence of nonbiface industries throughout the Middle Pleistocene in many areas of the Old World. In some instances these industries are clearly not simple extensions of the Lower Pleistocene chopper-tool complexes, such as the Oldowan, but have developed distinctive patterns of tool manufacture that differentiate them from both the earlier Oldowan and the contemporary hand axe industries. A well-known example of such a Middle Pleistocene nonbiface industry is the Clactonian, which has recently been contrasted with the Acheulian by Collins (14, p. 269). It is clear on the basis of earlier descriptions (9, 61), as well as Collins's typological and technological comparisons, that this industry is not simply a nonbiface facies of the Acheulian, but includes high frequencies of tool types that are rare to absent in Acheulian collections, as well as basic techniques of flake manufacture that contrast with the Acheulian. Therefore, the single factor of the presence or absence of hand axes is not sufficient to distinguish a Basal Paleolithic (characterized by a Lower Pleistocene Oldowan industry) from the more evolved Lower Paleolithic industries of the Middle Pleistocene.

A major barrier to the comparison of Lower Paleolithic industries in widely separated areas of the Old World is the present state of descriptive terminology and typology applied to these industries. At present two major systems of description and typology are being used, as well as several less widely applied systems. This diversity can be traced to formal differences in industries in different time periods and different regions of the Old World and to the accidents of historical tradition in the development of different "schools" of prehistoric archaeology. The major descriptive/typological traditions are the French school, derived largely from the taxonomic concepts of Breuil and Peyrony and presently best exemplified in the work of Bordes (4) and his students, and secondly, the British-African school whose influence can be seen in the work of M. D. Leakey (40) and that of J. D. Clark and M. Kleindienst (13). Classification based in the former tradition is widely employed in Europe, the Near East, and northwest Africa, while the influence of the latter school is chiefly seen in the description of material from sub-Saharan Africa.

These two traditions can be compared by examining the particular artifact typologies of the prehistorians just mentioned. Since Bordes's system is designed to include classification of both Lower and Middle Paleolithic collections and the Clark-Kleindienst classification spans the full range of the Paleolithic, this comparison will be restricted to only the categories of tools that occur in the Lower Paleolithic. Table 1 indicates the different basic emphases in taxonomic divisions in the three systems. It is clear that in each system there are types that span several typological categories in the other systems. In some cases, even basic terminological usage is inconsistent between systems, as in the complete absence of cores in Leakey's classification; all artifacts that would be classified as cores in the other systems are included in tools in this classification. In general, the Leakey system includes the fewest formal distinctions and the Bordes system the most detailed distinctions. Most tools classi-

Table 1 Relationship of some Lower Paleolithic artifact types in three classifications[a]

Bordes (4)	Clark-Kleindienst (13)	M. D. Leakey (40)
Chopping tools (bifacial) = ⟶ Choppers (unifacial)	Choppers[c] (mostly bifacial) 5 categories (grade into cores) ⟵—3—⟶	Choppers (mostly bifacial) 5 categories
Bifaces { Abbevillian, Ficron, Nucleiforme } ⟵—?—⟶	Some core-axes[c] ? ⟵—?—⟶	Proto bifaces
13 Shapes (outline + thickness) Partiels } ⟵——— =	{ Hand-axes[b] 8 shapes (outline) ⟵——2——, Lanceolates[b], Some core-axes[c] ? } =	Bifaces { Irregular ovates, Double pointed, Flat butted }
Hachereaux s. élats ⟵——— = 6 categories ? ⟵———	Cleavers[b], 4 shapes ⟵———, Chisels[c] ———⟶ ?	Cleavers
Pics = ⟶ Some bifaces ?	{ Picks[c], 4 categories ⟵—?—, Some core-axes[c] ? } =	{ Trihedrals, Oblong picks, Heavy duty picks }
Bifaces a dos ⟵—?—⟶	Knives[b] ———⟶ ?	
Boules polyédriques ⟵—?—⟶	{ Some cores ? ⟵—?—⟶, Spheroids[c] = ——— }	{ Polyhedrons, Spheroids, Subspheroids }
Bifaces discoides ⟵—?—⟶	{ Some disc cores ?, Discoids[d] } ⟵—?—⟶	Discoids
Scrapers { Racloir, 18 forms ⟵—?—⟶, Transversaux (3) ⟵———— =, Grattoirs (2) ⟵———⟶ }	Scrapers; large[b], small[d] { Side, indefinite number forms ⟵———, Side flake, End, some nosed ? ⟵———⟶ } =	Scrapers[e] { Side, some hollow and discoidal, End, some nosed ? }
Notches ⟵—?—⟶	Some notched scrapers ? ⟵—?—⟶	Some hollow
Denticulates ⟵—?—⟶	Some denticulate scrapers ? ———⟶ ?	
Rabot ⟵—?—⟶	Some core scrapers ⟵—?—⟶	{ Discoidal, Some peramital ? }

[a]Key: [b] Large cutting tools, usually > 100 mm.
[c] Heavy duty tools > or < 100 mm.
[d] Light duty tools, usually < 100 mm.
[e] Divided into heavy duty (> 50 mm) and light duty (< 50 mm).

=———⟶ Equivalent; fewer to more categories.
⟵——— Equivalent.
⟵—?—⟶ Some question of equivalence.
⟵—3—⟶ Number of equivalent categories.
———⟶ ? No apparent equivalent.

fied in the Leakey system can be fully accommodated in either the Clark-Kleindienst or Bordes system, but full equivalence is lacking between the latter two systems, since each includes more detail in some categories than does the other. In general, it is easier to translate a classification from the two more elaborate systems to the simpler Leakey system, but even here full equivalence is not assured, and the absence of formal distinctions held to be significant by most Paleolithic scholars reduces the utility and interest of comparisons within this system. The Clark-Kleindienst system can be seen as a promising effort in the direction of uniformity. Here equivalent terms from the Bordes typology were listed for each type seen as most closely resembling one in the Bordes classification. Despite these preliminary efforts at standardization, it is clear that to a significant degree comparative research in the Lower Paleolithic continues to be hampered by the barriers of provincial taxonomic systems which must be standardized before fully effective communication between scholars can be established. The present dilemma of the students of these industries is roughly comparable to that of comparative anatomists attempting to communicate in the absence of a standard Latin-Greek anatomical taxonomy.

The emphasis placed on the classification and comparison of chipped stone tools in Lower Paleolithic studies is, of course, a reflection of the fact that such materials form the overwhelming bulk of our evidence of the activities of man in this period. Two basic questions that must be dealt with by archaeologists when they use these materials for their interpretation of the life ways of Lower Paleolithic man are: (*a*) what significance did these artifacts have for the people who made them; and (*b*) what relationship do the remains of these lithic industries that are accessible to the archaeologist have to the full cultural system in which they were manufactured?

In order to answer the first question we invariably make assumptions relating to the cognitive abilities of the hominids who produced the artifacts. Some of these assumptions can be based upon the uniformity of the industries over periods of hundreds of thousands of years. The absence of evidence of innovation and differentiation in the tool forms that can be observed over these prolonged intervals can be taken as evidence against the presence of the conceptual abilities relating to abstraction and synthesis that characterize modern *Homo sapiens*. One important implication of this evidence relates to the role of verbal communication based upon these conceptual abilities. With regard to stone tools, the repetition of patterns and lack of innovation suggest that they may have been the product of complex forms of imitative behavior in a pattern no longer to be found among the hominidae, and that verbal direction played a minimal role in the learning processes associated with tool manufacture. The learning abilities of the Pongidae suggest a propensity among man's ancestors for the development of complex imitative behavior. It is interesting in this regard that in the replication of chipped stone tools in experimental archaeology, demonstration and imitation play a far more significant role than description. In fact, difficulty in describing precisely the techniques employed in such manufacture is a common frustration among modern lithic technologists.

It seems evident that the most desirable qualities of chipped stone for Paleolithic man were sharp and durable edges for the cutting, piercing, and abrasion of softer materials. The extent to which Lower Paleolithic man manipulated and modified materials other than stone remains a matter of speculation due to the almost complete lack of preservation of most organic substances in Lower and Middle Pleistocene contexts. One clue in this regard is afforded by the relatively extensive preservation of bone, ivory, and enamel in some Lower Paleolithic sites. While these materials are amenable to shaping and modification by cutting, chiseling, and abrasion, there is virtually no evidence for the employment of these techniques on what must have been relatively abundant raw material. Instead, when bone is employed for tool manufacture, it appears to have been worked by the same techniques that we see employed in the shaping of stone, i.e. by chipping. Probably because deliberately chipped bones appear somewhat similar to bones smashed for marrow or otherwise broken in butchering, extensive studies of deliberately shaped bone in the Lower Paleolithic are rare. Nevertheless, some examples of Lower Paleolithic chipped bone have been reported from as widely scattered localities as central Spain (2) and Northern China (10), suggesting that bone may have been a more important item in the technology of these early hominids than has been appreciated by lithic-oriented prehistorians. But the restriction of shaping techniques to breaking and chipping suggests a limited awareness of the potential of this qualitatively distinct material in artifact manufacture. Earlier suggestions that the Australopithecines of South Africa had developed an industry of modified bone tools now seem refuted by studies of bone alteration by hyaenas (56, 58). Beyond these infrequent reports of bone artifacts there is an almost complete absence of direct evidence of nonlithic tool manufacture in the Lower Paleolithic. Exceptions to this are the two well-known pointed wooden shafts from a Middle Pleistocene context in England (60) and early Late Pleistocene Germany (50), which are generally interpreted as deliberately shaped spears, and several wooden tools (not yet fully reported) from the Kalambo Falls site in southeast Africa (30, p. 521). How extensively, and with what techniques for modification, wood, hide, and animal and vegetable fiber were employed in the technology of Lower Paleolithic man remains unknown. It is curious that if as has been supposed the wooden shafts mentioned above were shaped by shaving and scraping with stone tools, there is virtually no evidence of the employment of these useful techniques on ivory, antler, or bone. This suggests that the woodworking technology of Lower Paleolithic man may have been fairly rudimentary and confined to the removal of inconvenient branches and nodes by chopping, with fire employed to some degree for shaping and hardening.

The utility of chipped stone for Lower and Middle Pleistocene hominids and the significance of its employment for their evolution should not be underestimated. It seems unlikely that the omnivorous diet of the Australopithecines could have led to a successful utilization of large game without these supplementary teeth and claws of stone for butchering their kills. The extent to which tools were used in gaining access to otherwise unavailable vegetal resources and to small game and nonmammalian fauna is another aspect of technological development that awaits exploration.

Assuming that the above is a reasonable appraisal of the role of stone tools in the technology of Lower Paleolithic man, we can now examine the collections of these artifacts available to the archaeologist as indicators of the life-ways of the hominids that made them. One aspect of our interpretation is related to the kinds of planning and intelligence that we attribute to these hominids. Once these creatures became dependent upon the use of stone in the procurement and processing of food, it became necessary for them to integrate these variables in order to obtain food; sufficient anticipation was necessary to insure the presence of both meat and stone at the same place in order to utilize the protein effectively. Where game was abundant and useful stone infrequent, there must have been considerable selective advantage for those hominids who could best anticipate how to bring these resources together. It seems likely that the development of these kinds of abilities played a significant role in the development of the kind of conceptualization upon which much of the success of man's later cultural adaptation is based. There is little doubt that these abilities changed through the Lower Paleolithic and that Late Middle Pleistocene man was far more efficient in this regard than his early Lower Pleistocene antecedents. Thus in some respects it is difficult to generalize about the significance of stone tool collections and assemblages for the whole of the Lower Paleolithic.

One area in which some generalization is possible concerns the nature of these artifacts in relation to their place in a fully functioning technological system. It is evident that most of the artifacts in an archaeological site were deliberately abandoned. The chief exception to this would be material lost or misplaced before the termination of the occupation. Possible causes for the abandonment of artifacts may have been that they were seen as exhausted in terms of function in the technology; others may have been too bulky or heavy for the anticipated move. Depending upon the degree of anticipation of future activities that we attribute to the inhabitants of the site, it is possible that objects were abandoned because they would not be appropriate to subsequent activities, because sufficient similar material would be available at future sites when it was needed, or more promising material was available en route. It is also possible, if return visits to the site were anticipated, as in a regular seasonal round, that the material left at the site was to some extent seen as a cache from which future implements could be made and was more conveniently left where it was until needed. It is from collections resulting from these problematical circumstances of deposition that prehistorians have reconstructed the activities and historical traditions of Lower Paleolithic man. The inability of the archaeologist to identify the circumstances under which the artifacts were abandoned inhibits his ability to interpret them. In the absence of some understanding of the environmental and social variables affecting the prehistoric men who left the artifact concentration it is difficult for the archaeologist to establish the significance of these artifacts to those extinct hominids.

To some degree, experimental studies of lithic technology and careful analysis of the context and character of later industries have contributed to our ability to interpret these most ancient artifacts. Here also our additional knowledge may raise more questions than it answers. As an example, we may consider the "spheroids" which occur frequently in the Lower and Middle Pleistocene industries of Africa. Many workers interpret these chipped ball-like specimens as deliberately manufactured implements; in extreme instances they are seen as components of complex tools such as the bolas (40, p. 266). Occasionally they exhibit signs of abrasion as though they had been used for pounding or hammering on other stones. The lithic technologist's interpretation of these objects, however, may be quite different. By experimentation it can be established that the angles between the numerous flake scars that form the surface of the spheroid are too wide to serve as platforms from which further flakes can be struck, so that the spheroid can be viewed as an exhausted core from which every possible flake has been struck. It is reasonable to suppose that such symmetrical exhausted cores might have been used as convenient pounders, hammers, or even missiles, although this may not have been the original intent of their fabricators. This kind of interpretation leads to the very large question of the multiple use of artifacts and the implications of this multiple use for the final character of the assemblage that remains for the archaeologist.

There is a tendency on the part of prehistorians to compartmentalize the artifacts they recover into formal types and to use this classification in their interpretation in such a way as to view each artifact as a tool made for one particular purpose. In part this is probably at the least an unconscious extension of the specialized nature of tools in modern technology. Chipped stone tools, on the other hand, can be viewed as temporary stages in the reduction of pieces of raw material. Each specimen has the potential of assuming a succession of forms through modification dictated by convenience or a changing succession of tasks at hand. This tendency for a metamorphosis of tools through a succession of modifications has been referred to as the *Frison effect* in a previous paper (34), following the clear demonstration by Frison (22) of these patterns in a late prehistoric site in western North America. The dilemma introduced into archaeological interpretation by the Frison effect is that it is seldom possible to distinguish the full sequence of modifications (typological transitions) through which a particular piece of stone has passed. The form of the tool seen by the archaeologist is that of the last modification prior to its abandonment, and it may not be possible to identify previous uses of the specimen on the site—uses that represent different tool types. Thus the prehistorian probably seldom, if ever, sees a full and functional tool kit representing all or even most of the activities that have taken place on a site. Perhaps the best that we can hope for is that similar traditions of manufacture of tools for similar tasks will result in similar lithic refuse. Beyond these limitations we must also allow for the probable opportunistic behavior of prehistoric man. Ethnographic analogy (23, 62) suggests that frequent use was made of otherwise unmodified simple flakes which under most circumstances would not be considered as tools at all by the archaeologist. Thus the major body of artifactual materials upon which interpretations of the cultural activities of Lower Paleolithic man must be based can in most circumstances be expected to represent only a very incomplete picture of the employment of even this one substance (stone) in the technology, and much of even this limited aspect of the activities of these hominids seems inaccessible to us throughout the forseeable future.

There remains considerable disagreement among prehistorians regarding the significance of those patterns of artifact form that can be distinguished in the limited samples just described. The typological systems mentioned earlier for the classification of lithic artifacts are based on the recognition of repeated patterns of modification (e.g. the convex retouched edge of a flake paralleling the axis of flaking that signals "*racloir simple convexe*" to François Bordes.) All of the major typologies employed in the classification of Lower Paleolithic material at present are based on the intuitive recognition of attribute combinations related to manufacture or modification of the piece. The recognition of these patterns has resulted from the examination of large numbers of artifacts by the proponent of each typology. What kind of significance these classificatory units had for the manufacturers of the tools remains to be demonstrated. It seems likely on the basis of recent ethnographic work (23) that our present classifications are overly elaborated in terms of the kinds of tools that would be recognized by the authors of these industries. In fact, we have yet to see a clear demonstration that most of the distinctions made in our classification are of utility in distinguishing the repeated patterns of related types that we interpret as traditionally (stylistically) or functionally significant cultural units.

The one class of Lower Paleolithic chipped stone material that has probably been subjected to most careful and objective examination and classification includes the bifaces (or hand axes) that are the hallmark of most Middle Pleistocene cultures in the western Old World. While such studies (4, 18, 24, 54, 55, 63) suggest that some subclasses can be objectively defined in large populations of bifaces on the basis of attribute clusters, and that bifaces with certain attributes are largely restricted in time or space, prehistorians are still without firm evidence relating to the function of these first recognized and most elaborate of Lower Paleolithic stone tools. The wide variation in form of these tools suggests that a bifacial mode of manufacture was employed as a basic pattern into which variations for slicing, piercing, chopping, and abrading tools could be introduced; i.e. particular kinds of bifaces were produced for different functional purposes, or certain kinds of bifaces could have been reshaped by several successive modifications for a series of different tasks. The possibility that these bifaces were also ready sources (as specialized cores) for thin sharp flakes has been given little consideration in the literature. An additional complicating factor is the probability that some differences in the patterns of biface manufacture were primarily matters of stylistic preference and were largely irrelevant to function.

Thus the prehistorian is limited in the kinds of interpretations he can make of the Lower Paleolithic record by the nature of the artifactual evidence, which is largely confined to the stone tools, cores, flakes, and debris that were abandoned following the final occupation of a site by hominids whose ways of thinking may have differed to a significant degree from our own. A further difficult and crucial problem in this interpretation relates to the question of obtaining evidence beyond the artifacts themselves—the context of the material and the implications of this context for the length of time the site was occupied and the environmental conditions at the time of occupation. In few Lower Paleolithic sites can we state with certainty that the accumulation of artifacts represents a single undisturbed short-term occupation— the kind of occupation that could be expected to result in the spatial segregation of functionally related artifacts that in turn might provide clues to the social patterns of the group that occupied the site. Instead there is every reason to believe that we are in most cases dealing with repeated brief utilization of environmentally favorable localities that resulted in the gradual accumulation of artifacts and reutilization of artifacts on the occupation surface and that repeatedly disturbed previous functionally related spatial relationships. At the least it may be assumed that these occupation surfaces were, for some unknown period following their abandonment, subject to scavenging for tools and raw materials. Our sample is further limited by the fact that preservation of these early prehistoric remains was limited to those contexts that escaped the destructive forces of weathering and erosion. Chiefly represented are situations in topographic lows where water transport of sediments was responsible for covering and protecting occupation surfaces. In rare instances in Lower and Middle Pleistocene contexts we find artifacts in cave and rock shelter deposits; here the limitations on space and apparent frequent reutilization over long periods of time pose special problems in interpretation. It is a maxim in Paleolithic archaeology, as in paleontology, that we will never know what was going on on the hilltops (or even in the uplands in most instances). Conversely, coastal environments have also lost most of their Lower Paleolithic sites through marine erosion during periods of eustatic and tectonically caused fluctuation in sea level. In many areas coastal occupations of interglacial date remain submerged below 100 or more meters of ocean.

In a general sense, as we come up through time in prehistory we see an increasing abundance of preserved sites, although in the Lower Paleolithic random factors of destruction have removed all sites in many areas through great periods of time and we are left with isolated concentrations of remains in a few favored localities representing widely disparate spatial and temporal contexts. When we consider the limited time represented by any single occupation by the small bands of food collectors that were responsible for the Lower Paleolithic cultural record we can see just how limited our evidence is for the interpretation of this early phase of hominid behavior and cultural development.

Our knowledge of man's cultural activities in the 3 million or so years of the Lower Pleistocene is based largely on the excavation of just over a dozen sites in the restricted locality of Olduvai Gorge in northern Tanzania and about a dozen more throughout the rest of the Old World. The entire excavated area of occupation surfaces is well under the size of a modern football field. We are fortunate in that virtually all of these excavations have been conducted with full use of the meticulous techniques of spatial recording and ancillary analysis developed over the last three decades. We are not so fortunate in our knowledge of Middle Pleistocene prehistory, where a substantial portion of our knowledge is based upon earlier excavations and extensive surface collections in which controls and appreciation of nonartifactual materials varied considerably. This period of approximately half a million years is represented by excavations of perhaps four dozen in situ deposits of cultural material, less than half of which were conducted with modern techniques of recording and ancillary analysis. Also, large geographical areas known from scattered finds to have been inhabited are completely without excavated sites.

In addition to the internal chronological problems of length of time and number of occupations represented by each concentration of artifacts, there remains the major chronological challenge of relating these isolated sites to each other through the relatively enormous expanse of time included in the Lower and Middle Pleistocene. In a few restricted localities, such as Olduvai Gorge and Ubeidiya, these relationships can be determined by direct stratigraphic superposition in a well-controlled section. Here, however, major portions of the geologic structure may reflect relatively short periods of deposition, leaving us with no knowledge of much of the time sequence represented by the interval between the lowest and highest sites in the sequence. At Olduvai, for instance, a recent estimate (26) suggests that the whole deposition of Bed I took place over an interval of approximately 100,000 years, or less than 4% of the estimated time span of the Lower Pleistocene. Yet this particular section has provided us with 80% of the occurrences of Oldowan industries at the Gorge (41). Beyond these exceptional stratigraphic controls broader stratigraphic correlations have been employed in the East Rudolf and Omo areas of northeast Africa. Here relative chronological position is based upon the position of sites with respect to major stratigraphic boundaries, resulting in more general and scattered relationships of equivalence and succession than is the case at Olduvai. When we look for correlations beyond those areas within which regional stratigraphic controls are possible we find ourselves on less firm ground. The two major methods of relating widely separated deposits to a common chronological sequence are: (*a*) the use of absolute dating techniques, and (*b*) the placing of sites within a sequence of environmental and/or geological events of broad global extent.

The most extensively employed absolute dating technique for Lower Paleolithic remains is the potassium-argon radioactive decay series. While there have been instances of misleading results from the application of this technique, as in the recent dating of the KBS tuff in the East Rudolf area, it is generally accepted as reliable for Lower and Middle Pleistocene dating. Since its initial application to deposits at Olduvai Gorge in 1961 (39), potassium-argon dating has revolutionized our conception of the length of the period of man's development by extending the age of the Pleistocene back beyond 3.5 million years. Unhappily the archaeological use of this technique depends upon the presence of volcanic extrusives from eruptions contemporary with or (less desirable stratigraphically) bracketing artifactual materials. It is therefore limited to relatively few of the situations in which Lower Paleolithic remains are found. We are, in fact, fortunate that so many of our Lower Pleistocene finds occur in areas of extensive vulcanism during that period in East Africa. Outside of this area, direct applications of the technique to the dating of archaeological remains have been few and in most instances somewhat unsatisfactory. Another technique which appears to promise wider application, though much more general time placement, is paleomagnetic dating, based upon periods of reversal in the polarity of the earth's magnetic field (16). The absolute time scale for these magnetic episodes has been determined by potassium-argon dating of volcanic materials whose crystalization preserved the magnetic polarity at the time of eruption. The fact that heating to relatively low temperatures can cause magnetic realignment suggests that this technique ultimately can be applied on a worldwide scale to the study of sites where fire was in contact with magnetic minerals. The promise of this technique for widespread correlation has recently led to the eminently sensible proposal that the boundary between the Lower and Middle Pleistocene be taken as the point of change between the Matuyama Reversed Epoch and present-day Brunhes Normal Epoch, about 700,000 years ago (11). The acceptance of such a proposal will require the reevaluation of faunally based sequences that previously provided the basis for major subdivisions within the Pleistocene. Olduvai Gorge can again furnish an example. Here earlier correlations based on the time of replacement of a Villafranchian fauna suggested that the Lower Pleistocene ended with the deposition of the lower portion of Bed II; the paleomagnetic correlations would place the Lower/ Middle Pleistocene boundary between Beds III and IV. The advantage of taking the single event of a paleomagnetic transition rather than faunal changes as the chronological anchor for a major time boundary is that since faunal extinctions and appearances did not occur simultaneously throughout the world, this type of biostratigraphic evidence may be misleading when used as the basis for widespread time correlations. The difficulty with paleomagnetic dating in the correlation of Lower Paleolithic cultures is that the major periods of stable paleomagnetic polarity are too long to be of much use except in determining very general time placement (Lower vs Middle Pleistocene) and they are punctuated by brief periods of apparent short reversals called "events." While the probability of a site dating within one of these brief abnormal events is small, the possibility of a misleading paleomagnetic placement, in the absence of other dating evidence, must always be considered. It may, however, ultimately be possible, with the aid of supporting chronological evidence, to employ these events in more accurate paleomagnetic dating of sites whose time of occupation coincides with them.

Both of the dating techniques discussed above have had relatively limited application outside of the northeast African area where they have been extensively employed in the study of Lower Pleistocene sites. By far the majority of Lower Paleolithic sites in the Old World have been correlated both relatively and absolutely through the use of biostratigraphic or paleoclimatically related sequences. The basic shortcoming of the broad use of biostratigraphic evidence for the relatively brief (in terms of biological evolution) spans of time represented by the Lower Paleolithic is the insupportable assumption of synchronous faunal changes mentioned above. Beyond this, the time span of most identifiable species allows only a very general time placement for the kind of faunal assemblage normally associated with a Paleolithic site. Thus a particular assemblage may be said to characterize the early or late Middle Pleistocene but is seldom diagnostic beyond that level of difference, and even here there is occasional disagreement. The use of paleoclimatically linked evidence for Lower Paleolithic correlation, since the formulation of the Alpine sequence of four major glaciations early in this century (52), has been dominated by the basic four-glacial concept.

The early attempts at paleoclimatic correlation now seem naive, with all of the Lower Paleolithic compressed into the Last (Riss-Würm) Interglacial (51, p. 108), but within a decade the careful work of such stratigraphers as Commont in the north of France had shown that the hand axe industries had their beginnings at least as early as the penultimate interglacial (Mindel-Riss). The subsequent extension of this chronology to areas outside of western Europe through the use of glacially related phenomena such as raised marine beaches and evidence of changes in temperature and precipitation have led to a common employment of Alpine Glacial chronological terms in areas well removed from continental Europe, as well as assumptions of equivalence for local terminology. A challenge to this four-glacial (later modified to six glacials) model of Pleistocene climatic change has emerged from extensive recent paleoclimatic studies based on temperature changes reflected in microorganisms and chemical changes in deep sea deposits. It is assumed that the closely correlated temperature fluctuations seen in widely distributed deep sea cores reflect synchronous global oscillations in climate, which recent studies tend to link to astrophysical mechanisms responsible for continental glaciation (27).

In contrast to the four- or six-glacial mode for all of the Pleistocene, these cores suggest a prolonged sequence of alternately warm and cold periods of roughly equal intensity, with perhaps as many as eight over the last 700,000 years (since the onset of the Middle Pleistocene) (19). Since the Late Pleistocene is defined as including only the last major glaciation and the preceding interglacial, which can be dated to correspond with the last of these eight major oscillations, it would appear that we may have as many as seven glacial events comparable to the Würm in the Middle Pleistocene. It is interesting that recent studies of cycles of loess deposition in central Europe appear to support the climate sequence seen in the deep sea cores (36, pp. 169–70). This new evidence suggests that the traditional model of climatic succession based on evidence of Alpine and continental glaciation is oversimplified (36, p. 178), and has resulted from the destruction of a substantial portion of continental sediments through glacial removal and erosion, and that the chronological arrangement of sites in the Middle Pleistocene, particularly in Europe and adjacent areas, will require serious reexamination. We can no longer with any confidence refer a site with an "early Middle Pleistocene" fauna and evidence of a cold environment to a Mindel Glacial time, sites with cold "late Middle Pleistocene" fauna to a Riss Glacial time, or all sites with a "warm Middle Pleistocene" fauna to a "Great Interglacial" or Mindel-Riss interglacial (or Hoxnian or Holstenian) time. Instead it appears that there may have been six warm interglacials and seven glacials in the Middle Pleistocene during the time span previously assigned to the two glacials and one interglacial in the traditional sequence.

The implications of this postulated sequence beyond the temperate areas are equally profound, since such factors as sea level and atmospheric circulation patterns can also be expected to have fluctuated many more times than had previously been suspected. It is likely, for example, that previous correlations of particular cool pluvial conditions in the Levant with the Mindel and Riss glaciations will need further examination, as will the correlation of Middle Pleistocene industries with the Mindel-Riss Interglacial on the basis of particular raised marine beaches.

In view of the relatively slow evolution of the fauna during the Middle Pleistocene, it appears that the most promising solution to the correlation of Middle Pleistocene sites lies in linking archaeological sites to more detailed local stratigraphic and climatological sequences and in the development and wider application of such absolute dating techniques as paleomagnetic and thermoluminescence dating. At present all we can say is that many of the correlations proposed in recent syntheses are probably incorrect (at least in a detailed sense) and their revision will require considerable new evidence. We are probably most secure in our Middle Pleistocene correlations at the upper end of the time scale, where effects of the penultimate glacial ("Riss") can, in many instances, be isolated from earlier cold periods. Prior to this last cold phase of the Middle Pleistocene we now have a much broader range of possible time positions for our cultural evidence. Yet within this time range lie many sites whose relative chronological positions have been the subject of recent controversy. In Europe, these sites and localities would include Swanscombe, Terra Amata, Torralba and Ambrona, Torre in Pietra, Clacton, Hoxne, Mauer, Vértesszöllös, and the Carpentier pit at Abbeville.

Granted the limitations mentioned in the preceding discussion of the nature of our evidence of Lower Paleolithic man, what *do* we know about man's early development as a tool-making creature? The earliest evidence for the manufacture of stone tools at the time of this writing is based on a find by J. Chavaillon dated to approximately 2.5 million years and derives from Member C of the Shungura Formation of the Lower Omo River valley in southern Ethiopia (32, p. 487). Earlier reports of stone tools of a similar age in the KBS industry from the east Rudolf area of Kenya have been revised, and the age of this industry is now considered to be about 1.6–1.8 million years (17). Thus, by shortly after two million years ago, we have firm evidence of the use of stone tools in a broad area of east Africa extending from Olduvai Gorge in northern Tanzania, through the east Rudolf area of Kenya, and into the Southern Omo valley of Ethiopia. The evidence for these early cultures, associated hominids, and their geological and environmental setting have recently been treated in detail in two important volumes of collected papers (15, 33). In a provocative paper, Isaac (32) attempts to reconstruct as much as possible of what the current evidence from the Koobi Fora formation in the east Rudolf area suggests about the life ways of the hominids responsible for the early archaeological sites. These are the more important points in his treatment:

(a) By that time there were already several well-defined formal categories of chipped stone tools. This may imply a significant period of development of tool use prior to the appearance of these industries.

(b) Artifact concentrations are suggestive of a "home base" which served as a focal point for cultural activities. Important here is the notion that at least some of the products of the food quest were brought back to the base camp to be divided among the band. It is certain that many if not all artifacts were transported here. The relatively small size of these concentrations (5 to 20 meters in diameter) suggests that relatively small populations were involved, and this is emphasized when we consider that we really have no way of distinguishing single from multiple occupations in these sites. Further evidence in this regard may be seen in the work of Merrick at the FtJi2 occurrence in the Omo area, where there is some evidence for two closely superimposed lenses of artifacts in a concentration with a maximum extent of 20 meters (47). It is tempting to speculate that these larger concentrations may reflect periodic re-use of a favorable locality in a restricted territory.

(c) The association of artifact concentrations with stream channel deposits suggests a preferred habitat relating to the exploitation of ecotonal environments in the vicinity of gallery forest and adjacent savannah. Here Isaac recognizes the selective nature of the depositional forces that have preserved his material, but he feels the evidence is sufficiently strong to warrant his interpretation of a culturally significant association. An additional relevant factor might be the probable preference by the hominids for sites near a water supply.

Within about half a million years of the appearance of these widespread early manifestations of tool use, the first evidences of the manufacture of bifaces are apparent in the Developed Oldowan industries at Olduvai (especially at site MNK and the Lower Floor at TK) (41, p. 484), and are probably associated with the Karari Industry in the east Rudolf area (25). In the Olduvai sequence their appearance is accompanied by an increase in spheroids and battered pieces. If they are associated with the Karari industry, it is possible to say that in both areas they coincide with a generally wider range of distinct tool forms, suggesting that they are part of an overall elaboration of the technological system. In view of a recent report of the discovery of a hominid provisionally classified as early *Homo erectus* (KNMER 3733) from the east Rudolf area in this time horizon (42), it may be that these more elaborate industries reflect the presence of more advanced hominids than those responsible for the earlier Oldowan industries.

The time of the earliest appearance of Lower Paleolithic industries in the rest of the Old World is still relatively unknown. There is increasing evidence for a middle Lower Pleistocene arrival of man in Europe; e.g. the Sandalja I Cave (Yugoslavia) human incisor and chopper associated with a Middle Villafranchian fauna (45), and the recent finds of pebble tools near Cadiz, in a depositional context comparable to that in which similar material was reported by Biberson, from an apparently middle Lower Pleistocene context in Morocco (8; F. Bordes, personal communication). Recent evidence from Iran suggests a Lower Pleistocene date for the appearance of man in Southwest Asia (59); however, no firm evidence has yet appeared to support a comparable date for early tool manufacture in other areas of Asia. Aside from these brief glimpses of Lower Pleistocene man beyond Africa, there is still so little evidence, despite extensive examination of many Lower Pleistocene localities, that we are forced to conclude that hominid populations were thinly scattered in Europe and Asia at that time. Probably they were confined to warmer southern regions of these continents, and perhaps then only preceding glaciation or during interglacial periods. In contrast, during the Middle Pleistocene there is fairly abundant evidence of Lower Paleolithic man from the temperate latitudes of north China to Great Britain.

There is little question that this successful adaptation to cooler environments is related to the control of fire. The full implications of the incorporation of fire into the technology of Middle Pleistocene man have yet to be understood. Most obviously it was used to modify the temperature of habitation areas and allow biological survival in environments otherwise untenable for an essentially tropical adapted hominid. Beyond this, however, the use of fire in shaping wood and the influence on utilization of wood resulting from continuing collection of fuel are important considerations. Probably of widest interest, and most likely to be accessible to present analytical techniques, are the effects of the deliberate employment of fire in hunting practices. That the use of fire in hunting may be a very ancient practice seems suggested by the perhaps unique evidence of burned wood preserved at Torralba (29), although even here the possibility that the fire was accidental or simply a defense against the glacial climate cannot be eliminated. Whether Middle Pleistocene man ever consciously appreciated the advantages of improving the forage for the animals he hunted by deliberate burning is open to question, but with this force in his control the possibility for increased survival through the use of these techniques must be considered. Perhaps it is not too far-fetched to suggest that examination of the palynological record in favorable localities may reveal evidence of unexpectedly frequent environmental alteration attributable to fire in this period.

One aspect of the Lower Paleolithic in the Middle Pleistocene that has been the focus of considerable attention on the part of prehistorians is the diversity of lithic industries. By the 1940s a basic geographical division was recognized between the "hand axe" industries of the western Old World and Peninsular India and the "chopper/chopping-tool" industries of northern India and east Asia (49). More recently it has been recognized that bifaces similar or identical to western examples are present in the late Lower Paleolithic of Java (6) and, apparently in small numbers, in Middle Pleistocene industries in China (e.g. 37). In the latter case especially, these kinds of tools appear to occur so infrequently that their significance is open to question. Certainly the interpretation of Laritchev (37) that "Hand axes . . . are in the same extent characteristic for East and Southeast Asia as for South Asia (India), Near East, Africa and Europe" is a clear overstatement in the light of present evidence. The few widely scattered (in space and time) bifaces from China that he cites do not convey the impression of a thriving Acheulian industry. It seems likely that such tool forms may have resulted (though rarely) from the range of lithic manufacturing techniques employed in that area. Here the danger of using a single tool form as a diagnostic index fossil is particularly apparent. A study of the full industry, including frequencies of tool types, techniques of flake extraction, etc would quickly serve to demonstrate the profound differences between the northern Chinese industries and the Acheulian of the western Old World.

It has long been obvious that the western Lower Paleolithic is not a uniform group of industries. Specifically, there appear to be several manifestations of nonbiface industries in Europe in circumstances that suggest that the two kinds of industries may be contemporaneous. A discussion incorporating several interpretations of the significance of these different industries was recently initiated by Collins (14) and illustrates the divergence of opinions currently held by prehistorians on this question. Unfortunately, as Frenzel noted perceptively in his "Comment" (20), this discussion suffers from a heavy reliance on the now questionable evidence for correlation based on the traditional interpretation of Middle Pleistocene glacial succession (see above). The same uncertainties affect the otherwise useful and very thorough discussion of many of these industries by Howell (28). It is clear that most of the arguments raised in these discussions cannot be resolved until better agreement has been reached on the chronological relationships of the sites and industries. Even among the Acheulian biface industries of western Europe there appears to be some geographically consistent variability: occasional flake cleavers similar to those of the African Acheulian are associated with high frequencies of relatively crude hand axes and little Levallois technique in Spain and the southwest of France; in contrast, there is general absence of flake cleavers, more frequent refined bifaces, and a greater use of Levallois technique in northern France and England (5–7). Whether this difference relates to an African influence via Gibraltar, as has been suggested (1, 5), or whether the prevalence of more massive raw material sources (quartzites in Spain and Bergerac flint in southwest France) stimulated independent invention remains an open question. Certainly the presence of immense flat ovate flakes with the platform trimmed away in a bifacial "retouch of accommodation" in Locality 15 at Choukoutien (personal observation) suggests an independent development of a flake cleaver technique in northern China. The presence of African-style flake cleaver and biface industries at Jisr Banat Yaqub in the Levant (57), where massive basalts were available, and in massive quartzite on the Indian Penninsula, both quite distant from similar industries in Africa, suggests that raw material resources may have been an important factor in the development of such industries. This raw material association is particularly evident in the Levant, where other Acheulian industries (all made on nodular chert) show little evidence of these African techniques.

Variability in the African industries is best examined for the Lower Paleolithic in the well-controlled sequence at Olduvai Gorge. Here there is a relatively prolonged period of contemporaneity of two distinct industries: the Achuelian, characterized by hand axes and other tools made on large flat flakes, and the Developed Oldowan, in which such tools and flakes are absent and there is a prevalence of choppers and spheroids. M. D. Leakey (41) refers these industries to distinct traditions, apparently related to independent populations of hominids. She also sees distinctive variability within the Acheulian; this suggests "that the artifacts from each site or level were made by a group of people who had their own tradition in tool making and standard tool kit from which they did not deviate to any appreciable extent" (41, p. 492). In the absence of any clear trend toward increasing refinement in biface manufacture (41), as had originally been proposed by L. S. B. Leakey (38), the general picture that emerges is a period of perhaps a million years in which the only variability in the stone tool technology of Acheulian hominids seems to have been an apparently random fluctuation in the relative frequencies of particular artifact forms. Possibly more insight into this variability can be gained through a look at the somewhat later African Acheulian manifestations at Isimila or Olorgesailie. Here in two areally and temporally restricted sequences of late Acheulian industries we can see considerable variability in the tool forms produced.

At Isimila 3 types of industries were described (35) based on the relative frequencies of small tools, large sharp-edged tools, and large blunt-edged or "heavy duty" tools. While these industries would all be classified as Acheulian by M. D. Leakey on the basis of the presence of bifacial hand axes and cleavers, the kinds of differences that they exhibit are to some extent reminiscent of the Acheulian-Developed Oldowan variation. One interpretation of the Isimila evidence might be that each of the samples represents a point on a continuum of variability within a single basic industry, with each of the three variants showing a predominance of certain task-specific elements. Given the rather small sample size ($\overline{X} = 90$ for the nine cases) and the presence of some elements in each class in each sample, this does not seem to be an unreasonable assumption. If we examine the ratios of two sets of pairs of variables examined by Kleindienst for the stratigraphic sequence at Isimila and Olorgesailie (35) as shown in Table 2, it appears that: (a) a rather close correlation exists between the presence of shaped tools and larger implements on the one hand and waste and small implements on the other, and (b) at Olorgesailie there is a clear trend through time in the eleven strata from high ratios of waste and small tools to high ratios of shaped tools and large tools and then a gradual return to the original pattern. At Isimila there is a suggestion of a trend from more waste and small tools to more shaped tools and large tools, but it is not as clear as the trend at Olorgesailie. Such differences may indicate shifts in the kinds of tasks performed in a given locality as resources changed over time, the Olorgesailie evidence indicating a possible full cycle in this kind of change. Detailed environmental analysis might substantiate this hypothesis. It does seem likely on the basis of variation in styles of hand axe and cleaver manufacture between samples that many of these occupations may represent distinct limited traditions of implement manufacture within distinct social groups. Perhaps if similarly abundant samples in comparable restricted time periods and spatial loci were available in the million year sequence of Acheulian at Olduvai, similar trends or cyclical patterns might be evident there as well.

In terms of more specific interpretations of social patterns and way of life of Middle Pleistocene man we are limited to too few examples of in situ artifact distributions to make meaningful generalizations. The evidence of Lazaret (44) and Terra Amata (43) is stimulating in this regard, but too limited to warrant a discussion of such variables as group size, domestic patterning, and seasonal scheduling with any degree of confidence. In considering the example of Lazaret in particular, it is worth remembering that caves and rock shelters tend to shape the patterns of occupation by constricting the space within which domestic activities can be carried out. Here the freedom of separation of activities that characterizes an open site may be sacrificed in order to take advantage of the protection afforded by the restricted space of the shelter.

In conclusion, it may be useful to summarize some overall impressions of the Lower Paleolithic on the basis of our present evidence and to review several of the outstanding problems that can now be perceived. The overriding impression of the technological evidence in the archaeological record is one of almost unimaginable monotony. Perhaps the most overwhelming example of this is the Acheulian of Olduvai Gorge, where for approximately a million years no significant innovation is discernable. In other areas, such as western Europe, some gradual trends which appear to represent refinements in man's ability to control the results of his techniques of stone flaking are evident. But even these innovations take place over hundreds of thousands of years; this means that we are talking about tens of thousands of generations of hominids maintaining patterns of technological traditions without discernable change. When, by contrast, we view the diverse succession of industries and proliferation of areally distinct patterns of the Upper Paleolithic, which may in its totality represent between 1200 and 1300 generations, the distinctive character of the Lower Paleolithic becomes evident. The evidence strongly suggests a more limited capacity for the control of variables upon which synthesis and innovation are based and suggests a qualitatively different kind of cultural activity from that familiar to us in the activities of *Homo sapiens sapiens.* There is thus good reason to refer to this Lower Paleolithic pattern as representing a *paleocultural* behavior which differed significantly from the cultural behavior of modern man. One aspect of this difference may have been the absence of the kind of linguistic communication that characterizes modern man. While this limitation has been suggested previously for Lower and Middle Pleistocene hominids it is notoriously difficult, if not impossible, to demonstrate anatomically; perhaps here our technological evidence is the best we will have on the behavior and abilities of these early men.

If we accept such behavioral differences for the Lower Paleolithic men, it follows that attempts to reconstruct their ways of life must, as Isaac has suggested (31), take

Table 2 Ratios of some basic classes of lithic materials from two late Acheulian sites in East Africa

Stratigraphy	Waste (%)	N1	Small tools (%)	N2
Isimila				
SST. 1a; up. J6–J7	42.7	233	9.5	95
SST. 1a; H9–J8	41.9	186	5.3	95
SST. 1a; K14	60.6	434	21.6	125
SST. 1b; lo. J6–J7	76.1	932	42.0	88
SST. 1b; K6	36.4	305	2.6	177
SST. 2; J12	68.2	148	7.5	40
SST. 3; lo. H15	77.4	328	12.2	41
SST. 3; lo. K18 TR2	84.8	1546	54.9	93
SST. 3; K19	71.6	528	23.4	90
Olorgesailie				
L.S. 13	72.7	278	100.0	17
L.S. 12	75.0	88	100.0	3
L.S. 11	70.0	434	81.3	59
L.S. 10	68.2	890	47.9	148
L.S. 9	40.9	215	6.0	99
L.S. 8	58.7	443	14.0	135
L.S. 7	40.5	205	8.1	112
L.S. 6	65.9	740	50.0	150
L.S. 3	61.5	465	73.5	87
L.S. 2	64.3	451	69.8	106
L.S. 1	74.5	428	98.2	70

[a] N1 = number of tools + waste; N2 = number of shaped tools. From Kleindienst (35).

into account the fact that their activities were not completely analagous to those of modern hunter-gatherers, but were distinct from those of any creatures we can presently observe. There is every likelihood that by the Middle Pleistocene, if not before, these hominids were the most intelligent and effective predators on the earth. Even without language they were surely more aware of the potentials of their environment and their fellows than any previous animal population. The adaptations that occurred in these tens of thousands of generations are part of the foundation that underlies modern man's behavioral and cognitive systems.

The Lower Paleolithic does see a transition from man's first use of deliberately fragmented pieces of stone to the manufacture of fully conceived implements whose final form is regularly patterned and in no way suggested by the shape or exterior texture of the stone from which they were made. This is certainly a significant step in conceptualization and foreshadows the more complex innovations of the Middle and Upper Paleolithic. It occurs, however, in the context of the very slow and gradual change that characterizes the whole of this period.

The problems that confront the prehistorian attempting to interpret the Lower Paleolithic are typical of those met by any young branch of science. The few scattered occupation sites that have been subjected to careful excavation are spread over immense distances of space and time. The remainder of our data are from early and less adequate excavations and materials naturally transported from their place of manufacture or use. We are continually attempting to extract any regularities from this slender evidence that we can relate to hypotheses about the activities of these long extinct hominids, beyond the forces that they applied to make their stone tools and the kinds of animal bones that they left as refuse in their camps. In order to see these regularities it is important that we develop a common language to discuss our evidence concerning tool manufacture. Agreement on a universally applicable descriptive vocabulary for the definition of artifact variability should be one of the strongest priorities for Lower Paleolithic research. Such a descriptive system is a necessary foundation for the comparative studies that will enable us to begin to generalize about this aspect of our evidence. It is very unfortunate that we have not yet reached agreement on this fundamental aspect of research. A second major problem area in Lower Paleolithic studies concerns the refinement of chronological relationships between sites and industries; until we are fully aware of the complexity of the Pleistocene record and develop techniques to link our archaeological evidence to an absolute time scale we will be unable to make more than the most general hypotheses concerning the changes occuring in early cultural development. Another area in need of clarification, and barely touched upon in this paper, is the relationship between fossil hominids and the Paleolithic industries. With every new find of *Homo erectus* and similar fossil men in the Middle Pleistocene [such as the recent discovery at Blizingsleben (46)] the specter of "Pre-Sapiens," fostered by spuriously dated fossils such as Galley Hill and Piltdown, becomes less viable, and a gradual evolution paralleling the cultural record seems more likely. There is, however, still much work to be done to clarify this biological and cultural sequence.

Ultimately our aim is to provide a better understanding of the meaning of the variability and conservatism that we can observe in the paleocultural record ot the Lower and Middle Pleistocene in terms of the behavior and development of the fossil men that preceded *Homo sapiens.* In order to do so we must continually reexamine the nature of our evidence and the assumptions that we are making in our interpretation of this record.

Literature Cited

1. Alimen, H.-M. 1975. Les "isthmes" Hispano-Marocain et Siculo-Tunisien aux temps acheuléens. *Anthropologie* 79:399–436
2. Biberson, P. 1964. Torralba et Ambrona. Notes sur deux stations acheuléens de chasseurs d'éléphants de la Vielle Castille. *Inst. Prehist. Arqueol. Barcelona Monogr.* 6:201–48
3. Bordes, F. 1950. Principes d'une méthode d'étude des techniques de débitage et de la typologie du Paléolithique ancien et moyen. *Anthropologie* 54: 19–34
4. Bordes, F. 1961. Typologie du Paléolithique ancien et moyen. *Publ. Inst. Préhist. Univ. Bordeaux Mém.* 1, Vols. 1, 2. 85 pp., 108 pp.
5. Bordes, F. 1966. Acheulian cultures in Southwest France. In *Studies in Prehistory,* ed. D. Sen, A. K. Ghosh, pp. 49–57. Calcutta
6. Bordes, F. 1968. *The Old Stone Age.* New York: McGraw-Hill. 255 pp.
7. Bordes, F. 1971. Observations sur L'Acheuleen des grottes en Dordogne. *Munibe* 23:5–24
8. Bordes, F., Viguier, C. 1971. Sur la

présence de galets taillés de type ancien dans un sol fossile à Puerto de Santa Maria au Nord-Est de la baie de Cadix (Espagne). *C.R. Acad. Sci. Paris Ser. D* 272:1747–49

9. Breuil, H. 1932. Les industries à éclats du Paléolithique ancien I—Le Clactonien. *Préhistoire* 1:125–90

10. Breuil, H. 1939. Bone and antler industry of the Choukoutien *Sinanthropus* site. *Paleontol. Sin.* n.s. D, 6

11. Butzer, K. W., Isaac, G. Ll. 1975. Delimitation of the geologic time term "Middle Pleistocene." In *After the Australopithecines: Stratigraphy, Ecology, and Culture Change in the Middle Pleistocene,* ed. K. W. Butzer, G. Ll. Isaac, pp. 901–3. The Hague: Mouton. 911 pp.

12. Clark, G. 1969. *World Prehistory: A New Outline.* Cambridge Univ. Press. 331 pp.

13. Clark, J. D., Kleindienst, M. R. 1974. The Stone Age cultural sequence: terminology, typology and raw material. In *Kalambo Falls Prehistoric Site,* Vol. 2, ed. J. D. Clark, pp. 71–106. Cambridge Univ. Press

14. Collins, D. 1969. Culture traditions and environment of early man. *Curr. Anthropol.* 10:267–316

15. Coppens, Y., Howell, F. C., Isaac, G. Ll., Leakey, R. E. F., eds. 1976. *Earliest Man and Environments in the Lake Rudolf Basin.* Univ. Chicago Press. 615 pp.

16. Cox, A. 1969. Geomagnetic reversals. *Science* 163:237–45

17. Curtis, G. H., Drake, X., Cerling, T., Hampel, X. 1975. Age of the KBS tuff in the Koobi Fora formation, East Rudolf Kenya. *Nature* 258:395–98

18. Doran, J. E., Hodson, F. R. 1975. *Mathematics and Computers in Archaeology.* Edinburgh Univ. Press. 381 pp.

19. Emiliani, C., Shackleton, N. J. 1974. The Brunhes epoch: Isotopic paleotemperatures and geochronology. *Science* 183:511–14

20. Frenzel, B. 1969. Comment. *Curr. Anthropol.* 10:304–5

21. Fridrich, J. 1976. The first industries from eastern and south-Eastern Central Europe. *Colloq. 8, 9e Congr. Int. Sci. Préhist. Protohist., Nice,* pp. 8–23

22. Frison, G. C. 1968. A functional analysis of certain chipped stone tools. *Am. Antiq.* 33:149–55

23. Gould, R. A., Koster, D. A., Sontz, A. H. 1971. The lithic assemblage of the Western Desert Aborigines of Australia. *Am. Antiq.* 36:149–69

24. Graham, J. M. 1970. Discrimination of British Lower and Middle Paleolithic handaxe groups using canonical variates. *World Archaeol.* 1:321–37

25. Harris, J. W. K., Bishop, W. W. 1976. Sites and assemblages from the Early Pleistocene beds of Karari and Chesowanja. *Colloq. 5, 9e Congr. Int. Sci. Préhist. Protohist., Nice,* pp. 70–117

26. Hay, R. L., 1971. Geologic background of Beds I and II stratigraphic summary. See ref. 40, pp. 9–18

27. Hayes, J. D., Imbrie, J., Shackleton, N. J. 1976. Variations in the Earth's orbit: pacemaker of the Ice Ages. *Science* 194:1121–32

28. Howell, F. C. 1966. Observations on the earlier phases of the European Lower Paleolithic. *Am. Anthropol.* 68 (2–2): 88–201

29. Howell, F. C., Butzer, K. W., Aguirre, E. 1962. Noticia preliminar sobre el emplazamiento acheulense de Torralba (Soria). *Excavaciones Arqueol. Esp.* 10: 1–38

30. Howell, F. C., Clark, J. D. 1963. Acheulian hunter-gatherers of sub-Saharan Africa. In *African Ecology and Human Evolution,* ed. F. C. Howell, F. Bourlière. *Viking Fund Publ. Anthropol.* 36:458–533

31. Isaac, G. Ll. 1975. Stratigraphy and cultural patterns in East Africa during the middle ranges of Pleistocene time. See Ref. 11, pp. 495–542

32. Isaac, G. Ll. 1976. The activities of early African hominids: A review of archaeological evidence from the time span two and a half to one million years ago. See Ref. 33, pp. 483–514

33. Isaac, G. Ll., McCown, E. R. 1976. *Human Origins: Louis Leakey and the East African Evidence.* Menlo Park: Benjamin. 589 pp.

34. Jelinek, A. J. 1976. Form, function, and style in lithic analysis. In *Cultural Change and Continuity: Essays in Honor of James Bennett Griffin,* ed. C. E. Cleland, pp. 19–33. New York: Academic. 378 pp.

35. Kleindienst, M. R. 1961. Variability within the late Acheulian assemblage in Eastern Africa. *S. African Archaeol. Bull.* 16:35–52

36. Kukla, G. J. 1975. Loess Stratigraphy of Central Europe. See Ref. 11, pp. 99–188

37. Laritchev, V. E. 1976. Discovery of hand-axes in China and the problem of local cultures of Lower Paleolith of East

Asia. *Colloq. 7, 9e Congr. Int. Sci. Préhist. Protohist., Nice,* pp. 154–78

38. Leakey, L. S. B. 1951. *Olduvai Gorge.* Cambridge Univ. Press. 164 pp.

39. Leakey, L. S. B., Evernden, J. F., Curtis, G. H. 1961. Age of Bed I, Olduvai. *Nature* 191:478–79

40. Leakey, M. D. 1971. *Olduvai Gorge, Vol. 3: Excavations in Beds I and II, 1960–1963.* Cambridge Univ. Press. 306 pp.

41. Leakey, M. D. 1975. Cultural patterns in the Olduvai sequence. See Ref. 11, pp. 477–93

42. Leakey, R. E. F., Walker, A. C. 1976. *Australopithecus, Homo erectus* and the single species hypothesis. *Nature* 261:572–74

43. Lumley, H. de 1969. A Paleolithic camp at Nice. *Sci. Am.* 220 (5):42–50

44. Lumley, H. de, ed. 1969. Une cabane acheuléenne dans la grotte du Lazaret (Nice). *Mémoires de la Société Préhistorique Française 7.* 234 pp.

45. Malez, M. 1976. Excavation of the Villafranchian Site Šandalja I near Pula (Yugoslavia). *Colloq. 8, 9e Congr. Int. Sci. Préhist. Protohist., Nice,* pp. 104–23

46. Mania, D. L. 1976. Altpaläolithischer Rastplatz mit Hominidenresten aus dem Mittelpleistozänen Travertin-Komplex von Bilzingsleben (DDR). *Colloq. 9, 9e Congr. Int. Sci. Préhist. Protohist., Nice,* pp. 35–47

47. Merrick, H. V. 1976. Recent archaeological research in the Plio-Pleistocene deposits of the Lower Omo, Southwestern Ethiopia. See Ref. 33, pp. 461–81

48. Mortillet, G. de 1872. Classification des diverses périodes de l'Age de la Pierre. *C. R. 6e Congr. Int. Anthropol. Archeol. Préhist., Bruxelles,* pp. 432–44

49. Movius, H. L. 1949. Lower Paleolithic archaeology in Southern Asia and the Far East. *In Studies in Physical Anthropology, No. 1., Early Man in the Far East,* ed. W. W. Howells, pp. 17–81

50. Movius, H. L. 1950. A wooden spear of Third Interglacial age from Lower Saxony. *Southwest J. Anthropol.* 6:139–42

51. Osborn, H. F. 1916. *Men of the Old Stone Age.* New York: Scribner's. 545 pp. 2nd ed.

52. Penck, A., Brückner, E. 1909. *Die Alpen im Eiszeitalter.* Leipzig: Tauchnitz. 1199 pp.

53. Radmilli, A. M. 1976. The first industries of Italy. *Colloq. 8, 9e Congr. Int. Sci. Préhist. Protohist., Nice,* pp. 35–74

54. Roe, D. A. 1968. British Lower and Middle Palaeolithic handaxe groups. *Proc. Prehist. Soc.* 34:1–82

55. Roe, D. A. 1970. Comments on the results obtained by M. J. Graham. *World Archaeol.* 1:338–42

56. Shipman, P., Phillips, J. E. 1976. On scavenging by hominids and other carnivores. *Curr. Anthropol.* 17:170–72

57. Stekelis, M. 1960. The Paleolithic deposits of Jisr Banat Yaqub. *Bull. Res. Counc. Isr. Sect. G* 9:63–90

58. Sutcliffe, A. J. 1970. Spotted hyaena: crusher, gnawer, digester and collector of bones. *Nature* 227:1110–13

59. Thibault, C. 1976. Decouverte de Paléolithique Archaique dans le Nord-Est de l'Iran. *Résumé Commun. 9e Congr. Int. Sci. Préhist. Protohist., Nice,* p. 117

60. Warren, S. H. 1922. The Mesvinian industry of Clacton-on-Sea, Essex. *Proc. Prehist. Soc. East Anglia* 3:597–602

61. Warren, S. H. 1951. The Clactonian flint industry: a new interpretation. *Proc. Geol. Assoc.* 62:107–35

62. White, J. P. 1968. Ston niap bilong tumbuna: the living Stone Age in New Guinea. *In La Préhistoire: Problèmes et Tendances,* ed. F. Bordes, D. de Sonneville-Bordes, pp. 511–16. Paris: Centre Natl. Rech. Sci. 526 pp.

63. Wymer, J. J. 1968. *Lower Paleolithic Archaeology in Britain: As Represented by the Thames Valley.* London: Baker. 429 pp.

Ann. Rev. Anthropol. 1977. 6:33–56

CROSS-CULTURAL COGNITIVE STUDIES

❖9586

Carol R. Ember[1]

Department of Anthropology, Hunter College of the City University of New York, New York, NY 10021

In undertaking a review of cross-cultural cognitive studies, one is naturally inclined to ask what anthropologists have done in this area. The answer unfortunately is very little. This is in spite of the fact that an interest in cognition has recently gained popularity among anthropologists. We have seen the emergence of the fields of *cognitive* and *structural anthropology,* yet studies in these fields have by and large avoided systematic cultural comparisons. Psychologists, on the other hand, have been taking to the field in increasing numbers, and have explicitly and deliberately sought to be cross-cultural (in the minimal sense of comparing two or more cultures). The growth of the field of cross-cultural psychology is attested to by two new journals, the *Journal of Cross-Cultural Psychology* and the *International Journal of Psychology,* and much of cross-cultural psychology is devoted to cognitive pursuits. By necessity then, this review is largely an evaluation of the research done by psychologists.

But before turning to that body of research, I shall address myself to some of the major differences between the anthropological and psychological approaches to cognition, the pros and cons of each strategy, and what I think each can learn from the other. I shall devote some time to this subject because I think it unfortunate that, save for a few individuals and a few collaborative efforts, the two fields are worlds apart. I shall then critically examine some of the substantive areas of cognition that have been investigated cross-culturally. Finally, I will try to make some suggestions about how research in this area might be improved.

COMPARING COGNITIVE APPROACHES IN ANTHROPOLOGY AND PSYCHOLOGY

The goal of cognitive anthropology is to discover the cultural rules or oganizing principles underlying the cultural behavior of particular peoples (100). While this

---

[1]I wish to thank the interlibrary loan staff at Florida Atlantic University for their help in obtaining library material for me while I was there on research leave (1976–77).

33

goal certainly does not by itself preclude comparison, certain attitudes of cognitive anthropologists seem to have contributed to their extremely relativistic and noncomparative orientation.

One of the major impetuses to the development of the "new ethnography" or the "ethnoscience" approach was the belief that traditional ethnography had failed to describe adequately how people cognized their world. Hence the "new ethnographers" renounced "etic" (imposed) categorizations and stressed the need to describe the "emic" view of a group of people. This emphasis on description has tended, I think, to inhibit comparison. For some, this may have been simply because they were too busy describing. For others, a noncomparative view of things appears to be associated with the belief that cultures should not be compared until cultural descriptions are "replicable and accurate" (95) or until the things compared are shown to be "truly comparable" (100). Much the same view characterized Boas's historical particularism. As I shall argue later, in my opinion the noncomparative approach of most anthropologists is unfortunate. Although we may pile up formal descriptions of kinship terminologies, folk taxonomies, etc, just as Boas's students recorded volumes of ethnographic detail, nothing much seems to be done with all the data. The collectors, I submit, do not know what to do with the data because they do not envision any purpose beyond description.

In contrast, the two major goals of cross-cultural psychologists are explicitly comparative (10). One goal is to determine whether different peoples process information differently, and if so why. Are there differences in perception, imagery, recall, problem-solving, learning, categorization, etc? A second goal is to discover whether relationships or principles "demonstrated" in the Western world obtain in other parts of the world. For example, are Piaget's postulated stages of cognitive development found in other cultural contexts? While these goals obviously require the collection of descriptive materials, the comparative frame is explicit. That frame has almost always been "etic" or, rather, "emically Western," which is not surprising since psychologists typically take previously developed measuring devices and findings from "here" to "there."

Advantages and Disadvantages of the Two Approaches

As I see it, the advantage of the psychological approach over the anthropological approach for the most part is that it has been comparative and quantitative. As such I would maintain that it is more likely to lead to explanatory understanding. The anthropological approach on the other hand has the advantage of being concerned with natural categories, cultural context, and the validity of different styles of life. As such I think it is more likely to lead to humanistic understanding. Needless to say, it would be nice if the two could be put together more often.

Although I shall argue that the psychologists have the advantage of being comparative, I think their comparisons have often suffered from latent, if not explicit, ethnocentrism. Whether an individual psychologist means it or not (and I am not claiming intentional bias), most comparisons between "us" and "them" have involved measures and tests developed here. It is not surprising, therefore, that "we" almost always do "better," i.e. score higher, than "they." If psychologists believe (as I think they often do) that their measures are valid for assessing abilities, then their comparisons may become invidious. So, for example, if one believes that classifying objects by form instead of color indicates more "abstract" thinking, African adults seem to think less abstractly than American children! Such comparisons make most anthropologists cringe, and I think rightly so. For almost any anthropologist can probably point to (for a particular people) any number of subject areas in which "they" will be "better" than "we." In fact, in the few instances in which psychologists have developed measures "there" and used them back here (21, 55), Americans fare less well. For example, Americans are more apt to classify leaves or rice "concretely" rather than "abstractly." What is wrong with this type of comparison is not comparison itself but the interpretation put on the comparison. As Campbell has pointed out (18), a difference in scores is not interpretable by itself. Aside from the possibility that there may be a difference in ability, there are at least three equally likely if not more likely possibilities: 1. the measure is not tapping the same ability in the two places; 2. one group may not understand what is expected of them; and 3. one group is not as motivated as the other to "perform" for the investigator. Because of these problems, some cross-cultural psychologists (22) have advocated that we avoid comparisons of degree of "ability." Rather, investigators should try to understand why a given "ability" is applied differently in different situations.

In spite of the unintended ethnocentrism that seems to characterize some of the research in cross-cultural psychology, I think that its comparative approach is and will be more productive than the noncomparative approach that characterizes most of cognitive anthropology. I think so because the finding of differences is thought-provoking and leads to more questions and more research, *even if the interpretations of those differences are faulty.* For example, take the finding that Africans classify more by color than by form, and the probably biased interpretation that they think less abstractly! A myriad of questions arise: Could the difference be due to the fact that we learn more about geometric forms in our schools? Do others classify more "abstractly" than we do in certain domains? If classification varies by domain in different cultures, why does it vary? Do people classify more "abstractly" when they are more familiar with a domain or when it is more important to them? Does type of classification in one domain generalize to other domains? If so, which ones? The questions could continue, but the point is that once the questions are asked, better comparisons can be designed.

With some exceptions of course [see for example (3, 4, 106)], most cognitive anthropologists have chosen not to be comparative, and are content to provide a formal (not quantitative) analysis of the way in which a particular people presumably cognizes a particular semantic domain. But why is there so little curiosity about why some societies utilize certain components for classification and others use others? Perhaps it is because cognitive anthropologists believe it is premature to compare. However, I think that such a belief rests on a faulty notion of what comparison means (see also 40). To compare things does not require that they be the same or completely described. In point of fact, nothing in the world is exactly the same as anything else, and nothing is ever completely describable. To compare means simply that one is able to describe some differences between things in some quantitative or qualitative way. When a componential analyst says that a particular people uses components x, y, and z to classify their kinsmen, there is already a basis of comparison. We can say that another people only uses x, but not y and z. All we have to do to compare is to ask whether two or more cases are the same or different and why.

Comparison, I submit, is possible whenever one wishes to compare. If cognitive anthropologists have chosen generally not to compare, I do not believe it is because comparison is not possible. Comparing and theorizing about differences or similarities does not naturally emerge when the facts are in, only when one believes it is possible. One cannot perceive laws until one looks for them. So it takes a believer in generalizations to discover them. I would venture to say that unless and until cognitive anthropology shakes off its antipathy to cross-cultural comparisons and to quantification, it cannot contribute to an explanatory understanding of how different cultures vary in cognition.

The psychologists are by no means without their faults, and these will, I think, become more obvious as I review some of the substantive areas of research undertaken in the 1970s. Their most serious fault is that they generally fail to realize that the testing situation and their measures are cultural phenomena, which may not be so comprehensible or appropriate in other cultural contexts. (To be sure, many psychologists would argue that many of their "tests" are not even appropriate in all of our subcultural contexts!) In comparison, with all of their faults anthropologists do have an advantage over psychologists. Anthropological training teaches us to be more aware of things from another culture's point of view; therefore anthropologists may be more able to think of reasons for the cognitive differences that are measured by the psychologists. Above all, anthropologists would be cautious about concluding or implying that deficiencies exist in some other population. Perhaps that caution makes anthropologists reluctant to compare altogether. But comparison need not imply "better" or "worse" unless one chooses to interpret the results that way.

Let me now turn to the kinds of cross-cultural cognitive studies that have been conducted in the 1970s. By and large I address myself to studies done since the Triandis, Malpass & Davidson (99) review, mentioning earlier work only where it appears to be particularly influential or unusual. Rather than review this literature exhaustively or by substantive categories per se (e.g. perception, classification, intellectual tasks), I focus on three types of studies. Each of these types in my opinion is characterized by certain faults or advantages. The first type consists of studies that have presumably found differences in "ability" or "skill," which are almost always in the direction of deficiencies for non-Westerners. The second type consists of atheoretical studies of differences and universals in semantic meaning. The third type consists of studies that have been designed to test theories.

COMPARISONS OF "ABILITY" OR "SKILL"

There are very few social scientists today who are not aware of the "culture bias" inherent in the various "intelligence" tests that have been developed. Indeed, it has become increasingly clear that all groups do less well (93) than those for whom the tests were normed in the first place. For this and other reasons, most researchers have ceased to compare the "intelligence" of different cultural groups.

I bring up the issue of intelligence testing first because I think that some of the same issues must be raised with respect to other tests of "cognitive abilities," although the need to do so has not appeared as pressing. Perhaps this is because the comparisons have not appeared as invidious. Yet without evidence that the measures developed here are validly tapping the same abilities elsewhere, we must be skeptical when non-Westerners more or less consistently show "deficiencies" compared with "us." Moreover, as I suggest below, the "deficiencies" may be due to the fact that the cross-cultural psychologists' measures often build in a bias against non-Westerners. I am not suggesting that the observed differences do not tell us anything, but they may suggest that some other difference is being measured than "deficient" cognitive ability.

Findings

PICTORIAL PERCEPTION   Since Hudson's studies in Africa in the 1960s, subsequent research has tended to support the notion that non-Westerners do not perceive depth in pictures or identify the orientation of the picture (where it was taken from) particularly well. [For a review of studies by Hudson and others before 1973, see (71); for subsequent studies, see (69, 101).] Deregowski (34) has attempted to show that non-Western subjects display somewhat more 3-D knowledge if they are asked to build models of pictures rather than respond verbally. Nonetheless, they still do less well than Westerners. The only "superiority" in pictorial perception found so far in non-Westerners, as far as I know, is that when shown an ambiguous "trident" figure Zambians were superior in drawing it precisely because they saw it as flat, not as three-dimensional (35)! As for what may correlate with differential "ability" to perceive depth and orientation in pictures, the most suggestive evidence is that education generally enhances performance [referred to in (71).]

MEMORY   On the basis of anecdotal evidence collected by anthropologists and others, nonliterate peoples have been traditionally expected to excel in memory (21, 22). However, the little systematic research that has been conducted does not generally support that contention, nor the contention that nonliterate peoples would tend to remember by rote (20, 21, 60, 70, 90).

As for factors that might influence memory, there appears to be some appreciable effect of education and urbanism on memory performance of the Kpelle (21). Contrary to what was traditionally expected, educated Kpelle appear to be "superior" on memory tasks as compared with nonliterate Kpelle. A few studies have shown that different stimuli are remembered relatively better than others in different cultures (70, 90), suggesting that the cultural importance of the stimuli may influence memory. I shall return to this point later.

COGNITIVE DEVELOPMENT   A large number of cross-cultural studies have been carried out to examine whether or not postulated stages of cognitive development occur in other societies, and whether or not they are attained by children at similar ages. The bulk of this research deals with Piaget's stages of cognitive development [for recent reviews see (1, 23)]. By and large, researchers have tended to focus on Piaget's stage of concrete operations, and within that on children's notions of conservation. First, I shall deal with the results on rates of development, inasmuch as they relate to the establishment of "ability" differences. I will return later to the results of tests of theory about the supposed sequence of development.

Conservation   The acquisition of the concept of conservation, the idea that certain properties (quantity, number, length) remain invariant in the face of transformations, is one of the major components of concrete-operational thought, according to Piaget (43). This means that the child has the ability to reverse mental operations. If, for example, a child sees water poured from a fat beaker to a tall, skinny cylinder, and when asked says there is the same amount of water in the cylinder as before, then he or she understands the concept of conservation of quantity. The conserver is mentally able to reverse the process and see that the amount is the same both ways.

By and large, most cross-cultural studies find that the attainment of conservation is delayed among non-Westerners, although there are some exceptions with some conservation tests and some subgroups (see 1, 23). In some studies, schooling seems to affect performance positively, in other cases not at all, and in some cases negatively (1, 44). It has been suggested that schooling has little effect on the conservation of weight and mass and more effect on those tasks that require words, drawings, or visual imagery (1, 45). Or it may be that school affects conservation when school involves the active manipulation of objects (1, 32).

Causality   Piaget's theory postulates a developmental increase in causal thinking. Although little research has been done in this area, there is some indication of a developmental "lag" in causal thinking in India (102), Mexico (62), and Western Samoa (62), as compared with children in the United States. In both the United States and Mexico, "advantaged" schoolchildren show more causal thinking than "disadvantaged" (62).

Spatial concepts   Piaget and Inhelder postulated that topological concepts of space (being able to see the relationships within a figure) will develop before projective concepts (being able to see figures related to each other according to a point of view) and Euclidean concepts (being able to locate things in relationship to a coordinate system). Comparing Zulu and white South African children, one study (33) found that the order of development was supported, but Zulu children lagged behind whites. Only on two tasks (out of many) did half the Zulu children attain the stage of "concrete operations." Another study (58) found that Euclidean responses were more likely to be made in more industrialized countries. And in a more limited study looking only at a judgment of perspective, rural Africans lagged behind Europeans (72).

Morality   As with causality and spatial concepts, comparatively little cross-cultural research has been done on moral development, and most has come out of Kohlberg's laboratory. Elaborating on Piaget's suggestions, Kohlberg claims to have shown invariant sequences of development in five different countries—United States, Britain, Taiwan, Mexico, Turkey (61). However, outside of the United States and Britain, boys of 16 do not get to stage 5 or 6 (the "highest" stages). Taiwanese and Mexican boys are not beyond stages 3–4; and in isolated villages in Turkey and Yucatan, 16-year-old boys generally are at stages 1–2. In the Bahamas, White (103) finds that children of 14 are not beyond stages 1–3.

Classificatory ability   In studying classificatory ability, researchers have either used Bruner's developmental framework or Piaget's as a basis for their testing procedures. Bruner [referred to in (22)] suggests that as the child matures there is a shift from the perceptual basis of classification (size, color) to a functional basis of classification. Many researchers speak of a developmental shift from "concrete" to "abstract" principles of grouping. Working in this framework, researchers have usually asked subjects to sort predetermined objects or pictures that vary on two or three dimensions like color, form, and function. Piaget also deals with classificatory abilities and their development. In the phase of concrete operations, classificatory skills involve the ability to reclassify or to use multiple classificatory criteria.

In the cross-cultural studies done in the 1960s, non-Westerners were found generally to lag behind in the development of classificatory skills. Using Western-derived tests, some subsequent studies also show that non-Westerners tend to sort more by color (36) and lag somewhat in "operational" classificatory ability (29, 31); but the differences tend to be erased or lessened when there is similar socioeconomic background (30), high contact with Europeans (30), or when the stimulus materials are varied (25) or made more familiar (55, 77). Education seems to enhance ability to classify cards by form and function rather than by color (21, 41, 47, 54, 89) and seems to enhance verbalization of classificatory criteria (54, 55).

Problems in the Studies of "Ability" and "Skill"

One of the purposes of the research just reviewed was to see if there are differences in cognition or rates of "maturation" from one group to another. Most of the studies reviewed did find differences, largely in the direction of "deficiencies" for non-Westerners. There is no question that differences were observed; the question is how to interpret these differences. As the comparisons stand, there is no way to assess the meaning of the observed differences. They may reflect difference in "ability." But I think a more likely explanation for most of these findings is that the measures do not tap ability equally in all cultures; rather they may be tapping some differences in experience or knowledge which should not be equated with differential "ability" or "skill."

If a measure is tapping difference in experience, which is often culture-specific experience, then the validity of the measuring instrument must be questioned, just as many have questioned the standard intelligence tests as appropriate instruments for cross-cultural comparisons. The charge that the instruments are culturally biased in favor of the place they were developed cannot be dismissed lightly. I submit that this is likely to be the case with most of the research cited above, because the differences largely lie in one direction ("they" usually do worse), and on the few occasions when researchers use "emically" salient domains the differences largely disappear. A further piece of evidence is the role played by factors such as education.

In most developing countries, education is styled after European-American schools. If formally educated individuals in other countries do better than their noneducated contemporaries, then the evidence is suggestive that something learned in school (implicitly or explicitly) is being measured.

The possibility that researchers have simply been measuring unfairly with culturally biased instruments is perhaps greatest in the case of pictorial perception, classificatory ability, and moral development. In the case of pictorial perception, Miller (71) has hypothesized that non-Westerners seem less able to perceive depth or orientation in pictures because they have not learned the *conventions* or *techniques* we use in interpreting such representations. Dawson's (26) finding, that teaching sessions (primarily of drawing) significantly improved the 3-D perception of an experimental group of Temne, supports Miller's suggestion. The fact that increasing education usually increases pictorial perception also gives weight to this suggestion. However, education may exert its effect only if school curricula teach drawing or provide considerable access to pictorial materials.

There may be bias in the measures of classificatory ability for two reasons. First, in most studies the stimuli to be classified are presented on cards and are pictures or drawings of things. Second, very often the objects portrayed are triangles, circles, squares, or other geometric objects. I have already indicated why drawings or pictures may cause trouble for those who have little experience with them. Similarly, lack of experience with geometric figures may hamper classification. If ease of classifying and reclassifying depends on familiar objects, then those who have gone to school, have learned how to draw pictures, and have learned about triangles, circles, and squares may have an advantage. How can people classify "abstractly" when they do not recognize or understand what something is? Price-Williams' (82) early and innovative study of Tiv children's classification of native animals and plants strongly suggests that "classificatory ability" depends on familiarity. Indeed, the few subsequent comparative studies that utilize materials familiar to the subjects found classificatory "ability" that is comparable or superior to that of Europeans (21, 55, 77).

The studies that deal with the development of spatial concepts may suffer from problems that I have already discussed, since they employ tasks involving pictures or geometric figures, the interpretation of which may require familiarity.

The work done on moral development suffers from a different problem, one more properly associated with "culture bias." Simpson (92) points out the ethnocentrism inherent in Kohlberg's stages of "moral development," arguing that a person cannot be coded (according to Kohlberg's manual) as being in "Stage 5" unless his or her society is a constitutional democracy. Similarly, Simpson notes that a person cannot be said to be in "Stage 6" unless he or she is verbally facile with analytical and theoretical words like "justice" and "equality," a facility which may be largely acquired in college courses.

The possibility of measurement bias is less obvious, I think, in tests of conservation, memory, and causality. Nonetheless, that possibility cannot be dismissed. First, the types of instruments or objects used may be strange (for example, beakers and cylinders of water). Second, the testing situation itself or the strangeness of experimenters and experiments may be intimidating to someone who is not familiar with them. For example, Greenfield (46) reports that some Wolof children thought that the experimenter had somehow altered the amount of water in a conservation experiment, but the children did not think so when they poured the water themselves.

That familiarity of material has an effect on conservation attainment is suggested also by Price-Williams (81). He found no difference between Tiv and European children in understanding the conservation of earth, nuts, and number. And Price-Williams, Gordon & Ramirez (84) found (using clay test materials) that children from pottery-making families were significantly more likely than children not from pottery-making families to be "conservers." Of course, it is possible that children familiar with pottery making develop the "conservation" ability earlier than other children, but it is also possible that they just do better because the tests use materials with which they are familiar. Unfortunately, the question is moot, since few subsequent studies have used "emically" familiar materials.

In studies of memory, some researchers have tried to use objects familiar to their subjects (21). But that does not necessarily preclude the possibility of measurement bias. For it is possible that other peoples may not be as attentive to objects as Americans would be. Americans may be particularly fond of objects. A Kenyan student remarked to me one day when we were visiting a museum in this country, "Why do Americans revere objects so much that they have to put them in guarded places in glass cases?" Her comment was very telling about an American value. Why don't Americans feel that they live in a place until they hang pictures or put out decorative objects? If researchers measured memory of things or concepts that are salient in another culture (but not salient to Americans), comparison might show the people in that other culture to be superior. I think it is very suggestive that Ghanaians remember oral prose better than Americans (85) and that Guatemalan schoolchildren remember places better than objects, in contrast to American children who remember objects better than places (70).

In addition to the problem of possible culture bias in measures, there is another serious shortcoming in the studies that have compared "abilities" or "skills." They have not generally addressed themselves to why the observed differences might exist. If one of the goals of cross-cultural psychology is to understand how different cultural or environmental factors may influence cognitive processes, then the finding of differences should be the starting point, not the end point, of investigation (37, 68, 83, 99).

ATHEORETICAL STUDIES OF SEMANTIC DIFFERENCES AND UNIVERSALS

The studies reviewed here, like those of the previous section, are also atheoretical; they contrast with the previous studies in being concerned with semantic distinctions rather than with mental "abilities" or "skills." Not all of the comparative semantic studies have been atheoretical; those that are theoretical will be reviewed in the next section, along with other theoretical studies. Because the semantic studies do not compare people from different cultures with respect to how "well" they do, these studies do not suffer from the possible problems of culture bias.

Findings

THE AFFECTIVE STRUCTURE OF SEMANTIC SPACE   On the basis of research in more than 20 nations, Osgood, May & Miron (78) have suggested that there are certain universal factors in the attribution of "affective" as opposed to denotative meaning. That is, they suggest that all people feel about things along three dimensions—evaluation (e.g. "good" versus "bad"), activity (e.g. "active" versus "passive"), and potency (e.g. "strong" versus "weak"). If there are these universal dimensions of affective meaning, as Osgood and his collaborators suggest, these dimensions can be used to see if particular concepts are viewed similarly in different cultures. To do this they ask subjects to rate concepts on polar-opposite adjectives representing each of these dimensions. (This is called the semantic differential technique.) They have found, for example, that certain colors are viewed in certain affective ways in many cultures (see 78).

PERCEPTION OF PERSONALITY   There has been an attempt to use the semantic differential technique to see if there are cultural universals or differences in the way people perceive the structure of personality. In the United States, Norman (76) asked male college students who knew each other to rate each other on a series of adjectival dimensions of personality. Factor-analyzing the ratings, Norman suggests that there are five independent dimensions in terms of which his subjects rate personality. One study (49) replicated Norman's results in Manila; and another study (12) replicated them in Japan. On both of the replications, Norman's first two factors appeared to emerge—extroversion and agreeableness (which may correspond to Osgood's activity and evaluative dimensions, respectively)—suggesting some universality. But not all of the factors Norman found emerged in the replications.

BODY-BUILD STEREOTYPES   In the United States it has been shown that certain behavioral and personality characteristics are stereotypically associated with different body types. Recently, investigators have begun to look at other cultural settings to see if the same kinds of stereotyping occur. Mexican children (65) and Japanese adolescents and university students (56, 64) seem to report similar associations between various body builds and certain personality or behavioral characteristics.

JUDGMENT OF EMOTION   There have been two approaches with regard to whether or not there are universals in the judgment of emotions. One approach uses semantic-differential contrasts, and it appears that there is some cross-cultural consistency in the rating of emotional expressions (reviewed in 87, also 86). The second approach is to ask people from different cultures to label the affect in pictures. Ekman and his associates (reviewed in 38) have reported substantial agreement across six cultures in such labeling. However, there may not be as high a degree of agreement in nonliterate as opposed to literate societies (39).

Problems With Atheoretical Semantic Studies

Most of the research described in this section has been concerned with universals of semantic meaning. Unfortunately, there is some question as to how universal the findings are, since most of the research has relied on testing highly educated individuals with paper and pencil tests. And even though Osgood, May & Miron (78) studied over 20 nations, most of them were Indo-European speakers. If a claim is to be made for universality, the pursuit has to be carried to many populations speaking languages from many different language families. In addition, the individuals sampled should not all be literate and highly educated. Obviously, measures other than paper and pencil tests have to be devised to give nonliterate populations a chance to show whether or not certain semantic phenomena are universal. Word-association tasks might be used profitably in this regard, although to date they also have been limited to literate samples (97).

The heavy reliance on factor analysis in the studies just reviewed also presents a problem. First, although factor analysis is a valuable technique for summarizing data, there is a certain amount of subjective judgment involved in deciding what a factor "means." Second, since in two different cultures the "loading" on a supposed factor is never quite the same, a judgment of universality must also be somewhat subjective. If the investigator is prone to see universality, he or she might be more likely to find it. Research seeking universals would profit therefore from the use of additional measures to corroborate the factor-analytic findings.

Although the search for universals is a legitimate pursuit, I personally feel that a good deal more mileage could have been obtained from the studies reviewed above if the authors had explored how some of the differences found might be explained. For example, Bond, Nakazato & Shiraishi (12) found in personality ratings that the factor of agreeableness appeared to be more important in the Philippines and the factor of extroversion appeared to be more important in Japan. These differences, they suggest, might be related to the fact that "getting along with others" is more valued in the Philippines while "fitting into the hierarchy" is more valued in Japan. This suggestion could be tested cross-culturally, and probably also intra-culturally. For example, are hierarchical societies more attentive to some aspects of personality than to others? One could investigate such a question at the same time one looks for universals, if the researcher has some idea of what makes for differences in semantic saliences in the cultures under study.

THEORETICAL STUDIES

We now turn to research which is more explicitly oriented to testing theory. There are two types of theory-testing studies—those that test theories supposedly explaining universals and those that test theories supposedly explaining differences. Because these two types of theory-testing research do not have quite the same problems, I shall deal with them separately.

Studies of Presumed Universal Principles

One of the aims of social science is to see if principles which have been shown to obtain in one cultural setting work in others. If we are to have a science of *human* (not specifically Western) behavior, this is obviously a necessary aim. However, difficulties in interpretation arise if principles do not work out the same in other places. If there are differences, it is difficult to know how to interpret them—they may be due to problems of measurement, problems of research design, or to the possible nonuniversality of the principles. To illustrate these difficulties of interpretation, let us examine the cross-cultural attempts to test Piaget's theory of stages of cognitive development.

Aside from comparing *rates* of cognitive development, most of the cognitive development studies referred to earlier also had a second purpose—to see if the sequence of theoretical stages postulated by Piaget is universal. However, the problems of measurement that we discussed earlier may seriously impede that purpose, particularly since most studies relied only on one (or a few) measures of a particular supposed stage of development, and those measures were developed in Geneva.

If a particular test is not appropriate for the culture studied and does not adequately measure the ability in question, one cannot be sure what the results mean. How do we know if a test is appropriate for a particular culture? One strategy is to employ a battery of items, as Super (96) has done in Zambia. Comparing children of different ages, many of the tests showed significant changes between 5–7 years of age, as theory would suggest. Not all tests indicated this, but a general pattern emerged. Another strategy is to combine testing with extensive interviewing in the more clinical tradition of Piaget, as Bovet (14) has done in Algeria. The researcher thereby has a chance to explore how the child responds (or does not respond) to the "test." But one of the most useful strategies may be to look for shifts in development using "emic" materials as part of the testing procedure. Innovative in this regard is the study by LeVine & Price-Williams (67) of children's handling of their own kinship system to indicate changes in cognitive development. For example, young children can indicate how someone relates to them, but cannot until a later age indicate how two others relate to each other.

There is another problem with these studies, which stems from their usual design. Since most studies have looked at just one stage (usually "concrete operations") in the presumed sequence, most have not in fact been able to falsify or confirm the postulated sequence. Only measures for each of several stages can do that. However, even if measures for different presumed stages are used, and even if children of different ages show the predicted differences on these measures, we would still not have evidence that individual children do in fact develop cognitively, as theorized. What we need are either longitudinal studies or the kind of comparison across ages that Feldman et al (42) employed. They used "hierarchical" tests in which the operations required at a theoretically "higher" level incorporate the abilities at a presumed "lower" level. Thus, if children show the profile of abilities predicted by the theory, we can be more sure that they have in fact developed in the way Piaget postulated.

What then do the cross-cultural studies that have been done suggest about Piaget's theory? Generally the age trends that have been found, particularly those regarding the attainment of "concrete operations," are not inconsistent with Piaget's theory—older children are more likely than younger children to attain that stage as measured. But, as I have pointed out, the many problems of measurement and research design may make it difficult to interpret these results as necessarily indicating that children pass through these stages in sequence. Piaget has also theorized about the sequence of cognitive development within the major stages. Here the evidence, at least with reference to the sequence of conservation concepts (within "concrete operations"), is somewhat contradictory to his theory (14, 32; see also 24).

Studies of "universals" must try to adapt their measures to the culture under study. If not, the results will be largely uninterpretable, as I have argued the comparisons of "abilities" and "skills" are uninterpretable by themselves.

Explanations of Differences

Although problems of measurement and research design obviously do not disappear when one attempts to test theories that explain differences in cognition, the problems associated with such studies are, I think, fewer and less serious than the problems associated with the other kinds of studies reviewed above. First, there is more assurance that a measure is valid if the researcher finds the difference predicted by his or her theory. Second, when one attempts to explain a difference in cognition as a function of different life conditions, experiences, adaptational requirements, or physiology, there is usually no evaluative component attributed to the cognitive difference (although, as we shall see, some of the evaluation problem still remains). Third, and perhaps most important, the postulation of an explanation, even if it turns out to be incorrect, seems to provoke alternative explanations and further research.

In asking why people in different societies perceive or cognize their world in different ways, most cross-cultural studies with a theoretical bent have looked to socio-environmental factors to explain variability. Most recently, however, some researchers have suggested that psychophysiological differences among populations may, in part, account for differences in perception and cognition.

SOCIETAL COMPLEXITY   In the few instances where comparisons of semantic domains were made by anthropologists, the major independent variable proposed to account for the difference is cultural or societal complexity. Berlin & Kay (4) proposed that, as societies increase in complexity, they acquire additional basic color terms in a certain more or less fixed sequence. Berlin (3) has also proposed, with reference to plant taxonomies, that different levels of classification are added in an evolutionary sequence correlated with increasing development. And Witkowski (106) has shown that, within the domain of kinship, societal complexity correlates with some increases in semantic distinctions.

The Berlin & Kay (4) formulation of a theory about why different societies encode color in different ways provides a very striking example of how productive the formulation of a theory (with some supportive data) can be. Not only did it generate criticism, it also generated further testing (50, 51, 53, 74), speculation as to how societal complexity might exert its effect (50, 107), and an alternative psychophysiological hypothesis (reviewed later). Although there has not yet been any formal test of the relationship between societal complexity and growth of plant taxonomies, Berlin's (3) work has generated a great deal of comment, as can be judged by the fact that in a recent issue of the *American Ethnologist* devoted to folk biology, almost all the articles referred to that work. Others have started to generalize about additional types of folk classification (16, 17).

Subsequent research has given substantial support to Berlin & Kay's (4) theoretical speculations about basic color terms. First, Berlin & Kay postulated that, regardless of variation in terms, there would be cross-cultural agreement on the foci of colors. Their own evidence consisted of the colors bilingual students in the United States picked out as "best colors" for their native languages. Although it could be argued that such students may have been affected by U.S. conceptions of color, two studies conducted elsewhere support the notion of basic focal colors. E. R. Heider (53) found that the Dani (a New Guinea group which has only two basic color terms) remembered the supposedly universal focal colors significantly better than nonfocal colors, and Harkness (50) found that, in spite of different color lexicons, Spanish and Mam (a Mayan language) speakers agreed on best examples of colors.

One of the problems with most of the anthropological work on semantic domains is that the cognitive data are elicited from just one or, at best, a few informants [but see (50, 53) for more adequate samples]. While the semantic distinctions of a few informants may be widely shared, particularly in less complex societies, they may not be. Even in an unstratified society like the Dani, E. R. Heider (52) has pointed out that informants varied in their color lexicons. All her informants in a large sample agreed on two basic terms, but half used a third term as well. Given then that individuals may differ even in a less complex society, field-workers eliciting cognitive materials should use a (preferably random) sample of informants. An additional reason for employing a sample of informants is that variation among individuals can be used to advantage. For example, Harkness (50) found that Berlin & Kay's (4) "earliest" basic color terms seem to be learned first by children.

The studies just discussed will probably stimulate more theorizing and research. One of the major questions is to ask what it is about cultural complexity that affects the size and structure of semantic domains. Other questions include (see also 106): Do these supposed effects apply to the population as a whole or only to specialists? Do some domains of cognition increase in complexity while others diminish? How and why does cognitive encoding change? What other aspects of culture might variation in encoding relate to? Do societies more dependent on plants than animals, for example, differ in the size and complexity of plant versus animal taxonomies?

VISUAL ENVIRONMENT Segall, Campbell & Herskovits (88) have hypothesized that a people's "visual environment" will influence their susceptibility to different illusions. In particular, they proposed that people from "carpentered" environments would tend to be more susceptible to the Müller-Lyer and Sander parallelogram illusions and that people who live in "open vistas" would tend to be more susceptible to the horizontal-vertical illusion. These hypotheses have prompted a great deal of discussion and subsequent research (8, 11, 15, 28, 59, 63, 94). Although subsequent studies have given qualified support to this interpretation (8, 11, 28, 59, 94), there are two alternative hypotheses. One, which Segall et al (88) themselves discussed, is that susceptibility to some illusions, particularly those like the Müller-Lyer illusion, may depend upon prior experience with pictures and the conventions of interpreting two-dimensional drawings as three-dimensional (see also 63). The second alternative hypothesis, which I shall discuss later, suggests that psychophysiological differences may account for the results. [For descriptions of the illusions mentioned, see (88).]

The hypothesis that certain illusion susceptibilities may be influenced by familiarity with drawings and pictures is not necessarily alternative to the "carpentered-world" hypothesis, because both conditions may be part of the more general visual environment to which a person is exposed. Pictures and drawings may be displayed in the school environment. However, it is possible that just one of the factors (e.g. knowledge of pictures) is the critical part of the visual environment, not the other. And since "carpenteredness" and exposure to conventions of 3-D representation in pictures largely co-occur, the "familiarity with pictures" hypothesis could account for the previous results. Suggestive as this hypothesis is, no research has explicitly compared the two hypotheses. To do so one would have to measure susceptibility to illusions, 3-D pictorial representations, and "carpenteredness" of the environment, simultaneously.

SOCIALIZATION AND ADAPTATION   A theoretical orientation that I think has a great deal of potential is the ecological/adaptational orientation. Berry has advocated this theoretical model as it might be applied to understanding variation in perceptual and cognitive processes (9). He suggests that different perceptual and cognitive processes may be selected and trained for in societies that differ in their adaptational requirements. Berry's model has obvious parallels to the Whiting & Child (104) model of how ecology, largely through socialization, affects modal personality.

The major application of this orientation to date has been with respect to societal and subcultural variation in what is referred to as "field independence" and "field dependence." As formulated by Witkin and his colleagues (105), "field independence" and "field dependence" theoretically refer to different perceptual "styles," each of which is believed to be a general response tendency to a variety of perceptual experiences. Field independence refers to the "tendency for parts of the field to be experienced as discrete from the field as a whole," whereas in field dependence parts are "fused with field, or experienced as global."

Berry (5, 7) has argued that differences in perceptual style might be selected for by different ecological demands. For example, he suggests that the demands of a hunting ecology would require field independence: hunters must develop the ability to see things such as animals in visual isolation from their backgrounds, and must learn to visualize themselves in precise relation to their surroundings so they can find animals and get back home. Enlarging his 1966 (5) two-sample comparison between the Temne and the Eskimo to eight samples of subsistence-level peoples (one traditional and one transitional community in each of four societies), Berry (7) predicted and found that degree of dependence on hunting correlated with greater field independence.

Differential socialization has also been used to explain variation in field dependence/independence. Expanding on Witkin's intracultural findings, Dawson (26) postulated that people in societies with "stricter" child-rearing would be more field dependent. Both on the basis of intra- and inter-cultural comparisons, Dawson's (26) and Berry's (5, 7) studies support that relationship. However, the socialization hypothesis is by no means alternative to the ecological/adaptational hypothesis. As Barry, Child & Bacon (2) suggested, different socialization practices may be adaptive in different economies. In particular, they argued that hunter-gatherers are likely to train children to be individualistic and assertive, and agriculturalists/herders are likely to train children to be compliant and obedient (presumably by "stricter" training). Berry (7) expects both child-training and subsistence to work similarly in determining field independence or dependence—hunters should be more field independent both because their mode of subsistence requires that "style" and because their child-training would not be as strict.

With respect to more commercialized societies, it has been argued that the demands of "economic development" require more "field independence" (48). Indeed, in a cross-national study of managers and technicians in 22 non-Western countries, Gruenfeld & MacEachron (48) found such a correlation—the more "developed" the nation, the more field independence.

Although I have argued that theoretical studies (because they try to explain differences) do not usually involve an evaluative comparison, unfortunately that has not been quite true for some of the field independence/dependence studies. Witkin thinks of field independence as more "developed" than field dependence inasmuch as he believes that psychological development proceeds from lesser to greater differentiation; for example, children in this country have been observed to become more field independent as they grow older. However, as Cohen (19) has pointed out, this trend might appear in our society precisely because our school system pushes (and is biased toward) the "analytic" (or "independent") style in its curriculum and tests. If different styles are adaptive for different conditions, there should be no connotation that one is "better" than another. Field dependence may be adaptive in societies in which social context and smooth relations are of primary importance (73, 98).

Although field independence/dependence appears to be predictively associated with theoretically postulated variables, problems of measurement validity do not necessarily "go away." For example, I think that some question needs to be raised about two of the most frequently used measures of field independence/dependence —the embedded figures test (EFT) and Kohs block design test (BT), both of which involve pictures or drawings which may be more familiar to some people than to others (see also 66). There is some suggestion that EFT and BT may reflect "educational ability" since Siann (91) found that those two tests correlate more highly with a test of "verbal ability" than with another presumed test of field independence/dependence—the rod-and-frame test (RFT). Another possibility is that EFT (and probably also BT) is an appropriate measure of field independence/dependence only in people who are educated (and presumably familiar with pictures and drawings). I say this because RFT is sometimes not correlated with EFT in subsamples which seem to me to be less educated [see the review of studies in (105)]. The rod-and-frame test may be a generally more appropriate measure of field independence/dependence because it involves an apparatus rather than pictures or drawings. Unfortunately, it has not been employed extensively as yet in cross-cultural studies.

Most of the studies of field independence/dependence I have just discussed compare more than two societies. But they were unusual—a majority of the studies in this area [for references see (105)] compare just two cultures. But a comparison of just two cultures cannot show convincingly whether the observed difference is likely to be an effect of the presumed cause, because a two-culture comparison could by chance support a theoretical prediction more often than the comparison of a larger number of cultures. To be sure, a two-culture comparison can show a significant difference between the two cultures (e.g. by t-test), but the presumed independent variable cannot be significantly linked to the difference since the independent variable has not been manipulated experimentally. When a larger number of cultures is compared, even without experimental manipulation, we can test for the statistical significance of the relationship between the supposed cause and supposed effect. All of this suggests that researchers in this area should consider doing one or both of two kinds of study that allow for statistical testing of the postulated linkage between supposed causes and effects (37, 66). Either they can capitalize on intracultural variation to test for such linkages (e.g. 5, 26), and/or they can use a number of cultures in their comparison (e.g. 7). Doing research in a number of societies is obviously very costly and time-consuming, but perhaps researchers could use the data collected by others, as the cross-cultural anthropologists have been doing for years.

PSYCHOPHYSIOLOGICAL FACTORS   In Berlin & Kay's (4) explanation of differences in color lexicons and in Segall, Campbell & Herskovits' (88) interpretation of differential illusion susceptibility, the researchers assumed that there were no physical differences in ability to perceive color or length of lines. Recently this assumption has been questioned by Bornstein (13) with reference to color lexicons and by Pollack (80) and Bornstein (13) with respect to illusion susceptibility. Variation in eye pigmentation and pupil size may affect both abilities.

There is some evidence (reviewed in 13) that more pigmented peoples (with their more pigmented eyes) have reduced sensitivity to the short wavelength (the blue) side of the color spectrum. This difference may affect color terminology. Bornstein shows that there are more semantic equations between blue and green and blue-green-black on the average in those societies closer to the equator. Evaluating cross-cultural data statistically, M. Ember (*Am. Anthropol.* 79. In press) finds that peoples closer to the equator are indeed significantly more likely to have fewer basic color terms.

Although the Bornstein hypothesis is not presented necessarily as alternative to the Berlin & Kay hypothesis, it is possibly alternative since more complex cultures tend to be farther away from the equator. Hence differences in eye pigmentation could account for Berlin & Kay's results. It seems, however, that there may be an interaction between biological and cultural factors. In a control analysis, M. Ember (*Am. Anthropol.* 79. In press) has found that cultural complexity predicts number of basic color terms only at higher latitudes. Thus cultural complexity may influence the number of color terms *only* when a people can readily perceive differences at the "blue" end of the spectrum.

While greater eye pigmentation may decrease sensitivity to certain colors, it may enhance the ability to judge line lengths in the Müller-Lyer (M-L) illusion because of reduction in chromatic aberration and an increase in directed light paths due to decreased pupil size (13). Highly pigmented peoples, then, would be expected to be *less* susceptible to the M-L illusion. Does the "retinal pigmentation" hypothesis explain the cross-cultural differences better than the "carpentered-world" hypothesis of Segall, Campbell & Herskovits?

Some suggestion that the retinal pigmentation hypothesis works better comes from Berry (8), who found that pigmentation (judged from photos) was a stronger predictor of susceptibility to the M-L illusion than "carpenteredness" (also measured judgmentally); and when Berry did a partial control analysis, pigmentation was a more powerful predictor. There are other indications that retinal pigmentation may be more important than visual experience. First, the color of the M-L illusion affects illusion susceptibility (57, 80). Second, susceptibility to that illusion declines with age (80). These two findings are not consistent with the visual experience hypothesis.

However, some evidence contrary to the pigmentation hypothesis comes from two intracultural comparisons. Stewart (94) compared blacks and whites in the United States and found no significant difference in illusion susceptibility. And the data in Bolton et al (11), comparing two Peruvian communities at different altitudes, were more in accord with the Segall, Campbell & Herskovits hypothesis than with the pigmentation hypothesis. More comparisons of the two hypotheses are clearly called for.

It seems apparent that the postulation of a biological explanation as an alternative to a cultural explanation has provoked researchers to begin to design research to evaluate the two alternatives explicitly. However, more attention should be paid to measuring eye pigmentation directly [as Stewart (94) has done]—distance to the equator or altitude or inspection of photographs are indirect measures. With respect to illusion susceptibility, the possible confounding effect of differences in familiarity with pictorial material (and interpreting two dimensions as three dimensions) must also be considered.

The possible influence of biology on the production of color lexicons and illusion susceptibility certainly is provocative. Might eye pigmentation also affect the abilities portrayed in certain pencil and paper tests that depend on contours or are portrayed in different colors? Jahoda's (57) finding that students from Malawi did better on judging geographical contours in red rather than blue (whereas Scottish students were not affected) suggests that color of testing materials might affect many of the results of other studies. The possible effects of physical differences are by no means limited to eye pigmentation. Recently some have suggested that degree of lateralization of the brain may also affect cognitive styles (27, 28, 79). Such a suggestion is at this time highly tentative, but such lines of inquiry need to be pursued.

SUMMARY AND CONCLUSIONS

At the outset I noted that anthropological and psychological approaches to cognition have tended to be extremely divergent. Cognitive anthropologists have by and large avoided comparison and quantification, stressing the need to describe "emic" categories and classification. Cross-cultural psychologists have been explicitly comparative, most often using measures elsewhere that were developed in their native countries. Thus their comparative frame has almost always been "etic," or rather "emically Western."

This difference between the two approaches underlies, I think, some of the most fundamental problems in cross-cultural research on cognition. On the anthropological side, the sin is largely one of omission. Having seemingly chosen *not to compare* (perhaps out of a fear of being evaluative), cognitive anthropologists usually have not involved themselves in trying to explain differences and similarities in cognition, nor even in helping psychologists do a better job of designing more appropriate testing materials. On the psychological side (where it is easier to be more critical of sins of commission), the most fundamental problems seem to result from a lack of awareness or understanding of the other culture. Most seriously, there seems to be little awareness that the measures used may be full of our cultural biases and therefore highly inappropriate to the task of comparing across cultures. Psychologists, I have argued, would do well to consider actively the hypothesis that their measures may be biased. To this end, researchers should employ a variety of measuring instruments, including at least some that use "emic" domains or at least have "emic" salience [see (6) and (83) for suggestions]. Or measures based on behavior observations might be used (75). And if researchers feel obliged to compare "abilities," it would be well for them to develop yardsticks "there" and bring them back "here" to see if the "abilities" still differ in favor of Westerners.

In one sense psychologists have been too comparative, and in another sense not comparative enough. The sense in which they have been too comparative is in the comparison of "abilities" or "skills" between "us" and "them." As I have tried to show, such comparisons suffer from the most serious problems, and lend themselves too easily to the facile finding of "deficiencies" on the part of others. A more profitable (and more ethical) strategy is to design research to test ideas about *why* there might be differences, even if the hypothesis is simply that lack of familiarity accounts for the differences or that the test is measuring something we pick up in our school system. Unfortunately, few studies have been explicitly designed to test theories or even simple hypotheses. As I think my review indicates, the relatively few theory-testing studies have been most productive in stimulating alternative explanations and additional research. Moreover, if a theory provides an explanation for *why* differences in life conditions may lead to differences in performance on cognitive tasks, the possibility of negative or ethnocentric evaluation is minimized.

The sense in which psychologists have not been comparative enough is that by and large comparisons have been limited to two cultures at a time (usually "us" versus one other culture). Even if the psychologist has a theory about what feature of the other culture might account for the difference, he or she does not gain much mileage out of the comparison even if the difference is in the expected direction, for any aspect of the other culture might account for the difference! Even if the researcher does not have the funds (and the time) to conduct fieldwork in additional cultures, the theoretical prediction could be tested directly by making an intracultural comparison to see if individuals or groups differing on the presumed independent variables differ as predicted on the dependent variables (see also 37, 66). I suspect that intracultural tests have not been conducted often for much the same reasons that sampling designs have not usually been adequate—namely, studying intracultural variation and obtaining representative samples both require a good deal of time in the field, primarily because of the need to determine background characteristics. Of course, the best comparative strategy—the one most appropriate for testing theory about cross-cultural variation—is to look at many more than two cultures in which intracultural comparisons could also be made.

In spite of the problems discussed here, comparative studies (even those with the most serious problems) have provoked many interesting questions. Many of those questions are specific to particular areas of research, but we can point to a number of general issues. One of the most potentially interesting is the possible effect of Western style education on cognition. We really do not know much about how schooling affects "thinking" in our society, since school universally correlates with age. However, given the variable attendance at school in many parts of the world, and given that education often relates in some way to the various "abilities" that have been studied, we should now begin directly to investigate the effects of schooling. The possible influence of differences in eye pigmentation, not only perhaps on color terms and illusion susceptibility, but also on how different people respond to test materials, suggests that biological differences cannot be ignored. It may be that many cognitive differences are produced by an interaction between cultural and biological factors.

Cross-cultural psychologists have made us aware of many apparent cognitive differences that need to be explained. Cognitive anthropologists have collected extensive data on native semantic domains. Although anthropologists have not generally done comparative studies or tried to explain differences, their data are available for comparison. What we need now is more studies that try to test explanations. If such studies increase, the field of cross-cultural cognitive studies could become very exciting. Curiosity has no limits.

Literature Cited

1. Ashton, P. T. 1975. Cross-cultural Piagetian research: an experimental perspective. *Harv. Educ. Rev.* 45:475–506
2. Barry, H., Child, I., Bacon, M. 1959. Relation of childtraining to subsistence economy. *Am. Anthropol.* 61:51–63
3. Berlin, B. 1972. Speculations on the growth of ethnobotanical nomenclature. *Lang. Soc.* 1:51–86
4. Berlin, B., Kay, P. 1969. *Basic Color Terms: Their Universality and Evolution.* Berkeley: Univ. California Press. 178 pp.
5. Berry, J. W. 1966. Temne and Eskimo perceptual skills. *Int. J. Psychol.* 1: 207–29
6. Berry, J. W. 1969. On cross-cultural comparability. *Int. J. Psychol.* 4:119–28
7. Berry, J. W. 1971. Ecological and cultural factors in spatial perceptual development. *Can. J. Behav. Sci.* 3:324–36
8. Berry, J. W. 1971. Müller-Lyer susceptibility. Culture, ecology, or race? *Int. J. Psychol.* 6:193–97
9. Berry, J. W. 1976. *Human Ecology and Cognitive Style.* New York: Wiley. 242 pp.
10. Berry, J. W., Dasen, P. R., eds. 1974. *Culture and Cognition: Readings in Cross-Cultural Psychology,* p. 13. London: Methuen. 487 pp.
11. Bolton, R., Michelson, C., Wilde, J., Bolton, C. 1975. The heights of illusion: on the relationship between altitude and perception. *Ethos* 3:403–24
12. Bond, M. H., Nakazato, H., Shiraishi, D. 1975. Universality and distinctiveness in dimensions of Japanese person perception. *J. Cross-Cult. Psychol.* 6: 346–57
13. Bornstein, M. H. 1973. The psychophysiological component of cultural difference in color naming and illusion susceptibility. *Behav. Sci. Notes* 8:41–101
14. Bovet, M. C. 1974. Cognitive processes among illiterate children and adults. See Ref. 10, pp. 311–34
15. Brislin, R. W. 1974. The Ponzo illusion: additional cues, age, orientation, and culture. *J. Cross-Cult. Psychol.* 5: 139–61
16. Brown, C. H. 1976. General principles of human anatomical partonomy and speculations on the growth of partonomic nomenclature. *Am. Ethnol.* 3: 400–24
17. Brown, C. H., Kolar, J., Torrey, B. J., Truong-Quang, T., Volkman, P. 1976.

Some general principles of biological and non-biological folk classification. *Am. Ethnol.* 3:73–85
18. Campbell, D. T. 1964. Distinguishing differences of perception from failures of communication in cross-cultural studies. In *Cross-Cultural Understanding: Epistemology in Anthropology,* ed. F. S. C. Northrop, H. H. Livingston, pp. 308–36. New York: Harper & Row. 396 pp.
19. Cohen, R. 1969. Conceptual style, culture conflict and non-verbal tests of intelligence. *Am. Anthropol.* 71:828–56
20. Cole, M., Gay, J., Glick, J. 1968. A cross-cultural investigation of information processing. *Int. J. Psychol.* 3:93–102
21. Cole, M., Gay, J., Glick, J., Sharp, D. W. 1971. *The Cultural Context of Learning and Thinking.* New York: Basic Books. 304 pp.
22. Cole, M., Scribner, S. 1974. *Culture and Thought: A Psychological Introduction.* New York: Wiley. 227 pp.
23. Dasen, P. R. 1972. Cross-cultural Piagetian research: a summary. *J. Cross-Cult. Psychol.* 3:23–39
24. Dasen, P. R. 1972. The development of conservation in Aboriginal children: a replication study. *Int. J. Psychol.* 7: 75–85
25. Davidoff, J. 1972. The effect of colour distraction on a matching task in Ghanaian children. *Int. J. Psychol.* 7:141–44
26. Dawson, J. L. M. 1967. Cultural and physiological influences upon spatial-perceptual processes in West Africa. Parts I and II. *Int. J. Psychol.* 2:115–28, 171–85
27. Dawson, J. L. M. 1972. Temne-Arunta hand-eye dominance and cognitive style. *Int. J. Psychol.* 7:219–33
28. Dawson, J. L. M. 1973. Temne-Arunta hand-eye dominance and susceptibility to geometric illusions. *Percept. Mot. Skills* 37:659–67
29. deLacy, P. R. 1970. A cross-cultural study of classificatory ability in Australia. *J. Cross-Cult. Psychol.* 1:293–304
30. deLacy, P. R. 1971. Classificatory ability and verbal intelligence among high-contact Aboriginal and low-socioeconomic white Australian children. *J. Cross-Cult. Psychol.* 2:393–96
31. deLacy, P. R. 1971. Verbal intelligence, operational thinking and envi-

ronment in part-Aboriginal children. *Aust. J. Psychol.* 23:145–59

32. deLemos, M. M. 1969. The development of conservation in Aboriginal children. *Int. J. Psychol.* 4:255–69

33. deLemos, M. M. 1974. The development of spatial concepts in Zulu children. See Ref. 10, pp. 367–80

34. Deregowski, J. B. 1968. Difficulties in pictorial depth perception in Africa. *Br. J. Psychol.* 59:195–204

35. Deregowski, J. B. 1972. Pictorial perception and culture. *Sci. Am.* 227:82–88

36. Deregowski, J. B., Serpell, R. 1971. Performance on a sorting task: a cross-cultural experiment. *Int. J. Psychol.* 6: 273–81

37. Eckensberger, L. H. 1973. Methodological issues of cross-cultural research in developmental psychology. In *Life-Span Developmental Psychology: Methodological Issues,* ed. J. R. Nesselroade, H. W. Reese, pp. 43–64. New York: Academic. 364 pp.

38. Ekman, P. 1973. Universal facial expressions in emotion. *Stud. Psychol. Bratislava* 15:140–47

39. Ekman, P., Sorenson, E. R., Friesen, W. V. 1969. Pan-cultural elements in facial displays of emotion. *Science* 164:86–88

40. Ember, M. 1970. Taxonomy in comparative studies. In *A Handbook of Method In Cultural Anthropology,* ed. R. Naroll, R. Cohen, pp. 697–706. Garden City, NY: Natural History. 1017 pp.

41. Evans, J. L. 1975. Learning to classify by color and by class: a study of concept discovery within Colombia, S. America. *J. Soc. Psychol.* 97:3–14

42. Feldman, C., Lee, B., McLean, J., Pillemer, D., Murray, J. 1974. *The Development of Adaptive Intelligence.* San Francisco: Jossey-Bass. 142 pp.

43. Flavell, J. H. 1963. *The Developmental Psychology of Jean Piaget,* p. 245. Princeton, NJ: Van Nostrand. 472 pp.

44. Furby, L. 1971. A theoretical analysis of cross-cultural research in cognitive development: Piaget's conservation task. *J. Cross-Cult. Psychol.* 2:241–55

45. Goodnow, J. 1969. Problems in research on culture and thought. In *Studies in Cognitive Development: Essays In Honor Of Jean Piaget,* ed. D. Elkind, J. Flavell, pp. 439–62. New York: Oxford Univ. Press. 303 pp.

46. Greenfield, P. M. 1966. On culture and conservation. In *Studies In Cognitive Growth,* ed. J. S. Bruner et al, pp. 225–56. New York: Wiley. 343 pp.

47. Greenfield, P. M., Reich, L. C., Olver, R. R. 1966. On culture and equivalence: II. See Ref. 46, pp. 270–318

48. Gruenfeld, L. W., MacEachron, A. E. 1975. A cross-national study of cognitive style among managers and technicians. *Int. J. Psychol.* 10:27–55

49. Guthrie, G. M., Bennett, A. B. 1971. Cultural differences in implicit personality theory. *Int. J. Psychol.* 6:305–12

50. Harkness, S. 1973. Universal aspects of learning color codes: a study in two cultures. *Ethos* 1:175–200

51. Hays, D. G., Margolis, E., Naroll, R., Perkins, D. R. 1972. Color term salience. *Am. Anthropol.* 74:1107–21

52. Heider, E. R. 1972. Probabilities, sampling and ethnographic method: the case of Dani color names. *Man* 7:448–66

53. Heider, E. R. 1972. Universals in color naming and memory. *J. Exp. Psychol.* 93:10–20

54. Irwin, H. M., McLaughlin, D. H. 1970. Ability and preference in category sorting by Mano schoolchildren and adults. *J. Soc. Psychol.* 82:15–24

55. Irwin, H. M., Schafer, G. N., Feiden, C. P. 1974. Emic and unfamiliar category sorting of Mano farmers and U.S. undergraduates. *J. Cross-Cult. Psychol.* 5: 407–23

56. Iwawaki, S., Lerner, R. M. 1974. Cross-cultural analyses of body-behavior relations: I. A comparison of body build stereotypes of Japanese and American males and females. *Psychologia: Int. J. Psychol. Orient* 17:75–81

57. Jahoda, G. 1971. Retinal pigmentation, illusion susceptibility and space perception. *Int. J. Psychol.* 6:199–208

58. Jahoda, G., Deregowski, J. B., Sinha, D. 1974. Topological and Euclidean spatial features noted by children. *Int. J. Psychol.* 9:159–72

59. Jahoda, G., Stacey, B. 1970. Susceptibility to geometrical illusions according to culture and professional training. *Percept. Psychophys.* 7:179–84

60. Kagan, J., Klein, R. E., Haith, M. M., Morrison, F. J. 1973. Memory and meaning in two cultures. *Child Dev.* 44:221–23

61. Kohlberg, L. 1968. The child as a moral philosopher. *Psychol. Today* 2:25–30

62. Langgulung, H., Torrence, E. P. 1972. The development of causal thinking of children in Mexico and the United States. *J. Cross-Cult. Psychol.* 3:315–20

63. Leibowitz, H., Pick, H. 1972. Cross-cultural and educational aspects of the

Ponzo illusion. *Percept. Psychophys.* 12:430–32

64. Lerner, R. M., Iwawaki, S. 1975. Cross-cultural analyses of body-behavior relations: II. Factor structure of body-build stereotypes of Japanese and American adolescents. *Psychologia: Int. J. Psychol. Orient* 18:83–91

65. Lerner, R. M., Pool, K. B. 1972. Body-build stereotypes: a cross-cultural comparison. *Psychol. Rep.* 31:527–32

66. LeVine, R. 1970. Cross-cultural study in child psychology. In *Carmichael's Manual of Child Psychology,* Vol. 2, ed. P. Mussen, pp. 559–612. New York: Wiley. 872 pp.

67. LeVine, R., Price-Williams, D. R. 1974. Children's kinship concepts: cognitive development and early development among the Hausa. *Ethnology* 13:25–44

68. Lloyd, B. B. 1972. *Perception and Cognition: A Cross-Cultural Perspective.* Harmondsworth, England: Penguin. 190 pp.

69. McGurk, H., Jahoda, G. 1975. Pictorial depth perception by children in Scotland and Ghana. *J. Cross-Cult. Psychol.* 6:279–96

70. Meacham, J. A. 1975. Patterns of memory abilities in two cultures. *Dev. Psychol.* 11:50–53

71. Miller, R. J. 1973. Cross-cultural research in the perception of pictorial materials. *Psychol. Bull.* 80:135–50

72. Mottram, S., Faulds, B. D. 1973. An adaptation of a Piagetian spatial perception study applied cross-culturally. *Percept. Mot. Skills* 37:348–50

73. Munroe, R. L., Munroe, R. H. 1975. *Cross-Cultural Human Development.* Monterey, Calif: Brooks/Cole. 181 pp.

74. Naroll, R. 1970. What have we learned from cross-cultural surveys? *Am. Anthropol.* 72:1227–88

75. Nerlove, S. B., Roberts, J. M., Klein, R. E., Yarbrough, C., Habicht, J. 1974. Natural indicators of cognitive development: an observational study of rural Guatemalan children. *Ethos* 2:265–95

76. Norman, W. T. 1963. Toward an adequate taxonomy of personality attributes. Replicated factor structure in peer nomination personality ratings. *J. Abnorm. Soc. Psychol.* 66:574–83

77. Okinji, O. M. 1971. The effects of familiarity on classification. *J. Cross-Cult. Psychol.* 2:39–49

78. Osgood, C. E., May, W. H., Miron, M. S. 1975. *Cross-Cultural Universals of Affective Meaning.* Urbana: Univ. Illinois. 486 pp.

79. Paredes, J. A., Hepburn, M. J. 1976. The split brain and the culture-and-cognition paradox. *Curr. Anthropol.* 17:121–27

80. Pollack, R. 1970. Müller-Lyer illusion: effect of age, lightness, contrast, and hue. *Science* 170:93–94

81. Price-Williams, D. R. 1961. A study concerning concepts of conservation of quantities among primitive children. *Acta Psychol.* 18:297–305

82. Price-Williams, D. R. 1962. Abstract and concrete modes of classification in a primitive society. *Br. J. Educ. Psychol.* 32:50–61

83. Price-Williams, D. R. 1975. *Explorations in Cross-Cultural Psychology.* San Francisco: Chandler & Sharp. 128 pp.

84. Price-Williams, D. R., Gordon, W., Ramirez, M. III. 1969. Skill and conservation: a study of pottery-making children. *Dev. Psychol.* 1:769

85. Ross, B. M., Millsom, C. 1970. Repeated memory of oral prose in Ghana and New York. *Int. J. Psychol.* 5:173–81

86. Saha, G. B. 1973. Judgment of facial expressions of emotion: a cross-cultural study. *J. Psychol. Res.* 17:59–63

87. Saral, T. B. 1972. Cross-cultural generality of communication via facial expressions. *Comp. Group Stud.* 3:473–86

88. Segall, M. H., Campbell, D. T., Herskovits, M. J. 1966. *The Influence of Culture on Visual Perception.* Indianapolis: Bobbs-Merrill. 268 pp.

89. Serpell, R. 1969. Cultural differences in attentional preference for colour over form. *Int. J. Psychol.* 4:1–8

90. Shepherd, J. W., Deregowski, J. B., Ellis, H. D. 1974. A cross-cultural study of recognition memory for faces. *Int. J. Psychol.* 9:205–12

91. Siann, G. 1972. Measuring field dependence in Zambia: a cross-cultural study. *Int. J. Psychol.* 7:87–96

92. Simpson, E. L. 1974. Moral development research: a case study of scientific cultural bias. *Hum. Dev.* 17:81–106

93. Smith, M. W. 1974. Alfred Binet's remarkable questions: a cross-national and cross-temporal analysis of the cultural biases built into the Stanford-Binet intelligence scale and other Binet tests. *Genet. Psychol. Monogr.* 89:307–34

94. Stewart, V. M. 1973. Tests of the "carpentered" world hypothesis by race and environment in America and Zambia. *Int. J. Psychol.* 8:83–94

95. Sturtevant, W. C. 1964. Studies in ethnoscience. In *Transcultural Studies in*

Cognition, ed. A. K. Romney, R. D'Andrade, pp. 99–131. *Am. Anthropol.* 66 (No. 3, Part 2).

96. Super, C. M. 1972. Cognitive changes in Zambian children during the late preschool years. *H.D.R.U. Rep. No. 22.* Human Development Research Unit, Univ. Zambia. 70 pp.

97. Szalay, L. B., Maday, B. C. 1973. Verbal associations in the analysis of subjective culture. *Curr. Anthropol.* 14:33

98. Triandis, H. C. 1972. *The Analysis of Subjective Culture.* New York: Wiley-Interscience. 383 pp.

99. Triandis, H. C., Malpass, R. S., Davidson, A. R. 1972. Cross-cultural psychology. In *Bien. Rev. Anthropol. 1971:* 1–84

100. Tyler, S. A., ed. 1969. *Cognitive Anthropology,* pp. 3, 15. New York: Holt, Rinehart & Winston. 521 pp.

101. Waldron, L. A., Gallimore, A. J. 1973. Pictorial depth perception in Papua New Guinea, Torres Strait, and Australia. *Aust. J. Psychol.* 25:89–92

102. Walker, C., Torrence, E. P., Walker, T. S. 1971. A cross-cultural study of the perception of situational causality. *J. Cross-Cult. Psychol.* 2:401–4

103. White, C. B. 1975. Moral development in Bahamian school children: a cross-cultural examination of Kohlberg's stages of moral reasoning. *Dev. Psychol.* 11:535–36

104. Whiting, J. W. M., Child, I. 1953. *Child Training and Personality.* New Haven: Yale Univ.

105. Witkin, H. A., Berry, J. W. 1975. Psychological differentiation in cross-cultural perspective. *J. Cross-Cult. Psychol.* 6:4–87

106. Witkowski, S. R. 1977. Semantic complexity and societal complexity. *Behav. Sci. Res.* In press

107. Witkowski, S. R., Brown, C. H. 1977. An explanation of color nomenclature universals. *Am. Anthropol.* 79:50–57

Ann. Rev. Anthropol. 1977. 6:57–67
Copyright © 1977 by Annual Reviews Inc. All rights reserved

LINGUISTICS: THE RELATION OF PRAGMATICS TO SEMANTICS AND SYNTAX

❖9587

Jerry L. Morgan
Department of Linguistics, University of Illinois, Urbana, Illinois 61801

INTRODUCTION

In the past few years there has been a remarkable growth of research on the topic of pragmatics. In this review I will sketch and discuss some developments in conversational pragmatics and their impact on syntactic and semantic studies. Before proceeding to this task, though, some discussion of the term "pragmatics" is in order.

THE RANGE OF THE TERM "PRAGMATICS"

The term "pragmatics" is in wide and fashionable use today in linguistics, philosophy, psychology, and adjoining fields. Its applications range from the narrow scope of the study of the meaning of deictic expressions to use as a catch-all category covering all aspects of communication that cannot be analyzed as literal meaning, including even matters of turn-taking and social interaction.

Morris (28) used "pragmatics" to describe those aspects of language which involve users, and contexts of use, of linguistic expressions. He opposed pragmatics to syntax (the study of linguistic form) and semantics (the study of the literal meaning of expressions). But Morris's discussion of pragmatics was programmatic and not very specific. Bar-Hillel (3) proposed more specifically that pragmatics be concerned with indexical expressions; that is, expressions whose meaning or reference cannot be determined without reference to context—the pronoun *I* and the adverbs *here, now,* and *then,* for example. Despite such discussions, the study of pragmatics in linguistics received little attention until strong interest in it was provoked in the early 1970s, when the interests of philosophers and linguists (especially, but not exclusively, those associated with "generative semantics") converged on the topics of presupposition and conversational implicature (these terms will be explained below).

57

Stalnaker (40), motivated by an interest in presupposition and its relation to semantics, gives a broader characterization of pragmatics as "the study of linguistic acts and the contexts in which they are performed." In his influential program, semantics is the study of "propositions," not sentences. Sentences are not propositions, but are used to express them. Thus one cannot directly speak of the truth or falseness of a sentence like "they are here now" without constructing from context of utterance particular values for "they," "here," and "now"; the result is a proposition whose truth can be evaluated. Pragmatics, then, is the study of "the ways in which the linguistic context determines the proposition expressed by a given sentence in that context," and includes the study of speech acts, indexicals, knowledge, beliefs, expectations, and intentions of the speaker and hearer, and other aspects of context that bear on the determination of the proposition expressed by a sentence. On top of this, the term "pragmatics" has come to be used also for the study of meaning *implied* by the proposition the sentence is used to express. The philosopher H. P. Grice (14), in an extremely important and influential paper (circulated underground for several years prior to publication), gave an insightful account of aspects of indirectly conveyed meaning ("conversational implicatures") that cannot be considered part of the literal meaning of the sentence, but are the result of inferences about the speaker's intentions in saying what he says. Grice's paper has led to a gradual broadening of interest in matters of context, communication, and intention, so that now the term "pragmatics" is applied even to studies of discourse structure, politeness, and social interaction in conversation. What unites all these apparently disparate areas under the same term is the crucial role in each of inference, in context, about the intentions of the speaker. Whether this blanket characterization covers a genuinely unified set of phenomena, or is merely so vague and general as to be vacuous, will probably not become obvious for several years.

HIGHLIGHTS OF RECENT WORK ON PRAGMATICS

J. L. Austin's (2) concept of the "speech act" has had a pervasive influence in linguistics in the past few years. Austin's basic observation is different from the usual view of sentences as formal objects to be treated as well-formed formulae of a logico-mathematical semantic system, independent of speaker, hearer, and context. Austin observes that many sentences—"performative" sentences—of deceptively declarative form, are nonetheless not regardable as true or false; rather, they must be described in terms of "illocutionary acts" on the part of the speaker which may succeed or go awry in various ways, depending on matters of intention and context that he calls "felicity conditions." For example, the sentence "I christen this ship the USS Esmerelda" seems not to be a sentence one could appropriately describe as true or false. Rather, one could most appropriately speak of it as succeeding or failing as (part of) an act of christening, depending on the authority of the speaker to christen, the presence of the right ship, and so on. Austin raises the question whether *all* sentences ought not to be considered as instances of various kinds of speech acts, for which he provides a classification system. His work has inspired an extensive literature on theoretical problems of the notion "speech act"; for example, Cohen (5), Searle (37), Strawson (42), McCawley (22), and Stampe (41).

Austin's work has also inspired an influential transformational theory of the performative sentence—the "performative hypothesis" put forth by Ross (30) and Sadock (32). In this theory every sentence has as its highest verb in deep structure a "performative verb" (roughly, a verb that names the speech act the sentence can be used to perform). Thus a declarative sentence like "It's raining in Philo" would have an underlying structure like "I say to you that it's raining in Philo," and "Is it raining in Philo?" would have an underlying structure of the same sort as "I ask you whether it is raining in Philo." This theory was originally framed as an explanation for certain apparently syntactic phenomena (a goal it has never completely achieved), all syntactic arguments for it being of the same general form. The distribution of some lexical element, or the application of some syntactic rule, is shown to consist of two environments: 1. embedded, with certain restrictions on the embedding environment, involving either some co-reference condition between main and embedded clauses or some restriction on the verb in the main clause; and 2. unembedded, in the main clause of sentences with certain speech act properties, perhaps including some peculiar constraints on matters of reference. For example, the idiomatic expression ". . . be damned if . . ." with the meaning (roughly) of emphatic denial, is sometimes described in these terms; it can occur embedded as a complement of a verb of stating as in 1 but not 2 below, as long as the subject of the idiom is identical to that of the verb of stating, a condition violated in 3.

1. John says he'll be damned if he'll eat there again.
2. *John regrets that he'll be damned if he'll eat there again.
3. *John says you'll be damned if you'll eat there again.

Second, the idiom can occur with its nonliteral meaning in main clauses, but only if the sentence is one that would be used to perform an act of stating, as in 4 but not 5,

4. I'll be damned if I'll eat there again.
5. *Will I be damned if I'll eat there again?

and only if the subject is first person, as in 4 but not 6.

6. *You'll be damned if you'll eat there again.

Under the performative hypothesis, 2 and 5 are considered anomalous for essentially the same reason, as are 3 and 6. This result is achieved in the following way: if we assume that this problem is to be described in syntactic terms, then we are faced with a nonunified account, consisting of one statement describing the distribution of ". . . be damned if . . ." in subordinate clauses, and another apparently unrelated statement describing the distribution of the idiom in main clauses. We can give a unified account by reducing one of these environments to a subcase of the other. To do this, we hypothesize that the apparent main-clause instances are in fact cases of embedding where the underlying main clause has been deleted. Thus the underlying structure of cases like 4, 5, and 6 would be something like 7, 8, and 9, respectively:

7. I say to you that I'll be damned if I'll eat there again.
8. I ask you whether I'll be damned if I'll eat there again.
9. I say to you that you'll be damned if you'll eat there again.

Thus 8 and 9 can be seen to violate the now *general* condition 10, and the ungrammaticality of 5 and 6 is thereby accounted for.

10. The idiom "... be damned if ..." can occur only embedded in the complement of a verb of stating, and the subject of the idiom must be identical in
reference to that of the verb of stating.

The performative hypothesis has been attacked on various grounds by Anderson (1),
Fraser (9), Morgan (26), and Searle (39), among others. There are three important
lines of attack. First, there are a large number of apparent counter-examples to the
hypothesis that the performative verb is always the highest verb in underlying
structure, as exemplified in 11 through 15, where the verb that names the act the
sentence is used to perform is not in the main clause, but in a subordinate clause,
thus not "highest."

11. I'm afraid I must ask you to leave.
12. May I offer you a cookie?
13. Your behaviour leaves me no alternative but to sentence you to 20 years.
14. The university takes great pleasure in announcing that there will be no raises
this year.
15. I regret to announce that the King is dead.

Some or all of these counter-examples could be dealt with, at least in principle,
in either of two ways: first, by claiming that a particular case is an *indirect* speech
act (see discussion below) and therefore not a genuine counter-example. This approach seems appropriate for cases like 12, which one might plausibly say is really
a question and only indirectly an offer. Second, one could attempt for a given
counter-example an analysis wherein it is only at the level of surface structure that
the performative verb is in a subordinate clause. For 15, for example, one might
propose an underlying structure like 16, which does not count as a counter-example
to the condition, which says only that the performative verb must be highest in
underlying structure, not necessarily in surface structure.

16. I announce that the King is dead, and I say that I regret it.

But entirely satisfactory accounts in these terms have not yet appeared, and the
counter-examples remain a problem.

A second, more difficult problem for the performative hypothesis is data that
suggest that a syntactic approach to such phenomena is a mistake in the first place.
Examples like 17 and 18 point to the conclusion that it is the speech act nature of
the sentence, not its syntactic properties, that determines the distribution of the
elements in question.

17. I want you to know that I'll be damned if I'll ever eat there again.
18. I hope it's obvious to everybody that I'll be damned if I'll eat there again.

It would seem that in cases like this one must either abandon the assumption that
the solution is a syntactic environment, or reduce the notion "syntactic environment" to vacuity. But if the correct conclusion is that the distribution of such
elements, and the application of some syntactic rules, is determined not by syntactic
properties (or even semantic properties, apparently) of the sentences involved, but
by the nature of the speech act purposes for which the sentence is used, then the
result is a theory of grammar of a radically new and unfamiliar nature.

The third major problem for the performative hypothesis, or indeed for any
analysis of such matters, is providing an account of the relation between semantic
properties of linguistic elements and the speech act properties of the sentences in

which they occur. The relation is sometimes construed as an automatic one; that the truth-condition semantics of a given word allows one to predict its speech act properties. For example, knowing the meaning of 19 allows one to know that 20 can be used to apologize.

19. John apologized.

20. I apologize.

In knowing the regular English semantic rules of combination and the meanings of the words, *I, christen,* etc, one knows *thereby* that 21 can be used to christen a ship with the name *Thelma.*

21. I christen this ship Thelma.

But this construal of the relation between semantics and speech acts is probably mistaken; at least there are some severe difficulties in making it work. For example, one would suppose from the meaning of *fire* in 22 that 23 ought to be a way of firing people. But 24 is used instead.

22. John fired Bill.

23. I fire you.

24. You're fired.

Similarly, the semantic approach to speech act properties seems to imply that 25 can be used to divorce; but it can't, at least in this culture.

25. I divorce you.

And it is hard to see how a semantic approach can possibly yield a perspicuous account of the situation in a culture where 26 is used to divorce. Is each sentence one-third performative?

26. I divorce you. I divorce you. I divorce you.

It appears from such cases that a semantic analysis provides neither necessary nor sufficient conditions for a given expression to be usable performatively. Rather, semantic criteria [of the sort discussed by McCawley (22), for example] characterize only a class of *natural candidates* for use as performative formulae. But the natural candidate may not be actually usable, because no performative formula is used in performing the act, or because some other natural candidate is used, or because (conceivably) some expression which is *not* a natural candidate is used, perhaps by some historical accident. For example, a culture could just as well establish a convention whereby boats must be christened not by saying "I christen . . .", but by saying the boat's name twice, reciting the Lord's Prayer, and spitting in a porthole. So it appears that knowledge of language per se must be distinguished from knowledge of another kind of convention, conventions about certain ways in which expressions can be used. Knowledge of language provides only a class of expressions that *could* be used, *by virtue of their meaning,* as performative formulae; knowledge of culture (law, religion, etc) tells us which (if any) of the natural candidates is actually recognized as a valid performative formula. But there do seem to be sentences whose speech act potential is a matter of knowledge of language, rather than knowledge of culture. It is knowledge of English that tells us that 27, 28, and 29 can be used to state, question, and order, respectively.

27. It's five o'clock.

28. Is dinner ready?

29. Sit down!

PRAGMATICS AND SEMANTICS

Conversational Implicature

Grive (14) makes clear that much more is conveyed in the utterance of a sentence than merely the literal meaning of the sentence. For example, if upon being asked to a late party I reply, "I have an eight o'clock class," I will probably succeed in conveying a refusal of the invitation, even though the literal meaning of my reply is not the same as that of the sentence "I won't come to your party." Or, in Grice's example, if someone asks me how a friend is doing in his new job at a bank, and I reply "Oh quite well, I think; he likes his colleagues, and he hasn't been to prison yet," then I will probably convey the opinion that the friend's honesty is open to question, though it would be entirely implausible to attribute that meaning directly to any part of the sentence I uttered.

Grice offers an informal account of conversational implicature that can be described as a framework for inferring the speaker's intentions in saying what he says, with the literal meaning it has. Grice's account has as its basis the "Cooperative Principle": "Make your conversational contribution such as is required, at the stage at which it occurs, by the accepted purpose or direction of the talk exchange in which you are engaged" (14, p. 45). From this he derives conversational "maxims" of four categories—Quantity, Quality, Relation, and Manner—such as "make your contribution as informative as is required," do not say what you believe to be false," "be relevant," and "avoid ambiguity of expression." Grice takes pains to point out that these maxims are not unique to language use, but are instead the general means by which any form of behavior is understood as rational, a point often overlooked in subsequent literature on conversational implicature.

It is clear that we spend most of our waking hours interpreting the behavior of other people by assigning intentions to their saying and doing. The process is usually not entirely conscious, and much of the behavior we observe does not attract our conscious notice as long as we are able to classify it as non-threatening. But if we encounter behavior that is not easily classifiable, it catches our direct attention until we are able to form some hypothesis about the nature of the intentions behind it. In this light Grice's maxims can reasonably be considered from the hearer's viewpoint as a set of rules for making inferences about the speaker's intentions in the linguistic acts he performs, and from the speaker's viewpoint as a set of rules for selecting linguistic acts that make his intentions clear.

Grice's maxims sometimes seem trivial to the casual reader, but in fact their beauty lies in their obvious simplicity. Grice and others show convincingly that nontrivial results can be derived from these seemingly trivial principles. Horn (16), for example, attacks some difficult problems of quantifiers and scalar predicates from a Gricean viewpoint, and derives important results. One result is a demonstration that certain classical problems of entailment between quantified statements can be reduced to conversational implicature; for example, that the problematic relation between instances of existential quantification as in "some men are mortal" and "some men are not mortal" is not a relation of entailment, but a conversational implicature that can be naturally accounted for by Grice's maxims and the notion "scalar predicate." In Horn's analysis, if one has good reason to believe 30, then to say 31 is a violation of Grice's maxim of quantity.

30. All linguists are human.
31. Some linguists are human.

If what's at issue is the membership of the set of human linguists, then to say the true sentence 31 is nonetheless to be insufficiently informative. From the hearer's viewpoint, if one assumes that the speaker of 31 is adhering to conversational maxims—in particular, giving as much relevant information as one has evidence for—then it would follow that the speaker has no reason to believe 30, or he would have said it instead of 31. The utterance of 31 thus conveys by implicature that some linguists are *not* human.

Indirect Speech Acts

Grice's notion of conversational implicature has also been proposed as an account for what Gordon & Lakoff (11) call "indirect speech acts"; that is, conversational implicatures wherein a sentence with a certain speech act nature is used to convey what amounts to a second speech act, perhaps of a different kind. There are many examples of this sort. For example, a yes-no question can be used to indirectly make assertions, offers, requests, or wh- questions, among other things. Thus the *a* examples below might, on occasion, be used with the effect of the *b* examples.

32a. Would I lie to you?
32b. I wouldn't lie to you.
33a. Wouldn't you like a drink?
33b. Have a drink.
34a. Can you please hand me that hammer?
34b. Please hand me that hammer.
35a. Do you know where the bathroom is?
35b. Where's the bathroom?

Sadock (31), Davison (7), Gordon & Lakoff (11), Searle (38), Green (12) and Fraser (10) provide detailed discussions of various kinds of indirect speech acts.

Semantics vs Pragmatics

The difficult and controversial issues in this literature revolve around the problem of distinguishing conversational implicature from literal meaning. For example, in saying 36 one usually conveys clearly that disrobing preceded getting into bed.

36. I took off my clothes and got in bed.

But should this be dealt with as part of the literal meaning of the sentence, or as conversational implicature? One could construct an initially plausible case for either approach. It is clear that semantic and pragmatic analyses compete as accounts of many phenomena, raising questions as to how much of the traditional territory of semantics is to be taken over by pragmatics. Many problems of reference—Donnellan's (8) attributive-referential distinction is a good example—can be more appropriately described in pragmatic, not semantic, terms [see Stalnaker (40) for discussion]. Nunberg & Pan (29) propose an analysis of generic nominal expressions (as in the subject noun phrases in "a symphony has four movements" or "elephants never forget") in which the analytically troublesome "all"-like quantifiers involved in the understanding of these sentences are not part of the literal meaning of the expressions, but are inferred via pragmatic principles. Horn (17) and Halpern (15) have discussed pragmatic accounts of the semantico-syntactic rule of negative-transportation that is often proposed as an account of the fact that a sentence like 37 can be understood to mean 38.

37. I don't think it's raining.
38. I think it's not raining.

Presupposition, often taken to be a semantic problem, has recently been discussed as at least partially pragmatic in nature [Stalnaker (40), Morgan (23), Karttunen (18, 19)]. But reliable tests for distinguishing pragmatic from semantic properties have not yet been established. Grice's discussion provides some informal tests for conversational implications, but Sadock (33) shows they are not sufficient as tests. The problem is made especially difficult by the fact, pointed out by Cole (6) and Sadock (32), that conversational implicature can become "grammaticalized" as literal meaning, no doubt a common source of semantic change. This kind of diachronic development is frequent in the fossilization of euphemisms, to choose a common example, so that the very meaning the euphemism is employed to avoid is later grammaticalized as the literal meaning of the expression. Thus "go to the bathroom," originally a device to discuss taboo bodily functions without directly mentioning them, for many speakers now means literally what it formerly only hinted at. So some speakers now say 39 or 40 without any sort of contradiction or semantic anomaly.

39. The dog went to the bathroom on the living room rug.
40. The baby went to the bathroom all over me.

Given the possibility of this kind of diachronic development, it follows that it will often be difficult to distinguish a genuine case of conversational implicature from a case where implicature has been "frozen" as literal meaning, so that the expression wears its history on its sleeve. This is in fact Sadock's position on such sentences as "can you pass the salt". *Can you* is now an idiom, with a literal meaning closely related to, and historically arising from, the conversational implicature of a request. Motivations for this position arise from two interesting facts: First, *can you* is intuitively more direct as a request than other expressions with similar meanings. Thus 41 is felt to be a fairly direct request, but 42 and 43 are more in the way of hints.

41. Can you pass the salt?
42. Are you able to pass the salt?
43. Is it possible for you to pass the salt?

Second, *can you,* but not its apparently synonymous expressions, has some of the syntactic earmarks of a direct request; for example, preverbal *please,* as in 44 through 46.

44. Can you please pass the salt?
45. *Are you able to please pass the salt?
46. *Is is possible for you to please pass the salt?

PRAGMATICS AND SYNTAX

There is a common (though by no means universal) assumption among generative grammarians that the application of a syntactic rule can be conditioned only by elements or structures that are present at some stage in the derivation of the sentence in which the rule applies. Given this assumption, it follows that something about the (presumably underlying) structure of 44 conditions the application of the rule that places *please* in preverbal position. But one need not accept this assumption. Gordon & Lakoff (11) in fact propose that certain rules are conditioned by the presence of some conversational implicature. Morgan (24, 27) proposes that it is not conversational implicature, but the communicative intentions of the speaker that trigger such rules, so that the rules can be considered to have the function of signaling intentions. At any rate, it is slowly becoming clear that there are various kinds of correlations between pragmatics and syntactic form, ranging from the role pragmatic considerations play in the determination of stress and intonation [Bolinger (4), Schmerling (36), Sag & Liberman (34)] and rule application [Schmerling (35), Green (13), Kuno (20, 21), for example] to less obvious matters like Ross constraints [Morgan (25)].

Schmerling (36), for instance, discusses (among other matters) the fact that the different stress patterns assigned by speakers to 47 and 48, when the content of these sentences was "news," depended on their assumptions about whether the events referred to were expected or not.

47. Trûman díed.
48. Jóhnson dîed.

A variety of pragmatic considerations have been seen to affect rule application. (Put another way, rule application has been seen as reflecting speakers' attitudes, assumptions, and/or intentions.) Kuno (20, 21), for example, discusses the roles that such notions as topicality and empathy have in determining permissible syntactic relations between a pronoun and the noun phrase it refers to. Green's (13) discussion of inverted sentences like 49 suggests that the rules which define such sentences and what kinds of clauses they may occur in must be sensitive to the speaker's intentions in using the particular clause.

49. In came the dog.

But it should not be concluded that pronominalization and inversion are unusual in being sensitive to pragmatic factors; current work by a number of linguists indicates that many supposedly optional syntactic rules are conditioned by such factors.

Though this work is still rather fragmental and not based on a unified and coherent theory of discourse pragmatics, it has already demonstrated that some syntactic phenomena can only be fully understood in the light of pragmatic analysis.

Literature Cited

1. Anderson, S. 1968. *On the linguistic status of the performative/constative distinction.* Bloomington: Indiana Univ. Ling. Club
2. Austin, J. L. 1962. *How to do Things with Words.* Oxford Univ. Press
3. Bar-Hillel, Y. 1954. Indexical expressions. *Mind* 63:359–79
4. Bolinger, D. 1972. Accent is predictable (if you're a mind reader). *Language* 48:633–44
5. Cohen, L. J. 1964. Do illocutionary forces exist? *Philos. Q.* 14:118–137
6. Cole, L. J. 1975. The synchronic and diachronic status of conversational implicature. In *Syntax and Semantics,* Vol. 3: Speech acts, ed. P. Cole, J. Morgan, pp. 257–88. New York: Academic
7. Davison, A. 1975. Indirect speech acts and what to do with them. See Ref. 6, pp. 143–86
8. Donnellan, K. 1966. Reference and definite descriptions. *Philos. Rev.* 75: 281–304
9. Fraser, B. 1971. *An examination of the performative analysis.* Bloomington: Indiana Univ. Ling. Club
10. Fraser, B. 1975. Hedged performatives. See Ref. 6, pp. 187–210
11. Gordon, D., Lakoff, G. 1975. Conversational postulates. See Ref. 6, pp. 83–106
12. Green, G. M. 1975. How to get people to do things with words: The whimperative question. See Ref. 6, pp. 107–42
13. Green, G. M. 1976. Main clause phenomena in subordinate clauses. *Language* 52:382–97
14. Grice, H. P. 1975. Logic and conversation. See Ref. 6, pp. 41–58
15. Halpern, R. 1976. The bivalence of neg raising predicates. In *Studies in the Linguistic Sciences,* ed. C. Kisseberth et al, 6(1):69–81
16. Horn, L. 1973. *On the semantic properties of logical operators in English.* PhD thesis. Univ. California, Los Angeles, Calif.
17. Horn, L. 1975. Neg-raising predicates: Toward an explanation. In *Papers from the eleventh regional meeting, Chicago Linguistic Society,* ed. R. Grossman, L. San, T. Vance, pp. 279–94. Chicago Ling. Soc.
18. Karttunen, L. 1973. Presuppositions of compound sentences. *Ling. Inq.* 4: 169–93
19. Karttunen, L. 1974. Presuppositions and linguistic context. *Theor. Ling.* 1:182–94
20. Kuno, S. 1975. Three perspectives in the functional approach to syntax. In *Papers from the Parasession on Functionalism,* ed. R. Grossman, L. San, T. Vance, pp. 276–336. Chicago Ling. Soc.
21. Kuno, S. 1976. Subject, theme, and the speaker's empathy—a reexamination of relativization phenomena. In *Subject and Topic* ed. C. Li, pp. 417–44. New York: Academic
22. McCawley, J. D. Remarks on the lexicography of performative verbs. In *Proceedings of the Austin Conference on Presuppositions, Implicatures, and Performatives,* ed. A. Rogers et al. To appear
23. Morgan, J. L. 1973. *Presupposition and the representation of meaning: prolegomena.* PhD thesis. Univ. Chicago, Chicago, Ill.
24. Morgan, J. L. 1975. Remarks on the notion 'sentence'. See Ref. 20, pp. 433–49
25. Morgan, J. L. 1975. Some interactions of syntax and pragmatics. See Ref. 6, pp. 289–304
26. Morgan, J. L. 1976. *Pragmatics, common sense, and the performative analysis.* Presented at 12th Reg. Meet., Chicago Ling. Soc.
27. Morgan, J. L. 1977. Conversational postulates revisited. *Language.* In press
28. Morris, C. 1938. Foundations of the theory of signs. *Int. Encycl. Unified Sci.* 1(2):77–138
29. Nunberg, G., Pan, C. 1975. Inferring quantification in generic sentences. See Ref. 17, pp. 412–22
30. Ross, J. R. 1970. On declarative sentences. In *Readings in English Transformational Grammar,* ed. R. Jacobs, P. Rosenbaum, pp. 222–72. Waltham: Ginn
31. Sadock, J. M. 1970. Whimperatives. In *Studies Presented to R. B. Lees,* ed. J. Sadock, A. Vancek, pp. 223–38. Edmonton: Ling. Res.
32. Sadock, J. M. 1975. *Toward a Linguistic Theory of Speech Acts.* New York: Academic
33. Sadock, J. M. 1976. Methodological problems in linguistic pragmatics. In *Problems in Linguistic Metatheory,* pp. 1–27. East Lansing: Dep. Ling., Michigan State Univ.

34. Sag, I., Liberman, M. 1975. The intonational disambiguation of indirect speech acts. See Ref. 17, pp. 487–97
35. Schmerling, S. F. 1975. Asymmetric conjunction and rules of conversation. See Ref. 6, pp. 211–32
36. Schmerling, S. F. 1976. *Aspects of English Sentence Stress.* Austin: Univ. Texas Press
37. Searle, J. R. 1969. *Speech Acts.* New York, London: Cambridge Univ. Press
38. Searle, J. R. 1975. Indirect speech acts. See Ref. 6, pp. 59–82
39. Searle, J. R. 1976. Review of J. Sadock: Toward a linguistic theory of speech acts. *Language* 52:966–71
40. Stalnaker, R. 1972. Pragmatics. In *Semantics and Natural Language,* ed. D. Davidson, G. Harman, pp. 380–97. Boston: Reidel
41. Stampe, D. W. 1975. Meaning and truth in the theory of speech acts. See Ref. 6, pp. 1–40
42. Strawson, P. F. 1971. Intention and convention in speech acts. In *Logico-Linguistic Papers,* ed. P. F. Strawson, pp. 149–60. London: Methuen

Ann. Rev. Anthropol. 1977. 6:69–101
Copyright © 1977 by Annual Reviews Inc. All rights reserved

NUTRITIONAL ANTHROPOLOGY AND BIOLOGICAL ADAPTATION

❖9588

Jere D. Haas [1]

Division of Nutritional Science, Cornell University, Ithaca, New York 14853

Gail G. Harrison [1]

Departments of Family and Community Medicine and Pediatrics, College of Medicine, University of Arizona, Tucson, Arizona 85724

INTRODUCTION

Adaptation is a pervasive theme in biological anthropology. The recent anthropological literature has produced several theoretical papers that discuss the concept of adaptation and its application in sociocultural and biological anthropology (3, 4, 9, 10, 16, 36, 37, 91, 111, 176). A significant feature of these discussions is the treatment of population and even individual adaptation as neither solely biological nor social in origin or effect. The role of the nutritional environment in human adaptation may serve as an organizing framework for this broad area of multidisciplinary research. However, we will limit our discussion here to the interface of nutrition with biological anthropology. For the reader who wishes to explore the literature in the sociocultural aspects of food and nutrition, we suggest the bibliography compiled by Wilson (189) and the review by Montgomery (112), as well as the recent volume on food and food habits edited by Arnott (7). Fitzgerald's (42) reader includes papers on nutrition in both cultural and biological adaptation. And the bibliography by Rechcigl (139) is an extensive compilation of references to food, nutrition, and health which can be of great value to the anthropologist.

By restricting our review to the area of nutrition and biological adaptation we do not plan to ignore the important interactions that occur between social and biological components of the adaptive process. However, since the roots of nutrition are in the biological sciences, we feel that much can be learned about the anthropological value of nutrition research through an understanding of its interface with human biology and biological anthropology.

[1] We gratefully acknowledge the assistance of Cathy Campbell and Linda Jackson in searching the literature for this review, and Eleanor Parker for typing the manuscript.

69

THE ROLE OF NUTRITION IN HUMAN ADAPTATION

Human adaptation studies in physical anthropology grew naturally out of the foundations of evolutionary biology and human variability that characterized the discipline through the first half of this century. The work of environmental physiologists during the 1940s and 1950s contributed a methodological sophistication to human variation studies, resulting in a redefinition of the terminology of adaptation and its use in human population studies (9, 134). One major development of this collaboration of physiologists and anthropologists was the move from the single stress, individual response model of adaptation to an attempt at understanding how individuals and populations adapt to multiple stress environments. Reviews of the role of nutrition in physical anthropology (51) and human biology and adaptation (36, 89, 122, 171, 173) placed nutrition in a key position as a critical component of the complex multistress human environment. Some of the best attempts at viewing human nutrition within a broader conceptual framework of human adaptation have been presented recently by Mazess (110, 111), Thomas (176), and Stini (171, 173). Their contributions will be mentioned throughout this review.

The conceptualization of human adaptation by Mazess (110), emphasizing the importance of viewing adaptation at several levels of biological organization, underlies a large part of this review and thus deserves extensive comment. Mazess notes that one can observe the effects of a stress or several stressors at levels of biological organization ranging from biochemical function, through responses of cells, tissues, organ systems, the individual, the population, or the ecosystem. Each higher level serves as the immediate environment for the level of organization directly below it. The environmental physiologist is primarily interested in describing adaptive responses at the biochemical, cellular, organ, and individual level, where the maintenance of physiological homeostasis is of prime importance in determining the effectiveness of the adaptation (11). However, anthropologists and population biologists are more concerned with adaptive responses at the population or ecosystem level where changes in the gene pool, sociocultural processes, or ecological successions reflect the effectiveness of the adaptive response. Mazess notes that population adaptations are usually observed as an extrapolation of individual adaptive responses and thus provide only a limited view of how the population as a unit may respond to environmental constraints.

Mazess (110, 111) goes on to describe yet another set of organization categories which he calls "adaptive domains," that permits adaptation to be evaluated within any one of these hierarchical levels of biological complexity. At the level of the individual the adaptive domains are: physical performance, nervous system functioning, growth and development, nutrition, reproduction, health, cross-tolerance and resistance, affective functioning, and intellectual ability. A response to any stress, if it is to be termed "adaptive" for the individual, must be shown to be necessary or beneficial to the functioning of one or more of these adaptive domains. This review deals with the factors that influence and may be influenced by variation in one of these adaptive domains—nutrition.

Another approach to human adaptability which may be useful in the study of nutrition has been proposed by Slobodkin (165) and modified for human groups by

Thomas (176). Thomas uses a systems approach to identify various stressors and the forms of behavioral or biological "buffers" that permit the population to adapt (Figure 1). The adaptive strategy employed by the group is established in a feedback system that relies on such characteristics as the demographic structure of the group, the availability of vital resources, and the relative effect of the behavioral buffers to reduce the stress so that the usually more costly biological (genetic) adaptations need not be utilized. Within this model, nutrition may serve as a stressor in the form of a nutrient deficiency or as a vital resource in the human environment that is necessary to activate a behavioral or biological buffering system in response to other stresses. In this way one can use the model to view population level "adaptive domains" such as intragroup and intergroup behavior, demographic processes, technology, and phenotypic variability within the group, in relation to nutritional variation imposed from within the group or from outside.

Thomas's model is especially useful in evaluating adaptation to multistress environments. Several single stresses can each be followed through the system and behavioral, biological, demographic, and resource response can be monitored. Where changes in certain components differ or become incompatible with efficient adaptive responses to any other stress, one can predict potential risk or problem areas when the environmental stresses become more severe. Changing dietary patterns due to demographic or social change, environmental catastrophe, or periodic fluctuations in food availability could become very important to a high risk population, especially if food resources are already scarce or unreliable or nutrition plays an important part in the adaptive strategy to another stress.

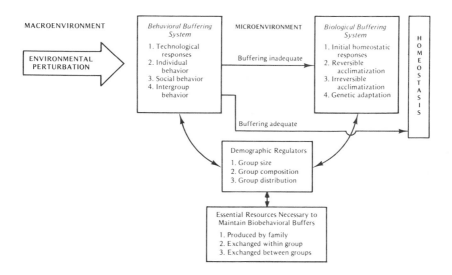

Figure 1 Factors influencing the maintenance of homeostasis. From *Physiological Anthropology,* edited by A. Damon. Copyright © 1975 by Oxford University Press, Inc. Reprinted by permission (see 176, p. 70).

Considering the conceptual models of Mazess and Thomas, we can assess the role of nutrition in human adaptation as either a stressor in its own right or as part of an adaptive strategy to single or multistress environment.

To demonstrate the role of nutrition in human adaptation to climatic stress we would like to review several of the classic "single stress" studies, where physiological responses may be highly dependent upon variability in the nutritional environment. These studies have dealt with such stresses as cold, heat, ultraviolet radiation, and high altitude hypoxia.

Cold Stress

The nutritional environment has been frequently studied in relation to biological responses to low ambient temperatures. Steegmann (167) carefully reviewed a large portion of the literature on human morphological and physiological responses to cold stress. Little & Hochner (97) reviewed basically the same literature but approached the problems of thermal stress with an emphasis on growth and development. Both reviews emphasize, as do others (44), that metabolic responses are a major mechanism for adaptation where thermogenesis must compensate for heat loss to the environment. In this regard the state of the nutritional environment must be considered as an important element of the adaptive strategy to cold stress.

There are at least three important areas of research in cold stress studies that involve nutritional status and metabolic response. These are the effects of dietary quality and nutritional status on (*a*) the maintenance of an adequate adipose layer for insulation to heat loss and as an energy reserve; (*b*) the efficiency of metabolic responses to hypothermia; and (*c*) growth and development of children under cold stress as it relates to the development of an adult phenotype that may be more effective at reducing heat loss. The first area has been studied only peripherally in attempts to correlate heat loss with variation in skinfold thickness as a measure of subcutaneous fat (13). If the subcutaneous adipose layer is in fact an important adaptive mechanism in the cold, it is highly dependent upon an adequate caloric intake by the individual.

The thermogenic quality of the Eskimo diet with its high proportion of animal protein and fat has been linked to the very active metabolic response of this population to total body cold exposure (65, 148). The metabolic adaptations through increased gluconeogenesis, which account for efficient utilization of diets with extremely high amounts of protein and fats, is an interesting phenomenon in its own right (35). However, the additional heat generated through the specific dynamic action of foods is presumably the reason why the Eskimo has an unusually high metabolic rate, and can maintain high skin temperature under chronic cold exposure (148).

Much has been written about the application of Bergman's and Allen's rules regarding surface-area-to-weight relationships and efficiency of metabolic heat conservation in man (91, 97, 146). Although never demonstrated to be adaptive in that it confers benefits for the functioning of any of Mazess's adaptive domains, the low surface-area-to-weight relationship of many individuals in cold-stressed populations is still a truism to biological anthropology. One must be careful not to present "evidence" for adaptation based on these rules without demonstrating that they are in fact adaptive or beneficial to the group.

The role of nutrition during growth and development in molding the adult phenotype has been well recognized (70, 122, 175) and the processes that link nutrition, growth, and potentially adaptive morphological traits to cold response are equally viable areas for human adaptability research (97). Research should now focus on the developmental aspects of physiological responses to cold to assess whether metabolic responses to variation in nutrient intake in growing children have any effect on adaptability to cold stress at all stages of the life cycle. Little et al (99) have suggested that developmental acclimatization to peripheral cold stress among Peruvian Quechua may have a developmental component; however, the mechanism of this adaptation in relation to diet or nutritional response during growth has not been demonstrated for any population.

Heat Stress

The role of nutrition in heat adaptation has been less well established than in cold adaptation. Human adaptation to hot environments is not so dependent on a metabolic response except where a high heat load accumulates through muscular exercise or other forms of thermogenesis and must be lost to the environment to maintain thermal balance. The reader may consult the reviews of Folk (44), and Little & Hochner (97) for coverage of the physiological mechanisms of heat adaptation.

Although the direct relationship between nutrition and heat adaptation may not be readily apparent, there are several areas of nutrition research that are clearly related to heat stress. Just as with cold stress, human morphology in terms of surface-area-to-weight ratio and subcutaneous fat thickness have been implicated in heat adaptation (15, 97, 146). However, in these studies the nutrition component of human plasticity has been more explicitly studied, probably because heat stress and problems of protein-energy malnutrition are both common in the tropical developing countries. In an analysis of physique among genetically homogenous Nilotic tribal subgroups, Roberts (145) suggests that extreme intergroup nutritional variations does account for some variation in weight-to-height relationships but that the general maintenance of a linear physique still persists, presumably due to adaptation to a common hot climate. It remains to be tested whether the slight variation in physique within these groups, which is probably diet-related, results in differences in response to heat stress. If at least adequate protein, energy, mineral, and vitamin sources are needed for linear growth then a deficit in any of these nutrients may not only limit linear growth but also affect metabolic responses to heat stress, either directly or through the influence of body morphology.

Other nutritional aspects of heat tolerance are related to dietary mineral availability and water loss through perspiration (44). Effects of dehydration or physiological response to heat and nutrient utilization have been examined in various settings. Early workers noted that losses of nitrogen through sweat increased substantially when healthy adults were subjected experimentally to high ambient temperatures; the conclusion was made that protein requirements per kilogram of body weight may be higher in the tropics than in temperate climates (28a). Recent work in

Thailand, however, has more closely approximated natural conditions by studying well-acclimatized subjects at temperatures in the range of the real environment and consuming diets containing realistic amounts of protein (69). Under these conditions, urinary nitrogen losses decreased as skin losses rose, resulting in no net change in protein requirements. The authors attribute the conflicting results of earlier studies to the use of nonacclimatized subjects, unusually high temperatures, hard physical work, and high dietary protein intakes. There remains the possibility that this compensatory mechanism may be inadequate in the face of hard physical labor at high temperature. Also of significance is the observation that energy requirements are increased as ambient temperature increases above 40°C (29).

Adaptation to multistress environments in the tropics is particularly important to biological anthropologists who are interested in understanding the patterns of adaptation that accompanied our hominid ancestors during their evolutionary progression in Africa and South Asia. Much speculation has been made in this regard (123, 127, 171), but we are in need of adequate research on contemporary hunters and gatherers where multistress adaptation can be observed firsthand (185).

Ultraviolet Radiation

One area indirectly relating diet and heat adaptation is the reported relationship between biosynthesis of Vitamin D and skin color on one hand and skin color and protection of subcutaneous sweat glands on the other.

The hypothesis proposed by Loomis (100) that attempts to explain the distribution of human skin color is based primarily on a nutritional argument for both extremes of the skin color spectrum. Light skin is considered to be adaptive in upper latitudes where it serves to absorb more ultraviolet (UV) radiation and thus promote Vitamin D synthesis in the epidermal layer of the skin. Furthermore, Loomis proposes that dark skin is adaptive in the lower latitudes where it serves to screen out dangerously high levels of UV radiation and thus provides protection from hypervitaminosis D. Hamilton (61), in his treatise on coloration in animals and man, suggests that a Vitamin D explanation is more plausible for adaptation in depigmented populations but argues that the quantitative aspects of the hypervitaminosis hypothesis for tropical man are uncertain. To our knowledge there is no evidence of pathological overproduction of Vitamin D due to excessive UV radiation in the tropics, so this mode of selection is unrealistic. Hamilton presents several plausible alternatives to explain skin color variations, one of which relates to the efficiency of dark skin in maintaining homeothermy under a marginal dietary energy intake by maximizing absorption of radiant heat.

Hypoxia

Hypoxic stress, which affects populations living at extreme high altitude, elicits metabolic responses in individuals which are important in determining human nutrient requirements under environmental stress. One of the most significant nutrients involved in adaptation to hypoxia is iron with its role in hemoglobin synthesis and oxygen transport. Considering the amount of research conducted on high altitude populations, there has been relatively little attention given to iron metabolism.

Picon-Reategui (130) contends that the native diets of highland Peruvian Indians in the community of Nuñoa meet iron requirements for all age groups and during pregnancy. However, there is a limited base for extrapolating these findings from one region to other high altitude areas. It does appear that the traditional Andean diet of wheat, barley, and chenopodia, even when it provides a marginal caloric intake, will still supply adequate iron to meet low altitude recommended intakes. However, with a greater dietary contribution from tubers and less from grains and little animal protein certain individuals in the population could easily approach deficiency levels defined by a greater requirement at high altitude.

One must also consider the availability of the iron in relation to its dietary source. This is especially true if iron intake is solely from nonmeat sources, from which its biological availability is low. Also, erythropoitic activity under conditions of acute protein deficiency has been shown to be reduced, thus leading to reduced oxygen carrying capacity through reduced red blood cell production (41).

Whereas high levels of red blood cell and hemoglobin concentration are considered to be a major mechanism for physiological adaptation to hypoxia (110), there has been little effort to establish the lower limits of hemoglobin that may signify an anemic condition in native populations. Future research should examine the role of iron metabolism in adaptation to such conditions as pregnancy and low-iron and low-protein diets.

Other nutrient requirements may also be affected by hypoxia. There is some question as to whether energy requirements are increased or not affected (12, 26, 130) by hypoxic stress or whether they may be influenced by cold stress interacting with hypoxia. Energetic efficiency in relation to small body size is yet another area of research being pursued at high altitude. The contention that small body size may be adaptive under marginal nutritional condition as well as at high altitude (47, 48, 177) requires that dietary and nutritional factors during growth be evaluated in light of the morphology and adaptability of the small adult.

This limited review of nutritional involvement in several metabolic stresses suggests that multiple stress models for the study of human adaptability must be developed. Furthermore, at least one of the additional components of these models must be nutrition, especially if it presents itself as an obvious stress or a constraint to the overall adaptive strategy.

BEHAVIORAL RESPONSES AND NUTRITIONAL VARIATION

Since the dietary environment both serves as a constraint and provides means by which adaptation to other constraints may be accomplished, the use of foods by human populations offers a particularly fertile area for biocultural investigation. A few areas in which there have been recent anthropological interest and which have practical implications include behavioral responses to nutritional limitations of staple energy sources, the use of foods and food supplements as pharmacologic agents, behavioral responses to scarcity and to abundance of food resources, and the role of food energy in assessing energy-flow relationships of human populations within ecosystems.

Behavioral Responses to Nutritional Limitations of the Staple Crop

Since the advent of agriculture, most human populations have relied on cereal cultigens for their major source of energy. The domestication of wheat in the Middle East, then of rice in Western Asia, and finally of maize in the Western Hemisphere are commonly referred to as "agricultural revolutions," closely associated with the origins of great civilizations, rapid population growth, and major changes in social and cultural organization (85). In spite of their advantages in supplying a high yield of food energy, each of the staple cereal crops has nutritional limitations, and none can be depended upon as a sole source of energy and nutrients. Yet in much of the nonindustrialized world, the staple cereal supplies 70 percent or more of caloric needs. Under these circumstances the nutritional limitations of the staple cereals become critical, and biological and cultural means of coping with these constraints must be developed.

In the case of rice-based diets, the chief limitations are in the quantity of the protein (and thus the volume required to meet protein needs for the growing child) and in the vitamin content of milled rice which is preferred over unmilled rice in most areas. Milling and washing, practices which are almost universal in rice-eating areas, remove most of the thiamine and other water-soluble vitamins in rice. Protein content may also be decreased significantly. The results in populations which subsist on milled rice have been endemic beriberi and protein-energy malnutrition.

Practices which tend to increase the amount and quality of available protein and to improve the supply of vitamins in rice diets include the very common consumption of dried or fresh fish, fish sauces, soy products, and fresh vegetables with rice. Another beneficial practice, which is centered in India, is the practice of parboiling, in which the unhusked rice is steamed and then dried before milling. The technique diffuses water-soluble nutrients through the grain so that a smaller proportion of these nutrients is lost in subsequent milling and washing; adult beriberi is much less common in areas where rice is parboiled than in rice-eating areas which do not practice this custom (83).

Corn-based diets present equally complicated biological problems for the populations which are dependent upon them. Zein, the principal protein component of corn, is relatively low in the amino acids lysine and tryptophan and high in leucine; corn is also relatively low in niacin and most of the niacin present is in a form which cannot be utilized. Thus the quality of the protein is low and corn-eating populations additionally run a high risk of pellagra. The high-leucine/isoleucine ratio in corn has been reported to have an antagonistic effect on the conversion of tryptophan to niacin, thus further enhancing the niacin shortage (88). However, the original research is this area has been criticized, and the role of leucine and isoleucine in this conversion is at best unclear.

In spite of the considerable antiquity of maize cultivation in the New World, pellagra is a relatively modern disease which has appeared in areas where corn has become a staple crop. The disease has now disappeared from France and Italy, and from the southern United States, where in the first several decades of the 20th century it was a severe scourge, but pellagra still persists in Romania and in parts of Africa south of the Sahara and in the Middle East (149). However, pellagra has been and still is rare in Central and South America.

The apparent immunity of New World populations to endemic pellagra can be attributed to two practices which improve the value of their corn-based diets. One is the consumption of maize with beans, whose amino acid composition complements that of maize; the other is the practice of treating the corn with alkali (lye, lime, or wood ashes) before grinding. It has long been known that alkali treatment has a beneficial effect on the availability of niacin in maize and on the essential amino acid composition and concentration. Katz et al (85) have recently proposed that the widespread alkali treatment of maize in the New World represents a cultural means of overcoming the limitation of a critical level of maize consumption beyond which, without such treatment, a maize subsistence might result in a high prevalence of malnutrition.

Diets based on wheat are less often productive of protein-energy malnutrition and vitamin deficiencies than those based on corn or rice, in part because they are more often supplemented by animal products and other foods. However, recent evidence indicates that diets based on unrefined wheat may pose problems of mineral nutriture. In rural Iran, where flat breads made from whole wheat meal supply at least 50 to 70 percent of the energy intake (105), wheat is ground into whole meals locally by stone mills and is sifted minimally, with the siftings often being recycled and included in the whole meal. The result is a product which contains virtually all of the fiber and phytate of the original kernel (141). Phytate combines with calcium, iron, zinc, and other divalent metals to form poorly soluble compounds which are not readily absorbed from the intestine (141, 142). Recently it has been suggested that dietary fiber may also be responsible for interference with mineral absorption (140). Thus the high-fiber, high-phytate diet may contribute to the high incidence of rickets and osteomalacia, hypogonadal dwarfism of zinc deficiency, and iron-deficiency anemia that afflict many in this area.

While cereal crops provide the bulk of energy and protein for most of the world's population, many tropical groups (consisting of an estimated 5 percent of the world's population) subsist on a diet in which manioc is the primary source of energy. Moran (114) has provided a useful overview of the role of manioc in human subsistence, and makes the point that greater attention should be focused on the advantages of manioc as a staple crop under certain conditions. Manioc produces high energy yields, requires less labor, and requires less of soil nutrients than do cereal crops; further, it is tolerant to drought, pests, weeds, and adverse soil conditions. Cultivation of manioc as a staple crop can free both labor and capital to develop sources of high-quality protein. Further, manioc can be used successfully to feed livestock. Thus, manioc may become an important crop in an ecologically deteriorating world.

The major limitations of manioc are its very low protein content compared to cereals and the fact that it contains, to varying degrees, the highly toxic compound prussic acid. The concentration of prussic acid varies from harmless to lethal amounts, with so-called "sweet" manioc containing lower concentrations than "bitter" manioc. The correlation with variety and appearance, however, is loose and unreliable, and there is considerable variability even within the same field. Populations which subsist on manioc have devised a variety of processes for grating, heating, and soaking to reduce the prussic acid content to safe levels.

Manioc contains significant amounts of calcium, ascorbic acid, thiamine, riboflavin, and niacin; it is very low in protein. The amount of nutrients lost in the extensive processing needed to detoxify the product is not known since there have been very few nutrient analyses of processed manioc products (125).

Foods and Supplements with Pharmacologic Effects

The line between nutrients and drugs is a hazy one, and one fruitful area for research in population adaptation is the use of foods and food supplements for their pharmacologic effects in mitigating stresses imposed by disease, malnutrition, or other factors.

One area of current controversy is the possible role of cassava (manioc)- based diets in providing a buffer against the effects of sickle-cell anemia. The hypothesis is that the sickle-cell heterozygote is at an advantage in an environment in which falciparum malaria is endemic has been accepted by many anthropologists as the best-supported example of disease acting as a selective agent in humans. In any case, it is certain that many African and Mediterranean groups have for many generations lived with high frequencies of the sickle-cell allele. Since the homozygote for hemoglobin-S (Hb-S) generally dies before reproductive age, there would seem to be strong pressure to develop behavioral or biological buffers to blunt the effects of the disease. It has long been known that "mild" or "benign" sickle-cell anemia occurs in some individuals from north Africa, the Mediterranean, and Jamaica, and there have been reported cases of such individuals whose disease worsened appreciably upon migration to the United States and in whom return to the original environment resulted in moderation of symptoms (160).

A possible explanation for this phenomenon has grown out of attempts to treat sickle-cell crises clinically (23). First urea, and then its breakdown product cyanate, have been used to treat sickle-cell crises. It was found that cyanate was effective in disrupting the hydrophobic bonding holding the Hb-S molecules together, in inhibiting sickling, in extending the life of red cells containing Hb-S, and in decreasing the frequency of painful crises in homozygotes. This effect could be shown at doses of cyanate well below the toxic level.

The significance of this clinical work for human adaptability is that many populations in malarial, sickle-cell regions consume diets which contain substantial amounts of compounds which are precursors to cyanate—thiocyanate. They yield cyanate in the red cell and have been shown to work effectively as a cyanate source in treating sickle-cell anemia. Cassava is the richest known source of preformed thiocyanate, and yams, sorghum, and millett—all integral parts of tropical African diets—are also significant sources of thiocyanate. The amount of thiocyanate consumed in a diet based on cassava is of the order of the therapeutic dosage and below the toxic dose; the US diet, in contrast, yields less than one-quarter as much thiocyanate, well below doses shown to be therapeutically effective (68).

On this basis, it has been proposed that a major advantage of manioc-based diets in some tropical areas is their ability to effectively mitigate the severe effects of sickle-cell anemia. The fact that sickle-cell anemia in Africa is relatively rare in adults but common in infants has been taken to indicate that most cases in adults are clinically moderated by consumption of cyanate-yielding foods (68). However, it has been argued that most homozygotes die in infancy before they are old enough to consume significant amounts of cassava or other cyanate-yielding foods (90). There is no logical reason to suppose that heterozygotes would benefit from cyanate, since sickle-cell heterozygotes generally do not have any difficulty unless they are hypoxic stressed, such as at high altitudes.

Another food-drug adaptation under current investigation is the role of coca (*Erythroxylon coca*) chewing in the biological adaptation of marginally nourished highland Peruvian groups. Burchard (22) has studied the role of coca in maintaining blood glucose levels and in nutritional supplementation of the diet. Coca is chewed at frequent intervals throughout the day, and results in rapid elevation of blood glucose levels after chewing. Further, coca in the amounts chewed adds significant amounts of calcium, thiamine, riboflavin, and ascorbic acid to the diet. However, it can be questioned just how much of these nutrients are absorbed considering the leaf is never swallowed. There are other pharmacologic effects hypothesized, including the slowing of intestinal motility, tolerance and energy conservation in the cold, and increased endurance to work (62).

Another example of the possible use of nonfood items to supplement a deficient diet is that of geophagy—the form of pica (the eating of nonfood items) in which earth or clay is consumed. Hunter (72) has suggested that geophagy arose and became institutionalized because it had biologically adaptive value for the individual in its original environment, and that the practice became maladaptive for Africans who brought the custom with them to North America.

Geophagy is common among children and adults in much of Africa, and is an integral part of the folk medical system of many groups. Earth is often dug from a shrine or the grave of an ancestor or holy person and is widely used as medicine to control diarrhea, gastric irritation, and syphilis. The practice is universally more common in women than in men, and in all groups geophagy is associated to one degree or another with pregnancy or lactation.

According to Vermeer's (182) account of geophagy among the Tiv of Nigeria, clays are dug from local sites, especially termite mounds (which concentrate minerals) and consumed locally without any processing or entering of the exchange economy. However, some groups have developed complex economic systems around the practice. Among the Ewe, geophagy is deeply embedded as a cultural practice. Vermeer reports that 14 percent of men and 46 percent of women he interviewed reported eating clay, and he estimated a mean daily consumption of 13 grams for men and 30 grams for women. Chemical analysis of Ghanian clays indicates that significant mineral supplementation may occur through this practice (183). The mineral content of clays varies widely, but on the basis of in vitro digestion, Hunter estimates that if an individual consumed 30 grams of clay per day, iron supplementation would range from 16 to 66 percent of the Recommended

Dietary Allowance, copper up to 33 percent, calcium 4 percent, magnesium and zinc 4 and 9 percent. The bioavailability of minerals from the clay is not known, and experimental evidence is conflicting; availability may vary a great deal depending on the clay.

Hunter has proposed, on the basis of these data, that in parts of Africa a long period of trial and error has institutionalized a nutritionally valuable practice. The "biological wisdom" argument is difficult to prove or disprove. There is a clear association in many areas between pica and malnutrition, especially anemia; but the association does not answer the crucial question: which came first, the pica or the anemia? Some studies in children have reported that treatment with iron has removed the craving for earth. On the other hand, there is evidence that clay binds minerals ingested through food and makes them unavailable biologically, and that excessive clay intake reduces motility of the gastrointestinal tract and can even cause blockage of the colon. No doubt the properties of clays from different locations vary widely. A definitive study has not yet been done of the mineral nutriture of clay-eating versus non–clay-eating individuals in the same environment; further careful studies of mineral absorption from clay and from food in the presence of clay-eating are needed.

Effects of Chronic and Acute Undernutrition on Social Organization

The biological and social consequences of severe quantitative undernutrition, whether chronic or acute, offer a direction for research which is of more than academic interest. In general, the existing literature in this field falls into three categories: (a) the study of experimental starvation; (b) studies of societies in which the food supply is quantitatively and chronically inadequate; and (c) studies of the effects of famine.

The major body of literature on experimental starvation is based on the Minnesota studies conducted on conscientious objectors during World War II (87). Such studies will probably never be repeated, nor should they be, but the careful documentation of biological and behavioral changes in previously well-nourished men fed low-calorie rations over a period of months is invaluable. The richness of biological information is limited only by the state of the science at that time; the observations on behavior are informative although they deal with individuals living in artificially isolated and supportive conditions. Careful reading of this classic work should be regarded as essential for any anthropologist interested in populations experiencing short- or long-term inadequacy of food supply.

Studies of societies in which food is chronically inadequate because of extremely marginal environmental conditions are limited. Holmberg's account of the Siriono of Eastern Bolivia portrays a society in which food predominates as a focus for individual behavior (66). Mates are selected on the basis of their ability to procure food; food sharing is very limited; and priorities for food go to those most able to impose their will. Bolton's description of the "Qolla," a South American Aymara group under chronic hypocalorie stress, attempts to link chronic hypoglycemia to what he sees as normative aggressive behavior (20). Perhaps the most provocative recent work in this area is Turnbull's controversial account on the Ik of northern Uganda (181). The social disorganization in this society of gatherer-hunters transplanted to a totally inadequate environment was so severe that Turnbull was moved to question whether some of the basic characteristics which have conventionally defined humanity (such as family structure of some type and ritual disposal of the dead) are necessary conditions of humanness after all.

The study of famine provides a richer literature, although it has not been primarily the work of anthropologists. Famine, defined as the semistarvation or starvation of large numbers of people, can be conceptualized as a failure of the behavioral and biological buffering systems in Thomas's concept of human adaptation, because the stressor (lack of food) is too extreme or its onset is too sudden for effective adaptive mechanisms to evolve. Famine has not been an infrequent occurrence for human populations; Keys et al (87) documented some 500 recorded famines in historic times. Almost all recorded famines have resulted from widespread crop failure due to drought or other natural disaster, with the notable exception of the Great Plague of 1345 in Europe, which was precipitated by an epidemic, and of famines in recent history induced by warfare. Mayer has provided a thorough review of recent famines and their biological and social consequences (109). The recent famines in Bangladesh (21, 166), Biafra (1) and the Sahel (56, 106, 159) have resulted in a growing literature related to the effects and the effective relief of famine situations. Stein & Susser's (169) massive retrospective analysis of the Dutch famine of 1944–45 is perhaps the most detailed analytic work on biological and social effects of famine, although care must be exercised in extrapolating from this short-term crisis in a previously affluent population to the more common condition of acute deprivation superimposed upon varying degrees of chronic malnutrition.

Responses to Abundant Food Supplies

Of perhaps less immediate concern are the responses of human populations to abundant food supplies. The social organization of northwest coast American Indians has long been a subject of anthropological interest, with controversy centered on the role of the potlatch as a ceremonial mechanism for the redistribution of resources (131). Abundance of food supplies, coupled with uneven access to these supplies, is the situation of most industrialized countries today, and research is needed on behavioral responses to abundance and diversity. Jerome (79) has proposed that urban United States families utilize the diversity of food products available to them to reinforce the high-priority cultural value of individuality, through catering to individual likes and dislikes within the family. Rathje et al (64, 137) have used archaeological techniques to monitor trends in food use and discard in an urban US population, and have proposed that increase in food wasted is a predictable response not only to abundance but to diversity.

The interplay of behavioral and biological responses to the food supply under conditions of affluence poses many questions of anthropological interest, and as anthropologists turn more and more to our own cultures as field laboratories we are likely to see further development of theory and data in this area.

Energy Flow in Human Population Studies

Food energy, while a vital nutrient to human survival, is a small portion of the total energy which is responsible for sustaining a population within an ecosystem. Recently anthropologists have expanded upon the early ideas of White (188) regarding the role of energy in cultural evolution to examine the ecological concept of energy flow in human communities. Several studies on energy flow in anthropological populations have been published in the past 10 years. The most interesting ones have focused on behavioral, technological, and biological phenomena that influence and are influenced by energy flow systems (57, 86, 93, 136, 177).

The concept of energy flow permits biobehavioral interrelationships to be reduced to common caloric units of productivity, consumption, and expenditure. Input and output of energy are observed for a group so that efficiency of energy captured or produced as food versus energy expended in the process of producing the food can be documented. The maintenance of a caloric balance may suggest an adapted state, but should not necessarily lead to such simplistic conclusions. The real value of these studies is that they provide a methodology for studying a large number of interrelated components and processes within a community model. The studies of the Peruvian Quechua by Thomas (177) and the Iniut Eskimo by Kemp (86) are the most complete from the point of view of quantification of energy production, consumption, and expenditure and the application of energy flow to the study of biobehavioral adaptation.

Odum (124) has presented an interesting application of energy flow to the study of human cultural behavior and the development of religion, political organization, social structure, and economic exchange. This volume by a community ecologist is an excellent source of information on nomenclature and model construction but often oversimplifies the complex nature of human cultural behavior. The recent module by Little & Morren (98) provides an excellent introduction to energy flow in human adaptation studies. Anthropologists interested in energy flow should consult the monograph edited by Jamison & Friedman (74) which presents 11 papers under the title, *Energy Flow in Human Communities.*

BIOLOGICAL VARIABILITY AND THE NUTRITIONAL ENVIRONMENT

The nutritional environment plays an important role in defining the limits of human biological adaptation. Individuals and populations may differ in the way they respond to variations in the nutritional environment in ways that reflect their adaptability. Two important areas of research in human adaptation studies deal with the variations in nutrient utilization and variation in functional responses in several "adaptive domains" for individuals and populations under nutritional stress.

Population Differences in Nutrient Utilization

Variability among human populations in requirements for and utilization of food energy and other nutrients is central to the study of biological adaptation. The high prevalence of the so-called "hyperefficiency diseases" (94) of obesity, diabetes, and cardiovascular disease in some groups undergoing relatively severe and rapid dietary change has been attributed to previously adaptive mechanisms for efficient metabolism and storage of food energy. Neel (120) postulated that adult-onset diabetes mellitus is due to a "thrifty" diabetic genotype which evolved because it was advantageous in populations whose food supply was of a feast-then-famine nature. He postulated that a genotype which permits rapid and elevated insulin release in response to incoming nutrients would facilitate synthesis and storage of fat. More recent work (144) indicates that environmental factors related to overcrowding and infection may also be etiologically important, but such an hypothesis does not rule out a genetic susceptibility to an environmental agent. Other examples of possible adaptations for efficient energy metabolism and/or storage include the apparent efficiency of gluconeogenesis in Eskimos (35), for which selection can be logically postulated due to a long history of a high-protein, high-fat diet and the requirement of the central nervous system for glucose as a metabolic substrate. The predisposition of many Polynesian populations to efficient fat storage has also been noted (133). However, in this case neither a metabolic mechanism nor an adaptive advantage relative to the environment has been demonstrated. The significance of population differences in the efficiency of energy utilization and storage is enormous in terms of morbidity and mortality patterns of groups undergoing acculturation. There is a great need for studies of groups undergoing dietary change both in situ and as migrants, such as the work of Prior (133) on the Maori and Tokelauans and of Lieberman & Baker (95) on Samoan migrants.

Perhaps the best-studied characteristic in which human populations differ in their ability to utilize a particular source of nutrients is that of continued production of intestinal lactase in the adult. This enzyme enables the utilization of lactose, the carbohydrate source in mammalian milk. Population differences in the prevalence of primary adult lactase deficiency and lactose intolerance are well documented (63, 101, 161–163). It is clear that except for relatively low prevalences of lactase deficiency in some pastoral groups in Africa, high rates of lactase sufficiency in adults are characteristic only of groups whose ancestors come from a zone covering northern and western Europe including Scandinavia and the Slavic countries and extending as far south as Spain. The rest of the world seems to exhibit, in general, low rates of lactose tolerance among adults. Genetically mixed groups show intermediate prevalences of the traits.

While a genetic etiology for adult lactase sufficiency has not been proven, the majority of the data support a genetic hypothesis of causation (52, 151). It has been suggested by some authors that selection for the allele in certain environments was due to a nonspecific nutritional advantage conferred upon the lactase-sufficient adult in a dairying culture (101, 162). Flatz & Rotthauwe (43) have offered a more specific hypothesis based on the action of lactose in facilitating the absorption of calcium. A major action of Vitamin D is the facilitation of the absorption of calcium by the intestinal mucosa. Lactose enhances calcium absorption, and this action has been shown to depend upon the hydrolysis of lactose to glucose and galactose. Thus Flatz & Rotthauwe propose that maintenance of the ability to hydrolyze lactose, in the sunlight-poor environment of Northern Europe and with dairy animals available, would have conferred protection against rickets and osteomalacia and the consequent ill effects on viability and fertility. This hypothesis is consistent with experimental work which shows that lactase-deficient adults substantially decrease their absorption of calcium when fed lactose (28).

It is evident that populations in environments other than Northern Europe have devised practices which enable them to avoid the adverse effects of lactase deficiency and still derive nutritional benefit from milk where dairying is practiced. Cheese, yogurt, sour milk, ghee, and other products have been developed which allow utilization of milk while lowering its lactose content. There is evidence that many lactose-intolerant adults in the milk-drinking culture of the contemporary United States simply restrict the amount of milk they drink at any one time to an amount which does not provoke symptoms, thus deriving some benefit from the available food without suffering adverse effects (63).

Population differences in nutrient requirements other than those mediated by body size have been little studied. Ascorbic acid requirements would offer a logical route for such research, since the nutrient is stored only to a very limited extent in the body, human intakes vary widely, and the phylogenetic distribution of ability to synthesize ascorbic acid is fairly well understood.

Optimal human intakes of ascorbic acid under varying conditions have not been established and are the subject of some controversy. Documented intakes in apparently healthy people range from less than 10 milligrams to several grams per day in individuals self-dosing with vitamin pills. It has been suggested, on the basis of a lack of correlation between dietary intake and milk secretion of vitamin C in lactating women, that humans may retain the ability to synthesize ascorbic acid under some conditions. Rajalakshmi et al (135) have reported that 27 out of 40 human placentas they examined immediately postpartum showed evidence of ascorbic acid synthesis. Their studies have not been confirmed, to our knowledge, but offer an intriguing area for further research. It has been shown that embryonic guinea pig liver possesses the enzyme necessary for ascorbic acid synthesis, while the liver of the adult guinea pig does not (25); in a German study human fetal livers did not show evidence of ascorbic acid synthesis (67).

The phylogenetic distribution of ability to synthesize ascorbic acid has been worked out in some detail, thanks to the development of a method for testing for synthetic ability in vitro (150). Among mammals, the fruit-eating bat of India (*Pteropus medicus*) and the guinea pig, as well as higher primates, require dietary sources of the vitamin while other mammals, including at least some prosimians (39), synthesize it in the liver.

Nutrient Deficiencies and Behavioral Disorders

Studies of the role of specific nutrient deficiencies in certain behavioral disorders has drawn the attention of anthropologists. Most notable are the examples of iodine deficiency and cretinism, and calcium deficiency and arctic hysteria.

Iodine deficiency is a major cause of the endemic goiter and cretinism found predominantly in mountainous regions such as New Guinea, Nepal, and the Andes. Although goiter (an enlarged thyroid gland) is not necessarily harmful to the individual, it can alert public health workers that a far more critical problem of iodine deficient cretinism may also be present in the population. A study on the social impact of cretinism in an Ecuadorian Indian community has been reported by Greene (55). This study presents good evidence on the social cost of maintaining a high percentage of mentally retarded cretins in the village where 17.4 percent of the normal adult population also exhibit symptoms of neurological dysfunction. Greene observed that many factors contribute to the poor socioeconomic status of this Indian population. They live on the least productive land and are economically exploited by a mestizo class who view the Indians' poor intellectual performance as genetically based and thus justify their dominance over the Indian. As Greene notes, "the mestizos do not view these (behavioral and social) phenomenon as possibly neurologically based behavioral deficits produced by nutritional factors which themselves have been produced, to a great degree, by the nature of the social arrangements and the uneven distribution of economic resources" (55, p. 132).

In a study of the arctic hysterias among the Alaskan Eskimo, Foulks (46) has suggested that calcium deficiency is a contributing factor in the etiology of several psychological disorders. Foulks found that serum calcium levels were normal in the general population and marginally low in patients who reported frequent attacks of hysteria. Through a combination of factors related to diurnal variation in calcium metabolism, anxiety, and hyperventilation, Foulks suggests conditions by which low dietary calcium may account for the common occurrence of this psychosis among selected groups of Arctic Eskimos.

Another mechanism to explain low calcium levels is suggested by data from Mazess & Mather (111a) on bone loss among Canadian Eskimos. Other studies have observed negative calcium balance in persons on high protein diets. Mazess & Mather note that the high protein diet was until recently part of the traditional way of life of most Arctic Eskimos.

Functional Correlates of Nutritional Variation

If nutritional variation is to be understood within the context of adaptation, we must recognize its role in the maintenance of as many adaptive domains as are feasible to observe for a given population or group. Much of the work in human nutrition has viewed the functional correlates of nutritional variation at the infraindividual and individual level of organization with some interesting but limited work attempted at the population and ecosystem level. The most productive research that is of value to anthropology are the studies of relationships between human nutritional variation and such spheres of individual functioning and behavior as growth and development, reproduction, physical performance, intellectual ability, and disease and health. Additional functional correlates at the population level could also be examined for social organization, intergroup and intragroup interaction, mating and reproductive behavior, and mortality and morbidity. Nutritional sciences generally have not dealt with these population problems and it is here that the anthropologist can make a major contribution. Keeping in mind that population responses are not a simple extrapolation of individual response, we present several examples of the interrelation of nutrition with individual adaptive domains.

GROWTH AND DEVELOPMENT   Studies of human growth and development have long been a cornerstone of physical anthropology. Growth studies still dominate the research journals in human biology and physical anthropology as they have for half a century. Most of anthropological research in growth has been aimed at explaining adult morphological variation within and among populations in relation to the events of early life that mold the adult phenotype (70). The effect of nutrition on growth has been recognized by many as the major factor influencing adult phenotypic plasticity (121, 175). Only recently has child growth been investigated as a mechanism by which major physiological and behavioral adaptation may be developed in individuals living under environmental stress.

Human studies of nutritional adaptation during growth and development are best exemplified by the work of Stini (172, 173) and Frisancho et al (47), and much related literature has been recently reviewed by Newman (122). These studies focus on the role of phenotypic plasticity in maintaining the growth processes at a functional level in spite of severe caloric or protein deprivation. Alterations in protein anabolism which conserve vital hepatic function at the expense of skeletal muscle development have been viewed by Stini (172, 173) as an important developmental adaptation to chronic low levels of dietary protein. Although this anabolic response may apply to adaptation during growth, it is important to evaluate any such adaptation in light of the functional capacity of the adult who has developed and grown while nutritionally stressed. In viewing growth of muscle mass, for example, it must be documented that such conservation of protein during early growth really does prevent the compromising of other functional demands, such as immunocompetence, that must be maintained during infancy or childhood, or adult functional demands, such as reproductive performance or work capacity which are usually considered essential for population adaptation. One must continually keep in mind that adaptation is a compromise of responses that must be evaluated *in toto* and not limited to a specific time frame of several years during infancy. Future research with nutritional influences on this adaptive domain should emphasize not only the immediate short-term influences of nutritional status on functional capacity but also should consider the long-range effects which may even extend beyond one or two generations.

The anthropological study of human growth has contributed a great deal to our knowledge of non-nutritional factors that may affect human development. Most notable are the climate studies cited earlier (97, 146) and the studies of developmental genetics which deal with intragroup and intergroup variations in development (71). These studies have served as one focus in a current debate by anthropologists, public health workers, and development planners over the use of international versus local growth standards to assess nutritional status in underdeveloped countries (40, 53, 59, 78, 184). Nutritional anthropometry is an extremely useful tool for the diagnosis of acute and chronic PEM. However, the anthropometric assessment of nutritional status depends upon the use of reference standards for "normal" children. The Third Commission of the International Union of Nutritional Sciences (40) felt that there was a need for an international series of anthropometric reference standards based upon ". . . studies (to) be carried out in as large a variety of countries as possible. Each country's own standards must be derived from carefully selected samples representing children growing in an optimal environment for that country. Genetic and racial factors must be defined and appropriately represented in the sample" (p. 218). The Commission recognized that the term "optimal environment" was complex and difficult to define. A similar problem exists in defining optimal growth. Using standards of growth based on an elite upper class group could create two problems. The standards may be undesirably high and impossible to achieve within the capability of a poor child's growth potential as well as within the capability of most intervention programs to supply the environment necessary to support such a growth pattern. This could be true regardless of whether the upper class has a different ancestry than the poor lower class as you find in many developing countries. Secondly, the elite class may actually be represented by a reasonable number of children with pathologically excessive growth which may predispose them to obesity, diabetes, or heart disease as adults. Thus by forcing the poor children to achieve these elite class standards we may be imposing an additional health burden on the population when they become adults (78). Also the small body size in some groups may in fact be adaptive for that child within his poor environment, since he requires less protein and calories to support maintenance of a small metabolic mass (47, 53, 173, 177).

The opposition to local standards is not debating these issues. However, the proponents of a single universal growth standard point toward the expense and effort necessary to establish these local standards, which, for best application, should be based on costly longitudinal or large cross-sectional studies. The recent trend of devoting relatively large amounts of scarce resources to data collection in developing countries rather than to the pressing need to alleviate malnutrition itself has been a real concern for international nutritionists. It is clear that if local standards are not available, individual diagnosis or national policy decisions must recognize the limitations of using a reference standard that may be based on children that differ from the target population in ethnic, genetic, socioeconomic, climatic, and health background. Valuable resources can be poured into programs to increase stature or weight to an unattainable level or in treating children who are healthy but "small" and thus diagnosed as malnourished. The utility and application of these measurements under specific research, clinical and public health situations have been evaluated by McLaren & Burman (104), Jelliffe (76), and several authors in the volume edited by Roche & Falkner (147). These and related references should be consulted by anyone who plans to assess nutritional status in children.

REPRODUCTION   Variation in reproductive performance as observed by the social scientist has usually been associated with nonbiological variables. Human biologists have recognized that a significant biological component must also be included in the study of human fecundity and fertility (6, 54, 77, 192).

An analysis of nutrition and fertility requires investigation into many facets of the past and present social and biological environments of the specific population under study. Current research in this area covers the entire life cycle from female sexual maturation and preconception nutrition to prenatal nutrition, postnatal morbidity, and interconception nutrition.

The effect of nutrition on fecundity and fertility has received increased attention in recent years. Stein & Susser (168) have presented rather convincing evidence of reduced fertility under a condition of acute famine in Holland during 1944 and 1945. They suggest that reduced fecundity may also result from acute rationing of food in this population and thus account in part for the reduced fertility.

Several studies reviewed by Keys et al (87) suggest that starvation affects spermatogenesis and sperm motility and lifetime. The delayed menarche and earlier menopause observed in developing countries certainly reduces the period of female fecundability. Frisch (49) and colleagues have proposed that the initiation of menstruation (menarche) and the attainment of reproductive capacity that follows may be observed when a woman reaches a critical body weight. This critical weight presumably reflects a critical metabolic mass or a degree of fatness that is dependent upon nutritional status among other factors. The critical weight hypothesis has drawn considerable debate since it first appeared in 1970. Johnston et al (80) challenged it on statistical grounds; Welon & Bielicki (187) found it untenable when tested with longitudinal data from Poland; and Billewicz et al (19) call attention to additional statistical irregularities when the hypothesis is tested with data from Newcastle-upon-Tyne. The debate continues with rebuttals by Frisch to several of her critics (50).

One other area of nutritional involvement in fecundability involves lactation amenorrhea. Continuous breast feeding from 10 to 26 weeks postpartum suppresses normal hypothalamic—pituitary—ovarian function resulting in amenorrhea (77, 129). Therefore, infant feeding practices which involve variation in length of breast feeding not only affect infant morbidity and mortality but also other demographic parameters such as fecundability, birth interval, and fertility (77). The review of nutrition and lactation by Thomson & Black (179) along with the model proposed by Habicht et al (58) present valuable insight into the interrelationship of preconception, prenatal and postpartum nutritional status, weight loss, and lactation interval in providing an optimal environment for pregnancy and lactation.

Reproductive performance is classically measured through fertility or capacity for child bearing. By definition, once a child is delivered alive the period designated for the measure of female reproductive functions ends. The effect of nutritional deprivation during pregnancy may result in early fetal loss (abortion) if the stress is severe, or fetal growth retardation if dietary intakes are marginal. If a fetus is stillborn (delivered dead between 20 weeks and term), it is reflected in the fertility estimates since preconception or prenatal factors resulted in the death. However, if the live born infant dies in the first few hours or the first postnatal month, this is not reflected in the estimate of reproductive performance in spite of the fact that the principal cause of death was probably a problem during prenatal development that produced an infant poorly adapted for extrauterine life. In this context, malnutrition which can be linked to poor fetal development, and increased risk of neonatal death (18, 115) should be assessed as having an effect on reproductive function. This would include the studies of neonatal mortality in developing countries where malnutrition during pregnancy is common.

From this work in nutrition and reproductive performance several conclusions can be drawn. First, acute malnutrition with severe rationing of calories will significantly reduce fertility. Stein & Susser (168) have observed that this occurs across socioeconomic classes. Second, poor preconception nutrition, which may extend back to the mother's infancy and childhood, has long-term effects on the pregnancy. Although Stein & Susser state that "chronic malnutrition in populations has not been shown to be a limiting factor on fertility" (p. 132), the severity of acute malnutrition during pregnancy most certainly depends upon the chronic nutritional conditions that preceded the pregnancy (115, 138, 178). Third, in acute malnutrition such as the Dutch famine there may be a minimal threshold level of nutritional deprivation below which fertility is highly correlated with caloric intake, and above which the association between birth rate and calories is weaker (168). It can be assumed that various levels of fetal growth retardation may also be related to critical levels of maternal caloric intake which are higher than the critical level associated with reduced fertility. Studies in Guatemala have attempted to reduce the incidence of low birth weight infants born to poor rural familes through caloric supplementation during pregnancy (60). The caloric supplementation above 20,000 Kcal throughout pregnancy has been shown to increase mean birth weight by about 250 grams and reduce the incidence of low birth weight in supplemented pregnancies to one-third the incidence observed for nonsupplemented pregnancies.

PHYSICAL PERFORMANCE   Most texts in exercise or work physiology (8, 82) include nutrition in terms of such topics as cellular metabolism and athletic training diets. Work capacity and physical performance play an important role in population adaptation studies, and a better understanding of the effects of nutritional status and dietary variation on performance is essential for adequate interpretation of these studies. Two types of studies on physical performance and adaptation have recently become an important area for anthropological investigation. Both have grown out of the earlier concern of physical anthropologists for an assessment of variations in maximal work capacity under environmental stress exemplified by the work of environmental physiologists working in anthropological projects (12, 14, 110, 116). One recent area of concern deals with studies of human productivity under limited energy availability; the other deals with problems of work efficiency in relation to body size and morphology.

The studies of productivity in relation to diet incorporate many of the principles used in energy flow studies. The usual objective of these studies is the determination of variations in productivity measured by crop yield, energy expenditure, or daily work output as a function of energy consumed from traditional or supplemented diets (65a, 183a). Some of these studies can be criticized in terms of methodology, and most lack sensitivity to non-nutritional variables that may affect productivity. Methodological difficulties of assessing dietary intake and measuring caloric expenditure are being resolved slowly with each new study. Perhaps the application of these methods by anthropologists and other social scientists will help to alleviate problems of oversimplification of the nutritional and physiological explanations for worker productivity.

Studies of human mechanical efficiency in relation to body size have been conducted in an effort to explain the adaptive significance of small body size in chronically undernourished populations. Just as small body size is hypothesized to be adaptive due to reduced biomass and nutritional requirements, it can be at the same time maladaptive if it significantly reduces individual productivity and work capacity. This is another good example of how adaptations are generally compromise solutions which optimize functional capacity within a system of multiple constraints. A study by Frisancho et al (48) on body size and aerobic capacity of high altitude Peruvian natives demonstrates that maximal aerobic capacity (ml O_2/kg/min) is greater in short versus tall highland natives, while short and tall subjects of low altitude origin do not differ in aerobic capacity. Thomas (177) reports that small highland Peruvian men expend less energy but do not show a reduced capacity to sustain work when the tasks involved are typical or work levels observed for normal subsistence activities. This point is an important one if the net effect of maintaining a small body size is to be demonstrated as an adaptive strategy for populations under hypocaloric stress.

NEUROLOGICAL FUNCTION AND INTELLIGENCE   Some of the most recent developments in human nutrition research have focused on malnutrition, brain development, and learning. The research has generally concerned itself with two major themes: the identification of organic damage or poor growth of the brain in malnourished fetuses and infants (34, 190) and the identification of learning disabilities that may be related to either the social and biological factors that lead to malnutrition in young children or the poor brain development that results from malnutrition (30, 33). This research has recently been extensively reviewed by Latham (92), and various symposia on the topic have been published (32, 157).

The work in this area during the 1960s focused primarily on the effects of nutrient deficiencies, primarily protein deficiency, on brain development with an attempt to link malnutrition to brain damage, which presumably in turn would affect learning and intelligence. The work by Dobbing (34) on critical stages of brain growth, and Winick (190) on the effects of malnutrition on brain cell division and biochemical composition are good examples of this approach. The proceedings of the 1967 MIT conference on malnutrition, brain growth, and behavior represent the state of knowledge up to that time (157).

More recent work has recognized the complex interactions of social, biological, and environmental factors that lead to protein-energy malnutrition (PEM) and how these same factors also affect learning and behavior. As Latham (92) points out, "many authors go beyond (experimental evidence) and imply that research shows that protein caloric malnutrition *causes* a retardation in intellectual development" (p. 551). The work of Levitsky et al (96) provides an insight into the role of environmental stimulation in enhancing the learning abilities of malnourished laboratory animals. With cautious interpretation, these animal studies can serve to direct human research. Although longitudinal human studies of the behavioral consequences of PEM have been conducted in Guatemala, Colombia, Peru, India, and South Africa, the work in Mexico has specific relevance to anthropological studies. Many of these studies confirm the results of animal studies by emphasizing that the environment which leads to malnutrition is also a poor learning environment (143). The work of Chavez (24) in Mexico demonstrates that nutritional supplementation with maternal stimulation of malnourished infants improves the learning environment and reverses previous retardation in learning to a greater extent than when nutritional supplementation alone is employed. In another Mexican study, Cravioto & DeLicardie (31, 33) have observed a similar role of stimulation through enriched parent-offspring interaction. They conclude that the maintenance of a poor learning environment is closely related to the ecological factors that also maintain PEM in the same population.

These human studies have generally been conducted with children who have been severely malnourished. However, such children represent about 5 percent of the early childhood population in developing countries and are only the tip of the malnutrition iceberg. Subclinical malnutrition may affect as much as 40 to 70 percent of the children in developing countries, and it is these children who as adults will be the major contributors to the next generation. We still understand very little about the long-range implications of PEM and even less about the long-range effects of subclinical malnutrition. The environment that leads to PEM and poor learning may not differ significantly from family to family within a community. Indeed Cravioto & DeLicardie (31) have shown that PEM often affects only one child within a family and macroenvironmental factors such as family size, parity, education, or income do not serve to distinguish which child or even which family may be affected. The persistence of a poor learning environment may exist without the occurrence of PEM, and the effects of this poor environment on the learning capabilities of subclinically malnourished children may be of great concern to the anthropologists who study population adaptation.

Adult mental function has been studied by Keys et al (87) under short-term acute malnutrition, but the applicability of this research to human population adaptation is limited. Future research should focus on problems of this nature in an anthropological context.

IMMUNE FUNCTION   The fact that malnutrition and infectious disease interact significantly has long been recognized (158); but only in the last few years have the basic mechanisms begun to be elucidated. The area is one of great practical as well as theoretical importance. The evidence accumulated to date includes (a) epidemiologic data which focuses almost entirely on the interactions of protein-energy malnutrition and infectious disease, and (b) a growing body of clinical and experimental data on the effects of various types of malnutrition on immune function. For a general review, the reader is referred to Worthington (191) and to papers by Scrimshaw (155), by Sirisinha (164) and Edelman (38); for an overview of malnutrition and infection in pregnancy and their effects on fetal growth and development, see Katz et al (84); for an evolutionary view of infection and disease in human populations, see Allison (5).

The known mechanisms by which infection worsens protein and energy status include increased metabolic rate due to fever, increased urinary nitrogen losses, and decreased nutrient absorption if the infection involves the gastrointestinal tract; more indirect but equally important effects occur through loss of appetite, a tendency for solid foods—especially those of animal origin—to be withdrawn in many cultures, and the use of remedies and drugs which interfere with absorption. The known effects of severe PEM on immune function include impairment of both cell-mediated and humoral immune response, impairment of leukocyte function, and interference with the integrity of epithelial surfaces. Less well established but under active investigation are effects on lysozymes, complement and gastrointestinal flora. Not only are the frequency and severity of infectious episodes increased in malnutrition (107), but the clinical pattern, which reflects the nature of host response, is altered. Certain organisms, such as gram-negative bacteria and yeast, are more likely to flourish; fever, inflammation, and rash responses are diminished or absent; leukopenia is typical; gangrene occurs more often than normally. The fact that both PEM and measles depress cell-mediated immunity may explain the particularly high case-fatality rate for measles in malnourished children (155).

The effects of deficiencies of single nutrients on immune function are not consistent; synergy or antagonism occurs depending on the function of the nutrient (191). Of particular interest is the complex and not yet well understood relationship between iron status and infection. Iron-deficient individuals exhibit several defects in immune function. On the other hand, high serum levels of free (non–transferrin-bound) iron facilitate bacterial growth and are correlated with severity of infection. This may be particularly important in PEM, where serum transferrin levels are low (102).

NUTRITIONAL SURVEYS OF ANTHROPOLOGICAL POPULATIONS

For the anthropologist wishing to assess nutritional status or interpret published reports on nutritional status, it is important to have some familiarity with methods and standards. Often this need will be best met by collaboration with a nutritional scientist. However, a familiarity with the literature in this area is a decided advantage in interpreting data and formulating research problems.

The ICNND *Manual for Nutrition Surveys,* published first in 1957 and revised in 1963 (73), served for many years as the standard work in the field. It has been largely replaced by Jelliffe's WHO Monograph, *The Assessment of the Nutritional Status of the Community,* which in spite of its age remains an extremely useful reference (76). More recent works include the proceedings of a recent symposium by Roche & Falkner (147) and a manual for nutritional status assessment adapted specifically to the US (27). The volume by Sauberlich et al (152) on laboratory methods serves as an up-to-date reference on this particular aspect of assessment. A recent paper by Stini (174) on the concept and measurement of nutritional status provides an overview specifically written from an anthropological viewpoint. The US Recommended Dietary Allowances (117) are in wide use; for international use the recent FAO/WHO standards are recommended (128).

Area, regional, and problem-centered syntheses of data on nutrititional status of human populations are scarcer than one would wish. However, there are some sources which provide an entry into the nutritional data for many regions. The ICNND survey series provides data for more than 30 countries, collected since 1955 by the Interdepartmental Committee on Nutrition for National Defense (now the Nutrition Program of the US Public Health Service). These surveys include medical, biochemical, and dietary examination and evaluation of local resources for food production, processing, and distribution. Many of the ICNND surveys are sufficiently out of date so that the conclusions drawn are of limited value, but the detailed data may be of use in tracing the history of nutritional problems in a given area.

A more recent, and more ecologically oriented, series of regional syntheses is that by Jacques May. He and his colleagues have produced am impressive series of 14 volumes on the ecology of malnutrition in various regions, which include available clinical and biochemical data as well as relevant ecological and demographic information [see (108) for citations to other volumes published by Hafner, New York].

The Human Adaptability project of the International Biological Program produced several interdisciplinary works which contain a great deal of nutritional information. A summary of the IBP may be found in the National Academy of Sciences report (116), while the nutritional data are summarized by Kline & King (89). The US program has produced to date one synthesis volume on Andean populations (14), with another, on Eskimo populations, in press (75), as well as a methodological manual (186).

The reader who is is interested in nutritional status in the US will find substantial information in the reports of several recent surveys. The Ten-State Nutrition Survey was conducted between 1968 and 1970, and concentrated on assessing the nutritional status of areas containing an excess of families below the poverty level (153). More recently, the HANES (Health and Nutrition Examination Survey) report has provided data on a more representative sample of the US population (119). The National Preschool Nutrition Survey provides data on this vulnerable section of the population (126). Data on nutritional status of North American Indian populations is dispersed; however, a 1972 volume by Moore, Silverberg & Read (113) synthesizes much of the available information on native American children.

For detailed data on nutritional status in particular areas, the researcher is obliged to delve into the primary literature. For access to unpublished and ongoing work, directories of institutions such as the one published by FAO for Latin America (45) are a great help.

CURRENT ISSUES IN WORLD FOOD PROBLEMS

The production and distribution of adequate food for the world's population may be the most serious health-related problem which faces national and international policymakers today. The crux of the problem from an anthropological point of view is the issue of how to translate productivity gains in agriculture into meaningful gains in nutritional status among those most in need. Addressing that issue requires a conceptual framework which emphasizes the interdependence among biological and cultural aspects of nutrition. It is to be expected that the skills of anthropologists will be increasingly in demand as governments and scientific groups address nutrition issues more explicitly.

The National Academy of Sciences/National Research Council has recently completed a detailed set of recommendations for the deployment of US research efforts so as to maximize impact on world food and hunger problems (118). The report of the Nutrition Overview section of that study specifies several major areas for needed research, all of which will benefit from strong anthropological contributions. The first major area, and most fundamental, directs research toward understanding the functional consequences of malnutrition on an individual and a societal level. Individual and social cost are to be measured in terms of work performance, disease resistance, learning and behavioral adaptation, fertility, mortality, and other functional measures.

Other high priority areas for research include social and cultural determinants of what people actually eat—especially those which determine intrahousehold distribution of food—and the effects of direct and indirect intervention efforts on nutritional status. In these areas, the perspective of the applied anthropologist is necessary and most appropriate.

Recommendations such as those of the NAS/NRC group represent a shift away from the point of view lamented by Adams that "the major preoccupation of those concerned with development (has been) how to make more of it" (2, p. 85). There are several reasons for the shift toward a more hopeful and rational approach. A lesson not to be ignored is that the People's Republic of China, through strength of political will, has managed virtually to eradicate overt malnutrition in its population (180). While few in the western development community would want to emulate the Chinese methods, the example of possibility is strong; and the fact that the solutions, however little may be known of the details, have largely not been technological ones, also holds a lesson. A second reason for a shift in focus is the increasing recognition that the actual cost of feeding the world by North American industrialized agricultural methods may be prohibitively expensive in terms of energy costs and environmental impoverishment (132, 170). Pleas for concentration on maximizing the production and value of indigenous food crops are making increasing sense in this context.

It is clear that there will continue to be a need for the cultural anthropologist in implementing programs of nutritional change. What is new about the world food and nutrition situation today is that the nature of the problems—the allocation of scarce resources—demands the perspective of the biological anthropologist, since human adaptation to nutritional stress is at the center of the decision-making process. For example, it may be crucial to know, in a given situation, whether increased availability of staple cereals or fortification of existing products with amino acids will have the greater payoff in terms of well-being for the greatest number of people. A controversy over the "protein gap" is raging in nutritional circles (103, 156, 188a). Some scientists feel that international requirements are too low and that the protein problem has been eradicated falsely by the stroke of a pen, while others believe that the focus on protein in the past few decades has been in part a fight with a paper dragon, since the limiting factor for most of the world's malnourished is energy, and concentration on protein has possibly done a great disservice by focusing on technological solutions for what is essentially a social problem. Whatever the ultimate resolution of this particular question, it is clear that the matter of adaptation to nutritional stress is central. Issues in distribution of food resources are receiving serious attention from planners (17, 81). Anthropologists, with their population focus and time perspective, have never had a clearer role to play in the solution of real and pressing problems.

Literature Cited

1. Aall, C. 1970. Relief, nutrition, and health in the Nigerian/Biafran war. *J. Trop. Pediatr.* 16:70–90
2. Adams, R. N. 1974. Some observations on the inter-relations of development and nutrition programs. *Ecol. Food Nutr.* 3:85–88
3. Alland, A. 1975. Adaptation. *Ann. Rev. Anthropol.* 4:59–73
4. Alland, A., McCay, B. 1973. The concept of adaptation in biological and culture evolution. In *Handbook of Social and Cultural Anthropology,* ed. J. J. Honigmann, pp. 143–78. Chicago: Rand-McNally
5. Allison, A. C. 1975. Interactions of genetic predisposition, acquired immunity and environmental factors on susceptibility to disease. In *Man-made Lakes and Human Health,* ed. N. F. Stanley, M. P. Alpers, pp. 401–26. New York: Academic
6. Anderson, R. K. 1975. Nutrition, fertility, and reproduction. In *Prognosis for the Undernourished Surviving Child,* ed. A. Chavez, H. Bourges, S. Basta. pp. 7–10. Basal: Karger
7. Arnott, M. L., ed. 1975. *Gastronomy: The Anthropology of Food and Food Habits.* The Hague: Mouton
8. Astrand, P.-O., Rodahl, K. 1970. *Textbook of Work Physiology.* New York: McGraw-Hill
9. Baker, P. T. 1967. Human biological variation as an adaptive response to the environment. *Eugen. Q.* 13:81–91
10. Baker, P. T. 1968. Multidisciplinary studies of human adaptability. *Mater. Pr. Antropol.* 75:321–31
11. Baker, P. T. 1974. An evolutionary perspective on environmental physiology. In *Environmental Physiology,* ed. N. B. Slonin, pp. 510–22. St. Louis: Mosby
12. Baker, P. T. 1976. Work performance of highland natives. See Ref. 14, pp. 300–14
13. Baker, P. T., Danials, F. Jr. 1956. Relationship between skinfold thickness and body cooling for two hours at 15°C. *J. Appl. Physiol.* 8:409–16
14. Baker, P. T., Little, M. A., eds. 1976. *Man in the Andes: A Multidisciplinary Study of High Altitude Quechua.* Stroudsburg, PA: Dowden, Hutchinson & Ross
15. Bar-Or, O., Lundegren, H. M., Buskirk, E. R. 1969. Heat tolerance of exercising obese and lean women. *J. Appl. Physiol.* 26:403–9
16. Bennett, J. W. 1976. Anticipation, adaptation, and the concept of culture in anthropology. *Science* 192:847–53
17. Berg, A. 1973. *The Nutrition Factor: Its Role in National Development.* Washington DC: Brookings
18. Bergner, L., Susser, M. W. 1970. Low birth weight and prenatal nutrition. An interpretive review. *Pediatrics* 46:946–66
19. Billewicz, W. Z., Fellowes, H. M., Hytten, C. A. 1976. Comments on the critical metabolic mass and age of menarche. *Ann. Hum. Biol.* 3:51–59
20. Bolton, R. 1973. Aggression and hypoglycemia among the Qolla: A study in psychobiological anthropology. *Ethnology* 12:227–57
21. Brown, R. E. 1972. Some nutritional considerations in times of major catastrophe. Observations following a recent visit to the Bangladesh refugee camps in Northeastern India. *Clin. Pediatr.* 11:334–42
22. Burchard, R. 1975. Coca chewing: a new perspective. In *Cannibas and Culture,* ed. V. Rubin, pp. 463–84. The Hague: Mouton
23. Cerami, A., Peterson, C. M. 1975. Cyanate and sickle-cell disease. *Sci. Am.* 232(4):44–50
24. Chavez, A., Martinez, C., Yaschine, T. 1975. Nutrition, behavioral development, and mother-child interaction in

young rural children. *Fed. Proc.* 34:1574–82

25. Chenoy, N. J. 1972. Ascorbic acid levels in mammalian tissues and its metabolic significance. *Comp. Biochem. Physiol.* 42A:945–52

26. Chinn, K. S. K., Hannon, J. P. 1969. Efficiency of food utilization at high altitude. *Fed. Proc.* 28:944–47

27. Christakes, G. 1973. Nutritional assessment in health programs. *Am. J. Public Health* 63 (Suppl.)

28. Condon, J. R., Nassim, J. R., Hilbe, A., Millard, F. J. C., Stainthorpe, E. M. 1970. Calcium and phosphorus metabolism in relation to lactose tolerance. *Lancet* 1:1027–29

28a. Consolazio, C. F., Nelson, R. A., Matoush, L. O., Harding, R. S., Canham, J. E. 1963. Nitrogen excretion in sweat and its relation to nitrogen balance requirements. *J. Nutr.* 79:399–406

29. Consolazio, C. F., Shapiro, R. S., Masterson, J. E., McKinzie, P. S. L. 1961. Energy requirements of men in extreme heat. *J. Nutr.* 73:126–34

30. Cravioto, J. 1970. Complexity of factors involved in protein-calorie malnutrition. In *Malnutrition Is A Problem of Ecology,* ed. P. Gyorgy, O. L. Kline, pp. 7–22. Basel: Karger

31. Cravioto, J., Delicardie, E. R. 1975. Mother-infant relationship prior to the development of clinically severe malnutrition in the child. *Proc. West. Hemisphere Nutr. Congr., 4th,* pp. 126–36

32. Cravioto, J., Hambraeus, L., Vahlquist, B., eds. 1974. *Early Malnutrition and Mental Development.* Uppsala, Sweden: Alquist & Wiksell

33. Delicardie, E. R., Cravioto, J. 1974. Behavioral responsiveness of survivors of clinically severe malnutrition to cognitive demands. See Ref. 32, pp. 134–53

34. Dobbing, J. 1974. Prenatal nutrition and neurological development. See Ref. 32, pp. 96–110

35. Draper, H. H. 1974. Aspects of adaptation to the native Eskimo diet: Energy metabolism. *Am. J. Phys. Anthropol.* 41:475 (Abstr.)

36. Dubos, R. 1965. *Man Adapting.* New Haven: Yale Univ. Press

37. Durham, W. H. 1976. The adaptive significance of cultural behavior. *Hum. Ecol.* 4:89–121

38. Edelman, R. 1975. Cell-mediated immunity in protein-calorie malnutrition. In *Protein-Calorie Malnutrition,* ed. R. E. Olson, pp. 377–81. New York: Academic

39. Elliot, O, Yess, N. J., Hegsted, D. M. 1966. Biosynthesis of ascorbic acid in the tree shrew and slow loris. *Nature* 212:739

40. Falkner, F. 1972. The creation of growth standards: a committee report. *Am. J. Clin. Nutr.* 25:218–20

41. Finch, C. A. 1975. Erythropoiesis in protein-calorie malnutrition. See Ref. 38, pp. 247–57

42. Fitzgerald, T. K., ed. 1976. *Nutrition and Anthropologie in Action.* Assen (Netherlands): Van Gorcum

43. Flatz, G., Rotthauwe, H. W. 1973. Lactose nutrition and natural selection. *Lancet* 2:76–77

44. Folk, G. E. 1974. *Textbook of Environmental Physiology.* Philadelphia: Lea & Febiger. 2nd ed.

45. Food and Agriculture Organization 1976. *Directorio de los Centros Latinoamericanos de Investigacion en Tecnologia Alimentaria y Nutricion Humana.* Santiago: FAO Regional Office for Latin America

46. Foulks, E. F. 1973. *The Arctic Hysterias of the North Alaskan Eskimo.* Anthropol. Stud. No. 10. Washington DC: Am. Anthropol. Assoc.

47. Frisancho, A. R., Sanchez, J., Pallardel, D., Yanez, L. 1973. Adaptive significance of small body size under poor socio-economic conditions in southern Peru. *Am. J. Phys. Anthropol.* 39: 255–61

48. Frisancho, A. R., Velasquez, T., Sanchez, J. 1975. Possible adaptive significance of small body size in the attainment of aerobic capacity among high-altitude Quechua natives. In *Biosocial Interrelations in Population Adaptation,* ed. E. S. Watts, F. E. Johnston, G. W. Lasker, pp. 55–64. The Hague, Paris: Mouton

49. Frisch, R. E. 1975. Critical weights, a critical body composition, menarche and the maintenance of menstrual cycles. See Ref. 48, pp. 319–52

50. Frisch, R. E. 1976. Letter. *Ann. Hum. Biol.* 3:489–491

51. Garn, S. M. 1966. Nutrition in physical anthropology. *Am. J. Phys. Anthropol.* 24:289–92

52. Gilat, T., Benaroya, Y., Gelman-Malachi, E., Adam, A. 1973. Genetics of primary adult lactase deficiency. *Gastroenterology* 64:562–68

53. Goldstein, H. Some statistical considerations on the use of anthropometry to assess nutritional status. See Ref. 147, pp. 221–30

54. Gopalan, C., Naidu, A. N. 1972. Nutrition and fertility. *Lancet* 2:1077–79
55. Greene, L. S. 1973. Physical growth and development, neurological maturation, and behavioral functioning in two Ecuadorian Andean communities in which goiter is endemic. I. Outline of the problem of endemic goiter and cretinism. Physical growth and neurological maturation in the adult population of La Esperanza. *Am. J. Phys. Anthropol.* 38:119–34
56. Greene, M. H. 1974. Impact of the Sahelian drought in Mauritania, West Africa. *Lancet* 1:1093–97
57. Gross, D. R., Underwood, B. A. 1971. Technological change and caloric costs: Sisal agriculture in northeastern Brazil. *Am. Anthropol.* 73:725–40
58. Habicht, J.-P., Delgado, H., Yarbrough, C., Klein, R. E. 1975. Repercussions of lactation on nutritional status of mother and infant. See Ref. 6, pp. 106–14
59. Habicht, J-P., Martorell, R., Yarbrough, C., Malina, R. M., Klein, R. E. 1974. Height and weight standards for preschool children: How relevant are ethnic differences in growth potential? *Lancet* 1:611–14
60. Habicht, J-P., Yarbrough, C., Lechtig, A., Klein, R. E. 1974. Relation of maternal supplementary feeding during pregnancy to birth weight and other sociobiological factors. In *Nutrition and Fetal Development*, ed. M. Winick, pp. 127–47. New York: Wiley
61. Hamilton, W. J. 1973. *Life's Color Code*. New York: McGraw-Hill
62. Hanna, J. M. 1974. Coca leaf use in southern Peru: Some biological aspects. *Am. Anthropol.* 76:281–96
63. Harrison, G. G. 1975. Primary adult lactase deficiency: a problem in anthropological genetics. *Am. Anthropol.* 77:812–35
64. Harrison, G. G., Rathje, W. L., Hughes, W. W. 1975. Food waste behavior in an urban population. *J. Nutr. Educ.* 7:13–16
65. Hart, J. S., Sabean, H. B., Hildes, J. A., Depocas, F., Hammel, H. T., Anderson, K. L. 1962. Thermal and metabolic responses of coastal Eskimos during a cold night. *J. Appl. Physiol.* 17:953–60
65a. Heywood, P. F. 1974. *Malnutrition and Productivity in Jamaican Sugar Cane Cutters*. PhD thesis. Cornell Univ., Ithaca, NY
66. Holmberg, A. R. 1950. *Nomads of the Long Bow: The Siriono of Eastern Bolivia*. Washington, DC: Smithsonian Inst.
67. Hornig, D. 1975. Metabolism of ascorbic acid. *World Rev. Nutr. Diet.* 23:225–58
68. Houston, R. G. 1973. Sickle cell anemia and dietary precursors of cyanate. *Am. J. Clin. Nutr.* 26:1261–64
69. Huang, P. C., Lo, C. C., Ho, W. T. 1975. Protein requirements of men in a hot climate: Decreased urinary nitrogen losses concomitant with increased sweat nitrogen losses during exposures to high environmental temperature. *Am. J. Clin. Nutr.* 28:494–501
70. Hunt, E. E. 1958. Human growth and body form in recent generations. *Am. Anthropol.* 60:118–31
71. Hunt, E. E. 1966. The developmental genetics of man. In *Human Development*, ed. F. Falkner, pp. 76–122. Philadelphia: Saunders
72. Hunter, J. M. 1973. Geophagy in Africa and in the United States: A culture-nutrition hypothesis. *Geogr. Rev.* 63:171–95
73. Interdepartmental Committee on Nutrition for National Defense 1963. *Manual for Nutrition Surveys*. Washington, DC: GPO. 2nd ed.
74. Jamison, P. L., Friedman, S. M., eds. 1974. *Energy Flow in Human Communities*. University Park, PA: Human Adaptability Coord. Off.
75. Jamison, P. L., Zegura, S. L., Milan, F. A., eds. 1977. *The Eskimo of Northwestern Alaska: A Biological Perspective*.
75. Stroudsburg, PA: Dowden, Hutchinson & Ross. In press
76. Jelliffe, D. B. 1966. *The Assessment of the Nutritional Status of the Community*. Geneva: World Health Organ. Monogr. Ser. 53
77. Jelliffe, D. B., Jelliffe, E. F. P. 1975. Interrelationships of lactation, conception and the nutrition of the nursing couple. See Ref. 6, pp. 11–15
78. Jelliffe, E. F. P., Gurney, M. 1975. Definition of the problem. See Ref. 147, pp. 1–14
79. Jerome, N. 1975. On determining food patterns of urban dwellers in contemporary United States society. See Ref. 7, pp. 91–111
80. Johnston, F. E., Roche, A. F., Schell, L. M., Wettenhall, H. N. B. 1975. Critical weight at menarche: Critique of a hypothesis. *Am. J. Dis. Child.* 129:19–23
81. Joy, J. L. 1975. Planning to reduce nutritional deprivation. *Food Nutr.* 1:10–17

82. Karlsson, J., Saltin, B. 1971. Diet, muscle glycogen, and endurance performance. *J. Appl. Physiol.* 31:203–6
83. Katsura, E., Oiso, T. 1976. Beriberi. In *Nutrition in Preventive Medicine*, ed. G. H. Beaton, J. M. Bengoa, pp. 136–45. Geneva: World Health Organ.
84. Katz, M., Keusch, G. T., Mata, L. 1975. Malnutrition and infection during pregnancy: Determinants of growth and development of the child. *Am. J. Dis. Child.* 129:419–63
85. Katz, S. H., Hediger, M. L., Valleroy, L. A. 1974. Traditional maize processing techniques in the New World. *Science* 184:765–73
86. Kemp, W. B. 1971. The flow of energy in a hunting society. *Sci. Am.* 225: 104–15
87. Keys, A., Brozek, J., Hanschel, A., Mickelsen, O., Taylor, H. L. 1950. *The Biology of Human Starvation.* Minneapolis: Univ. Minnesota Press. 2 vols.
88. Kies, C., Fox, H. M. 1972. Interrelationships of leucine with lysine, tryptophan, and niacin as they influence the protein value of cereal grains for humans. *Cereal Chem.* 49:223
89. Kline, O. L., King, C. G., eds. 1976. *Nutritional Adaptation to the Environment.* University Park, PA: Human Adaptability Coord. Off.
90. Lambotte, C. 1974. Sickle-cell anemia and dietary precursors of cyanate. *Am. J. Clin. Nutr.* 27:765–66
91. Lasker, G. W. 1969. Human biological adaptability: the ecological approach in physical anthropology. *Science* 166: 1480–86
92. Latham, M. C. 1974. Protein-calorie malnutrition in children and its relation to psychological development and behavior. *Physiol. Rev.* 54:541–65
93. Lee, R. B. 1969. !Kung Bushman subsistance: An input-output analysis. In *Environment and Cultural Behavior*, ed. A. P. Vayda, pp. 47–49. Garden City, NY: Natural History Press
94. Lieberman, L. S. 1976. *Diet, natural selection and adaptation in human populations.* Presented at Ann. Meet. Am. Anthropol. Assoc., 75th, Washington DC
95. Lieberman, L. S., Baker, P. T. 1976. *The Samoan Migrant Project: Preliminary Report* (Monogr.). University Park: Pennsylvania State Univ.
96. Levitsky, D. A., Massaro, T. F., Barnes, R. H. 1975. Maternal malnutrition and the neonatal environment. *Fed. Proc.* 34:1583–86
97. Little, M. A., Hochner, D. H. 1973. *Human Thermoregulation, Growth and Evolution.* Addison-Wesley Module Anthropol. No. 36
98. Little, M. A., Morren, G. E. B. 1976. *Ecology, Energetics and Human Variability.* Dubuque, Iowa: Brown
99. Little, M. A., Thomas, R. B., Mazess, R. B., Baker, P. T. 1971. Population differences and developmental changes in extremity temperature responses to cold among Andean Indians. *Hum. Biol.* 43:70–91
100. Loomis, W. F. 1967. Skin-pigment regulation of Vitamin-D biosynthesis in man. *Science* 157:501–6
101. McCracken, R. D. 1971. Lactase deficiency: an example of dietary evolution. *Curr. Anthropol.* 12:479–517
102. McFarlane, H., Reddy, S., Adcock, K. J., Adeshina, H., Cooke, A. R., Akene, J. 1970. Immunity, transferrin, and survival in kwashiorkor. *Br. Med. J.* 4:268–70
103. McLaren, D. S. 1974. The great protein fiasco. *Lancet* 2:93–96
104. McLaren, D. S., Burman, D., eds. 1976. *Paediatric Nutrition.* Edinburgh: Churchill-Livingstone
105. Maleki, M. 1973. Food consumption and nutritional status of 13 year old village and city schoolboys in Fars Province, Iran. *Ecol. Food Nutr.* 2:39–42
106. Mason, J. B., Hay, R. W., Holt, J., Seaman, J., Bowden, M. R. 1974. Nutritional lessons from the Ethiopian drought. *Nature* 248:646–50
107. Mata, L. J., Urrutia, J. J., Lechtig, A. 1971. Infection and nutrition of children of a low socioeconomic rural community. *Am. J. Clin. Nutr.* 24:249–59
108. May, J. M. 1974. *The Ecology of Malnutrition in Eastern South America.* New York: Hafner
109. Mayer, J. 1975. Management of famine relief. In *Food: Politics, Economics, Nutrition and Research*, ed. P. H. Abelson, pp. 79–84. Washington DC: Am. Assoc. Adv. Sci.
110. Mazess, R. B. 1975. Human adaptation to high altitude. In *Physiological Anthropology*, ed. A. Damon, pp. 167–209. New York: Oxford Univ. Press
111. Mazess, R. B. 1975. Biological Adaptation: aptitudes and acclimatization. See Ref. 48, pp. 9–18
111a. Mazess, R. B., Mather, W. E. 1975. Bone mineral content in Canadian Eskimos. *Hum. Biol.* 47:45–63
112. Montgomery, E. 1977. Anthropological contributions to the study of food-

related cultural variability. In *Progress in Human Nutrition,* Vol. 2, ed. S. Margen. Westport, Conn: Avi. In press

113. Moore, W. M., Silverberg, M. M., Read, M. S., eds. 1972. *Nutrition, Growth and Development of North American Indian Children.* DHEW Publ. (NIH)72–76. Washington DC: GPO

114. Moran, E. F. 1975. Food, development, and man in the tropics. See Ref. 7, pp. 169–86

115. National Academy of Sciences 1970. *Maternal Nutrition and the Course of Pregnancy.* Washington DC: Natl. Res. Counc., Natl. Acad. Sci.

116. National Academy of Sciences 1974. *U. S. Participation in the International Biological Program.* Report No. 6, US Natl. Comm. Int. Biol. Program. Washington DC: Natl. Res. Counc., Natl. Acad. Sci.

117. National Academy of Sciences 1974. *Recommended Dietary Allowances.* Washington DC: Natl. Res. Counc., Natl. Acad. Sci. 8th ed.

118. National Academy of Sciences 1977. *The World Food and Nutrition Study.* Washington DC: Natl. Res. Counc., Natl. Acad. Sci. In press

119. National Center for Health Statistics 1974. *Preliminary Findings of the First Health and Nutrition Examination Survey, United States, 1971–1972. Dietary Intake and Biochemical Findings.* Rockville, Md: Natl. Center Health Stat.

120. Neel, J. V. 1962. Diabetes mellitus: A "thrifty" genotype rendered detrimental by "progress." *Am. J. Hum. Genet.* 14:353–62

121. Newman, M. T. 1960. Adaptations in the physique of American Aborigines to nutritional factors. *Hum. Biol.* 32:288–314

122. Newman, M. T. 1975. Nutritional adaptation in man. See Ref. 110, pp. 210–59

123. Newman, R. W. 1970. Why man is such a sweaty and thirsty naked animal: A speculative review. *Hum. Biol.* 42:12–27

124. Odum, H. T. 1971. *Environment, Power and Society.* New York: Wiley-Interscience

125. Oke, O. L. 1968. Cassava as food in Nigeria. *World Rev. Nutr. Diet.* 9:227–50

126. Owen, G. M., Kram, K. M., Garry, P. J., Lowe, J. E., Lubin, A. H. 1974. A study of nutritional status of preschool children in the United States, 1968–1970. *Pediatrics* 53:597–646

127. Otten, C. M. 1967. On pestilence, diet, natural selection, and the distribution of microbial and human blood group antigens and antibodies. *Curr. Anthropol.* 8:209–26

128. Passmore, R., Nicol, B. M., Rao, M. N. 1974. *Handbook on Human Nutritional Requirements.* Geneva: World Health Organ. Monogr. Ser. 61

129. Perez, A., Vela, P., Potter, R., Masnick, G. S. 1971. Timing and sequence of resuming ovulation and menstruation after childbirth. *Popul. Stud.* 25:491–503

130. Picon-Reategui, E. 1976. Nutrition. See Ref. 14, pp. 208–36

131. Piddocke, S. 1965. The potlatch system of the southern Kwakuitl: A new perspective. *Southwest. J. Anthropol.* 21:244–64

132. Pimentel, D., Hurd, L. E., Bellotti, A. C., Forster, M. J., Oka, I. N., Sholes, O. D., Whitman, R. J. 1973. Food production and the energy crisis. *Science* 182:443–49

133. Prior, I. 1971. The price of civilization. *Nutr. Today* 6:2–11

134. Prosser, C. L. 1964. Perspectives of adaptation: Theoretical aspects. In *Handbook of Physiology,* ed. E. B. Dill, E. F. Adolf, C. G. Wilber, Sect. 4:11–25. Washington DC: Am. Phys. Soc.

135. Rajalakshmi, R., Subbulakshmi, G., Ramakrishnan, C. V., Joshi, S. K., Bhatt, R. V. 1967. Biosynthesis of ascorbic acid in human placenta. *Curr. Sci.* 36:45–46

136. Rappaport, R. A. 1971. The flow of energy in an agricultural society. *Sci. Am.* 224:116–29

137. Rathje, W. L., Harrison, G. G. 1977. *Le projet du garbage: a new methodology for monitoring trends in consumer behavior. Fed. Proc.* (Abstr.) In press

138. Read, M. S. 1970. Nutrition and ecology: crossroads for research. See Ref. 30, pp. 202–18

139. Rechcigl, M. 1973. Reviews relating to food, nutrition and health: a selected bibliography. *World Rev. Nutr. Diet.* 16:398–445

140. Reinhold, J. G., Ismail-Beigi, F., Faradji, B. 1975. Fiber vs phytate as determinant of availability of calcium, zinc, and iron of breadstuffs. *Nutr. Rep. Int.* 12:75–85

141. Reinhold, J. G., Nasr, K., Lahimgarzadeh, A. 1973. Zinc, calcium, phosphorus and nitrogen balances of Iranian

villagers following a change from phytate-rich to phytate-poor diets. *Ecol. Food Nutr.* 2:157–62

142. Reinhold, J. G., Lahimgarzadeh, A., Nasr, K., Hedayati, M. 1973. Effects of purified phytate and phytate-rich bread upon metabolism of zinc, calcium, phosphorus, and nitrogen in man. *Lancet* 1:283–88

143. Ricciuti, H. N. 1977. Adverse social and biological influences on early development. In *Ecological Factors in Human Development,* ed. H. McGurk, pp. 157–72. Amsterdam: North-Holland

144. Ritenbaugh, C. K. 1974. *The Pattern of Diabetes in a Pima Community.* PhD thesis. Univ. California, Los Angeles

145. Roberts, D. F. 1960. Effects of race and climate on growth of African children. In *Human Growth,* ed. J. M. Tanner, pp. 59–72. London: Pergamon

146. Roberts, D. F. 1973. *Climate and Human Variability.* Addison-Wesley Module Anthropol. No. 34.

147. Roche, A. F., Falkner, F., eds. 1974. *Nutrition and Malnutrition: Identification and Measurement.* New York: Plenum

148. Rodahl, K. 1952. Basal metabolism of the Eskimo. *J. Nutr.* 48:359–68

149. Roe, D. A. 1973. *A Plague of Corn: The Social History of Pellagra.* Ithaca, NY: Cornell Univ. Press

150. Roy, R. N., Guka, B. C. 1958. Species difference in regard to the biosynthesis of ascorbic acid. *Nature* 182:319–30

151. Sahi, T. 1974. The inheritance of selective adult-type lactose malabsorption. *Scand. J. Gastroenterol.* 9 (Suppl. 30): 1–73

152. Sauberlich, H. E., Skala, J. H., Dowdy, R. P. 1974. *Laboratory Tests for the Assessment of Nutritional Status.* Cleveland: CRC Press

153. Schaefer, A. E. 1969. Testimony before the U.S. Senate Select Committee on Nutrition and Human Needs. Part 3— *The National Nutritional Survey,* pp. 370–79. Washington DC: GPO

155. Scrimshaw, N. S. 1975. Interactions of malnutrition and infection: advances in understanding. See Ref. 38, pp. 353–68

156. Scrimshaw, N. S. 1976. An analysis of past and present recommended dietary allowances for protein in health and disease. *N. Engl. J. Med.* 294:136–42

157. Scrimshaw, N. S., Gordon, J. E., eds. *Malnutrition, Learning and Behavior.* Cambridge, Mass: MIT Press

158. Scrimshaw, N. S., Taylor, C. E., Gordon, J. E. 1968. *Interactions of Nutrition and Infection.* World Health Organ. Monogr. Ser. 57

159. Seaman, J., Holt, J., Rivers, J., Murlis, J. 1973. An inquiry into the drought situation in Upper Volta. *Lancet* 2:774–78

160. Serjeant, G. R. 1973. Sickle-cell anemia: clinical features in adulthood and old age. In *Sickle Cell Disease,* ed. H. Abramson, J. F. Bertles, D. L. Wither, p. 252. St. Louis: Mosby

161. Simoons, F. J. 1969. Primary adult lactose intolerance and the milking habit: a problem in biological and cultural interrelations. I. Review of the medical research. *Am. J. Dig. Dis.* 14:819–36

162. Simoons, F. J. 1970. Primary adult lactose intolerance and the milking habit: A problem in biological and cultural interrelations. II. A culture historical hypothesis. *Am. J. Dig. Dis.* 15:695–710

163. Simoons, F. J. 1973. Progress report. New light on ethnic differences in adult lactose intolerance. *Am. J. Dig. Dis.* 18:595–611

164. Sirisinha, S. 1975. Immunoglobulins and complement in protein-calorie malnutrition. See Ref. 38, pp. 369–75

165. Slobodkin, L. B. 1967. Toward a predictive theory of evolution. In *Population Biology and Evolution,* ed. R. C. Lewontin, pp. 187–205. Syracuse, NY: Syracuse Univ. Press

166. Sommer, A., Mosley, W. H. 1972. East Bengal cyclone of November, 1970. Epidemiological approach to disaster assessment. *Lancet* 1:1029–36

167. Steegmann, A. T. 1975. Human adaptation to cold. See Ref. 110, pp. 130–65

168. Stein, Z., Susser, M. 1975. Fertility, fecundity, famine: food rations in the Dutch famine 1944/5 have a causal relation to fertility and probably to fecundity. *Hum. Biol.* 47:131–54

169. Stein, Z., Susser, M. 1976. *Famine and Human Development: The Dutch Hunger Winter of 1944/45.* New York: Oxford Univ. Press

170. Steinhart, J. S., Steinhart, C. E. 1974. Energy use in the U.S. food system. *Science* 184:307–16

171. Stini, W. A. 1971. Evolutionary implications of changing nutritional patterns in human populations. *Am. Anthropol.* 73:1019–30

172. Stini, W. A. 1972. Reduced sexual dimorphism in upper arm muscle circumference associated with protein-deficient diet in a South American population. *Am. J. Phys. Anthropol.* 36:341–52

173. Stini, W. A. 1975. Adaptive strategies of populations under nutritional stress. See Ref. 48, pp. 19–42
174. Stini, W. A. 1977. The concept and assessment of nutritional status. In *Anthropological Aspects of Human Nutrition*, ed. F. E. Johnston. Santa Fe: School of American Research. In press
175. Tanner, J. M. 1962. *Growth at Adolescence*. Oxford: Blackwell
176. Thomas, R. B. 1975. The ecology of work. See Ref. 110, pp. 59–79
177. Thomas, R. B. 1976. Energy flow at high altitude. See Ref. 14, pp. 379–404
178. Thomson, A. M., Billewicz, W. Z. 1963. Nutritional status, maternal physique and reproductive efficiency. *Proc. Nutr. Soc.* 22:55–60
179. Thomson, A. M., Black, A. E. 1965. Nutritional aspects of human lactation. *Bull. World Health Organ.* 52:163–77
180. Timmer, C. P. 1976. Food policy in China. *Food Res. Inst. Stud.* 15, No. 1
181. Turnbull, C. M. 1972. *The Mountain People.* New York: Simon & Schuster
182. Vermeer, D. E. 1966. Geophagy among the Tiv of Nigeria. *Ann. Assoc. Am. Geogr.* 56:197–204
183. Vermeer, D. E. 1971. Geophagy among the Ewe of Ghana. *Ethnology* 10:56–72
183a. Viteri, F. E., Torun, B. 1975. Ingestion calorica y Trabajo fisilo de obreros agricolas en Guatamala. *Bol. Of. Sanit. Panam.* Washington DC (January)
184. Walker, A. R. P., Richardson, B. D. 1973. International and local growth standards. *Am. J. Clin. Nutr.* 26:897–900
185. Weiner, J. S. 1975. Adaptation and variation among hunters and gatherers. In *The Natural History of Man,* ed. J. S. Weiner, Chap. 4. New York: Universe Books
186. Weiner, J. S., Lourie, J. A. 1969. *Human Biology: A Guide to Field Methods.* IBP Handbook No. 9. Philadelphia: Davies
187. Welon, Z., Bielicki, T. 1973. The adolescent growth spurt and the "critical body weight" hypothesis. *Mater. Pr. Antropol.* 86:27–33
188. White, L. A. 1959. *The Evolution of Culture: and the Development of Civilization to the Fall of Rome.* New York: McGraw-Hill
188a. Williams, C. D. 1975. On that fiasco. *Lancet* 1:793–94
189. Wilson, C. S. 1973. Food habits: A selected annotated bibliography. *J. Nutr. Educ.* 5(1)Suppl. 1:39–72
190. Winick, M. 1976. *Malnutrition and Brain Development.* New York: Oxford Univ. Press
191. Worthington, B. S. 1974. Effect of nutritional status on immune phenomena. *J. Am. Diet. Assoc.* 65:123–29
192. Wray, J. D. 1975. Will better nutrition decrease fertility? See Ref. 6, pp. 16–31

Ann. Rev. Anthropol. 1977. 6:103–19
Copyright © 1977 by Annual Reviews Inc. All rights reserved

PSYCHOLOGICAL ANTHROPOLOGY

❖9589

Christie W. Kiefer

Human Development Program, University of California, San Francisco, California 94143

Applying the term "psychological anthropology" to a special subfield of ethnology used to make more sense than it does now. To be sure, there has always been a liberal amount of psychological thinking—either implicit or explicit—throughout the theoretical literature on the evolution and nature of man, but most ethnologists used to hope they could identify biological, ecological, and cultural laws that operated—or that could be studied—independently of the workings of the human mind. This hope has faded for most of us in the last decade or two, due especially in the United States to large-scale government support of our science.

One reason for this trend has been the necessity—imposed by granting agency standards—of a clearer sense of problem. Whether we are interested in technology or in religion, we are required to anticipate the questions of interdisciplinary review committees about "overlooked variables." Since psychologists greatly outnumber anthropologists on most committees (as in the universe), there are almost certain to be some questions about psychology. Another reason has been our very obvious failure to develop a predictive science of man of the sort that public sponsors would like ideally to see. Rather than reject the possibility of a predictive science, and rather than scrap our theories altogether, we are tempted to look for complications at the level of psychology that might indicate where we have missed the mark. If, for example, we find that some individuals and communities are greatly upset and disorganized by rapid social change, and others of the same cultural type are not, we become more curious about cognitive, situational, and personality variables (cf 20, 62, 93). Whether or not this is the most productive direction for anthropology to take, it has the happy result of generating a great many researchable questions.

At any rate, we have been thrown into competition with psychologists and sociologists for research funds, and have had to become much more self conscious about our methods. We have seen how difficult it is to get two or more subjects, or two or more observers, to agree on a description of anything, much less an interpretation of it (cf 13, 69). We have become more aware that observing and participating are themselves very complex and poorly understood processes of perception, thinking and communication. In building the mirror for man, we have found that the image of the builder himself looms large therein. One sees three tendencies resulting from this: (*a*) an interest in the dynamics of perception, cognition, and communication; (*b*) a borrowing of "hard" experimental and statistical methods from other disciplines and especially psychology; and (*c*) a vigorous quest for a philosophy of method, especially phenomenology. I will say more about each of these tendencies later on.

In short, it has become almost impossible to be an ethnologist and *not* to be concerned about psychology. In his recent essay on theories of culture, for example, Keesing (60) assigned the term "sociocultural system" to the idea of shared behavior patterns, and reserved the term "culture" for the deep ideational structures, the sort of generic mental codes, that generate the observable level of behavior. Even a materialist like Marvin Harris (47) must nowadays spend a great deal of time explaining his lack of mentalism. On the whole, then, I agree with Honigmann (49) and Bourguignon (16) that the term "psychological anthropology" makes most sense when used to designate the psychological concerns of anthropologists. It strikes me as silly to claim, for instance, that it is "really" the study of the individual in relation to the cultural (111), or to exclude the rich variety of psychological interpretation found in most recent ethnographic studies.

Psychological anthropology then is a large and loosely organized realm of ideas about the mental background of behavior; and in this realm I have sought the outlines of a larger view of human mind and culture, keeping especially alert for what seems new. I have not attempted a detailed review of the literature, and I have dealt only peripherally with recent developments in methods (see 3, 11, 18, 25, 72, 98), or with the application of psychological anthropology to other fields such as psychiatry and education (see 37, 61, 84, 94). Far from lagging behind the generally rapid growth of the behavioral sciences, these areas have become, to the eye of the casual reviewer, extensive and complicated in their own right.

In trying to pull together the key substantive and theoretical concerns of psychological anthropology proper, I have found (as have other reviewers) persistent differences of viewpoint and terminology within specific areas of interest, as well as widely diverging interests. While some ethnologists appear to be contented with highly parochial psychological views based on one or two cultures or a limited range of behavior, there are also many who read widely in psychology and are self-reflective and self-critical. I find the search for order easier, therefore, after some thought about the historical and philosophical context of the field.

THE CLIMATE OF PSYCHOLOGICAL THOUGHT

The search for universal and useful laws of human psychology has been extremely discouraging in our century. The effects on rates of psychopathology and social chaos of the availability of psychoanalysis, behavior modification, transactional analysis, and even chemotherapy are less than inspiring (cf 2). Clinicians, social planners, and psychologists themselves find very little of value in the research that psychologists do (41, p. 191; 55, p. 408; 106, p. 141). Even the elegant and convincing work of Piaget has been very hard to evaluate, largely because of the problematic nature of the relationship between language and thought (see 46, 83, 85). One result of this has been an increasing distance between what William James used to call "tough-minded" and "tender-minded" approaches to psychology. If it appears that the organization of human thought and behavior is too complex and changeable to yield to understanding at the level of persons and groups, the researcher is tempted to seek a predictive science at lower levels and in the "increasing division of subject matter into smaller and smaller segments" (114, p. 16) or at the level of social trends on a vast scale which obscures the effects of immediate context. Tangential escape routes lead into the phenomenological and existential views of the "tender" methodologists (see 58), where individual uniqueness and the inevitable subjectivity of knowledge are emphasized.

In psychological anthropology, tough-mindedness is easily recognizable in survey research on such topics as child rearing (109, 110) subsistence (33), perception(12, 92), and cognition (24, 28). The emphasis on measurement in such studies encourages the division of behavior into discrete variables and the summarizing of many individual behaviors into group profiles on each of these variables. This is what Bourguignon (16) refers to as the "generalizing" tendency. In such studies, individual behavior tends to be seen as a dependent variable, shaped by forces larger than the individual and his immediate social nexus. These larger forces may be mainly (a) biological or biosociological, as in the case of psychoanalytically inspired theory and the genetic approaches to perception (12); (b) ecological as in Marvin Harris's (47) work and the ecological theories of perception (92); (c) some combination of these, as in the work of Edgerton (33), the Whitings (109, 110), and to some extent DeVos (30) and LeVine (72); (d) historical, such as the followers of Max Weber (e.g. 86); or (e) social-structural, as in the work of Hsu (50, 51), Douglas (32), and Kearney (59).

The "tender" or "particularizing" tendency represents an alternative attempt to make useful generalities about the human mind in the absence of a truly predictive psychology. It seems to be based partly on the relativism of Franz Boas and his intellectual descendants in anthropology, and encouraged by configurational and phenomenological psychologists like Allport (1) and May (77), and the interactionists in social psychology like Mills (82), Becker (7), and Goffman (42). In this group I put those who emphasize the self-consciously purposeful nature of human life, and who regard purposes as things that are constantly emerging out of the histories, immediate concerns, and intimate social surroundings of individuals. Geertz's (38) approach to ethnology is of this sort, as is Berreman's (10), Bateson's (6), Plath's (88), Kaplan's (58), Henry's (48), and sometimes Wallace's (104). Implicit or explicit in their work is the idea that individuals and situations can be *understood* (not predicted or controlled) as complex idiosyncratic and highly changeable configurations, and that this is what *should* be achieved by social science.

We will not improve our understanding of everything in psychological anthropology by applying the tough-tender code to it. Many writers incorporate a little of both, and many are concerned about issues that run at right angles to this polarity. I think it is an important polarity because it illustrates nicely the depth and breadth of disagreement among us. Another good illustration is the oft-noted lack of widely accepted scientific vocabulary. The lack of theory-building which disturbs observers Honigmann (49), Campbell & Naroll (18), Bourguignon (16), and Cole & Scribner (25) results partly from the wide divergence of interests in psychological anthropology, but partly also from the fact that we cannot agree on what constitutes a personality trait or how to measure it (72, p. 98) or even whether the concept of personality is useful or not (51, 58, 96). When there is a green isle of agreement in the sea of controversy it often gets lost in the fog of terminology. For example, many modern writers follow the practice of dividing personality into what Kluckhohn (64, p. 179) called "nuclear" and "peripheral" areas, the nuclear areas being relatively stable throughout life and the peripheral areas being greatly influenced by socializing forces. However, terminology obscures the agreement. LeVine (72) uses the terms "genotype" and "phenotype"; Edgerton (33) speaks of "intrapsychic events" and "values"; Bell (8) says "modal personality" and "national creed"; DeVos(30) prefers "affective concerns" and "values"; Turner (99) uses "impulsive" and "institutional selves"; and so on. Needless to say, there is little specification of what behavior belongs to which sphere of personality, and little comment by these writers themselves on their mutual area of agreement.

The Tower of Babel effect is inevitable because there are no generally superior models of the mind or of culture; and there are no generally superior strategies for how to get these models. Any attempt to dig channels of theoretical direction in the swamps of description and speculation will fail unless some large consensus is found regarding what is interesting and important versus what is dull and trivial. We do not know how to respond to the injunction to ". . . concentrate upon those aspects [of behavior] on which we can get agreement . . ." (18, p. 444) until we can get agreement on the *usefulness* of a measurement, an observation, or a theory. Should we make bold to overlook, for example, the very considerable shortcomings of quantitative cross-cultural studies because they are subject to tests of reliability and validity accepted by the other sciences? Bochner, Brislin & Lonner (11) suggest that these virtues should be weighted, along with the novelty of results and the difficulty of getting them, as a temperate solution to the rigor problem. Unfortunately, things can be novel, rigorous, and difficult and still be oppressively boring.

THE NEED FOR A NEW PHILOSOPHY

I am not very worried about this state of affairs. As theories, techniques, and observations pile up in the study of man, one is more and more impressed, as one ought to be, with human complexity, variety, and ingenuity. However, the disunity of anthropological theory in general levies an increasing burden on the teacher, who must try to reduce it all to coherent proportions. A bad but tempting solution is to lop off great pieces of a subject and cast them out, as some have attempted to cast projective testing out of psychological anthropology (98). Such measures only postpone the difficulty. Students want to know, for example, where the recent projective work of DeVos (30), Maduro (76), Fromm & Maccoby (36), the Spindlers (95), Bushnell & Bushnell (17), Edgerton (33), Day, Boyer & DeVos (26), Kiefer (62) and others belongs in the universe if it is not psychological anthropology. A far better solution to the problem is to take what I call the "pragmatic" position: that is, to admit that *a diversity of interests among anthropologists leads inevitably to a diversity of conclusions* and to insist that *each investigator should make clear what questions he is asking and why he thinks these questions are interesting.* These steps will improve psychological anthropology in several ways, which I must discuss in some detail.

First, this is a more philosophically acceptable view than the currently widespread one that we should aim at general laws of human behavior in the manner of the physical sciences. Many major philosophers—Husserl, Heidegger, Sartre, Whitehead, Wittgenstein, Cassirer, Ortega y Gasset, Polanyi, Habermas, Wilden, Ryle, and Langer among them—have exposed as unproductive the positivist position that there are truths "out there" which must be discovered by a purely logical mind. I think I can illustrate the importance of the postpositivist position for psychological anthropology by applying that position to the much belabored issue of human universals.

Obviously, no two human acts are in fact the *same* act. They occur, at the very least, at different times or at different places or in different realms of reality (for example, "mating" and "consummating a marriage"). Human acts then are more or less mutually similar or dissimilar. Similarity is a comparative concept like goodness, and implies its opposite—dissimilarity. Only in a universe where there are differences is the concept of similarity useful. Further, the usefulness of the concept is determined by the importance of the differences, which is to say, by the interest of an observer in them. Things devoid of differences in moral, aesthetic, or practical value are "all the same." Beef and lamb curry are interchangeable to a starving Presbyterian, but not to a fastidious Brahmin. If we are confronted with, say, the contents of a Mexican *mercado* and asked to group them by similarity, the first question we must ask is, "For what?" The same question applies to the classification of human acts. Are a bullfight, Hesiod's *Theogony*, a Japanese high school exam, and playing the dozens in Harlem variations on a single Oedipal theme, are they microcosmic models of the social organization and values of their inventors, or both or neither? The only conceivable answer to such questions must refer to the *use* of the analysis. It does not help to say that one analysis or the other explains the facts more thoroughly, because the interest of the observer determines what facts are relevant and what constitutes an explanation. As for the notion that one set of interests is more scientific than another, that position rests on the belief that scientific knowledge is cumulative, which in fact it is not (45, 66, 89). Our sense of what is scientific is constantly evolving out of the ongoing activity of people we take to be scientists.

We need not be impressed by the philosophical respectability of the pragmatic position, but we should be interested in whether it will make psychological anthropology any clearer. I think it will. Once the idea of a cumulative science is abandoned, each scientist is free—in fact obligated—to formulate his personal interest in his subject, to communicate this to his colleagues and students, and to ask them to do the same. Each of us will then be in a better position to decide whether our interest coincides with that of another thinker, and whether his efforts are in fact successful in serving his—and our—interests. Relations with research sponsors could become much more honest. So far, sponsors and researchers have generally avoided discussions of personal interest, and I think this has often resulted eventually in mutual disappointment and mistrust.

The greatest benefit of the pragmatic position, however, is found in its effect on teaching. At the moment it is very difficult for students to make sense of theory and methodology in psychological anthropology. Most of them have been brought up on the idea of a cumulative science, and they want to arrange all the theories in the world into an absolute hierarchy. But no existing model of the mind is so elegant that a clever detractor cannot make it look ridiculous. The best solution is to teach the *uses* of theories, and let them stand side by side. The problem of choosing one's own methods and hypotheses is also much simplified for the student who is trained to think carefully about his or her personal interests. Let us take the tough-tender controversy as a rough illustration. If upon reflection a student finds that he or she is *not interested* in explaining particular concrete individuals, communities, or cultures, but that the search for cross-cultural universals is interesting enough that he or she is willing to live with the epistemological limitations of survey methodology, a great deal of effort will be saved that would otherwise be wasted trying to discover logical ways to make and defend the choice.

FOCI AND TRENDS

Having discussed some of the historical and philosophical problems of psychological anthropology as a whole, we may now look more closely at its various facets and their recent development before attempting an overview of the current state of the field.

Personality

Interest in the relationship between personality and culture has always included a certain curiosity about the role of individual motivation in social change (e.g. 75). However, aside from certain modernization studies—whose applicability to other kinds of social change is doubtful (78)—and studies of charismatic leaders (34, 103), there has until recently been relatively little research on the issue and little in the way of evolutionary theory. In the last few years, several inroads have been made into this problem. Whiting (108), Ingham (52), and LeVine (72) have proposed general models of the relationship between personality and cultural evolution of a sort which are likely to generate research. Edgerton (33), Inkeles (53), Fromm & Maccoby (36), and DeVos (30) have done research on personality using projective techniques in which they have sought relationships between ecological and technological changes on one hand and specific personality traits on the other. At the same time, detailed studies of *acculturation* have brought that concept under fire, suggesting that it has been far too simplistic to be useful in making sense out of the details of historical processes (23, 62, 70, 87). On the whole, the effect of these studies has been to cast further doubt on models of social change which are narrowly psychological and based on modern Western examples (e.g. 79), as well as on patently nonpsychological theories (e.g. 47). Styles of childrearing and ways of viewing human society and the natural order apparently do make a difference for kinds and rates of social change—but a knowledge of these things will not get us very far when it comes to predicting or explaining change. The odd historical current or the rare inexplicable personality too often looms large in the macrocosm of history; and in the microcosm of biography we find that individuals are remarkably flexible and many-faceted.

Perhaps for this reason, a growing number of anthropologists have become interested in developmental changes throughout the human life cycle. The work of Kagan (56), for example, shows the resiliency of older children in overcoming cognitive deficits related to early deprivation. Inkeles's work (54) shows how adult experience can greatly affect self-perception and other personality traits. Plath (88), Clark (22), Kiefer (62), and Erikson (35) have begun to look closely at the socializing effects of middle and late life roles and relationships. Maduro (76) has looked at the development of creativity as a lifelong process in India. Levy has looked at changes in adult personality in Tahiti as the products of a historical process which has deprived adult men of "power, ceremony, wisdom, and adventure" (73, p. 196). Bourguignon (16) has criticized the anthropological habit of confounding historical and developmental change, and Clark (21) has called for an "anthropology of middle age." In October 1976 the Harvard Center for Community Health and Medical Care issued a list of 53 American anthropologists interested in the study of aging.

The concept of *identity* has also found an increasing role in anthropological studies of personality. This trend has recently been well reviewed by Robbins (91), but I would like to add a few comments to that review. Questions about the reality and validity of the self often become particularly acute under conditions of cultural contact and rapid cultural change. As DeVos & Romanucci-Ross (31) and Barth (4) have shown, self-identification as a member of a cultural group can be both a liability and a resource where the group in question occupies a low-status position in an ethnically mixed society. Where there is no such status deprivation, moreover, ethnic identification can help to strengthen an individual's sense of personal cohesiveness and continuity, as well as opening opportunities for real participation in meaningful social interaction. In my own work with Japanese Americans, I found that periods of anxiety surrounding ethnic identity and social worth were resolved for some people by conversion experiences. Among those who had immigrated to this country during a time when being Japanese carried very low status, the conversion was often to Christianity, albeit of an ethnically segregated variety. The children of the immigrants tended to think of their own generation as unique, and to view themselves as neither Japanese nor American, but as "Nisei," Americans of Japanese ancestry. The third generation in America, however, arrived at maturity during a period of strong racial protest and the growing prestige of their ancestral homeland. Conversion experiences tended to reveal to them their basic Japaneseness.

I agree with Robbins that the concept of identity has much to offer, especially as anthropologists become more concerned with problems of cultural change and complex, multiethnic societies. However, the study of identity reveals once again the essential plasticity and complexity of cognitive functioning which plagues our efforts to build general laws. Green (44), myself (62), and Gergen (39) independently found that healthy people, especially bicultural people, often have more than one distinct and fairly well integrated identity when they are involved in distinct social roles which require potentially conflicting perceptions, values, and commitments. In rare cases, individuals may even be aware of their dual identities, but more often they are not. How this is possible should become clearer in the discussion of cognition which follows.

Symbols, Thought, and Social Action

One of the most engaging problems in cultural anthropology (indeed, in the human sciences at large) is the relationship between symbols and social action. The relationship is often not a conscious, or at least not a verbal one; and the explanations of it given by our subjects are rarely consistent or convincing enough to yield good theory. The relationship between symbols and the things they symbolize, after all, is determined largely by convention and only slightly by any intrinsic properties of the symbols themselves. And yet there seem to be semiconsistencies in the way people use and react to these semiarbitrary stimuli, both over time and across individuals and cultures. It is obvious that human beings are moved by symbols to the most extreme sorts of behavior, and that nearly every human act, no matter how simple, mundane, or "instinctive," involves a symbolic component. The situation would be much easier to deal with if only there was some observable set of experiences, affecting large numbers of people, that would severely limit the number of possible associations or "meanings" a symbol might have. Social structure, history, and biological development have been put forward as limiting factors, chiefly by Durkheim, Weber, and Freud, respectively—and for a long time these three provided much of the direction for symbolic anthropology. More recently, a fourth possibility has appeared in the form of "deep structure," as revealed by transformational linguistics (60).

However, in the last few years several lines of thought have begun to converge on a new attitude about symbols: namely, that the important thing about them is their plasticity, their situational variability, their inherently unstable relationship to thought and action. Among the sources of this trend are the works of philosophers Wittgenstein (112, 113), Cassirer (19), and Langer (67); the sociology of George Herbert Mead (81) and his descendants; the influx of anthropologists into complex and rapidly changing situations; and recent research in cognition and ethnographic semantics.

Among philsophers, Wittgenstein has perhaps gone farthest in demonstrating that there is no fixed mental equivalent of a symbol or of a symbolic or grammatical structure. Communication evolves out of ongoing situations made up of symbols, feelings, actors, objects and inarticulate mental processes, all of which interpret one another reciprocally. We can easily see the parallel between this view of language and the symbolic interactionist approach to social behavior (e.g. 42). One reason it has begun to interest psychological anthropologists is the relatively new necessity of theorizing about extremely complex and unstable situations. Turner, for example, has turned his attention to symbols "as instrumentalities of various forces—physical, moral, economic, political, and so on—operating in isolable, changing fields of social relationships" (101, p. 143). In this context, he tells us that symbols ". . . can be detached from abstract systems of symbols . . . with which they have been previously connected, and 'hooked in' to new ad hoc combinations of symbols to constitute, legitimate, or undermine programs and protocols for collective action . . ." (p. 148). Turner's examples of this come from episodes of rapid social change, such as the Hidalgo insurrection of 1810 in Mexico.

To the extent that the meaning of symbols is situational, of course, their relationship to social institutions, to broad historical forces, and to biological events is problematic. This is recognized in a number of recent works which aim to classify societies according to a variety of types with respect to the relationship between symbol, thought, and action. Somewhat parallel efforts have been made by Douglas (32), Peacock, (86), Kearney (59), Barth (5), and Hall (46) to show that the relative stability of symbols, and their embodiment in social institutions, varies according to aspects of religion, social organization, and techno-social change. Douglas and Kearney use the term "strong grid" and Hall the term "high context" to refer to those societies in which there is relatively extensive sharing of meanings attached to symbols, and where therefore relationships between symbols and social institutions tend to be rich, complex, and stable. Barth characterizes these societies as either "elementary," "replicating," or "involute," depending on their complexity, and distinguishes them from "contract" systems, which are low-context or weak-grid. Peacock attempts a kind of evolutionary classification in which "primitive" and "modernizing" societies seem to be characterized by strong grids and "archaic" and "modern" societies by weak grids. In all these studies, the relative instability and lack of meaningful collective rituals in modern Western nations is seen partly as a function of the highly tentative and situational quality of their symbols.

Turner's (100) and Douglas's (32) studies on rituals give us many examples of the tightly interconnected webs of meaning that can be spun in small homogeneous societies. Interesting further bits of support for distinguishing between the primitive and the modern as modes of symbol use come from work on color naming and from a variety of studies on cognitive styles and brain physiology. Berlin (9) shows that primitive societies generally use only two or three basic color terms (such as black, white, and red), but tend to have a very large number of secondary terms for specific color shades (such as deer-colored, sky-colored, and so on). This makes it possible for primitive people to describe nuances of color very effectively, but it is also an example of how symbols become knit together into richly interlocking systems. Since the number of objects which can be used for secondary color names is of manageable size, and since everyone speaking the language is familiar with most or all of the objects, the system is useful. Meanwhile, objects often become linked symbolically when they share the same color. Presumably this system of naming applies to other qualities of objects and people as well, with the result that words and things are rich in associative nuances.

A great deal of cross-cultural work on cognitive style has been admirably summarized by Cole & Scribner (25). In a moment I will discuss the overall importance of this work, but here I want to comment on its relevance to the symbolism problem.

There is a tendency for people in nonliterate societies to perform better on tasks that involve the use of visual, tactile, and kinesthetic skills than the use of verbal skills. Kpelle men, for example, have difficulty describing objects to one another in such a way that the described object can be found in a mixed group; and yet there is no evidence that they have difficulty *perceiving* subtle differences among objects with which they are familiar (25, pp. 178–79). Studying adults and children with little education in Zambia, Deregowski (29) found that they tended to respond verbally to line drawings as though they could not see perspective in them; but when asked to construct stick-models of other line drawings, they often constructed three-dimensional models. Similarly, the Trukese are excellent navigators but cannot describe how they navigate (40), and the Kpelle are excellent house builders but cannot say how to build a house (25). A wide variety of studies indicates that this sort of distinction between verbal and nonverbal skill tends to disappear with Western-style education.

Primitive societies apparently depend for their survival on their ability to transmit and retain complex skills and thinking habits more or less intact without completely verbalizing them. How this is done is of course still something of a mystery, Bateson (6) having produced the only detailed example of which I am aware. However, it seems reasonable to suppose that in such societies, symbols are more "locked-in" to matrices of meaning which are at best only partly verbal or verbalizable; and that the ability to verbalize thought thoroughly may be a prerequisite for the ability to detach specific symbols from their matrices and recombine them, as Turner says, ". . . to constitute, legitimate, or undermine programs and protocols for collective action." Freud said much the same thing when he found that the most persistent and consequential thoughts of his patients were those least accessible to consciousness—or as I would say, to speech.

This brings us back to the Wittgensteinian problem of the relationship between speech and thought. As Cole & Scribner (25) point out, this problem is generally glossed over in studies of cognition because of the difficulty of obtaining nonverbal information about how people think. Moreover, in our own culture, the relationship between thinking and talking is so close that we tend to consider the former a silent version of the latter. The results of cognitive research I have just mentioned, however, reveal how inaccurate this assumption often is. Another set of revealing findings comes from neurophysiology. There is now a large body of literature (see 83, 85, 97) demonstrating that the cognitive functions of the two cerebral hemispheres tend to differ, especially in right-handed people. Thinking in the right hemisphere tends to be well suited for the solution of spatial, kinesthetic, and musical tasks, whereas verbal analytic tasks tend to be the specialty of the left hemisphere. Morrison & Durrenberger (83) note that right-brain thinking may be essentially apropositional rather than analytic, and that left-brain thinking might involve the dismantling of right-brain structures and their reassembly according to grammatical rules. If this is the case, the search for "deep structures" of behavior through the analysis of linguistic material might be misplaced.

To summarize the bearing of cognitive research on the problem of symbolism then: Modern Western nations may have evolved a very special way of symbolic thinking that has separated us from the rest of mankind while at the same time giving us science (anthropology included) and technology. This view is supported by the widespread finding (see 25) that exposure to Western style education correlates with improved performance on verbal tasks in developing cultures. The Western nations have a long literate tradition; an extreme sense of individuality rather than a merging of self and environment; complex and rapidly changing cultures with functionally specific social relations and extensive role specialization which are based upon and in turn necessitate "weak-grid" or verbally explicit and precise communication styles; and the tendency to standardize experience through mass education and print rather than through mass ritual. One is intrigued by the suggestions of McLuhan (80), Peacock (86), and others that we are drifting again toward nonliterate modes of consciousness and ritualism as we pass from a print-dominated to an electronics-dominated culture. It may be partly in response to this possibility that anthropologists have lately become more interested in altered states of consciousness—a subject to which I will return in a moment.

Pinning down the elusive speech-thought relationship would certainly improve the study of cognition, but there is yet another powerful obstacle to be considered, namely the problem of the interactions of emotion and thinking. Here again a large and growing literature indicates that speed and accuracy of intellectual performance (57), information retention (107), and even style of perception and thinking (27) are strongly influenced by central nervous system arousal, which is in turn closely related to subjective emotional state. Weingartner & Murphy (107) found that information given to subjects in one emotional state was retrieved better in the same state than in a different state. Deikman (27) summarizes evidence that sympathetic nervous system arousal tends to be associated with an "action mode" of perception—in which conceptual and perceptual boundaries become clear and thinking tends to be analytic and manipulative—and parasympathetic arousal with a "receptive mode," in which there is a more diffuse deployment of attention, decreased boundary perception, and "paralogical" thought processes.

Furthermore, there is some good evidence that states of emotional arousal during psychological testing may be culturally specific. Lazarus and his colleagues (68) found that anxiety levels as measured by galvanic skin response (GSR) were strikingly different in Japanese and American subjects under matched experimental conditions. One would expect that nonliterate African tribesmen, literate African urbanites, and middle class Americans might very well respond to similar test conditions with very diverse emotions, and that their performance would differ accordingly. The interpretation of cognitive tests is further complicated by possible important differences between cultural groups in affect tone related to nutrition, disease, and social and environmental stress—and their variability from day to day and person to person. As far as I know, there have been no cross-cultural studies of cognition which directly address the problem of emotion, although it should not be difficult to get crude measures of emotional arousal using GSR, heart rate, deep body temperature, muscle tension, or some combination of these.

In its present state of development, cross-cultural research on cognition can sometimes provide useful information about barriers to intercultural communication, and about areas of perception and thinking where education is needed in industrializing societies. It cannot tell us much about how people actually think in the course of their daily lives, or about the range and variety of possible ways of thinking available to mankind. Perhaps an attempt to comprehend the human brain through the medium of language is a little like a blind man's attempt to understand a herd of elephants.

Altered States of Consciousness

The recent great increase in the variety of psychotropic drugs in our society, and the growth in the frequency of their use, has stimulated everyone's interest in so-called nonordinary or altered states of consciousness. An added stimulus, as I mentioned earlier, may very well be a resurgence among educated Americans of parapsychological beliefs and practices and of mind-altering psychotherapeutic and religious practices (90). These trends are probably related to a certain loss of faith in the narrow scientism of the past century or so—a loss in turn brought on by the persistence of political, economic, and health problems, the threat of ecological disaster, and the *rapprochement* between certain branches of science and the occult. At any rate, we now have a great deal of laboratory research on drugs, sleep, hypnosis, and parapsychological phenomena; and anthropologists have increased their activity in the areas of trance, psychosis, and drug use in other cultures.

Leaving aside the large cross-cultural literature on drugs—a literature which I am not qualifed to evaluate—notable examples of altered-states research and theory have been produced by Wallace (105), Lewis (74), Bourguignon and her colleagues (14, 15, 43), S. G. Lee (71), Kiev (63), Koss (65), and Bateson (6). There is widespread agreement among these writers that the achievement of altered states of consciousness in ritual (often called "dissociation" or "trance") usually has a therapeutic or instructional function. The altered state is said to give the individual who achieves it an alternative identity in which he or she can act out otherwise forbidden impulses (14), or to eradicate some maladaptive psychological set so that a new set can be learned (63, 65, 105), or to allow feats of prowess to be performed (74). This idea is clearly formulated in Wallace's "law of dissociation." Wallace holds that most rituals function to prepare their participants for a radical departure from previous behavior or thought habits:

> "Any given set of cognitive and affective elements can be restructured more rapidly and more extensively the more of the perceptual cues from the environment associated with miscellaneous learning of other matters are excluded from conscious awareness, and the more of those new cues which are immediately relevant to the elements to be reorganized are presented" (105, p. 239).

There is now a good deal of evidence from experimental psychology and neuro-physiology that this is a sound theory. Cowan and I[1] have summarized this evidence under the rubric of "state/context dependence." Changing the chemical/hormonal

[1]Kiefer, C., Cowan, J. "State/Context Dependence and Theories of Ritual Behavior." Manuscript in preparation, Human Development Program, University of California, San Francisco, December 1976.

status of the brain, or the perceptual environment, results in a decrement in the ability to recall or recognize information learned before the change. Physiological findings suggest that the brain stores information in dispersed "networks" of neurons, and that changing brain chemistry or context reduces the accessibility of these networks for retrieval. To the extent that the state/context of the learning situation is restored, the retrievability of information improves again. Rituals involving altered states of consciousness, or even moderately strong emotional arousal, together with the establishment of a special perceptual and cognitive context, should indeed tend to decrease the effects of previous learning.

However, there is still the problem of how new perceptions learned during the ritual altered state are transferred to the postritual ordinary state. At least three factors which are characteristic of many rituals have been shown experimentally to reverse the state/context dependence effect. These are (a) repetition of the information to be learned; (b) the focusing of attention on the information to be learned (which tends to happen during states of moderately high anxiety); and (c) the "encoding" of discrete bits of learned information into larger and more complex units. It is possible that each of these factors increases the size of the neuron networks that carry the learned information, thereby making retrieval easier.

We could speak with more confidence about such theories if we had data on physiological changes occurring during altered states in various cultures. The views of Bourguignon on spirit possession (15) and of Goodman on glossolalia (43) also remain tantalizing speculations until we have more physiological evidence. Now that miniature electronic equipment is being used to monitor physiological functions of animals and astronauts in a variety of situations, we may see the technique being used more widely in anthropology in the next decade.

The study of altered states of consciousness may contribute a good deal to the understanding of social change in modern urban societies. Earlier I mentioned the relationship between industrialization, print, and the decline of ritualism in the West, and noted that we may have entered a period wherein this trend is being reversed. The increased attention to altered states of consciousness on the part of millions of Americans seems to agree with this interpretation. The idea that the self-environment relationship can be improved through internal experience rather than external action strikes me as characteristic of belief systems in which overt ritualism plays an important part. It might not be a coincidence that the interest in altered states and in the preservation of the natural environment have developed together. Both place man in a relatively passive or at least interdependent role in relation to the universe, and both tend to be conservative, evoking values of less mechanized times and places.

SUMMARY

Anthropology as a whole has become more psychological in recent years as a result of the structure of research funding and the great accumulation of psychological research results of possible relevance to the science of culture. The difficulty of achieving a unified science of man, or even a widely accepted theory or set of observations, has led on one hand to the search for more respectable positivist methods, and on the other hand to the search for an antipositivist epistemology upon which to push forward. In addition to this basic difference in attitude, there are many minor differences among psychological anthropologists in substantive interest, theoretical bias, and simple terminology.

We have become accustomed to dealing in great detail with complex and rapidly changing human situations. As a result of this, and of the picture of the human brain emerging from experimental psychology and physiology, we have come to view man as more complex and more elastic than we suspected a decade or two ago. He continues to develop mentally and to be resocialized throughout life. He adapts to bewildering change. He manages two or more cultural identities simultaneously. He has at his disposal a range of states of consciousness, each with its own cognitive and perceptual peculiarities. His thought is not strictly determined by his speech habits or social organization, but makes use of shifting nonverbal structures which neither he nor we can verbalize. He can redefine his symbols to suit his causes. If we can sum him up at all, it will be in Kurt Vonnegut's epitaph for him: "Not even the creator of the universe knew what [he] was going to say next" (102, p. 175).

Literature Cited

1. Allport, G. 1937. *Personality: A Psychological Interpretation.* New York: Holt, Rinehart & Winston
2. Andreski, N. 1973. *Social Science as Sorcery.* New York: St. Martin's
3. Barnouw, V. 1973. *Culture and Personality.* Homewood, Ill: Dorsey. Rev. ed.
4. Barth, F. 1969. Introduction. In *Ethnic Groups and Boundaries,* ed. F. Barth, pp. 9–38. Boston: Little, Brown
5. Barth, F. 1972. Analytical dimensions in the comparison of social organizations. *Am. Anthropol.* 74(1,2):207–20
6. Bateson, G. 1975. Some components of socialization for trance. *Ethos* 3(2): 143–55
7. Becker, H. 1953. Becoming a marijuana user. *Am. J. Sociol.* 59:235–42
8. Bell, D. 1968. National character revisited. A proposal for renegotiating the concept. In *The Study of Personality: An Interdisciplinary Appraisal,* ed. E. Norbeck, D. Price-Williams, W. McCord, pp. 103–20. New York: Holt, Rinehart & Winston
9. Berlin, B. 1970. A universalist-evolutionary approach in ethnographic semantics. In *Current Directions in Anthropology,* ed. A. Fischer, Special issue of Bull. Am. Anthropol. Assoc. 3(3) part 2:3–18
10. Berreman, G. D. 1972. Social categories and social interaction in India. *Am. Anthropol.* 74(3):567–87
11. Bochner, S., Brislin, R. W., Lonner, W. J., eds. 1975. Introduction. *Cross Cultural Perspectives on Learning,* pp. 3–36. New York: Wiley
12. Bornstein, M. 1975. The influence of visual perception on culture. *Am. Anthropol.* 77(4):774–98
13. Bott, E. 1972. Psychoanalysis and ceremony. In *The Interpretation of Ritual: Essays in Honor of A. I. Richards,* ed. J. S. LaFontaine, pp. 205–38. London: Tavistock
14. Bourguignon, E. 1965. The self, the behavioral environment, and the theory of spirit possession. In *Context and Meaning in Cultural Anthropology,* ed. M. Spiro, pp. 39–60. New York: Free Press
15. Bourguignon, E. 1973. Dreams and altered states of consciousness in anthropological research. In *Psychological Anthropology,* ed. F. L. K. Hsu, pp. 403–34. Cambridge, Mass: Schenkman. 2nd ed.
16. Bourguignon, E. 1973. Psychological anthropology. In *Handbook of Social and Cultural Anthropology,* ed. J. J. Honigmann, pp. 1073–118. Chicago: Rand McNally
17. Bushnell, J., Bushnell, D. 1975. Projective doll play reconsidered: The use of a group technique with rural Mexican children. In *Psychological Anthropology,* ed. T. R. Williams, pp. 163–220. The Hague: Mouton (World Anthropol. Ser.)
18. Campbell, D. T., Naroll, R. 1973. The mutual methodological relevance of an-

thropology and psychology. See Ref. 15, pp. 435–63
19. Cassirer, E. 1944. *An Essay on Man.* New Haven, London: Yale Univ. Press.
20. Chance, N. A. 1965. Acculturation, self-identification, and personality adjustment. *Am. Anthropol.* 67(2):372–93
21. Clark, M. 1973. Contributions of cultural anthropology to the study of the aged. In *Cultural Illness and Health,* ed. L. Nader, T. Maretzki. Anthropol. Stud. Ser., Am. Anthropol. Assoc. (9): 78–88
22. Clark, M., Anderson, B. 1967. *Culture and Aging.* Springfield: Thomas
23. Clark, M., Kaufman, S., Pierce, R. 1976. Explorations of acculturation: Toward a model of ethnic identity. *Hum. Organ.* 35(3):231–39
24. Cole, M., Gay, J., Glick, J. A., Sharp, D. W. 1971. *The Cultural Context of Learning and Thinking.* New York: Basic Books
25. Cole, M., Scribner, S. 1974. *Culture and Thought: A Psychological Introduction.* New York: Wiley
26. Day, R., Boyer, B., DeVos, G. A. 1975. Two styles of ego development: A cross-cultural, longitudinal comparison of Apache and Anglo school children. *Ethos* 3(3):345–74
27. Deikman, A. 1971. Bimodal consciousness. *Arch. Gen. Psychiatry* 25:481–89
28. de Lacy, P. R. 1970. A cross-cultural study of classificatory ability in Australia. *J. Cross-Cult. Psychol.* 1(4):293–304
29. Deregowski, J. B. 1968. Difficulties in pictorial depth perception in Africa. *Br. J. Psychol.* 59:195–204
30. DeVos, G. A. 1973. *Socialization for Achievement.* Berkeley: Univ. Calif. Press
31. DeVos, G. A., Romanucci-Ross, L. 1975. Instrumental and expressive uses of ethnicity. *Ethnic Identity: Cultural Continuities and Change,* pp. 378–89. Palo Alto, Calif: Mayfield
32. Douglas, M. 1970. *Natural Symbols.* London: Cresset
33. Edgerton, R. B. 1971. *The Individual in Cultural Adaptation.* Berkeley: Univ. Calif. Press
34. Erikson, E. H. 1958. *Young Man Luther.* New York: Norton
35. Erikson, E. H. 1969. *Gandhi's Truth.* New York: Norton
36. Fromm, E., Maccoby, M. 1970. *Social Character in a Mexican Village.* Englewood Cliffs, NJ: Prentice-Hall

37. Gearing, F. 1973. Anthropology and education. In *Handbook of Social and Cultural Anthropology,* ed. J. J. Honigmann, pp. 1223–50. Chicago: Rand McNally
38. Geertz, C. 1973. *The Interpretation of Cultures.* New York: Basic Books
39. Gergen, K. J. 1972. Multiple identity—the healthy, happy human being wears many masks. *Psychol. Today* 5(12):31
40. Gladwin, T. 1964. Culture and logical process. In *Explorations in Cultural Anthropology: Essays Presented to George Peter Murdock,* ed. W. H. Goodenough, pp. 167–77. New York: McGraw-Hill
41. Glock, C. V. 1967. *Survey Methods in Psychological Research.* New York: Sage
42. Goffman, E. 1961. *Asylums.* New York: Doubleday
43. Goodman, F. 1972. *Speaking in Tongues: A Cross-Cultural Study of Glossolalia.* Univ. Chicago Press
44. Green, V. 1971. *Situational Change and Selection Versus Assimilation in Understanding Multi-Ethnic Societies.* Presented at Ann. Meet. Am. Anthropol. Assoc., New York
45. Habermas, J. 1971. *Knowledge and Human Interests.* Transl. J. J. Shapiro. Boston: Beacon Press
46. Hall, E. T. 1976. *Beyond Culture.* Garden City, NY: Anchor-Doubleday
47. Harris, M. 1968. *The Rise of Cultural Theory.* New York: Crowell
48. Henry, J. 1973. *On Sham, Vulnerability, and Other Forms of Self-Destruction.* London: Penguin
49. Honigmann, J. J. 1975. Psychological anthropology: Trends, accomplishments, and future tasks. See Ref. 17, pp. 601–26
50. Hsu, F. L. K. 1961. Kinship and ways of life: An exploration. In *Psychological Anthropology,* ed. F. L. K. Hsu, pp. 400–56. Homewood Ill: Dorsey
51. Hsu, F. L. K. 1973. Psychological anthropology in the behavioral sciences. See Ref. 15, pp. 1–15
52. Ingham, J. 1976. *Toward a Psychoanalytic Materialism in Anthropology.* Presented at conference on "American Social and Cultural Anthropology: Past and Future," Wayzata, Minn.
53. Inkeles, A. 1969. Making men modern: On the causes and consequences of individual change in six developing countries. *Am. J. Sociol.* 75:208–25

54. Inkeles, A. 1975. Becoming modern: Individual change in six developing countries. *Ethos* 3(2)323-42
55. Jones, M., Bayley, N., MacFarlane, J., Honzik, M. 1971. *The Course of Human Development.* Waltham, Mass: Xerox Publ.
56. Kagan, J. 1975. Resilience in cognitive development. *Ethos* 3(2):231-47
57. Kahneman, D. 1973. *Attention and Effort.* Englewood Cliffs, NJ: Prentice-Hall
58. Kaplan, B. 1968. The method of the study of persons. See Ref. 8, pp. 121-33
59. Kearney, M. 1975. World view theory and study. *Ann. Rev. Anthropol.* 4: 247-70
60. Keesing, R. M. 1974. Theories of culture. *Ann. Rev. Anthropol.* 3:73-97
61. Kennedy, J. G. 1973. Cultural psychiatry. See Ref. 37, pp. 1119-98
62. Kiefer, C. W. 1974. *Changing Cultures, Changing Lives.* San Francisco: Jossey-Bass
63. Kiev, A. 1964. The study of folk psychiatry. In *Magic, Faith, and Healing,* ed. A. Kiev, pp. 3-35. New York: Free Press
64. Kluckhohn, C. K. 1949. *Mirror for Man.* New York: McGraw-Hill
65. Koss, J. D. 1975. Therapeutic aspects of Puerto Rican cult practices. *Psychiatry* 38:(2)160-71
66. Kuhn, T. S. 1962. *The Structure of Scientific Revolutions. International Encyclopedia of Unified Science* 2(2)
67. Langer, S. 1957. *Philosophy in a New Key.* Cambridge, Mass: Harvard Univ. Press
68. Lazarus, R. S., Tomita, M., Opton, E. Jr., Kodama, M. 1966. A cross-cultural study of stress-reaction patterns in Japan. *J. Pers. Soc. Psychol.* 4(6):622-33
69. Leach, E. 1972. The structure of symbolism. See Ref. 13, pp. 239-76
70. Lebra, T. 1972. Acculturation dilemma: The function of Japanese moral values for Americanization. *Counc. Anthropol. Educ. Newsl.* 3(1):6-13
71. Lee, S. G. 1974. Spirit possession among the Zulu. In *Culture and Personality: Contemporary Readings,* ed. R. Edgerton, pp. 387-407. Chicago: Aldine.
72. LeVine, R. A. 1973. *Culture, Behavior, and Personality.* Chicago: Aldine
73. Levy, R. I. 1973. *Tahitians: Mind and Experience in the Society Islands.* Univ. Chicago Press
74. Lewis, I. M. 1971. *Ecstatic Religion.* London: Penguin
75. Linton, R. 1945. *The Cultural Background of Personality.* New York: Appleton-Century-Crofts
76. Maduro, R. 1974. Artistic creativity and aging in India. *Int. J. Aging Hum. Dev.* 5(4):303-29
77. May, R. 1969. *Love and Will.* New York: Norton
78. McClelland, D. 1961. *The Achieving Society.* Princeton, NJ: Van Nostrand
79. McClelland, D., Winter, D. 1969. *Motivating Economic Achievement.* New York: Free Press
80. McLuhan, M. 1965. *Understanding Media.* New York: McGraw-Hill
81. Meltzer, B. 1964. *The Social Psychology of George Herbert Mead.* Kalamazoo: Western Michigan University, Center for Sociological Research
82. Mills, C. W. 1959. *The Sociological Imagination.* New York: Grove
83. Morrison, J. W., Durrenberger, E. P. 1976. Comment on "split brain research, culture and cognition." *Curr. Anthropol.* 17(3):506-8
84. Nader, L., Maretzki, T., eds. 1973. *Cultural Illness and Health.* Anthropol. Stud. Ser., Am. Anthropol. Assoc. No. 9
85. Paredes, J. A., Hepburn, M. J. 1976. The split brain and culture-and-cognition paradox. *Curr. Anthropol.* 17(1): 121-27
86. Peacock, J. L. 1975. *Consciousness and Change: Symbolic Anthropology in Evolutionary Perspective.* New York: Wiley
87. Pierce, R., Clark, M., Kiefer, C. 1973. A bootstrap scaling technique. *Hum. Organ.* 31(4):403-10
88. Plath, D. W. 1973. Cares of career, and careers of caretaking. *J. Nerv. Ment. Dis.* 152(5):346-57
89. Polanyi, M. 1958. *Personal Knowledge: Towards a Post-Critical Philosophy.* Univ. Chicago Press
90. Price-Williams, D. 1975. Primitive mentality—civilized style. See Ref. 11, pp. 291-303
91. Robbins, R. 1973. Identity, culture and behavior. See Ref. 16, pp. 1199-1222
92. Segall, M. H., Campbell, D. T. Herskovits, M. J. 1966. *The Influence of Culture on Visual Perception.* Indianapolis: Bobbs-Merrill
93. Spindler, G. D. 1968. Psychocultural adaptation. See Ref. 8, pp. 326-47
94. Spindler, G. D., ed. 1974. *Education and Cultural Process.* New York: Holt, Rinehart & Winston
95. Spindler, L. 1975. Researching the psy-

chology of culture change. See Ref. 17, pp. 137–62

96. Spiro, M. E. 1954. Human nature in its psychological dimensions. *Am. Anthropol.* 56(1):19–30

97. ten Houton, W., Morrison, J. W., Durrenberger, E. P., Korolev, S. I., Scheder, J. 1976. More on split-brain research, culture, and cognition. *Curr. Anthropol.* 17(3):503–11

98. Triandis, H. C., Malpass, R. S., Davidson, A. R. 1972. Cross-cultural psychology. *Bien. Rev. Anthropol. 1971:* 1–84

99. Turner, R. H. 1976. The real self: From institution to impulse. *Am. J. Sociol.* 81(5):989–1016

100. Turner, V. 1969. *The Ritual Process.* Chicago: Aldine

101. Turner, V. 1975. Symbolic studies. See Ref. 59, pp. 145–61

102. Vonnegut, K. Jr. 1973. *Breakfast of Champions.* New York: Dell

103. Wallace, A. F. C. 1956. Revitalization movements. *Am. Anthropol.* 58(2):264–81

104. Wallace, A. F. C. 1961. *Culture and Personality.* New York: Random House

105. Wallace, A. F. C. 1966. *Religion: An Anthropological View.* New York: Random House

106. Wallach, M. 1967. Thinking, feeling, and expressing: Toward understanding the person. In *Cognition, Personality, and Clinical Psychology,* ed. R. Jessor, S. Feshbach, pp. 141–72. San Francisco: Jossey-Bass

107. Weingartner, H., Murphy, D. 1974. *State Dependent Recall in Manic Depressive Disorders.* Presented at Ann. Meet. Am. Psychol. Assoc., New Orleans

108. Whiting, J. W. M. 1974. A model for psychocultural research. *Ann. Rep. 1973:* 1–14. Washington DC: Am. Anthropol. Assoc.

109. Whiting, J. W. M., Whiting, B. B. 1973. Altruistic and egoistic behavior in six cultures. See Ref. 84, pp. 56–66

110. Whiting, J. W. M., Whiting, B. B. 1975. Aloofness and intimacy of husbands and wives: A cross-cultural study. *Ethos* 3(2):183–207

111. Williams, T. R. 1975. Introduction. See Ref. 17, pp. 1–41

112. Wittgenstein, L. 1958. *The Blue and Brown Books: Preliminary Studies for the Philosophical Investigations.* New York: Harper & Row

113. Wittgenstein, L. 1966. *Philosophical Investigations,* ed. G. Pitcher. New York: Doubleday

114. Wyatt, F. 1967. How objective is objectivity? *J. Proj. Tech. Pers. Assess.* 31(5):3–19

Ann. Rev. Anthropol. 1977. 6:121–35
Copyright © 1977 by Annual Reviews Inc. All rights reserved

SEMIOTICS OF CULTURE: ❖9590
GREAT BRITAIN AND
NORTH AMERICA[1]

D. Jean Umiker-Sebeok

Research Center for Language and Semiotic Studies, Indiana University,
Bloomington, Indiana 47401

Despite a long tradition of anthropological studies of signification and communication on both sides of the Atlantic, it is only in the last two decades that semiotics has moved from the periphery of exploratory anthropological concern into the core of the field, where it has become a part of the self-conscious definition of the ethnographer's subject matter, methodology, and theory, especially macrotheory [see the recent reviews by Schwimmer (73), Singer (80), and Turner (87)].

> At no time in the history of anthropology has interest in the symbolic character of cultural phenomena been more clearly pronounced than during the last two decades; and at no time has it been pursued more skillfully or with such provocative results. So fundamental, in fact, has the concern with meaning become that it now underlies whole conceptions of culture, conceptions that are explicitly grounded in the premise that the semiotic dimension of human affairs—the full array of signs and concepts men use to communicate with each other and to interpret themselves and the world around them—should be the central object of description and analysis (8, p.l).

In the rush to explore the implications of a semiotic approach to human culture (e.g. 32) anthropologists have proposed a stupefying array of terms by which the new territory might be designated. The most widespread of these, *symbolic anthropology*, was introduced by J. L. Peacock and D. W. Crabb (see 61, p. x, fn. 3) as a parallel to other subfields within anthropology, and has been taken up by others in Canada, [e.g. Schwimmer's *Journal of Symbolic Anthropology* (70), now to begin a new life as the *Yearbook of Symbolic Anthropology* (72)] and in the United States [e.g. Schneider et at (68)]. Geertz (27) advocates the use of *interpretive anthropology,*

---

[1] It was originally planned to have the literature of Continental Europe (East and West) and the Soviet Union covered by a second author. However, the manuscript was not received in time for inclusion in this volume.

stressing less the institutional framework of this new discipline or the types of objects studied than the dynamics of textual creation within and between individuals and groups. Turner (86, 88) proposes (*comparative*) *symbology* for the study of the form and function of certain types of significative phenomena—namely, "symbols," or, citing an *Oxford English Dictionary* definition, things "regarded by general consent as naturally typifying or representing or recalling something by possession of analogous qualities or by association in fact or thought" (87, p. 151). Douglas (19) has adopted Turner's term. Singer (80, 81) calls for a *semiotic anthropology*, in a conscious and much needed attempt to apply a Peircean semiotic perspective to the problems of meaning and communication in anthropology.

The term chosen for the title of this review, *semiotics of culture*, is borrowed from the work of the brilliant group of Soviet semioticians, the so-called Moscow-Tartu School, who define it as ". . . the study of the functional correlations of different sign systems . . . [attaching particular importance to] . . . questions of the hierarchical structure of the languages of culture, of the distribution of spheres among them, of cases in which these spheres intersect or merely border upon each other" [Lotman et al (48, p. 57)]. In the view of this group, culture is a universe created by a plurality of mutually interacting and mutually supportive sign systems which may be studied from the point of view of the definition and structuring of different types of cultural "texts," the latter term being given a broad interpretation similar to Geertz's use in his discussion of "deep play" (26) [but see (97) for a discussion of the differences between Geertz and the Moscow-Tartu school on the question of the relation between the underlying cultural sign systems and their textual manifestations].

Some of the notions of the Moscow-Tartu school have been borrowed in British and North American anthropological circles, primarily in regard to literary and folkloric texts (e.g. 42) and aesthetic theory [for the latter see (96)], while both the term *semiotics of culture* and the broad semiotic theory of culture which it designates have been largely ignored. Recently, however, the term, if not the concepts behind it, was adopted for the title of a Burg-Wartenstein conference attended by an international group of anthropologists and linguists [see the report by Lamb & Makkai (40) and the proceedings (41)].

For a concise presentation in English of the basic principles of the Soviet theory of semiotics of culture, see Lotman et al (48); Winner & Winner (97) present a lengthy *explication du texte* of this article, including a list of English language publications and translations of this group. Baran (3, 4) provides a succinct summary of the background and principal contributions of the Moscow-Tartu School, and Shukman (77) gives a detailed account of the work of one of the leading members of the group, Yu. M. Lotman. [See also (64) and the bibliography of Soviet semiotics by Eimermacher (22).] The impact of the ideas of the Russian Formalists, especially the folklorist Propp, ancestors of the current Moscow-Tartu group, on the anthropological study of narratives has been enormous, the references to kindred British and North American analyses of folklore being by now too numerous to mention here [see e. g. Köngas Maranda & Maranda (38) and Maranda & Köngas Maranda (51)]. For reviews of the implications of such analyses for a general theory of culture, see Schwimmer (73) and (71), the latter a review of (50). Soviet work on nonverbal sign systems is less well known, but see Glassie's review (30) of Bogatyrev's (14) analysis of Slovakian costume.

The Soviet term recommends itself by the fact that it does not specify a particular academic discipline, important in that a unified semiotic theory of culture precisely calls for an interdisciplinary approach. In addition, by employing *semiotics* instead of *semiology*, it avoids the possible interpretation that *semiotics of culture* is a language-dominated theory of signs. [See M. Singer's (80) comparison of the two traditions of semiotics and semiology, as well as T. A. Sebeok's (74) description of the historical development of these two terms and J. Culler's (18) discussion of the logocentrism of Saussure's semiology.]

Perhaps the most compelling reason for adopting the Soviet term, however, is that promising new theoretical statements coming from British and North American centers exhibit a remarkable degree of convergence with trends in Soviet theory, particularly regarding the necessity of creating a semiotic theory of culture born of the marriage between the francophonic semiological tradition of first-order analysis of semiotic codification, stemming from the work of F. de Saussure, and the anglophonic semiotic tradition, following Locke and Peirce, of second-order analysis of the interweaving of semiosis and the fabric of social order [see Jakobson's fascinating account (36) of general lines of development in semiotics]. The Moscow-Tartu school has shown itself to be a leader in this respect. In the process of elaborating a semiotic theory of culture, a new model of man—as a semiotic animal par excellence—is being fashioned as a substitute for the traditionally coupled pair of concepts—"symbolic" and "economic" man.

Singer (80) argues that the coming of age of a semiotic anthropology had to await the evolution, during the first half of this century, away from a global, Tylorian concept of culture toward a narrower one, complementary to the concept of society. He traces the slow path toward a redefinition of culture as a system of meanings and values principally in the work of Kroeber, Parsons, Radcliffe-Brown, and Redfield [for additional insights into Redfield's contributions, see Singer (79)]. This revised concept of culture, making feasible an autonomous science of culture, now a science of meanings and values, had become widespread by the mid-1950s, laying the foundation for a feverish exploitation of a "new" domain in the nomothetic sciences of man.

The specification of what kinds of symbol systems cultures were made up of and how these were related to social action, to individual personalities, and to ecological conditions begins to be explored in the 1960's and 1970's in the work of Lévi-Strauss, Geertz, Schneider, Leach, and Victor Turner, among others (80, p. 50).

The unfortunate result of the culture-society split was that those who focused on "what kinds of symbol systems cultures were made up of"—on semiotic codes— and those interested in "how these were related to social action"—on messages— have tended to view each other as opponents. Often cited is Geertz's (27, but see also 28) characterization of the weaknesses of the early attempts within anthropology to go beyond either a view of culture as a superorganic reality or as simply behavioral events—on the one hand "ethnoscience, componential analysis, or cognitive anthropology" (27, p. 11) and, on the other, those who treat culture "purely as a symbolic system," the latter being discussed as follows:

> Though a distinct improvement over "learned behavior" and "mental phenomena" notions of what culture is, and the source of some of the most powerful theoretical ideas in contemporary anthropology, this hermetical approach to things seems to me to run the danger . . . of locking cultural analysis away from its proper object, the informal logic of actual life (27, p. 17).

This critique is repeated in Turner's recent review of "symbolic studies" (87), where what is called the "abstract systems" group [including "linguistic, structural, and cognitive anthropology," (p. 145)] is contrasted with the "symbols and social dynamics" group [including those working at the interface of anthropology, microsociology à la Goffman, sociolinguistics, folklore, literary criticism, and semiotics (p. 150)]. For an interesting collection of papers by young anthropologists who imaginatively draw from the approaches of Geertz, Lévi-Strauss, Schneider, and Turner, see (95); also to be recommended are the earlier articles by Ortner (57–59).

Schwimmer (73, p. 7), in his discussion of the "new ethnography" coming from the United States, also calls certain theoreticians to task (e.g. Goodenough and Keesing) for equating culture "to a summation of a large but finite number of semiotic domains." But he is careful to point out that not all ethnoscience practitioners have adopted this *deus ex machina* theory. Furthermore, he notes that both ethnoscience and the later cognitive anthropology "apart from cultural classifications in a variety of domains . . . led to important advances in kinship studies, both in respect of mathematicization and the construction of adequate rewrite rules . . . Here the advances were in processual analysis, optimization analysis, graph theory, matrix analysis and various kinds of mathematical modeling . . ." (73, fn. 3). See also reviews by D. R. White (93) and M. Black (13).

Turner's characterization of the countermovement to "abstract systems" analysis —"processual symbology"—draws heavily from the arguments put forth in linguistics during the last half of the 1960s [e.g. Weinreich et al (92)] in support of a concentration on linguistic performance in contrast to the then popular Chomskyan emphasis on competence—or the ideal knowledge of a language which any native speaker has. While having been influenced by Roland Barthes's work [see Turner's "Introduction" to (88)], Turner nevertheless expresses a dissatisfaction with the semiological tradition of Saussure, where the logical outcome of his theory is that what is social about a sign system (language or otherwise) is precisely a shared code, which can be studied through the investigation of any individual member of the culture, and what is not social must be investigated through the examination of many different individuals in different contexts [see Weinreich et al (92)]. As Singer points out (80, p. 53), the dyadic concept of the sign, plus the emphasis on conventional as opposed to natural sign relations, tends to exclude both externally real objects and empirical subjects or egos from semiological analyses, relegating them to the domain of other scientific disciplines. Culler (18, p. 116), describing Saussure's notion of semiology, cites the painter G. Braque's modernistic credo: "I do not believe in things; I believe in relationships." Context in the semiological tradition, in other words, is more accurately named "co-text" [a term proposed by Bar-Hillel (5)].

The movement to describe symbols "in action" centers around the demonstration of "natural" relations between sign vehicles and either the sign user or objects in the external world—particularly social institutions and groups. Interest is turned toward the motivation of signs in terms of the internal context of the interpreters or the external context of the outside world. Within a Peircean framework (see 63), this might be expressed as the discovery of iconic and indexical relations between the sign itself and the sign's object or interpreter. Lévi-Strauss, it will be remembered [see Leach's discussions (39, 43–45)], placed great emphasis on metaphoric (iconic) and metonymic (indexical) relations, but on the level of the relationship between the sign and its interpretant (or other signs, interpretants being other signs). Firth, in fact, states that ". . . one of the main tasks of anthropology is the reduction of arbitrariness as it appears in symbolic allocation" (24, pp. 62–63). In this vein, see the early work by Bateson [reprinted in (11)] as well as more recent contributions to the study of iconicity by Basso (6, 7), Eco (21), Fernandez (23), Munn (54), Ojo (56), Sebeok (75), Thom (84), and Watt (90, 91). The notion of indexicality is central to ethnomethodology (see 25, 52), since it is concerned with the way, in everyday life, "everything appears firmly attached to its meaning" despite the conventional nature of the signs in use (49, p. 118). However, outside of ethnomethodology and the recent pragmatics movement in linguistics and philosophy [for example, see (78), which follows Jakobson], problems of indexicality have not received the attention they deserve. Turner discusses the motivation of what he calls *signs* in terms of indexical relations between messages and the outside world ["we master the world through signs" (87, p. 159)], *symbols* in terms of iconic relations between messages and the internal experiences of individuals ("we master . . . ourselves by symbols"). Reminiscent of Turner's conception of symbols mediating between the poles of personal experience and normative reason, Willis sees meaning as emerging from "the tension between opposed aspects of experience, an ultimate awareness beyond a merely rationalist comprehension" (94, p. 128).

Sahlins (66) criticizes attempts to describe the motivation of signs without first determining the first-order semiotic infrastructure:

> Douglas is actually concerned with the functioning of already symbolic elements (affinal relationships, lineages, concepts of animals, food taboos, etc.) as *signs* for one another . . . (indeed most anthropological studies addressed to the "symbolic" are similarly preoccupied with this second-order sign function rather than with the constitution of symbolic form and meaning) (66, p. 120).

As Sahlins points out, this type of analysis permits "most of the cultural content to evaporate." Each such symbol may act alternatively as the signifier or the signified of the other, "yet each remains beside the sign of the other, a symbol in its own domain, whose concept also depends on differential relations within that domain."

Sahlins' analyses of clothing and color sign systems (65, 66) provide examples of the importance of exploring the artifice beneath the appearance of the "natural" [cf Sperber's similar discussion of olfactory signs (83)].[2]

Sperber's (83) critique of exegetical studies of symbolism such as are found in the work of Turner follows closely, although implicitly, the ideas of C. S. Peirce concerning the iconic and indexical relations underlying the symbolic relationship:

> The motivation of symbols is traditionally taken as the criterion which contrasts them to signs, which are considered to be non-motivated. On closer inspection, this criterion is not very clear: firstly, for a great number of symbols no motivation is given. Secondly, etymology may constitute a sufficient symbolic motivation . . . Therefore the criterion, far from distinguishing signs from symbols, seems to oppose all words and some symbols on the one hand, to non-motivated symbols on the other (83, pp. 23–24).

Motivations, according to Sperber, are not generalizable, and should be treated not as interpretations of discourse but as discourse to be interpreted (p. 29). Sperber would have us do away with the notion of a separate, physical "symbol" (p. 50), retaining only the cognitive or interpretive processes performed by various sign relations.

As Singer (80) makes clear, the Anglo-Saxon orientation in semiotic anthropology is toward the *actor* (as opposed to *message*), to the *message* (as opposed to *code*). The work reviewed by Turner (87) follows a restatement of the biases of this tradition, where emphasis is on *symbolic interaction*, or *symbols in action*, e.g. the dramaturgical models of Burke, Duncan, and Goffman and those anthropologists who follow their lead—such as Geertz (27, chap. 8), Hymes (34, 35), and Peacock (60–62); *symbolic action* [e.g. Hill (33), Munn (54, 55), Spencer (82), Turner (86)]; and *symbolic "potency"* [Turner (89)], *symbols and power* (e.g. 53). Geertz's statement, originally published in 1964 [see chap 8 of (27); also (33)], that social scientific theory "has . . . been virtually untouched by one of the most important trends in recent thought: the effort to construct an independent science of what Kenneth Burke . . . has called 'symbolic action' " (33, p. 17) would hardly be appropriate today.

The emphasis on *performance*, as opposed to competence, borrowed by folklorists and anthropologists from linguistics (see also 12), is yet another form of this bias, evidence of a basic reluctance of letting "culture" stray too far from "nature."

> It seems that wherever one turns in American anthropology one meets . . . some incompleteness in the appropriation of the cultural object by meaning. The impressive ethnoscience developed by Goodenough, Lounsbury, Conklin, and others, especially out of the linguistic legacy of the Boas school, has been shackled by a positivist concept of culture as behavioral competence or ethnography, therefore of meaning as referential significance and of analysis as translation—in terms of an apparently objective code whose "objectivity" encodes a theory. Or to take examples of a very different kind (if equally impressive in intellectual quality), the efforts of Geertz or Schneider, each in their own way, have

[2]In his study of gender advertisements (30a), seen only after the completion of this article, Goffman points to the social definition of what is often taken to be "natural expression."

likewise turned on a specific limitation of the symbolic, as is built into the distinction between action and ideology, society and culture. This particular distinction has been characteristically European, and more immediately the tenent of British than of American social anthropology [Sahlins (66, p. 106)].

Geertz's criticism [reprinted in (27); see also p. 449, fn. 38] of Lévi-Strauss's "cerebral savage" and his cryptological approach to social life, which attempts to understand "myths, totem rites, marriage rules, or whatever . . . entirely in terms of their internal structure, independent de tout sujet, de tout objet, et de tout contexte," rather than treating them, as would Geertz, "as texts, as imaginative works built out of social materials . . . ," is to a certain extent still valid, despite Sperber's argument that Lévi-Strauss goes beyond the semiological tradition of analysis of symbol systems as codes. The proposal for a textual, "interpretive" approach, a "thick description" of culture, viewed as an "acted document" is laudable. However, the approach to the Balinese cockfight as a "Balinese reading of Balinese experience, a story they tell themselves about themselves" (27, p.448), that is as a message "saying something of something" is stimulating but cannot replace the detailed first-order analysis of the semiotic structures underlying the message or text; the "social materials" used are themselves culturally—semiotically—organized [see e.g. Sperber (83, p.70), where context should be interpreted by means of symbolic elements, not vice versa].

While recognition of the importance of going beyond the separation of co-text and context theories of meaning is becoming commonplace in recent years, it should be noted that Bateson's early conception of culture as a mechanism for the generation and transmission of information (e.g. 9–11) anticipated many of the issues which are only now drawing the attention of the mainstream of anthropology. A brief allusion to the impact of Bateson's contribution to a semiotic theory of culture is found in Schwimmer's review (73), but a full account needs to be made.

As an example of recent efforts toward a new paradigm for studies of meaning, Halliday (31) indicates that if code and behavior are divorced, it is only the behavior that has a social context, and social context then means no more than "situation of the communicative act," whereas it is crucial to view code and behavior as one, thereby placing both in a properly social context. Halliday points to several linguistic theories which attempt to place performance and competence in proper perspective—e.g. conversational-, discourse-, stratificational-, systemic-, and variation-analysis.

The impetus for a change in theoretical outlook comes from a reevaluation of the modern, Western cultural concepts which have influenced the development of anthropological theories of meaning. Sahlins (66), for example, shows that the arbitrary separation of practical reason and culture, and the priority given to the former, common to our own cultural semiotics, has been projected onto primitive cultures.

At first glance the confrontation of the cultural and material logics does seem unequal. The material process is factual and "independent of man's will"; the symbolic, invented and therefore flexible. The one is fixed by nature, the other is arbitrary by definition.

Thought can only kneel before the absolute sovereignty of the physical world. But the error consists in this: that there is no material logic apart from the practical interest, and the practical interest of man in production is symbolically constituted. The finalities as well as the modalities of production come from the cultural side: the material means of the cultural organization as well as the organization of the material means (66, p. 207).

What is unique to bourgeois society, Sahlins continues, "consists not in the fact that the economic system escapes symbolic determination," as has sometimes been maintained, "but that the economic symbolism is structurally determining" (66, p. 211). We must not automatically assume, in other words, that each culture emphasizes the same arrangement of semiotic domains. Rather, "the cultural scheme is variously inflected by a dominant side of symbolic production, which supplies the major idiom of other relations and activities. One can thus speak of a privileged institutional locus of the symbolic process, which emanates a classificatory grid imposed upon the total culture" (66, p. 211). The exploration of the shape which "the dialectical process by which this apotheosis of ourselves as human and godlike and other than animal is formed and reformed and bent back upon itself" [Leach (43, p. 34)] takes in different cultures should not be prejudiced by our own culture's seemingly "natural" concepts of work versus play, nature versus culture, etc. Willis's (94) insightful description of animal symbolism within the broad context of three African cultures offers an example of how a fresh look at semiotic hierarchies leads to a critique of accepted modern social theory—in this case, that of Weber (see, e.g., pp. 126–27).

Schneider (67, p. 207) also criticizes the anthropologist's acceptance of the received distinction between "expressive" and "practical" as a basis for the division of ethnographic description into the traditional areas of "religion," "art," "politics," etc. Similarly, the culture-nature distinction cannot be presumed universal (67, p. 211; cf 19). The only way in which the natives' own cultural logic can be discovered is, he points out, through the study of culture as a total system of symbols and meanings, not through the accretion of isolated studies of cultural symbols:

> The analysis of cultural symbols is not the same thing as the study of culture as a total system of symbols and meaning. These are not unrelated endeavors, but they are not identical. The problem of deciphering religious symbols, for example, is not the same thing as the problem of analyzing the total culture as a system of symbols and meanings. The one simply analyzes certain symbolic sets for their meanings. The other is based on a total social theory in which the concept of culture plays a significant part (67, p. 208).

A similar view is expressed by Eco (21) and Schwimmer (73). But Schneider, unlike Sahlins or Sperber, is unwilling to give up the distinction between culture and society. In response to criticism that his theory does not pay enough attention to action, he merely places his own concept of culture within T. Parsons's general theory of social action, the parallel systems of culture and society being mediated by what he calls norms, or moral propositions operating as templates for social action. "The study of culture is concerned . . . with the study of social action as a meaningful system of action, and it is, therefore, by definition, concerned with the question of 'meaning-in-action' (67, p. 198–99). Peacock (61) also expresses dissatisfaction with traditional approaches to the relationship between society and culture. Like Schneider, he borrows from Parsons and, like Hymes (see 34) and Geertz (see 27), from K. Burke. It would appear that in British and North American anthropology Sahlins is alone in pursuing Lévi-Strauss's ideas concerning communication to their logical conclusion [but compare, in Italy, Eco (21) and, in France, Sperber (83)]. Others, while recognizing the arbitrary distinction between practical and symbolic, refuse to make a total commitment to a theory which does away with it, so that analyses tend to focus on an isolated set of symbols, such as a corpus of myths or rituals, the "symbolic," with an explicit attempt to point out the "practical" or "functional" nature of the set in relation to "society" and/or ways in which society is reflected in symbolic practices.

Since Lévi-Strauss's assertion (47) that anthropology is a branch of semiology, the debate has raged whether semiotics should be viewed as a method which may be applied fruitfully to anthropological subjects or as a basic science, delimiting a definite subject matter which could be approached, among other ways, by the application of anthropological methods of observation. A recent contributor to this debate, Eco (21, p. 28) follows in great part Lévi-Strauss's ideas concerning the exchange theory of messages, concluding that "the laws of signification are the laws of culture. For this reason culture allows a continuous process of communicative exchanges, insofar as it subsists as a system of systems of signification. *Culture can be studied completely under a semiotic profile*" (cf 20). Schwimmer, on the other hand, maintains that "there is little support for a reduction of anthropology to a domain of semiotics . . . In anthropology, semiotic analysis is a useful, often indispensable method, but it does not presuppose or entail any specific theory of culture" (73, p. 8;cf 37). Although in the same article Schwimmer warns that general semiotics should not be confused with the narrower *sémiologie* pursued by francophonic scholars such as Barthes, Greimas, Kristeva, and others, he appears to view semiotics more or less as a method—such as structuralism—rather than as a general science. Peirce (63), as Singer (80) makes clear, viewed semiotics as a part of his overall Logic—as a normative science—with ethnography serving as a specialized discipline with its own peculiar methods and forms of disciplinary training. While advocating the adoption of this view of semiotics, as well as Peirce's triadic concept of the sign which yields a pragmatic semiotics, Singer would not do away with the distinction between society and culture which is fundamentally foreign to Peirce's system. By *semiotic anthropology,* Singer means specifically the explicit application of *Peircean* semiotic to anthropological problems. While recognizing that "the results of applying semiotics to anthropology, or to any other empirical field are not easily predictable," he is "betting that there will be a strong empirical component in the resulting mix, as well as a logical and rational component" (personal communication 2-18-77). Another candidate is *anthropological semiotics,* which stresses the use of the special techniques and tools of ethnography in the pursuit of an understanding of the semiotic behavior of man. In either case, I agree with Singer that what is important is the adoption of Peirce's integrating framework [cf the even broader theories of natural semiotics of Sebeok (76) and Thom (84)] in an attempt to avoid the splitting of the anthropologist's personality into the empiricist vs rationalist perspectives described by Leach (46).

The year 1976 saw the publication of at least two studies [by Bouissac (16), see also (17), and by MacCannell (49)] demonstrating the feasibility of a combination of the structural method with a pragmatic semiotic. In a masterful investigation of the modern world through tourism as a semiotic activity crucial to modern man's cultural system, MacCannell shows that, contrary to Lévi-Strauss's belief that one cannot do an ethnography of modernity, this can be accomplished without resorting to the traditional methodologies of taking a limited "symbolic" domain or a single community and extrapolating to the entire social system. [See Geertz's criticism of such methods in (27, chap. 1).] Stimulated by the work of Redfield and Singer, MacCannell offers us a rich picture of modern culture on the level of a social totality in flux. Using Peirce's notion of the sign for tourist attraction and Lévi-Strauss's structural method, he incorporates "Goffman's front vs. back distinction into differentiation, to link it up to Marxist and semiotic theory, and to ethnomethodological studies of behavior" (49, p. 179). MacCannell describes the transition from an urban-industrial society to a modern one in the following terms:

> As urban-industrial society develops, it seems to arrive at a point beyond which it can go no further: it runs out of resources, gets hemmed in or absorbed by other regions, or it is rendered obsolete by superior organization elsewhere. If it continues to differentiate beyond this point it turns in on itself. Each earlier differentiation develops a reflexive self-consciousness at the group level. Factories construct models of themselves just beside themselves for use by tourists. Automobiles (sports cars) and bridges split into dual functions, as transportation devices and as touristic experiences. The human group itself becomes conscious of itself as the source of the fulfillment of the human potential and arbitrary, intentional groupings appear and experimentally vary the theme of fulfillment (49, p. 182).

The Tourist provides ample evidence of the fruitfulness of considering culture and practical reason as arbitrary divisions of a human logic—or semiotic, in Peirce's sense.

Bouissac (16), in his brilliant analysis of the semiotic complexities of the multimedia texts of circus performances, provides another example of a "thick" description of a modern institution which is "interpretive" without neglecting the structural analysis of the underlying internal logic of the semiotic material. Drawing from several current semiotic and semiological methodologies, as well as Lévi-Straussian structural anthropology, Bouissac teases from circus performances extremely subtle indications of the text as a peculiar representation of our cultural logic: "A circus performance tends to represent the totality of our popular system of the world, i.e., it actualizes all fundamental categories through which we perceive our universe as a meaningful system" (16, p. 7). He also continually reminds us—in semiotic terms —of the semirejection of the circus by the culture, the circus's ambiguous status owing to its free manipulation of cultural elements. As a metacultural code, "a code that implicitly refers to the cultural codes" (16, p. 7), we find "some of the cultural elements . . . combined differently in the system of the circus than in the corresponding everyday instances" (p. 8).

While not the self-conscious variety of reflexivity familiar to modern society, the dynamic interplay of primitive and traditional social structures, together with the changes they may engender, have become increasingly important in recent anthropological literature. V. Turner's (88, 89) discussions of his concepts of *communitas* and *liminality*, for example, continue to stimulate interest in cultural sign systems "where the codes on which the communication depends are difficult to establish and highly ambiguous or open-ended . . . [such as], for example, with literature" [Culler (18, pp. 100-1)]. The now common treatment of art and ritual as culturally rich, metacultural sign systems similar to literature [see e.g. Boon (15), Firth (24), Geertz (29), Peacock (61), Turner (88)], stressing the great variety and complexity of allusion—their texture as well as their structure—marks the extent to which traditional typological classification of sign systems, and the corresponding specialization of semioticians, are dissolving, for in Saussure's day ritual was seen as belonging to a class of sign systems distinct from "open-ended" forms like literature [see Culler (18)].

In his discussion of revelation and divination in Ndembu culture, Turner (88) once again takes up the notion of the creative impulse of performative communitas reality, "from which all social structures may be endlessly generated."

> Communitas is the primal ground, the *urgrund* of social structure. Chihamba is an attempt to transmit to Ndembu the inherited wisdom of their culture about this primal ground of experience, thought, and social action and about its fitful intrusions into the ordered cosmos which native models portray and explain (88, p. 23).

Turner's conception of culture's evolution through the process of pushing back boundaries, including those between symbol systems (88, p. 33), brings to mind Bateson's notion of play and other meta-communicative behavior as "peeling the cognitive onion" (see 11), as, in fact, does much of recent work in the play of cultural codes, especially in ritual [e.g. Babcock (1, 2); see also proceedings of the 1976 Annual Meeting of the American Anthropological Association session on symbolic reflexivity]. For an example of the application of the notion of semiotic creativity to socialization, see (69). Turner himself (85) has discussed the phylogenetic development of man in such terms.

The new appreciation of a creative manipulation of semiotic codes, conscious or unconscious, owes a great deal to the changing perspective on man's relationship to his codes which has been developing in modern society [see Firth's discussion (24)]. As both MacCannell (49) and Peacock (61) have shown, the modern quest par excellence is not for the fundamental meaning of our everyday lives and beliefs —not, that is, for a unitary, transcendant identity—but for a constant expansion and reorganization of consciousness, in semiotic terms for ever new and shifting sets of signifiers and signifieds. Life in the postindustrial world is discussed in terms of life "styles" and the self "images" around which they revolve.

Our industrial forebears seemed to struggle endlessly with the problem of their identity. They elaborated theories to account for their own motives as being hidden deep in mysterious religious and sexual impulses. The modern consciousness builds images and remodels them to suit changing moods, creating new religions, making a recreation out of sex and rewriting history to make it accord with new reality. It is also making a routine out of the controversy and conflict accompanying this process [MacCannell (49, p. 142)].

In a world of protean selves [Peacock (61, p. 221)] ever hungry for new meanings, the ethnographer's excursions into exotic cultures may unexpectedly influence the lives and expectations of his countrymen as well as of those people who are the object of his study [see Eco's (21) discussion of the impact of semiotic on the very forms which it studies). MacCannell (49, pp. 173–74) even goes so far as to predict that "ethnography will eventually occupy a position in the modern world similar to the one occupied by psychoanalysis in the industrial world." The semiotic analysis of ethnography, in other words, may provide the raw material for a reconstruction of reality in the shifting hierarchy of semiotic systems in modern society. Whether or not ethnography does come to fulfill such a service role in the modern world, the ethnographer's own conception of the types of behavior in other cultures to be studied has been altered by the direction of his own society, and while he may now enjoy the process of discovering new and dynamic aspects of man's systems of representation and communication heretofore undervalued, he must be careful not to project his own culturally determined image of man as a self-consciously semiotic animal onto men in premodern societies, just as he must avoid the more frequently encountered images of man as an economic animal versus a symbolic one [Sahlins (66)].

The ongoing transition from individual applications of semiotic methods and concepts to anthropological materials to the creation of a unified semiotic theory of culture has been marked by two principal debates. The first chronologically involved the primarily North American dissatisfaction with language-dominated approaches to signs, both Saussurian semiology and the various formal methods derived from structural linguistics, which seemed to stress co-text at the expense of context, competence over performance, thought over action, code over behavior. Numerous calls were made for the inclusion of the sign user and the outside world in semiotic analysis. Examples of such interpretive and pragmatic descriptions emphasized the discovery of natural as opposed to conventional sign functions, otherwise referred to as sign "motivation."

The second, more recent bone of contention concerns the place of the traditional society-culture split in a semiotic theory of culture. Spurred by a reanalysis of Western notions of the "symbolic," some researchers claim that the first debate could be resolved by doing away with the culture-bound oppositions which stem from the society-culture distinction and around which both sides built their theoretical statements. The study of natural and conventional sign relations becomes, as in the semiotics of C. S. Peirce, one integrated part of a general logic once that division is eliminated. The first-order determination of significance and the second-order description of communication must, in this view, be considered as one.

Efforts toward a creation of a semiotic theory of culture have just begun. The liveliness of the discussions described in this review can be taken as a sign that the field is healthy and promises much for the future. Especially favorable to the continued progress of this line of inquiry is the active participation of an increasingly large number of anthropologists in the recently created national semiotic societies of the United States and Canada, as well as the International Association for Semiotic Studies, which draw their members from a wide variety of scholarly disciplines and semiotic schools. Anthropological semioticians can no doubt be counted upon to take advantage of this influx of new concepts and methods derived from the contacts provided by such institutions by fashioning a set of tools uniquely suited to the demands of cross-cultural field investigations.

Literature Cited

1. Babcock, B. B., ed. 1977. *The Reversible World: Essays in Symbolic Inversion.* Ithaca: Cornell Univ. Press. In press
2. Babcock, B. B. 1978. Too many, too few: Ritual modes of signification. *Semiotica* 19. In press
3. Baran, H. 1975. A review of structural semiotic research in the Soviet Union. *Sov. Stud. Lit.* 9:3–16
4. Baran, H., ed. 1976. *Semiotics and Structuralism. Readings from the Soviet Union.* White Plains: Int. Arts Sci. Press
5. Bar-Hillel, Y. 1970. *Aspects of Language.* Jerusalem: Magnes Press
6. Basso, K. H. 1976. 'Wise words' of the Western Apache: Metaphor and semantic theory. See Ref. 8, pp. 93–121
7. Basso, K. H. 1977. Metaphor, meaning, and language use. See Ref. 41
8. Basso, K. H., Selby, H. A., eds. 1976. *Meaning in Anthropology.* Albuquerque: Univ. New Mexico Press
9. Bateson, G. 1936. *Naven.* Cambridge, England: Cambridge Univ. Press
10. Bateson, G. 1966. Information, codification and communication. In *Communication and Culture,* ed. A. G. Smith. New York: Holt, Rinehart
11. Bateson, G. 1972. *Steps to an Ecology of Mind.* New York: Ballantine
12. Bauman, R., Sherzer, J. 1975. The ethnography of speaking. *Ann. Rev. Anthropol.* 4:95–119
13. Black, M. B. 1974. Belief systems. In *Handbook of Social and Cultural Anthropology,* ed. J. J. Honigmann, pp. 509–77. Chicago: Rand McNally
14. Bogatyrev, P. 1971. *The Functions of Folk Costume in Moravian Slovakia.* The Hague: Mouton
15. Boon, J. A. 1972. *From Symbolism to Structuralism. Lévi-Strauss in a Literary Tradition.* Oxford: Blackwell
16. Bouissac, P. 1976. *Circus and Culture: A Semiotic Approach.* Bloomington: Indiana Univ. Press
17. Bouissac, P. 1977. A semiotic approach to nonsense, clowns, and limericks. In *Sight, Sound, and Sense: Contributions to the 1975–76 Indiana University Pilot Program in Semiotics for the Humanities,* ed. T. A. Sebeok. Bloomington: Indiana Univ. Press. In press
18. Culler, J. 1976. *Saussure.* London: Fontana
19. Douglas, M. 1970. *Natural Symbols.* London: Cresset
20. Eco, U. 1973. Social life as a sign system. In *Structuralism: An Introduction,* ed. D. Robey, pp. 57–72. Oxford: Clarendon
21. Eco, U. 1976. *A Theory of Semiotics.* Bloomington: Indiana Univ. Press
22. Eimermacher, K., ed. 1974. *Arbeiten Sowjetischer Semiotiker der Moskauer und Tartuer Schule (Auswahlbibliographie).* Kronberg Ts.: Scriptor Verlag
23. Fernandez, J. 1974. The mission of metaphor in expressive culture. *Curr. Anthropol.* 15(2):119–45
24. Firth, R. 1973. *Symbols: Public and Private.* Ithaca: Cornell Univ. Press
25. Garfinkel, H. 1967. *Studies in Ethnomethodology.* New York: Prentice-Hall
26. Geertz, C. 1972. Deep play: Notes on the Balinese cockfight. *Daedalus* 101: 1–37
27. Geertz, C. 1973. *The Interpretation of Cultures.* New York: Basic Books
28. Geertz, C. 1976. "From the natives' point of view": On the nature of an-

thropological understanding. See Ref. 8, pp. 221–37

29. Geertz, C. 1976. Art as a cultural system. *Mod. Lang. Notes* 91:1473–99
30. Glassie, H. 1973. Structure and function, folklore and the artifact. *Semiotica* 7(4):313–51
30a. Goffman, E. 1976. *Gender Advertisements.* Studies in the Anthropology of Visual Communication 3(2). Philadelphia: Soc. Anthropol. Visual Commun.
31. Halliday, M. A. K. 1977. Language as code and language as behaviour: A systemic-functional interpretation of the nature and ontogenesis of dialogue. See Ref. 41
32. Hanson, F. A. 1975. *Meaning in Culture.* London: Routledge & Kegan Paul
33. Hill, C. E., ed. 1975. *Symbols and Society. Essays on Belief Systems in Action.* Athens: Southern Anthropol. Soc.
34. Hymes, D. 1968. Review of Kenneth Burke, *Language as Symbolic Action. Language* 44:664–69
35. Hymes, D. 1969. Review of H. D. Duncan, *Symbols in Society. Science* 164:695–96
36. Jakobson, R. 1975. *Coup d'oeil sur le développement de la sémiotique.* Bloomington: Indiana Univ. Res. Cent. Lang. Semiotic Stud.
37. Jarvie, I. C. 1976. On the limits of symbolic interpretation in anthropology. *Curr. Anthropol.* 17(4):687–91
38. Köngas Maranda, E., Maranda, P. 1971. *Structural Models in Folklore and Transformational Essays.* The Hague: Mouton
39. La Fontaine, J. S., ed. 1972. *The Interpretation of Ritual. Essays in Honour of A. I. Richards.* London: Tavistock
40. Lamb, S. M., Makkai, A. 1976. Semiotics of culture and language. *Curr. Anthropol.* 17(2):352–54
41. Lamb, S. M., Makkai, A., eds. 1977. *Semiotics of Culture and Language.* Proc. Burg Wartenstein Symp. 1975. In preparation
42. Lane, M., ed. 1970. *Introduction to Structuralism.* New York: Basic Books
43. Leach, E. 1970. *Claude Lévi-Strauss.* New York: Viking
44. Leach, E. 1972. The structure of symbolism. See Ref. 39, pp. 239–76
45. Leach, E. 1973. Structuralism in social anthropology. See Ref. 20, pp. 37–56
46. Leach, E. 1976. *Culture and Communication. The Logic by which Symbols Are Connected.* Cambridge, England: Cambridge Univ. Press

47. Lévi-Strauss, C. 1966. The scope of anthropology. *Curr. Anthropol.* 7(2): 112–23
48. Lotman, J. M., Uspenskij, B. A., Ivanov, V. V., Toporov, V. N., Pjatigorskij, A. M. 1975. Theses on the semiotic study of cultures (as applied to Slavic texts). In *The Tell-Tale Sign. A Survey of Semiotics,* ed. T. A. Sebeok, pp. 57–84. Lisse: de Ridder Press
49. MacCannell, D. 1976. *The Tourist.* New York: Schocken
50. Maranda, P., ed. 1974. *Soviet Structural Folkloristics.* The Hague: Mouton
51. Maranda, P., Köngas Maranda, E., eds. 1971. *Structural Analysis of Oral Tradition.* Philadelphia: Univ. Pennsylvania Press
52. Mehan, H., Wood, H. 1975. *The Reality of Ethnomethodology.* New York: Wiley
53. Moore, S., Myerhoff, B. 1975. *Symbol and Politics in Communal Ideology.* Ithaca: Cornell Univ. Press
54. Munn, N. 1973. *Walbiri Iconography: Graphic Representation and Cultural Symbolism in a Central Australian Society.* Ithaca: Cornell Univ. Press
55. Munn, N. 1974. Symbolism in a ritual context: Aspects of symbolic action. See Ref. 13, pp. 579–612
56. Ojo, J. R. 1977. Semiotic elements in Yoruba art and ritual. *Semiotica* 19. In preparation
57. Ortner, S. B. 1972. A kernel of truth: Some notes on the analysis of connotation. *Semiotica* 6:324–43
58. Ortner, S. B. 1973. On key symbols. *Am. Anthropol.* 75:1338–46
59. Ortner, S. B. 1975. Gods' bodies, Gods' food. A symbolic analysis of a Sherpa ritual. See Ref. 95, pp. 133–69. New York: Wiley
60. Peacock, J. L. 1975. Weberian, Southern Baptist, and Indonesian Muslim conceptions of belief and action. See Ref. 33, pp. 82–92
61. Peacock, J. L. 1975. *Consciousness and Change. Symbolic Anthropology in Evolutionary Perspective.* New York: Wiley
62. Peacock, J. L. 1976. Expressive symbolism. In *Explorations in General Theory in Social Science. Essays in honor of Talcott Parsons,* ed. J. J. Loubser, pp. 264–76. New York: Free Press
63. Peirce, C. S. 1965–1966. *Collected Papers of C. S. Peirce,* ed. C. Hartshorne, P. Weiss, A. W. Burks. Cambridge: Harvard Univ. Press
64. Rewar, W. 1977. Notes for a typology of culture. *Semiotica* 18: In press

65. Sahlins, M. 1976. Colors and cultures. *Semiotica* 16:1–22
66. Sahlins, M. 1976. *Culture and Practical Reason.* Univ. Chicago Press
67. Schneider, D. M. 1976. Notes toward a theory of culture. See Ref. 8, pp. 197–220
68. Schneider, D. M. et al, eds. 1977. *Symbolic Anthropology.* New York: Columbia Univ. Press
69. Schwartz, T., ed. 1976. *Socialization as Cultural Communication. Development of a Theme in the Work of Margaret Mead.* Berkeley: Univ. California Press
70. Schwimmer, E. G., ed. 1973–1974. *Journal of Symbolic Anthropology.* The Hague: Mouton
71. Schwimmer, E. G. 1976. Folkloristics and anthropology. *Semiotica* 17(3): 267–89
72. Schwimmer, E. G., ed. 1977. *Yearbook of Symbolic Anthropology.* London: Hurst
73. Schwimmer, E. G. 1977. Semiotics and culture. In *A Perfusion of Signs,* ed. T. A. Sebeok. Bloomington: Indiana Univ. Press. In press
74. Sebeok, T. A. 1976. 'Semiotics' and its congeners. In *Contributions to the Doctrine of Signs,* pp. 47–58. Bloomington: Indiana Univ. Press
75. Sebeok, T. A. 1976. Iconicity. *Mod. Lang. Notes* 91:1427–56
76. Sebeok, T. A. 1977. Semiosis in nature and culture. In *Semiotics and Theories of Symbolic Behavior in Eastern Europe and the West,* ed. T. G. Winner. Lisse: de Ridder Press. In press
77. Shukman, A. 1977. *Literature and Semiotics. A Study of the Writings of Yu. M. Lotman.* Amsterdam: North-Holland
78. Silverstein, M. 1976. Shifters, linguistic categories, and cultural description. See Ref. 8, pp. 11–55
79. Singer, M. 1976. Robert Redfield's development of a social anthropology of civilizations. In *American Anthropology: The Early Years,* ed. J. V. Murra, pp. 187–260. 1974 Proc. Am. Ethnol. Soc. New York: West Publ. Co.
80. Singer, M. 1977. Culture theory's tilt to semiotics. See Ref. 17. In press. Also to appear as a chapter in Ref. 81
81. Singer, M. 1977. *Man's Glassy Essence. Explorations in Semiotic Anthropology.* Bloomington: Indiana Univ. Press. In preparation
82. Spencer, R. F., ed. 1969. *Forms of Symbolic Action. 1969 Proc. Am. Ethnol. Soc.* Seattle: Univ. Washington Press
83. Sperber, D. 1975. *Rethinking Symbolism.* Cambridge, England: Cambridge Univ. Press
84. Thom, R. 1973. De l'icône au symbole: Esquisse d'une theorie du symbolisme. *Cahiers Int. de Symbolisme* 22/23:85–106
85. Turner, V. W. 1969. Forms of symbolic action: Introduction. See Ref. 82, pp. 3–25
86. Turner, V. W. 1974. *Dramas, Fields, and Metaphors: Symbolic Action in Human Society.* Ithaca: Cornell Univ. Press
87. Turner, V. W. 1975. Symbolic studies. *Ann. Rev. Anthropol.* 4:145–61
88. Turner, V. W. 1975. *Revelation and Divination in Ndembu Ritual.* Ithaca: Cornell Univ. Press
89. Turner, V. W. 1975. Ritual as communication in potency: An Ndembu case study. See Ref. 33, pp. 58–81
90. Watt, W. C. 1975. What is the proper characterization of the alphabet: I. Desiderata. *Visible Lang.* 9:293–327
91. Watt, W. C. 1977. Of semiotic evidence. See Ref. 41
92. Weinreich, U., Labov, W., Herzog, M. 1968. Empirical foundations for a theory of language change. In *Directions for Historical Linguistics,* ed. W. Lehmann, Y. Malkiel. Austin: Univ. Texas Press
93. White, D. R. 1974. Mathematical anthropology. See Ref. 13, pp. 369–446
94. Willis, R. 1974. *Man and Beast.* London: Hart-Davis, MacGibbon
95. Willis, R., ed. 1975. *The Interpretation of Symbolism.* New York: Wiley
96. Winner, I. P. 1977. The semiotic character of the aesthetic function as defined by the Prague linguistic circle: Implications for structural anthropology. In *Language and Thought,* ed W. C. McCormack, S. Wurm. The Hague: Mouton. In press
97. Winner, I. P., Winner, T. G. 1977. The semiotics of cultural texts. *Semiotica* 18:101–56

Ann. Rev. Anthropol. 1977. 6:137–59
Copyright © 1977 by Annual Reviews Inc. All rights reserved

CHINESE ❖9591
PALAEOANTHROPOLOGY

K. C. Chang

Department of Anthropology, Harvard University, Cambridge, Massachusetts 02138

INTRODUCTION

This paper will review the important results of palaeoanthropological study in China in the last decade. Palaeoanthropology refers to the study of human and cultural history during the Pleistocene and its immediately preceding and succeeding periods. To give historical backgrounds of current issues wherever desirable, Chinese palaeoanthropology in earlier years will be discussed, but the reader's attention is called to earlier review papers (2, 7, 8, 54) for the period prior to the 1960s.

BRIEF HISTORY AND CURRENT STATE OF THE DISCIPLINE

The study of Early Man in China was in the first decades of its history the study of Peking Man (*Homo erectus pekinensis*), and that study was until 1949 dominated by Western scientists. It was Max Schlosser of München who, in 1903, first identified the "dragon bones," used for centuries by the Chinese as medicine, as fossils of ancient animals. J. G. Andersson, a Swedish geologist, was led to Chou-k'ou-tien in 1918 on a dragon bone hunt, and in 1921 he identified Dragon Bone Hill at Chou-k'ou-tien as a potential Early Man site. Otto Zdansky, another Swede, excavated at Locality 1 of Chou-k'ou-tien in 1921–23, and C. Wiman of Uppsala recognized two human teeth among the excavated fossils. When Andersson announced this find in Peking in 1926, A. W. Grabau, a German geologist teaching at Peking University, proposed the name Peking Man.

As a result of the keen interest aroused by this new find, the Geological Survey of China, in cooperation with the Department of Anatomy of the Union Medical College, and supported by a grant from the Rockefeller Foundation, organized a two-year research program at Chou-k'ou-tien. In spring 1927, a well-preserved left lower molar was found by Birger Bohlin, and Davidson Black of the Peking Union Medical College first coined a Latin name for it, *Sinanthropus pekinensis*. Additonal teeth were found in 1927 and 1928, and the cave deposits proved much richer than a two-year project could tackle.

137

"Further, it became obvious that correlated field work elsewhere in China and in the neighbouring regions would be necessary before many of the geological, palaeontological and physiographic problems raised at Choukoutien could be answered. . . . In order to meet this situation the Cenozoic Research Laboratory was organized as a special department of the Geological Survey of China, both to carry on field work at Choukoutien and to investigate general Cenozoic geology and palaeontology throughout China. Funds in support of such investigation over a period of years being generously granted by the Rockefeller Foundation, the Cenozoic Research Laboratory began its activities in the spring of 1929" (6).

The research work spurred on by the new laboratory and new funds soon became intense and productive: the discovery of the first skull by P'ei Wen-chung in 1929 and the recognition of a lithic industry and evidence of fire in 1931 were the most dramatic. The subsequent results in additional discoveries of human fossils and cultural remains, their significance to the prehistory of China and that of the world, and the final fate that came upon the human fossils in 1941, all are now too well known to warrant another recounting here (see 82).

But this early chapter in the history of the Chou-k'ou-tien work merits a brief retelling because several major elements of the story continued to play important roles in Chinese palaeoanthropology after 1949, the year when the People's Republic of China was founded. First of all, the study of Early Man in China continued to be the charge of the Cenozoic Research Laboratory and its direct descendants. The laboratory, which resumed field research at Chou-k'ou-tien and elsewhere in 1949, was assigned to the Institute of Palaeontology of the Academia Sinica, and its name was changed to Laboratory of Vertebrate Palaeontology. In 1953, the Laboratory of Vertebrate Palaeontology became an independent institute within the Academia Sinica, and in 1957 it was further expanded into a new Research Institute of Vertebrate Palaeontology and Palaeoanthropology (IVPP). The IVPP now has four laboratories: I. Lower Vertebrates; II. Higher Vertebrates; III. Cenozoic Geology and Palaeontology; and IV. Palaeoanthropology and Palaeolithic Archaeology. Laboratory IV had a staff of 28 as of May, 1975.[1] Thus palaeoanthropological study remains in close collaboration with Cenozoic geologists (both stratigraphers and glacial geologists) and palaeontologists. Moreover, Palaeolithic archaeology remains to be carried out in a setting in which the major intellectual stimuli come more from Cenozoic scholars than from post-Palaeolithic archaeologists.

Secondly, the domination of the Western scientists in the Cenozoic Research Laboratory and the financial backing of palaeoanthropological research by the Rockefeller Foundation—not to mention the loss of Peking Man fossils in the hands of American officials of the Peking Union Medical College—naturally led to Chinese resentment. Furthermore, independence and self-reliance are now national policies

[1]This information was based on a lecture given by Woo Ju-k'ang on May 16, 1975, to members of the United States Palaeoanthropology Delegation. The delegation (of which I was a member) visited China for 30 days in May and June, and its official report is in the course of being edited and published. Other than the above piece of information, this review has not utilized any technical data obtained by the delegation but has been based exclusively on published material. However, no essential information has been left out.

with regard to scientific research as well as economic development. Consequently, international collaboration (in developing nations very often a disguise for Western domination) became a thing of the past, and Chinese palaeoanthropology is now in the hands of Chinese scientists. Western scholars have been able to visit palaeoanthropological sites and examine the fossils, and excellent casts of the fossils are widely available, but Chinese publications must now be relied upon outside China as the principal source of information.

On the basis of reports by outsiders as well as Chinese publications, one finds that the current practice of palaeoanthropological research differs significantly from that of Old China and of the West. Palaeoanthropology is now combined with production and construction on the one hand, and politics and the education of the masses on the other. The research process may be described as follows. New data (human fossils and lithic remains) may be brought to light under three different conditions: (a) Accidental discoveries may be made by farmers and workers, who are now palaeoanthropologically aware and are constantly on the lookout, and the finds are then reported upward through science and cultural relics channels. At the province level or even occasionally at the county level, there are trained scientists capable of assessing the significance of the find. (b) In major construction projects in regions with known history or likelihood of finds, palaeoanthropologists are a part of the regular work crew, ensuring that important finds will be salvaged. (c) Discoveries may be made as the result of purposeful search under scientific projects.

When finds are made and judged significant, they may be investigated at the local or provincial level (by staff members of scientific and archaeological bureaus or commissions or of local museums of history and natural history), or the fact will be reported to the IVPP in Peking. Individual specialists or teams of them will visit the site and decide on its proper investigation. Since the IVPP has on its own staff geologists, geomorphologists, and palaeontologists, IVPP teams are often interdisciplinary to begin with. When additional scientific specialties are required at important sites, research personnel from other research institutes of the Academia Sinica and from local museums and research institutes (such as the Institute of Geology and Palaeontology of Nanking) will join the investigation.

Local "peasants, workers, and soldiers," who are often responsible for the new discovery to begin with, are further involved with the investigation throughout. They provide excavation crews. They participate in educational sessions—conducted in the course of the excavation—in such themes as "labor created man," "primitive society," and "primitive people's struggle against nature." Similar themes will dominate museum exhibits that are put up after the excavation is completed. Casts of fossils and stone implements will be made in quantity so that important finds will be displayed in museums throughout the country. Pamphlets are prepared to explain the finds. A new journal, *Hua Shih* (*Fossils*), was launched recently to popularize the whole field of palaeontology and palaeoanthropology. In all these activities palaeoanthropologists participate, but they are also responsible for studying the finds and reporting them in scientific language. In technical publications they join with the rest of the world's palaeoanthropologists in discussing issues of common interest.

The principal technical publication in Chinese palaeoanthropology is the journal *Vertebrata Palasiatica,* published quarterly since 1957 by the IVPP, which also puts out occasional monographs. Another important journal, *Quaternaria Sinica,* was published by the Committee for Chinese Quaternary Studies (Peking) from 1958 through 1965; in it were papers in many scientific fields (geology, soil studies, palynology, geomorphology, and so forth) essential for stratigraphical and environmental studies of Early Man. After the Cultural Revolution (1966–71), *Quaternaria Sinica* did not resume publication as did many other scientific journals, but scientific papers are now published by several new journals, the most important being: *Acta Geologica Sinica* (edited by The Geological Society of China), *Scientia Geologica Sinica* (The Institute of Geology, Academia Sinica), *Acta Palaeontologica Sinica* (The Institute of Palaeontology, Academia Sinica), *Acta Geophysica Sinica* (The Geophysical Society of China), and *Geochimica* (The Kuei-yang Institute of Geochemistry, Academia Sinica). (All of the above journals are published by the Science Press in Peking).

All of the principal publications carry titles and very often summaries in English. Chinese palaeoanthropologists also make an effort to make their study results known internationally through their writings in Western languages (17, 100, 102), and they have received several foreign groups of visiting specialists whose reports are also useful in publicizing China's considerable progress in this field in recent years (42, 68; Lisowski, unpublished communication).

One word about Taiwan: known palaeoanthropological data on the island are relatively scarce, and they have been pursued by the staff members of the Departments of Geology and of Anthropology and Archaeology, National Taiwan University.

PLEISTOCENE STRATIGRAPHY, CHRONOLOGY, AND PALAEOENVIRONMENT

The system of subdivision of Pleistocene in China has undergone several important revisions since before the second World War. Teilhard de Chardin's (88) and Movius's (73) syntheses in the 1940s represent the results of several decades of pioneer work, mainly by scientists of the Geological Survey of China. Extensive research undertaken since the founding of the People's Republic of China culminated in a vastly more sophisticated scheme, with both broad divisions and finer subdivisions, described in the 1960s by Liu Tung-sheng of the Institute of Geology and his colleagues, a scheme which is widely adopted in its broad outline by palaeoanthropologists today. After the Cultural Revolution, detailed studies at many localities have resulted in still finer characterizations of individual geological units.

The pre-War subdivision as synthesized by Movius (73) is as follows. Pleistocene deposits are grouped into three broad units, Lower Sanmenian Red Clay, Upper Sanmenian Choukoutienian Reddish Clay, and Malan Loess; each adjacent pair of these units is separated by an erosional interval: Fenho, Huangshui, Ch'ingshui, and Panch'iao. The three major depositional units were associated with three major faunas: the *Proboscidipparion-Equus* fauna of Lower Sanmenian (Nihowan), the *Sinanthropus-pachyosteus* fauna of Upper Sanmenian (Chou-k'ou-tien), and the *Elephus-ultima* fauna of loessic times (Sjara-osso-gol) (54, 76).

This broad subdivision has continued to serve as the basis of stratigraphical studies after 1949, but in the 1950s, with vastly increased geological prospecting and industrial construction, relevant data fast became available from many parts of China, including palynological data, available here for the first time. In 1959, at the First All-China Stratigraphical Conference, Quaternary was subdivided into Q_1, Q_2, Q_3, and Q_4, the first three equivalents of the Lower, Middle, and Upper periods of Pleistocene and Q_4 being Holocene, and stratigraphies from the following regions of China were correlated according to this fourfold subdivision: Sinkiang, Tsaidam basin, Chinghai-Kansu, Inner Mongolia-northern Northeast, North China, lower Yangtze, Fukien-Chekiang, middle Yangtze, Kwangtung-Kwangsi, the southwest, Tibet, and Taiwan (26, 36). At the same conference, Liu Tung-sheng reported on his studies of the loess stratigraphy in North China and proposed to correlate it with pluvials and interpluvials; expanded versions of this report were published in 1962 (71) and 1964 (72). The 1964 version of the scheme, based upon such explicitly stated criteria as biology (mammals, invertebrates, plants), palaeolithic cultures, climatic changes (glacial moraines, periglacial remains, loess, lake shoreline changes, old soils, erosional remains, karst and limestone sinters), structure and geomorphology, and absolute dating, is summarized in Table 1.

The years in the mid- and late sixties saw the Great Proletarian Cultural Revolution, in which the position of scientific research in society and the societal priorities with regard to various scientific pursuits underwent fundamental reexamination, and no scientific work pertaining to Quaternary stratigraphy and palaeobiology was published. But work apparently continued at least in some areas and was being carefully planned in others, for early in 1972 the results of new studies began to see the light of print on a broad front. The pre-Cultural Revolution Quaternary division continues to be employed for palaeoanthropological purposes, but refined regional studies are being undertaken. In September 1975 another Quaternary Conference on North China was held in P'ing-shan, Hopei, and a revised stratigraphical chart is said to have been prepared (63).

Significant new work may be described under the following headings:

Absolute Dating

Until recently Chinese Pleistocene chronology had been based almost exclusively on relative dating, and interregional and intercontinental correlations were primarily attempted through the matching of faunas. The single absolute date was a uranium-thorium date of 210,000–500,000+ for Peking Man published by V. V. Cherdyntsev (14). Since the Cultural Revolution, results of radiocarbon and palaeomagnetic datings have come to light. As of this writing (November 1976), radiocarbon determinations of 67 archaeological and 6 geological samples have been reported by the Laboratory of the Institute of Archaeology, Academia Sinica (28–31); those of 3 archaeological and 3 geological samples have been reported by the C^{14} Laboratory

Table 1 Regional Quaternary Stratigraphies in China [Liu et al (72)]

	Quaternary			
Stratigraphic Divisions / Region	Lower Pleistocene Q₁	Middle Pleistocene Q₂	Upper Pleistocene Q₃	Holocene Q₄
North China Stratigraphies				
Middle Huangho Basin	Wu-ch'eng loess; Ni-ho-wan group (San-men group)	Shan Hsien group (Ko-ho group); Lower Li-shih loess; Ting-ts'un group; Upper Li-shih loess group	Chien Hsien group (Sjara-osso group); Malan loess	Lower terrace and peats
Chou-k'ou-tien Cave Deposits	Locality 18 (Hui-yü)	Locality I; Localities 3 and 15; Locality 13	Upper Cave	
Hopei Plain	Volcanic deposits; Clays of various colors and sand- and gravels	Volcanic deposits; Brown-red loess-like deposits; Volcanic deposits; Brown-yellow loess-like deposits	Volcanic deposits; Modern river beds and gray-yellow deposits	
Northeast	Pai-t'u-shan group; Basalt (Lower / Upper)	Huang-shan group (Lower / Upper)	Ku-hsiang-t'un group (Hailar group); Basalt (Lower / Upper)	Riverine alluvium, eolian sands, lacustrine and marsh deposits
South China Stratigraphies				
Szechwan Basin	Shan-shang gravels (Chang-la gravels)	Ya-an gravels (Ch'ung-ch'ing gravels); Calcareous sinters and Yen-ching-kou cave deposits	Chiang-pei gravels; Ch'eng-tu clay	Riverine alluvium
Southern Caves	Formation of caves at 110 m	"Giganto-pithecus" deposits; Formation of caves at 85-90 m	Yellow and red deposits (Giant panda, Stegodon deposits); Formation of caves at 35-40 m; Light gray and light red deposits	Gray deposits (Neolithic); Formation of caves below 20 m
Southern Glaciers	Dark red mud and gravels (Po-yang Glacial)	Dark red mud and peat layers(?) (Po-yang--Ta-ku Interglacial); Dark brown mud and gravels (Ta-ku Glacial)	Red mud (Ta-ku--Lu-shan Interglacial); Orange mud and gravels (Lu-shan Glacial); Yellow-brown earth (Lu-shan--Ta-li Interglacial?)	(Ta-li glacial?)
Middle and Lower Yangtze	Yü-hua-t'ai gravels (Pai-sha-ching gravels?)	Red earth with net patterns	Red earth with net patterns; Iron concretions; Red earth without net patterns; Gravels and slope deposits (iron concretions)	Hsia-shu clay; Riverine alluvium
Huai River Plain	First Sedimentary Cycle (Lower)	Second Sedimentary Cycle (Upper / Lower)	Third Sedimentary Cycle (Upper; Middle and Lower)	Fourth Sedimentary Cycle (Upper; Middle; Lower)

Table 1 *(Continued)*

Stratigraphic Divisions	Paleoclimate	Faunas: Northeast	North China	Huai River	South China	North China Stratigraphies: T'ien-shan Glaciation	Ho-hsi Corridor	Loess Plateau
Holocene Q₄						Post-glacial	Riverine alluvium, eolian sands, Secondary loess / Slope and erosional deposits	Secondary loess
Upper Pleistocene Q₃	Moist (Pluvial?)	Sha-kuo-t'un fauna				Glacial retreat		Slope and erosional deposits
	Dry (Interpluvial III')	Djalai-nor fauna (Yü-shu fauna)	Upper Cave fauna		Tze-yang fauna	Aktashya glacial (Moraines III') / Glacial retreat	Loess and loess-like rocks	Malan loess
	Moist (Pluvial III)	Ku-hsiang-t'un fauna	Sjara-osso fauna			Taitok Glacial (Moraines III)	Lacustrine deposits / Gobi gravels	(Ch'ing-shui erosion)
Middle Pleistocene Q₂	Dry (Interpluvial II'')		Chou-k'ou-tien fauna	Hsia-ts'ao-wan fauna	Wan Hsien fauna	Second Interglacial		Upper Li-shih loess (T'ung-ch'üan erosion)
	Moist (Pluvial II) / Dry (Interpluvial II'₂) / Moist (Pluvial II₂) / Dry (Interpluvial II'₁) / Moist (Pluvial II₁)		Ni-ho-wan fauna		Liu-ch'eng fauna	Chikdapan Glacial (Moraines II) / Glacial retreat / First Interglacial / Glacial retreat	Chiu-ch'üan gravels	Lower Li-shih loess (Huang-shui erosion) / Wu-ch'eng loess
Lower Pleistocene Q₁	Dry (Interpluvial I') / Moist (Pluvial I)					Kokodipusang Glacial (Moraines I)	Yü-men gravels	(Fenho basin)

of the Institute of Geology, Academia Sinica (35), and those of 3 archaeological and 20 geological samples have been reported by the C^{14} Laboratory of the Kuei-yang Institute of Geochemistry, Academia Sinica (33, 34). Of these, only 4 of the archaeological samples pertain to Pleistocene studies, but many of the geological ones are useful for cross-dating early Holocene deposits. According to an Australian report (42), Peking University has also set up a radiocarbon laboratory, but none of its work has yet been reported. In the summer of 1976, a news dispatch of New China (Hsin-hua) Agency (74) reported the application of palaeomagnetic dating to the geological formations at Yüan-mou in Yunnan (see below) by the Institute of Geomechanics, Academia Sinica, in Peking. The same dispatch further reported that the palaeomagnetism of Yüan-mou materials had also been worked on by the Institute of Geology and the Kuei-yang Institute of Geochemistry, with identical results. Subsequent personal communication with Wu Hsin-chih at the IVPP confirmed these news reports, but scientific papers are as yet unavailable.

New Studies of Glaciations

Studies of Pleistocene glaciations were undertaken before the war, most ardently by J. S. Lee (59), and more recently (37, 85, 92, 110), but greater vigor in this field has been shown in the last decade. In a recent correlation (64), glacial remains in the Ta-pieh mountains, the T'ai-hang mountains, the Tsin-ling mountains, the T'ien-shan mountains, northwest Szechwan, southwest Szechwan, southeast Kuei-chou, and the Mount Jolmo Lungma (Mt. Everest) area were correlated into a reaffirmed 4-glacial/3-interglacial series (Po-yang, Ta-ku, Lu-shan, Ta-li). The most important new research took place in the Jolmo Lungma area during 1966–68 (53). Observations of geological profiles and analyses of faunal and palaeobotanical (including palynological) collections at a number of glacial-related locations have resulted in the recognition of three Pleistocene glaciations, two interglaciations, and three postglacial phases. This may be compared with the glacial studies of Helmut de Terra and H. H. Patterson in the Kashmir area of the Himalayas, which have frequently been used as the standard glacial sequence of East Asia (39).

Palynological Studies of Pleistocene Geological Samples

The palynological study of Pleistocene samples was begun in China in the 1950s, and important results were achieved in the next decade, including those of long sections or cores (27, 48, 70, 109), Peking Man cave deposits (45, 84), and Holocene peats (24, 69), all suggestive of past climatic changes. In recent years, two areas of palynological research are worth special mention. The first is the palynological study of glacial-related samples in the Jolmo Lungma area, resulting in substantial information on climatic change and the raising of the Himalayas in Pleistocene (25, 46). The second is the sporo-pollen analysis of long geological cores, often taken from lake bottoms and peat deposits, resulting in important data on past vegetational and climatic histories. Some of these cores are exceedingly deep, such as a Shanghai core of 300 meters (64), and many were dated by the carbon-14 method (90, 91). A core from Liao-ning provides the first Chinese data outside Taiwan for Postglacial climatic history, including data for a hypsithermal dated to 2500–7500 B.P. (89).

Interdisciplinary Studies of Regional Geohistories

Both for geohistorical study and for palaeoenvironmental reconstruction for Early Man research, interdisciplinary expeditions have in recent years taken place at important localities in various parts of China, such as the Jolmo Lungma area of Tibet (27a), Yüan-mou in Yunnan, Lan-t'ien in Shensi (32), Chou-k'ou-tien in Peking, and the Choshui and Tatu river valleys in Taiwan (9). These expeditions have resulted in detailed reconstructions of Pleistocene histories (including geology, palaeogeomorphology, palaeontology, and palaeobotany-palynology) of small regions, which will eventually constitute the basic building blocks of a Pleistocene stratigraphy of all China.

Attempts at Eurasian Correlation

Chinese Pleistocene events traditionally have been correlated with the much more refined European sequence through faunal history and glacial chronology (55, 56, 75), but until detailed chronologies of Chinese Pleistocene can be established from internal evidence on a regional if not local basis throughout China, any such correlation can only be undertaken at a very broad level (49). The more refined Pleistocene stratigraphical sequences of Europe and Siberia have been used by Jean Aigner to suggest relative dating of Chinese Pleistocene localities whose internal evidence has only enabled chronological placements that she characterizes as "gross" and "oversimplistic" (1). Aigner also takes exception to the correlation of glacial-pluvial and interglacial-interpluvial phases, favored by Chinese geologists in the 1960s, on the ground that glacial intervals are considered "dry" in Siberia. Her views, however, have not met wide acceptance.

EARLIER HOMINIDS

From Late Miocene or Early Pliocene beds in the coalfields at Hsiao-lung-t'an in K'ai-yüan, Yunnan, a number of mammalian fossil teeth were discovered in February 1956. Of these, five molars were identified as Dryopithecine; Woo Ju-k'ang coined a new species name for them, *D. keiyuanensis* (94). Five additional molars of the same creature were found from the same beds in 1957 (95). In an extensive reclassification of Dryopithecines throughout the Old World, Simons and Pilbeam (83) have reclassified the Yunnan teeth as *Ramapithecus punjabicus* (Pilgrim 1910), which is a member of Hominidae. This new classification has been favorably received by Chinese palaeoanthropologists (16, 102). In July 1976 a new find of *Dryopithecus* fossils was reported in the coalfields in Lu-feng Hsien, again in Yunnan. The find is reported to have come from Pliocene beds and to consist of "more than a hundred teeth, a complete mandible, and deformed maxilla fragments" (74). We await a more complete report of this new discovery as well as more specific scientific identification of the fossils.

From South Chinese deposits described as Lower Pleistocene and early Middle Pleistocene teeth and mandibles of *Gigantopithecus blacki* have now been found from one locality in Hupei (44) and at least four localities in Kwangsi (12). The most recently (1973) discovered teeth in Pa-ma, Kwangsi, were among the largest *Gigantopithecus* teeth that have been found, but they are dated to Middle Pleistocene, giving further support to the view that *Gigantopithecus* was an extinct member of Pongidae (80).

Associated with fossil teeth of *Gigantopithecus* and those of more than 20 mammals at the Dragon Bone Cave at Kao-p'ing in Chien-shih Hsien, western Hupei, were found, in 1970, three molars that have been identified as australopithecine. Another molar of the same general morphology had before this been found among the fossils collected in Pa-tung Hsien, western Hupei (51). Associated fauna indicates a late Early Pleistocene date of these teeth. Chinese scientists have compared these molars with known African australopithecines and conclude that they are closest to *A. africanus,* although they may represent a new Asian species or may even be those of a *Homo* species.

Homo fossils have indeed been brought to light in South China, from Lower Pleistocene deposits in Yüan-mou, Yunnan, which will be described below. These indicate that in South China during Lower Pleistocene not fewer than three newly discovered hominoid species lived side by side, namely, *Gigantopithecus,* at least one australopithecine, and *Homo erectus.* Their phylogenetic as well as ecosystemic interrelationships are of the greatest interest. No comparable fossils are yet known from North China, but stone pieces that have been described as artifacts have been reported from Lower Pleistocene deposits at Hsi-hou-tu, in Jui-ch'eng Hsien, Shansi (17, 19) and at Ni-ho-wan, Hopei (50).

HOMO ERECTUS AND HOMO SAPIENS FOSSILS

A fair number of post-australopithecine fossils have come to light since 1949 (7, 8, 67). Table 2 lists all important finds from credible Pleistocene strata, grouped into late Early, early Middle, Middle, late Middle, and late Pleistocene periods.[2] Of these, the finds at Yüan-mou, Lan-t'ien, Chou-k'ou-tien, and Tze-yang deserve some additional comments.

Yüan-mou

As early as 1926–27, Yüan-mou (or Ma-kai) of Yunnan was known as an important palaeontological locality, where Walter Granger made a large collection of mammalian fossils. This fauna E. H. Colbert (38) attributed to Early Pleistocene. During the war years, Bien Mei-nien (5) undertook geological studies of the Cenozoic strata in Yüan-mou, also believing that the Yüan-mou beds were Early Pleistocene. Addi-

---

[2]In a recent issue of *Vertebrata Palasiatica* (Vol. 14, No. 3, 1976, inside backcover), S. T. Wang of Museum of Hupei reports the discovery in 1975 of three fossil teeth of "ape-man" (*Homo erectus*) type "earlier than Peking Man of Chou-k'ou-tien," in Mei-p'u People's Commune, Yün Hsien, Hupei. Sufficient details are still lacking to warrant the placement of this find in the chart at this time.

Table 2 Important Chinese human fossils discovered since 1949

Period	Name	Location	Fossils	Year found	Reference
Late Early Pleistocene	Yuan-mou	Shang-na-pang, Yuan-mou, Yunnan	2 teeth	1965	47
Early Middle Pleistocene	Lan-t'ien	Kung-wang-ling, Lan-t'ien, Shensi	Skull	1964	101
Middle Pleistocene	Lan-t'ien	Ch'en-chia-wo, Lan-t'ien, Shensi	Mandible	1963	99
	Chou-k'ou-tien	Locality 1, Chou-k'ou-tien, Peking	Teeth, tibia, mandible, skull	1949, 1951, 1959, 1966	22
	Chou-k'ou-tien	Unnamed new locality	Unspecified human fossils	1971	Unpublished communication
	T'ung-tzu	Yen-huei Cave, T'ung-tzu, Kueichou	2 teeth	1971	108
Late Middle Pleistocene	Ch'ang-yang	Lung-tung, Hsia-chung-chia-wan, Ch'ang-yang, Hupei	Left maxilla, a premolar	1956	15
	Ma-pa	Shih-tzu-shan Cave, Ma-pa, Kwangtung	Skull	1958	105
Late Pleistocene	Chien-p'ing	Chien-p'ing, Liaoning	Humerus	1957	98
	Hsia-ts'ao-wan	Hsia-ts'ao-wan, Ssu-hung, Anhwei	Femur	1954	104
	Hsin-t'ai	Wu-chu-t'ai, Hsin-t'ai, Shantung	Molar	1966	107
	Lai-pin	Ch'i-lin-shan Cave, Lai-pin, Kwangsi	Skull	1956	20
	Li-chiang	Li-chiang, Yunnan	3 femurs	1960	62
	Liu-chiang	Tung-t'ien-yen, Liu-chiang, Kwangsi	Skull and part of postcranial skeleton	1958	97
	Ordos	Ti-shao-kou-wan-ts'un, Wu-shen Ch'i, Ikchao League, Inner Mongolia	Parietal bone, femur	1956	96
	Shih-yü	Shih-yü, Shuo Hsien, Shansi	Occipital bone	1963	18
	Ting-ts'un	Ting-ts'un, Hsiang-fen Hsien, Shansi	3 teeth, parietal	1954, 1976	74, 79
	Tso-chen	Ts'ai-liao-hsi, Tso-chen, T'ai-nan, Taiwan	Parietal fragment	1970	66
	Tu-an	Cave at Chia-kuei, Tu-an, Kwangsi	2 teeth	1971	57
	Tze-yang	Huang-shan-hsi, Tze-yang, Szechwan	Skull	1951	78

tional fossils were collected here in 1960 (77), 1965 (47), and 1967 (116); among the 1965 collections made from the Yüan-mou red clay near Shang-na-pang, were identified two human incisors, said to exhibit features of *Homo erectus*. The Yüanmou stratum, from which the human teeth and other mammalian fossils were found, is now believed wholly to date to Early Pleistocene and represents a riverine-lacustrine deposit that is at places as thick as 371 meters. Three sections are distinguished on exposed surfaces; the human teeth and such other mammalian fossils as *Equus yunnanensis* and *Stegodon* sp. came from the lower layers of the upper section. Additional mammals identified in 1967, such as *Hyaena licenti, Rhinocerus sinensis,* and *Vulpes chikushanensis,* further strengthened the Early Pleistocene dating. In July 1976 the Institute of Geomechanics in Peking announced that the Yüan-mou group was dated by palaeomagnetism to 1.5 to 3.1 million years B.P., and that the stratum of the human teeth was dated to 1.7 million years B.P. (74). It is also stated that evidence of the use of fire and Palaeolithic implements were also brought to light in 1971–73 in the same locality. It appears that much fresh research work is going on at Yüan-mou and that additional interesting and important finds can be expected.

Lan-t'ien

The two localities where the human fossils were found—Ch'en-chia-wo and Kung-wang-ling—have been well reported as to their geomorphology, geology, palaeontology, and palynology (32). The latest Chinese opinion is that these two localities are roughly contemporaneous (103) and that both predate Peking Man (17), although Chou Ming-chen (32) was of the opinion that "Kung-wang-ling was, on the whole, probably somewhat earlier than the fauna of the Peking Man locality at Chou-k'ou-tien," and that "the Ch'en-chia-wo fauna was probably contemporaneous with, or slightly later than, Kung-wang-ling." Aigner & Laughlin (3), however, prefer to see a much wider temporal distance between skull and mandible: "We have assigned the Kungwangling cranium to the Chinese lower Pleistocene (Mosbachium-equivalent) on the basis of our interpretation of the faunal and geological evidence. . . . We have temporally separated the Chenchiawo mandible from the Lantian cranium, and on the basis of geologic and faunistic comparison assigned it (as with Choukoutien I) to the Holstein equivalent in China." To a large extent many scholars find reasonable a Kung-wang-ling—Djetis equivalence and Ch'en-chia-wo/Chou-k'ou-tien Locality 1—Trinil equivalence on faunal grounds (43, 81). But since the Pleistocene subdivision of China has yet to be further refined on internal evidence one is reluctant to accept the Aigner-Laughlin revision, which is based primarily on the faunal lists of these two localities. It has been reported (42) that palaeomagnetic data processed at the Institute of Geomechanics Laboratory have shown that the Brunhes-Matuyama boundary of age about 0.69 million years occurs in the lower part of the lower Li-shih Loess. If the correlation of the Kung-wang-ling stratum with lower Li-shih Loess (32) stands up, the Lan-t'ien skull should then indeed be dated to a period after the Brunhes-Matuyama boundary, namely Middle rather than Lower Pleistocene.

Chou-k'ou-tien

In 1966 new excavations at Locality 1, Chou-k'ou-tien, brought to light two pieces of cranial fossil bones, one a frontal and the other an occipital, both attached with small portions of adjoining bones. These have proved to belong to the same individual whose left temporal (and adjoining portions of parietal and occipital bones) was found in 1934 and designated as skull V. The Chinese scientists who described the new fossils in 1973 (22) regard skull V (as augmented) as that of a middle-aged male, with a cranial capacity of 1140 cc. The locus from which the new fossils were found was located in layer 3 as designated in 1934, which puts the skull in a later period of the deposition of the Peking Man cave. Associated fauna includes *Crocuta ultima* and *Cervus elaphus*, suggesting that by the time of the skull V deposits the fauna of the area had begun to exhibit Late Pleistocene elements.

Skull V has characteristic *Homo erectus pekinensis* features, according to the Chinese scientists: low and flat skull vault, reclining forehead, maximum breadth of skull being at a low plane, and developed supraorbital, occipital, and other prominences. On the other hand, they point out, Skull V exhibits a number of "progressive" features: occipital prominence is less pronounced than that of the other skulls; the sphenoidal and the parietal margins of the temporal squama exhibit an arch-shaped prominence; the end of the frontal crest shows a tendency to fork; the distance between the internal and the external occipital protuberances is shortened; the pyramidal axis tends to be horizontal; the supraorbital prominence is relatively fine; the walls of the skull vault tend to be vertical; and the skull walls appear thinner than the other skulls. On the basis of these latter features, the Chinese scientists take issue with Weidenreich's (93) contention that Peking Man underwent no appreciable physical evolutionary change during his long occupation of the cave.

The Upper Cave remains at Chou-k'ou-tien have variably been dated to late Pleistocene and early Postglacial. The Institute of Archaeology reported in 1976 a radiocarbon determination of 18340 ± 410 on a piece of deer bone from the site (31).

Tze-yang Man

Reportedly found in association with fossils of now extinct Pleistocene mammals, the Tze-yang skull has been regarded as possessing primitive *Homo sapiens* features and dating from late Pleistocene (78). In 1972 and 1974, the Institute of Archaeology reported that two pieces of wood, said to have occurred in the same stratum as that of Tze-yang Man skull, yielded the following two radiocarbon determinations: ZK-19: 7270 ± 130; ZK-256: 6650 ± 120 (half-life = 5568 ± 30) (28, 30). These dates have led archaeologists to question the Pleistocene dating of the Tze-yang skull (4). Beginning in 1962, the staff members of the Quaternary Group at the Geological College in Ch'eng-tu have undertaken extensive studies of the peat layers in the Tze-yang area from which the human skull and the mammalian fossils were found, arriving at the conclusion that the deposits were in fact early Holocene rather than late Pleistocene (13).

PALAEOLITHIC ARCHAEOLOGY

In a previously published article (11) I have listed in detail Chinese Palaeolithic sites that had been known to 1960. Newer discoveries and studies are summarized below (Figure 1).

Lower Palaeolithic Remains

NI-HO-WAN   A single quartzite chopping tool was collected in 1972 from a bed of unquestionably Ni-ho-wan stratum, in association with Ni-ho-wan fauna, at Ni-ho-wan, Hopei (50).

LAN-T'IEN   New data of stone implements were excavated in March-June 1966 by members of the IVPP at Lan-t'ien. Thirteen implements were excavated at Kung-wang-ling, 7 more from 5 other localities nearby, and 35 were collected on the surface. All of them were made of quartzite, vein quartz, and quartzite sandstone pebbles. Flake implements predominate, and flaking was done unilaterally in most cases. Recognized types include large pointed implements (Abbevillian hand-ax-like), large discoidal scrapers, chopping tools, small choppers, pointed scrapers, flakes with wears from use, and stone balls (87).

CHOU-K'OU-TIEN   The excavation of 1966 at Locality 1 brought to light 173 pieces of stone. The materials were predominantly vein quartz (57.3%) and flint (26.3%), and they include many secondarily retouched artifacts, both those assignable to clear types (40.7%) and those that are not (35.8%). Of this new assemblage, the Chinese archaeologists (22) thought that the following points were notable: a rectangular core with faceted striking platforms is reported to be the first such specimen from the Chinese Lower Palaeolithic; the typology of tools is complex and diverse, including various scrapers, points, and burins; and both technology and typology indicate that the Chou-k'ou-tien industry underwent continuous change during the long occupation at the cave (a point that relates to the change in physical characteristics of Peking Man himself).

KO-TZU-TUNG   A new site, Ko-tzu-tung (The Cave of Pigeons), is located at Wa-fang Brigade, Shui-ch'üan People's Commune, K'o-tso Mongolian Autonomous Hsien, Liaoning. It was found in 1956 and excavated in May–June 1973. Sixty-eight pieces of stone were found here and considered as Palaeolithic implements, and remains of fire and fossils of no fewer than 22 kinds of mammals were also uncovered. Both cores and flakes were found. Among stones regarded as artifacts, 15 are scrapers, 3 are points, 1 is a chopper, most made of flint. Associated animal fossils include those of *Crocuta ultima, Coelodonta antiquitatis, Ochotona daurica, Marmota robusta, Canis* cf. *chiliensis, Felis* cf. *microtis, Equus* cf. *hemionus,* and *Gazella* sp. This fauna suggests to the authors who reported the material (52) that the debris were deposited during late Middle Pleistocene under semiforest, semisteppe conditions.

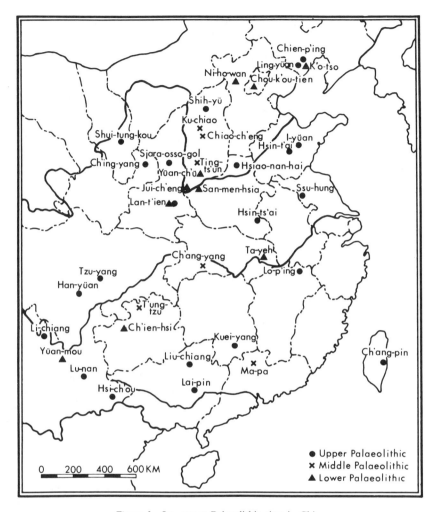

Figure 1   Important Palaeolithic sites in China.

SHIH-LUNG-T'OU   Another new Lower Palaeolithic site, the limestone cave at Shih-lung-t'ou, is located in Chang-shan People's Commune in Ta-yeh Hsien, Hupei. Eighty-eight stone implements—mostly of quartzite and flint—were found with mammalian fossils that include *Hystrix subcristata, Ailuropoda melanoleuca, Hyaena sinensis, Felis tigris, Stegodon orientalis, Rhinoceros sinensis,* and boar, deer, sika deer, and cattle, which seem to indicate a late Middle Pleistocene age. The lithic materials are characterized by cores, flakes, choppers, chopping tools, and scrapers, types that, according to the authors (61), find the closest affinity in the Chou-k'ou-tien industry. If the age of the find proves to be firm, this would be the best Lower Palaeolithic site ever found in South China.

Middle and Upper Palaeolithic Remains

T'UNG-TZU   A cave site, Yen-hui-tung is located in Yün-feng Brigade, Chiu-pa People's Commune, T'ung-tzu Hsien, Kueichou, in southwestern China. Found in 1971, it was excavated in 1971 and 1972. In addition to the human teeth described earlier, the site has also yielded 12 stone implements and some burned bones (108).

SHANG-SUNG-TS'UN   Eleven stone implements, mostly of the pebble tool variety, were found in river terraces near Shang-sung-ts'un, Pai-se Hsien, Kwangsi, in 1973. They are classified as late Palaeolithic (60).

PAI-LIEN-TUNG   A cave site, Pai-lien-tung, in Liu-chou city, Kwangsi, was found as early as 1956. A new excavation in 1973 brought to light a pebble chopper, remains of hearth and mammalian fossils (*Macaca, Paguma larrata, Rhizomys* sp., *Cervus* sp.), and fish bones (58).

PA-HSIEN-TUNG   Several caves with stone implement-bearing deposits were located in 1969 in the hills in the northern part of T'ai-tung Hsien, Taiwan, on the east coast. Excavations brought to light a lithic assemblage with both pebble tool and small quartz flake components. Radiocarbon dates show that the lithic industry here began somewhere in late Pleistocene but persisted into only a few thousand years (86).

PA-CHIEN-FANG   Fifty-one stone implements came to light in 1972 and 1973 from a riverine terrace near Pa-chien-fang village in Ling-yüan Hsien, Liaoning. They are of the flake and blade varieties, and associated fauna indicates a late Pleistocene age (65).

SHIH-YÜ   One of the more important Palaeolithic sites in China, the Shih-yü site (located in Shuo Hsien in northern Shansi), was found and excavated in 1963. Brought to light were: a human occipital bone, more than 15,000 pieces of stone, many burned rocks and bones, one perforated stone disc, more than 5000 animal teeth, and many broken animal bones. The lithic assemblage is typically Ordosian (with blades and microblades) and the fauna is characteristically Sjara-osso-gol, which dates the assemblage to Upper Pleistocene (18). A piece of cattle bone has yielded a radiocarbon date of 28,135 ± 1330 B.P. (31).

The fact that the lithic industry of Chou-k'ou-tien and that at Lan-t'ien and K'o-ho exhibit significant differences has long been noted (7). As a result of their studies of the very rich finds at Shih-yü, Chia Lan-p'o, Yu Yü-chu, and Kai P'ei at the IVPP have proposed to see the differences between the two traditions, which they maintain were continuous and persistent throughout the Palaeolithic periods, as representing two adaptive patterns and two ways of life. The first tradition, the K'o-ho–Ting-ts'un series, or the "large flake chopper–large prismatic point tradition," is characterized by large choppers of various types made of broad and large flakes, large prismatic points, and stone balls. Small ("microlithic") implements are few and include limited types in this series, which is typified by the sites at K'o-ho, San-men-hsia, and Ting-ts'un. The second tradition, the Locality 1–Shih-yü series, or the "keel-scraper–burin tradition," is distinguished by the small implements ("microlithic") made of irregular small flakes, of a great diversity of types, with small and careful retouch. Important sites of this series are Locality 1 and Locality 15 of Chou-k'ou-tien, Sjara-osso-gol, Shih-yü, and Hsiao-nan-hai (18). In their view, this contrast persisted into terminal Pleistocene or even the Postglacial period. A newly reported "mesolithic" workshop site at Eh-mao-k'ou in Huai-jen Hsien, northern Shansi, with large flakes, thick pointed implements, hand-axes, and "tortoise shell-shaped axes," is regarded as a late manifestation of the K'o-ho–Ting-ts'un series. Chia & Yu (21), in observing this persistence of the contrastive traditions, believe that "such differences reflect the differences in their economic life ways. Under the microlithic [Locality 1—Shih-yü] tradition, people's lives leaned toward hunting and fishing, only to be supplanted with gathering and other means of livelihood. Early on in late Palaeolithic period (e.g. at the Shih-yü site in Shansi) chipped arrowheads appeared. In later periods, when microlithic elements became even more conspicuous, arrowheads became more abundant, indicating a heavier reliance upon hunting. Animal domestication eventually grew out of an intensified hunting way of life. On the other hand, the large flake-chopper—thick point series suggest gathering as the primary way of life, supplemented by hunting and other means of subsistence. The subsequent beginning of agriculture was probably based upon a further development of gathering."

EARLY POSTGLACIAL ANTHROPOLOGY AND ARCHAEOLOGY

A Chinese early Postglacial hypsithermal that has long been postulated (11) but hotly contested (41) now has received undisputable support from palynological studies (89–91). The Palaeolithic-Neolithic continuum in North China is reinforced by the new studies of the Upper Cave skulls (106) and by the finds of new Postglacial nonceramic lithic assemblages that show Ordosian continuities (21, 23).

New archaeological data unearthed in the last decade or so and the newly available radiocarbon dates suggest that early Postglacial inhabitants of at least two or possibly three regions in China crossed the threshold to agricultural ways of life. They centered in the middle Yellow River valley of North China, the southeastern coastal areas, and the lower Yangtze and the Huai river plains, and their cultures in these areas are known respectively as Yang-shao, Ta-p'en-k'eng, and Ch'ing-lien-kang (10, 11).

Physical anthropological data are available from the Yang-shao and Ch'ing-lien-kang cultures. In the 1960s, three groups of skeletons were uncovered at three Yang-shao cemeteries in P'an-po [61 individuals (115)], Pao-chi [136 individuals (114)], and Hua Hsien [99 individuals (111)], all in Shensi. According to anthropometric studies of these skeletons by the late Yen Yen of the Institute of Archaeology and his associates, these three populations exhibit striking resemblances among themselves, as could be expected, and they also show the closest similarity, among comparative modern populations, with such "southern Mongoloid" groups as southern Chinese, some Indo-Chinese peoples, and Indonesians. In the 1970s, studies by Yen Yen and others of three Ch'ing-lien-kang populations were published: Ta-wen-k'ou of Shantung [79 individuals (112)], Hsi-hsia-hou of Shantung [27 individuals (113)], and Ta-tun-tzu of Kiangsu [113 individuals (40)]. Anthropometric studies show that these three populations cluster into a single group that shows some distance from the Yang-shao group, and that among the modern populations with which they have been compared the Polynesian samples come closest to the Ch'ing-lien-kang group. Such studies are apparently of great interest in assessing the interrelationship of the early farming cultures of China mentioned above, and also in regard to the question of the origins of some Southeast Asian and Oceanic populations.

CONCLUDING REMARKS

China has not yet produced an Olduvai Gorge or an Omo Valley, but what has been found so far (Figure 1) shows that China's palaeoanthropological resource is rich and that man's story here is already sketched by a variety of fossils and many Palaeolithic sites. In the Miocene and Pliocene beds of Southwest China there are fossils of *Dryopithecus* and *Ramapithecus,* and *Australopithecus* teeth have been recognized as far north as to the middle Yangtze. *Homo erectus* apparently appeared on the scene in Yüan-mou perhaps 1.7 million years ago in Early Pleistocene, and both they and their northern contemporaries are thought to be makers of stone implements. *Homo erectus* continued into Middle Pleistocene (Lan-t'ien, Chou-k'ou-tien, and others); there is now evidence of their use of fire (which has also been reported from Yüan-mou stratum), and their lithic industry exhibits considerable sophistication and complexity. Chopper-chopping-tools (as defined by Movius) characterize many assemblages, but they are far from the dominant types, and the difference of the Chinese assemblages from contemporary cultures in the western parts of the Old World may in the past have been somewhat exaggerated. Within China itself, separate, persistent traditions, regional in scope and possibly adaptive in nature, have been recognized by Palaeolithic archaeologists.

By the middle of Upper Pleistocene, fossils of *Homo sapiens* began to appear widely in China, some earlier ones described as neanderthaloid. After a brief and still ill-defined Middle Palaeolithic interval (represented by the finds at Ting-ts'un), the Chinese Palaeolithic developed its blade technology to account for a characteristically Upper Palaeolithic industry found in many areas of China, especially the North. After the final retreat of glaciers, some 10,000 years ago, an agricultural way of life was developed in two or possibly three areas of China (with millet the central crop in the Yang-shao area, rice in the Ch'ing-lien-kang area, and perhaps taro and yam in the Ta-p'en-k'eng area). Anthropometric studies of the skeletons of the early farmers in North and East China show them to be qualified to be the ancestors of the modern inhabitants of South China, Southeast Asia, and parts of Oceania.

This sketchy outline of Early Man in China will surely be enriched with important details with additional discoveries and researches in the decades to come. Discoveries there will undoubtedly be, and the whole country is potentially productive, but South China in particular, with its abundant hills and caves, will probably prove to be the most important source of finds to come. Because of China's current scientific priorities, large teams of scientists have only rarely been organized into expeditions to poke into potentially fossiliferous grounds full time, but when they do so in the future they will undoubtedly be rewarded. Furthermore, the masses of people have been fully sensitized into palaeoanthropologically aware citizens and virtually serve as permanent Early Man scouts in the field. It is certain that the next decade will see more discoveries, including very important ones, and their competent study by a growing, interdisciplinary group of Chinese scientists. It is also hoped that we will see far more extensive international exchange of information in this field.

Literature Cited[1]

1. Aigner, J. S. 1972. Relative dating of North Chinese faunal and cultural complexes. *Arct. Anthropol.* 9 (2):36–79
2. Aigner, J. S. 1974. Pleistocene archaeological remains from South China. *Asian Perspect.* 15:16–38
3. Aigner, J. S., Laughlin, W. S. 1973. The dating of Lantian Man and his significance for analyzing trends in human evolution. *Am. J. Phys. Anthropol.* 39:97–109
4. An, C. M. 1972. *Discussion concerning the chronology of certain primitive society cultures in China. *K'ao-ku* 1972 (1):57–59
5. Bien, M. N. 1940. Geology of the Yuanmo basin, Yunnan. *Bull. Geol. Soc. China* 20:23–31
6. Black, D., Teilhard de Chardin, P., Young, C. C., P'ei, W. C. 1933. Fossil Man in China: The Choukoutien cave deposits with a synopsis of our present knowledge of the late Cenozoic in China. *Geol. Mem. Geol. Surv. China, Ser. A,* no. 11, Peiping
7. Chang, K. C. 1962. Prehistoric archaeology in China: 1920–60. *Arct. Anthropol.* 1 (2):29–61
8. Chang, K. C. 1962. New evidence on fossil man in China. *Science* 136:749–60
9. Chang, K. C. 1974. Man and land in central Taiwan: The first two years of an interdisciplinary project. *J. Field Archaeol.* 1:265–75

10. Chang, K. C. 1975. *Radiocarbon dates in Chinese archaeology and their significance. *Bull. Dep. Archaeol. Anthropol. Natl. Taiwan Univ.* 37/38:29–43
11. Chang, K. C. 1977. *The Archaeology of Ancient China.* New Haven, London: Yale Univ. Press. 3rd ed.
12. Chang, Y. Y., Wang, L. H., Tung, H. J., Ch'en, W. C. 1975. *Fossil teeth of *Gigantopithecus* discovered in Pa-ma, Kwangsi. *Vertebr. Palasiat.* 13:148–53
13. Ch'eng-tu Geological College, Quaternary Study Team 1974. *A discussion of the chronological problem of the geological stratum containing the Tze-yang Man fossil. *K'ao-ku Hsüeh Pao* 1974 (2):111–23
14. Cherdyntsev, V. V. 1961. *Voprocy Geologii Antropogena.* Moscow: Isd. AN
15. Chia, L. P. 1957. *The fossils of Ch'ang-yang Man and the associated mammalian fauna. *Vertebr. Palasiat.* 1:247–57
16. Chia, L. P. 1974. *Some issues on human origins. *Vertebr. Palasiat.* 12: 165–73
17. Chia, L. P. 1975. *The Cave Home of Peking Man.* Peking: Foreign Languages Press. 52 pp.
18. Chia, L. P., Kai, P., Yu, Y. C. 1972. *Report of the excavation of the palaeolithic site at Shih-yü, Shansi. *K'ao-ku Hsüeh Pao* 1972 (1):39–58

[1]To facilitate reading and save space, Chinese titles will be given only in their English translations. An asterisk * will be placed at the beginning of such titles.

19. Chia, L. P., Wang, C. 1962. *Present status of palaeolithic research in Shansi and its prospects. *Wen-wu* 1962 (4/5): 23–27

20. Chia, L. P., Woo, J. K. 1959. Fossil human skull base of late palaeolithic stage from Chilinshan, Leipin district, Kwangsi, China. *Vertebr. Palasiat.* 3: 27–39

21. Chia, L. P., Yu, Y. C. 1973. *The stone workshop site at Eh-mao-k'ou, Huai-jen, Shansi. *K'ao-ku Hsüeh Pao* 1973 (2):13–26

22. Ch'iu, C. L., Ku, Y. M., Chang, Y. Y., Chang, S. S. 1973. *Peking Man fossils and cultural remains newly discovered at Chou-k'ou-tien. *Vertebr. Palasiat.* 11:109–31

23. Chou, K. H. 1974. *Stone Age remains at Ling-ching, in Hsü-ch'ang, Honan. *K'ao-ku* 1974 (2):91–98

24. Chou, K. S. 1965. *The investigation of two peat deposits near Peking and their pollen-spore analysis. *Quat. Sin.* 4 (1): 118–34

25. Chou, K. S., Ch'en, S. M., Yeh, Y. Y., Liang, H. L. 1973. *Some problems of Quaternary palaeogeography in Mount Jolmo Lungma region from sporo-pollen analysis data. *Sci. Geol. Sin.* 1973 (2):133–51

26. Ch'üan Kuo Ti-ts'eng Wei-yüan-huei (All China Stratigraphy Commission) 1963. *Chinese Cenozoic: Proc. All China Stratigraphy Conf.* Peking: Science Press. 31 pp.

27. Chung-kuo K'o-hsüeh Yüan (Academia Sinica), Chih-wu Yen-chiu Suo (Institute of Botany), and the Cenozoic Palynology Team of the Institute of Geology of the Ministry of Geology 1966. *Palaeobotanical studies of the Cenozoic in the Lan-t'ien area of Shensi. See Ref. 32, pp. 157–82

27a. Chung-kuo, K'o-hsüeh Yüan, Hsi-tsang K'o-hsüeh K'ao-cha Tui (Scientific Expedition in Tibet) 1976. *Report of Scientific Investigations in the Jolmo Lungma Region, 1966–68, Quaternary Geology.* Peking: Science Press. 112 pp.

28. Chung-kuo K'o-hsüeh Yüan K'ao-ku Yen-chiu Suo (Institute of Archaeology) Shih-yen-shih (Laboratory) 1972. *Report of radiocarbon determinations (1). *K'ao-ku* 1972 (1):52–56

29. Ibid 1972. *Report of radiocarbon determinations (2). *K'ao-ku* 1972 (5): 56–58

30. Ibid 1974. *Report of radiocarbon determinations (3). *K'ao-ku* 1974 (5): 333–38

31. Ibid, and Laboratory of the Institute of Vertebrate Palaeontology and Palaeoanthropology, Academia Sinica 1976. *Carbon-14 dating method for bone samples. *K'ao-ku* 1976 (1):28–30

32. Chung-kuo K'o-hsüeh Yuan Ku Chi-chuei Tung-wu Yü Ku Jen-lei Yen-chiu Suo (IVPP) 1966. *Cenozoic in Lan-t'ien, Shensi: Proc. Field Conf.* Peking: Science Press. 311 pp.

33. Chung-kuo K'o-hsüeh Yuan Kuei-yang Ti-ch'iu Hua-hsüeh Yen-chiu Suo C¹⁴ Shih-yen-shih (C-14 Laboratory, Kueiyang Institute of Geochemistry) 1973. *Radiocarbon determinations of some archaeological samples. *Geochimica* 1973 (2):135–37

34. Ibid 1974. *Report of age determinations of natural radiocarbons (2). *Geochimica* 1974 (1):28–31

35. Chung-kuo K'o-hsüeh Yuan Ti-chih Yen-chiu Suo C¹⁴ Shih-yen-shih (C-14 Laboratory, Institute of Geology) 1974. *Age determinations of natural radiocarbons. *Sci. Geol. Sin.* 1974 (4):383–84

36. Chung-kuo K'o-hsüeh Yuan Ti-chih Yen-chiu Suo Kou-tsao Ti-chih Yen-chiu Shih (Laboratory of Structural Geology, Institute of Geology) 1966. *Characteristics of the geological structure and change in the Mesozoic and the Cenozoic in North and South China.* Peking: Science Press. 105 pp.

37. Chung-kuo Ti-ssu-chi Yen-chiu Wei-yuan Huei (Chinese Quaternary Research Committee) and Chung-kuo Ti-ssu-chi Ping-ch'uan Yen-chiu Kung-tso Chung-hsin Lien-lo Tsu (Liaison Team, Center for Glacial Studies of the Chinese Quaternary) 1964. *Studies of Glacial Remains of the Chinese Quaternary.* Peking: Science Press. 168 pp.

38. Colbert, E. H. 1940. Pleistocene mammals from Ma Kai valley of northern Yunnan, China. *Am. Mus. Novit.* 1099:1–10

39. de Terra, H., Patterson, T. T. 1939. *Studies on the Ice Age in India and Associated Human Cultures.* Carnegie Inst. Washington Publ. 493

40. Han, K. H., Lu, C. W., Chang, C. P. 1974. *A study of the Neolithic skeletons from Ta-tun-tzu, P'i Hsien, Kiangsu. *K'ao-ku Hsüeh Pao* 1974 (2): 125–40

41. Ho, P. T. 1969. *Loess and the Origin of Chinese Agriculture.* Hong Kong: Chinese Univ. Hong Kong. 228 pp.

42. Hope, J., ed. 1976. *Australian Quaternary Newsletter,* No. 7

43. Howells, W. W. 1966. Homo erectus. *Sci. Am.* 215:46–53

44. Hsu, C. H., Han, K. H., Wang, L. H. 1974. *Gigantopithecus fossils and associated fauna in western Hupei. *Vertebr. Palasiat.* 12:293–306

45. Hsü, J. 1965. *Climatic conditions at Peking at the time of Peking Man. *Quat. Sin.* 4 (1):77–83

46. Hsü, J., Kung, C. C., Sun, H. C., T'ao, C. J., Tu, N. C. 1973. *Quaternary Palaeobotanical studies on the Mount Jolmo Lungma region and the Himalayan uplift. *K'o-hsüeh T'ung-pao* 1973 (6):274–77

47. Hu, C. C. 1973. *Fossil teeth of Homo erectus discovered in Yüan-mou, Yunnan. *Acta Geol. Sin.* 1973 (1):65–71

48. Huang, T. C. 1975. Palaeoecological study of Taiwan (4)—Waichiataokou profile. *Taiwania* 20:1–22

49. Isaac, G. L., Pilbeam, D. R. 1975. Correlation charts compiled at the symposium. In *After the Australopithecines: Stratigraphy, Ecology, and Culture Change in Middle Pleistocene,* ed. K. Butzer, G. Isaac, pp. 889–99. The Hague: Mouton

50. Kai, P., Wei, C. 1974. *The discovery of an Early Pleistocene stone implement at Ni-ho-wan. *Vertebr. Palasiat.* 12: 69–72

51. Kao, C. 1975. *Australopithecine teeth associated with Gigantopithecus in western Hupei. *Vertebr. Palasiat.* 13: 81–88

52. Ko-tzu-tung Excavation Team 1975. *Report of the excavation at the palaeolithic site in Ko-tzu-tung, Liaoning. *Vertebr. Palasiat.* 13:122–36

53. Kuo, H. T. 1974. *Climatic changes in the Mount Jolmo Lungma region, southern Tibet, China, during the Quaternary period. *Sci. Geol. Sin.* 1974 (1): 59–80

54. Kuo, M. J., Young, C. C., P'ei, W. C., Chou, M. C., Woo, J. K., Chia, L. P. 1955. *Discovery and Research of Human Fossils in China: Proc. Conf. in commem. 25th anniv. discovery first Peking Man skull.* Peking: Science Press. 104 pp.

55. Kurten, B. 1957. Mammal migrations, Cenozoic stratigraphy, and the age of Peking Man and the Australopithecines. *J. Palaeontol.* 31 (1):215–27

56. Kurten, B. 1961. An attempted parallelization of the Quaternary mammalian faunas of China and Europe. *Soc. Sci. Fenn.: Commentat. Biol.* 23 (8)

57. Kwangsi Chuang Autonomous Region Museum 1973. *Human teeth and mammalian fossils found in Tu-an, Kwangsi. *Vertebr. Palasiat.* 11:221–23

58. Kwangsi Liu-chou City Museum 1975. *Vertebrate fossils from the late palaeolithic site at Pai-lien-tung, Liu-chou city. *Vertebr. Palasiat.* 13:137

59. Li, S. K. (J. S. Lee) 1975. *Quaternary Glacials in China.* Peking: Science Press. 160 pp.

60. Li, Y. H., Yu, Y. C. 1975. *Palaeolithic implements discovered in Pai-se, Kwangsi. *Vertebr. Palasiat.* 13:225–28

61. Li, Y. H., Yüan, C. H., Tung, H. J., Li, T. Y. 1974. *Report of the excavation of the palaeolithic site at Shih-lung-t'ou, Ta-yeh, Hupei. *Vertebr. Palasiat.* 12:139–57

62. Li, Y. H. 1961. *A locality of Quaternary mammalian fossils in the Li-chiang basin, Yunnan. *Vertebr. Palasiat.* 1961:143–49

63. Li, Y. H. 1976. *The North China Quaternary Conference held at P'ingshan, Hopei. *Vertebr. Palasiat.* 14 (3), inside back cover

64. Li, Y. C., P'an, C. Y., Ts'ao, C. Y., Hu, C. C., Chou, M. L., Ch'en, M. N., Wang, S. F., Chang, C. L. 1973. *A study of Quaternary glaciations in China. *Acta Geol. Sin.* 1973 (1):94–101

65. Liaoning Province Museum 1973. *A palaeolithic location at Hsi-pa-chienfang, Ling-yüan. *Vertebr. Palasiat.* 11:223–26

66. *Lien Ho Pao* (United Daily), August 15, 1975, Taipei, Taiwan

67. Limbrey, S. 1975. China. In *Catalogue of Fossil Hominids, Part III: Americas, Asia, Australia,* ed. K. P. Oakley, B. G. Campbell, T. I. Molleson, pp. 49–87. London: British Museum

68. Lisowski, F. P. 1965. Human fossils recently discovered in Shensi Province, China. *Man* 65:119

69. Liu, C. L., Li, W. C., Sun, M. J., Liu, M. L. 1965. *Pollen and spore assemblage in the peat deposits south of Mount Yen. *Quat. Sin.* 4 (1):105–17

70. Liu, M. L. 1965. *Preliminary study of the pollen and spore assemblage in the early Pleistocene deposits at Huei-shing-kou, Huei-hsing-chen, in Shan Hsien, Honan. *Quat. Sin.* 4 (1):145–47

71. Liu, T. S., Liu, M. H., Wu, T. J., Ch'en, C. H. 1962. *The climatic marker and the division of the Quaternary strata in China. *Acta Geol. Sin.* 1962 (6)

72. Ibid 1964. *On the stratigraphic division of the Chinese Quaternary. In

*Problems of the Geology of the Quaternary, ed. Inst. Geol. Acad. Sin., pp. 45–64. Peking: Science Press
73. Movius, H. L. Jr. 1948. The lower palaeolithic cultures of southern and eastern Asia. Trans. Am. Philos. Soc. n.s. 38, Part 4:329–420
74. New China News Agency, July 25 and November 22, 1976, dispatches
75. P'ei, W. C. 1939. An attempted correlation of Quaternary geology, palaeontology, and prehistory in Europe and China. Inst. Archaeol., Univ. London, Occasional Papers No. 2, Geochronological Table No. 1, pp. 3–16
76. P'ei, W. C. 1957. The zoogeographical divisions of Quaternary mammalian faunas in China. Vertebr. Palasiat. 1: 9–24
77. P'ei, W. C. 1961. *Fossil mammals of early Pleistocene age from Yuan-mou (Ma-kai) of Yunnan. Vertebr. Palasiat. 1961 (1):16–30
78. P'ei, W. C., Woo, J. K. 1975. *Tze-yang Man. Peking: IVPP. 71 pp.
79. P'ei, W. C., Woo, J. K., Chia, L. P., Chou, M. C., Liu, H. T., Wang, T. I. 1958. *Report of the Excavation of the Palaeolithic Site at Ting-ts'un, Hsiangfen Hsien, Shansi. Peking: Science Press. 111 pp.
80. Pilbeam, D. R. 1970. Gigantopithecus and the origins of hominidae. Nature 225:516–19
81. Pilbeam, D. R. 1975. Middle Pleistocene hominids. In After the Australopithecines, ed. K. Butzer, G. Isaac, pp. 809–56. The Hague: Mouton
82. Shapiro, H. 1974. Peking Man. New York: Simon & Schuster. 190 pp.
83. Simons, E. L., Pilbeam, D. R. 1965. Preliminary revision of the Dryopithecinae (Pongidae, Anthropoidea). Folia Primatol. 3:81–152
84. Sun, M. J. 1965. *The spore and pollen assemblage in the strata of Peking Man fossils at Chou-k'ou-tien. Quat. Sin. 4 (1):84–96
85. Sun, T. C. 1957. *Important Remains of Quaternary Glaciations in China. Peking: Science Press. 60 pp.
86. Sung, W. H. 1969. *Ch'ang-pin culture. Newsl. Chinese Ethnol. 9:1–27. (See a review article on the Ch'ang-pin culture by K. C. Chang, based on this reference by Sung, in Asian Perspect. 1971, 12:133–36)
87. Tai, E. C., Hsü, C. H. 1973. *New palaeolithic finds in Lan-t'ien and the culture of Lan-t'ien Man. K'ao-ku Hsüeh Pao 1973 (2):1–11

88. Teilhard de Chardin, P. 1941. Early Man in China. Institut de Géo-Biologie Pekin. 99 pp.
89. Ti-ssu-chi Ti-chih-tsu chi C¹⁴-tsu (Quaternary Geology Team and C-14 Team of the Kuei-yang Institute of Geochemistry) 1974. *Preliminary results on Holocene geochronology in southern Liaoning. Geochimica 1974 (1):25–27
90. Tsukada, M. 1966. Late Pleistocene vegetation and climate in Taiwan (Formosa). Proc. Natl. Acad. Sci. 55:543–48
91. Tsukada, M. 1967. Vegetation in subtropical Formosa during the Pleistocene glaciations and the Holocene. Palaeogeogr., Palaeoclimatol., Palaeoecol. 3:49–64
92. Wang, M. Y., Cheng, M. P. 1965. *Remains of Quaternary glaciations in Tibetan plateau. Acta Geogr. Sin. 31 (1):63–72
93. Weidenreich, F. 1935. The Sinanthropus population of Choukoutien (Locality) with a preliminary report on new discoveries. Bull. Geol. Soc. China 11:427–68
94. Woo, J. K. 1957. Dryopithecus teeth from Keiyuan, Yunnan province. Vertebr. Palasiat. 1 (1):25–31
95. Woo, J. K. 1958. New materials of Dryopithecus from Keiyuan, Yunnan. Vertebr. Palasiat. 2:38–43
96. Woo, J. K. 1958. *Fossil human parietal bone and femur from Ordos, Inner Mongolia. Vertebr. Palasiat. 2:208–12
97. Woo, J. K. 1959. Human fossils found in Liu-kiang, Kwangsi, China. Vertebr. Palasiat. 3:109–18
98. Woo, J. K. 1961. *Fossil human humerus from Chien-p'ing, Liaoning province. Vertebr. Palasiat. 1961 (4):287–89
99. Woo, J. K. 1964. *A mandible of the Homo erectus type discovered in Lan-t'ien, Shensi. Vertebr. Palasiat. 8:1–12
100. Woo, J. K. 1965. Recent advances of palaeoanthropology in China. Homenage a Juan Comas en su 65 aniversario, Vol. 2: Antropologia fisica, pp. 403–13. Mexico City
101. Woo, J. K. 1966. *A Homo erectus skull discovered in Lan-t'ien, Shensi. Vertebr. Palasiat. 10:1–16
102. Woo, J. K. 1971. Discoveries of prehistoric man in China. China Reconstructs December 1971, pp. 24–27
103. Woo, J. K. 1973. *Lan-tien ape man. Wen-wu 1973 (6):41–44
104. Woo, J. K., Chia, L. P. 1955. *Fossil human femur fragment of Hsia-ts'aowan. Acta Palaeontol. Sin. 3:67–69

105. Woo, J. K., P'eng, J. T. 1959. *Fossil human skull of early palaeoanthropic stage found at Mapa, Shao-kuan, Kwangtung province. *Vertebr. Palasiat.* 3:175–82

106. Wu, H. C. 1961. *A study of the human fossils at the Upper Cave, Chou-k'ou-tien. *Vertebr. Palasiat.* 1961:181–203

107. Wu, H. C., Tsung, K. F. 1973. *Human tooth and mammalian fossils of late Pleistocene age at Wu-chu-t'ai in Hsin-t'ai, Shantung. *Vertebr. Palasiat.* 11: 105–6

108. Wu, M. L., Wang, L. H., Chang, Y. Y., Chang, S. S. 1975. *Early Man fossils and cultural remains discovered in T'ung-tzu, Kweichou. *Vertebr. Palasiat.* 13:14–23

109. Yang, H. C., Chiang, T. H. 1965. *The spore and pollen assemblages from the Quaternary deposits of the Chinghai Lake basin and their significance. *Acta Geogr. Sin.* 31 (4):322–35

110. Yang, H. J., Ch'iu, S. C. 1965. *Climatic fluctuations during the Quater-nary glaciations and the postglacial period in the upper Urumchi valley. *Acta Geogr. Sin.* 31 (3):194–211

111. Yen, Y. 1962. *A study of the Neolithic skeletons from Hua Hsien. *K'ao-ku Hsüeh Pao* 1962 (2):85–104

112. Yen, Y. 1972. *Report of a study of the Neolithic skeletons from Ta-wen-k'ou. *K'ao-ku Hsüeh Pao* 1972 (1):91–122

113. Yen, Y. 1973. *Report of a study of the neolithic human skeletons from Hsi-hsia-hou. *K'ao-ku Hsüeh Pao* 1973 (2): 91–125

114. Yen, Y., Liu, C. C., Ku, Y. M. 1960. *Report of a study of the neolithic human skeletons from Pao-chi. *Vertebr. Palasiat.* 4:103–11

115. Yen, Y., Wu, H. C., Liu, C. C., Ku, Y. M. 1963. *A study of the human skeletons at Pan-p'o. In *Hsi-an Pan-p'o*, pp. 234–54. Peking: Wen-wu Press

116. Yu, Y. C., Ch'i, K. C. 1973. *New mammalian fossils from the Pleistocene in Yüan-mou, Yunnan. *Vertebr. Palasiat.* 11:66–80

Ann. Rev. Anthropol. 1977. 6:161–79
Copyright © 1977 by Annual Reviews Inc. All rights reserved

CURRENT DIRECTIONS IN   ❖9592
MIDWESTERN ARCHAEOLOGY

James A. Brown

Department of Anthropology, Northwestern University, Evanston, Illinois 60201

INTRODUCTION

Ten years ago James B. Griffin (62) observed that three themes dominated eastern North American prehistory: 1. the gradual evolution from hunting and gathering bands to settled agricultural societies over a period of 15,000 years; 2. the achievement of two cultural "climaxes"; and 3. the strong impact on cultural evolution of cultivated plant introductions from Mesoamerica. Subsequent research in the Midwest has continued to focus primarily on these themes or on issues and problems derived from them. The historical roots of these themes reach back to a period before serious archaeology existed when the central intellectual questions were the origins and fate of the Mound Builder race. Since then, scholarly attention has turned to an anthropological concern for the processes and conditions promoting cultural evolution in the Midwest as determined by investigations based on a sound regional prehistory. The original issues, however, find echoes in those problems that revolve around the fate of Mississippian high culture in the Midwest and the relationship of historic tribes to this past stage of greater complexity.

I have chosen a topical approach here in order to emphasize the central features of Midwestern archaeology, although I am aware of the fact that my overview is limited in scope and inevitably biased in favor of materials that I know best. Since a limited number of topics can be broached in a review of this length, my choice was limited to topics focusing on processes and interconnections. In accordance with this topical organization, I have brought to bear the research contributions of allied disciplines that have come to play an increasing role in regional research. The contributions of geomorphology, ecology, climatology, and bioanthropology have greatly strengthened our understanding of prehistoric social organization and subsistence economy.

Since a topical organization governs this review, I suggest consulting the summaries of Griffin (62), Ford (48), and Dragoo (39) for a current overview of culture history from a chronological point of view. On the state and local level a list is available in Ford's (48) summary, to which can be added two other works (26, 98).

The geographical limits of concern here are the states of Minnesota, Wisconsin, Michigan, Ohio, Indiana, Illinois, Iowa, and Missouri—more specifically, the region encompassed within these states that belongs to the Till Plains physiographic province.

This paper is written with the purpose of reviewing current directions in major research approaches as well as current thought on the major factors underlying Midwestern cultural evolution.

RESEARCH ORIENTATIONS

Culture and Environment

PALEOENVIRONMENT   Starting from a crude environmentalist stance founded in the natural area approach to culture areas, the investigation of environmental bases of cultural adaptations has reoriented itself in keeping with advances in the discipline of ecology. The ecological and geographical approach has been widely promoted in the writings of Butzer (23a), who emphasized the necessity for detailed modeling of past environments through a multitude of complementary sources that monitor the local site setting, economic resource base, and regional environment. Physics, biology, and ecology are heavily drawn upon for modeling. The study of Midwestern paleoenvironments has just begun. Recent studies draw on the evidence from faunal and floral remains (93, 135), geomorphology (24) pollen analysis (19, 112), and other environmental indicators (20, 93, 113).

The potential importance of paleoenvironmental studies is probably clearest for the late Pleistocene and early Holocene periods, since major changes in the potential of subsistence resources occurred then in response to deglaciation (24, 48, 93). For instance, the major riverine environments that were productive for Archaic hunter-gatherers (19, 48, 134) have undergone a transformation in resource potential created as a response to the evolution of river systems. As clearly argued by Butzer (24) in the case of the Illinois River, the long-term ongoing trend there is toward a straight, fixed position to the river bed and more pronounced natural levees. As a consequence, larger tracts of bottoms are flooded, thus expanding the highly productive riparian and aquatic habitats (121). This evolution has been taking place since the Mississippi River system adjusted to the eustatic rise of the seas, an estimated 11,000 years ago (24). But the impact on Archaic hunter-gatherers' adaptations in the riverine areas is not clearly registered until the Middle Archaic (ca 6000 B.P.) (19, 24).

THE CLIMATIC MODEL   Environment is viewed in Midwestern studies more through the lens of a climatic model than any other. Considerable progress has been made toward compiling a climatic history of eastern North America through more sophisticated paleoclimatic modeling and the accumulation of better quality data (9). Recent gains have been made through the application of a circulation model to the summertime climatic record and to the greater control exercised over chronology from tree core and laminated lake core records.

The conclusion that can be drawn from this research is that past changes have occurred and that they have been of sufficient magnitude to have affected cultural subsistence (9, 68).

Subsistence Studies

Interest in determining subsistence practices has encouraged the collection of animal bones, mussel shells, and charred plant remains. As knowledge has accumulated on subsistence, it becomes increasingly clear that if these investigations are the powerful vehicles that they are thought to be in uncovering prehistoric subsistence, then food residues must be collected systematically in order to reduce bias and to facilitate comparison between sites. The techniques of sampling and recovery for food remains have begun to be widely adopted. For instance, it has only been recently that flotation techniques have been incorporated into excavation programs with the purpose of increasing the representation of fragile and small scale remains (129). These remains are especially important for documenting evidence of early plant domestication and cultivation. A growing corpus of research reports on food remains exist covering a range of time from the Early Archaic to the Historic periods. During this time the subject of subsistence has moved beyond the narrow perspective it started out with, i.e. to document the historically important subsistence modes, although this concern remains important (e.g. 49). But as yet there have been no systematic regional summaries that have incorporated flotation data since the summaries of Yarnell (138) and Cleland (28). Several enlightening reports on specific research have appeared that have broader implications and pose more general questions concerning the evolution of subsistence systems (e.g. 6, 103, 128). Other uses have been made of faunal remains, particularly as sources of seasonal determination (11, 71).

Subsistence data have now been used to investigate hunting and gathering strategies (6, 30, 114) and to investigate a wide range of ecological relationships (71, 114, 130). Of theoretical significance here is the adoption of a maximization (or least effort) model as an approach to subsistence modeling (114) suitable for explaining many subsistence patterns noted in the literature (6, 27, 28, 30, 104, 133, 134). It is useful in assessing position on the scale of focal-diffuse economies (or narrow-broad spectrum) and the factors promoting the particular combination of resource patterns observed in the archaeological record. Second, subsistence data have been used to document season of occupation in a region in which winter dormancy in the latitude of the Midwest imposes significant constraints on human occupation (cf 28, 42, 71, 85, 130, 133, 134).

Ford (48) has summarized subsistence trends: 1. New species were acquired to the subsistence base during the Early and Middle Archaic in consequence of post-Pleistocene environmental change. 2. The Late Archaic saw the inception of an expansion of the food base through intensification of foraging within shrinking territories. 3. The process continued and as a consequence promoted the adoption of Mesoamerican cultivated plants. 4. Over a long span of time corn agriculture supplemented by beans created a more substantial resource base that led to reduced reliance on wild nuts and seeds. Each of these points has been affirmed by recent work in Archaic (20, 87), Late Woodland (81, 83, 104, 126, 130) and Historic sites (22).

Settlement Analysis

SITE STRUCTURE   The study of settlement plans and patterns of settlement has been the major approach to providing access to past sociocultural systems (14, 38, 43, 50, 105, 121).

The study of site plans takes as its primary point of departure Binford's proposition that the overall content and spatial distribution of material remains are dependent on the tasks performed and the social composition of the group engaged in these tasks (13). The first concrete exposition of this position took place in the context of his case study of Hatchery West Site, which revealed that a settlement structure adhered in the partitionable distribution of cultural features and material remains (14). In this case study an examination of the subsurface features separately from the surface middens led him to observe that an excavation strategy devoted to the collecting of objects from the middens would miss a major dimension of site patterning and hence would misconstrue the occupation type. This perspective is essentially represented in large block excavations undertaken since then (10, 21, 99).

Another investigation into site structure was undertaken by Brose (17), in an effort to apply the Deetz-Longacre model (36) of style groupings to determine the social composition of the coresidential unit. He investigated patterns of co-occurrence of pottery classes by frequency in a seasonal Middle Woodland base camp. His model of social residence, however, conflicts with Martin's (88), derived from the consequences of male cooperative requirements on coresidential patterns. In consequence of the attention presently paid to the operation of functional factors in conditioning the archaeological record, greater care is exercised in extracting temporal trends that are the building blocks of chronology (121, 133). The methodologies used to construct chronologies from short site sequences have come to reflect this new awareness (76).

SETTLEMENT PATTERNS AND SYSTEMS   When projected on a larger area than the site, Binford's propositions can be usefully employed to define a settlement system in the number and distribution of sites according to differences in season of occupation, degree of specialization, and relative complexity (121, 133).

Of these, variations in site complexity relate more directly to sociocultural complexity. Fowler (50) has classified Mississippian agriculturally based settlements along this dimension. These sites are permanent locations from which more specialized foraging and extraction activities take place. At an earlier period, when the contribution of cultivation to subsistence was much less, the dimension of complexity is less evident. However, Struever & Houart (122) have shown that a rank order of mound sites can be identified during the Hopewellian period in the Lower Illinois on the basis of location and presence of special earthworks. The determination of the seasonality limits to an occupation has usually been accomplished from the evidence of faunal remains (104, 130, 133, 135).

The degree of specialization obtaining at a site has received greater attention since it is thought to be determinable empirically. The focus of Fitting's (43) classification was on specialization since it ignored site structure. He developed three measures on which distinctions could be made: 1. occupational intensity; 2. site activity orientation; and 3. sexual bias in group composition. Although these measures monitor variability, the lack of sampling control in the first place introduces uncontrolled bias in these measures. Even with sampling control, however, these measures are untested.

A similar approach was used by Farnsworth (41) to classify sites by surface evidence in an effort to test Struever's (121) settlement patterning hypothesis for Middle Woodland.

Winters (133) tackled the problem by devising an index of activity specialization, based on a ratio of specific categories of artifact types, namely the sum of fabricating, processing, and domestic equipment to the number of weapons. In applying this measure to other Archaic sites, he discovered reasonable conformity to expectations and, in addition, he found that certain categories such as wood-working implements were concentrated in base camps of the Green River Archaic (134).

T. G. Cook (34) has further elaborated this approach. He examined the presence of functionally specific tool categories in Archaic occupations to determine settlement type. In the meantime, Ahler (1, 2) discovered a complex relationship between artifact form and tool function in a study of a single multifunctional form, the "projectile point." Armed with preliminary results, he developed a more sensitive functional classification. He used key, functionally dependent attributes to govern his types rather than depending on form, which as a categorical basis for classification may incorporate several conflicting key attributes, even on a single specimen. His functional classes were defined independent of form (2).

Each of these approaches has limited utility in the absence of sampling control. Sampling problems have plagued intersite comparison and determination of seasonal patterns of site use. The need for adequate control is underscored by the fact that variation—seasonal occupation in an annual cycle—is an important variable in the Midwest.

In addition to these direct approaches that make use of artifactual data to define settlement types, there is the indirect, locational approach. The latter makes use of a geographical classification of sites (by period or phase) to infer a site typology. This line of reasoning was applied by Struever (121), Fitting (43, 44), and Winters (133). A more refined direct approach to this research perspective was developed by Roper (109, 110), employing a cluster analysis on factor scores of site locational attributes. She discovered that the constraints to location imposed by stream distribution with a valley could be isolated. Site survey analyses have likewise revealed patterns of land use, especially sensitive to patterns of agricultural exploitation (3, 18, 52, 74, 86).

The Ethnohistoric Approach

Research directed toward the discovery of the historic ethnic connections with prehistoric complexes has repeatedly found complexity and ambiguity where simplicity was assumed (137). Long experience with the problems of early historic research in the Midwest has led to a refinement of methodology and a critical reevaluation of the older ethnic determinations (89, 91). More secure determinations have been the result (12, 22, 42). However, the assumption that there is a direct correspondence of one tribe to one archaeological complex can be shown to be unwarranted. Rather, ethnohistoric archaeologists have concluded, in essential agreement with the conclusion of other archaeologists, that a trait list approach to "cultures" in the archaeological record is unsuitable. Basically it fails in not considering the structure and composition of the social group responsible for the manufacture, use, and disposal of the material remains linked with them. For example, the structure of the Chippewa tribe is quite different from the settled Iroquoian and Siouan tribes, even bearing in mind the emergent aspect to the Chippewa tribe (15, 137). In consequence, the degree to which each group should have its own distinctive material culture exclusively should vary greatly in accordance with its social structure. Also, the quantity of grave objects has been found to relate to availability and volume of supply of such goods in aboriginal bands (46). Due to the social structure of historic Midwestern tribes, the model that each tribe should have its own material complex is found to fail (22). The ceramic associations of early Central Algonkian tribes reflect their patrilineal band organization more than some ideal correlation of ethnicity to material culture (90, 91). An important contribution of these investigations into archaeology of early historic groups is the finding that stylistic structure of our material remains can usefully monitor different social structures (36).

Recent research has emphasized the strength of an archaeological record that has an historical and ethnologic context since historic control makes the archaeological data far more useful in monitoring social processes. An historic record is made more intelligible by increasing its information content and reducing the ambiguity inherent in inadequate description. In fact, Baerreis (7) has argued that a synthetic ethnohistoric approach combining archaeological, ethnological, historical, and bioanthropological approaches would be far stronger than the narrower discipline-specific approach that uses other data as supplementary sources only.

Other Approaches

BIOANTHROPOLOGICAL   Osteological investigations into demography, nutrition, epidemiology, and biodistance determinations have contributed a control on subsistence and feature of social organization not otherwise ascertainable (16, 23, 32, 55).

MORTUARY PRACTICES   Standing closer to traditional archaeology, but nonetheless specialized in its perspective, is the sociological approach to practices for the disposal of the dead (57, 58, 111, 125). Neither of these specializations can be given the extended treatment necessary to understand their approaches thoroughly. Instead their findings are employed as independent contributions.

DIMENSIONS OF CULTURAL CHANGE

Trends in Settlement Patterns

In the evolution of subsistence-settlement systems, the appearance of sedentary occupations marks an important stage of development. It is customary in the Midwest to point to the Late Archaic shell middens as the earliest evidence of multiseasonal occupation of a single site (25, 39). Paleo-Indian and Early Archaic (i.e. Dalton) settlement systems appear to lack a single base camp occupied throughout the growing season (107). Such stable multiseasonal base camps make their appearance in the Middle Archaic in the major river valleys of the southern portion of the Midwest where winters are milder and the annual resource minimum is relatively short. Base camps with permanent shelters appear ca 4000 B.C. at the Koster site (20); housing with prepared floors appears in the Riverton culture during the Late Archaic of the Wabash valley. By the Middle Woodland Period in this same environmental zone, year-round occupation of permanent base camps was common (79, 104). To the north the appearance of permanent base settlements can only be confirmed after corn agricultural economies appear with the Mississippian Period. However, distinctive shifts in the direction of longer warm weather occupations in a single location accompany the more intensive utilization of aquatic resources during the Middle Woodland Period in the midlatitudes (42) and as far north as Saginaw Bay (44).

Year-round subsistence economies were sustained through broad-spectrum hunting and gathering supplemented with the cultivation of squash and plants of the Eastern Agricultural Complex. At least some districts did not rely on maize cultivation. With this broad and diffuse economic base a relatively compact distribution of base settlements existed in favored areas in the Mississippi and Illinois valleys (79, 122). In the Lower Illinois valley a substantial population of about one person per square mile has been estimated by different methods (4, 37). Groups were organized in territories that map onto the local resource potential. Style analysis of Havana ware decorative patterns confirms this model in these respects: (a) style variability in the main river valley is far greater along the valley floor than that for corresponding distances in the uplands; and (b) the greatest discontinuities in style occur at the major environmental breaks between the Lower and Middle Illinois Valley. Kay's (79, 80) analysis of Havana sites on the Missouri conforms to the same model. Confirmation of this model lies in the clustering and relative density of bluff-top mounds, which vary roughly in proportion to the bottomland acreage between river and bluffs. And again, genetic distance studies in Middle Woodland skeletal series match the pattern of microstyle variability to the extent that materials are available (23, 72).

In accordance with this evidence for relatively intense foraging adaptation, a major component of the residential population was subjected to biological stresses initiated by food shortages or disease. Elites, who were given more elaborate mortuary treatment, were sheltered from such stress (23).

The crises that accompanied the onset of the Late Woodland Period led to even more circumscribed territories in the Lower Illinois Valley (33). Early Late Woodland plant and animal exploitation was extremely localized and oriented toward limited selection of resources in the immediate proximity of the settlements. Emphasis on labor-intensive foraging strategies is evidenced by quantities of harvested wild seeds (6, 83, 97, 121). A mound survey reveals that the density of Late Woodland type mounds is far greater per linear mile per century than the Middle Woodland (37). Territorial packing and curtailment of the resource diversity has the expectable impact on mortality and nutrition. Mortality, incidence of dental disease, and traces of protein-calorie malnutrition are much more pronounced in Late Woodland skeletons (23, 32).

In consideration of the early appearance of sedentary occupation in the region, it is not surprising that burial mound construction can be pushed back in time to around 2000 B.C. (26). This age is sufficiently early to cast doubt on diffusion of mound construction from the North; likewise the appearance of pottery in the region follows a progression from south to north (84a). The North does not appear to be a source for the diffusion of pottery (117).

Expansion of the Food Base

Although the beginnings of plant cultivation were believed to have preceded the introduction of Mesoamerican cultigens (maize, beans, and squash), only recently has evidence accumulated to support the notion that local wild plants, collectively known as the Eastern Agricultural Complex, were the object of early cultivation in the eastern United States (123). The importance of this conclusion is that early cultivation is connected to indigenous processes promoting plant domestication instead of to outside stimuli.

Until recently, however, the priority of the Eastern Complex was questionable because the early dated contexts for native plants included squash and gourd as well (48). Thus the local plant foods which were unquestionably important to diet in Late Archaic and Early Woodland Periods could have been conceived of as local responses to the diffusion of agricultural practices. The research of Watson and her associates (128) clearly demonstrates from study of human feces recovered in Mammoth Cave that a consistent plant food diet centering on hickory nuts, sunflower, sumpweed, and chenopod seeds existed in the first millenium B.C. Since that study the age of squash has been pushed back to around 2000 B.C. (87). However, it is important to bear in mind that early squash was thick-shelled, implying a utilization in the manner of gourds and less as a food proper (140).

Yarnell (140) concluded from a review of the Eastern Complex that only sunflower (*Helianthus annus*), sumpweed (*Iva annua*), and perhaps a species of *Chenopodium* were domesticated among the many plants affected ecologically by human manipulation. Of the three native species, the evidence for domestication is best for sumpweed and sunflower, which he thought were domesticated by the early second millenium B.C. (139, 140). Sumpweed is present in a number of pre-Hopewellian period sites (e.g. 82), occurring as early as the late Middle Archaic (ca 3500–3000 B.C.) at the Koster site during a period of expansion of the resource base (20).

Although the amount of *Iva* is small, it cannot be attributed to natural deposition since the site is well removed from the plant's natural habitat. The harvesting of *Iva* in the Midwestern riverine area prior to certain evidence of Mesoamerican plant use confirms the prediction of Struever & Vickery (123), following Struever's model (121), that the origins of plant cultivation were connected with intensive wild plant harvesting in floodplain habitats. However, Struever's (121) singling out of riparian mud flats as the primary habitat of early plant collecting is questionable on two counts: 1. the Ohio River Valley has to be excluded from consideration because flooded bottomlands do not occur (115); and 2. the weedy species (*Polygonum erectum, Iva* sp., and *Chenopodium* sp.) identified in Archaic and Woodland contexts are neither found in mud-flat habitats nor is their abundance sufficient in this habitat to be the focus of a harvesting strategy (5, 96, 139). Although sumpweed appears in damp and marshy habitats, knotweed (*Polygonum erectum*) occurs most abundantly in open trampled areas of the sort found around human settlements (96). In consideration of the habitat preferences of the early harvested species, floodplain environments may have been important in the inception of native plant collecting. But during the Middle and early Late Woodland Periods when the Eastern Complex plants were harvested most intensively, other habitats appear to have been specifically prepared to foster the abundance of native plants. The mud-flats model, however, is not an essential element to early independent evolution of native plant collecting. More generally, plant cultivation can be conceived of as a consequence of intensive harvesting in the trend toward broadening the hunting and gathering food base (48). Since sumpweed harvesting coincides with a period of increased foraging for aquatic and riparian animals, wild plant harvesting is linked probably to year-round exploitation of floodplain habitats (20, 134). Hence concentration of foraging activity over most of the year in an area supporting economic plants responsive to selection probably accounts for the appearance of the Eastern Agricultural Complex in the Archaic.

Consequences of Corn Agriculture

Although the history of squash in the Midwest is secure, that of maize and beans is much more uncertain. Many of the associations reported for early maize in Early and Middle Woodland contexts (123) have proved to be suspect (140), although there remain some that have withstood scrutiny to date. Late Woodland use seems to date around A.D. 500 from evidence in the Lake Erie area (120). But generally speaking, the stress responses noted for Middle and early Late Woodland (see above) are indicative of pre-agricultural responses (31). Middle Woodland maize is not securely established in the Midwest. It has not been recovered so far in Middle Woodland sites that have been systematically collected for charred plant remains. The flotation recovery technique is particularly sensitive to the presence of corn since a single cob breaks into a large number of small, easily recognized pieces. Where corn is documented by cobs and kernels in Mississippian sites, these pieces are ubiquitous in the midden (N. Asch, personal communication). Various explanations have been offered to account for the scarcity of Middle Woodland maize in the Midwest, including unfavorable growing environments (123) and specialized use preventing preservation (95). The common occurrence of corn by the Mississippian Period is usually not conceived of as inconsistent with long prior experience in corn cultivation. New maize strains are thought to have been introduced at the beginning of the Mississippian Period (63).

The common bean has an early confirmed context around A.D. 1070 from a New York site (140), but it becomes more common only about A.D. 1300. In the large Mississippian settlement of Cahokia, beans have not been found although corn is abundant (27, 35). Although the age of earliest use of corn in the Southeast is unknown, this plant would have to have been acclimated to that latitude before it could be grown in the Midwest. The priority of maize there has been argued from the presumed rate required to adapt maize genetically to shorter growing seasons obtaining north of its original tropical habitat (63).

The lag in the introduction of Mesoamerican cultigens north of the Ohio River has been partially corroborated by Munson (95) in a study of linguistic cognates for these plants in eastern language stocks. Maize, squash, and gourd were oldest in the great Southeast, with squash being the first to associate with groups north of the Ohio Valley, at an age estimated glottochronologically at 1500 B.C. Maize has a time depth of around A.D. 1, which it shares with beans. This linguistic model is in accordance with archaeological evidence as to the order in which these cultigens were introduced north, with the exception of beans.

Whatever the early history of corn eventually may be, corn agriculture becomes a major subsistence orientation in the Midwest only with the Mississippian cultural system. In the far southern end of the Midwest, maize is established just prior to this period (N. Asch, personal communication). The inception of the Mississippian Period (ca A.D. 1000) is marked by an increase in cultural complexity and new technology (64, 99, 100) along the southern border of the Midwest. In the St. Louis area, within a relatively short period of time, rapid change had brought a transformation to a complex society around A.D. 1100. At this time the primate town of Cahokia had grown to a maximum aggregation of 5 square miles (50) with a large population (59). It dominated a settlement heirarchy that included secondary and tertiary towns with mounds and a fourth level consisting of moundless villages (50). Excavations at Cahokia (27, 50, 99), satellite, second rank mound centers (105), and small villages (10) constitute the current source for understanding of Mississippian settlement at its peak (50). Population growth led to nutritional stress, different mortality curves, and great incidence of disease (16, 92). Hunting pressure had an impact on local resources around Cahokia that is revealed in the numbers of small-bodied birds and mammals present in the food remains (27, 102). The social stratification accompanying this increase in the size of the social community was clearly developed (50, 94). Separate disposal of the elite dead occurred in the central precincts (50); nonelites were interred in village cemeteries (57, 67). Great disparities in the distribution of grave goods among the dead in both cemeteries and mounds are typical (111).

A state level of political organization has been proposed (100), although features generally associated with this level of complexity are absent at Cahokia (48). Others have preferred to draw parallels with the organizational and economic response of Cahokia and its satellites to the processes of population aggregation found in the

Valley of Mexico (50, 54, 105). The causes of Mississippian development in the St. Louis area is a contested problem. Although a corn agricultural food base is commonly accepted as a necessary condition, some lean to the subsistence economy as a sufficient prime mover for local evolution (50, 63, 64), whereas others stress the stimulus of an outside tradition on Mississippian development (100, 105, 106). The former view Mississippian cultural elements as syncretized from numerous sources; the latter tend to view these elements as having basically a single origin to the south. Arguments based on stratigraphy do not adequately resolve the issue (51, 65, 66, 105, 106). There is no evidence for widespread migration of people, however (40), although a movement of small numbers of elite has been hypothesized by some (e.g. 67). To the hinterland north of Cahokia the spread of corn agriculture around A.D. 1000 is associated with technological changes, including the adoption of large globular vessels, that are incorporated into Late Woodland technologies (38, 45, 53, 54, 67, 69, 70, 83, 84, 118). In settlements where corn is archaeologically very visible, there is convincing evidence of its dietary impact on human nutrition (55). The subsequent penetrations of corn agriculture are not well known. During a period of favorable climate (ca A.D. 1300) agriculture penetrated in new northern areas (9) and probably had an impact on other areas where agriculture was previously unsuccessful (cf 73). Within this milieu northern flint corn became more common due to its hardy growing and preservation qualities. This strain is thought to have promoted a fully agricultural Oneota economy and indirectly undermined the domination of Cahokia on its hinterland (63). It presumably promoted successful establishment of agriculture in the Lower Great Lakes area by the Historic Period.

Environmental Factors

The climate control model was initially formulated by Griffin (61) to the effect that (a) climatic change was instrumental in terminating the Hopewellian cultural horizon, at least along its northern border; and (b) that climatic factors were instrumental in the northern spread and subsequent alteration of Mississippian cultures.

The weight of climatic evidence confirms that the period in which Mississippian culture arose and spread northward in the Midwest (A.D. 700–1200) had especially favorable summer growing climate for corn. It was followed by a cooler period (1200–1300) that was briefly replaced in the northern Midwest by a warm/dry period (1300–1450) before returning to a cool episode (9). Paleoclimatic data also confirm that the Hopewell period coincided with a cool and wet episode between A.D. 1 and 400 (9).

The difficulty with this model of climatic control over culture histories (via its effects on subsistence productivity) is that it attempts to explain too much without adequate articulation with subsistence-settlement strategies in general as well as other variables of social control, political alliance, and exchange. The model plausibly explains change in agricultural productivity in marginal areas where the effects of climatic change can be clearly foreseen (48). It is not surprising that the climate control model is widely used to explain the expansion and contraction of agricultural systems in marginal situations (8, 53, 54, 69, 70, 77). But the application of the model to the "rise and fall" of cultural systems is quite another matter, especially in the case of Hopewell. Here it is not clear how climatic change in general would affect a diversified resource base that is not as specialized overall as Mississippian agriculture, even if corn was cultivated in some localities.

The long protracted warm dry episode in the mid-Holocene left strong evidence in both pollen cores (136) and in other environmental indicators of the Archaic Period (19, 93, 113). However, to adopt a simple climate control model to explain the effects of environment on subsistence-settlement patterns requires more than simply predicting the abundance of sensitive plants and animals (93). First, the consumer demands of Archaic hunter-gatherers were probably easily met in the relatively well-watered and resource-rich Midwest. Hence they would be less vulnerable to the environmental impact of mid-Holocene drying than peoples living in resource-poor areas to begin with (19). Second, the effect of climatic change on hunter-gatherers in as diverse an environment as riverine areas of the Midwest is to lead to changes in the mix of existing hunting strategies rather than to adopt fundamentally different strategies. A weakness of the paleoclimatic perspective is illustrated by the connection between climate and change in the Illinois River (see above). The changes in river regimen are a lagged response to climate to the degree that there is any relationship at all. Mechanical factors are more immediate.

In general, however, there is a growing awareness that a more complete ecological approach is necessary to model the man-land relationships, and that this approach should draw its principles from animal ecology to model adequately the dependency of subsistence on the physical environment.

The Rise of Exchange Networks

Beginning around 4000 B.C. in the Midwest, a pattern of exchange developed that attained over the course of several thousand years a peak in scale and intensity of interregional exchange identified with the Hopewellian "climax" in eastern North America. This period, occurring between A.D. 1 and 400, capped a long-term growth trend in the number of communities evolved in interregional exchange and in the number of items used in exchange (121). Afterwards, evidence for long-distance trade in the Midwest disappeared for a period of 500 years and with it the material remains of relative cultural complexity associated with Hopewell.

The spectacular scale on which earthworks were constructed and the vast area over which trade was maintained have established the distinctive identity of Hopewell, the more tangible expression of which is contained in its typical artifacts, symbols, and art styles. Our conception of Hopewell was advanced in a major way with the recognition that the widely occurring trade objects and their attendant horizon style markers pertained to cultural contexts different from subsistence-related artifacts. The latter are indicative of local Middle Woodland subsistence-settlement orientations that are presently organized into the Havana, Crab Orchard, Scioto, and Lake Forest traditions (39, 122, 124). The overall affinity of these distinct, regionally circumscribed cultural traditions is due to local level participation in multiregional cultural interaction. There is no evidence that connections were due to population movements (108, 131). The distinctive trade goods are now thought to be status-conferring objects that served to sustain trade relations under conditions of irregular local production of foodstuffs and other economic goods for exchange. The objective of the exchange of exotic goods was to maintain ties between regions and districts through trade relationships (122). Hence, Hopewell amounts to a weakly institutionalized intersocietal network of exchange ties. The level of interregional coherence attained in the Hopewellian network is attested to by its stylistic unity and its overall panregional organization, most clearly indicated by the size, wealth, and complexity of the great interior Ohio Valley mound centers. They lie athwart the major axis of exchange between the Southeast and the Midwest.

The degree of complexity achieved in Hopewell is the subject of continuing debate (48, 122). The study of disposal of the dead patterns reveals the existence of rank in the form of graded statuses (58, 125). In the Lower Illinois Valley the higher ranking dead were the best nourished (23, 125). The burial treatment of Middle Woodland peoples is more complex and recognizes more status positions than the late Middle Archaic (20, 125).

The Hopewellian level of exchange organization emerged by degree from more modest scale exchange networks of the Early Woodland and Late Archaic. Fitting & Brose (47) have argued that the Adena burial mounds and the Early Woodland burial "cult" complexes going under the names of Old Copper (in its later phases), Glacial Kame, Red Ocher, and Meadowwood should be regarded as products of the same conditions that promoted Hopewellian exchange. The grave goods were status-defining exotics or "wealth," whose interment validated relations among the living. The differences in the form and elaboration of burial reflect regional preferences, different degrees of social complexity, and differential participation in exchange. They found that a major change in the organization of these networks took place around 1000 B.C. with the submergence of an east-west trade pattern by a north-south pattern. The conditions giving rise to these exchange patterns were foreshadowed in the Archaic. Winters (132) found that exchange of exotic goods was erratic in the Green River Late Archaic and indicative of an unstable system. But signs of a trend toward increasing concentration of marine shell wealth in fewer burials obtained through time. The early evidences of long-distance trade are attested to by artifacts of native copper, ca 3000 B.C. (34, 116).

The end of the Middle Woodland/Hopewell Period is marked by the cessation of interregional exchange and the breakup in the fabric of stylistic continuity over the northern half of the eastern United States. Numerous explanations have been offered for this change (63). They divide into outside (exogenous) causes and internal causes. Representative of the former is the climatic deterioration explanation, which has won the most adherents since first proposed by Griffin (61; e.g. 9, 123, 127). His thesis has climatic change around A.D. 400 interfering with local subsistence productivity, which for him meant corn yields. Although the degree to which corn productivity was central to Middle Woodland subsistence varies, there is evidence for a shift in orientation by later times (75, 81). Others have held that the breakup in Hopewellian interaction was largely due to internal causes that reduced the need for trade as local subsistence self-sufficiency rose (28). This line of argument emphasizes the divisive role that increased productivity plays in undermining an exchange system used to offset local food shortages. Increased productivity has been tied to corn agriculture (28, 41) or to the appearance of bow-and-arrow technology (48, 63, 75). It should be noted that the cultivation of maize does not appear in the lower Illinois valley until several centuries after the end of the Middle Woodland (97, 123,

130). However, an increase in the importance of corn agriculture in the South may have had a decisive effect in terminating networks in the Midwest until subsistence resources were upgraded there later.

Exchange networks were resumed in the Midwest with the establishment of Mississippian cultural systems. In keeping with the scale of cultural complexity that prevailed, trade was more clearly differentiated into economic goods and items of social display having explicit overtones of rank and military prowess. Specific quarries were systematically exploited for hoe blades, and workshops existed for the production of marine shell artifacts (50). The latter and native copper were heavily drawn upon as material for prestige objects, which occurred in far more limited contexts than before and were usually absent in villages (57). Wealth was clearly concentrated in primate centers, although in respect to this conclusion Cahokia has produced far less than expected. However, the political effects of having a large population and economic base can be seen in the influence Cahokia exercised over its northern hinterland from A.D. 1000 to 1200. In addition to the economic reorientations made by Midwestern groups, most also adopted a Mississippian-type technology (57, 63) that varied in respect to its similarity to Cahokian technology. These effects were once attributed to actual population migrations (60). Better dating, however, has revealed that numerically important variants (e.g. Oneota, Mill Creek) were established before A.D. 1100 (54, 69) when Cahokia achieved its zenith and created even closer stylistic ties to the hinterland (119). No population movements can be documented from the Cahokia heartland, but there is ample evidence of virtually in situ genetic continuity within districts of the hinterland reaching to the Historic Period in places (56, 101). The eclipse of Cahokia ca 1300 did not bring a central place back to the Midwest (63, 64). In its stead came a regionally self-contained cultural orientation (Oneota) that maintained a minimal interaction with the South. In sum, the cultural composition of the Midwest at the dawn of the Historic Period showed the dominating effects of a regionally oriented subsistence-settlement system that followed in the wake of the effects of a strong political hegemony 500 years earlier.

Literature Cited

1. Ahler, S. A. 1971. Projectile point form and function at Rodgers Shelter, Missouri. *Mo. Archaeol. Soc. Res. Ser. 8*
2. Ahler, S. A., McMillan, R. B. 1976. Material culture at Rodgers Shelter: a reflection of past human activities. See Ref. 135, pp. 163–99
3. Anderson, A. D., Zimmerman, L. J. 1976. Settlement-subsistence variability in the Glenwood locality, southwestern Iowa. *Plains Anthropol.* 21:141–54
4. Asch, D. L. 1976. The Middle Woodland population of the lower Illinois valley. *Northwest. Archeol. Prog. Sci. Pap. 1*
5. Asch, D. L., Asch, N. B. 1977. Chenopod as cultigen: a re-evaluation of some prehistoric collections from eastern North America. *Midcont. J. Archaeol.* 2:3–45
6. Asch, N. B., Ford, R. I., Asch, D. L. 1972. Paleoethnobotany of the Koster site: the Archaic horizons. *Ill. State Mus. Rep. Invest. 24*
7. Baerreis, D. A. 1961. The ethnological approach and archaeology. *Ethnohistory* 8:49–77
8. Baerreis, D. A. 1971. Summary of discussion and appended remarks. *J. Iowa Archeol. Soc.* 18:22–28
9. Baerreis, D. A., Bryson, R. A., Kutzbach, J. E. 1976. Climate and culture in the western Great Lakes region. *Midcont. J. Archaeol.* 1:39–57

10. Bareis, C. J. 1976. The Knoebel site, St. Clair county, Illinois. *Ill. Archaeol. Surv. Circ. 1*
11. Benn, D. W. 1974. Annuli in the dental cemetum of white-tailed deer. *Wis. Archeol.* 55:90–98
12. Bettarel, R. L., Smith, H. G. 1973. The Moccasin Bluff site and the Woodland cultures of southwestern Michigan. *Anthropol. Pap. Mus. Anthropol. Univ. Mich. 49*
13. Binford, L. R. 1972. *An Archaeological Perspective.* New York: Seminar
14. Binford, L. R., Binford, S. R., Whallon, R., Hardin, M. A. 1970. Archaeology at Hatchery West. *Mem. Soc. Am. Archaeol. 24*
15. Bishop, C. A., Smith, M. E. 1975. Early historic populations in northwestern Ontario: archaeological and ethnohistorical interpretations. *Am. Antiq.* 40:54–63
16. Blakely, R. L. 1971. Comparison of the mortality profiles of Archaic, Middle Woodland, and Middle Mississippi skeletal populations. *Am. J. Phys. Anthropol.* 13:567–98
17. Brose, D. S. 1970. The Summer Island site, a study of prehistoric cultural ecology and social organization in the northern Lake Michigan area. *Case West. Reserve Univ. Stud. Anthropol. 1*
18. Brose, D. S. 1976. Locational analysis in the prehistory of northeast Ohio. See Ref. 29, pp. 3–18
19. Brown, J. A. et al 1977. Preliminary contributions of Koster site research to paleoenvironmental studies of the Central Mississippi Valley. *Mem. Soc. Am. Archaeol.* In press
20. Brown, J. A., Bebrich, C. A., Struever, S., eds. 1977. Archeological investigations at the Koster site: a progress report. *Northwest. Archaeol. Prog. Prehist. Rec.* In press
21. Brown, M. K. 1973. *Cultural transformation among the Illinois: the application of a system model to archaeological and ethnohistorical data.* PhD thesis. Michigan State Univ., East Lansing, Mich.
22. Brown, M. K. 1975. The Zimmerman site: further excavations at the grand village of the Kaskaskias. *Ill. State Mus. Rep. Invest. 32*
23. Buikstra, J. E. 1976. Hopewell in the lower Illinois valley. *Northwest. Archeol. Prog. Sci. Pap. 2*
23a. Butzer, K. W. 1971. *Environment and Archeology, An Ecological Approach to Prehistory.* Chicago: Aldine-Atherton. 2nd ed
24. Butzer, K. W. 1977. Geomorphology of the lower Illinois valley as a spatial-temporal context for the Koster Archaic site. *Ill. State Mus. Rep. Invest.* In press
25. Caldwell, J. R. 1958. Trend and tradition in the prehistory of the eastern United States. *Am. Anthropol. Assoc. Mem. 88*
26. Chapman, C. H. 1975. *The Archaeology of Missouri, I.* Columbia: Univ. Missouri Press
27. Chmurny, W. W. 1973. *The ecology of the Middle Mississippian occupation of the American Bottom.* PhD thesis. Univ. Illinois, Urbana, Ill.
28. Cleland, C. E. 1966. The prehistoric animal ecology of the Upper Great Lakes region. *Anthropol. Pap. Mus. Anthropol. Univ. Mich. 29*
29. Cleland, C. E., 1976. *Cultural Change and Continuity, Essays in Honor of James Bennett Griffin.* New York: Academic
30. Cleland, C. E. 1976. The focal-diffuse model: an evolutionary perspective on the prehistoric cultural adaptations of the eastern United States. *Midcont. J. Archaeol.* 1:59–76
31. Cohen, M. N. 1975. Archaeological evidence for population pressure in pre-agricultural societies. *Am. Antiq.* 40:471–75
32. Cook, D. C. 1976. *Pathologic stress and disease process in Illinois Woodland populations: an epidemiologic approach.* PhD thesis. Univ. Chicago, Chicago, Ill.
33. Cook, S. F. 1975. Subsistence ecology of Scoville. *Am. Antiq.* 40:354–56
34. Cook, T. G. 1976. *Koster: An artifact analysis of two Archaic phases in West-central Illinois.* PhD thesis. Univ. Chicago, Chicago, Ill.
35. Cutler, H. C., Blake, L. W. 1973. *Plants from archaeological sites east of the Rockies.* Mimeo. rep. Mo. Bot. Garden, St. Louis
36. Deetz, J. 1965. The dynamics of stylistic change in Arikara ceramics. *Ill. Stud. Anthropol. 4*
37. DeRousseau, C. J. 1976. *Mortuary site survey and paleodemography in the lower Illinois river valley.* Presented at 41st Ann. Meet. Soc. Am. Archaeol., St. Louis
38. Douglas, J. G. 1976. *Collins: A Late Woodland ceremonial complex in the Woodfordian Northeast.* PhD thesis. Univ. Illinois, Urbana, Ill.

39. Dragoo, D. W. 1976. Some aspects of eastern North American prehistory: a review 1975. *Am. Antiq.* 41:3–27
40. Droessler, J. G. 1976. *Change and continuity: biocultural interaction at the Late Woodland-Mississippian interface.* Presented at 41st Ann. Meet. Soc. Am. Archaeol., St. Louis
41. Farnsworth, K. B. 1973. An archaeological survey of the Macoupin valley. *Ill. State Mus. Rep. Invest. 26*
42. Faulkner, C. H. 1972. The late prehistoric occupation of northwestern Indiana: a study of the Upper Mississippi cultures of the Kankakee valley. *Indiana Hist. Soc. Prehist. Res. Ser. 5*
43. Fitting, J. E. 1969. Settlement analysis in the Great Lakes region. *Southwest. J. Anthropol.* 25:360–77
44. Fitting, J. E. 1970. *The Archaeology of Michigan.* New York: Nat. Hist. Press
45. Fitting, J. E. 1975. Climatic change and cultural frontiers in eastern North America. *Mich. Archaeol.* 21:155–205
46. Fitting, J. E. 1976. Patterns of acculturation at the Straits of Mackinac. See Ref. 29, pp. 321–34
47. Fitting, J. E., Brose, D. S. 1971. The northern periphery of Adena. See Ref. 124, pp. 29–55
48. Ford, R. I. 1974. Northeastern archaeology: past and future directions. *Ann. Rev. Anthropol.* 3:385–413
49. Ford, R. I., Brose, D. S. 1975. Prehistoric wild rice from the Dunn Farm site, Leelanau county, Michigan. *Wis. Archeol.* 56:9–15
50. Fowler, M. L. 1974. Cahokia: ancient capitol of the Midwest. *Addison-Wesley Modules Anthropol. 48*
51. Fowler, M. L., Hall, R. L. 1975. Archaeological phases at Cahokia. *Ill. Archaeol. Surv. Bull.* 10:1–14
52. Geier, C. R., Loftus, M. K. 1976. Preliminary notes on prehistoric settlement behavior in a section of the Mississippi valley in Southwest Wisconsin. *Wis. Archeol.* 57:58–129
53. Gibbon, G. E. 1972. Cultural dynamics and the development of the Oneota lifeway in Wisconsin. *Am. Antiq.* 37:166–85
54. Gibbon, G. E. 1974. A model of Mississippian development and its implications for the Red Wing area. See Ref. 78, pp. 129–37
55. Gilbert, R. I. 1975. *Trace element analyses of three skeletal Amerindian populations at Dickson Mounds.* PhD thesis. Univ. Massachusetts, Amherst, Mass.
56. Glenn, E. J. 1974. Physical affiliations of the Oneota peoples. *Off. State Archaeol. Iowa 7*
57. Goldstein, L. G. 1976. *Spatial structure and social organization: Regional manifestations of Mississippi Society.* PhD thesis. Northwestern Univ., Evanston, Ill.
58. Greber, N. M. 1976. *Within Ohio Hopewell: Analysis of burial patterns from several classic sites.* PhD thesis. Case-Western Reserve Univ., Cleveland, Ohio
59. Gregg, M. L. 1975. A population estimate for Cahokia. *Ill. Archaeol. Surv. Bull.* 10:126–36
60. Griffin, J. B. 1960. A hypothesis for the prehistory of the Winnebago. In *Culture in History: Essays in Honor of Paul Radin,* ed. S. Diamond, pp. 809–65. New York: Columbia Univ. Press
61. Griffin, J. B. 1961. Some correlations of climatic and cultural change in eastern North American prehistory. *Ann. NY Acad. Sci.* 95:710–17
62. Griffin, J. B. 1967. Eastern North American archaeology: a summary. *Science* 156:175–91
63. Hall, R. L. 1973. *An interpretation of the two-climax model of Illinois prehistory.* Presented at 9th Int. Congr. Anthropol. Ethnol. Sci., Chicago
64. Hall, R. L. 1974. *Some problems of identity and process in Cahokia archaeology.* Presented at Adv. Semin. Mississippian Dev., Sch. Am. Res., Sante Fe
65. Hall, R. L. 1975. Chronology and phases at Cahokia. *Ill. Archaeol. Surv. Bull.* 10:15–31
66. Hall, R. L. 1974. Review of P. J. O'Brien's "A formal analysis of Cahokia ceramics from the Powell tract" (Ill. Archaeol. Surv. Monogr. 3). *Am. Anthropol.* 76:956–57
67. Harn, A. D. 1975. Cahokia and the Mississippian emergence in the Spoon river area in Illinois. *Trans. Ill. State Acad. Sci.* 68:414–34
68. Hastenrath, S. 1972. The influence of the climate of the 1820's and 1830's. *Wis. Archeol.* 53:20–39
69. Henning, D. L. 1970. Development and interrelationships of Oneota culture in the lower Missouri river valley. *Mo. Archaeol. 32*
70. Henning, D. L. 1971. Origins of Mill Creek. *J. Iowa Archeol. Soc.* 18:6–12
71. Hill, F. C. 1975. *Effects of the environment on animal exploitation by Archaic inhabitants of the Koster site.* PhD thesis. Univ. Louisville, Louisville, Ky.

72. Houart, G. L. 1976. *Micro-style analyses of ceramics and the identification of social groups for Middle Woodland communities in the Illinois valley.* Presented at 41st Ann. Meet. Soc. Am. Archaeol., St. Louis

73. Hurley, W. M. 1974. Culture contact: Effigy Mound and Oneota. See Ref. 78, pp. 115–28

74. Hurley, W. M., Lee, G. B., Storck, P. L. Prehistoric cultural sites in relation to soils and other physical features of the landscape in part of the Kickapoo valley, Wisconsin. *Ont. Archaeol.* 19:39–47

75. Johnson, A. E., ed. 1976. Hopewellian archaeology in the Lower Missouri Valley. *Univ. Kan. Publ. Anthropol. 8*

76. Johnson, A. E., Johnson, A. D. 1975. K-means and temporal variability in Kansas Ctiy Hopewell ceramics. *Am. Antiq.* 40:283–95

77. Johnson, E. 1971. The northern margin of the Prairie Peninsula. *J. Iowa Archeol. Soc.* 18:13–21

78. Johnson, E., ed. 1974. *Aspects of Upper Great Lakes Anthropology: Papers in Honor of Lloyd A. Wilford.* St. Paul: Minn. Hist. Soc.

79. Kay, M. 1975. *Central Missouri Hopewell subsistence-settlement system.* PhD thesis. Univ. Colorado, Boulder, Colo.

80. Kay, M. 1975. Social distance among Central Missouri Hopewell settlements: a first approximation. *Am. Antiq.* 40:64–71

81. King, F. B., Roper, D. C. 1976. Floral remains from two Middle to early Late Woodland sites in central Illinois and their implications. *Wis. Archeol.* 57:142–51

82. Klippel, W. E. 1972. An Early Woodland Period manifestation in the Prairie Peninsula. *J. Iowa Archeol. Soc. 9*

83. Kuttruff, L. C. 1974. *Late Woodland settlement and subsistence in the lower Kaskaskia River valley.* PhD thesis. Southern Illinois Univ., Carbondale, Ill.

84. Lewis, R. B. 1975. The Hood site, a Late Woodland hamlet in the Sangamon valley of central Illinois. *Ill. State Mus. Rep. Invest. 31*

84a. Linder, J. 1974. The Jean Rita site: an Early Woodland occupation in Monroe county, Illinois. *Wis. Archaeol.* 55:99–162

85. Lippold, L. K. 1973. Animal resource utilization at Wisconsin Effigy Mound sites. *Wis. Archaeol.* 54:135–52

86. Lovis, W. A. 1976. Quarter sections and forests: an example of probability sampling in the northeastern woodlands. *Am. Antiq.* 41:364–75

87. Marquardt, W. H., Watson, P. J. 1977. Excavation and recovery of biological remains from two Archaic shell middens in western Kentucky. *Southeast. Archaeol. Conf. Bull.* In press

88. Martin, M. K. 1974. The foraging adaptation—uniformity or diversity? *Addison-Wesley Modules Anthropol. 56*

89. Mason, C. I. 1976. Historic identification and Lake Winnebago. See Ref. 29, pp. 335–48

90. Mason, R. J. 1974. Huron Island and the Island of the Poutouatamis. See Ref. 78, pp. 149–56

91. Mason, R. J. 1976. Ethnicity and archaeology in the Upper Great Lakes. See Ref. 29, pp. 349–61

92. Masset, C. 1976. Sur la mortalité chez les anciens Indiens de l'Illinois. *Curr. Anthropol.* 17:128–32

93. McMillan, R. B., Klippel, W. E. 1977. Environmental change and hunter-gatherer adaptation in the southern Prairie Peninsula. *Mem. Soc. Am. Archaeol.* In press

94. Mochon, M. J. 1972. Language, history and prehistory: Mississippian lexico-reconstruction. *Am. Antiq.* 37:478–503

95. Munson, P. J. 1973. The origins and antiquity of maize-beans-squash agriculture in eastern North America: some linguistic implications. In *Variation in Anthropology: Essays in Honor of John C. McGregor,* ed. D. W. Lathrap, J. Douglas, pp. 107–35. Urbana: Ill. Archaeol. surv.

96. Munson, P. J. n.d. Censuses of weedy plants on disturbed areas in the central Illinois river valley. Unpublished manuscript

97. Munson, P. J. et al 1971. Subsistence ecology of Scoville, a terminal Middle Woodland village. *Am. Antiq.* 36:410–31

98. Murphy, J. L. 1975. *An Archaeological History of the Hocking Valley.* Athens: Ohio Univ. Press

99. O'Brien, P. J. 1972. A formal analysis of Cahokia ceramics from the Powell tract. *Ill. Archaeol. Surv. Monogr. 3*

100. O'Brien, P. J. 1972. Urbanism, Cahokia and Middle Mississippian. *Archaeology* 25:188–97

101. Ossenburg, N. S. 1974. Origins and relationships of Woodland peoples: the evidence of cranial morphology. See Ref. 78, pp. 15–39

102. Parmalee, P. W. 1975. A general summary of the vertebrate fauna from

Cahokia. *Ill. Archaeol. Surv. Bull.* 10:137–55
103. Parmalee, P. W., Klippel, W. E. 1974. Freshwater mussels as a prehistoric food resource. *Am. Antiq.* 39:421–34
104. Parmalee, P. W., Paloumpis, A. W., Wilson, N. 1972. Animals utilized by Woodland peoples occupying the Apple Creek site, Illinois. *Ill. State Mus. Rep. Invest. 23*
105. Porter, J. W. 1974. *Cahokia archaeology as viewed from the Mitchell site: A satellite community at A.D. 1150–1200.* PhD thesis. Univ. Wisconsin, Madison, Wis.
106. Porter, J. W. 1976. *Thin section analysis of prehistoric ceramics from the Cahokia site, Collinsville, Illinois.* Presented at 10th Ann. Meet. Geol. Soc. Am., Kalamazoo, Mich.
107. Price, J. E., Krakker, J. J. 1975. Dalton occupation of the Ozark border. *Univ. Mo. Mus. Brief 20*
108. Reichs, K. J. 1975. *Biological variability and the Hopewell phenomenon: An interregional approach.* PhD thesis. Northwestern Univ., Evanston, Ill.
109. Roper, D. C. 1974. The distribution of Middle Woodland sites within the environment of the lower Sangamon river, Illinois. *Ill. State Mus. Rep. Invest. 30*
110. Roper, D. C. 1975. *Archaeological survey and settlement pattern models in central Illinois.* PhD thesis. Univ. Missouri, Columbia, Mo.
111. Rothschild, N. A. 1975. *Age and sex, status and role, in prehistoric societies of eastern North America.* PhD thesis. New York Univ., New York, NY
112. Shay, C. T. 1971. *The Itasca Bison Kill Site, An Ecological analysis.* St. Paul: Minn. Hist. Soc.
113. Shutler, R. Jr. et al 1974. The Cherokee Sewer Site (13CK405): a preliminary report of a stratified Paleo-Indian/Archaic site in northwestern Iowa. *J. Iowa Archaeol. Soc. 21*
114. Smith, B. D. 1975. Middle Mississippi exploitations of animal populations. *Anthropol. Pap. Mus. Anthropol. Univ. Mich. 57*
115. Snook, J. C., Swartz, B. K. Jr. 1975. An over extension of the mud-flats hypothesis?: a comment on the Struever-Vickery hypothesis. *Am. Anthropol.* 77:88
116. Steinbring, J. 1974. The preceramic archaeology of northern Minnesota. See Ref. 78, pp. 64–73
117. Stoltman, J. B. 1973. The Laurel culture in Minnesota. *Minn. Prehist. Archaeol. Ser. 8*
118. Stoltman, J. B. 1976. Two new Late Woodland radiocarbon dates from the Rosenbaum rockshelter (47DA411) and their implications for interpretation of Wisconsin prehistory. *Wis. Archeol.* 57:12–28
119. Stoltman, J. B. 1977. A new temporal model for eastern North America prehistory. Submitted to *Curr. Anthropol.*
120. Strothers, D. M. 1974. *The Princess Point complex.* PhD thesis. Case-Western Reserve Univ., Cleveland, Ohio
121. Struever, S. 1968. Woodland subsistence-settlement systems in the lower Illinois valley. In *New Perspectives in Archaeology,* ed. S. R. Binford, L. R. Binford, pp. 285–312. Chicago: Aldine
122. Struever, S., Houart, G. L. 1972. An analysis of the Hopewell interaction sphere. *Anthropol. Pap. Mus. Anthropol. Univ. Mich.* 46:47–79
123. Struever, S., Vickery, K. D. 1973. The beginnings of cultivation in the Mid-west-Riverine area of the United States. *Am. Anthropol.* 75:1197–1220
124. Swartz, B. K. Jr., ed. 1971. *Adena: The Seeking of an Identity.* Muncie, Ind: Ball State Univ.
125. Tainter, J. A. 1975. *The archaeological study of social change: Woodland systems in west-central Illinois.* PhD thesis. Northwestern Univ., Evanston, Ill.
126. Tiffany, J. A. 1974. An application of eigenvector techniques to the seed analyses of the Brogley rockshelter (47GT156). *Wis. Archaeol.* 55:2–41
127. Vickery, K. D. 1970. Evidence supporting the theory of climatic change and the decline of Hopewell. *Wis. Archeol.* 51:57–76
128. Watson, P. J., ed. 1974. *Archaeology of the Mammoth Cave Area.* New York: Academic
129. Watson, P. J. 1976. In pursuit of prehistoric subsistence: a comparative account of some contemporary flotation techniques. *Midcont. J. Archaeol.* 1:77–100
130. Whatley, B. L. 1976. *Subsistence practices in the Woodland Period.* Presented at 41st Ann. Meet. Soc. Am. Archaeol., St. Louis
131. Wilkinson, R. G. 1971. Prehistoric biological relationships in the Great Lakes region. *Anthropol. Pap. Mus. Anthropol. Univ. Mich. 43*
132. Winters, H. D. 1968. Value systems and trade cycles of the Late Archaic in the Midwest. See Ref. 121, pp. 285–312
133. Winters, H. D. 1969. The Riverton culture. *Ill. State Mus. Rep. Invest. 13*

134. Winters, H. D. 1974. Introduction to the new edition. In *Indian Knoll,* by W. S. Webb, pp. v–xxvii. Knoxville: Univ. Tennessee

135. Wood, W. R., McMillan, R. B., eds. 1976. *Prehistoric Man and his Environment, A Case Study in the Ozark Highland.* New York: Academic

136. Wright, H. E. Jr. 1974. The environment of early man in the Great Lakes region. See Ref. 78, pp. 8–14

137. Wright, J. V. 1968. The application of the direct historical approach to the Iroquois and the Ojibwa. *Ethnohistory* 15:96–111

138. Yarnell, R. A. 1964. Aboriginal relationships between culture and plant life in the Upper Great Lakes region. *Anthropol. Pap. Mus. Anthropol. Univ. Mich. 23*

139. Yarnell, R. A. 1972. *Iva annua* var. *macrocarpa:* extinct American cultigen? *Am. Anthropol.* 74:335–41

140. Yarnell, R. A. 1976. Early plant husbandry in eastern North America. See Ref. 28, pp. 265–74

Ann. Rev. Anthropol. 1977. 6:181–225
Copyright © 1977 by Annual Reviews Inc. All rights reserved

ANTHROPOLOGICAL STUDIES ON WOMEN'S STATUS

♦9593

Naomi Quinn
Department of Anthropology, Duke University, Durham, North Carolina 27706

INTRODUCTION

The feminist movement of the 1960s has had a striking influence on female anthropologists in this country. Apart from their personal interest in women's status, the movement itself has cast them in the key intellectual role of defining women's place in a revised theory of the evolution of human society. Beginning in the early 1970s and rising to a current crescendo of books and articles, anthropologists representing all theoretical persuasions, most of them American and most of them women, have produced an entire new literature on the status of women cross-culturally. This literature has proliferated so rapidly that apparently competing views, and in some cases compatible and mutually supporting ones, have gone unacknowledged; publication dates of some works are virtually simultaneous. The result is a bewildering number of disconnected hypotheses about the status of women.

A first, and obvious, purpose of this review is to catalog the various explanations which have been proposed to account for observed similarities and differences in women's status from society to society. The second aim of this review will be an attempted evaluation of the logic of different hypotheses, evidence bearing on them, the points at which they are mutually reinforcing or conflicting, and any common themes which underly them.

One theme common to a number of theoretical treatments to be reviewed deserves comment. While the opportunity to bring personal commitment and professional interest to bear on a single problem has been uniquely rewarding and inspirational, the feminist stimulus for current investigations of women's status has had an important hidden consequence. The political issue, of course, revolves around the conditions which perpetuate the low status of women today, both in Western and in underdeveloped countries. This concern shows plainly in the concluding recommendations many writers feel called upon to make, for bettering the present-day condition of women in our own society (e.g. 25, 29, 37, 48, 64, 70). In addition, much

181

anthropological discussion of women's status has borrowed this political conceptualization of the problem as a basis for analysis. Though writers may begin by carefully defining what they take to mean "women's status," in terms of female political participation, economic control, personal autonomy, interpersonal equality, legal adulthood, ideological position, or other specific indices, for the purpose of testing a particular hypothesis, they often lapse into much looser usage in nearing their conclusions, and speak broadly of "women's low status," "female subjugation," "female oppression," or "male dominance." The appeal of such a construct is understandable. For if women's status can be treated as a unitary construct, and diverse measures of this status as so many related and covarying symptoms, then it is logical to seek a "key" to lower status across societies. If such a "key" explanation can be found, it follows that eradication or modification of this or that particular economic, social, or ideological evil thought to explain women's low status, will bring about their ultimate equality. The unicausal explanations which result from such attempts to diagnose and prescribe for women's low position in society thus bear a resemblance to other, more familiar theories which have attributed this universally inferior status to some one or another biologically determined sex difference, although, of course, explanations of this latter type treat women's resultant position as immutable rather than alterable.

A clear example of this type of reasoning is provided by Rosaldo (68, pp. 19–21), who strings together a series of superficially similar ethnographic examples to demonstrate that "an asymmetry in the cultural evaluations of male and female, in the importance assigned to women and men, appears to be universal." Rosaldo notes that in societies in New Guinea, the Philippines, and Australia, the food grown or hunted by men is a prestige food in contrast to that produced by women; that among the Arapesh a wife is regarded as a "daughter" to her husband and required to act like an ignorant child during the male flute ceremony; that Yoruba women (in spite of their considerable economic importance in trade) must kneel to serve men; that Iroquois women (in spite of their widely remarked political control) could not occupy chiefly office; that among the Merina of Madagascar women are considered not to know the subtleties of polite language; that Jewish *shtetl* women of Eastern Europe (in spite of their economic control over the household) were required to defer to their husbands and that scholarly men represented the highest cultural ideal in these Jewish communities. Rosaldo (68, p. 22) then asks, "Why is sexual asymmetry a universal fact of human societies?" The rest of her piece is an attempt to explain this universal fact in terms of a division between the public and the domestic spheres of life present to some degree in all societies, and she ends by proposing that men must be brought into the domestic sphere.

Writers surveying the existing ethnographic evidence thus tend to bring to notice, and accentuate, instances of exceptionally low (and much rarer instances of exceptionally high) female status. As does Rosaldo, a writer can readily assemble a wide variety of instances in which women in a number of societies are disadvantaged in comparison to men, to convey an impression of consistently low female status; at the same time, the ways in which women in these same societies have equal or even higher status than men are easily ignored, or even, as in the cases of Yoruba,

Iroquois, and Jewish *shtetl* women described by Rosaldo, employed to stress the discrepancy between their political or economic importance and what is pictured as their overall lot. This review will suggest that it may be more accurate, and more helpful to future research, to treat women's status as a composite of many different variables, often causally independent one from another. Thus in any given society, this status may be very "low" in some domains of behavior, approach equality in others, achieve equality with men's status in others, and even, in some domains, surpass the status of men. The possibility that women's status may be a complex outcome of two or more independent variables has not gone entirely unnoted by other writers (e.g. 5, 32, 43, 62, 72, 75, 81); but none has developed the implications of this approach for cross-cultural research. If the various hypotheses which have been proposed as "keys" to women's universally low status are entertained, not as competing explanations, but as explanations which separately account for different aspects of women's position in society, then future research should be directed to the specific conditions which influence women's political participation, or their control over economic matters, or their personal autonomy, or the degree of deference they owe to men, or the level of prestige attached to their persons or their occupations, or ethnotheories about them, or stylistic differences which characterize their language and behavior—and away from the search for conditions purported to influence women's status overall. This is certainly not to claim that different aspects of women's status are never interrelated (e.g. 72), but such interdependencies must be specified, not assumed.

A trend away from "key" theorizing and toward the definition and investigation of more particular aspects of women's position seems already detectable in the latest literature on the subject, although it is early to tell. This new, narrower focus seems motivated less by an explicit rejection of current theory, as by the infusion of new ethnographic data, in a quantity and detail to encourage refined examination of particular domains of women's lives and activities and appreciation of the complexity and multiplicity of women's roles across these domains. If this trend persists, then the "key" theories which have initiated the anthropological study of women's status, and with which this review is largely concerned, will simply lapse or be incorporated into explanations of more restricted scope.

Another, more direct challenge to "key" theories about women's status is posed by the mushrooming number of claims to bias in the ethnographic literature. Such bias is attributed to the combined distortions of male-oriented ethnographers and their male informants. For example, while men may paint a picture of the women in their society as unclean or uncouth, feeble-minded or uncontrollable, women may have an equally uncomplimentary picture to paint of their men (6, 55, 80). The evidence is lacking because ethnographers (both male and female) do not talk to women (62, 67), and women may be unwilling or unable to generalize to ethnographers (1, 81). Additionally, men may have an unequal opportunity for impression management because they deal with outsiders and monopolize the contact language (55).

Enthnographers, it is also charged by the new critics, have been overly ready to perceive an asymmetrical picture of men and women where such asymmetry does not exist. Leacock (37) has noted that women's isolation in menstrual huts is commonly interpreted as their exclusion from society, while men's parallel isolation in men's houses is interpreted as the exclusion of women from the men's world. Faithorn (22) disputes the traditional anthropological treatment of female pollution in highlands New Guinea, pointing out that for one eastern highlands group, the Kafe, it is not women per se who are regarded as polluting, but certain reproductive substances such as menstrual blood and semen. Because they too may pollute, men must take care to keep their semen-stained bodies and clothing from touching, and must avoid stepping over, other people or their food. Faithorn charges that because New Guinea ethnographers have conceptualized women themselves rather than their bodily excretions as the agents of pollution, they have paid no systematic attention to taboos surrounding male sexuality. Rohrlich-Leavitt, Sykes & Weatherford (67) have detailed the bias of male ethnographers in treating Australian aboriginal women as profane, ritually unclean, and economically unimportant. Female ethnographers cited by these authors (27, 32) have painted a different picture of aborigine life, in which women play a central role in subsistence, perform their own important rituals, and are treated by men with respect and dignity. Briggs (6) differs with earlier ethnographers in claiming that Eskimo men do not devalue women or their economic contribution.

Linton (46) has attacked the male bias contributing to an undue theoretical emphasis given hunting in anthropological reconstructions of the evolution of hunting-gathering groups. Draper (17) has pointed out that among the foraging !Kung Bushmen she studied, the return of women from gathering expeditions is greeted by just as much excitement and anticipation as the arrival of men from the hunt, contrary to the common ethnographic representation of the latter activity as being more highly culturally valued. She also counters the ethnographic stereotype of female foraging, in contrast to men's work, as individualized, repetitious, and boring. Rather, !Kung gatherers must command the ability to discriminate among hundreds of plant species at different stages of their life cycle, and must also collect information as to the "state of the bush," crucial to band movements and hunting decisions.

Anthropologists generalizing from others' ethnographic accounts may contribute another level of male bias. Di Leonardo (15), for example, critiques Goodenough's (28) definition of marriage as universally entailing a man's unilateral acquisition of sexual rights in a woman. Di Leonardo returns to the primary ethnographic sources on which Goodenough has drawn to show that he has neglected the appreciable sexual rights which women have in their husbands, reported for these societies. Likewise Bossen (5) faults Evans-Pritchard (21) and others for characterizing women in traditional societies as wholly devoted to domestic activities, in spite of women's roles as traders and subsistence producers in so many of these societies.

Other writers have pointed out that the penetration of Western colonialism, and with it Western practices and attitudes regarding women, have so widely influenced women's role in aboriginal societies as to depress women's status almost everywhere in the world. Boserup (4) has called attention to the detrimental influence colonial practices had on the economic position of women in agriculture, restructuring traditional land tenure systems to preclude female inheritance, everywhere encouraging men to take over farming, and introducing cash crops and new farming technologies exclusively through men. In a pastoral economy, Bossen (5) has noted the similar role of government policy in transferring livestock rights and grazing land ownership to Navaho men. Mintz (51) points to a similar reduction in women traders' traditional share of the West African and Haitian markets as men's commercial activities expanded—possibly because of the preference of European representatives for dealing with men. In another context, Leacock (38) has described the impact of the fur trade on the Naskapi, eastern Canadian hunter-gatherers. The fur trade disrupted the collective economy and put ownership of trap-lines, furbearing animals, and the commodities for which fur was exchanged in the hands of individual men. Martin (48) has pointed out that cash cropping, industrial wage labor, and other colonial practices which encouraged portable wealth and the accumulation of this wealth by men not only decreased the productive importance of women but also fostered the development of the independent nuclear family, which in turn has accentuated the domestic isolation of women.

Everywhere under the modernization of traditional economies, opportunities for wage labor, higher-paying jobs, and training for skilled and supervisory positions in the modern labor force favored men. Women were either relegated to marginal wages or left behind in noncompetitive and shrinking traditional sectors, or at best channeled into "women's professions" (4, 5, 65). This pattern reflects employer preferences imported from the developed countries. Women in both low-skill wage labor and traditional work thus find themselves in oversupply, and in effect, suffer disguised unemployment (5). Unlike men with higher pay, women are unable to accumulate capital for investment in large-scale trade and other economic enterprises (5, 65). Additionally, because of the experience and travel they gain in their jobs, men become more knowledgeable about the modern world (4, 5).

Perhaps less attention has been paid to the consequences of colonialism for women's political position. Van Allen (83) has discussed one case: the British misinterpretation and consequent suppression of the traditional practice of "sitting on a man," by which Igbo women applied political influence within their communities. Leacock (38, pp. 608–11) maintains that under the influence of wage labor and trade, North American Indian "chiefs and other men of influence began to play roles beyond that of spokesmen, often as entrepreneurial go-betweens in commercial matters, or leaders of resistance, and the masculine 'authority' of ethnographic accounts took shape." She argues from colonial accounts that egalitarian societies such as the Naskapi were not governed by male authority; instead, decision making was widely dispersed among adults of both sexes, and the twin ethic of group solidarity and individual autonomy enforced through ridicule and teasing deterred anyone from forcing his will on others. Sacks (73) has suggested that while women did occupy positions of authority on a par with men in some prestate societies, male and female forms of authority differed. For example, Iroquois and Delaware men initiated and executed policy concerning war and peace, whereas women exercised veto power over these decisions. Men dealt with external, women with internal relations. To view these kinds of authority as unequal rather than simply different, reflects not the views of the participants in prestate polities, but a "state bias" in Western anthropological interpretation of these political systems, Sacks argues.

Martin (48) notes the parallel effects of Christian and Islamic theology, which taken together blanket large portions of the modern world, in fostering domestic, subordinate roles and sexual restrictions for women. Goodale (27) has described the loss of domestic influence suffered by Tiwi women because government and mission officials considered the husband to be the boss of the family, and interpreted attempts by his mother or mother-in-law to arbitrate marital disputes as unwarranted interference. Similarly, Leacock (38) reports, the Jesuits taught the Naskapi the importance of permanent monogamy, wifely obedience, and a husband's exclusive sexual rights over his wife.

Together, the bias of male informants in reporting, ethnographers in describing, and cross-cultural workers in interpreting various disparate customs as evidence of women's universally low status, and the depressive effects of colonialism on many aspects of women's lives, may seem to leave very little cross-cultural female subordination to explain. Certainly an awareness of such potential distortions instills caution toward some of the most widely and firmly held anthropological truths about women; and new examples challenging these generalizations are accumulating in the literature.

The next section will deal with universals, variously biological, psychological, and economic, which are currently entertained as viable explanations for the universal disparity in the roles and statuses of the two sexes. [Arguments against some earlier notions about universal sex differences are effectively marshalled by Linton (46), Rosaldo & Lamphere (69), and Martin & Voorhies (48)]. The section following the next will treat a number of variables which have been proposed to explain cross-cultural differences in the status of women. Throughout, the specific effects which particular universals or variables are purported to have on women's status will be distinguished from any general claims that these factors lower women's overall status.

UNIVERSAL DETERMINANTS OF WOMEN'S STATUS

Men's Greater Physical Strength

It is undisputed that men have greater physical strength then women. Men are larger, although this difference holds only within, not across, populations (14). Men have longer arms and sprint-adapted pelves (30). And a large number of physiological sex differences, summarized by Hutt (31), equip men for a more active and strenuous life: greater caloric intake, greater potassium needs after puberty, higher basal metabolism, proportionally larger hearts and lungs, larger, stronger muscles and less fat, continued development in strength after puberty (girls reach a plateau), and the promotion of tissue growth and repair, particularly in muscle and bone, by the male hormone testosterone. Other hormonal effects are:

Boys and men have a lower resting heart-rate but a higher systolic blood pressure, which means the heart has more 'room for manoeuver' in cases of stress or physical exertion. They are also able to carry more oxygen in the blood and have a considerable increase of haemoglobin particularly after puberty . . . This increase in red cells is due directly to the action of the male hormone. Males are also more efficient at neutralizing metabolites like lactic acid which are the by-products of exercise and work (31, pp. 78–79).

Not so widely agreed upon are the differences in behavior which result from these physiological and skeletal differences. One obvious consequence of the male advantage in strength and energy is the ability of men to carry out more arduous physical tasks. This ability is viewed, in turn, as an adaptation complementary to women's biological role as bearers and nursers of children in early human societies subsisting by hunting and gathering. Most writers agree that hunting is incompatible with pregnancy, carrying small infants, and child care, although they are not always agreed as to whether is is the actual physical exertion which hunting demands, the danger it involves, or the long-distance travel it engenders which is most critical to this incompatibility. A similar argument can be made for the incompatibility of childbearing, nursing, and rearing with female participation in defense. Friedl (25) has pointed out, in addition, that female exclusion from warfare may be adaptive to the female role in human reproduction: since a man may father large numbers of offspring but a women bears few children over her lifespan, men's lives can be more readily expended without threatening population maintenance. Thus men are thought to have evolved specialized adaptations to the tasks of hunting and warring which devolved upon them. Liebowitz (42) has cautioned by analogy to nonhuman primates, however, that greater male size and strength may be a female adaptation to reproduction rather than a male adaptation to roles involving protection, aggression, leadership and provision. Once females begin to reproduce they cease to grow, thus insuring efficient energy allocation; there is no such adaptive advantage for the cessation of male growth.

Whatever the evolutionary history behind men's greater size, strength, and energy, writers (e.g. 14, 53) have considered that these characteristics suit men for heavy labor and thus help explain the near-universal exclusion of women from such tasks as tree felling, plowing, and the operation of heavy agricultural machinery as well as hunting and warfare. And the resulting division of labor between the sexes has been argued by some to initiate far-reaching effects on the status of women. These hypotheses will be considered in the section on Cross-Cultural Variability in Women's Status. More directly, the physical advantage of males has been construed by some as an explanation of the universal dominance of men over women. In this connection, greater male strength and energy are no more relevant than another documented physiological sex difference with behavioral consequences: greater male aggressiveness.

Men's Greater Aggressiveness

In a cautious reevaluation of the psychological literature, Maccoby & Jacklin (47) overturn or call into question most of the sex differences which have been raised in this literature, by the simple strategy of tallying studies in terms of positive and negative findings. One of the few behavioral differences which survives this test is the finding that males are more aggressive than females. This difference extends to both physical and verbal aggression, begins at ages 2 to 2½, and holds cross-culturally. Analyzing behavioral observations of children in seven widely separated societies, Whiting & Edwards (88) found that boys engaged in more rough-and-tumble play, exchanged more verbal insults, and were more likely to counterattack physically or verbally if aggressed against. An exception is reported by Draper (18) for foraging !Kung Bushman children; possibly because play groups are heterosexual and children are not expected to do chores which would put different demands on girls and boys, 4 to 7-year-old sample girls actually exceed boys of the same age in amount of roughhousing. Inexplicably, this trend is reversed by ages 8 to 14. Physiologically, levels of aggression have been convincingly tied to levels of male hormones in both humans and subhuman primates and both males and androgenized females. This evidence is evaluated by Maccoby & Jacklin.

Voorhies (48) considers the aggressiveness of human males to be an adaptation to their role in defense, analogous to its adaptive function in some primate species. Maccoby & Jacklin (47) speculate further that another consistent finding of aggressiveness studies—boys aggress primarily against one another and seldom against girls—is adaptive to species survival because it insures that a higher proportion of females will survive to reproductive maturity.

Hutt (31) argues that aggressiveness is closely linked physiologically to two other male behavioral characteristics: ambition and drive. But this conclusion is jeopardized by Maccoby & Jacklin's summary of findings from experimental studies. In these studies, the trend for male subjects to be more competitive is not consistent and the various measures of competitiveness are not free of contamination by other motivations; and boys and girls through college age show similar levels of achievement motivation. Voorhies (48), in rejecting a physiologically based interpretation of male ambitiousness, points to the early cross-cultural finding of Barry, Bacon & Child (2) that boys are trained in achievement and self-reliance. In the latter authors' sample of 31 societies for which the socialization of achievement was adequately reported, fully 87% pressured boys more than girls to be achievers. Achievement training was defined (3, p. 249), for purposes of rating ethnographic materials, as "usually on the basis of competition, or imposition of standards of excellence in performance." Such training is gained, presumably, in the actual performance of chores, and also in games, informal play, ceremonies, and other opportunities to watch and imitate adult male models. Barry, Bacon & Child (2, 3) consider that the training of boys in achievement and self-reliance functions as preparation for male tasks requiring skill and separation from home, particularly large game hunting and fishing, which also require individual initiative to replenish storable food supplies daily. By contrast, girls are trained in nurturance, responsibility, and obedience, traits which suit them for their economic role in child care and domestic routines. Moreover, these authors [(2); discussed in D'Andrade (14)] show that overall sex difference in socialization is greater in those types of economy which put a premium on male strength and skill, a finding which bolsters an interpretation of male achievement motivation as a product of socialization. The absence of a sex difference in the achievement motivation of Western children, based on experimental studies, is consistent with this interpretation; for the subject boys and girls, most achievement occurs in the context of school, where both are equally pressured to so achieve (88, 89).

Like male physical advantage, male aggressiveness has often been used to explain the universal dominance of men over women. But "dominance" is used, in the literature on women's status, to mean a wide range of behaviors and institutional arrangements including, for instance, men's monopoly over political office-holding, their claim to female deference, and their right to exchange women in marriage. Implicit in these usages is the notion that men are somehow able to gain such rights and monopolies by aggressive use of force. There are two sources of evidence against such an assumption.

The first evidence comes, once more, from Maccoby & Jacklin's review of the psychological literature on aggressiveness. These authors claim that

> in adolescence and adulthood, aggression declines as the means for achieving dominance (or leadership). As the power to influence others comes to depend more and more upon competencies and mutual affection and attraction, rather than simple power assertion by force, equality of the sexes in power-bargaining encounters becomes possible (47, p. 274).

While dominance among groups of primates or young boys is largely attained by fighting or threats, studies show that among girls such attributes as attractiveness, popularity, style-setting ability, special interests, and social skills are influential, and increasingly among male adolescents and adults, popularity and leadership qualities such as the ability to achieve group goals displace fighting prowess and compete with athletic ability as marks of leadership. Dominance in adulthood may derive from such diverse social talents as flattery, deception, competence, or supportiveness toward other group members; and interpersonal aggression may be detrimental to effective leadership. Thus Maccoby & Jacklin doubt that men monopolize positions of status and authority in any society by means of their naturally greater aggressiveness.

Gough (29) has indeed speculated that, to the limited extent that men do hold power over women in hunting societies, this power derives from their monopoly over weapons and their physical strength, which give them ultimate control of force. But Webster (86) notes the lack of evidence that men in hunting-gathering societies ever turn their weapons or their strength against women or use this strength as means of social control. Moreover, while sex may be the overriding basis for the formation of interest groups in some societies, among which the Mundurucú are described as an extreme example (55), it is usual in many other societies for disputes to align mixed-sex groups of kin against one another. Friedl (25) points out that conflicts within hunting-gathering bands or between intermarrying bands are most frequently settled by departure of one disputant, with his followers, or engagement in public ritual contests, such as song competitions. This picture of conflict management accords well with Maccoby & Jacklin's discussion of the social means by which adults in Western society gain dominance and leadership.

A possibility which writers on this subject have overlooked is that the greater verbal aggressiveness of males, rather than their strength and physical aggressiveness, may help to explain their assumption of formal leadership roles cross-culturally. Verbal assertiveness seems more compatible with the other interpersonal skills which leadership demands than the exercise of physical force. A description of the sex difference in verbal participation in Israeli kibbutz assemblies is instructive: ". . . when women do take the floor in formal situations they talk briefly and to the point . . . It is men who often repeat themselves and argue ponderously and bombastically" [Tiger & Shepher (82, p. 136)]. A conclusion whether this is a Western sex difference or a pancultural one awaits anthropological attention. Varied ethnographic observations that men preempt the role of spokesmen vis-à-vis outsiders (38, 55, 66) are again only suggestive.

Is there any sense in which their greater physical strength and aggressiveness does permit men to "dominate" women? Maccoby & Jacklin (47) admit that dominance in some adult relationships does depend upon brute force. Most suggestively, the illustration they choose is a British newspaper account of chronic wife-beating. While Maccoby & Jacklin consider that the use of force is rare in modern marriages, presumably because of social opinion and legal sanctions, anthopological reports of wife-beating come from many societies. The use of physical force by men against women may be prototypical of the one-to-one, intimate relationship of marriage. Schlegel (76) discovered this when she compared matrilineal societies in which authority over women is exercised by their brothers, to those in which such authority is exercised by their husbands. In coding one index of the locus of male authority, socially tolerated "aggression" on the part of either or both of these men, Schlegel found that ethnographic reports of husbands' and brothers' behavior were qualitatively different. While a husband's physical aggression might be tolerated, a brother's right to threaten or punish his adult sister seemed rarely to rest on his potential or actual use of physical force, but depended rather on his recognized claim to authority.

This is not to argue that the marital relationship is the only one in which male aggression against women is practiced or licensed; in some societies, it is reported, individual women may be beaten by their kin or gang-raped by their husband's age-mates. It is indicative that Mundurucú women avoid gang rape by traveling together in bands outside the settlement (55). The relatively high frequency of wife-beating among forms of physical aggression against women, may simply reflect, as well as the intimacy of the marital relationship and the inevitable tensions which arise within it, the greater opportunity which men have to aggress against women when they are alone with them in the privacy of their households. Kafe women protect themselves against this eventuality by avoiding private quarrels and airing marital grievances at public gatherings (23). Male strength and physical aggressiveness, while not plausible explanations of men's collective preemption of political offices and authority, are plausible factors in the power of men over individual women, often when these women are socially isolated, and notably in the domestic context.

Women's Role in Childbearing and Childrearing

Like men's advantage in strength and aggressiveness, women's role in childbearing and childrearing is argued to affect their economic role. Friedl (25) has suggested an interconnected set of conditions related to women's reproductive functions which select for a fixed division of labor between the sexes in hunting-gathering societies. Since carrying burdens would interfere with a hunter's ability to run long distances and to use weapons, any particular foraging expedition is devoted exclusively either to hunting or to gathering. Because of the unreliable supply of game, hunters must be free to keep hunting until they meet with success, a condition best met if provisions of regularly available gathered food are the responsibility of others. Women's unsuitability for hunting, and thus their availability for gathering, is determined by the large amount of time they are either pregnant or nursing small children who must be carried on long trips. The early marriage and continuous childbearing and nursing of women in hunting-gathering bands makes it unfeasible for women to take part in hunting for any appreciable length of time in their adult lives, and insures that no sizeable pool of mature, strong women is ever available for the hunt. White et al (87) have further proposed that women beyond childbearing age or those who do not produce children are still excluded from male tasks because they have not learned the necessary skills, while investment has already been made to train them in the skills they need to perform women's tasks. Spiro [(79), quoted by D'Andrade (14)] has remarked, in the context of the reemerging sexual division of labor on an Israeli kibbutz, that when a sizeable proportion of the women are on pregnancy leave they must be replaced in their productive jobs by men, and women seem to have difficulty regaining these jobs once men preempt them. However, Tiger & Shepher (82) raise a question as to why women do not similarly preempt the jobs of kibbutz men called away on military duty.

That women nurse children and do not roam as far from home apparently overdetermines their role in childrearing as well; everywhere, women are primarily responsible for child care (8). There is also some evidence, summarized by Maccoby & Jacklin (47), implicating female hormones in maternal responsiveness, and male hormones in the suppression of maternal behavior; such hormonal effects presumably also predispose women to take on the role of child care. Tiger & Shepher (82, p. 272) have argued that this "species-wide attraction between mothers and their young" explains the initiative taken by the kibbutz women they studied to institute the "hour of love," a practice whereby mothers interrupt their work schedules to spend an hour each day with their children, and familism, whereby children sleep at home rather than in the children's houses. Mothers have agitated for familism even though their work load is much heavier in familistic kibbutzim.

Tiger & Shepher conclude rather grandly that kibbutz women

> have acted against the principles of their socialization and ideology, against the wishes of the men of their communities, against the economic interest of the kibbutzim, in order to be able to devote more time and energy to private maternal activities rather than to economic and political public ones (82, p. 272).

Thus maternal responsiveness is made to seem the "key" to women's apparent disinterest in occupational equality and political participation, reflected in the evidence that women pass up opportunities to occupy "male" jobs and fail to participate as fully as men in the general assembly and kibbutz committees. However, it would seem less tortured to treat the findings regarding motherhood, political participation, and the sexual division of labor independently. In particular, it is difficult not to conclude from the material presented by these writers that kibbutz residents retain a persistent and pervasive ideological bias toward a traditional European division of labor by sex, in spite of the authors' disclaimers and the self-consciously egalitarian official ideology of the kibbutzim.

The demands of child care place restrictions on the energy, mobility, and attention women can deploy at other pursuits. Brown (8) has argued that it is the special demands of child care, rather than women's inability to perform heavy physical labor, that determines whether they are able to participate in any particular subsistence task. She concludes (8, pp. 1085–86) that subsistence activities in which women can participate are those which "do not require rapt concentration and are relatively dull and repetitive; they are easily interruptible and easily resumed once interrupted; they do not place the child in potential danger; and they do not require the participant to range very far from home." Brown points out that these restrictions alone account for the universal pattern of women's exclusion from large animal herding, large game hunting, deep-sea fishing, and plow agriculture. Murdock & Provost (53), in an analysis of coded data for 185 societies, found that "quasi-feminine" activities, assigned predominantly or exclusively to women in a number of societies, fit Brown's description well: fuel gathering, preparation of drinks, gathering of wild vegetal foods, dairy production, spinning, laundering, water fetching, cooking, and preparation of vegetal food. These authors argue, however, that Brown neglects another feature of such activities: the daily attention they require makes them incompatible with men's tasks such as warfare, hunting, fishing, and herding, all of which commonly require long absences from the household. Murdock & Provost also identify a set of "strictly masculine activities"—hunting large aquatic fauna, smelting ore, metalworking, lumbering, hunting large land fauna, woodworking, fowling, musical instrument making, trapping, boatbuilding, stoneworking, work in bone, horn, and shell, mining and quarrying, and bonesetting. The male advantage for performance of most of these activities, they say, resides in men's great physical strength and capacity for bursts of energy, coupled with their ability to travel distances from home unfettered by pregnancy and infant care.

Friedl (25) considers it more instructive to examine the ways in which child care is accommodated to women's customary work. She feels that Brown overstates the constraint on women's mobility, in view of the large number of societies in which female gatherers, cultivators, or traders do walk long distances either daily, sporadically, or seasonally. The pace and strenuousness of the travel must be taken into account. Trading, for example, nicely complements the care of infants still small enough to be carried on long walks; much of a trader's time may be spent sitting in the marketplace, attending to buyers only intermittently. C. Smith (personal communication) relates that in western Guatemala, marketing is done exclusively by women, and peddling, except for an occasional postmenopausal woman, exclusively by men. This pattern, which may be duplicated elsewhere, probably reflects the greater difficulty and hazard of travel and transport over peddling routes. Likewise, large game hunting and large animal herding, as well as being strenuous, preoccupying, and hazardous, require fast-paced travel.

Friedl (25) notes that shifts in body balance during the latter stages of pregnancy bar women from hunting as effectively as the burden of transporting nursing infants after birth. Not only the necessity of nursing their infants, but other considerations regarding infants' physical and emotional well-being, may determine how long they will be carried. Lee (39, p. 331) relates that !Kung infants and young children have an extremely close relationship with their mothers and that, while children are carried by their mothers less and less and babysat by others more and more between the ages of two and four, "at age four, well after they have been weaned from the breast, they are weaned from the back." Thus while older children and elderly people in many societies provide substitute child care for periods as long as a day, freeing mothers to carry out distant, laborious, or time-consuming subsistence tasks (25), clearly this is truer of the care of older children than that of younger ones who still need to nurse and who are still regarded as requiring maternal contact.

Friedl suggests that one adaptation to the requirements of women's tasks among some hunter-gatherers and horticulturalists is low fertility and wide spacing of children. Lee (39) argues that the particular feature of gathering to which child spacing is a response is the physical impossibility of one woman carrying two children (or a child and a fetus) at once. Thus !Kung births are spaced an average of 4 years apart.

Nerlove (56) has pointed out that some degree of flexibility is also introduced into the subsistence roles open to women by the practice of supplementing mother's milk. Nerlove hypothesizes that early supplementary feeding of infants is a strategy more likely to be adopted by women who are required to participate heavily in subsistence. Testing her hypothesis on a sample of 83 societies for which pertinent information was available, she found that the greater women's participation in a society's subsistence activities, the more likely are infants to be started on supplementary foods before they are a month old. As Nerlove is careful to say, this finding does not invalidate observations about the pattern of subsistence tasks from which women are excluded, but applies within these constraints on women's activities.

Children's Socialization

Since women are the bearers, nursers, and primary caretakers of children, the role of primary child socializers also devolves upon them. As elaborated by Chodorow (11), this role accounts for further, far-reaching differences between male and female personalities. Chodorow develops the implications of the fact that, universally, both boys and girls are brought up by women. Both sexes must learn their appropriate gender identity, but a girl accomplishes this simply by modeling after her mother; as has long been recognized by psychoanalytic theorists, a boy, in order to become a man, must give up a primary identification with his mother and shift to an identification with his father or other salient adult males. Chodorow argues that because a man does not play a caretaking role and because in most societies his male activities take him away from home, he is relatively inaccessible to his son.

> As a result, a boy's male gender identification often becomes a "positional" identification, with aspects of his father's clearly or not-so-clearly defined male role, rather than a more generalized "personal" identification—a diffuse identification with his father's personality, values, and behavioral traits—that could grow out of a real relationship to his father (11, p. 49).

Consequences of the boy's struggle to define his gender under these conditions are denial of femininity, denial of attachment to and dependence upon his mother (coupled with her tendency to push him into the male role), and in the attempt, devaluation of whatever he considers feminine. By contrast, the development of a girl's gender identity is continuous, unproblematic, and mediated by the real affective relationship with her mother. The explicit training boys receive reinforces their differential development: it is oriented toward achievement and self-reliance rather than nurturance and responsibility [a conclusion based on the cross-cultural study of Barry, Bacon & Child (2)]; it is delayed rather than continuous; and it entails a transitional period of universalistic membership in a group of peers rather than particularistic role relations. While women's particularistic interactions cut across generational lines and encompass diffuse relationships and responsibilities, men's interactions are likely to crosscut kinship units, to be restricted to a single generation, to be recruited along universalistic criteria, and to invoke highly specific relationships and responsibilities.

From the complex of effects Chodorow describes, Rosaldo (68, p. 25) singles out as significant this experience of "horizontal and often competitive peer groups, which cross-cut domestic units and establish 'public' and over-arching ties." Consequent are the boy's need to achieve status as a peer and as a man rather than assume it naturally, and his knowledge of this status as an abstract set of rights and duties, associated with formal authority and formal roles, in contrast to a young girl, who "probably has more experience of others as individuals than as occupants of formal institutionalized roles; so she learns how to pursue her own interests by appeals to other people, by being nurturant, responsive, and kind" (68, p. 26). Together these features of boys' upbringing cause them to prize achievement, seek out competition for status, and maintain the social distance requisite to authority. These traits in turn account for the universal monopoly of men over the public world and the relegation of women to the domestic world. Politically, this means that men occupy, and women are excluded from, the ranked, institutionalized positions. In economic terms, it means that women's work is relatively less public, and done individually or in small, loosely organized groups. The products of this work are used within the family and household or, if distributed more widely, appropriated by men in their pursuit of prestige. The more marked the differentiation between domestic and public spheres of activity in a given society, the more women's political and economic status will suffer.

Ortner (60) argues further that along with women's unalienable biological function in reproduction and their domestic confinement as a result of their nursing and child care responsibilities, women's personality contributes to their symbolic identi-fication with nature and their consequent exclusion from the realm of culture. The feminine personality traits of personalism and particularism, which result from the socialization experience detailed by Chodorow, lead women to enter into direct, relatively unmediated relationships "embedded in things as given" (60, p. 82). Thus women lend themselves to a universal interpretation as closer to nature than men, whose propensity to superimpose on relationships "abstract categories and transper-sonal values" identifies them as products of culture. Chodorow's argument can be made to bear implications of the broadest scope.

The claim that their socialization by women has sharply different effects on boys and girls must be evaluated cautiously however. Chodorow's psychoanalytically based picture of sex differences is largely clinically supported; experimental and cross-cultural research aimed at isolating the socialization experiences and the psychological consequences described by Chodorow, Rosaldo, and Ortner is lack-ing. Their picture may be biased by the distinctively Western ideology which emerged with the industrial revolution (see section on *Economic Variables*) and which emphasizes women's place in the home and their expressive role in the family.

One body of experimental data (47) contradicts this picture. This research sug-gests that males no less than females, and perhaps more so, employ "Machiavellian" strategies—that is, act accomodating and even submissive as part of a plan to influence another's behavior. On a "Mach" scale measuring the extent to which a subject uses exploitative and manipulative behavior in interpersonal relations, and predicting success in bargaining with others for desired ends, adult men have generally proven more Machiavellian than women. A sample of 10-year-old children tested on a modified version of the scale, while showing a great deal of variability, did not differ by sex. This finding does not jibe with Rosaldo's (68, p. 26) delineation of the young girl, in contrast to the boy, learning "to pursue her own interests, by appeals to other people."

Chodorow views the content of task socialization as contributory to sex differ-ences in interpersonal involvement, although it requires a somewhat broad construc-tion of nurturance, responsibility, achievement and self-reliance to allow that differential training in these behaviors contributes to a more general pressure on girls "to be involved with and connected to others, boys to deny this involvement and connection" (11, p. 55). In experimental studies on altruism (47), children of both sexes are found to be equally helpful; however, Maccoby & Jacklin cite the cross-cultural evidence (2, 88) that girls are more helpful and responsible. In Whiting & Edwards' (88) analysis of behavioral observations of children in seven cultures, girls show more help-giving behavior and offer more emotional support than boys, and this tendency becomes stronger with age, suggesting that it is socialized rather than innate. Girls also "suggest responsibly" more than do boys. Maccoby & Jacklin interpret this cluster of feminine behaviors as relating to the more frequent assign-ment of girls to babysitting responsibilities. Of course, a greater maternal responsive-ness on the part of girls (section on *Women's Role in Childbearing and Childrear-ing*) might predispose them to accept babysitting assignments more readily than boys, and therefore to develop the behaviors elicited by this task. Whiting & Edwards draw attention to the fact that the American girls in their cross-cultural sample score low in offering help and support, and because of the small size of families and the time occupied at schoolwork, do very little infant care compared with girls in other societies. Correspondingly, boys in the Kenyan community studied, many of whom care for infants and perform domestic chores, more frequently offered help and support than boys in other societies. In a separate study (19), sisterless boys in a western Kenyan community who did child care, cooking, and other domestic chores proved to be more like girls over a range of behaviors, although this particular study did not measure differences in nurturance; these boys were more responsible, less aggressive both physically and verbally, less "dependent" in the senses of seeking help, support, attention, information or material goods, and less "egoistically dominant" in the sense of dominating, reprimanding, or prohibiting others' actions nonresponsibly. Interestingly, boys who did women's work outside the homestead, such as fetching wood and water, digging root crops, picking vegetables, and taking flour to be milled, did not score more feminine than boys who did no "feminine" work at all, indicating the specificity of the context in which this complex of behaviors is learned.

This cross-cultural evidence supports a view of nurturance and responsibility as learned in the context of specific tasks. As pointed out earlier (section on *Men's Greater Aggressiveness*), the cross-cultural association of achievement and self-reliance training with male subsistence tasks demanding skill and initiative, and the experimental evidence that American middle-class boys are not more achievement oriented than girls who experience the same pressure to achieve at school and the same exemption from subsistence chores at home, equally support an interpretation of achievement and self-reliance as sex differences learned in the performance of different tasks. The evidence that American boys are any more competitive than girls is equivocal (section on *Men's Greater Aggressiveness*), presumably also because both are socialized to compete in school. Thus cross-cultural differences in task socialization of boys and girls seem less to support sex differences in nurturance, responsibility, achievement, self-reliance, and competitiveness as to fully explain these differences. When differences in task socialization are narrowed or obliterated, these sex differences in behavior are not maintained by the differential opportunities of girls and boys to interact with and model after same-sex adults, as Chodorow's argument requires.

Lastly, Maccoby & Jacklin (47) conclude that there is no consistent tendency across relevant studies for girls to be more dependent, as might be expected from Chodorow's (11, p. 51) suggestion that boys' sex-role learning "involves denial of attachment or relationship, particularly of what the boy takes to be dependence or need for another," while girls continue to be dependent on their mothers in adulthood. Anthropological studies, however, provide some support for this aspect of Chodorow's hypothesis. Anthropologists (88) have found that boys do roam farther from home during free time. This difference has been viewed by some as reflecting not necessarily girls' greater dependence but boys' greater investigativeness and aggressiveness (52), coupled with their assignment to chores which require self-reliance and mobility (88) and grant them greater opportunity for exploration (57), while the chores of girls keep them close to home. But Draper (18) provides a critical test of these alternative interpretations, with an analysis of differences between bush !Kung boys and girls. She holds that differential socialization for task performance cannot account for sex differences between these children, since they perform virtually no chores in this unusually leisured economy. Nevertheless, bush girls stay inside the camp or outside it within view and earshot of adults more than boys. They interact with adults more often, particularly with women, and interact with peers less often. Supporting this picture are the behavioral observations from seven societies, analyzed by Whiting & Edwards (88), who found that younger girls sought help more often than did younger boys, and girls as a whole sought and offered physical contact more often than boys, a difference which decreased with age. Whether the sex difference in dependency is innate, or whether it is due to the particular socialization experience proposed by Chodorow, remains unresolved.

Women's Compliance

At the end of their lengthy review of the psychological literature on sex differences, Maccoby & Jacklin (47) hazard a novel hypothesis about universal feminine subjugation, one which has not yet received consideration from anthropologists. Their argument stems from their discussion of sex differences in the dominance behavior of children. Boys do not dominate girls because they do not play with them; they tend instead to play in large all-boy groups and dominate one another. However, Maccoby & Jacklin remark on the tendency of girls to comply more readily, not to dominance attempts by other children, but to directives from parents and teachers. Maccoby & Jacklin consider several interpretations of this finding: perhaps adults deliver requests to girls with more assurance; or perhaps girls seek coalitions with adults in order to cope with the greater aggressiveness of boys. Interestingly, Draper finds it equally puzzling that girls in settled !Kung villages become the chief butt of their mothers' demands for the performance of frequent small tasks such as pounding grain, child care, and fetching. She concludes that

> little girls are usually on the premises and easy targets for their mothers' commands; little boys seem to be either gone from the village (on errands already described) or else visible but distant enough from the women so that their help cannot be enlisted conveniently (17, p. 102).

It is not clear from this description whether mothers single out their daughters for chores because they are conveniently close, or as Whiting & Edwards (88) suggest in relation to other cross-cultural data, whether they keep them close by so as to be able to recruit them as needed. But Draper's (18) observations of differences between foraging !Kung boys and girls suggest to her the former interpretation. As noted earlier (section on *Children's Socialization*), bush girls, although they are not sent on errands or set to do small chores, also stay closer to adults and interact with them more frequently than do boys. Because of girls' proximity and their preference for adult company, adults may interrupt and redirect them more frequently, Draper argues, reinforcing their tendency to stay close by. Thus girls are predisposed to be "ready targets for heightened pressure for cooperation, errand running, and child tending," the need for which arises in sedentary !Kung villages and settled communities elsewhere. Task assignment, in turn, fosters compliance. Draper (18, p. 611) tenders a final speculation: "the notion that females are more sensitive to social cues and to the needs of others may have its origins in the restricted mobility and greater orientation to adults of females."

Maccoby & Jacklin suggest:

> Perhaps the traditional assignment of certain jobs to men and others to women has come about not so much because men are in jobs that call for aggressiveness as because women, being slower to anger, are less likely to protest onerous assignments. We have seen that girls are more likely than boys to comply with demands that adults make upon them; although it has not been demonstrated, it appears likely that in adulthood as well they will "take orders" from authority figures with less coercion. To put the matter bluntly, they are easier to exploit (47, p. 371).

What is perhaps unusual about this hypothesis is that it locates a cause of women's "oppression" not in some objectionable quality of men—their aggressiveness, their competitiveness, their inability to enter into intimate, particularistic relationships, their unwillingness to participate in the domestic sphere—but rather, in a psychological trait of women themselves. Presently, the hypothesis is wholly untested.

CROSS-CULTURAL VARIABILITY IN WOMEN'S STATUS

Economic Variables

In the literature on women's status, hunting-gathering groups in which women's gathering supplies a substantial proportion of subsistence (25) have come to represent one end of a continuum, at which women's status is as nearly equal to men's as in any society in the world. Certainly this situation is related to the absence in such societies of well-defined male-held political offices, and the restraint frequently placed on any form of authority over others, political conditions which make it easier for women to participate in group decisions and to exercise individual autonomy (34, 38). Important also may be the fact that many hunter-gatherers seem to lack even an incipient division of men's and women's worlds into public and domestic domains (34). Draper (17) points out that, unlike sedentary !Kung, foraging Bushmen live under conditions which permit no distinction between the domestic and the public sphere. Camp inhabitants live in a wholly public world, sleeping and eating outside in a small circular clearing, within which all activities are visible and normal conversations audible. Women and men mix freely, and both are about equally absent from camp on foraging expeditions.

Thus while Rosaldo (68) discusses the division between public and domestic domains as a universal focus for the sexual division of labor, entailed by women's role in child-bearing, nursing, and rearing, other writers have preferred to stress the particular economic conditions which enhance the "inside-outside dichotomy" (48, p. 290). Draper's comparison between seminomadic and settled !Kung suggests to her that the dichotomy arises as a consequence of settlement. Permanent settlement leads to a much greater investment in habitations; and doors and encircling fences, which create inner courtyards around the houses, are built to keep out unpenned domestic animals. Sedentism also invites the accumulation of possessions; and, as a result of the architectural changes, new differences in material wealth which would not be tolerated in the bush can be privated in houses. Somehow, and Draper is not sure why, "men, more than women are defined as the managers or owners of the property" (17, p. 108); houses, goats, and children are referred to as belonging to adult males, and women are attached to men's households. Moreover, there is a growing disparity in the mobility of men and women. Men are more often away from home, caring for animals, clearing fields, working for wages, and interacting with Herero men. Women, in turn, are at home more than formerly. Their gathering activities curtailed, they spend much more time processing and preparing domesticated foods than was necessary for gathered foods. And the houses and possessions which come with the settled way of life require time-consuming upkeep.

Draper's account of changes in !Kung Bushman life does not contradict Martin's (48) thesis, that the sharpest isolation of women from public life arose with developed agriculture. Martin invokes some of the same changes, intensified under agriculture, which are incipient in the Bushman case. As Boserup (4, see also 25) has earlier pointed out, women play an important role in shifting cultivation; while men clear the land for planting, women are often the sole cultivators of the staple crops planted, and almost always share in their cultivation. "With the innovation and spread of intensive cultivative techniques, however, women dropped out of the mainstream of production for the first time in the history of cultural evolution" (48, p. 290). As Boserup has argued, weeding, a time-consuming female horticultural task, is reduced or eliminated by plowing. Plowing itself, as well as the construction and maintenance of irrigation works used in some systems of intensive agriculture, are men's work—presumably because of the demand for physical strength and perhaps also, as Brown has suggested (section on *Women's Role in Childbearing and Childrearing*), because of the interference with infant care which such labor entails. Thus women are excluded from agricultural labor in all but a minority of cases, notably East Asian paddy rice cultivation. The pattern observed by Boserup and Martin, women's high contribution to shifting cultivation and their low contribution to intensive agriculture, has been confirmed by Sanday (74) for a large cross-cultural sample.

Martin relates the sudden change in women's status which accompanies intensive cultivation to several concomitants of the new technology. The reduced need for female cultivative labor makes multiple wives an economic liability rather than an asset and renders the polygynous family obsolete. At the same time, the individuation of land tenure under intensive agriculture undermines the extended family, and the nuclear monogamy characteristic of newly emerged urban communities serves as a model, further encouraging the trend to nuclear families. In these small, self-sufficient units, women come to rely upon their husbands for subsistence. Women's labor, freed from cultivation, is absorbed by repetitive, monotonous tasks within the household, particularly food processing. Grain cultivation, and the storage of grain necessitated by the reduced mobility and limited growing season of agriculturalists, require hulling, washing, winnowing, and pounding into flour.

Their new economic role effectively isolates women from men and from public life. As Boserup (4) notes, the Islamic segregation of women is particularly compatible with such an economic arrangement, but certainly non-Islamic groups such as the southern French farming community described by Reiter (63) exhibit the same pattern. Martin speculates that this isolation and segregation of women in the domestic sphere insures their immobility and their exclusion from male activities, including politics, and keeps them in permanent adolescence. They remain minors who have no legal rights, whose sexual behavior must be closely circumscribed, who must be protected and supervised by men, and who owe these men, including their own grown sons, deference and submissiveness. This complex of customs spelling their immaturity arises from the fact that women have no direct access to the public sphere but must rely on men to mediate their social, legal, and economic affairs.

While Martin argues that the domestic isolation of women in industrial societies is a survival of the economic definition of sex roles arising from the practice of developed agriculture, others have held that this modern pattern of isolation is a direct outgrowth of new political conditions. Reiter (63), for example, implicates the rise of states, which subsume authority over legal matters, property, and labor power (e. g. conscription for public labor and war, taxation) formerly under the control of kin groups. In a similar argument, Sacks (72) emphasizes that the emergence of states represents the rise of class societies. In such societies the ruling class not only takes over functions formerly belonging to kin groups, but does so with the end of expropriating for rulers the surplus labor and goods which were formerly redistributed to the many. As men's labor is more intensively utilized in the public domain, all of the tasks related to household production are relegated to women (63). The function of kinship shrinks to that of reproducing and sustaining labor power; and these become defined as private matters. Reiter argues that the low status of women in state societies derives from the fact that the performance of these activities, unlike that of public ones, goes unrewarded by power and prestige. Sacks, like Martin, stresses that women are no longer even awarded adult status.

Sacks distinguishes between women's domestic status and their extradomestic status in society. But state societies so fully curtail women's adult status by excluding them from public production as to limit their power with regard to their husbands as well as their extradomestic power. An exception is the instance of precapitalist states in India, in which women did participate in public labor and, while suffering economic inequalities, did enjoy adult status. In prestate societies, Sack's examination of four African groups argues, women's public and domestic statuses are freer to vary independently, high domestic status depending primarily on the absence of private estates or the joint ownership of the estate by both spouses, and high public status depending upon women's participation in the productive activities which confer public power and prestige on society members.

Compatible as is Sacks's argument for the independence of women's social and domestic statuses with the position taken in this review, the ethnographic indices which she selects to measure these respective statuses seem ill chosen. She includes the freedom of women to enter into extramarital sex relations, to initiate divorce, and to seek extradomestic dispute settlement as measures of their public status, while treating a seemingly similar right to their own fertility (as reflected in the absence of any customary compensation for women's adultery) as an index of women's domestic status. Surely a double standard with regard to divorce and extramarital sex, just as much as a double standard with regard to adultery compensation, may be reflective of an unequal domestic power relationship. Again, Sacks (72, p. 226) uses the presence of menstrual and pregnancy restrictions as measures of women's domestic status, arguing that such taboos "seem to operate to separate women's reproductive functions from contact with the social production of exchange goods." Schlegel (76), for a much larger sample of (matrilineal) societies, found menstrual taboos to be unrelated to male domestic authority over women. Schlegel concludes that menstrual restrictions reflect something about women's extradomestic status, reaching the same conclusion as Sacks regarding the independence of women's statuses in these two domains, but differing as to which domain menstrual taboos should be assigned.

Why, Sacks and Reiter ask, do the activities of the domestic, private economy fall upon women in state societies? One answer seems to be that the earliest state projects are likely to be massive construction works and military expeditions, pursuits to which men are physically more suited, just as they are suited to large game hunting (63). Also, men are favored for public labor because they are more mobile, and can be more intensively exploited than women, who must interrupt their work to bear and nurse children. Sacks cites the historical example of seventeenth-century England, where women and children were deliberately excluded from wage work by employers under conditions of extreme oversupply of labor from the ranks of landless peasantry.

Reiter feels that industrial capitalism, with its ideology of the sanctity of the nuclear family and its radical separation of home and work place, further intensified the distinction between private and public domains. Zaretsky (91) develops this theme at length, arguing that by the nineteenth century the family under Western industrial capitalism, its productive functions attenuated and its reproductive role in the economy obscured, became a repository of emotional life and a bastion against the impersonality of large-scale industry and technology. Women, increasingly excluded from wage-labor, became identified with the home and with emotional life. By the time women reentered the labor force in large numbers, they were at a permanent disadvantage. Unemployment and underemployment had become structural features of capitalism, and the idea that women's real place was in the home helped define them as a marginal labor force. Sacks (72) similarly stresses the interaction of ideology and economic conditions in women's exploitation as a source of cheap labor.

Just as Sacks takes issue with Engels's notion that it is property ownership alone which determines women's status, so other writers (25, 74, 75) have argued with the assumption that participation in production is the key to this status. Once again, hunting-gathering groups, appealing because of their relative economic simplicity, have been used as a model. Friedl (25) and Rosaldo (68) point out that, despite the considerable importance of gathering, which may equal or outweigh that of hunting in the subsistence of such groups, it is hunting which confers power and prestige.

Friedl argues that this difference arises from the fact that large game, unlike vegetable food and small animals, is shared extradomestically. She attributes the extradomestic distribution of meat to its value as a scarce good; but surely also the size of individual kills and the threat of spoilage make their immediate distribution economically practical. Plant foods are regularly available and may be gathered in small quantities as needed. Friedl (25, pp. 21-22) claims that, because of the distribution of meat, "men have a larger circle of people with whom reciprocal relations exist. This is a major source of difference in the power of men and women." Those who distribute meat are highly valued, and generous givers are accorded honor and prestige. Further, such men "bind others to repay them and thereby exercise a kind of superior power as creditors until the return transaction takes place." Compared to the successful hunter, the most skillful gatherer and forceful personality among women has limited resources to parlay into recognition and debt. This difference explains any disparity between the sexes in the leadership of hunting-gathering bands.

Control over the production of subsistence foods, however narrowly they may be distributed, is not entirely irrelevant to the status women attain, however. Draper (17) comments that one factor contributing to the sexual egalitarianism of foraging !Kung, reflected in women's autonomy and their participation in group decisions, is the fact that these women do not need the assistance of men at any stage in the production of gathered foods, nor the permission of men to use any natural resources entering into this production. Friedl (25, p. 19) likewise points out that male dominance is greatest in hunting societies like the Eskimo, in which hunting is the sole source of food. Women's contribution to subsistence, in such groups, is limited to the processing of meat and skins, a role similar to the food processing role of women in developed agricultural societies; "a woman cannot initiate activities which independently provide her and her children with the staples of a livelihood." This is true even though, as Briggs (6) stresses, men recognize women's contribution as seamstresses and processors as vital to their own hunting success.

Among Eskimos, male dominance seems to consist in sexual aggression against women, the right of husbands to exchange sexual access to their wives, to beat them, to make travel and domestic decisions, and to veto women's plans, although women retain the freedom to initiate sexual encounters (though not always to repulse sexual advances), to leave their husbands, and to elect to stay behind when their husbands travel (25). Friedl does comment on two other features of Eskimo life which may have independent effect on the degree to which men dominate women: the importance of male competitive achievement, in which skill at obtaining sexual access to women is an element; and the social isolation of women, due to their food processing roles. The possible effects of female domestic isolation on licensed male aggressiveness, female submissiveness, and female exclusion from public activities have already been touched upon in this review; the effects of male competitiveness, in societies which give rein to this behavior, will be discussed below. The particular fate of Eskimo women may be a complex outcome of these several factors, not attributable solely to their role in production.

Friedl (25, pp. 8–9) comments that "those who work to produce goods have a greater chance to be assigned the control of distributing them, but do not automatically gain the right to do so." More particularly, Sanday (74) has drawn attention to an intriguing curvilinear relationship between women's participation in production and their status. As measures of women's status in a pilot sample of 12 societies Sanday selected four indicators, which could be arranged in a Guttman scale: (*a*) female control over produce; (*b*) external or internal demand or value placed on female produce; (*c*) female participation in at least some political activities; and (*d*) female solidarity groups devoted to political or economic interests. The scale suggested to Sanday that their ownership or control of strategic resources is a precondition to women's political power, a thesis developed in detail by Brown (7) to account for the striking political influence of women in one of Sanday's sample societies, the Iroquois.

Sanday found that in societies in which women's productive activities account for less that 30% of subsistence, women have predictably low status. Women's status is highest in those societies in which the sexual division of labor is fairly evenly balanced. Less accountably, women have low status in three societies in which they contribute predominantly to subsistence activities— Tikopia (75%), Azande (59%), and Somali (45%). In all these groups, women's efforts are confined to production of goods with low prestige and market value; men produce highly valued goods. Additionally, among the Azande and Somali, women are alienated from what they produce; they are, effectively, slave labor. Thus Sanday concludes, with Friedl, that their contribution to production is a necessary but not a sufficient condition for the improvement of women's status.

Sanday (75, pp. 194–95) argues that "initially female energy is concentrated in the reproductive and childrearing sphere, whereas male energy is concentrated mainly in the subsistence sphere," and men's resultant control over strategic resources confers on them political as well as economic advantage. It is only later, with the increased threat of human predation, that men move out of the subsistence sphere and into the defense sphere. Under conditions of prolonged warfare, women displace men in some subsistence activities, leading to a balanced division of labor and women's high public status. Sanday draws on a study by Ember & Ember (20) to document the relationship between men's involvement in warfare-related activities and women's greater participation in production. [As Friedl (25) has noted, endemic raiding may have an opposite effect, excluding women from cultivation altogether because of the danger of their working unprotected in the fields.] Sanday points out that other conditions, such as the long-distance sea trade of Pacific Islanders noted by Ember & Ember, require prolonged male absence and open the way for increased female participation in subsistence activities. Again, the Iroquois provide an example: not only were Iroquois men away at distant wars for years at a time (7); they also left home so often on hunting and trading expeditions and diplomatic missions, that Wallace (85, p. 369) was led to characterize them thus: "The Iroquois population was, in effect, divided into two parts: sedentary females and nomadic males." While men were in charge of preparing the fields, women carried out all the remaining agricultural activities. Sanday cites a further study by LeVine (41) which documents the relegation of traditionally male tasks to women and children due to the prolonged absences of migrant laborers under colonial rule in many parts of Africa. As LeVine's discussion of Gusii women illustrates, male absence need not result immediately in improvement of women's economic and political position. Gusii men retain their traditional rights over land and livestock, as well as control over cash income from their migratory employment and the sale of cash crops. On the other hand, women must work exceptionally hard because they have taken over additional tasks formerly done by men.

While Sanday is undoubtedly correct in treating prolonged male absence as an independent variable increasing women's participation in subsistence, she is unjustified in assuming that, prior to the emergence of warfare and other activities requiring male absence, men preempted the subsistence sphere. This assumption is at odds with Draper's and Friedl's picture of hunter-gatherers. Women in many foraging societies carry out vital subsistence activities compatible with their reproductive role; they may provide over half of the food eaten; and the economies of these societies seem to revolve around a sexual division of productive labor, rather than a division between male production and female reproduction. Friedl's (25) carefully reasoned argument (section on *Women's Role in Childbearing and Childrearing*) suggests why the division of labor between male hunting and female gathering is adaptive.

Sanday's sample societies are suggestive of factors other than male absence which facilitate female political participation. Of the three societies having both female political participation and female solidarity groups, Sanday notes that women's political position among the Iroquois seems to have been strengthened by men's prolonged absences; among the Yoruba by women's participation in long-distance trade and the resultant trade guilds in which female leadership was based; and among the Samoans, whose women did not hold political power traditionally, by women's movements growing out of European contact. The effect of trading, in particular, has been noted by several other writers. While trading does not always result in women's trade guilds and their entry into politics, it does consistently give women an unusual degree of economic autonomy—control not only of their own produce but of their own capital; and where warring is not endemic (75), great freedom of movement. As Friedl argues:

The independence from male control of a woman's trading activities is probably to be accounted for by the need for her working decisions about prices, quantities to buy or sell, and the like to be made right at the market place or on the way to it, where there is no opportunity to consult with a husband or other male relatives (25, p. 64).

The capability of supporting themselves through trade may also give women domestic equality vis-a-vis their husbands, as resulted in the Afikpo Ibo case (61). However, side by side with women's involvement in trade may persist men's traditional involvement in the production and exchange of prestige goods. Afikpo Ibo men grew yams for ceremonial exchange, and rejected the cultivation of the introduced cash crop, cassava, as beneath them (51). Production and marketing of cassava gave Ibo women a new-found economic freedom. While Mintz ties the failure of these women to achieve greater economic mobility to the relatively small-scale, short-range and part-time nature of their cassava marketing, and the low capital accumulation resulting from this activity, there is no reason to believe that marketing of any scale would have secured women entry into the traditional sphere of male prestige exchange. Economic independence of the sort women are able to derive from trading, and the prestige which they may be denied by their exclusion from ceremonial exchange activities, independently influence women's position.

The indispensability of female labor, the unavailability of male labor due to male absence, and the economic independence of women through trade may combine to explain cases in which women control their own production, and to set the stage for their political participation as well. But Sanday is understandably puzzled over the cases in which the disparity between women's heavy contribution to production, and their lack of economic control and low political status, is wide. She proposes (75, p. 200) that in these societies women's disproportionate contribution to production does not accord them power in relation to men because women are, or were at some time, "far more dependent on men to meet nonsubsistence survival needs than men are on women to meet subsistence needs." One such critical need men fulfill, Sanday suggests, is defense. She leaves to the imagination how one function strategic to the survival of a society becomes established, and accepted by both sexes, as more critical than other strategic functions. As Gonzalez (26, p. 44) comments, Sanday's argument

> misses the point that lives themselves may be strategic resources, especially in societies where population size itself is a crucial variable in determining survival for the entire group. Why, then, should women not have achieved a more prominent position as a result of their control in this domain?

Divale & Harris (16) provide a more detailed and complex scenario for the association between warfare and women's status. They suggest that "the number of males available may become the most critical factor determining the survivability of the entire population" (30, p. 268). This situation arises not because of the strategic role of men in defense itself (the argument admits that "in an energy-cost sense, women are almost universally a better energy bargain than men"), but because warfare in band and village societies supports a "male supremacist complex" which provides ideological justification for the practice of female infanticide, in turn critical to population control in the absence of modern contraception. Female infanticide is argued to be more economical than the death of adult women due to induced abortion, although the economic costs of raising men to die in war are not added into this equation; and both the disposal of females as infants and, more questionably, the death of adult men in battle (because such deaths can be blamed on outsiders) are held to be less costly emotionally than the death of adult women from abortion.

Warfare is argued, by a dubious chain of inference, to support a dazzling array of customs composing the "male supremacist complex" in band and village societies. These customs in turn, by reinforcing the low valuation of women, sustain the practice of female infanticide. Women are excluded from military training and possession of military weapons so that they can be reared to be passive, so that they will submit to decisions concerning the allocation of their sexual, productive, and reproductive services, so that sex can be used as the principal reinforcement for male military bravery. Divale & Harris consider that deprivation of food and shelter, which would impair warriors' physical fitness, are the only alternatives to sexual deprivation which would induce men to risk their lives in war. Polygyny is said to function as a reward for military prowess, and to intensify the shortage of females and reinforce such prowess, encouraging combat for the sake of wife capture. Supernatural ceremonial activities assist in rearing passive and submissive females. Patrilocality, patrilineality, male control over property, and the survival of male dominance in matrilocal, matrilineal societies are due to the solidarity of males with a joint interest in defense. Other practices which flow from this configuration are brideprice, male monopoly over hunting and weaponry, assignment of women to drudge work (an example of which is carrying infants), exclusion of women from headmanship and "big-man" status, and ideologies and rituals emphasizing the inferiority of women, including the beliefs that women are ritually unclean, menstrual blood is polluting, and female witches are more evil than their male counterparts, and the facts that supreme gods and legendary heroes greatly outnumber goddesses and heroines, men keep sacred items with which to menace women and children in men's houses, and widows are sent to the grave with their husbands. The Divale-Harris hypothesis, then, stands as a supreme example of a "key" theory, explaining all manifestations of women's low status across a wide range of societies. Indeed, these authors seem to regard its parsimony as one of the chief attractions of the theory. It must also be evaluated, however, both in terms of the inferences which its own internal logic requires, and in terms of the position taken in this review: that some of the ethnographic picture relied on by Divale & Harris is biased; many of the customs they cite are distributed independently across societies; these customs have widely different effects on the position of women and do not all spell women's devaluation; and convincing alternative hypotheses have been separately argued for many of the same customs.

Sanday (75, p. 200) speculates that even when warfare ceases and men's crucial role in defense is ended, they are able to retain their power advantage by instituting "expressive or actual mechanisms . . . to perpetuate female dependency." Women may be kept in a subordinate position by force or threat of force, or alternatively, by use of ideological devices, an example of which is the belief in romantic love. A similar notion of how ideology may be used to prepetuate female inferiority is developed by O'Laughlin (59), in a study of Kpau Mbum food prohibitions. The economic subordination of Mbum women is not explicable in terms of the division of labor, for the contributions of the two sexes to production are fairly equal. Yet female subordination is reflected in the organization of production—in predominantly male ownership of tools and breeding animals; greater male opportunities to inherit property and recruit surplus labor; and senior male authority over the distribution of grain, the cash revenues of household members, and the allocation of both household and recruited labor. O'Laughlin suggests that senior males maintain their advantage by controlling the various forces of production. They accumulate surplus, control over which is expressed by their consumption of beer, porridge, chicken, and goats, the prestige foods, and with this surplus they are able to trade for iron tools and to maintain a stock of seed grain. Male elders also have authority over the reproductive rights of female lineage members, and hence control over the labor force, the scarcest factor in Mbum production and the primary means of intensifying production. Senior males depend upon ideology to bolster their position. One such ideological elaboration of male dominance is the prohibition on female consumption of goats and chickens, a taboo which metaphorically equates women to other domesticated animals kept for breeding and exchange.

O'Laughlin explicitly disclaims the argument that ideological devices, such as the Mbum prohibition against women eating chicken, by themselves explain female subordination. Rather, she feels, the origin of women's subordination defies historical reconstruction; ideological mediation of contradiction is interdependent with the system of social relations itself—"power breeds power"—in maintaining this subordination once established. O'Laughlin thereby circumvents the most interesting and difficult question about the Mbum and similar societies in which women have an important subsistence role but a subordinate position.

What may be distinctive about such societies is that they feature pronounced male prestige-seeking activities. Competition for prestige involves men in the exchange of prestige goods; women are often excluded from the production (25,75) and always from the exchange of these goods. Typically, ceremonial exchange occupies a considerable amount of men's time and women's labor frees men for this activity (81). The suitability of women for almost all horticultural labor, and the slight demands on men's labor in many horticultural economies, allow the latter an unusual amount of leisure time for pursuit of prestige (35). Mount Hagen women, for instance, cultivate vegetables for subsistence and also raise the pigs which men distribute to gain "big-man" status (81). Notably, these women retain the exclusive right to harvest and allocate their own subsistence produce; it is only the prestige goods they produce which men control. Subsistence goods have low value in comparison with prestige goods, and women's role as producers of prestige goods is devalued in contrast to the role of men as transactors. Thus the variables which Sanday treats as measures of women's low status in such societies—their alienation from control of their own production and the relatively low prestige value assigned to this production—can be viewed, along with women's predominant role in subsistence, as a complex of outcomes arising from men's pristige-seeking activities.

Some writers on women's status have speculated about the conditions which foster or discourage competition for prestige among men. Draper (17), for instance, has suggested that the efforts of !Kung men to gain prestige through property accumulation are constrained, not only by the limits on accumulation imposed by the seminomadic life, but also by the social pressure for distribution of whatever belongings people do accumulate, because of the visibility of property. Leacock (38) has argued that among the Naskapi, the economic interdependence of the group enforces cooperation, sharing, and collective ownership. The Eskimo example suggests, however, that the noncompetitiveness of !Kung foragers and aboriginal Naskapi trappers is not characteristic of all hunting men. At the other end of a continuum, the emergence of hereditary office or class stratification may stifle male competition for prestige. Friedl (25) observes of egalitarian horticultural societies that distribution validates the right to prestige and rank, while in nonegalitarian horticultural groups, distribution is an entitlement of rank, which is validated on other grounds.

The residual question, and one which remains among the most puzzling in the literature, is why women are excluded from institutionalized competition for prestige whenever such institutions arise. If, as Friedl (25, p. 61) argues for hunter-gatherers, "rights of distribution and the control of channels of distribution of goods and services, rather than rights of control over production, are the critical elements for the understanding of differences in power between the sexes," it is unclear how men gain control of distribution in egalitarian horticultural societies. Among hunter-gatherers the distribution of the meat they hunt is said to give men an advantage in prestige and power over a larger circle of people. But a similar argument does not hold for horticulturalists, among whom men and women participate in different stages of production of the same foods (25).

Perhaps women are not so much forcibly excluded from prestige activities, as comparatively disinterested in pursuing them. Several ethnographic descriptions (6, 55, 81) suggest that while women may resent men's exemption from domestic drudgery and envy men's physical freedom or their involvement in exciting activities, they do not envy them their prestige. It seems reasonable that the differing socialization experiences of the sexes might lead them to have unequal interest in prestige-seeking. This difference might rest on Chodorow's assertion (section on *Children's Socialization*) that their socialization by women and their consequent struggle to achieve manhood causes boys to be more achievement-oriented and competitive, or it might be explained by the more direct effect of task performance in preparation for the adult male role (section on *Men's Greater Aggressiveness*). While boys receive more achievement training than girls in most societies, this difference is most pronounced in societies subsisting predominantly by large game hunting and fishing. Barry, Child & Bacon (3) go on to speculate, although not to test the relationship, that adult male participation in warfare will have an effect on boys' training similar to that of hunting and fishing. The competitiveness and drive to excel which boys learn in the course of such training may exhibit itself in prestige activities, in societies where a male prestige sphere is compatible with other features of the economic and political system discussed above. Research is needed to untangle these variables and test for relationships among them.

Women's greater compliance and willingness to take orders from those in authority (section on *Women's Compliance*) may contribute to the maintenance of male prestige activities. Strathern (81, p. 146) says of Mount Hagen women that they "accept, and do not denigrate, the ethos of exchange," accept their domestic, nonpolitical roles, and agree that men's strength gives them a prerogative over speech-making and fighting.

An important consequence of men's exclusive participation in competition for prestige and rank in egalitarian societies may be men's assumption of political authority as such societies become less egalitarian and more class-stratified. While, as Friedl (25) points out, women do have access to political office by hereditary principles, those women who gain office by such means are always in a small minority (68). It may be that their occupancy of "big-man" status makes men the natural heirs to chieftainship, and helps to explain the monopoly men hold over formal political office.

Social Structural Variables

In some societies, competition between males for prestige is tied to marriage; women are not only excluded from seeking prestige but are themselves objects of men's exchange and subject to men's disposal. They may, as among the Hageners, create avenues for ceremonial exchange. Or they may themselves be valuables, either producers of prestige goods which men require to enter competition, or exchangeable for some such goods. The study of societies in which marriage exchange is linked to male competition for prestige has led some writers to confound the effects, on women's status, of these two practices. But marriage exchange is also practiced in societies in which institutionalized competition for prestige is absent. Marriage is important in many societies as a means of alliance between households or descent groups to keep the peace or insure military support in case of war; to enable cooperative endeavors requiring pooled labor or other resources; or simply to provide a reliable source of future mates. Since it is such a multipurpose institution, marriage alliance is widely distributed among human societies, and has some distinctive and broadly similar effects on the position of women who are so exchanged.

To some degree the autonomy of women who circulate in marriage exchange is necessarily curtailed, it has been argued that such women "do not have full rights in themselves" (71, p. 177). Most obviously, exchanged women are said to lose autonomy with respect to selection of their marriage partners, although this claim needs qualification. Young men in such societies may suffer a similar loss of choice, and Strathern's (81) description suggests that young Mount Hagen grooms find their lot more difficult to bear than brides do theirs. Also, as Strathern shows by comparison of several highlands New Guinea groups, the degree to which women exercise choice of spouse in such systems may vary widely. Mount Hagen women can successfully resist particular selections made for them in favor of others, and can divorce early in the course of an unhappy marriage, because the ceremonial exchange which depends upon marital links is initiated after a marriage has proven stable. By contrast, Kuma marriage is strictly reciprocal between clans, so that any particular marriage is critical to the ongoing network of exchanges between men. A woman cannot object to the marriage planned for her, nor can she later appeal to her kin to support her divorce. Mount Hagen women, though, lose their options as their marriages mature; male kin may not back them in divorce if this would require the return of bridewealth which has already been distributed in ceremonial exchange; alternatively kin may encourage divorce if bridewealth payments are outstanding (71, 81). Depending upon the importance of the alliances their marriages establish, women may not only be encouraged, humored, and cajoled into entering into and staying in the marriages arranged for them; they may also be beaten and returned to their husbands, denied refuge by their kin (81), or even killed for their recalcitrance (78); alternatively, divorce may be quite easy (38). Divorced and widowed women may gain choice over whom they will remarry, although their loss of value for alliance making or bridewealth exchange may reduce their prestige and their attractiveness as marriage partners. And, as among the Nuer (73), marriages involving large bridewealth payments and committing brides to the legal jurisdiction of their husbands' kin groups may comprise a small minority of unions.

Rubin (71, p. 182) suggests that not only women's marital choice but their sexual freedom will be constrained in societies in which marriage exchange is practiced. Such a system would operate most smoothly "if the woman in question did not have too many ideas of her own about whom she might want to sleep with." Hence female sexuality in such societies is responsive rather than assertive; in this respect, societies in which marriage exchange is practiced resemble societies in which women's domestic segregation is marked. As Rubin points out, however, considerable variation with regard to women's sexual freedom may coexist with marriage exchange. Strathern (81, pp. 277, 299) cites the example of Kuma girls, whose desirability confers prestige on their sexual partners, and who enjoy courting parties and "take the initiative in sexual adventures." After their marriage, "men cannot afford their wives to be sexually desired valuables"; out of fear that they will persist in sexual adventuring, married women are proscribed from conversing with other men out of their husbands' presences. This drastic reduction in women's autonomy accounts for Kuma emphasis on the traumatic change of status which women suffer at marriage.

Although Rubin (71, p. 175) argues for marriage exchange as the "ultimate locus of women's oppression," other writers have emphasized that women in societies which practice marriage exchange are not particularly oppressed in other areas of their lives. Their role in carrying out subsistence activities may be unaffected, along with the community respect and domestic equality which this contribution earns them. They may have important rituals of their own (67). As Strathern (81) details for the Hageners, women take pride in their own work and in their reputations for industriousness and generosity, and their reputations as "important women" are based on these qualities as well as on the contributions they make to their husbands' successes in ceremonial exchange. Additionally, marriage exchange itself provides women with certain opportunities. Older women may take part in arranging marriages, setting up exchanges for their children (23, 27, 67) or influencing their daughters (11, 81). D'Andrade (14) has noted that systems in which a man marries his mother's brother's daughter, such as those of the Lovedu and the Tchambuli, may give women an advantage in negotiating marriages, and co-wives who are clan sisters a basis for banding together in coalitions against their husbands. Women also gain a kind of prestige by being valuable scarce goods and repositories of their families' prestige (84). And, by cooperating in marriage exchanges, women indebt, and thus gain power over, the men who give them away (84). They may threaten to leave their husbands in order to exact concessions from their kin. Thus marriage exchange, like other institutions, has specific and limited effects, not always negative, on women's status.

The marriage practice of polygyny has been said to have effects on the status of women. D'Andrade (14) cites findings that polygyny is associated with sexual restrictiveness, particularly with respect to women. The reason for this association is not obvious; perhaps their sexual restriction is a response to the relative scarcity of women which polygyny creates. Both D'Andrade and Schlegel (76) assume that sororal polygyny will enhance female autonomy because sisters can present a united front to their common husband; but Schlegel considers that jealousy is likely to arise between co-wives who are not sisters. She finds (76, p. 96) that in those matrilineal societies in which nonsororal polygyny is practiced, co-wife jealousy is significantly associated with a pattern in which their husbands have exclusive authority over women, and she concludes that "dependence of the wife upon the husband is a corollary of husband authority over the wife, so that competition threatens the wife's security with this authority pattern more than it does with other patterns." Martin (48) considers that co-wives who are not sisters will always be competitors for the economic resources of their husbands; Leis (40) argues that it is the economics of resource division which determines whether such competition will arise. In a controlled comparison of two Ijaw villages in the Niger Delta, Leis contrasts the situation of co-wives in Patani, the northern village, who farm the land of their husband's patrilineage, with that of co-wives in Korokorosei who acquire land from their respective mothers. Because the former receive equal shares of land, they are not in competition for their husband's financial assistance; the latter may have access to widely different amounts of land, and poorer women have to approach their husbands individually for help. Indicatively, Patani co-wives cook for their husband as a group, taking turns, while Korokorosei women cook individually; and Patani wives, unlike those of Korokorosei, sometimes join forces to register a common complaint against their husband. Clignet (12; see also 34) adds that polygynous wives will always have somewhat reduced domestic power over their husbands, compared to a monogamous wife, whose individual contribution to her husband is greater; in wholly monogamous societies, married men have no access to alternative sources of reward. On the other hand, a rate of polygyny which keeps wives in short supply may give women power over their husbands, especially if men are highly desirous of being polygynists (58).

Anthropologists have long noted that descent seems to have an independent effect on women's status, which is noticeably higher in matrilineal societies. For example, Martin (48, p. 224–25), discussing horticulturalists, who are distinguished by an unusually high frequency of matriliny, states that "whereas the position of females is quite variable in patrilineal societies, it is almost universally high in matrilineal ones." She considers that this is so because women in matrilineal systems are the "focus of the entire social structure," links through females channeling resource allocation and defining political and social relationships. The women who occupy these linking positions therefore wield considerable decision-making influence. Martin offers the Iroquois as an example. As noted (section on *Economic Variables*), others have identified prolonged male absence and women's consequent role in production and control of food as the key to Iroquois women's exceptional political influence. Martin (48, p. 226) argues that matriliny was a critical ingredient, since "a frequent accompaniment of matriliny—the manipulation of access rights to seeds and to arable land by matrilineal descent groups themselves—gave Iroquois women exclusive control over the production and storage of food. They were not only the primary producers, but collectively owned the means of production as well." However, others have emphasized that the Iroquois are unusual among matrilineal peoples. Friedl (25) stresses that in most matrilineal societies it is the men tracing descent through women who allocate land and oversee political and ritual affairs. The structural position of women in matrilineal descent groups, while facilitating the kind of economic control and political influence Iroquois women exercise, does not insure it.

Schlegel (76) has emphasized as well that matrilineal societies vary with regard to the domestic autonomy women possess. She found that in sample matrilineal societies in which domestic authority over women is divided between their brothers and their husbands, less overall authority is exercised over these women than in matrilineal societies in which either husband or brother has exclusive authority. Groups in which authority over women is divided are less likely to permit husbands to beat their wives and less likely to entitle brothers to threaten or punish their adult married sisters. Nonsororal polygyny, the form most divisive of co-wife solidarity, is unlikely to be practiced. The males in authority are less likely to punish women for adultery, and husbands are less likely to have the right to dispose of their wives' sexuality. Males do not have exclusive control of domestic property. On the other hand, divided authority over women does not correlate with some measures of female autonomy located outside the domestic sphere—the right of women to share important male-held positions outside the home, and the observation of menstrual restrictions. Thus Schlegel provides a demonstration, rare in the literature, of the independence of two aspects of women's status. Schlegel (76, p. 135) interprets her findings to mean that in matrilineal societies, and presumably in other societies as well, "domestic power declines as it disperses." Apparently it is more difficult for the men involved to exercise their share of authority when this authority is divided between them, but Schlegel does not hazard a guess about the interactional process. Are rights over women in such societies simply less important, and therefore unassigned? Or does each man encounter resistance from the other in attempting to exercise his authority over the woman in whom they both have rights? Something like the latter seems to take place among the Tiwi (27), for instance, among whom a husband must refrain from beating his wife too severely or too often lest her kinsmen, who are still considered her "boss," should come and take her away from him.

Schlegel also sheds light on the conditions under which women may owe deference to men. The distribution of women's deference to their husbands or brothers in matrilineal societies closely matches the distribution of tolerated force, either physical aggression by husbands or the right of brothers to use punishment and threat, which these men may exercise over them. Deference behavior in this context may constitute a culturally instituted strategy available to women for avoiding or minimizing aggressive behavior aimed at them.

The husband authority pattern in matrilineal societies, and the dependency of wives on their husbands which this pattern implies, casts doubt upon the widely held notion that the woman in matrilineal societies, because she is a central figure in her descent group, is relatively independent of her husband. What these findings suggest is that the critical factor is not the descent system per se but rather the organization of the domestic group (76, p. 96).

Schlegel concedes that husband authority may be comparatively less severe in matrilineal than in nonmatrilineal societies, though this comparison awaits further investigation.

Critical to the domestic position women occupy in matrilineal groups is the frequently associated practice of matrilocal residence. Friedl (25) contrasts the differing consequences of matrilineal descent with matrilocal residence, and patrilineal descent with virilocality. Under the former arrangement, the inmarrying husband is confronted with a lifelong domestic coalition between his wife and her mother and sisters, and broader kin relations which commit his wife's primary loyalty to her brothers and their matrilineage. Women in patrilineal, virilocal societies, residing with their husbands' kin, are unlikely to have their own patrilineal relatives nearby to support them in times of stress. Such a woman must face the loneliness of a new life among strangers and the scrutiny of her husband's relatives who are waiting to see whether or not she is hardworking and fertile.

In matrilocal households, Friedl continues, strains are slight; what strains are inherent in relationships between affines involve people living apart. Coresident women of a matriline have little basis for quarreling among themselves, unlike coresident males of a patriline and their unrelated wives who frequently quarrel over male-held patrilineal resources. The relations between the spouses themselves are less tense than in patrilineal societies, because unions are of less practical importance to the relatives of the couple. In patrilineal, virilocal groups, the strains between husband and wife may be further intensified when an older woman attempts to align her son against her husband and the other members of his descent group. And in these societies, women are likely to be considered kinds of property: wives work their husbands' land, bear the progeny of their husbands' descent groups, and may also marry in exchange for brideprice. In contrast, women have a greater opportunity, in matrilineal, matrilocal societies, for domestic equality. In case of divorce, a matrilocally resident woman need not shift households, nor find kin willing to take her back. However, Schlegel's findings (76) caution that matrilocality does not ensure women's domestic autonomy; while matrilocal societies rarely exhibit a pattern of husband authority and frequently exhibit one of divided authority, almost as frequently as Schlegel's sample of matrilineal societies, their brothers exercise exclusive authority over matrilocally resident women.

Matrilocal residence has extradomestic implications as well. Martin (48, p. 229) emphasizes that much of the influence of Iroquois women both within and without the longhouse derived not from their role as food producers alone, but from the additional fact that "related women remained together throughout life, forming tightly knit residential as well as social units." Related women of the same longhouse formed collective work groups and collective distribution groups, these latter being the means by which women asserted their control over food production and storage and its allocation to men and children. As Brown's (7) account makes clear, the group of women coresident in a longhouse, supervised by its elder matrons, were in a position to dispense or withhold daily meals, to evict inmarrying husbands and break up their marriages, and by withholding provisions, to hinder mens' organization of hunts and war parties. Brown sees this economic control as the key to Iroquois women's broad political power and influence. Thus, as Martin concludes, it is local group formation rather than descent group structure which determines women's economic control.

Matrilocality, among all types of residence associated with systems of descent, perpetuates the coresidence of related women after marriage. Matrilocality may facilitate the solidarity and influence of women even in the rare case where it is coupled with patrilineal descent (55). By contrast, the avunculate, where it is practiced in matrilineal societies, like virilocality in patrilineal ones, disperses related women and keeps together related men whose wives are outsiders to the residential group and strangers to one another (48). Martin also points out that matrilocality disperses related males, denying them a geographic basis for grouping. Also, she notes, if matrilocal polygyny is practiced it is likely to be sororal, a type favoring the formation of domestic coalitions among co-wives (this section).

Thus it would seem that while men are enabled to commit aggression against isolated women, women acting in groups are enabled to gain both domestic control and extradomestic political influence over men. D'Andrade (14) has pointed out the rarity across societies of matrilocal residence. The infrequency with which patterns of residence group together related women and disperse related men, rather than the other way around, helps to explain why the degree of political influence exercised by Iroquois women is characteristic of few societies.

Common interests among coresident women may foster women's solidarity, and their consequent political influence, even when they are not living matrilocally. In her comparision of two Ijaw villages, Leis (40) identifies the factors which account for the presence of strong women's associations only in the northern village, Patani. In both villages, virilocally married women are strangers to one another and to the community, and the only people with whom they have something in common are other inmarrying women. A similar argument is made by Wolf (90) to explain the strength of women's friendship ties in a Taiwanese community. But Patani women farm the land of their husband's patrilineage, and the authority of the patrilineage over all the women and children of a residence group provides a further basis for common interests. At the same time, Patani men spend their lives with their own kinsmen in the same village, a situation which encourages them to give their undiluted loyalty to their lineage group. In the other Ijaw village of Korokorosei, women are less integrated into their residence groups because their own farmland and that which their children will inherit lies elsewhere, encouraging them to maintain kin ties in other groups. Men continue close relationships with their matrikin and with their fathers, so that both sexes have diffuse kinship loyalties. Unlike Patani women, those of Korokorosei do not relate to the men of the village as a group, and do not orient themselves primarily toward one another. Other differences between women in the two communities rest in the relationships between co-wives (this section) and the commercial opportunities open to women. Patani women enter into marketing and trading, the income from which allows them, like Yoruba women, the domestic autonomy to join in activities and groups on their own without the permission of their husbands. Patani women's associations hold formal meetings; act as mediators in disputes between co-wives and other women, and sometimes between spouses; levy fines against women who commit certain offenses; pass laws that may affect nonmembers; lend money to men and women in and out of the association; and sanction those who refuse to accept their judgments or fail to pay debts owed to them. Sanctions may take the form of hazing, confiscating indispensable household items, or keeping offenders under siege in their houses; people do not resist the will of the association for very long. Thus, again, women's collective action brings them considerable political power.

Unrelated inmarrying women may have conflicts of interest which preclude collective action (34). By contrast with situations in which women's interests form a basis for their political organization, writers have characterized the especially weak position of wives marrying into patrilocal extended households. While such women may, as in the Taiwanese case (90), form neighborhood friendship networks which exert social pressure to support young wives against the unjust treatment of their affines, within the household itself these young wives are isolated. Such a bride suffers the loneliness and the scrutiny of her affines which typifies the lot of all virilocally married women (this section); in addition she may find herself under the authority of a hostile mother-in-law, whose interests are opposed to hers in competition for the affection and loyalty of her husband. Her only claim to status rests on her success in bearing and raising sons and her eventual position as a mother-in-law herself (13, 90). Typically, women can only gain power in such households indirectly, through men (13, 34), and their strategies for so doing may be characterized by gossip, persuasion, indirection, and guile. Collier (13) argues that such societies are marked by a distinctive ideology of women as irresponsible and sexually threatening, reflective of the divisive part young wives play in the household. At the same time mothers are idealized as warm and self-sacrificing, reflective of the loyalties which women engender in their sons.

Collier points out that the political acts of women in patrilocal extended households are individual rather than collective ones. Such acts may have extradomestic repercussions; for example, Collier notes, the divorces and household segmentation which Zinacanteco women cause account for the shallowness of lineages and the resultant importance of wealth and influence in a man's ability to attract a political following from among his relatives. But such community-wide political effects are incidental to the political ends toward which women work within their households. Unlike Iroquois or Patani women, Taiwanese and Zinacanteco women do not participate directly in events beyond the household.

Ideologies of Sexual Opposition

A distinctive complex of customs, which has been labeled "sex antagonism," has long been recognized as typical of societies in two widely separated regions of the world—the Brazilian Amazon and the New Guinea Highlands. Because the institutions associated with sex antagonism are unusual and extreme, these customs figure in composite pictures of male supremacy (16). From these two parts of the world come ethnographic accounts of institutionalized gang rape (45, 54). Other elements of the complex are a concern with female pollution; a preoccupation with male sexual depletion; and elaborate male ceremonial activities, knowledge of which must be kept secret from women. Faithorn (23, p. 87) has summarized ethnographic description of sex antagonism in New Guinea as centering on "the three interrelated themes of sexual segregation, male dominance/female subservience, and male purity/female pollution." Interpersonal relations between the sexes in these societies are also characterized as hostile and antagonistic.

Although, of course, customs such as gang rape and menstrual pollution are reported from other parts of the world, the confinement of the "sex antagonism" complex as a whole to the Amazon and highlands New Guinea ought to warn against treating sex antagonism as a universal feature of male-female relationships. Moreover, Meggitt (49) early observed that sex antagonism may underly very different relationships between men and women in different societies. He hypothesized that there are at least two separate complexes in New Guinea, the "Mae syndrome" in the western and southwestern highlands and the "Kuma syndrome" of the central highlands. The former stresses protection of men from contamination by women, and derives from the fact that groups like the Mae Enga recruit their wives from enemy clans; the latter syndrome is characterized by opposition of interests between the sexes, men continually striving to dominate women and women to escape this domination. Lindenbaum (44, 45) has suggested that this difference in emphasis may be linked to population density, representing adaptive strategies to cope with the threat of overpopulation, on the one hand, scarcity of women, on the other. Among the Enga, with high man-resource ratios, emphasis is on male chastity; among the Fore, with relatively low man-land ratios, beliefs in female pollution, while present, are deemphasized and do not inhibit male access to women; instead, male fears (like those of Kuma men) revolve around female sexual independence and the loss of one's wife to male competitors.

Recent ethnographic reports suggest an even more complex situation. Shapiro contrasts two well-studied Amazonian groups, emphasizing that Mundurucú women unlike Yanomama women engage in significant communal, cooperative labor and that Mundurucú women orient their lives around female relatives, Yanomama women toward their husbands. The Mundurucú cult of the sacred trumpets is necessary to keep these solidary women in control: "the fact that the trumpets must be hidden from them at all times seems to indicate the fear that if women were to see them, they would also see 'through' them" (77, p. 5; see also 55). While Yanomama women are excluded from male ceremonial life, they are not the targets of such a secret male cult. In New Guinea, equally, recent reports (9) stress the variable forms sex antagonism may take across groups. Some of the customs associated with the "sex antagonism" complex may be entirely absent in some societies, as is the belief in menstrual pollution among the Etoro (33). Not only do female pollution, male sexual depletion, secret male knowledge, and other customs in the complex receive widely different emphasis from society to society, but the same custom may figure symbolically in wholly different interpretations of women's role in nature and society. Thus Buchbinder & Rappaport (10) argue that marriage and sexual intercourse are threatening to Maring men because of the Maring association between fertility and decay. Kelly (33) interprets a similar Etoro ambivalence toward sexual intercourse as stemming from the belief in women's ability to deplete male life-force. And Meggitt (50) associates the same fear and ambivalence of Enga men toward marriage and sex to the aforementioned "enemy" origins of their wives. Each interpretation is embedded in a highly coherent analysis of an interrelated system of symbols. Thus different societies seem to incorporate common material into quite different conceptions of women's role.

Further, Langness (36) points out, interpersonal antagonism pertains, in different highland societies, not between the sexes in general but between men and women in particular roles. This antagonism may be confined to relations between husbands and wives (23). Or it may, as among the Maring, be more characteristic of relations between brothers and sisters, mothers and sons, due to a conflict of interests over marriage arrangements, while relations between spouses "in well-established marriages seem generally to be warm and unsuspicious" (10, p. 17). It is even possible that some of the strongest antagonisms between kin do not cross sex at all, but as among the Enga, pertain between fathers and sons (50). Equally, taboos may apply not to all members of the opposite sex, but to certain restricted categories of kin, such as the Kafe taboo prohibiting a man who has stepped over his food bag from giving that food to his wife, children, or affines of either sex (23).

In the face of evidence that features of the so-called "sex antagonism" complex are differently distributed and emphasized among societies sharing this complex, and incorporated into wholly different views of women, and restricted to different male-female relationships, it would be difficult to argue a unitary explanation for the complex as a whole.

One general explanation for a component of the sex antagonism complex is proposed by the Murphys (55, p. 139), who ask of Mundurucú women: "Why do not the women have rites and myths that validate their position and express their opposition to the men?" It is a major theme of their analysis that Mundurucú men harbor anxieties about women which are not reciprocated. This male anxiety is characterized (55, p. 95) in terms strikingly similar to Chodorow's (section on *Child Socialization*). The myth of the sacred flutes reflects the "uneasy overlordship, obtained only by expropriation from the original custody of the women," which men feel. The myth is an allegory of man's birth from woman, his early dependence upon his mother, and the necessity to break this bond and assert his autonomy and manhood. The male role can only be maintained by vigilance and self-assertion. Though the antagonism which Mundurucú men direct against women is not universal, where it exists its unidirectionality may be traceable to the fact that the men of such societies confront special difficulty in throwing off their attachments to women as they grow up. Briggs (6) has raised the same possibility to explain why Eskimo women are attributed with greater power to contaminate and subjected to more stringent taboos than men. The relationship of childrearing experiences which result in a difficult transition to manhood, and adult male antagonism toward women, requires cross-cultural verification. Alternatively, the Murphys suggest that Mundurucú men's antagonism toward women is accentuated by the struggle over social allocation of children, arising from the combination of patrilineal descent and matrilocal residence. This hypothesis relates sex antagonism once again to a real-life conflict of interests between adult men and women. Future research needs to inquire more systematically into the possible cross-cultural links between particular ideological themes of sexual opposition and different realistic concerns men have about women: for example, their enmity, as Meggitt has suggested, their scarcity, as Lindenbaum has suggested, the scarcity value of their production and reproduction, as O'Laughlin (section on *Economic Variables*) has suggested, their threat to the kin group, as Collier (section on *Social Structural Variables*) has suggested, or, as the Murphys propose, the affective control they exercise over their progeny.

The secret male cult of the Mundurucú is susceptible to a further interpretation with general implications. The cult is argued to maintain a precarious control over women that is necessary because in reality women have extreme autonomy in their daily lives and influence within their households. Men are interlopers in these households. Matrilocally related women are bound together by stronger emotional ties than men and have strong affective sway over their children. Women are not servile to men; they regard them as exploitative and dominant, but not superior. As a result of women's considerable autonomy and influence, men's ideology of dominance is defensive and uneasy, male status insecure. Women are regarded as unpredictable and difficult to manage, and the myth of the sacred trumpets, on which the ideology of male dominance rests, describes women as the original owners of these ceremonial objects and the secret knowledge pertaining to them. When women owned the trumpets, sex roles were reversed; men were made to submit to women's sexual advances and to do the housework. Similarly among the Fore of New Guinea, female challenge to male authority is a major cultural theme (although emphasis is on management of female sexuality rather than the threat of female solidarity), and a similar myth about sacred flutes, once in the hands of women but wrested from them by men, is reported (45).

There is a correspondence to be noted between this picture of male-female relations among the Mundurucú and a model of male-female relations which Rogers (66) has derived from ethnographic observations in a northwestern French village. Rogers and Friedl (24) attest to the power women exercise in European peasant households, in spite of the formal position and prestige of men and a pervasive ideology of male dominance. Women wield informal power over their children's marriage arrangements, their husbands' career choices and political activities, decisions about major household purchases, and the like. Men claim power in the village sphere, leaving women to control the less prestigious domestic sphere, which Rogers argues is the only domain over which villagers have effective control. The "myth of male dominance" serves to disguise this situation. While neither sex believes that the myth accurately reflects the actual situation, both sexes maintain the illusion of male dominance so that each can continue to exercise the forms of power allocated to them. Women retain control of their households and covertly manage their husbands' activities.

Rogers attempts to sketch some conditions leading to the "myth of male dominance" wherever it arises, not only in peasant, but in other traditional societies as well. She hypothesizes that such societies will be characterized by an association of women with the domestic sphere, a marked domestic orientation, the importance of informal relationships and forms of power, the greater accessibility of formal rights to men, and the approximately equal economic, social, and/or political dependence of men and women on each other. The latter condition insures that both groups will "play the game," maintaining an even balance of power. Contributing to the picture may be a felt lack of power on the part of men. Women's informal power in the domestic sphere is supported by the wider female solidarity groups often reported in peasant societies. Rogers reviews the literature to indicate the fit between her model and a wide variety of ethnographic descriptions of peasant communities. While the model is too exploratory to lend itself to a close analysis of nonpeasant societies, certainly some of its features—particularly, men's felt lack of power, the economic interdependence of the sexes, the importance of informal power and women's exercise of this power by means of female solidarity—are in conformity with the Mundurucú case, suggesting the profitability of a search for specific cross-cultural preconditions to ideologies of male dominance along the lines Rogers has initiated. It is noteworthy that by her interpretation, male dominance myths, far from reflecting women's overall low status, arise precisely because women have considerable economic importance, personal autonomy, and domestic influence.

CONCLUSION

To underline the argument for independence of different aspects of women's status, the hypotheses reviewed can now be rearranged. The components of women's position which have concerned anthropologists will be considered separately, and the specific conditions to which each component has been attributed will be summarized.

In the literature reviewed, male strength, maternal responsiveness, and the role of women in childbearing, nursing, and rearing have been proposed either singly or in combination to explain women's exclusion from warfare and a wide range of subsistence tasks and their exclusive assignment to other tasks. The willingness of women to comply with the commands of those in authority has been entertained in explanation of their tendency to accept assignment of unattractive tasks. However, the portrayal of at least one universally female task, gathering, as dull and repetitive has also been attributed to male ethnographer bias.

The universal female role in child socialization and the universal experience by which girls are socialized by women to be particularistic and personalistic have been invoked to account for the confinement of women to the domestic sphere. However, this confinement has also been treated as a consequence of sedentism and intensive agriculture, which reduce women's role in food production and increase their burden of food processing and household upkeep. In other views, the rise of the state and industrialization were critical in bringing about women's domestic isolation, because each of these developments expropriated men's labor (for the state or the capitalist) and relegated women to private production in the home.

While women's role in production does not necessarily guarantee them control over their products, such control may be augmented by the importance of women's contribution to subsistence and the unavailability of male labor due to male absence. On the other hand, institutionalized male prestige-seeking may mean that women's production, however important to the economy, is confined to the subsistence sphere or alienated from them to be circulated in men's prestige activities. In such societies women and their activities are granted low prestige by comparison to men and their activities.

The fact that women themselves do not participate in prestige activities may be explained by the different socialization experience of boys and girls. Either the effects attributed by Chodorow to the socialization of both sexes by women, or the cross-cultural pattern of task socialization by which children are prepared for their adult economic roles, might be invoked to explain why boys are socialized to be achievers and competitors. The greater compliance of girls may also explain their willingness to support men's prestige activities with their efforts.

Men's exclusive participation in prestige activities and their occupancy of "big-man" status, in turn, may help to explain their assumption of political office as societies develop hereditary political positions. Several other factors have been proposed to explain the monopoly men hold over formal political office. It has been suggested that because children of both sexes are brought up by women, boys but not girls learn to interact with others in the abstract, impersonal manner required of formal political roles. This reviewer, while rejecting the male advantage in physical strength and physical aggressiveness as an explanation of male political control, has suggested that the greater verbal assertiveness which is part of the picture of innate male aggressiveness may be implicated in men's assumption of political roles.

In more egalitarian societies without formal political offices, women have a more nearly equal part in domestic and extradomestic decision making, and this was truer of such societies before colonial contact. In many other societies women are said to exert informal political influence even though they are excluded from formal office. A crucial factor in women's ability to exercise political power is said to be their success in forming solidarity groups, whether these groups be facilitated by matrilocal residence or other kinship bonds, the lack of extraresidential kin to turn to, co-wife coalitions, or trading activities which foster trade associations and provide women with the independent means and economic autonomy to organize such associations. Conversely, any conditions which divide women's interests such as the competition for resources among co-wives or the unrelated wives of patrilineally related men, or the conflicts between inmarrying wives and their in-laws, will reduce women's chances of achieving collective political influence. Individual women lacking collective political bases are likely to adopt indirect strategies by which to manipulate events.

Separable from the degree to which women participate in prestige activities or exercise political influence is the question of how much individual autonomy they have, both extradomestically and within the domestic context. Women are thought to lose autonomy in societies which practice marriage exchange, although this constraint may apply narrowly to their marital choices and their sexual freedom, and may vary widely in different marriage alliance systems and for women of different ages and marital statuses in such systems. Sexual restriction of women is also associated with the practice of polygyny. Their sexual freedom, personal autonomy, and legal rights are also circumscribed wherever women are isolated and segregated in a domestic sphere and must rely on men to mediate their access to the public world. Women may gain autonomy through economic independence, for example as traders or as producers of important subsistence foods. And women's autonomy is high in hunting and gathering societies which lack male-held political offices and circumscribe the exercise of authority over others.

Women's domestic autonomy is threatened by men's greater strength and aggressiveness, since men are most likely to exercise this potentiality for physical aggression against isolated women, and domestic relations between spouses are frequently set in such isolation. In addition, social structural arrangements may affect the domestic position of women. In patrilineal societies women may be treated by their husbands and affines as male-owned property rather than autonomous group members. Virilocality may further weaken their autonomy because it isolates women from the support of their own kin and requires them to change residence in case of divorce. Women's domestic autonomy is also lessened in matrilineal societies by structural arrangements which place domestic authority in the hands of one man, either a woman's husband or her brother, rather than dividing it between them. On the other hand, women's autonomy and influence within marriage may be enhanced by sororal polygyny, which encourages co-wife coalitions, or monogamy, which increases a man's dependence upon his wife; nonsororal polygyny, while it may increase the competition for wives and hence their domestic power, may also foster competition among co-wives, increasing the dependency of each upon her husband and hence his power over her. Women also lost domestic autonomy under colonial policies which imposed Western Christian notions of wifely obedience on aboriginal marriage customs. Finally, women's loss of adult status in state societies is said to extend to their marital relationship.

Accompanying a loss of autonomy may be the requirement that women show deference to the men who control them. Thus women owe deference and submissiveness to men in societies which confine them to a domestic sphere and reduce them to legal and social minority. Women also owe deference to those men, whether their brothers or their husbands, who are permitted to use force against them in matrilineal societies; but women do not behave deferently toward either of these men when authority is divided between them and the use of force by either is not socially tolerated.

Ideologies which exalt men, denigrate women, or picture women as threats to men have been variously explained. Sex antagonism has been attributed to the anxiety men feel about women due to the difficulty boys experience in severing their initial attachment to their mothers. Antagonism toward women, reflected in various customs, has also been attributed to real-life conflicts between adult men and women over the allegiance of their progeny, or the women themselves to their husbands or their husbands' kin groups, for example. Others have described fearful male attitudes which invest women with dangerous powers as stemming from more primary beliefs associating fertility with death or sexual intercourse with depletion.

The "myth" of male dominance has been explained as a product of the balance of power between the sexes and the advantage which each sex gains by acting as if men are dominant. An ideology of women as irresponsible and sexually threatening has been suggested as an outcome of the real threat inmarrying wives pose to the unity of the household. An ideology of women as immature and requiring male protection and supervision is said to accompany the extreme domestic isolation of women associated with the rise of intensive agriculture and the state. An equation of women with domesticated animals has been argued to reinforce the arbitrary male control over women's scarce reproductive and productive contribution to the economy of one society. It has also been argued that women are everywhere ideologically devalued because of their universal identification with nature and their consequent exclusion from the world of culture. Men's devaluation of women, as well as their antagonism toward women, has also been attributed to the early difficulty men experience in breaking away from their mothers to achieve their manhood. Other writers caution against the generalization that ethnoideologies always devalue women or treat them as the objects of men's hostility; ethnographic reports generally omit the women's side of the picture.

The general observations which have most puzzled anthropologists are these: the universal monopoly men are said to hold over formal political office, the exclusion of women from prestige spheres, and the seemingly universal ideologies of sex differences favoring men. These generalizations, taken together and at face value, go far to create the compelling picture of universally low female status which has occupied so much anthropological attention. Taken separately, some of these observations may require revision under the impact of fresh ethnographic material and new perspectives, and each may prove susceptible to independent explanation. What is clearest in the literature reviewed is the need for further investigation into each of the separate claims which has been made about women's status, and the conditions under which each claim holds true. What is most impressive about this literature is the overwhelming number of specific researchable questions it has produced. Hopefully the social forces which inspired anthropological interest in women's status will sustain this interest through the long second stage of research fashioned to explore these new hypotheses.

ACKNOWLEDGMENTS

I have been fortunate in colleagues: Bonnie Erickson, Ernestine Friedl, Carol Smith, and Carol Stack have generously shared their reactions, ideas, and familiarity with the literature under review. Of course, any misinterpretations and omissions in this review are my own.

Literature Cited

1. Ardener, E. 1972. Belief and the problem of women. In *The Interpretation of Ritual: Essays in Honour of A. I. Richards,* ed. J. S. La Fontaine, pp. 135–58. London: Tavistock
2. Barry, H., Bacon, M. K., Child, I. L. 1957. A cross-cultural survey of some sex differences in socialization. *J. Abnorm. Soc. Psychol.* 55:327–32
3. Barry, H., Child, I. L., Bacon, M. K. 1959. Relation of child training to subsistence economy. *Am. Anthropol.* 61: 51–63
4. Boserup, E. 1970. *Woman's Role in Economic Development.* New York: St. Martin's
5. Bossen, L. 1975. Women in modernizing societies. *Am. Ethnol.* 2:587–601
6. Briggs, J. 1974. Eskimo women: makers of men. In *Many Sisters: Women in Cross-cultural Perspective,* ed. C. J. Matthiasson, pp. 261–304. New York: Free Press
7. Brown, J. K. 1970. Economic organization and the position of women among the Iroquois. *Ethnohistory* 17:131–67
8. Brown, J. K. 1970. A note on the division of labor by sex. *Am. Anthropol.* 72:1073–78
9. Brown, P., Buchbinder, G., eds. 1976. *Man and Woman in the New Guinea Highlands,* Spec. Publ. 8. Washington: Am. Anthropol. Assoc.
10. Buchbinder, G., Rappaport, R. A. 1976. Fertility and death among the Maring. See Ref. 9, pp. 13–35
11. Chodorow, N. 1974. Family structure and feminine personality. See Ref. 70, pp. 43–66
12. Clignet, R. 1970. *Many Wives, Many Powers: Authority and Power in Polygynous Families.* Evanston: Northwestern Univ. Press
13. Collier, J. F. 1974. Women in politics. See Ref. 70, pp. 89–96
14. D'Andrade, R. G. 1966. Sex differences and cultural institutions. In *The Development of Sex Differences,* ed. E. E. Maccoby, pp. 173–203. Stanford: Stanford Univ. Press
15. di Leonardo, M. Definitions of marriage and male dominance. Unpublished manuscript
16. Divale, W., Harris, M. 1976. Population, warfare, and the male supremacist complex. *Am. Anthropol.* 78:521–38
17. Draper, P. 1975. !Kung women: contrasts in sexual egalitarianism in foraging and sedentary contexts. See Ref. 64, pp. 77–109
18. Draper, P. 1975. Cultural pressure on sex differences. *Am. Ethnol.* 2:602–16
19. Ember, C. R. 1973. The effect of feminine task assignment on the social behavior of boys. *Ethos* 1:424–39
20. Ember, M., Ember, C. R. 1971. The conditions favoring matrilocal versus patrilocal residence. *Am. Anthropol.* 73:571–94
21. Evans-Pritchard, E. E. 1965. The position of women in primitive societies and our own. In *The Position of Women in Primitive Societies and Other Essays in Social Anthropology,* ed. E. E. Evans-Pritchard, pp. 37–58. London: Faber & Faber
22. Faithorn, E. 1975. The concept of pollution among the Kafe of the Papua New Guinea highlands. See Ref. 64, pp. 127–40
23. Faithorn, E. 1976. Women as persons: aspects of female life and male-female relations among the Kafe. See Ref. 9, pp. 86–95
24. Friedl, E. 1967. The position of women: appearance and reality. *Anthropol. Q.* 40:97–108
25. Friedl, E. 1975. *Women and Men: an Anthropologist's View.* New York: Holt, Rinehart & Winston
26. Gonzalez, N. L. 1974. Sex roles and cultural domains: review of *Woman, Culture, and Society,* ed. M. Z. Rosaldo, L. Lamphere. *Science* 186:43–44
27. Goodale, J. 1971. *Tiwi Wives: a Study of the Women of Melville Island, North Australia.* Seattle: Univ. Washington Press
28. Goodenough, W. 1970. *Description and Comparison in Cultural Anthropology.* Chicago: Aldine
29. Gough, K. 1971. The origin of the family. *J. Marriage Fam.* 33:760–71
30. Harris, M. 1975. *Culture, People, Nature: Introduction to General Anthropology.* New York: Crowell. 2nd ed.
31. Hutt, C. 1972. *Males and Females.* Baltimore: Penguin
32. Kaberry, P. M. 1939. *Aboriginal Woman: Sacred and Profane.* Philadelphia: Blakiston
33. Kelly, R. C. 1976. Witchcraft and sexual relations: an exploration in the social and semantic implications of the structure of belief. See Ref. 9, pp. 36–53

34. Lamphere, L. 1974. Strategies, cooperation, and conflict among women in domestic groups. See Ref. 70, pp. 97–112
35. Lancaster, C. S. 1976. Women, horticulture, and society in sub-Saharan Africa. *Am. Anthropol.* 78:539–64
36. Langness, L. L. 1976. Discussion. See Ref. 9, pp. 96–106
37. Leacock, E. B. 1972. Introduction. In *The Origin of the Family, Private Property and the State,* by F. Engels, pp. 7–67. New York: International Publ.
38. Leacock, E. B. 1975. Class, commodity, and the status of women. In *Women Cross-culturally: Change and Challenge,* ed. R. Rohrlich-Leavitt, pp. 601–16. The Hague: Mouton
39. Lee, R. B. 1972. Population growth and the beginnings of sedentary life among the !Kung Bushmen. In *Population Growth: Anthropological Implications,* ed. B. Spooner, pp. 329–50. Cambridge, Mass: MIT Press
40. Leis, N. B. 1974. Women in groups: Ijaw women's associations. See Ref. 70, pp. 223–42
41. LeVine, R. A. 1966. Sex roles and economic change in Africa. *Ethnology* 5:186–93
42. Liebowitz, L. 1975. Perspectives on the evolution of sex differences. See Ref. 64, pp. 20–35
43. Liebowitz, L. 1975. Changing views of women in society, 1975. *Rev. Anthropol.* 2:532–36
44. Lindenbaum, S. 1972. Sorcerers, ghosts, and polluting women: an analysis of religious belief and population control. *Ethnology* 11:241–53
45. Lindenbaum, S. 1976. A wife is the hand of man. See Ref. 9, pp. 54–62
46. Linton, S. 1971. Woman the gatherer: male bias in anthropology. See Ref. 64, pp. 36–50
47. Maccoby, E. E., Jacklin, C. N. 1974. *The Psychology of Sex Differences.* Stanford: Stanford Univ. Press
48. Martin, M. K., Voorhies, B. 1975. *Female of the Species.* New York: Columbia Univ. Press
49. Meggitt, M. J. 1964. Male-female relationships in the highlands of Australian New Guinea. *Am. Anthropol.* 66:204–24
50. Meggitt, M. J. 1976. A duplicity of demons: sexual and familial roles expressed in western Enga stories. See Ref. 9, pp. 63–85
51. Mintz, S. 1971. Men, women, and trade. *Comp. Stud. Soc. Hist.* 13:247–69

52. Munroe, R. L., Munroe, R. H. 1971. Effect of environmental experience on spatial ability in an East African society. *J. Soc. Psychol.* 83:15–22
53. Murdock, G. P., Provost, C. 1973. Factors in the division of labor by sex: a cross-cultural analysis. *Ethnology* 12:203–25
54. Murphy, R. F. 1959. Social structure and sex antagonism. *Southwest. J. Anthropol.* 15:84–98
55. Murphy, Y., Murphy, R. F. 1974. *Women of the Forest.* New York: Columbia Univ. Press
56. Nerlove, S. B. 1974. Women's workload and infant feeding practices: a relationship with demographic implications. *Ethnology* 13:207–14
57. Nerlove, S. B., Munroe, R. H., Munroe, R. L. 1971. Effect of environmental experience on spatial ability: a replication. *J. Soc. Psychol.* 84:3–10
58. Netting, R. McC. 1969. Women's weapons: the politics of domesticity among the Kofyar. *Am. Anthropol.* 71:1037–45
59. O'Laughlin, B. 1974. Mediation of contradiction: why Mbum women do not eat chicken. See Ref. 70, pp. 301–18
60. Ortner, S. B. 1974. Is female to male as nature is to culture? See Ref. 70, pp. 67–88
61. Ottenberg, P. 1959. The changing economic position of women among the Afikpo Ibo. In *Continuity and Change in African Cultures,* ed. W. R. Bascom, M. J. Herskovits, pp. 205–23. Chicago: Univ. Chicago Press
62. Reiter, R. R. 1975. Introduction. See Ref. 64, pp. 11–19
63. Reiter, R. R. 1975. Men and women in the south of France: public and private domains. See Ref. 64, pp. 252–82
64. Reiter, R. R., ed. 1975. *Toward an Anthropology of Women.* New York: Monthly Rev. Press
65. Remy, D. 1975. Underdevelopment and the experience of women: a Nigerian case study. See Ref. 64, pp. 358–71
66. Rogers, S. C. 1975. Female forms of power and the myth of male dominance: a model of female/male interaction in peasant society. *Am. Ethnol.* 2:727–56
67. Rohrlich-Leavitt, R., Sykes, B., Weatherford, E. 1975. Aboriginal woman: male and female anthropological perspectives. See Ref. 64, pp. 110–26
68. Rosaldo, M. Z. 1974. Woman, culture, and society: a theoretical overview. See Ref. 70, pp. 17–42
69. Rosaldo, M. Z., Lamphere, L. 1974. Introduction. See Ref. 70, pp. 1–16

70. Rosaldo, M. Z., Lamphere, L., eds. 1974. *Woman, Culture, and Society*. Stanford: Stanford Univ. Press

71. Rubin, G. 1975. The traffic in women: notes on the "political economy" of sex. See Ref. 64, pp. 157–210

72. Sacks, K. 1975. Engels revisited: women, the organization of production, and private property. See Ref. 64, pp. 211–34

73. Sacks, K. 1976. State bias and women's status. *Am. Anthropol.* 78:565–69

74. Sanday, P. R. 1973. Toward a theory of the status of women. *Am. Anthropol.* 75:1682–1700

75. Sanday, P. R. 1974. Female status in the public domain. See Ref. 70, pp. 189–206

76. Schlegel, A. 1972. *Male Dominance and Female Autonomy: Domestic Authority in Matrilineal Societies*. New Haven: Human Relations Area Press

77. Shapiro, J. 1973. *Male bonds and female bonds*. Presented at Ann. Meet. Am. Anthropol. Assoc., 72nd, New Orleans

78. Smith, C. A. 1973. *Why do men want power over women? The exogamy paradox*. Presented at Ann. Meet. Am. Anthropol. Assoc., 72nd, New Orleans

79. Spiro, M. E. 1956. *Kibbutz: Venture in Utopia*. Cambridge, Mass: Harvard Univ. Press

80. Stack, C., Caulfield, M. D., Estes, V., Landes, S., Larson, K., Johnson, P., Rake, J., Shirek, J. 1975. The anthropology of women. *Signs: J. Women Cult. Soc.* 1:147–60

81. Strathern, M. 1972. *Women in Between: Female Roles in a Male World: Mount Hagen, New Guinea*. London: Seminar Press

82. Tiger, L., Shepher, J. 1975. *Women in the Kibbutz*. New York: Harcourt, Brace, Jovanovich

83. Van Allen, J. 1972. "Sitting on a man": colonialism and the lost political institutions of Igbo women. *Can. J. Afr. Stud.* 6:165–81

84. van Baal, J. 1970. The part of women in the marriage trade: objects or behaving as objects? *Bijdr. Taal-, Land- Volkenkd.* 126:289–308

85. Wallace, A. F. C. 1971. Handsome Lake and the decline of the Iroquois matriarchate. In *Kinship and Culture*, ed. F. L. K. Hsu, pp. 367–76. Chicago: Aldine

86. Webster, P. 1975. Matriarchy: a vision of power. See Ref. 64, pp. 141–56

87. White, D., Burton, M., Brudner, L., Gunn, J. Implicational structures in the sexual division of labor. Unpublished manuscript

88. Whiting, B. B., Edwards, C. P. 1973. A cross-cultural analysis of sex differences in the behavior of children aged three through 11. *J. Soc. Psychol.* 91:171–88

89. Whiting, B. B., Whiting, J. W. M. 1975. *Children of Six Cultures: a Psycho-Cultural Analysis*. Cambridge, Mass: Harvard Univ. Press

90. Wolf, M. 1972. *Women and the Family in Rural Taiwan*. Stanford: Stanford Univ. Press

91. Zaretski, E. 1973. Capitalism, the family, and personal life. *Soc. Revolution* 13–14:69–125; 15:19–70

Ann. Rev. Anthropol. 1977. 6:227–54
Copyright © 1977 by Annual Reviews Inc. All rights reserved

BEYOND IDEOLOGY AND THEOLOGY: THE SEARCH FOR THE ANTHROPOLOGY OF ISLAM

Abdul Hamid el-Zein

Department of Anthropology, Temple University, Philadelphia, Pennsylvania 19122

In the course of our intellectual history, Islam came to be understood as a unified religious tradition and, in common with other institutional religions, taken as a guide to its own understanding (25). The concept of Islam thus defined the nature of the subject matter and its appropriate modes of interpretation or explanation, but discoveries emergent within this framework have begun to contradict these premises.

In order to reveal the significance and complexity of this problem, this review first examines two apparently opposed positions on Islam: the "anthropological" and the "theological." These perspectives emerge from different assumptions concerning the nature of Man, God, and the World, use different languages of analysis, and produce different descriptions of religious life. Five anthropological studies are taken here to represent the internal variation within the anthropological perspective, while a general commentary suffices to describe the more standardized theological paradigm. Of course, the works discussed here do not exhaust the relevant studies of Islam, but they exemplify certain major approaches well enough to allow discussion of the interaction of theoretical views and ethnographic description. In all approaches, the meaning of religion as a universal form of human experience and of Islam as a particular instance is presupposed, invariable, and incontestable. Consequently, all claim to uncover a universal essence, the real Islam. Ironically, the diversity of experience and understanding revealed in these studies challenges the often subtle premise of the unity of religious meaning. It then becomes possible to ask if a single true Islam exists at all.

By virtue of its scope and sophistication, the work of Clifford Geertz offers a suitable point from which to begin the investigation. Although he proceeds by assuming a single form of religious experience and a unity of meaning within Islamic tradition, Geertz simultaneously accentuates the diversity in the actual content of religious experience as lived in the everyday world. Although they are intricately imbedded in his most recent study on Islam (17), the theoretical notions which permit the eventual integration of this diversity are never systematically stated or elaborated. These crucial assumptions emerge clearly only through reconstructing implicit relationships between statements presented in other works.

For Geertz, human phenomena are simultaneously organic, psychological, social, and cultural. Certain universal problems and qualities of being human arise from the reality of man's biological condition and in necessary social and psychological processes. Yet when grasped by man's immediate consciousness, these existential problems and conditions appear plastic and elusive. It is through the dimension of culture, which is man's unique capacity, that these problems and processes are given meaning, organized and controlled (14, pp. 52–63; 15, p. 51; 16, p. 5; 17, pp. 16, 100; 18, p. 5). These four dimensions of human reality are mutually determinative, and therefore must ultimately be integrated within a single analytic framework. But because culture particularly is the means of interpretation of all experience, it becomes the central concept in Geertz's understanding of human existence. Culture lends both order and significance to man's direct and matter-of-fact apprehension of the reality of nature and existence. In this sense, culture does not refer to a set of institutions, traditions, or customs, but involves the conceptualization of life: an intersubjective process of the interpretation of immediate experience (17, pp. 93–94).

The cultural processes of giving meaning to the world are rooted in the human capacity for symbolic thought. All men impose thought or meaning upon the objects of their experience (events, images, sounds, gestures, sensations) which, when defined, become attached to symbols or the material vehicles of meaning (16, p.5). In turn, meaning arranges these objects in intelligible forms. This expressive capacity results in the creation of cultural systems understood as patterns of symbols which must possess a certain degree of coherence in order to establish for man the structure of his own existence (18, p. 17).

For Geertz, symbols and the meanings they carry are culturally defined and socially shared. An individual is born into an already meaningful world. He inherits cultural interpretations from his predecessors, shares them with his contemporaries, and passes them on to the following generations. Therefore, symbolic thought is always social, intersubjective, and public. It cannot escape into a mysterious and inaccessible domain of private subjective meaning.

So while man creates his own symbols, these symbols define for him the nature of his own reality. For Geertz, the analysis of culture consists of the study of these social, intersubjective, and culturally relative worlds. It is a positive science in the sense that it deals with symbols as empirical expressions of thought. And it is cast in phenomenological terms: his intention is to develop "a method of describing and analyzing the meaningful structure of experience . . . in a word, a scientific phenomenology of culture" (16, p. 7). The emphasis of this approach is on "meaning." Because it is impossible to discover directly the ontological status of events, actions, institutions, or objects, the problem lies in grasping their meaning when brought to consciousness.

The formation of different forms of cultural systems corresponds to certain levels of the organization of thought. Geertz refers informally to the variety of possible cultural systems throughout his studies: religion, art, common sense, philosophy, history, science, aesthetics, ideology (14, p. 62; 17, p. 94). In his study of Islam, common sense, religion, and science become the most essential symbolic forms in his analysis.

Common sense constitutes a primary dimension through which man gives meaning to his immediate experience (19). Common sense is not the mere matter-of-fact apprehension of reality but the judgments, assessments, or colloquial wisdom which structure a practical reality. This set of shared notions is not the outcome of deliberations or reflection, but emerges in the experiential engagement with reality. Common sense notions involve such basic aspects of survival that they are invariably taken for granted.

However, the relation between common sense notions, matter-of-fact reality, and human creativity is never stable. The nature of man's engagement with the world changes through time with increasing awareness and differs from place to place. Therefore, common sense notions differ and change accordingly—or when common sense simply fails to account for experience, its authority dwindles, and religion as a higher and more general interpretive order emerges (17, pp. 94–95). Religion, in Geertz's view, offers a wider interpretation of the world and serves as a correction of common sense. In this sense, religion and common sense enter into a continued dialectic and must be studied as reciprocal traits of man's experiential reality.

Geertz refers to religion as the synthesis of two dimensions of human experience: "world view" and "ethos." In any culture, the collective notions, images, and concepts of the world view establish the essential reality of nature, self, and society. They define the sheer actuality of existence (13, p. 421; 17, p. 97). Ethos constitutes the evaluative aspect of existence; it expresses the desired character, tone, style, and quality of social and cultural life. It concerns the way in which things are properly done (17, pp. 97–98). Ethos and world view, or values and the general order of existence, continually reaffirm each other. Their interrelationship is powerfully and concretely expressed in the form of sacred symbols which not only objectify but condense multiple rays of the universe of meaning and focus them in tangible and perceptible forms. Any culture will require only a limited number of synthesizing symbols due to their immense power to enforce this integration of fact and value (13, pp. 421–22).

Systems of religious symbols continually respond to the inevitable force of historical change. Geertz regards history as the continual process of formation and sedimentation of meaning. No laws or processes of history exist but the creation of meaning which, because meaning is intersubjective, constitutes a process of social transformation as well. To arrive at any general explanation, history is studied in reverse for there are no predictive and necessary sequences of meaning. Yet in spite of his rejection of grand-scale historical necessity, Geertz does impose the constraint of the concept of tradition. For most civilizations, the structure of possibilities of change is set in formative years (17, p. 11). Thus, traditions, such as Islam, emerge with the continuity of culturally shared meanings.

Yet the concept of history in Geertz's work contains an internal tension. On the one hand, historical change is the necessary field for man's continual creation of meaning through which he realizes himself as a human and cultural being. On the other hand, change is continually denied by man, whose very creation of symbols reflects the intention to fix and stabilize meanings in objectified forms. Religion reflects this struggle. In situations of extreme change such as foreign intrusion or conquest, religious symbols and beliefs may weaken in the face of upheaval and contradiction in previously coincident social conditions. Yet it is equally possible that by virtue of the commitment of faith, these symbols may persist by denying other forms of experience such as moral, aesthetic, scientific, or even practical considerations. In this sense, faith is the true counterpart of change. While belief may stabilize reality momentarily and partially, faith attempts to fix it absolutely.

It is through yet another mode of experience, science, that these other cultural systems may be understood. Because science is itself a cultural system, it too becomes a process of interpretation. Yet it constitutes a privileged mode of understanding in the sense that it grasps the reality of the entire process of human existence, unlike common sense and religion which remain limited to particular forms of experience. As a scientist, the anthropologist must not merely observe and report, he must interpret the native's interpretation of reality, or give a "thick" description (18). This thick description is achieved when the scientific imagination succeeds in suspending its own cultural attitudes in order to comprehend the essential nature of human experience. Scientific explanation in Geertz's view is a matter of discovering the intricacies of expression. To explain is to reorganize and clarify the complexity of meaning by revealing its order in symbolic forms (15, p. 47; 18, p. 16).

The scientific understanding of religious experience is perhaps the most difficult. These moments of subjective spiritual experience demand complete involvement, and therefore are never directly communicated between subjects. Rather, the immediate religious experience usually becomes translated into common sense terms. But science, as a privileged mode of interpertation, recognizes and accounts for this process of "secondary revision" and is capable of an indirect understanding of religious symbols. Furthermore, this very rephrasing into common sense reveals to the scientific mind the relevance of religion to social action.

In *Islam Observed* (17), it is this scientific phenomenology of culture which Geertz applies to the analysis of the diverse cultural expressions of Islam in Morocco and Indonesia. Geertz examines the interrelationship of sacred symbols with world view, ethos, faith, common sense, and social context which constitutes the total religious experience. The precise contents of the religious system and the social order vary through time and from culture to culture. In this study, the detailed and intricate variations in the meaning of the religious experience result from both the pressure of history and the already-given distinctions in cultural or social traditions. However, the complex diversity of meaning which emerges from the comparision of Indonesian and Moroccan Islam is always intended to reveal similarities at a higher analytic level which embrace the diverse processes of formation and transformation of cultural expressions or styles of a core tradition.

The first factor of variation is simply the accidental sequence of historical events. In Morocco, Islam was introduced as early as the seventh century by Arabic warriors who espoused the loosely defined concepts of a newly established religious community. The Indonesians, however, received a far more developed and well-ordered Islamic doctrine from traders who arrived in the fourteenth century. During these initial periods when Islam first put its roots into foreign lands, certain conditions in each society set the limits within which Islamic meaning might develop and change (17, p. 11). These constraints created the boundaries of possible variation which are the basis of the development of distinct "traditions" of meaning. Perhaps the most significant constraint in Geertz's analysis is the nature of the social order into which religious symbols and ideas must naturally fit in order to seem authentic (17, p. 20).

In the case of Morocco, the relevant social context consisted of an unstable pattern of settlement and continuous feuding. Religious symbols both defined and interpreted this social reality. In coincidence with a fragmented social structure, Moroccan Islam lacked a religious order or hierarchy which would determine who could and could not aspire to leadership and sainthood. Instead, personal charisma, which any man might possess regardless of social or religious status, became the sole criterion of authority and power. The symbol of authority, the saint, took on the image of the warrior zealously enforcing his own doctrine, continually striving to enhance his charisma by producing miracles, and demanding the blind obedience of as many followers as possible.

The Indonesian setting differed entirely. The population was quietly settled in towns or outlying agricultural villages, and their social relations were built upon a sense of order and cooperation. Their version of Islam involved a strict, hierarchical order of graded spirituality and corresponding rules determining who was to attain the highest stages. The saint became a symbol of self-contained order, inward reflection, and self-reform. His power lay not in the brute force of his authority but in the rewards of internal insight through years of meditation.

Geertz sees these saints as metaphors or cultural constructions in which society objectifies its values, norms, ideals, and notions defining significant actions. Each embraces and condenses thousands of meanings and is able to create a symbolic unity between otherwise discordant elements (14, pp. 58–59). Through the selection and comparison of these key synthesizing symbols, and through the investigation of particular historical and social dimensions of their expression, Geertz builds up the diverse patterns of existential meaning in these local *islams*. With precision, he locates the uniqueness which distinguishes one culture's experience of Islam from another's. While the saints of Morocco and the saints of Indonesia might play a similar role as condensing metaphors, their meanings will never be the same.

Despite his emphasis on the particularity and historicity of these religious experiences, Geertz continues to refer to them collectively as "Islamic" and to speak of "Islamic consciousness" and "Islamic reform." The unity which he thus imputes to the religious phenomena emerges as a consequence of his presupposed notions of human existence. For Geertz, human reality at its most fundamental level is unified. It involves the universal conditions of being. For all men, the lived-in world is an experienced world constituted through symbolically expressed meanings which are intersubjectively or socially shared. Geertz establishes not only the reality of shared experience but also the forms in which it is expressed. His work on Islam emphasizes the primacy of common sense, religion, and science. Although they vary according to the content of particular cultural expressions, the forms themselves and their interrelationships remain fixed and universal. The dynamics of these forms and the expression of their content yield the dimension of existence called history; and the continuity of meaning in time and space leads to the formation of historical traditions of meaning.

Thus all expressions of Islam find unity of meaning through two dimensions of these universal conditions: first as expressions of a particular form of experience, religion, with certain defined characteristics such as the integration of world view and ethos; and second as an historically continuous tradition of meaning in which the original expression and all those following it in time and space do not exist as complete distinct realities but as delicately related developments of an initial symbolic base linked by the social process of shared meaning. Islam is seen in terms of Wittgenstein's notion of family resemblances. Striking similarities seem to appear over many generations, yet a careful look shows that no one characteristic is held in common. Rather, features overlap and crisscross. There is less order than in a trend within a single tradition. Continuities arise in oblique connections and glancing contrasts (20). This unity of Islam established at the level of his philosophical premises allows Geertz to speak legitimately of an "Islamic" consciousness at the level of actual experience as well. Each individual experience contains the universal characteristics assigned to the religious form of experience and those particular shared meanings which recall an entire tradition of Islam.

It is this notion that the diverse expressions of Islam may be unified at the level of a universal meaning of human reality that links Geertz with otherwise opposed anthropological analyses. Crapanzano (8) in discussing the *Hamadsha* sect in Moroccan Islam addresses culture not as the intersubjective interpretation of experience but as the expression of a Freudian unconscious. From this psychological perspective all the consciously known and accepted meanings which make up culture become arbitrary and illusory. Their only reality lies in the fact that they repress and socially control the universal instincts and conflicts of the psyche. Therefore, Islam taken as a cultural and, in this case, religious expression constitutes an historical representation of these underlying tensions. At the level of conscious meaning, the diverse expressions of Islam are not considered as different cultural realities but as historically related ideologies or illusions built upon a single reality. This absolute truth which unifies all Islam, and all religion in general, lies in the unconscious and in the universal conditions of the human psyche.

Crapanzano's analysis focuses on a single Islamic order in Morocco, the *Hamadsha*. He intends to reveal how their expression of Islam is constructed in a way which resolves certain universal psychic conflicts manifest in the interrelationship of their social structure, values, and role expections. The followers of the *Hamadsha* consist mainly of Arabs. In their traditional family structure, males claim complete authority while women remain passive and submissive. However, the Arab father requests this same feminine submission from his sons, who wish to satisfy their father by complying with these demands and at the same time aspire to the ideal dominant behavior of the male. So the tension becomes apparent. A son is raised as a female and expected to behave as a male. If he realizes his male ideal, then he loses it by defying his father. In Crapanzano's view, these conflicts which arise from sexual instincts rooted in the Freudian psyche create the need for release achieved through the *Hamadsha's* religious expression.

Both legend and ritual are interpreted in order to uncover these hidden psychic meanings. The *Hamadsha* myths of the two dominant saints, *Sidi ᶜAli bin Ham-dūsh* and *Sidi Ahmed Dghughi* recreate the contradiction of dominance and submission, male and female. The saint's relationship mimics the bond between father and son. *Sidi Ali* takes an active, dominant role, while *Sidi Ahmed* affirms his manhood through passive submission to the orders of the other. The true meaning of rituals lies in the mediation of these conflicts. In the ritual of the *ḥadra*, the she-demon *ᶜAisha* functions as an externalized superego who enforces the position of the feminized male and at the same time reinforces his manhood. In this way she assists male participants in passing through the psychological trauma of the feminine role in order to recognize their ideal.

The above interpretations rest totally on two premises, one theoretical and the other ethnographic. First, Crapanzano assumes the Freudian hypothesis of the sexual tensions of the psyche. And secondly, he attributes a simplistic and clear-cut opposition of dominance and submission to the relationship between the Arab male and female which then confirms his theoretical position. Like Freud, Crapanzano forces extreme limitations on his material through seeking a single predetermined meaning. Because all consciously expressed cultural meanings are condemned as pure illusion, they must be reduced to the same underlying hidden reality. His Freudian assumptions restrict the universe of meaning to a limited and totally fixed vocabulary of symbols—the instincts—which determine the experience of all human beings regardless of their cultural background.

For this reason, Crapanzano's analysis never requires an interpretation of the many versions of the *Hamadsha* myths. He need examine only one, for all will ultimately reveal the same human truth. Yet these variations present significant questions. In one legend, *Sidi Ali* dies before *Sidi Ahmed* brings back the she-demon, and in another he dies after *Sidi Ahmed* returns. Such slight differences in the sequence of events may entail interpretations of the relationship of the saints or of the power of the she-demon which do not conform to the interpretation of reality given by Crapanzano.

However, from the perspective of the Freudian paradigm adopted by Crapanzano, these variations in cultural meaning add no new knowledge to the understanding of human experiences. Diverse cultural expressions do not distinguish different human realities, but merely provide an imaginary mode by which man escapes a single and universal reality: the unresolvable situation, the traumatic archaic experience where desires can neither be suppressed nor satisfied. So all apparently unique and diverse institutions, thoughts, and events merely repeat what man has always done before, and their variation through time or history is reduced to an endless sequence of recreations with no accidents and no surprises.

Reading Freud in this way gives the analyst the privileged power of seeing through illusion to a hidden reality. As Ricoeur puts it, "this can be understood as reduction pure and simple" (30, p. 192). However, Freud might be read in a different way—for instance, as Ricoeur reads him. Interpretation does not have to return to a single meaning. For if it is accepted that a symbol has one meaning, then all varying meanings at the level of consciousness are distortions hiding the real meaning which is *secret*, which cannot be grasped by those who actually live these meanings but only through the insight of the analyst. But if the symbol is left open, its real meaning is no longer a secret but an *enigma* to be restored by continual interpretation. Without these cultural interpretations the fixed content of the psyche is mute, and the symbolic relations are not yet in existence (29, pp. 91–98). Meaning then is not to be interpreted once, and correctly, but continually reinterpreted, as in Geertz's position, in order to reveal the significance of human life.

It is clear that Crapanzano's paradigm includes, beside the location of meaning in the primordial experience, definite assumptions about man, consciousness, and history. Man is imprisoned in a world which he did not create, and all his efforts to escape from it are doomed. In this view, history and change are mere illusions. Conscious meaning, or culture, which includes the religious expression of Islam, is a mechanism to cover and avoid the essential reality of the primordial experience (31, pp. 114–131).

This pessimistic view of life, history, and consciousness can be contrasted with the human reality addressed by Geertz. For Geertz, man's dialectical relation with the world transforms—through reflection and intention—the given, meaningless perceptions into a meaningfully lived human world. The mode of reflection and its intensity varies from the passive reflection on the socially given world to an active and critical reflection in which the world is not taken for granted but questioned, reinterpreted, and sometimes uprooted. But this critical and doubtful mood does not eliminate meaning or consciousness; rather, it expands both. There are no limits to man's abilities and creativity; progress itself is one of these meaningful concepts created by man in the course of his own history.

However, it is essential for man, in order to continue to produce meaning, to reflect upon his taken-for-granted reality, to modify it, transform it, and even deny it. In order to do this, he must view reality not as fixed and finished but as open to novel and new articulations. Social systems which hinder this openness will end in fossilizing man, history, and consciousness. Geertz alludes to the force of such restrictions when he describes stability in the Islamic societies which he studied: it will be a long time before someone in Morocco or Indonesia might declare that God is dead. In both societies, systems of meaning are socially and religiously imposed upon the members of the society to an extent which prohibits them from questioning or criticizing their reality.

Due to more frequent and more politically significant encounters with Western ideology and science, however, certain Islamic societies have begun to reflect criti- cally upon the religious assumptions at the base of their understanding of the world. The two monographs to be considered now both deal with the impact of social change on religious structure and with the changing shape of traditional society as a whole. Bujra's (7) contribution deals with the politics of social stratification in the southern Arabian town of Hureidah (in Hadramut). Gilsenan's (21) monograph investigates the formation of a mystical order and its relation to social and political change in twentieth century Egypt. Both analyze the response of religious systems to the dwindling of the social arrangements which once supported them. Although the ecology, social structure, and even the history of Islam in these two societies are different, both were characterized by well-defined, stable, and closed systems of traditional religious symbols and meanings which social upheaval now challenges.

In the case of Southern Arabia, it is the *Sadah*, or descendents of the Prophet Mohammed, who traditionally stand as the religious elite. The *Sadah* define themselves as a group according to their genealogical descent from the Prophet. Through claiming a necessary correspondence between religious knowledge and the concept of privileged descent, they possess the authority both to create the content of religious ideology and to enforce this ideology among the people.

According to the *Sadah*, descent from the Prophet passes on to them a superior knowledge with which they create the content of a system of religious symbols. They believe that their Islam is not a mere interpretation of the *Quran* or sacred tradition of the Prophet but rather that it is the real Islam inherited from their ancestor, Muhammed. They claim to be not only the mediators between man and God but the direct representation of God's reality on earth, restoring order to the world and defining the meaning of both nature and ordinary man according to the Word of God. Access to this knowledge is further controlled in a closed system of religious education. Although theoretically such training is open to all social groups by tradition, it is available only to the *Sadah* or to those whom they consider capable of religious knowledge, the *Mashaikh*.

The *Sadah* then enforce their own dominating position and perpetuate the religious ideology which they have constructed by means of certain social and political controls over the other groups within their society, and they legitimize these powers in terms of religious authority. They arbitrate continuous tribal feuds and establish sanctuary towns in which tribes may meet peacefully. In this way they also protect the rest of the population—the peasants and artisans known as *Masakin* (the poor) and *Du'fa* (the weak)—from the tribesmen's attacks. Although the *Sadah* are a unified group by virtue of the sacred symbol of descent, they have dispersed and settled over a large area in order to set up an extensive network of political relations with the many different tribes and segments of the *Masakin* stratum. They further infiltrate and control the other social groups through religious justification of the *Kafa'ah* marriage system which allows marriage only within the same social group or with women of a lower social stratum, in which case the children take the status of their father. No woman, however, may marry into a lower social group and diminish the social status of her children. By following this system, the *Sadah* create the delicate balance of being able to establish the controls of kinship within all social groups of lower birth and yet maintain their own higher status by claiming the children from such marriages as their own. By means of these controls based ultimately on religious ideology, the *Sadah* accumulated political power, social prestige, and economic superiority.

In a society constructed in this fashion, social change is completely curbed by the religious elite. If mobility is possible at all, it is downward and not upward (7, p.112). Bujra finds only two courses of potential change within this framework: first, the migration of the lower status groups to areas with a different social system and associated opportunities, and secondly, political intervention. Neither has totally erased the pre-established hierarchy, however; migrants often arrive in towns where the *Sadah* also settle and maintain economic advantages due to reputation. And although the British occupation disarmed and pacified the tribesmen, thus depriving the *Sadah* of a source of political power, the *Sadah* still dominate economic relations. Bujra assumes that real change will come only when this economic infrastructure is transformed by whatever means possible.

In his study, Bujra understands Islam as a set of ideas created by an elite and accepted by the masses, which enables its producers to enforce and manipulate social, economic, and political hierarchies. Islam is thus reduced to an instrumental ideology. According to his own understanding, Bujra interprets religious symbols as conscious means of achieving political and economic goals. The masses' reverence of the *Sadah* becomes a sign of submission which perpetuates the superior position of the *Sadah*. And the *Kafa'ah* marriage rules are understood only as a mechanism which allows the *Sadah* to marry into all groups and prohibits other groups from exercising the same right. Bujra, like Crapanzano, closes the system of meaning and interpretation. Crapanzano uses the idiom of the unconscious; Bujra uses the idiom of politics and domination. Bujra, who questions the significance of religious phenomena in the creation of a meaningful world in favor of a social and economic explanation of changing historical conditions, ends by interpreting the position of the *Sadah* and the meaning of their religious symbols within an analytic frame of reference which is imposed upon their cultural system rather than cast in the system's own terms.

To some extent, Gilsenan's analysis (21) of an expression of Islam in a changing society avoids this problem. He studies the emergence of a saint and his vision of God and human existence during a period of social upheaval in Egypt. He defines the saint as a charismatic leader, who, as Weber would have it, has a unique and personal power to shape the meaning of existence during a time of social crisis and to convince a group of people to commit themselves to his vision. Weber emphasizes, although Gilsenan does not, the revolutionary nature of the charismatic leadership and belief which "revolutionizes men 'from within' and shapes material and social conditions according to its revolutionary will" (40, p. 1116). Charisma starts as a conflict with the rational-legal norms: "Hence, its attitude is revolutionary and transvalues everything: it makes a sovereign break with the traditional or rational norms: 'It has been written, but I say unto you'" (40, p. 1115). The system of meaning which the charismatic leader creates must be clothed in novel, personal, and emotional insights which continuously capture the imagination of the believers and convince them to follow him without question. The essence of charisma arises in its spontaneity and dies as soon as it becomes routinized and depersonalized. Therefore, in its pure form, charisma opposes bureaucracy which represents formal, impersonal, and fixed systems of rules and meanings.

Gilsenan's analysis of the saint as a charismatic leader is more in line with the interpretation of Weber associated with Edward Shils, who emphasizes the extraordinary quality of charisma but then links it with established orders of society (4, pp.

570–614). The saint described by Gilsenan did not contest the existing social order. Instead, he appears to be a leader with a personal vision, arising at a time of crisis, and trying to establish a mystical order according to the organizational requirements created by the government. He intended social readjustment rather than revolution.

In Egypt, at the time of the appearance of the Saint *Sidi Salama ar-Radi* (1867–1927), the British occupation and the influence of technological and economic success in Western societies disrupted traditional values, social structure, and religious order, particularly the significance of mystical orders shattered in the face of the rising importance of secular means of achievement. The ᶜ*Ulama,* the religious elite whose authority rested upon legalistic and formal theological interpretations of the *Quran*, joined with the government in an effort to revive the image of Islam by purifying its concepts and formalizing its structure. Therefore, by official decision in 1903, the mystical orders were organized as a bureaucratic system. However, in spite of this, their inherently fluid notions of affiliation allowed continuous changes in membership and segmentation of the orders themselves. The political disfavor which this incurred, combined with competition from secular education, political parties, and social clubs, brought the entire rationale of mystical orders and knowledge into question.

The Saint *Sidi Salama ar-Radi* intended to reestablish the preeminence of mysticism through the creation of a new order which would satisfy the needs of the rising middle class and offer the working class a personal expression of religion. He possessed the traditional mystic criterion of leadership: he received the teachings of an already established line of religious leaders, and claimed the gift of supernatural power of God. In this sense, the Egyptian saint strikes a compromise between the miraculous charisma which Geertz finds in Morocco and the genealogically based charisma of the *Sadah.* His power is determined both by revelation and by a sacred lineage of teachers. Yet in this period of rapid modernization, the legitimization of sainthood also required formal theological knowledge. Although in the past mysticism was ambivalent concerning the worth of studying theology, it now claimed to include it. Thus, *Sidi Salama ar-Radi* incorporated miraculously the currently valued tenets of formal theology into a mystical tradition in which knowledge comes directly from God.

The order he established, the *Hamidiya Shadhiliya,* was based upon a corpus of laws which he decreed in order to define a strict hierarchy of roles and functions. Each member was responsible to the saint or to his representative. The actions of the members had to be watched carefully, and the branches of the order were to be inspected from time to time to secure their obedience of the laws. A sacred oath, the ᶜ*Ahd,* that enforced an irrevocable and life-long commitment to the order was required. A structure of the saint's religious innovations then fell directly into the existing pattern of the formal bureaucratic rigidity that mysticism claimed to challenge.

Perhaps the most puzzling aspect of Gilsenan's analysis is the use of the framework of charisma to elucidate the sociological power of this saint. If the investigation is pursued, the mystic appears to lack the requirements of the concept. First, the saint was originally a member of the *Qawigjiya-Shadhiliya* order, and from that group he drew the followers who constituted the core of his new order (27). Therefore, he did not found the order through the power of his personal charisma, but through systematic recruitment from members of a group already socially and politically predisposed to commitment. Secondly, the history of the *Shadhiliya* order in Egypt reveals a traditional compatibility between theological concepts and mystical knowledge (33, pp. 162–190). *Sidi Salama's* efforts to integrate theological formulations with mysticism were more a rephrasing of the content of an established pattern rather than a personal and revolutionary synthesis in line with Weber's definition of the charismatic leader.

And finally, the bureaucratic structure of the new order directly contradicts the nature of change which occurs through charisma. The saint, through his laws and through the sacred oath, abolished the vital process of continual reinterpretation that characterizes a charismatic message. Even Gilsenan admits that according to sociological criteria, the charisma of the saint failed to capture the nature, direction, and intensity of change in the social and political life of Egypt at that time. Instead his visions and organizations portrayed a static world which conformed to the traditional concept of formally structured religion.

Now the question of the proper role of religion in social processes arises. Unlike Bujra, who reduces religion and Islam to a political ideology which is used to manipulate a socioeconomic base, Gilsenan explores the power of religious meaning, through charisma, to create and define the nature and historical sense of social life. In this way, he brings out the cultural significance of religion which Geertz also has emphasized. Yet, as in Bujra's analysis, religion at base remains an ideological system designed to cover and justify a social reality. For Bujra, religion manipulates a social world; for Gilsenan, it merely defines and orders it. In the end, the role of the charismatic saint and of religion in general was to satisfy certain social and political conditions. The degree to which these demands were met determined the success of the saint and the legitimacy of the religious system. If religious means had failed to cope with changing social relations and attitudes, other institutions would have arisen as alternative solutions. So for both Bujra and Gilsenan the process of social change proceeds along a single path. And Islam constitutes a temporary ideological obstacle which will eventually be superseded by a more modern and rational form of society.

According to both Gilsenan and Bujra, religion constrains and stabilizes its social base. Islamic societies would have remained locked into a traditional form, determined by the rigidity of their religious world view, had it not been for the external forces of change arising through contact with the West. And even at that, the expressions of Islam in both Southern Arabia and in Egypt perpetrated their significance either by completely resisting change in other dimensions of society, as in the instance of the *Sadah*, or by readjustment to new social and political conditions with the foundation of a bureaucratic mystic order. In neither case did religion itself become an innovative force.

It is Eickelman's contribution to contest this notion of religion's inherently static form (9). He makes history the dominant theoretical perspective which views social reality and all cultural or symbolic systems, including religion, as in a continuous state of change. He criticizes other models of change as mere comparisions of two static states, the before and the after, without accounting for the social processes which make the transition possible. Certainly Gilsenan and Bujra fall into this category. They compare traditional and stable Islamic societies with new social forms conceived as the aftereffects of Western influence. Yet they ignore the immanent dialectic within each society which constitutes the basis of that change.

In order to reveal the complexity of these processes, Eickelman insists that social reality must be analyzed in both its synchronic and diachronic dimensions. A diachronic view of society over time preserves a sense of the uniqueness and particularity of its characteristics; a synchronic study uncovers the interrelationships among its elements that hold at one point in time but which, by virtue of a necessary incongruity between the symbolic and the social, inevitably lead to change. Thus these two points of view become complementary rather than contradictory as in many other anthropological approaches (32, pp. 153–164). In this respect, Eickelman claims to follow in the footsteps of Max Weber. He tries to refute those who find a basic conflict between Weber's sociological and historical analyses (3, pp. 518–528).

In Weber's own work, the immediately given reality is an essentially undefined, chaotic, and irrational stream of experience (6, pp. 77–93). Man selects and imposes meaning on certain aspects of life which then constitute his actual historical and social world. The range of possible meanings which he may choose to impose remains inexhaustible. Therefore, the creation of historical relevancies is also unlimited and "in flux, ever subject to change in the dimly seen future of human culture" (39, p. 111). In order to grasp and organize the concrete social and historical phenomena defined by the subjective meanings held by the actors themselves, the sociologist uses the concept of the ideal type which simplifies the complexity of the historical data by typification of subjective meaning. The ideal type itself is formed by the selection and exaggeration of one or several viewpoints. It is a thought-picture designed by the analyst. "In its conceptual purity, this mental construct cannot be found empirically anywhere in reality. It is a utopia" (39, p. 90). History and sociology then are combined in the sense that phenomena which conceptually change through time, or diachronically, are the source of the synchronic idealization of sociological understanding.

Eickelman's analysis of Maraboutism in Morocco reinterprets rather than reproduces these Weberian concepts. If he were to build his model on perpetual change in the strict Weberian sense, then the meanings, interests, and relevancies of the matter he studies must change. However, he states that "From an analysis of Maraboutism in its contemporary context and an attempt to comprehend the fundamental assumptions which Moroccans now make about social reality, one develops a sense of expectation of what is crucial and often absent in evidence concerning earlier periods" (9, p. 63). This implies the use of the present to reconstruct the past, which in turn suggests a continuity of values and interests which violate Weber's notion of historical change. Eickelman further remarks that after considerable immersion in the contemporary aspects of Maraboutism, "it became clear that something was missing, that what I saw were fragments of a pattern of beliefs, once solid, that was beginning to crumble" (9, p. 64). Again, a stable social and religious reality takes shape. Here the present is not conceived as a particular historical reality in its own right. Instead it is evaluated as incomplete against a reconstructed or presumed past totality.

Eickelman treats history as a real sequence of empirical events. He reconstructs historical facts according to documents, French travelogues, and observations of the present. These events are linked by an inherent continuum of meaning, values, and interests which reach from some point in the past into the present. This extension of historical meaning implies stability rather than change. The Moroccan cultural systems are not open to continual and unlimited variation but constrained by boundaries inherent in the notion of historical continuity.

If change takes place, it is within this bounded reality. For Eickelman the force of change in any society lies in the lack of fit between social conduct and symbolic systems which express the culturally defined universe of meaning. He feels that a tendency exists in anthropological analyses to place these two dimensions in perfect correspondence. Either the social structure is considered the essentially stable domain and the symbolic system becomes its reflection, or vice versa. In these cases, the problem of historical change is avoided. However, an interaction occurs between these two systems which indicates that they remain distinct and out of balance. This asymmetric relationship can be seen when the individual, Eickelman's basic unit of analysis, manipulates symbols in order to realize his social goals and interests, justify or acquire a social position, or accumulate power. Eickelman refers to the means of manipulation as ideologies which mediate the opposition of the symbolic and the social. Ideologies themselves must be conceived as social activities maintained through various forms of expression, including ritual action. In the process of expression and manipulation, ideologies change over time. In turn, they reshape and redefine the social order. Yet because ideology continually varies according to its historical moment of use, a social structure can never be in complete coincidence with its ideological counterpart.

All expressions of religion—in this case Islam—are dealt with in terms of the notion of "ideology" defined as an essentially instrumental and pragmatic function. Religious ideology works at two social levels: the explicit ideology articulated by intellectuals and the religious elite, and implicit ideology which consists of local and popular interpretations of religious tradition. Although they do share certain elements in common, these two dimensions continually come into conflict. With respect to a particular version of Moroccan Islam, Maraboutism, the local interpretations that Eickelman investigates are the outcome of a world view resting on five key concepts: God's will, reason, propriety, obligation, and compulsion. Although these concepts are not related to each other in any permanent pattern, they all serve to render social action both meaningful and coherent. For instance, God's will is considered to be the cause of all that happens in the world. Men of reason must continually modify their own course of action to accomodate that will (9, p. 126) in order to maximize their chances of worldly success. Those who are closer to God, as the Marabouts who are saints, will be able to decipher the acts of God and claim a privileged access to this knowledge. Therefore, "closeness" to a saint becomes the ideology used by the people to realize and justify any form of social gain.

The saint, at least for those who follow him, defines the initially unordered stream of reality by imposing meaning and coherence on the lived world. The vision of the world which he perpetuates is one of a fixed and universal reality where "everything is written from the eternity." Change becomes an illusion for the Marabout. Within this system, a player may gain or lose, reach the status of saint or be disgraced as a sinner. But in spite of these possibilities, he must remain within a total framework of the universe which he cannot change.

In order to analyze this religious ideology, Eickelman has placed it within the explanatory framework of history. However, on two accounts the very content of his study raises certain questions concerning the nature of this theoretical perspective. First, although history, and consequently all religion and Islam, are said to involve continual change, their study is based upon assumptions which claim to be universal and invariable; the fact of history itself does not change. And while the content of actual religious symbols may vary, religion is always defined as an ideology and ideology is defined as instrumental. The significance of all cultural expressions of Islam can then be interpreted in terms of these premises. It appears that in order to analyze change, the concept of change itself must be fossilized by presuppositions which define its nature and subject matter in order to make the recognition and description of any significant historical moment possible. Religion as an ideology of God's will as understood by the Moroccans dissolves history with the premise of eternity. The opposite notion, the validity of history, for Eickelman is perhaps ideology as well. A certain paradox then emerges. The study of religion as ideology must be conducted from another ideological position (24, pp. 287–99).

Not only Eickelman's work but all anthropological monographs reviewed here begin from certain fundamental, theoretical premises concerning the nature of human reality, conscious or unconscious experience, history, and religion. Each set of interdependent assumptions implies a corresponding mode of interpretation which will reveal the real meaning of the diverse cultural expressions of Islam. Yet in spite of their differences, all positions approach Islam as an isolable and bounded domain of meaningful phenomena inherently distinct both from other cultural forms such as social relations or economic systems and from other religions. Within the domain of Islam, they also construct an internal dichotomy between local or folk Islam and the Islam of the elite, or *Ulama*. However, the criteria of distinction differ in order to serve each view of reality, history, and meaning.

For Geertz, different societies transform Islam to fit their own unique historical experience, and therefore at the local level there exist as many meanings and expressions of Islam as historical contexts. However, the elite, the *Ulama,* separate themselves from the local interpretations or the specifications of particular historical embodiments of Islam. They reflect upon the sacred tradition with its unique experience in order to grasp the eternal essence of Islam. Yet their superior position, by definition one of separation from popular knowledge, makes it impossible for them to relate this universalism to the level of common experience. The Islam of the

Ulama is highly abstract, formal, and legalistic. Theology in this sense is more reflective than popular systems of religious meaning. At the same time it is less ritualistic and less bound to common sense experience and social action.

The mode of expression differs as well. Most folk interpretations of Islam dwell upon the meaning of natural phenomena conceived as the reflection of God and the authority of the saints. The power of these religious elements does not reside in their physical manifestation. The saint, for instance, is not the white-washed shrine or the person buried inside, but the system of meanings which differs from one society to another according to historical tradition and current circumstances. The theological versions deny the authority of these symbols. Their notion of Islam centers upon the reading of the *Quran* and the prophetic traditions which yield meanings intended to transcend any particular cultural idiom. Formal religious education becomes a process of repetition in which meanings are already defined and stabilized in the pretense of universality (23). These unchanging formulations of the essence of Islam and the folk concepts which change continually according to social usage in any particular circumstance exist simultaneously in all Islamic societies.

The anthropologist taking a phenomenological approach focuses on the daily lived experience of the local Islams and leaves the study of theological interpretation to the Islamists. Therefore, he faces the problem of grasping meanings which are fluid and indeterminant. He must stabilize these meanings in order to understand them and communicate them to others. Symbols then become finite and well-bounded containers of thought, and at the moment of analysis the continuous production of meaning is stopped. Meaning becomes static through its objectification in the symbol (38, pp. 267–85). In order to isolate these objectifications of subjective meaning, the analyst must regard the symbol itself as an objective reality which he can describe without the influence of his own symbolic patterns. Science then requires a disinterest and detachment, a certain neutrality common to the scientific community. Although the scientist's understanding is still a mode of interpretation which can only guess at the meaning of another's experience rather than enter it directly, it retains its superior validity by recognizing the process and structure of interpretation itself.

This notion of science contains certain internal contradictions. Science is considered a mode of interpretation and reflection on experience just as any other cultural form; therefore, the suspension of cultural attitudes can never be complete—the criteria of true objectivity must be a higher cultural form of experience. Furthermore, in the scientific process of reflection, not only experience but the conscious subjects as well must become objects of reflection. In this way the very creators of symbols under study become passive carriers of meaning, while the scientific and supposedly disinterested consciousness takes over the active role.

The phenomenological position implies a certain hierarchy of experience based on the degree and intensity of different forms of reflection. The greater the reflection on experience, the greater the order in the systems of meaning. And objective understanding lies in the recognition of the order of the complexity of meaning. The local *islams* involve accepted, taken-for-granted experiences, and little directed reflectivity. Theological Islam entails more reflectivity and a more ordered system of meanings. Finally, history, because it specifically requires reflection on the past, and science, in this case anthropological reflection on human experience, become the privileged mode of understanding due to their awareness of the nature of the processes of human experience. Yet within the total hierarchy, both theology and anthropology claim a higher degree of reflection than folk expressions of Islam. Therefore, they both regard these expressions as less ordered, less objective, and somehow less complete versions of the religious experience. Each, however, looks upon this diversity of experience in different ways. Theologians condemn it in order to enforce their view of the eternal meaning of Islam; anthropologists regard the various expressions as diluted forms, distorted by magic and superstition, and thus indirectly imply the existence of a pure and well-defined essence of Islam. Crapanzano, however, finds a different reality at the core of Islam. Instead of defining religious expression as an experiential form, he reduces it to the internal dynamics of the Freudian psyche. All religions, and thus all *islams,* become symbolic devices for the sublimation and expression of instinctual conflicts. Within this framework, both the Islam of the elite and the Islam of the folk serve the same existential function. However, the Islam of the *Ulama* provides the incontestable and formal explications, the norms of religious meaning, while folk expressions such as the *Hamadsha* act as particular therapeutic versions of real Islam which must disguise and legitimate their deviations from the "norm" by expressing certain elements of mythology and ritual in terms of formal Islam.

Therefore, the distinction between these two dimensions of Islam is based on the content of their expressions. Yet if both contents ultimately play the same role with regard to the reality of unconscious conflicts, if both attempt to normalize and socialize an otherwise neurotic tendency, then what exactly are the criteria used to distinguish the normal from abnormal or deviant content? According to Crapanzano's own premises, the content of both forms of Islam should be considered normal sublimations of abnormal tensions. This leads to the question of why the particularity of the *Hamadsha* order must be analyzed as "deviance." Crapanzano might have viewed the religious experience as a set of relations between the natural necessities imposed on man, his conflicting instincts, and the ideals developed on the superego. The uniqueness of any expression would be the result of the particular synthesis of these elements. But Crapanzano limits the real meaning of Islam both by reducing the function of religion to mediate conflicts of the unconscious psyche and by delineating an absolute standard of normal Islam. Indirectly, he rigidifies not only Islam, but the culture in which it exists and the symbols which express it. Moroccan society is portrayed in this paradigm as static and uninventive, constrained within a predetermined universe of meaning.

Like Crapanzano, Bujra regards the institutional expression of religious meaning as ideological illusion. The cause of its existence lies not in the tensions inherent in the human psyche but in conflicts rooted in the economic structure of society which embodies all essential human needs and values. Religion functions as the conscious reflection of social tension which results from material inequality and oppression. In the conservative and hierarchical society of Southern Arabia, the accepted form of Islam rationalizes and perpetuates the economic and political authority of the

Sadah. Here it is an ideology of domination. So religious meaning is not an experiential form as for Geertz, or a mask of the Freudian psyche, but the mode of legitimization of an existing social structure. Religious symbols are social signs which may be manipulated for purposes of power and therefore directly expressed in actual behavior. They are produced by the *Sadah* but passively taken for granted by the rest of the population who must accept the religious along with other forms of social control.

The distinction between elite and local Islam which must correspond with the notion of the meaning of religion takes a new turn. For Bujra, the elite version of the *Ulama* or *Sadah* does not constitute a privileged form of religious awareness as it does for Geertz, who insists that it is more reflective, or for Crapanzano, who refers to it as more "normal" than the local *islams*. Rather, he views the *Ulama's* Islam as merely another distorted ideology designed for the purposes of the manipulation of secular, social power, as are all other local expressions of Islam such as that of the *Sadah*. Both local and elite *islams* are compared to an ideal Islam which expresses the true and eternal principles of God found in the *Quran* and in the tradition of the Prophet which establish the reality of human freedom, equality, and justice. The problem becomes the recognition and actualization of this ideal Islam. Bujra optimistically predicts that the conflicts apparent in the current social order signal the inevitability of struggle and change towards this goal. Yet only the reorganization of the economic base will allow the complete overthrow of false ideology and realization of true Islam.

Gilsenan, in his analysis, reveals a distinction between elite and local Islam based not on opposition and domination, as in Bujra's definition of the role of the *Sadah*, but on complementarity. The formal and systematized laws of the *Ulama* differed in both content and style from the more mystical interpretation of the people. Yet both were traditionally opposed to the overriding authority of the ruling class. While the *Ulama* were considered a social minority with little claim to actual political power, the mystic orders (because they defined the popular notions and values of Islam) were capable of organizing a mass rebellion in response to any governmental threat. So in order to buttress their social power, the *Ulama* allied with the mystics. Even if these two approaches to Islam did not directly support each other's system of beliefs, they at least became noncontradictory. Both forms of Islam defined for society a stable and eternal vision of the world according to the all-pervasive order and meaning of God's will.

The breakdown of these two systems of belief came with the influence of Western technology, ideas, and values. The consequent drive for modernization allowed a situation in which the structure of secular bureaucracy, now considered to be the truly rational social order, challenged the traditional order built upon notions of a hierarchy designed by God which was inherent in all societies. Due to its own principles of formal and rigid order, the *Ulama* adjusted easily to the incoming social bureaucracy. However, they claimed the authority to redefine the spiritual premises on which that rational bureaucratic logic was based. Thus formal Islam is consonant with the new social order.

Along with the bureaucratic trend of modernization, the influence of other new systems of social relevance such as trade unions, political parties, and secular education caused the mystical orders, as well as the *Ulama*, to reevaluate their own concepts of meaning and order. The saint who was the center of Gilsenan's analysis attempted to show both the *Ulama* and secular forces that these rational principles could be gained only through mystical experience. Yet his own solution, to formalize and bureaucratize the mystical order, contradicted his intention to reinstate the authority of the immediate spiritual encounter. According to Gilsenan's own criteria, the saint is considered a failure. He could not adjust the preexisting structure of mysticism to the changing social order. For Gilsenan, religion is idle; it does not define true reality, but functions instead to support the pregiven reality of the social order. Both the elite and local version of Islam are ideologies, not of an ideal Islam as in Bujra's case, but of the rational order of secular society. Therefore, there exist two systems of meaning, the religious system and social reality. If the two systems correspond, the society remains stable; if they do not, the ideological system of religion yields to fundamental social conditions. The conflict is essential for it constitutes society's drive to modernize itself. It leads to the creation of historical consciousness, rationality, and individualism. From this perspective, the rational order of modern bureaucracy, competition, and secular life will eventually destroy and leave behind those other systems of meaning which cannot adjust to it. If in traditional society Islam defines the meaning and order of social reality, in modern society, the actual empirical conditions of social life determine the meaning of Islam.

This relation between Islam and social change forms the core of Eickelman's study of Maraboutism. He too distinguishes the elite Islam from its local expressions according to his own notion of the formation of ideological systems. In contrast to Gilsenan, Eickelman believes that any social structure, even in so-called "traditional" and conservative ones, never remains stationary but changes at each moment. This change results from the lack of fit between social conduct and symbolic systems. Their dialectical interaction produces ideological systems as a means of social manipulation manifest in actual social activities defined by specific historical contexts. In this framework, the Islam of the *Ulama* is considered an "explicit" ideology transcending the influence of culturally relative values and beliefs and therefore may legitimately be referred to as "religion." Local versions of Islam, however, are understood as "implicit" ideologies as they adhere to and are intertwined with common sense notions, the untutored and accepted assumptions concerning the nature of reality specific to each social group. These interpretations then vary according to cultural background and historical moment. Systems of religious meaning thus retain their social and historical particularity. Because they never rise to a level of cross-cultural application, like the Islam of the elite which gives them the status of true ideology, local Islam is always a very culturally specific set of beliefs, rather than a fixed and wholly coherent institutionalized religion.

Both forms of Islam coexist in a state of tension. The elite continually contest the local traditions of Islam. People acknowledge the general concepts dictated by the *Ulama*, but they choose to live according to more particularistic notions of Islam, which conform with the patterns of their daily experience.

This particular anthropological distinction appears to reinforce the *Ulama*'s claim to a superior religious position by treating the elite version as "religion," and reducing other interpretations to implicit ideology. These distinctions between elite and popular Islam are obviously derived from the fundamental assumptions defining each anthropological paradigm. Although all positions argue the objectivity and universality of their own premises, the mere fact of a multiplicity of possible meanings at the fundamental level of the nature of Man, God, and the World challenges the notion of a single, absolute reality. Rather than being accepted as given truths, these anthropological premises might be treated as anthropologists themselves treat the tenets of Islam: as diverse, culturally relative expressions of a tradition—in this case, a "scientific" one. If versions of Islam must be called ideology, then perhaps these various anthropologies demand the same understanding (11, pp. 183–206). It is hardly a new insight that scholars' own cultural ideas and values have molded the analysis of Islam. Even Weber, as Bryan Turner (35, p. 34) suggests, made "all the usual nineteenth century references to Mohammed's sexuality as an important factor in the shaping of the *Quran* and Muslim-teaching of family and marriage."

Recognition of the imposition of premises alien to the subject matter itself involves a reevaluation of the authority of scientific understanding. From this perspective, changes in the definition of the function or essence of Islam do not result from the accumulation of knowledge, but from the changing attitudes to religion in the West (37). The notion of the "disinterested observer" is, in fact, impregnated with the values of a scientific community. The self-declared superiority of such communities and their isolation from the common sense world promotes the development of a common reality, language, and system of values and interests labeled "scientific" and "objective." The criteria of certain knowledge pertinent to this shared vision of the world delineate and define the theoretical approach and subject matter of studies (12, pp. 18–19).

In terms of this supposedly scientific distinction between folk and elite Islam, anthropology studies the former, yet its principles of analysis resemble the latter.

Like science, theological positions which are referred to as elite Islam, regardless of how anthropologists define them in their different paradigms, assume the same detached attitude. In both science and theology, understanding the real meaning of religious phenomena comes only through a presumed separation from common subjective assumptions and from immediate involvement with the object of study. Both positions agree on the existence of a "folk" Islam as opposed to a formal Islam which, in order to be known, demands a greater degree of reflection and systematization of principles than found in popular expressions of belief. Anthropology and theology differ merely in the particular aspects of these local interepretations selected for analysis.

However, the authority claimed by theological Islam is contested by the recognition that in any given cultural system, a folk theology may be found which rivals formal theology in its degree of abstraction, systematization, and cosmological implication. It is even possible to argue that this folk Islam constitutes the real Islam and that the traditions of the *Ulama* developed historically out of already established principles of the nature of spiritual reality entwined with the life of the Islamic community (10). In fact, these opposing theologies are complementary. Because each form both defines and necessitates the other, the problem of determining a real as opposed to an ideological Islam becomes an illusion.

On the most general level of abstraction, folk theology involves reflection on principles of ultimate reality, nature, God, man, and history which are formally expressed in traditional literature, folk tales, heroic stories, proverbs, and poetry. For instance, in the tale of *Seif bin dhi Yazan,* the reality of the world according to Islamic principles and the existence of the Prophet was known before the actual historical birth of Mohammed and his articulation of that doctrine. Therefore, in the folk conception, counter to the view of historians and Islamicists, direct reflection upon the order of the world, rather than the actual statements of the Prophet and *Quran,* leads the mind to the origin of that order.

The order of both the natural and human world rests upon a hierarchical principle which arranges each thing or person continually in an ascending order: fire to water; the segments of a tribe, to the tribal section, to the tribe as a whole. *Ibn Khaldun,* better known in the West than any of the numerous folk writers on genealogy, pharmacology, folk tales, myths, etc, elegantly describes this cosmological progression: "Each one of the elements is prepared to be transformed into the next higher or lower one, and sometimes is transformed. The higher one is always lower than the one preceding it" (23, p. 194). At the end this order arrives at the World of Spirituality which both creates and maintains these connections. Arabic, the sacred language taught to Adam by God, expresses this eternal structure and all names reveal the original nature of things, *tabi'a* or *fitra.* The entire world becomes an open text where God reveals his language and his will. The *Quran* too is read and interpreted within this paradigm.

Ideally, the human mind must submit itself to this natural logic. However, because man deviates from this density by imposing false and alien concepts upon the world, mind and nature are not initially in correspondence. The role of the Prophet and the saints is to bring these two dimensions together (22, pp. 6–15). Yet this tension persists and manifests itself in the events of human existence called history. In this sense, the study of history becomes a moral science in which explication of the ethical meaning of the world points out the mistakes and achievements of man in relation to the ideal of perfect existence. History shows that although Adam attained complete knowledge, the passage of time brought about the misinterpretation and degeneration of his heritage. Mohammed and the first Islamic community which he established regained all that the descendents of Adam had lost. Now man must continually attempt to re-enact this fixed moment in time. So history in this paradigm never refers to the everchanging creation of new meanings of human life but to the struggle to recapture and immobilize an eternal experience.

While nature is continuous and ordered, history remains discontinuous and chaotic. In folk theology, the remembrance of the Prophet, the actions of the saints and all rituals attempt to transform the discontinuities of history into the natural order by processes of ritual repetition which stops the passage of time.

Historically, in the Western sense, an institutionalized form of theology developed in reaction to Greek philosophy and Aristotelian logic which challenged the notion of the complete omnipotence of God. Internal dialogues between the conflicting positions resulted also in the establishment of the actual discipline of theology which countered the principles of rationality with the ultimate authority of the *Quran* (36).

While in the folk tradition the order of nature and the *Quran* were regarded as metaphors, the strict and formal theological interpretation gave complete authority to the sacred book to define the order of the world (1, pp. 76–105).

This total focus on the sacred text led to the development of a strong formalism and traditionalism, a common language and the construction of a bounded universe of meaning (26). The *Quran* and prophetic tradition prescribed an absolute reality expressed in a privileged language in which true meaning exists. There arose an interpretive tradition for understanding the different usages of the terms of the *Quran* and the distinctions between clear and equivocal verses *(mutashabihat)*. This led to the development of the science of elucidation, *ilm al-Bayan*, designed to deal with the analysis of metaphor *(mjaz)* and metonymy *(kinaya)* as found in sacred texts (34, pp. 18–23). The construction of such devices is now thought to be governed simply by the relation of implication, whether the meaning of one word implies or is implied by another (28, pp. 184–98). These styles, used by God to express the final truth, allow the known to clarify and elucidate the unknown, and preserve both the known and unknown as real (2, pp. 251–412).

Therefore folk theology and formal theology developed from the same principle: that both nature and the *Quran* reflect the order and truth of God. Yet the two paradigms choose opposite priorities. While one locates meaning in nature and includes the *Quran* within that general order, the other finds truth first in the *Quran* and then extends that reality to the interpretation of the rest of nature. Their essential complementarity stems from a relation of mutual completion. Both seek to maintain the unity of God and the world, but both recognize processes which destroy that unity. Each position attempts to combat the other's point of dissolution. Formal theology begins from the unity of time and the word and combats the inevitable multiplicity of meaning in space—the fragmentation of local tradition (5, pp. 37–51). Folk theology begins from the acceptance of unity and order in space and combats the multiplicity of meaning created by the passage of time. Thus both attempt to contain the flux of experience: formal theology seeks to control space by fixing time, and the other to control time by fixing space.

In the end, there are no inherent differences in the content of either folk or formal theology to suggest that one is more objective, reflective, or systematic than the other. If Islamicists and theologians privilege the formal discipline, they do so only upon preconceived criteria of validity linked to their concept of truth. They claim an objectivity based upon systematic analysis of the *Quran* which is said to embody absolute truth. And they must therefore deny the legitimacy of an objectivity which bypasses the sacred text in favor of a direct insight into the order of the world. Actually, both forms of theology may be described as intricate systems of cosmological principles. They are complementary and equally "real." They differ only as modes of expression: one exists as an institution and the other as literature.

What unifies both expressions of theology with anthropology is the structure of their means of understanding Islam. All begin from positive assumptions concerning the nature of man, God, history, consciousness, and meaning. Their interpretations of the meaning of Islam depend themselves upon already presupposed and fixed meanings which determine the universality of Islam, define and limit properly "religious" and "Islamic" phenomena, and distinguish a folk from an elite, and a real from a false Islam. Only the specific content varies. Geertz begins from the reality of experience, Crapanzano from the psychic, Bujra and Gilsenan from the structure and function of social relations, Eickelman from a notion of history, and the theologies from God, nature, and the *Quran*.

Criteria of validity differ as well. The anthropological positions claim to be more objective than both the folk and the theological traditions. With respect to the folk expressions of Islam, they assume their scientific analyses to be more reflective and systematic. And although theology is recognized as highly reflective, it is not critical and therefore remains subordinate to the authority of anthropology which, being scientific, is critical as well. Anthropological analyses then establish their validity not only on the necessity of particular assumptions concerning the nature of reality but also on the epistemological criteria of scientific rationality. Theology, to the contrary, establishes truth on the incontestable basis of faith. So at the level of the content and form of knowledge, faith is opposed to science, theology and anthropology deny each other's capacity to grasp the final truth. Yet from the perspective of the structure of knowledge, their opposition is only apparent, for they both begin from and impose preconceived and positive meanings which necessarily frame their understanding of other experiences of Islam. Another form of contradiction emerges from this summary. All analyses are built upon the assumption of a single, absolute reality and seek to discover this reality in Islam. Yet when reviewed collectively, these studies reveal the incredible diversity of possible definitions and descriptions of Islam. This diversity is not due merely to differences in analytic perspective. Each paradigm, regardless of the nature of its premises, recognizes the uniqueness of religious expression at the level of the material it must analyze. Geertz works with different cultural and historical interpretations of experience; Crapanzano investigates the particularity of the *Hamadsha's* adjustment to their social relations; Bujra, Gilsenan and Eickelman deal with the inevitablity of historical change in the expression of Islam. And all approaches, including the theological, stress a distinction in the content of elite and folk Islam. Finally, the significance of the initial problem becomes clear. In the midst of this diversity of meaning, is there a single, real Islam?

Both the anthropological and theological approaches outlined here assume that there is a reality of Islam which may be derived from principles of an encompassing universal reality of the nature of man or God. The importance of diversity is then overriden at the level of both the religious and the total human experience which take on absolute, fixed, and positive meanings. Because they begin from such assumptions, actual interpretations of any particular cultural situation, symbol, or passage of the *Quran* will reflect pregiven meaning in two ways. First, although particular content may vary, it must always contain the characteristic of meaning specific to a form of experience. For Geertz the symbol of the saint in Morocco implies charisma and authority, while the Javanese is defined as meditative and withdrawn. However, according to his own paradigm, both symbols condense and synthesize world view and ethos. For Crapanzano, the different myths, legends, rituals, and orders of Islam all essentially serve to express psychobiological drives.

Therefore, the bounds and limits of such premises give each symbol, action or institution certain inherent and fixed characteristics. Further, even the culturally and historically relative dimensions of meaning which are said to change, change only in accordance with unchanging criteria of meaningfulness. For example, Eickelman is able to anticipate changes in ideological meaning only due to the continuous, perpetual state of imbalance in the relationship between the social and symbolic systems. So while diversity and fluidity of meaning are recognized at the level of actual cultural expression, synthesis is still the final purpose of analysis. When the essential and real principle governing this diversity is revealed, a web of frozen points of meaning is thrown over the subject's fluid meanings. It is impossible with such a rigid framework to suggest that each expression of Islam creates its own real world of meaning.

As the previously discussed positions would all agree, man does order his world through systems of meaning. Anthropologically, the problem now is to find a means of understanding that order which reaches the desired level of universality without diluting or destroying the significance of this diversity and the richness of meaning in human experience. The nature of the problem is exemplified in the various treatments of the Islamic saint. In the work considered here, the saint is alternatively viewed as a metaphor, a political man, an economic man, a survival, a fragment of ideology, or even an incoherence simply to be discarded. One thing emerges from the diversity of interpretation: each treated the saint as a thing and artificially added to it different dimensions of meaning which varied according to the investigator's interest. Each investigator selects from the multitude of possibly identifiable features and functions of the saint one or two which are deemed distinctive and which, in the subsequent analysis, are taken *as* the saint. Analysis based on such highly selective reading of ethnographic data artificially collapses the complexity of the "saint" to a single dimension, leaving unexplained many possible questions about the undeniable multiplicity of the cultural construct "saint."

Much of the behavior associated with the saint and his worshippers, along with the range of meaning signifiable through the saint, may appear to be spurious, idiosyncratic, and irrelevant. At the tomb of Egypt's most important saint, for example, Gilsenan observed what appeared to be wildly inappropriate behavior amongst the worshippers. Singing, dancing, shouting, joking, even cursing, accompanied the ritual of worship on the Saint's Day—behavior unexplainable either as piety of believers or as the intelligible actions of politically and/or economically rational actors. Indeed, the actions and modes described seem defiling in this religious context. It is not only in this Egyptian case where "defilement" makes an incongrous appearance. Westermarck observed an equally puzzling development in Morocco (41, pp. 177–78), where the tomb of the saint was periodically ritually smeared with blood, a consciously recognized mark of defilement. I observed similar procedures in Nubia and in the East African town of Lamu, where vistors to the saint's tomb smear the blood of sacrificed animals on the tomb walls. The analyst confronted with such material must either demonstrate its rational "fit" with what he has identified as the real significance of the saint, expand his definition of the "saint" to accomodate dimensions of meaning beyond simple political or economic manipulation or metaphoric condensation, or, as too often happens, he may find these data irrational and/or irrelevant accompaniments to the "essential" nature of the saint. It would seem most desirable to reexamine our original positive notion of "saint."

Elsewhere I have shown that the saint may be profitably viewed as a symbol, not in the sense of being a vehicle for meaning, but as a relational construct in which the dimension of purity/impurity, defilement and sacralization are articulated with a broad and variable range of content, including political, economic, and otherwise pragmatic aspects of life (10). The saint thus symbolically embodies fundamental properties of a system of classification in the matrix of which all institutions (politics, economics, etc) and institutionally related behavior (manipulation of power, disposition of resources, etc) are necessarily framed. The precise opposition embodied by the saint at this level may, of course, vary from place to place, just as the content apprehended therein varies. But it is only by going beyond institutions and functions, actors, and positive meanings to the relatively simpler complexity of categorical opposition that the richness of the saint or any other "religious symbol" emerges along with its position in the logic of culture.

The positions reviewed here all accept in some way the principle of objectivity based on a separation of realities in which the subject occupies the privileged position of being able to encompass within his consciousness the reality of the object. The object in each case is a thing or set of things whose order or ultimate meaning is to be discovered through techniques which identify systematic *connections* between *things*. The things may be symbols constructed as vehicles for otherwise disembodied but contained "meanings," institutions, domains, or any other entities whose existence as entities is unquestioned. That is, we have been treating analyses of Islam which accept as fundamental the existence of "Islam," "religion," "economy," "politics," and even "saints," whose relation to each other within a given culture may vary, but whose existential "truth" is not subject to question. The goal of such analysis then becomes one of finding the "essence" of things at hand and the kind of connection which seems best to explain how these things work in a "cultural system." The exact kind of relation (conceived as a connection) which emerges as dominant varies with the nature of things studied.

Thus for Geertz, symbols condense and convey meaning, while for Crapanzano they create and sustain an illusory relationship between history, culture, and the psyche. Bujra, Gilsenan, and Eickelman are concerned with demonstrating the role of "Islam" in directing the behaviorally realized interaction between political and economic institutions and in mediating the disjuncture between the reality of history and the deceit of ideology.

But what if each analysis of Islam treated here were to begin from the assumption that "Islam," "economy," "history," "religion" and so on do not exist as things or entities with meaning inherent in them, but rather as articulations of structural relations, and are the outcome of these relations and not simply a set of positive terms from which we start our studies? In this case, we have to start from the "native's" model of "Islam" and analyze the relations which produce its meaning. Beginning from this assumption, the system can be entered and explored in depth from any point, for there are no absolute discontinuities anywhere within it—there are no autonomous entities and each point within the system is ultimately accessible from every other point. In this view there can be no fixed and wholly isolable function of meaning attributed to any basic unit of analysis, be it symbol, institution, or process, which does not impose an artificial order on the system from outside. That is, the orders of the system and the nature of its entities are the same—the logic of the system is the content of the system in the sense that each term, each entity within the system, is the result of structural relations between others, and so on, neither beginning nor ending in any fixed, absolute point. The logic of such a system, the logic of culture, is immanent within the content and does not exist without it. But while the "content" might differ from one culture to another, the logic embedded in these various contents are the same. In this sense, both the anthropologist and the native share a logic which is beyond their conscious control. It is a logic which is embedded in both nature and culture, and which can be uncovered through the intricate analysis of content. Here the problem of objectivity which haunted all the studies discussed above disappears, and since it was a problem created by a notion of the transcendence of consciousness and subjectivity of the investigator, it will vanish as a phantom, leaving in its place a logic which is shared by both the subject and the object. Islam as an expression of this logic can exist only as a facet within a fluid yet coherent system; it cannot be viewed as an available entity for cultural systems to select and put to various uses. "Islam," without referring it to the facets of a system of which it is part, does not exist. Put another way, the utility of the concept "Islam" as a predefined religion with its supreme "truth" is extremely limited in anthropological analysis. Even the dichotomy of folk Islam/elite Islam is infertile and fruitless. As I have tried to show, the apparent dichotomy can be analytically reduced to the logic governing it.

The works we have discussed here seemed not to offer a means for uncovering the logic of culture or the principles which are immanent in culture and which order and articulate the thoughts and actions of culture bearers. In this sense we have not yet been led to the structure of "Islam," nor can we be, for it is a contradiction in terms to speak of the systemic "fit"—the structure—of an autonomous entity. The fact of structure can never be shown in an isolated state and is reached only by unfolding patterns of both actual and potential diversity of cultural content. In its totality, this variability reveals the absence of any positive, universal content. Working from this perspective, from which meaning is strictly relational, the analyst cannot select relevant material according to some standard of truth, but must consider systems in their entirety. In this way, the multiplicity of cultural meanings is explored and developed. There are no privileged expressions of truth. "Objectivity" must be bound to the shared structures of both the analyst and the subject regardless of the content of their respective cultural systems.

This logic of relations implies that neither Islam nor the notion of religion exists as a fixed and autonomous form referring to positive content which can be reduced to universal and unchanging characteristics. Religion becomes an arbitrary category which as a unified and bounded form has no necessary existence. "Islam" as an analytical category dissolves as well.

ACKNOWLEDGMENTS

I wish to thank Miss Sara Spang, who more than anyone else labored with the argument and style of this article. Charles Myers was also present throughout its preparation, and his suggestions were very valuable. My discussions with my wife concerning a religion in which we grew up were more enlightening than ever.

Literature Cited

1. Abu Zahra, M. 1970. *Usul al-Figh.* Cairo: Dar al-Fikr al Arabi. 415 pp.
2. Abu Zahra, M. 1970. *Al Quran, al-mujiza al Kubra.* Cairo: Dar al-Fikr al Arabi. 643 pp.
3. Bendix, R. 1945–1946. Max Weber's interpretation of conduct and history. *Am. J. Sociol.* 51:518–26
4. Bensman, J., Givant, M. 1975. Charisma and modernity: The use and abuse of a concept. *Social Res.* 42:570–614
5. Braune, W. 1971. Historical consciousness in Islam. In *Theology and Law in Islam,* ed. G. E. Von Grunebaum, pp. 37–51. Weisbaden: Harrassowitz. 105 pp.
6. Burger, T. 1976. *Max Weber's Theory of Concept Formation—History, Laws, and Ideal Types.* Durham: Duke Univ. Press. 231 pp.
7. Bujra, A. S. 1971. *The Politics of Stratification: A Study of Political Change in a South Arabian Town.* Oxford: Clarendon. 201 pp.
8. Crapanzano, V. 1973. *The Hamadsha: A Study in Moroccan Ethnopsychiatry.* Berkeley: Univ. California Press. 258 pp.
9. Eickelman, D. F. 1976. *Moroccan Islam.* Austin: Univ. Texas Press. 303 pp.
10. el-Zein, A. H. 1974. *The Sacred Meadows.* Evanston: Northwestern Univ. Press. 365 pp.
11. Fernea, R., Malarkey, J. 1975. Anthropology of the Middle East and North Africa: A critical assessment. *Ann. Rev. Anthropol.* 4:183–206
12. Feyerabend, P. 1975. *Against Method: Outline of an Anarchistic Theory of Knowledge.* London: NLB. 338 pp.
13. Geertz, C. 1957. Ethos, world view and the analysis of sacred symbols. *Antioch Rev.* 17:421–37
14. Geertz, C. 1964. Ideology as a cultural system. In *Ideology and Discontent,* ed. D. E. Apter, pp. 47–76. New York: Free Press. 342 pp.
15. Geertz, C. 1965. The impact of the concept of culture on the concept of man.
In *New Views of the Nature of Man,* ed. J. Platt, pp. 93–118. Chicago: Univ. Chicago Press
16. Geertz, C. 1966. Person, time and conduct in Bali: An essay in cultural analysis. Southeast Asian Stud., *Yale Univ. Cult. Rep. Ser. No. 14*
17. Geertz, C. 1968. *Islam Observed, Religious Development in Morocco and Indonesia.* New Haven: Yale Univ. Press. 136 pp.
18. Geertz, C. 1973. *The Interpretation of Cultures: Selected Essays,* pp. 3–30. New York: Basic Books. 470 pp.
19. Geertz, C. 1975. Common-sense as a cultural system. *Antioch Rev.* 33:5–26
20. Geertz, C. 1975. Mysteries of Islam. *NY Rev. Books* 22(20):18–26
21. Gilsenan, M. 1973. *Saint and Sufi in Modern Egypt: An Essay in the Sociology of Religion.* Oxford: Clarendon. 248 pp.
22. Hindam, A. A. 1939. *Hidayat al Qasideen.* Cairo: DAR al Anwar. 196 pp.
23. Ibn Khaldun 1967. *The Muqaddimah.* Transl. F. Rosenthal. Princeton Univ. Press. 2nd ed.
24. Lapidus, I. 1974. Notes and comments. *Hum. Islamica* 2:287–99
25. Levy, R. 1957. *The Social Structure of Islam.* Cambridge Univ. Press. 2nd ed.
26. Makdisi, G. 1971. Law and traditionalism in the institutions of learning in medieval Islam. In *Theology and Law in Islam,* ed. G. E. Von Grunebaum, pp. 75–88. Weisbaden: Harrassowitz
27. Mustafa, F. A. 1974. *The Social Structure of the Shadhilya Order in Egypt.* MA thesis. Univ. Alexandria, Egypt. 351 pp.
28. Nasif, M. 1965. *Nazariyat al Ma'na Fi al Naqd al Arabi.* Cairo: Dar al Qalam. 220 pp.
29. Ricoeur, P. 1970. *Freud and Philosophy: An Essay in Interpretation.* New Haven: Yale Univ. Press
30. Ricoeur, P. 1974. *The Conflict of Interpretations: Essays in Hermeneutics.* Evanston: Northwestern Univ. Press. 512 pp.

31. Rieff, P. 1951. The meaning of history and religion in Freud's thought. *J. Relig.* 31:114–31
32. Sahay, A. 1972. *Sociological Analysis.* London: Routledge & Kegan Paul. 212 pp.
33. al-Shayal, J. 1965. *Aalam al Askandriya.* Cairo: Dar al Maarif
34. Tabanah, B. 1962. *al-Bayan al Arabi.* Cairo: Egyptian Anglo Press. 325 pp. 3rd ed.
35. Turner, B. 1974. *Weber and Islam.* London: Routledge & Kegan Paul. 212 pp.
36. Van Ess, J. 1975. The beginning of Islamic theology. In *The Cultural Context of Medieval Learning,* ed. J. E. Murdoch, E. D. Sylla. Dordrecht: Reidel
37. Waardenburg, J. 1973. *L'Islam dans le miroir de l'occident.* The Hague and Paris: Mouton
38. Waardenburg, J. 1974. Islam studies as a symbol and signification system. *Hum. Islamica* 2:267–85
39. Weber, M. 1949. *The Methodology of the Social Sciences,* trans. and ed. E. A. Shils, H. A. Finch. Glencoe: Free Press. 188 pp.
40. Weber, M. 1968. *Economy and Society: An Outline of Interpretive Sociology.* New York: Bedminster. 1469 pp.
41. Westermarck, E. 1968. *Ritual and Belief in Morocco.* New Hyde Park: University Books

Ann. Rev. Anthropol. 1977. 6:255–81
Copyright © 1977 by Annual Reviews Inc. All rights reserved

SOCIAL EXCHANGE

♦9595

Harumi Befu

Department of Anthropology, Stanford University, Stanford, California 94305

INTRODUCTION

We have long been aware that exchange of goods, services, etc plays a vital part in our own social life as well as in the life of other peoples we study, and in fact, as Belshaw states (16, p. 7), that exchange penetrates through the social fabric and may be thought of as a network holding society together. Such awareness, however, was not translated into systematic thinking—with a few exceptions—until very recently. As for these exceptions, Ekeh (37, pp. 21–24) cites Sir James Frazer's *Folklore in the Old Testament* (49), published in 1919, and Chavannes's 1884 *Studies in Sociology* as representing early thinking on social exchange. While, as Ekeh points out, one may well find in these works features of exchange theory propounded by later theorists, their direct impact upon modern thinkers of social exchange is not very clear; it appears that they were the Mendels of exchange theory in that although they were on the right track, they were forgotten by more recent theorists who had to "rediscover" the concept.

Three anthropologists stand out as having had disproportionate influence in the development of exchange theory. The first is Mauss, who has carried on the Durkheimian French intellectual tradition and applied to it the phenomena of gift-giving in his essay on gift, first published in 1925 (89, 90). In seeing gift exchange as an obligatory act, Mauss focuses on normative rules. Pervasiveness of gift-giving in primitive societies leads him to propose the concept of "total prestation." These ideas provide some of the conceptual ingredients for Lévi-Strauss, the second major contributor to the anthropology of exchange, to develop a theory of cousin marriage (78, 80). Basic to the theory is the distinction between restricted exchange, which is only capable of connecting pairs of social groups, and generalized exchange, which integrates indefinite numbers of groups. The third major contributor is Sahlins (110, 111), whose conceptual distinction among *generalized exchange,* which (not to be confused with Lévi-Strauss's concept) parallels Mauss's "total prestation," *balanced exchange,* which is epitomized by monetized market exchange, and *negative exchange,* which is characterized in extreme by "something for nothing" stealth, has been widely taken up, applied, and tested with ethnographic data.

There are several empirically oriented studies which are to a major extent organized around the exchange concept. Probably the best known among them is Mali-

255

nowski's analysis of the Trobriand kula ring (87). In more recent years, Schwimmer (116) has conceptualized Orokaiva data in terms of a cycle of exchange which is mediated by objects such as land, pigs, etc, and causes social relations to move back and forth between hostility and reconciliation. Although very different in certain crucial details, both Strathern (127) and Young (132) see big-men's competition for status in Mt. Hagen and Kalauna, respectively, in Melanesia as played out in the arena of ceremonial exchange, known as *moka* among the Hagener and *abutu* in Kalauna. It is interesting that all these works and others (92, 94) which take exchange as an organizing concept come from Melanesia. Outside Melanesia, Kapferer (65) presents data from a factory from Africa, giving us a detailed and first-rate analysis in the framework of social exchange primarily derived from Blau (19). Barth's early analysis of Norwegian fishing crews and Swat Pathans (7, 8), couched in "transactional" terms, is essentially a study in social exchange, as is made evident in a volume edited by Kapferer (67), in which Barth's transactional approach is further developed and revised by a number of authors. Finally, Belshaw (16) in the mid 1960s and H. Schneider (115) some 10 years later have devoted considerable space to summarizing theoretical works and empirical studies on social exchange.

Turning to major contributions from social psychology, Homans and Blau systematically build their theories from experimental psychology and economies, Homans relying on psychology more than Blau, and Blau making more serious use of economics than Homans, as seen in his use of the concepts of marginal utility and indifference curves and his frequent reference to Boulding (23). Boulding himself has recently offered a theory of social exchange (25). Application of economic theory is further carried forth by Heath (56), whose central concept for building an exchange model is rationality. Less influential, but still systematic in constructing models of exchange, are Burns (28), Emerson (40, 41), Foa & Foa (44), Gergen (50), and Meeker (91).

In addition to these original contributions, a series of critiques of major works in social exchange have appeared. Since they are all in social psychology, I shall limit myself to merely mentioning them. *Sociological Inquiry* published a special issue dedicated to critiquing Homans' theory (124). This was later revised and published as a separate volume under the editorship of Turk & Simpson (130). Mulkay (93) has published a critical analysis of Homans' and Blau's theories of exchange. Finally, Ekeh (37) provides us with a penetrating and contrastive examination of the intellectual roots, philosophical foundations, and theoretical structure of Homans' and Lévi-Strauss's theories.

While psychological literature on exchange abounds, most of it, particularly experimental findings, are couched in such hypothetical terms that they are scarcely useful to anthropologists in helping analyze real-world data. These will be by and large omitted from this review. On the other hand, anthropologists can benefit from theoretical contributions in the social psychology of exchange and should be encouraged to be conversant with that segment of the literature which has potential relevance to analysis of real-life situations. Some of these materials will be reviewed here.

DOMAIN OF INVESTIGATION

There is temptation for anyone engrossed in construction of a theory to make it as comprehensive as possible. When this is carried too far, however, there is the danger of making the theory tautological. That is, when a supposed counter example is presented, concepts of the theory are often redefined and stretched to fit the facts. Altruistic and coercive acts are such "test cases" lying at the fringes of the domain of social exchange acts. This distinction among "altruistic," "exchange," and "coercive" parallels Etzioni's "normative," "remunerative," and "coercive" (42).

We may begin our consideration with Boulding's conceptualization of economic, political, and social systems (24). He suggests that human behavior, insofar as it involves necessity, chance, and freedom, should be seen as constituting population systems, exchange systems, threat systems, learning systems, and finally love systems, the last being added only tentatively because it has not been as well understood. What Boulding does here is to propose to exclude altruism (Boulding's "love") and coercion (his "threat") from the realm of social exchange, in contradistinction to many exchange writers who include either or both of these elements in their models. For example, Mauss (89, p. 71) regards as untenable Malinowski's contention (87, pp. 177–80) that some gifts are "pure gifts" not requiring reciprocation. For in Mauss's scheme there cannot be gifts which are "pure," i.e. which do not call for return, since he posits three obligations surrounding gifts, namely, to give, to receive, and to return. Meeker (91, p. 480) also considers altruism as a type of exchange. For her, altruism is an exchange rule which assigns maximum value to the total payoff of the receiver, which implies that in its limiting case, one would receive nothing at all for what he gives. This is tantamount to saying that social exchange can take place when there is no exchange taking place.

Blau acknowledges (19, p. 16) that there are "virtual saints" who "selflessly work for others without any thought of reward and even without expecting gratitude," but excludes such altruistic acts from the domain of exchange. Such saintly behavior may not be as rare as Blau thinks, if Titmuss's report of the motives of hundreds of blood donors in England is true. According to him, for most donors "there is no formal contract, no legal bond, no situation of power, domination, constraint, or compulsion, no sense of shame or guilt, no gratitude imperative, no need for penitence, no money, and no explicit guarantee of or wish for a reward or return gift" (129, p. 89).

Heath takes a stand that is essentially Blau's with respect to freely given gifts, excluding them from his consideration of social exchange, for "by definition these gifts are not given with an eye either to past or to future benefits but given out of a sense of altruism or of a wish to help those in need (56, p. 60)." In other words, from the point of view which Heath adopts—of rational choice and maximization as a conscious strategy—altruism does not make any sense. Gregory (54, p. 83), too, proposes a category of acts involving no obligation, asserting that there should be a place in the anthropological lexicon for such concepts as "pure gifts."

Finally, Simpson (121, p. 14) makes a clear and concise statement regarding this issue: "our theorists all indicate that altruistic behavior can be psychologically profitable; but its rewards come from inside the altruist himself and not from the beneficiary of the altruistic behavior, or else it is not altruism at all but approval seeking. There is no room for altruism in a theory that restricts the source of rewards to one's interaction partner."

At issue in this controversy is the status of intent on the one hand and of cultural norm on the other. The first question is whether or not, when people offer gifts or services, they indeed mean it to be a pure gift without any expectation of return. If the answer is "yes," and if the exchange model is to be based on a motivational system, the act should be excluded from the domain of exchange. We must not be too hasty, however. For as Parkin notes (101, p. 172), the ideal of altruism can act as an effective cover for utilitarian interests. Thus we should examine the case carefully both at the face value of what is proclaimed to be the intent of the give-and-take and also what is at the subterranean though not necessarily subconscious level of a self-serving scheme.

If one's interest is in constructing a systemic model, ignoring native's intent or taking native's intent only as partial data, then there is room to include free gifts and altruistic acts as relevant for the model. For example, native norms may proscribe desire to receive returns for gifts to certain categories of individuals, e.g. parents from their children for providing sustenance. Yet the norm of the same culture may demand the recipient of the gift to return the favor, e.g. for children to give some kind of return for the sustenance received. As a social system *qua* system, reciprocation does take place in such a situation, and the case should certainly be included in the model.

Turning now to the opposite end of the continuum from altruism, while Boulding admonishes us to leave coercion or threat out of exchange systems, many exchange theorists have included these and other "negative resources" as constituting elements of social exchange. Homans, for example, speaks of exchanging punishment to one another (59, p. 57). Blau, too, refers to punishment for wrongdoing, imprisonment of criminals, or employment office workers penalizing uncooperative clients (19, pp. 227–30). Sahlins (111, pp. 148–49), in his well-cited work on the model of primitive exchange, defines "negative reciprocity" as "the attempt to get something for nothing with impunity, the several forms of appropriation, transactions opened and conducted toward net utilitarian advantage," and in this rather broad and amorphous classification of acts, Sahlins includes "various degrees of cunning, guile, stealth, and violence to the finesse of a well-conducted horse-raid." The "flow" of resources here may be, as he admits, "one way."

What these examples indicate is that "negative" exchange as a category includes a variety of heterogeneous phenomena. It includes (*a*) physical coercion or threat thereof, (*b*) "something for nothing" stealth, and (*c*) withdrawal of positive rewards. Among them, I believe it is best to leave out of our consideration Sahlins' "one-way flow" of "something for nothing" and genuine physical coercion (and threat thereof). The former should be left out because it lacks the basic element of return, and the latter because it denies volition and hence room for operation of strategy, to be discussed below.

Concepts and constructs of exchange models are largely created for exchange of positive rewards—desired resources only if because, as Homans says (59, p. 57), "the exchange of rewards takes a larger share in social behavior than the exchange of punishments." Accordingly, none of the five propositions on human exchange on which Homans elaborates (59, Chap. 4) has to do directly with negative exchange. Ethnographic cases of exchange, too, by and large concern gift-giving, payment of bride price, potlatching, giving of armbands and necklaces in the kula ring, etc, which all illustrate exchange of desired goods. Conceptualization of negative exchange thus lags far behind that of positive exchange and is a task left for the future.

CONTEXT, NORM, RULES, AND STRATEGY

At this juncture I would like to introduce the concepts of *sociocultural context, the norm of reciprocity, cultural rules,* and *strategy.*

1. *Sociocultural context,* or the abbreviated term "cultural context," refers to the cultural and social environment within which a model of social exchange is constructed. It is that part of an exchange model which is assumed as given insofar as the model is concerned; it is the environment within which the model is embedded. No exchange model can operate in a cultural vacuum. Specification of the cultural context is what brings life to an exchange model. When Salisbury (113, p. 43) refers to "microeconomic analysis of transactions within a single moral community," as against transactions across moral communities, and when Kapferer (66, p. 12) exhorts us to pay attention "to particular cultural understandings which underlie maximization or any other tactic or strategy," they are pointing to the importance of cultural context in understanding exchange behavior.

To illustrate the concept with data from India, the jajmani system has often been analyzed as an exchange system in which higher and lower castes exchange goods and services (88, 97). In analyzing the give-and-take between jajmans and kamins, inequality in caste ranking as god-given, the ritual superiority of the Braman, specific caste ranking, economic superiority of Bramans stemming from ownership of land and other forms of wealth (in certain cases), paternalistic relationship obtaining between particular jajmans and their kamins, the cultural ascriptions of hereditary occupations to various castes constitute some of the major elements of the social and cultural context, without which discussion of exchanges between jajman and kamin is meaningless (70).

In short, the sociocultural context sets the stage on which participants can act out their exchange behavior according to "the script," i.e. dictates of the exchange model. Without the stage, actors cannot act; without the cultural context, exchange analysis is vacuous.

2. Gouldner, in his seminal work on the *norm of reciprocity,* posited the universal norm of reciprocity, which according to him, "makes two interrelated, minimal demands: 1. people should help those who have helped them, and 2. people should not injure those who have helped them" (53, p. 171). The norm as stated by Gouldner is an etic concept and an abstraction in approximation of culture-specific norms exhorting participants to reciprocate. These culture-specific norms are stated in varying degrees of explicitness. In the Philippines, the Tagalog concept of *utang na loob* (56, 58, 68) and the Tausug concept of *buddi* (69, pp. 65–66) both imply moral compulsion to return a favor. Similarly, the Japanese *on* and *giri* are concepts

implying normative necessity of one who has received a favor to give an appropriate return (12, 13, 74). American culture does not have an explicit normative concept of reciprocity which is as salient as the Tagalog *utang na loob* or the Japanese *on* and *giri.* That does not at all mean that Americans lack the norm. As exemplified in numerous experimental and field studies (e.g. 19, 59, 126), reciprocity is a powerful norm which plays a critical role in structuring the American society.

3. *Rules of exchange* refer to specific cultural rules governing what should or may be given or returned in a given type of situation defined in terms of the specific relationship between the participants, occasion for the exchange, etc. In contrast to the norm of reciprocity, which is a generalized expectation to reciprocate irrespective of what or how much is given or returned, rules of exchange specify what the norm leaves undefined.

In Hagen society, for example, the main items in *moka* exchange are specified as "pigs, six kinds of shell valuables, bird of paradise plumes and other feathers used for decorations, sale, decorating oil, stone axe-blades and hafted stone axes, marsupial furs, and red ochre paint" (127, p. 101). In many East African societies bride price is paid in cattle. These are cultural rules governing exchange behavior. Cultural rules need not define the precise kind and exact amount of goods and services to be given. Instead, generally they prescribe a range of acceptable kinds and quantities of resources. As a return for a dinner party, an American couple has a range of recipes to choose from. A Hagen chief giving a *moka* can vary the quantities of items to be given away. However, there is always a culturally prescribed limit to the range. An American couple cannot normally invite to a hamburger lunch a friend who invited them to a formal dinner and consider the exchange even. Hogbin tells us that a headman in Ontong Java became an object of ridicule by villagers because he was too ostentatious in giving a betrothal for his daughter (57, p. 37).

4. As rules of exchange define what the norm of reciprocity leaves undefined, so does the *strategy of exchange* specify the indeterminate part of cultural rules. Since cultural rules specify a range of possibilities as to what may be given and how it may be given, an individual must make decisions as to the exact content of the resource to be given, its quantity, and the manner of prestation. These decisions are often, if not always, made on the basis of the individual's desire to maximize the opportunity for his benefit/profit.

An individual normally exercises his strategy for a maximum return within the cultural context (which is to say, within the normative and institutional framework of the culture) and within the bounds set by cultural rules (31). It is important to distinguish between cultural rules and strategy. One refers to prescribed conventions, which for participants of a culture are by and large given; the other has to do with the operation of an individual's motivations by which cultural rules are exploited.

Anthropologists interested in exchange are generally concerned with constructing a model which manipulates cultural rules of exchange, such as rules of marriage, whereas social psychologists are interested in discovering strategies individuals use in exchange, either setting aside the question of cultural rules or by choosing a problem where explicit cultural rules do not exist and people behave at the dictates of the norm of reciprocity and within the framework of the cultural context. But such observation also applies to anthropologists interested in uncovering exchange strategies, as Parkins notes:

The central tenet of transactional analysis, however, appears to be that the maximization of self-interest is an axiomatic and universal feature of the human condition that underlies the exchange nature of social relations. Transactional analysis does not attempt to identify and analyze those social circumstances in which this supposed axiom of human behavior is raised to a level of cultural consciousness and identification (101, p. 173).

TYPOLOGY OF EXCHANGE RELATIONS

1. *Perceived dyadic exchange.* Normally in social exchange, one assumes a relationship to take place between two existing beings (individuals, groups, etc). However, if one were to analyze exchange as taking place strictly on the basis of "Person's" perception as to who "Other" is (to use Homans' jargon), Other need not physically exist as long as Person believes Other exists and behaves accordingly. Indeed, this is the very reason why in many psychological experiments on social exchange, subjects do not interact with any individuals, but are made to believe that they do through devious designs using confederates or simply written messages (presumably coming from subjects' partners, but in fact written before the experiment begins and simply handed over to subjects in outright deceit).

This consideration is relevant to ethnographic accounts of exchange in analyzing interaction with the supernatural world. For example, the Buddhist conception of merit, in which one accumulates merit through contribution to Buddhist institutions, giving of alms, etc, as a way of improving one's karma, implies an exchange relationship with the supernatural world (125). Again, Foster (46, 47) includes dealings with saints in his discussion of "dyadic contract." Although Foster does not formulate the concept in exchange framework, nevertheless the give-and-take of resources between the mortal and a saint and between mortals—in the "colleague" type contract, for that matter—can readily be reinterpreted in the light of exchange theory. In dealing with supernaturals, obviously, a saint's giving of resources such as blessings, curing of disease, bringing good fortune, etc are perceived acts: they are merely perceived by the mortal as a saint's doing. However, insofar as supernaturals are perceived to be real and certain phenomena are perceived as emanating from them as a result of the mortal's propitiation, promise, etc, such interactions are no different in substance from a mortal's interaction with another mortal, and the same theory of exchange should be applicable to both. Lebra's study (75) shows how reciprocity-based supernatural sanctions can effectively change human behavior.

2. *Motivational vs institutional.* Earlier we have referred to those interested primarily in elucidating strategy of exchange based on motivational process, compared with those interested in cultural rules constituting institutional process. I have elaborated on this distinction as "individualistic" vs "collectivistic" (37). Taking up Homans and Lévi-Strauss as representatives of these respective approaches, Ekeh

derives their approaches from the differing intellectual climates of Anglo-America and France. To him, the traditions of the individualistic and collectivistic approaches are traceable back to Calvinism and Catholicism respectively, Calvinism being characterized by atomistic world view, conception of the society as being posterior to the individual, realism, sobriety, and rationalism, and Catholicism by an organic world view, conception of the society as being prior to the individual, symbolism, emotionalism, and mysticism (37, pp. 14–19). It is these differences which are manifested in Homans' theory of social exchange on the one hand and Lévi-Strauss's on the other.

For Homans, and most social psychologists, social exchange is predicated upon human sentiment, and his theory is a theory of motivation. The starting point as such is obviously the individual. He is concerned with strategies of exchange for maximizing rewards and minimizing costs. Thus it is that Abrahamsson (2) has characterized Homans' utilitarian theory as "hedonistic," true to the Benthamian tradition. For Homans, norms and institutions arise out of the individual behavior, resulting from patterned relationships based on rewards and costs, and are maintained and supported only insofar as they are able to satisfy individuals. As such, Ekeh argues (37, p. 181), Homans' notion of group is derivable from and reducible to individual psychology.

Lévi-Strauss's theory, on the other hand, ignores human sentiment and motivational processes. It is satisfied that motivational processes exist and dictate human action in the form that complies with structural rules. The starting point for Lévi-Strauss is the group, and his concern is not the strategy of action but arrangements and interrelations of cultural rules of exchange and consequences of application of these rules. In all these respects, Lévi-Strauss is starting from a set of premises which at the very least have nothing to do with Homans, according to Homans & Schneider (61), or, as Ekeh would have it, are antithetical to Homans, not allowing any possible meeting ground. Lévi-Strauss's institutional approach has been followed up in a series of writings by Rosman & Rubel (105–108) and by Schwimmer (116).

Is the relation of group to individual to be conceptualized only as antithetical and contradictory? Or is there a possibility of bridging the gap? Several writers, all starting from the individualistic approaches, have proposed ways of dealing with this question. Blau's solution, espoused by Kapferer (65, pp. 6–7), is to posit the concept of "emergent" (19, p. 3): "Emergent properties are essentially relationships between elements in a structure. The relationships are not contained in the elements, though they could not exist without them, and they define the structure." The relationship which develops out of social exchange is emergent, as is the group defined by such relationships. But a crucial difference from Homans' approach is in Blau's contention (19, p. 4) that "the emergent properties of social exchange consequent to this interdependence cannot be accounted for by the psychological processes that motivate the behavior of the partners." Yet, as Ekeh points out (37, p. 185), this concept of emergent group should not be confused with Lévi-Strauss's concept of structure (79), which, derived from Durkheimian sociology, has an existence *sui generis.* As Kapferer notes (66, p. 15), intellectual derivation of the "emergent" concept is rather to be found in George H. Mead's social psychology, especially in his concept of "the definition of situation."

Paine also tries to cope with this "individual vs group" dichotomy by taking a hint from Barth's notion of "incorporation" and developing the concept of "*I* mode of exchange" in contradistinction to the "*T* (for transaction) mode of exchange." According to Paine, in the *I* mode of exchange, "value optimum" is sought for the sum of the partners, whose solidarity may be based on a contract or simply on common prior commitment to a certain value (100, p. 69). This concept closely parallels Meeker's definition of "group gain," namely "an exchange rule that assigns the maximum value to the sum of P's [Person's] and O's [Other's] total payoffs (91, p. 480)."

Somewhat different from the individual-group dichotomy, but still focusing on the same issue of how to conceptualize group in exchange terms, is Heath's distinction (55, p. 30), earlier developed by Kuhn (71) and also by Olson (96), of private and public good: "*A private good is one whose enjoyment can be restricted to those who have paid for it, whereas a public good is one which, if it is provided at all, must be made available to all potential beneficiaries whether they have contributed or not*" (italics original). The conventional consumer good is a private good. The classic example of a public good is national defense, which tax evaders and tax-exempted citizens as well as tax payers equally benefit from. However, in order for the theory of public good to work, according to Olson, there must be in addition "selective incentives" which differentially favor those who contribute more and/or differentially punish those who contribute less or do not contribute. In this system, those who contribute to the group cause most stand to gain most from the group benefit, and those who contribute the least benefit the least, giving rise to a hierarchy of statuses (i.e. differential reward system) in the group, based on the degree of contribution to the welfare of the group. This is essentially tantamount to exchange of prestige and other intangible "status" rewards with material resources, as Leach (73) has argued with respect to marital exchange and Cancian (30) with the Mesoamerican *cargo* system. If we are to use this line of thinking, blood donation in England (129) may be regarded as a public good. When Gregory defines "the expectation of circumstantially balanced reciprocity (ECBR) as "a belief that those having much (or having more) should share with those having none (or having less)" (54, p. 74), he is conceptualizing an exchange relationship between the individual and the community, since expectation of balance is not directed toward any particular individual, but to the pooling of the sum total of community resources. In short, balance is systemic at the group (community) level, not between any two individuals.

Another solution to this problem is offered by Ekeh, who first distinguishes between "mutual reciprocity" and "univocal reciprocity" (37, pp. 205–6), the former being dyadic exchange between two individuals and the latter involving at least three individuals in indirect exchange (to be discussed below). Ekeh's "univocal reciprocity" is somewhat like Lévi-Strauss's "generalized exchange" (80), but is crucially different in one respect. Namely, in generalized exchange there is an ordered transfer of resources from A to B, B to C, etc, and back to A. In Ekeh's univocal reciprocity, there is no such assurance. One can only hope someone would do you a favor of the kind you have done someone else. "If I see burglars in my neighbor's house, I have the duty of doing something about it . . . because I expect *any* neighbor of mine to do the same thing if he sees burglars in my own house. Thus the concept of univocal reciprocity leads directly to the conception of generalized duties and rights" (37, p. 206, italics original). According to Ekeh, it is only this concept of univocal reciprocity which can lead exchange theory to such high-order conceptions as citizenship. Thus Ekeh derives commitment to a group (nation state, in this case) through the concept of generalized duties; but he does not tell us how the concept of generalized duties is obtained through exchange, or whether it is part of the sociocultural context and must be accepted as a given.

3. *Generalized vs balanced exchange.* It was Sahlins (111) who introduced the tripartite division of exchange phenomena: generalized, balanced, and negative reciprocity, these being ends and a midpoint of a continuum. "Generalized reciprocity" here is essentially the same as Mauss's "total prestation" (89, p. 3) and should not be confused with Lévi-Strauss's concept of generalized exchange, which, as will be discussed below, is a different idea altogether. Concerning generalized reciprocity, Sahlins says:

"the expectation of a direct material return is unseemly. At best it is implicit. The material side of the transaction is repressed by the social . . . the counter is not stipulated by time, quantity, or quality, the expectation of reciprocity is indefinite . . . Receiving goods lays on a diffuse obligation to reciprocate when necessary to the donor and/or possibly for the recipient. The requital thus may be very soon, but then again it may be never" (111, p. 147).

Some of these descriptive features verge on pure altruism, as when Sahlins refers to the suckling of children as an extreme case, or when he admits "a sustained one-way flow of goods for a long period," suggesting that balancing of give-and-take is of little concern. I submit that in the long run, there is probably more balancing than meets the eye. For one thing, as I indicated above, even though it may be quite unseemly for the giver to expect a return, the receiver may be fully expected to return. Thus the imbalance from the perspective of the giver may well be corrected to a large measure from the receiver's perspective. A counter case given by Pryor & Graburn (104) will be discussed below.

In contrast to generalized reciprocity, balanced reciprocity is characterized by precise balance: "the reciprocation is the customary equivalent of the thing received and is without delay. . . . Balanced reciprocity may be more loosely applied to transactions which stipulate returns of commensurate worth or utility within a finite and narrow period" (111, p. 148). This distinction is to some extent echoed in Lebra's conception of exchange (76, p. 550). She uses the term "exchange" in a generic sense, and under it distinguishes between "market exchange" and "reciprocity," where the latter is characterized by "actor-loaded" or "socially charged" exchange. If we regard Lebra's distinction as being ends of a continuum, her pair of concepts parallel Sahlins' generalized-balanced pair. Sahlins' distinction between "generalized" and "balanced" also parallels Parkin's similar distinction between "altruistic" and "negotiable" ideologies of transaction. At one point Parkin (101, p. 172) equates his "negotiable" with Sahlins' "negative." But Parkin's conception of "negotiable" as everything having its price and having to be paid for (p. 187) is every bit like Sahlins' "balanced," and scarcely like the "something for nothing" negative exchange which Sahlins speaks of.

Sahlins offers the generalized and balanced reciprocity as an end and a midpoint of a continuum, implying, in his evolutionary, global-comparative thinking, different cultures to fall in different places along the continuum. But within a given space-time coordinate called a culture, different kinds of exchange patterns may be observable at the same time. It is not clear in such a situation whether exchange transactions are supposed to vary infinitely along the spectrum or whether they cluster and come in discrete types, as I think they do, representing separate spheres of exchange (to be discussed below).

Sahlins identifies the three variables of kinship distance, sociability, and generosity as determining the mode of exchange along the continuum of "generalized" through "balanced" to "negative" exchange. Lebra (76) criticizes Sahlins for treating these three variables as correlating in one-to-one fashion. She points out (76, p. 552) that "these variables are conceived as of unidimensional quantity progressing from the plus extreme to the minus extreme, whereas special attention should have been paid to the qualitatively different values involved in the variables, especially in sociability." Thirdly, Lebra feels that Sahlins' model suffers from not considering the interaction of two parties, and contingency of the actor's behavior upon the alter's, as Sahlins concentrates his attention upon the actor's behavior alone.

Many workers have used Sahlins' model as a framework of analysis for their own data (e.g. 12, 14, 34, 62, 64, 98) or to test it with their own field data. I shall review a few of the empirical tests. Among them, Brady's and Dama's tests only partially validate Sahlin's hypothesis. Subjecting the hypothesis to test with data from Ellice Islands, Brady concludes (26, p. 314) that "moderate support has been given for Sahlins' provisional hypothesis that the character of exchange events is likely to change in proportion to social and sectoral distance." However, Brady suggests (26, p. 314) that this hypothesis is likely to apply differentially "to individual as opposed to group exchange events, and that the most positive relationships tend to occur between generalized reciprocity and close-in social distance." His data tends to invalidate (26, p. 314) "the possibility of a strict linear transformation from generalized to negative reciprocity as social distance increases." Here Brady echoes Lebra's reminder that qualitative transformation along the spectrum should have been considered. Brady also found (26, p. 315) that "the generalized sphere of exchange for food is sometimes wider than the generalized sphere of exchange for other things, particularly in hospitality outputs," suggesting that perishables and durables should be considered to behave differently with respect to social distance.

Damas (33) finds in his Eskimo data that foodstuff is used for trade, i.e. balanced exchange, a good deal more than Sahlins' model would suggest. Secondly, among the Eskimo, kinship and community are not coterminous, and community considerations override kinship considerations in distribution of resources, contrary to Sahlins' hypothesis. Thirdly, Sahlins' model would have us believe that hunters and gatherers (such as Eskimos) should be primarily characterized by generalized reciprocity; but Damas finds a good deal of balanced and negative reciprocity as well as redistribution (which is supposed to be characteristic of a more complex, chiefdom level society) among them. In spite of these criticisms and suggestions for modifications, Sahlins' model at present stands as one of the most widely debated, along with Lévi-Strauss's.

The "generalized-balanced-negative" typology reminds us of another in the game theory: they are positive-sum, zero-sum, and negative-sum games. In a positive-sum game, as applied to exchange, both parties to an exchange relationship stand to gain through the give and take, for both sides give up certain resources which they need less in exchange for some other resources which they need more (and which the other party has and is willing to give). The perceived value of what one has obtained thus is greater than the perceived value of what he has given up or what he had before the exchange transaction. In this sense, exchange as a positive-sum game enables both parties to profit from the relationship. In a zero-sum game, an example of which is Foster's "image of limited good" (48), ego's gain is alter's loss in precise equivalence, a point of view which Parkin assumes with respect to exchange theory and leads him to assert that men in exchange are necessarily in competition for valued objects (101, p. 165). Lastly, the negative-sum game implies that loss or injury is sustained by each party through exchange, and is of course intimately tied in with the so-called "negative exchange." I have already noted the inadequate understanding or integration of negative exchange in the model for social exchange.

The game-theoretical typology above is not strictly a parallel of Sahlins' typology. Though it has seldom been used in exchange framework, it may prove to be a useful frame of reference in organizing exchange data and beckons further research in this area.

4. *Direct vs indirect exchange.* This distinction originates from Lévi-Strauss's "restricted-generalized" dichotomy (80). However, because Sahlins' usage of "generalized reciprocity" has been widely adopted, to avoid confusion we shall use the terms "direct" and "indirect." "Direct exchange" refers to exchange of resources between two parties whereby return of resources given by A to B is made directly back to A from B. In indirect exchange, at least three units are involved in exchange, such that A gives resources to B, who in turn gives resources to C, etc, until the last unit gives to A, thus completing the cycles. Lebra's "circular transference" corresponds to this type (76, p. 559).

As is well known, for Lévi-Strauss this distinction was applied to forms of cross-cousin marriage, such that bilateral cross-cousin marriage was an example of direct (or restricted) exchange, and unilateral (either patrilateral or matrilateral) cross-cousin marriage was a case of indirect (or generalized) exchange.

Ekeh considers Lévi-Strauss's concepts of direct (restricted) and indirect (generalized) exchange not refined enough and has offered further elaborations (37, p. 209). He suggests two forms of direct (restricted) exchange: *exclusive,* in which "the dyadic relationships are totally isolated"; and *inclusive,* in which "the dyadic relationships are implicated in a network with other dyadic exchange relationships." In my view, "exclusive, restricted exchange" is a vacuous category because except for dyads in imaginary worlds, such as Adam and Eve or Robinson Crusoe and Friday, no dyad exists totally isolated.

Ekeh also proposes a subdivision of "indirect (generalized) exchange" into "chain generalized exchange," which is the same as what we have defined as indirect exchange above, and "net generalized exchange," in which each unit of a group acts in relation to the rest of the group. There are two subtypes here. "Group-focused generalized exchange," which may be represented as: (A → BCD; B → ACD; C → ABD; D → ABC), meaning each unit contributes to the welfare of the group, but does this separately. In the other subtype, "individual-focused generalized exchange," represented as (ABC → D; ABD → C; ACD → B; BCD → A), the group helps each of its member units separately. Individual members of a group taking turns to stand in sentry may be an example of the group-focused generalized exchange. Villagers going from household to household helping in harvesting, as Embree reports of *kattari* (38, p. 135) in Japan, or a hunting band sharing the kill of a member [Denton (35), pp. 48–50] are instances of individual-focused generalized exchange.

While an indirect exchange such as cross-cousin marriage may appear to admit of one-way flow of women only, it should be remembered that in most such marriages, some form of bride compensation is given to the wife-giving group. This fact yields two consequences. One is that there are two cycles moving in opposite directions simultaneously, women moving in one direction and bride compensation in the other. The Trobriand kula ring, as reported by Malinowski (87), where arm bands circulate in one direction and necklaces in the opposite, is another example of double-cycled indirect exchange. A second consequence of this system is that each dyad in the system is engaged in direct exchange and that the whole cycle consists of a series of pairs connected like links in a chain.

5. *Horizontal vs vertical exchange.* Equal or egalitarian exchange is one in which values of resources exchanged are roughly the same, so that there is no enduring or clear-cut debt that one side owes the other. In egalitarian exchange, as between friends, there may be temporary "debt" but this is repaid in due course, restoring the balance. The balance restored or maintained need not be exact; in fact, in some respects it may be better not to strike the precise balance in that a small debt would be a symbolic reminder to the continuing relationship between the actor and alter (53). Such imbalance, however, is small enough and can be repaid easily with the resources one controls. Such is not the case with vertical or hierarchical exchange. Here resources controlled by the two parties are so vastly different in value that it would not be possible for the subordinate to pay back what the superior has given. What the superior controls may be employment opportunities, connection with government offices, money, and other material resources, of which the subordinate is in need, but to which he has no direct access.

If we combine the generalized/balanced dichotomy with the horizontal/vertical dichotomy, we have the following two-by-two table, with examples filling the appropriate cells (Figure 1). Close friends are horizontal in relationship and generalized in exchange, as defined by Sahlins, in comparison with a relationship which obtains between salesman and customer, where there is no super- or subordination any more

	Horizontal	Vertical
Generalized	Friend-friend	Melanesian big-man Polynesian Chieftainship Patron-client
Balanced	Salesman-customer	Employer-employee

Figure 1   Types of exchange relations.

than in a friendship, but the exchange relationship is strictly balanced. These relations again differ from vertical ones. The vertical-generalized category includes a kinship-based rank system of the kind Sahlins discusses (109; 111, pp. 158–64), examples of which are the Melanesian big-man and the Polynesian chieftainship. In the latter, "where kinship-rank reciprocity is laid down by office and political groupings, and becomes *sui generis* by virtue of customary duty" (111, p. 164), exchange takes on the character of chiefly redistribution, in the tripartite reciprocity-redistribution-market classification of the substantivist economic anthropology (102). Note that in this scheme of Sahlins', redistribution is no less an exchange relationship than reciprocity through gift exchange among kinsmen, even though the nomenclature juxtaposes "redistribution" with "reciprocity" as if they are antitheses. "Redistribution" in this scheme is a species of exchange imbedded in a hierarchical structure implying a resource differential. Incidentally, Sahlins' hypothesis concerning exchange and hierarchy receives confirmation from Brady (26, p. 314). In the Ellice Islands, he finds that with respect to the relationship between rank and reciprocity, "Greater existing rank, or aspirations for rank and prestige, lead some individuals to give away items through the morality of *noblesse oblige* when the initiator of a transaction intends to negotiate a 'trade' or obtain customary equivalence in a commercial exchange. The donor thereby transforms a potentially balanced exchange to a more generalized form."

Another generalized-vertical type of relationship, distinguished from big-man and chieftainship and occurring in the absence of kinship ties, is the patron-clientship and brokerage (131). Brokerage differs from patronage analytically in that a broker is able to obtain from another source (through personal contact, etc) whatever resources are desired by his client, whereas a patron possesses himself resources desired by his clients. Empirically, of course, one is likely to find the two roles combined in one person in varying degrees. The patron-client and brokerage relationships have been widely reported in ethnographic literature from Latin America (45, 83, 128), Asia (11, 18, 27, 103, 117–119), Europe (21, 29, 120), and North America (32, 99, 100).

Reinterpreting the traditional patron-client data in the exchange framework, however, is a new endeavor, and attempts are few and far between (81, pp. 5–9). Southeast Asian cases indicate changing relationship resulting from economic and political changes. Institution of electoral democracy in recent years there, for example, has necessitated erstwhile patrons, if they are to maintain a power base in the new political structure, to become patrons for a great many people at a grassroot level in an effort to secure a large electoral base. Befu (14) argues that bureaucratic structure is compatible with patron-client relationship, which may be a reason for the widespread persistence of patron-client relationships in developing countries. When a successful patron with much personal fund of resources and a loyal following becomes a bureaucrat, an office holder, he has two alternatives. On one hand, he can largely ignore the organizational goal of the bureaucracy and take advantage of the power and privilege ascribed to the office for personal gain at the expense of undermining the bureaucracy's goal. It is possible, on the other hand, for a patron-office holder to use his personal resources for the furtherance of bureaucratic goals.

BALANCING

The question of balance is inextricably tied in with the concept of social exchange. Balancing necessarily implies comparison of at least two elements. This comparison may be relative or absolute. In the former, A is said to be "greater" or "less" than B; in the latter, comparison is based on the difference between two numerical values assigned to A and B. Homans has opted for the former method (59, p. 43; 60, p. 221), Deutch's criticism (36, pp. 160–61) to the contrary notwithstanding. It is understandable that Heath, who adopts economic theory as his model for social exchange, would assume quantitative measurability, as when he asserts (56, p. 26) that "some *numerical* probability can be assigned to the likelihood that a particular outcome will follow a particular course of action" (italics added). Offhand it may seem plausible to assume, as Blau does (19, p. 171), that "the worth (utility) of the subordination he [a consultant] receives in terms of the worth of the cost in time he incurs, decreases at an accelerated rate with increasing consultations" and to plot this function in indifference curves (19, p. 173). This assertion assumes, however, that contents and quality of advice are uniform and that the nature of subordination does not vary from one case to another—an assumption which is not likely to receive empirical validation.

Whether one adopts quantitative or relative valuation, there seems to be at least two different approaches in assessing balance. One is to compare the cost one incurs with the reward he receives in a given exchange relationship (which may involve a number of transactions). "Cost" here may be defined as the resource one gives to the other party, or it may be defined, as Homans does (59, pp. 57–61), as alternative courses of action which one gives up in favor of the exchange one in fact has transacted. If one perceives the cost to be equal to the reward, then one may speak of a balance in this exchange relationship. A second way of conceiving balance is to compare one's own profit (reward minus cost) with the other party's profit. If the profit values are about the same, then a balance may be said to have been struck. It should be noted that valuation in this context refers to subjectively perceived valuation and comparison, and that the same resource may be differentially valued by the giver and the receiver. In fact, in many cases, Person gives up what he has because for him the resource for him is dispensable (i.e. in some sense unneeded), and gives it to Other because he believes Other will find it useful. Thus the same resource is more highly valued by the one who receives it than by the one who gives it. It is for this reason that social exchange is often regarded as a positive-sum game in which both sides end up having more value than before the transaction.

In anthropological literature, this notion of perceived valuation is not often used. Instead, objects to be exchanged are assumed to have some agreed upon, objective value which is the same for all concerned. There is no question that society defines the approximate "value" of exchange resources, whether it be a smile, a kiss, an overnight stay at a friend's house. However, it is worth repeating that this societal definition is only approximate, with a lattitude within which variation on the basis of subjective perception is legitimate.

Central to the process of balancing is the concept of distributive justice: justice in the distribution of rewards and costs (3, 59). In Homans' words (59, p. 75), "a man in an exchange relation with another will expect that the rewards of each man be proportional to his costs—the greater the rewards, the greater the costs—and that the net rewards, or profits, of each man be proportional to his investments." When distributive justice is realized, one may say that a balance is struck in the relationship. When not, according to Homans (59, p. 75), a man reacts with anger. Thus, to Homans, the question of whether a person is engaged in fair exchange with another is in the final analysis based on emotional reaction to his perception of cost accounting, and has nothing fundamentally to do with moral justice.

Anthropologists are not likely to be satisfied with Homans' psychological reductionism. Notion of normative standards—publicly agreed upon values of resources, approximate though they may be—weighs heavily upon ethnographic description. How much a kin group would pay another for bride compensation, how much assistance a revenge group would receive from friends, how willing a patron would be to help one of his clients, etc, are not basically an individual psychological matter, but a question about which there is considerable societal consensus. It is this consensus which I called "cultural rules." What we have not seen much and are badly in need of is an attempt at an ethnographic description which explicitly defines cultural rules and at the same time examines individual strategies in an exchange model.

Pryor & Graburn (104) raise a serious question regarding the nature and conception of balance. In their careful statistical analysis of Eskimo data on giving and receiving of resources, they discovered that by and large balance is not struck between a pair of giver and receiver, throwing grave doubts as to the utility of the concept of balance and to the nature of exchange in egalitarian societies. What they did find is that at an ideological level, Eskimos do exhort reciprocity and balancing of give-and-take. In fact, Pryor & Graburn maintain that the ideological conviction of reciprocity seems to serve as an effective cover or "blind" for empirical imbalance, enabling the imbalance to continue. This suggests the necessity of separating cultural ideology from actual practice, a rather elementary methodological point in anthropology which exchange theorists have neglected to observe.

RESOURCE TYPES

Since just about anything under the sun from smile and expression of respect to giving of advice and material rewards can all serve as resources for exchange, how are we to conceptualize or systematize all different kinds of resources? The most basic division in this respect is between positive and negative resources, the former being those which are sought after and the latter those avoided. We have already elaborated on the problematic nature of negative exchange and shall pass this topic here. One way of dealing with the question of typology is to reduce all resources to one category of phenomena. Nord (95), for one, argues that social exchange, in the final analysis, is a matter of seeking and conferring approval. Approval to him is the psychological currency of social exchange. On this assumption, be brings together a large body of research findings, mostly in social psychology, and reanalyzes them in an exchange framework. A problem with this approach is that people seek to obtain many other kinds of things in social exchange besides approval. A recent study by Hurlbert (63), for example, illustrates the importance of social status expressed in prestige, in faculty appointments and doctoral training in anthropology. Doctoral degrees are the valuables to be exchanged among departments. If two departments can give each other their products, then they each confer prestige upon the other. If a recipient department cannot reciprocate and give a PhD to the department from which it receives one, then prestige flows one way.

For cultural anthropologists, what is important is the realization that prestige, status approval, respect, love, affection, sympathy, etc, are English words, each of which has a somewhat different meaning. To try to group all these under a single heading of positive sentiment of some sort would do injustice to the semantic and symbolic realities of these expressions.

Another mode of conceptualizing resource types is Blau's pair, "intrinsic" vs "extrinsic" (19, pp. 35–38, 95–96), or Kapferer's pair, "sociational" vs "instrumental" (65, p. 164), the two pairs being essentially synonymous. The former, in Kapferer's words, refers to those transactions "which are ends in themselves and not detachable from their source," and the latter to those "which are essentially detachable from their source and are means to ends rather than ends in themselves." a difficulty of these schemes is that concrete behavior itself is being classified as being one or the other, when in reality concrete behavior is usually a combination of the two elements in varying degrees. Befu's (14) pair, "expressivity" vs "instrumentality," though in substance the same as Blau's and Kapferer's, avoids this difficulty by defining expressivity and instrumentality as aspects of an act and by assuming a given exchange act to manifest both qualities in varying proportion.

Using this distinction, Befu and his associates investigated the relationship between these two variables in Japan. Their as yet unpublished findings show that an exchange act (or resource) which is regarded as high in instrumentality, such as serving as guarantor or extending a personal loan, is also high in expressive value, and vice versa. Also, a person who is a source of much expressivity is one who provides a great deal of instrumental resources, and vice versa.

This set of findings contrasts with Foa & Foa's findings (44) from the United States indicating possible differences in cultural disposition toward social exchange. Foa & Foa classify resources into six categories: love, status, information, money, goods, and services. These six are arranged in a "circumplex (44, p. 82, see Figure 2), such that the two opposites (e.g. love and money or status and goods) are least likely to be exchanged for each other and that the two adjacent categories, such as

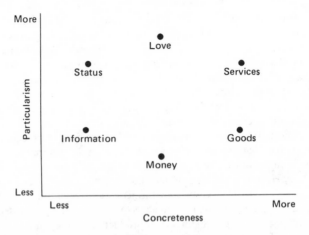

Figure 2   The cognitive structure of resource classes.

love and status or money and information, are most likely to be exchanged. Foa & Foa's findings are not directly comparable to those of Befu and his associates, thus requiring caution in interpretation. It appears, however, that Japanese tend to exchange instrumental values and expressive values simultaneously and that as their relationship becomes more and more intrinsically satisfying to one another, they become more and more useful to each other. Foa & Foa's findings suggest that in contrast to the Japanese pattern of exchange, in the United States instrumental relationship, for example involving exchange of money, is kept separate from expressive relationship where affect is exchanged.

SPHERES OF EXCHANGE

Bohannan (20) has divided Tiv economy into three spheres. The first, in order of moral ranking from the lowest to the highest, consists primarily of foodstuffs and is associated with the market. The second consists of prestige items, such as slaves, cattle, metal bars, ritual offices, etc. The third is largely restricted to rights in women, who are exchanged in marriage. Essential in Bohannan's definition of sphere are (*a*) moral ranking of spheres and (*b*) nonoverlapping of categories of resources among spheres. While exchange spheres manifesting these features are known elsewhere in the world, e.g. Tikopia (43) and New Guinea (112), they are far from universal. Barth (9, p. 157), for one, failed to find them among the Fur. Against Bohannan's definition, Kapferer (65, p. 190) uses the term "transactional sphere" to refer to a set of individuals involved in transactional activity who place similar value on the benefits and services transacted.

   Problems arise with Bohannan's definition in cultures, such as with the Pedi (114), where money is used both in market exchange and in bridal transactions. Kapferer's definition also has difficulty in that one pair of individuals can engage in exchange in two different spheres, as when they are employer and employee and are friends at the same time, thus engaging both in market and social exchange. My proposal is to define "sphere of exchange" in terms of a system of valuation of resources, such that a given resource would have approximately the same value in a given sphere, but receives a different valuation in another. Thus a cigarette would have a certain definable value in the market, but acquires a different one when given to a friend as a gift. Even money, when it enters a social sphere of exchange, is no longer interpreted on its face value but is evaluated in part on the basis of social circumstances (64). Distinction between the market and the social sphere of exchange is an important one, as Bennett has cogently pointed out (17, p. 305). Blau (19, p. 94) and Heath, following Blau (56, p. 56), have claimed that the two spheres are distinguished by the element of trust, being present in the social sphere and absent in the market. This is a gross distortion of the reality. Market transactions cannot be carried out without mutual trust among participants, be they bankers and account holders or buyers and sellers.

SYMBOLIC EXCHANGE

I have alluded to the importance of semantic and symbolic aspects of exchange above. Conceptualizing exchange in terms of transmission of messages is a tradition going back to Lévi-Strauss and Mauss on the one hand and to symbolic interactionists of the Chicago school on the other (1, 122, 123). Reflecting this interest, half of the papers contributed to the recent Kapferer volume deal with transaction of meanings and symbols (32, 51, 88, 100, 101, 114). Among them, Sansom's concept of "signal transaction" is of particular interest (114). Among the Pedi, as mentioned above, bridewealth is nowadays paid in cash. But in order to keep bridewealth payment out of the sphere of monetized market exchange, they use a metaphor of domestic animals like cattle and sheep in reference to units of money to be paid in bridewealth. In Jasper, according to Bennett (17), the reverse is true. There farmers exchange labor, borrow each other's equipment etc in a system of exchange entirely apart from the national market economy, but use the metaphor of the latter sphere, such as "buy," "sell," "loan," etc to refer to their intracommunity exchange transactions. Finally, Goody's analysis of greetings among the Gonja (52a) shows that they use greetings as symbolic gifts and gifts as symbolic greetings.

POWER

Though several definitions of power have been offered by exchange theorists, probably the most useful one is that proposed by Emerson (39–41) and essentially followed by Anderson & Befu (4), Blau (19), and Foa & Foa (44). Emerson conceives exchange relationship as being predicated upon dependence of two parties upon each other's resources. To the extent that Person is unwilling to voluntarily surrender resource desired by Other and able to use this resource as a "carrot," to force, coerce, or induce compliance upon the other party, one is said to have power over the other party. This fact then allows both parties to have power over each other.

Thus power is not conceived of as a unilateral relationship where if Person has power over Other, then Other does not have power over Person. Instead, power is a bilateral relationship of each potentially having power over the other. In contract negotiation between employer and labor union, for example, the former's resources include ability to improve labor conditions such as wage and fringe benefits and the latter's resources, power to withhold labor through strike. Thus both sides can be seen to have potential power over the other. When there is a clear differential between the degree of dependence of one party over the other, then one may say that there is power advantage of one over the other.

An important consequence of this definition of power is that the amount of power becomes a function of the availability of alternative sources from which the compliant can obtain needed resources. This is illustrated in Barth's analysis of the Swat Pathans (7), among whom the chief must be judicial in his exercise of power because his followers can leave him and go to another chief and receive protection. Similarly, in central Africa (52) when people are not confined to a village and instead can leave one and go to another if the village headman is too demanding, the headman's power is that much weaker. By the same token, for the power holder, availability of alternative sources of labor, service, etc increases his power. When there is a large pool of unemployed workers, it is the "buyer's market" in that the employer can demand and expect more from his workers because the employer can fire the recalcitrant and hire more obedient workers who are willing to work more for less reward. Patron-client relationship is a special type of power relation which we have already discussed above, and will not be taken up in this section.

Two sources of power must be clearly distinguished: personal and institutional. When the resources given out in exchange for compliance are personal possessions, as they are for a patron in most cases, we speak of personal power. Institutional power is found in an "office" which involves the right to exercise power. Thus anyone who assumes that office is entitled to exercise power as prescribed for the office, even though qualifications for assuming the office may not have anything to do with one's ability to exercise the power of the office. The distinction here is best illustrated with the Melanesian big-man and the Polynesian chieftain. The former acquires his position as a big-man by dint of his own effort. Being a son of a big-man often helps, as Strathern points out (127, pp. 210–11). "But a good start does not guarantee success, for a son must be a good manager and speaker on his own account if he is to become a big-man (127, p. 211)." On the other hand, when power is institutionalized in an office such as a chieftainship, one can hold the office and exercise the power of the office without having appropriate qualifications to do so, e.g. merely by being born a son of a chief. Appreciation of this distinction is crucial for a clear analysis of power in the context of social exchange. Another distinction to be noted has to do with kinds of powers. The big-man's exercise of power is clearly in the realm of social exchange in that his power is obtained, maintained, and exercised in exchange for various benefits he provides his followers and rival big-men. A chief or king's power, on the other hand, may not be entirely of this sort; most likely it is based on a combination of coercive, normative and remunerative sources, the first of which are, as we saw earlier, outside the domain of social exchange.

FUNCTION

Although as Mulkay (93) has demonstrated in his critique, social exchange theory has developed out of dissatisfaction and rejection of the conventional structural-functional approach, many empirical studies of exchange are still functionalist in approach . Two major functions of exchange identified here are (*a*) saving and investment and (*b*) social integration. These will be discussed in turn below.

To the extent that one has some control or knowledge as to what will be returned, giving serves the purposes of savings and investment. Although in social exchange, the giver is normally enjoined from specifying what is to be given back to him in return, in most cases cultural rules specify in varying degrees what are appropriate categories of resources to be returned. Thus by knowing what one may get in return and who is likely to provide maximum return, one can maximize the investment in the giving of one's resources. This saving function is well illustrated in reports by Beals (10), Bennett (17), Lombardi (82), Lomnitz (84–86), and Stack (126).

Lombardi's, Lomnitz's, and Stack's studies deal with the urban poor, and demonstrate the critical function which informal social exchange of material resources plays in keeping families above subsistence level, something which formal institutions such as employment and social security programs alone cannot accomplish. Bennett's study shows that North American farmers in Northern Plains are able to rely on assistance in labor and equipment from fellow farmers because they have provided similar assistance to them in the past. Similarly, in Oaxaca, according to Beals, gifts are given consciously as investment, to be returned at strategic moments. Although somewhat different, Gregory's reanalysis of Foster's concept of the image of limited good in terms of "expectation of circumstantially balanced reciprocity" is an attempt to see an exchange system as underwriting the economic security of the community.

If savings and investment are the major functions of social exchange from the "motivational" perspective, integration is the most obvious function in the "institutional" approach, as Lévi-Strauss has so abundantly shown in his theory of cross-cousin marriage. When Paine (100) argues that what he calls the "incorporation" mode, i.e. the institutional approach—but not the "negotiative" mode, i.e. the motivational approach—of analysis would throw light on group integration, he is echoing Lévi-Strauss's position. The theme of alliance between exchanging communities is seen in Malinowski's account of the kula ring (87) as well as in Strathern's analysis of *moka* in Mt. Hagen, New Guinea (127). The theme of community integration is evident also in Vatuk's study of gift-giving in an urban neighborhood in India and also in Rehfisch's study of competitive gift exchange between members of different villages among the Mambila (104a). Though somewhat different, Johnson's study of gift-giving among Hawaiian Japanese also falls in this category. Her findings that status maintenance, generational continuity, conflict resolution, and status equalization are accomplished by gift-giving indicate integrative functions of social exchange, as does Young's interpretation that the institution of *abutu* (competitive food exchange) serves the function of social control among the Kaluna in Massim (132).

CONCLUSION

Looking at the state of the field, one gets the distinct impression that theory has run ahead of empirical testing. A good deal of ink has been spilled over the conceptual status and theoretical nature of social exchange without sufficient empirical checking of the usefulness of concepts and models. We must make a concerted effort to gather data and test propositions generated from our models.

A major contribution of social exchange theory is that it has offered a frame of analysis at the collectivity level and also at the individual level and that it has at least attempted to bridge the two levels, in spite of claims by Ekeh and others that this is impossible. The field thus enables those working primarily in terms of cultural rules and those interested in strategy to converge and deal with common problems. In this attempt we have been able to combine the disciplines of psychology and anthropology without taking the conventional Freudian or neo-Freudian stand.

A strength of exchange theory is its linkage with economic and political anthropology. Relations to economics and economic anthropology are quite important. How important it is would depend on whose approach one takes. For those of Heath's persuasion, economics provides the foundation upon which social exchange theory is to be built. For those not so bent on the superiority of economics, social and market exchange are both species of exchange, perhaps of coequal level though belonging to different spheres. As such, at some abstract level, social and market exchange are encompassed by a common theoretical umbrella. A rapproachment between the two fields is inevitable as well as desirable.

Relationship to political science is also obvious from the point of view of the definition of power. If politics has to do with "who gets what, when, and how," then it is a question of acquiring resources and of strategies of acquiring them. Social exchange provides a framework in which strategies are to be analyzed. Its usefulness has been demonstrated by a number of empirical studies by political scientists (72, 77, 103, 117–119).

One of the areas in which little work has been done so far is the linkage of social exchange theory with network theory (e.g. 5, 6, 22). A fruitful start has been seen in Kapferer's study of African factory workers (65), but it remains the only major attempt in this direction. Social exchange theory focuses on dyads as dyads. Even when a third party is introduced, the basic framework is that developed in dyadic exchange. Social network theory, on the other hand, begins with the assumption that an individual is interacting simultaneously with a large number of people and develops its frame of analysis on this basis. It goes without saying that what network theory takes as given (multiple relations) is much more realistic than a series of dyads which exchange theory takes as the starting point. Moreover, network theory allows indirect relationships—friends of friends of friends—encompassed in its theoretical constructs, something which exchange theory cannot do very well except obliquely, for example, by linking a series of dyads in a chain. On the other hand, social exchange theory is better suited to analyzing processes, strategies, and functions, while network theory is better at developing structural framework. A combination of these two approaches then should yield a rather powerful theoretical basis to analyze social phenomena.

We hope that social exchange approach will receive more attention in the future and be further developed and revised in the areas and directions indicated above. There is no claim made here that social exchange theory will be a "unified theory" which would account for most of social and cultural phenomena. The claim made here is much more modest, yet even that modest degree of accomplishment awaits future research.

ACKNOWLEDGMENTS

I wish to thank George Dalton and Theodore Downing for discussing various issues in social exchange and offering helpful suggestions. I would also like to acknowledge with gratitude the generous grants and fellowships provided by the National Science Foundation (GS2370), the Japan Foundation, the John Simon Guggenheim Foundation, and Stanford University Center for Research in International Studies, whose sponsorship allowed me to carry out research which laid the basis for this paper.

Literature Cited

1. Abbott, C. W., Brown, C. R., Corsbie, P. V. 1973. Exchange as symbolic interaction: for what? *Am. Sociol. Rev.* 38(4):504–6
2. Abrahamsson, B. 1970. Homans on exchange: hedonism revisited. *Am. J. Sociol.* 76:273–85
3. Adams, J. S. 1965. Inequity in social exchange. *Adv. Exp. Soc. Psychol.* 2: 267–99
4. Anderson, S., Befu, H. 1970. Power in the context of social exchange. *Proc. Int. Congr. Anthropol. Ethnol. Sci., 8th, Tokyo* 2:247–49
5. Aronson, D. R., ed. 1970. Social networks. *Can. Rev. Sociol. Anthropol.* 7: No. 4 (entire)
6. Barnes, J. A. 1972. Social networks. *Addison-Wesley Module Anthropol. 26*
7. Barth, F. 1959. Political leadership among Swat Pathans. *Monogr. Soc. Anthropol. 19*
8. Barth, F. 1966. Models of social organization. *R. Anthropol. Inst. Occas. Pap. 23*
9. Barth, F. 1967. Economic spheres in Darfur. In *Themes in Economic Anthropology*, ed. R. Firth, pp. 149–74. Assoc. Soc. Anthropol. Monogr. 6. London: Tavistock
10. Beals, R. L. 1970. Gifting, reciprocity, savings, and credit in peasant Oaxaca. *Southwest. J. Anthropol.* 26:3:231–41
11. Befu, H. 1964. Ritual kinship in Japan: its variability and resiliency. *Sociologus* 14:150–69
12. Befu, H. 1967. Gift-giving and social reciprocity in Japan, an exploratory statement. *France-Asie/Asia* 188: 161–77
13. Befu, H. 1968. Gift-giving in modernizing Japan. *Monumenta Nipponica* 23: 445–56
14. Befu, H. 1974. Power in exchange: strategy of control and patterns of compliance in Japan. *Asian Profile* 2(5–6):601–22
15. Befu, H. 1977. Structural and motivational approaches to social exchange. In *Social Exchange: Advances in Theory and Research*, ed. K. F. Gergen, M. J. Greenberg, R. H. Willis. New York: Wiley. In press
16. Belshaw, C. S. 1965. *Traditional Exchange and Modern Markets*. Englewood Cliffs, NJ: Prentice-Hall
17. Bennett, J. W. 1968. Reciprocal economic exchanges among North American agricultural operators. *Southwest J. Anthropol.* 24:276–309
18. Bennett, J. W., Ishino, I. 1963. *Paternalism in the Japanese Economy: Anthropological Studies of Oyabun-kobun Patterns.* Minneapolis: Univ. Minnesota Press
19. Blau, P. 1964. *Exchange and Power in Social Life.* New York: Wiley
20. Bohannan, P. 1955. Some principles of exchange and investment among the Tiv. *Am. Anthropol.* 57:60–70
21. Boissevain, J. 1966. Patronage in Sicily. *Man* 1:18–33
22. Boissevain, J., Mitchell, J. C., eds. *Network Analysis: Studies in Human Interaction.* The Hague, Paris: Mouton
23. Boulding, K. 1955. *Economic Analysis.* New York: Harper

24. Boulding, K. E. 1962. The relations of economic, political and social systems. *Soc. Econ. Stud.* 11(4):351–62

25. Boulding, K. E. 1973. *The Economy of Love and Fear: A Preface to Grant's Economics.* Belmont, Calif: Wadsworth

26. Brady, I. 1972. Kinship reciprocity in the Ellice Islands: an evaluation of Sahlins' model of the sociology of primitive exchange. *J. Polynesian Soc.* 81(3):290–316

27. Breman, J. 1974. *Patronage and Exploitation: Changing Agrarian Relations in South Gujarat, India.* Berkeley: Univ. Calif. Press

28. Burns, T. R. 1973. A structural theory of social exchange. *Acta Sociol.* 19:188–208

29. Campbell, J. K. 1964. *Honour, Family, and Patronage, A Study of Institutions and Moral Values in a Greek Mountain Community.* New York, Oxford: Oxford Univ. Press

30. Cancian, F. 1965. *Economics and Prestige in a Maya Community: The Religious Cagro System in Zinacantan.* Stanford Univ. Press

31. Cancian, F. 1966. Maximization as norm, strategy, and theory: a comment on programmatic statements in economic anthropology. *Am. Anthropol.* 68(2):465–70

32. Cohen, A. P., Comaroff, J. L. 1976. The management of meaning: on the phenomenology of political transactions. See Ref. 67, pp. 87–107

33. Damas, D. 1972. Central Eskimo systems of food sharing. *Ethnology* 11(3):220–40

34. Davis, W. G. 1973. *Social Relations in a Philippine Market: Self-Interest and Subjectivity.* Berkeley, Los Angeles: Univ. Calif. Press

35. Dentan, R. K. 1968. *The Semai: A Nonviolent People of Malaya.* New York: Holt, Rinehart & Winston

36. Deutch, M. 1964. Homans in the Skinner box. See Ref. 130, pp. 81–90

37. Ekeh, P. P. 1974. *Social Exchange Theory, the Two Traditions.* Cambridge: Harvard Univ. Press

38. Embree, J. F. 1939. *Suye Mura, A Japanese Village.* Univ. Chicago Press

39. Emerson, R. M. 1962. Power-dependence relations. *Am. Sociol. Rev.* 27:31–41

40. Emerson, R. M. 1972. Exchange theory, part I: a psychological basis for social exchange. In *Sociological Theory in Progress,* ed. J. Berger, M. Zelditch, 2:38–57. Boston: Houghton Mifflin

41. Emerson, R. M. 1972. Exchange theory, part II: exchange relations and exchange networks. See Ref. 40, pp. 58–87

42. Etzioni, A. 1969. A basis for comparative analysis of complex organizations. In *A Sociological Reader on Complex Organizations,* ed. A. Etzioni, pp. 59–76. New York: Holt, Rinehart & Winston

43. Firth, R. 1939. *Primitive Polynesian Economy.* London: Routledge

44. Foa, U., Foa, F. 1974. *Societal Structures of the Mind.* Springfield, Ill: Thomas

45. Foster, G. M. 1953. Cofradia and compadrazgo in Spain and Spanish America. *Southwest. J. Anthropol.* 9:1–28

46. Foster, G. M. 1961. The dyadic contract: a model for the social structure of a Mexican peasant village. *Am. Anthropol.* 63:1173–92

47. Foster, G. M. 1963. The dyadic contract in Tzintzuntzan, II: patron-client relationship. *Am. Anthropol.* 65:1280–94

48. Foster, G. M. 1965. Peasant society and the image of limited good. *Am. Anthropol.* 67:293–215

49. Frazer, J. G. 1919. *Folklore in the Old Testament,* Vol. 2. London: MacMillan

50. Gergen, K. J. 1969. *The Psychology of Behavior Exchange.* Reading, Mass: Addison-Wesley

51. Gilsenan, M. 1976. Dying, honor, and contradiction. See Ref. 67, pp. 191–219

52. Gluckman, M., Mitchell, J. C., Barnes, J. A. 1949. The village headman in British Central Africa. *Africa* 19:89–106

52a. Goody, E. 1972. 'Greeting,' 'begging,' and the presentation of respect. In *The Interpretation of Ritual,* ed. J. S. Fontaine, pp. 39–71. London: Tavistock

53. Gouldner, A. W. 1960. The norm of reciprocity: a preliminary statement. *Am. Sociol. Rev.* 25:161–78

54. Gregory, J. R. 1975. Image of limited good, or expectation or reciprocity? *Curr. Anthropol.* 16:1:73–92

55. Heath, A. F. 1976. Decision making and transactional theory. See Ref. 67, pp. 25–40

56. Heath, A. F. 1976. *Rational Choice and Social Exchange: A Critique of Exchange Theory.* Cambridge Univ. Press

57. Hogbin, H. I. 1971. Polynesian ceremonial gift exchange. In *Polynesia: Readings on a Culture Area,* ed. A. Howard, pp. 27–45. San Francisco: Chandler

58. Hollnsteiner, M. R. 1967. Social structure and power in a Philippine munici-

pality. In *Peasant Society, A Reader,* ed. J. M. Potter, M. N. Diaz, G. M. Foster, pp. 200–12. Boston: Little, Brown
59. Homans, G. C. 1961. *Social Behavior: Its Elementary Forms.* New York: Harcourt, Brace & World
60. Homans, G. C. 1964. Commentary. *Sociol. Inq.* 34:221–31
61. Homans, G. C., Schneider, D. M. 1955. *Marriage, Authority and Final Causes: A Study of Unilateral Cross-cousin Marriage.* Glencoe: Free Press
62. Hostetler, J., Huntington, G. E. 1967. *The Huterites in North America.* New York: Holt, Rinehart & Winston
63. Hurlbert, B. M. 1976. Status and exchange in the profession of anthropology. *Am. Anthropol.* 78:272–84
64. Johnson, C. L. 1974. Gift-giving and reciprocity among the Japanese Americans in Honolulu. *Am. Ethnol.* 1(2): 295–308
65. Kapferer, B. 1972. *Strategy and Transaction in an African Factory: African Workers and Indian Management in a Zambian Town.* Manchester: Univ. Press
66. Kapferer, B. 1976. Introduction: transactional models reconsidered. See Ref. 67, pp. 1–22
67. Kapferer, B., ed. 1976. *Transaction and Meaning: Directions in the Anthropology of Exchange and Symbolic Behavior.* Assoc. Soc. Anthropol. Commonwealth, Essays in Soc. Anthropol., Vol. 1. Philadelphia: Inst. for Study Human Issues
68. Kaut, C. 1961. *Utang na loob,* a system of contractual obligation among Tagalogs. *Southwest. J. Anthropol.* 17: 256–72
69. Kiefer, T. M. 1972. *The Tausug: Violence and Law in a Philippine Moslem Society.* New York: Holt, Rinehart & Winston
70. Kolenda, P. M. 1963. Toward a model of the Hindu Jajmani system. *Hum. Organ.* 22(1):11–31
71. Kuhn, A. 1963. *The Study of Society, A Unified Approach.* Homewood, Ill: Irwin-Dorsey
72. Lande, C. H. 1973. Networks and groups in Southeast Asia: some observations on the group theory of politics. *Am. Polit. Sci. Rev.* 67:103–27
73. Leach, E. R. 1951. The structural implications of matrilateral cross-cousin marriage. *J. R. Anthropol. Inst.* 81: 24–53
74. Lebra, T. S. 1969. Reciprocity and the asymmetric principle: an analytical

reappraisal of the concept of "on." *Psychologia* 12:129–38
75. Lebra, T. S. 1972. Reciprocity-based moral sanctions and messianic salvation. *Am. Anthropol.* 74:391–407
76. Lebra, T. S. 1975. An alternative approach to reciprocity. *Am. Anthropol.* 77:3:550–65
77. Lemarchand, R., Lemarchand, K. L. 1972. Political clientism and development. *Comp. Polit.* 4:149–78
78. Lévi-Strauss, C. 1949. Les Structures Élémentaires de la Parenté. Paris: Presses Univ. de France
79. Lévi-Strauss, C. 1953. Social structure. In *Anthropology Today,* ed. A. Kroeber, pp. 524–53. Univ. Chicago Press
80. Lévi-Strauss, C. 1969. *The Elementary Structures of Kinship.* Boston: Beacon
81. Lewis, H. S. 1974. Leaders and followers: some anthropological perspectives. *Addison-Wesley Module Anthropol. 50*
82. Lombardi, J. R. *Reciprocity and Survival.* Unpublished manuscript
83. Lomnitz, L. 1971. Reciprocity of favors in the urban middle class of Chide. In *Studies in Economic Anthropology,* ed. G. Dalton, pp. 93–106. Washington DC: Am. Anthrol. Assoc.
84. Lomnitz, L. 1974. The social and economic organization of a Mexican shantytown. In *Anthropological Perspectives on Latin American Urbanization,* Vol. 4, Chap. 6. LAUR: Sage Publications
85. Lomnitz, L. 1977. Survival and reciprocity—the case of urban marginality in Mexico. In *Extinction and Survival in Human Populations,* ed. C. D. Laughlin, A. I. Brady. New York: Columbia Univ. Press
86. Lomnitz, L. 1977. *The Survival of the Unfittest.* In press
87. Malinowski, B. 1922. *Argonauts of the Western Pacific.* New York: Dutton
88. Marriott, M. 1976. Hindu transactions: diversity without dualism. See Ref. 67, pp. 109–42
89. Mauss, M. 1954. *The Gift: Forms and Functions of Exchange in Archaic Societies.* Glencoe: Free Press
90. Mauss, M. 1925. Essai sur le don: forme et raison de l'echange dans les societes archaiques. *Annee Sociol.* n.s. 1:30–186
91. Meeker, B. F. 1971. Decisions and exchange. *Am. Sociol. Rev.* 36:485–95
92. Meggitt, M. 1977. *Blood is Their Argument: Warfare Among the Mae Enga Tribesmen of the New Guinea Highlands.* Palo Alto: Mayfield

93. Mulkay, M. J. 1971. *Functionalism, Exchange and Theoretical Strategy.* New York: Schoken. 220 pp.
94. Newman, P. L. 1965. *Knowing the Gururumba.* New York: Holt, Rinehart & Winston
95. Nord, W. R. 1969. Social exchange theory: an integrative approach to social conformity. *Psychol. Bull.* 71(3):174–208
96. Olson, M. 1965. *The Logic of Collective Action: Public Goods and the Theory of Groups.* Cambridge: Harvard Univ. Press
97. Orans, M. 1968. Maximizing in Jajmaniland: a model of caste relations. *Am. Anthropol.* 70:875–97
98. Paine, R., ed. 1971. *Patrons and Brokers in the East Arctic.* St. John's Memorial Univ. Newfoundland Inst. Soc. Econ. Res.
99. Paine, R. 1971. A theory of patronage and brokerage. See Ref. 98, pp. 8–21
100. Paine, R. 1976. Two modes of exchange and mediation. See Ref. 67, pp. 63–86
101. Parkin, D. 1976. Exchanging words. See Ref. 67, pp. 163–90
102. Polanyi, K. 1957. The economy as instituted process. In *Trade and Market in the Early Empires: Economics in History and Theory,* ed. K. Polanyi, C. M. Arensberg, H. W. Pearson, pp. 243–70. Glencoe: Free Press
103. Powell, J. D. 1970. Peasant society and clientelist politics. *Am. Polit. Sci. Rev.* 64(2):411–25
104. Pryor, F. L., Graburn, N. H. 1977. The myth of reciprocity. In *Social Exchange: Advances in Theory and Research,* ed. K. J. Gergern, M. S. Greenberg, R. Willis. New York: Wiley. In press
104a. Rehfisch, F. 1962. Competitive gift exchange among the Mambila. *Cah. Estud. Afr.* 3(9):91–103
105. Rosman, A., Rubel, P. G. 1972. *Feasting With Mine Enemy: Rank and Exchange Among Northwest Coast Societies.* New York: Columbia Univ. Press
106. Rosman, A., Rubel, P. G. 1972. The potlatch: a structural analysis. *Am. Anthropol.* 74(3):658–71
107. Rubel, P. G., Rosman, A. 1970. Potlatch and Sagali: the structure of exchange in Haida and Trobriand societies. *Trans. NY Acad. Sci.* 32(6):732–42
108. Rubel, P. G., Rosman, A. 1971. Potlatch and hakari: an analysis of Maori society in terms of the Potlatch model. *Man* 6:4:660–73

109. Sahlins, M. D. 1963. Poor man, rich man, big-man, chief, political types in Melanesia and Polynesia. *Comp. Stud. Soc. Hist.* 5:285–303
110. Sahlins, M. D. 1965. Exchange value and the diplomacy of primitive trade. *Proc. Am. Ethnol. Soc.,* pp. 95–129
111. Sahlins, M. D. 1965. On the sociology of primitive exchange. In *The Relevance of Models for Social Anthropology,* ed. M. Banton, pp. 139–236. New York: Praeger
112. Salisbury, R. F. 1962. *From Stone to Steel.* Cambridge Univ. Press
113. Salisbury, R. F. 1976. Transactions or transactors? an economic anthropologist's view. See Ref. 67, pp. 41–59
114. Sansom, B. 1976. A signal transaction and its currency. See Ref. 67, pp. 143–61
115. Schneider, H. 1974. *Economic Man: The Anthropology of Economics.* New York: Free Press
116. Schwimmer, E. 1974. *Exchange in the Social Structure of the Orokaiva, Traditional and Emergent Ideologies in the Northern District of Papua.* New York: St. Martin's
117. Scott, J. C. 1972. The erosion of patron-client bonds and social change in rural Southeast Asia. *J. Asian Stud.* 32(1):5–37
118. Scott, J. C. 1972. Patron-client politics and political change in Southeast Asia. *Am. Polit. Sci. Rev.* 66:91–113
119. Scott, J. C., Kerkvliet, B. J. 1973. How traditional rural patrons lose legitimacy: a theory with special reference to lowland Southeast Asia. *Comp. Stud. Soc. Hist.* 5:501–40
120. Silverman, S. F. 1965. Patronage and community-nation relationships in central Italy. *Ethnology* 4:172–89
121. Simpson, R. L. 1972. *Theories of Social Exchange.* Morristown, NJ: General Learning Press
122. Singlemann, P. 1972. Exchange as symbolic interaction. *Am. Sociol. Rev.* 37:414–24
123. Singlemann, P. 1973. On the reification of paradigms: reply to Abbott, Brown, and Crosbie. *Am. Sociol. Rev.* 38(4):506–9
124. Sociological Inquiry 1964. Research and commentary on the theorems and perspectives of George C. Homans. *Sociol. Inq.* 34:2
125. Spiro, M. E. 1966. Buddhism and economic action in Burma. *Am. Anthropol.* 68:1163–73

126. Stack, C. 1974. *All Our Kin: Strategies for Survival in a Black Community.* New York: Harper & Row

127. Strathern, A. 1971. *The Rope of Moka, Big-men and Ceremonial Exchange in Mount Hagen, New Guinea.* London: Cambridge Univ. Press

128. Strickon, A., Greenfield, S. M. 1972. *Structure and Process in Latin America, Patronage, Clientage, and Power Systems.* Albuquerque: Univ. New Mexico Press

129. Titmuss, R. M. 1971. *The Gift Relationship, From Human Blood to Social Policy.* New York: Random House

130. Turk, H., Simpson, R. L. 1971. *Institutions and Social Exchange. The Sociologies of Talcott Parsons and George C. Homans.* Indianapolis: Bobbs-Merrill

131. Wolf, E. 1966. Kinship, friendship, and patron-client relations in complex societies. In *The Social Anthropology of Complex Societies,* ed. M. Banton, pp. 1–22. London: Tavistock

132. Young, M. W. 1971. *Fighting with Food: Leadership, Values and Social Control in a Massim Society.* Cambridge Univ. Press

Ann. Rev. Anthropol. 1977. 6:283–314
Copyright © 1977 Annual Reviews Inc. All rights reserved

MOUNTAIN OF TONGUES: THE   ❖9596
LANGUAGES OF THE CAUCASUS

J. C. Catford

Department of Linguistics, University of Michigan, Ann Arbor, Michigan 48104

INTRODUCTION

The Great Caucasus mountain range strides for 500 miles across the isthmus from the Black Sea to the Caspian, forming a massive barrier between Europe and Asia. To the ancient Greeks, these mountains and the lands that lay below and around them were a place of mystery and legend. They dominated the farthest recess of the Euxine Sea; to Greek mariners the voyage to the Colchidian city of Phasis (the modern Poti) and up the like-named river (now known by the Svan name of "Rioni") was the Ἔσχατος δρόμος, the "uttermost run." Thither the Argonauts went in quest of the Golden Fleece, and in the mountains behind Phasis, and behind the Greek city of Dioscurias (the modern Sukhumi) Prometheus was chained, and there, too, in the words of Herodotus, there dwelt "many and all manner of nations."

Again and again in the two and a half millenia since Herodotus's day, writers have commented on the ethnic and linguistic diversity of the Caucasus. Strabo, writing about four and a half centuries later, having discounted more exaggerated estimates, affirms that 70 tribes, all speaking different languages, would come down to trade in Dioscurias, and a few decades after Strabo, Pliny claimed that the Romans carried on business in the same city by means of 130 interpreters. Arab travelers in the middle ages bore continuing witness to Caucasian polyglossia, and it was one of them, the tenth century geographer al-Mas'udi, who named the Caucasus *Jabal al-alsun,* "mountain of tongues."

At the present day we count more than 50 languages in the Caucasian mountain valleys, in the foothills, and in the closely adjoining plains. Some of these languages belong to well-known language families. Thus, Indo-European is represented by Armenian and by the Iranian languages Ossetic, Kurdish, Tat, and Talysh, not to mention Russian, the principal *lingua franca* of the area, and small enclaves of Greeks and speakers of other IE languages. The Turkic languages are Azeri (Azerbaijani), Turkoman, Karachay-Balkar, Nogai, and Kumyk. Mongolic is represented by Kalmyk, and Semitic by "Neo-Assyrian" or Aisor.

283

All these languages belong to families which have their most characteristic habitat elsewhere and the bearers of which are known to have migrated into the area at various historically attested times. There is, however, a residue of 37 languages which were not imported into the area in historical times and which are believed to have been spoken in the Caucasus area for at least 4000 years. These "indigenous" or "autochthonous" languages comprise the group generally called Caucasic or Caucasian in Western European publications, and most commonly "Ibero-Caucasian" (iberijsko-kavkazskie) in modern Russian sources. It is important to note that the prefix *ibero-* in this Russian term has absolutely no reference to the Iberian peninsula at the opposite end of Europe: it refers strictly to Caucasian Iberia, an ancient transcaucasian state in part of what is now Georgia. Some western scholars, it is true, have used the term Ibero-Caucasian to refer quite explicitly to a presumed relationship between Caucasian and Basque, as did Holmer (32), but there is no such presumption behind the Russian term.

There are two major groups of Caucasian languages, Northern and Southern. The North Caucasian languages fall into three groups: Abkhazo-Adyghan or North West Caucasian (NWC), Nakh or North Central Caucasian (NCC) and Dagestanian or North East Caucasian (NEC). The South Caucasian languages (SC), also known by the Georgian-derived name Kartvelian, form a single major group. Within each of these groups there are subgroups of closely related languages, as well as a few isolated languages.

In the following list the languages are placed within their appropriate groups and subgroups, but are numbered consecutively from 1 to 37. After the name of each language, or in some cases after the name of a whole subgroup, I give a brief indication of where the language is spoken and the number of its speakers in the Soviet Caucasus. These figures are chiefly taken from the *Encyclopaedia Britannica* (25), which quotes the 1970 Soviet Census, supplemented by reference to (40). The Ubykh language is now spoken by only a handful of people at Manyas, Turkey, south of the Sea of Marmara. According to Vogt (87), in 1962 there were no more than 20 speakers, all rather old. I, perhaps optimistically, have guessed the current number to be "about 10."

A few Caucasian languages have fairly well recognized English names, and in most cases I use these. For the rest I use slightly anglicized Russian forms—which, incidentally, often differ very widely from the native name. Two of the Tsez languages, Hinukh and Hunzib, are often literally transliterated from Russian as Ginukh and Gunzib: I spell them with "H" since this is one of those cases where "G" is used in Russian to represent an [h] sound.

North West Caucasian (Abkhazo-Adyghan)
   Abkhaz-Abazan: 1. *Abkhaz* (Abkhazian ASSR—80,000), 2. *Abaza* (Karachay-Cherkess AO—25,000).
   3. *Ubykh* (near Manyas, Turkey, about 10).
   Adyghan or Circassian: 4. *Adyghe* (formerly in most of the region between the Kuban River and the Black Sea; now chiefly in Adygej AO and a few villages near Tuapse and in the Karachay-Cherkess AO—100,000), 5. *Kabardian* (chiefly in Kabardino-Balkar ASSR and in Karachay-Cherkess AO—320,000).

North Central Caucasian (*Nakh*)
6. *Chechen* (Chechen-Ingush ASSR—613,000), 7. *Ingush* (Chechen-Ingush ASSR—158,000), 8. *Batsbiy* (Tusheti, N. Georgian SSR—3000).
North East Caucasian (*Dagestanian*)
Avaro-Andi-Dido: 9. *Avar* (chief language of the Dagestan Highlands—400,000). *Andi group* (in the western salient of the southern half of Dagestan): 10. *Andi* (9000), 11. *Botlikh* (3000), 12. *Godoberi* (2500), 13. *Karata* (5000), 14. *Akhwakh* (5000), 15. *Bagwali* (4000), 16. *Tindi* (5000), 17. *Chamali* (4000), Dido or Tsez group (immediately south of Andi group), 18. *Tsez* (7000), 19. *Khwarshi* (1000), 20. *Hinukh* (200), 21. *Bezhti* (2500), 22. *Hunzib* (600).
Lak-Dargi: 23. *Lak* (Dagestan highlands—86,000), 24. *Dargi* (E. of Lak—231,000). Lezgian group
25. *Artchi* (detached, between Lak and Avar—1000), 26. *Tabasaran* (S. Dagestan—55,000), 27. *Agul* (S. Dagestan—9000), 28. *Rutul* (S. Dagestan—12,000), 29. *Tsakhur* (S. Dagestan—11,000), 30. *Lezgi* (S. Dagestan and N. Azerbaijan—300,000), 31. *Krytz* (N. Azerbaijan—6000), 32. *Budukh* (N. Azerbaijan—1000), 33. *Khinalug* (N. Azerbaijan—1000), 34. *Udi* (N. Azerbaijan and one village in E. Georgia—4000).
South Caucasian (*Kartvelian*)
35. *Georgian* (Georgian SSR—2,792,000), 36. *Svan* (in the mountains of N.W. Georgia—43,000), 37. *Zan* with two major dialects: *Megrelian* (W. Georgia and E. Abkhazia—360,000) and *Laz* or *Chan* (on the Black Sea coast of East Anatolia, abutting on Georgia—50,000).

From the above, we see that there are about 5,660,000 speakers of Caucasian languages in the Soviet Caucasus. Outside of the USSR there are perhaps 80,000 Georgian speakers (about 70,000 of them in Turkey and Iran), 50,000 Laz speakers in Turkey, and about 170,000 speakers of NWC languages throughout the Middle East. These last are the people generally known throughout the area as "Circassians," but include about 10,000 Abazans as well as speakers of Circassian (Adyghan) dialects. They are the descendants of the great number (estimated at nearly half a million) of NWC Moslems who migrated into Turkey around 1865 when the Russians invaded their NWC homeland. Great numbers were settled in Anatolia, where their descendants still live. The Turks settled others around the eastern borders of the Ottoman Empire as frontier guards, hence the present-day Circassian colonies in the Middle East. The 1964 *Atlas of Peoples of the World* (3) enumerates 105,000 Circassians in Turkey, 25,000 in Syria, 20,000 in Jordan, and 8000 in Iraq. In addition, there are about 2000 in Israel. In the United States there is a small Circassian community in New York City and in New Jersey.

Adding the 300,000 or so Caucasian speakers outside the USSR to the number living in the Soviet Caucasus, we reach a grand total of about 6 million speakers of Caucasian languages.

For an overall view of Caucasian languages very little is available in English. The Dutch linguist Aert Kuipers contributed a survey to the first volume of *Current Trends in Linguistics* (54). Also valuable, though brief, is the article on Caucasian languages by the Georgian linguists Gamkrelidze & Gudava in the latest edition of the *Encyclopaedia Britannica* (25). *Peoples and Languages of the Caucasus* by Geiger et al (27) is a useful reference work, though in some respects (e.g. population statistics) out of date, and, of course, it gives no descriptions of the languages.

For general descriptions of Caucasian languages one must turn to works in languages other than English. Dirr's 1928 *Einführung* (21) is outdated, though the section on the Caucasian verb is still a useful summary. Deeters' 79-page survey "Die Kaukasischen Sprachen" in the 1963 *Handbuch der Orientalistik* (15) is quite useful, but the best short introduction to Caucasian languages as a whole is Klimov's *Kavkazskie jazyki* (Caucasian Languages), published in Russian in 1965 (50) and in German translation in 1969. The German version is more useful in some respects than the original. It contains a much fuller bibliography, better maps, and a useful list of Caucasian alphabets with transliterations. For the reader of Spanish there is Bouda's 85-page "Introducción" (8), which includes texts.

Undoubtedly the most useful general introduction is Volume 4 of the Russian series *Jazyki narodov SSSR* (*Languages of the Peoples of the USSR*) (40). This 700-page work contains general introductory material and a short descriptive sketch of from 15 to 22 pages in length of every Caucasian language. These descriptions, covering chiefly phonology and morphology (with a few paragraphs on syntax, lexis, and dialects), are written according to a uniform plan by leading Soviet Caucasologists.

Since the major works just mentioned (25, 40, 50) between them provide a fairly complete bibliography up to 1969, I make no attempt to do the same here, mainly citing publications only when they are relevant to the discussion in hand. What I attempt to do in this survey is to provide a general account of Caucasian languages topic by topic rather than language by language.

PHONOLOGY

There is a widespread belief among linguists that Caucasian languages are characterized by enormous numbers of consonants but minimal vowel systems. This is more or less true only of the NWC languages. Among these, Ubykh apparently holds a world's record with 80 consonant phonemes and probably two vowels. The Bzyb or northwest dialect of Abkhaz has 67 consonants (and two vowels), though literary Abkhaz has only 58 consonants. The Bzhedukh dialect of Adyghe has 64 consonants, literary Adyghe only 52, while Kabardian has 47 consonants. Both the Adyghan languages have minimal vowel systems. The remaining 32 Caucasian languages, however, have a much more "ordinary" ratio of consonants to vowels. With three exceptions, the 26 Dagestanian languages have from 30 to 46 consonants and from 5 to 10 basic vowel phonemes. These exceptions are the Andi language Akhwakh and the Lezgian languages Artchi and Khinalug. Akhwakh has 50 consonants, as against the 38 to 45 of other Andi languages, chiefly because of its full set of 7 laterals, and 4 uvular stop and affricate phonemes. In general, Lezgian consonant systems run from 30 to 46. According to Khajdakov (42), Artchi has 51 consonants, although Mikailov (65) lists only 46. Khinalug appeared already to have some unusual consonantal features for a Lezgian language among its 44 or 45 consonants in Dešeriev's grammar (16). The most recent description of Khinalug by a Moscow State University team (47) indicates that at least one consonant /ɬ/ has disappeared from Khinalug. On the other hand, Kibrik et al (47) elaborate the system, chiefly by recognizing a series of palatalized consonant phonemes, bringing the total inventory to 76. The Kartvelian languages have 28 (Georgian) and 30 (Zan and Svan) consonants plus 5 (Georgian) and basically 6 (Zan and Svan) vowels, though the number of vowel phonemes is higher in some dialects of Svan. There is as yet no general work on the phonetics and phonology of Caucasian languages, though this is a project toward which the present author is working, but there are, of course, phonological sketches in descriptions of particular languages, notably those in *Jazyki narodov* (40). We mention here, however, some particularly informative special works on the phonetics/phonology of single languages or language groups.

For the NWC languages there is a useful phonological sketch in French, with tables of the consonant phonemes of Ubykh, Abkhaz, Adyghe, literary Kabardian, and the Bes(le)ney dialect of Kabardian in Catherine Paris' book on the latter dialect (69). The phonetics of all dialects of the Adyghan languages have been treated by Balkarov (4), the special features of Adyghe dialects by Rogava & Keraševa (72), and of Kabardian dialects in the 1969 symposium edited by Kumakhov (62).

For the NCC (Nakh) languages we have Sommerfelt's studies published (in French) in 1934, 1938, and 1947 (78). These, like Deseriev's 1963 book in Russian (18), have a comparative-historical orientation but also give descriptive information. The most recent work on general NCC phonology is Crelašvili's *System of Consonants of the Nakh Languages* in Georgian (14), but available also in Russian in the same author's 81-page "avtoreferat" or dissertation resumé. There are several descriptive works on Chechen phonetics, notably by Deseriev (17) and in Deserieva's (19) "contrastive analysis" of the phonetics of Chechen and Russian.

Apart from some of the older work of Trubetskoy, such as his "Die Konsonatensysteme der ostkaukasischen Sprachen," published in 1931 (84), there are no purely descriptive works on Dagestanian (NEC) languages as a whole. Bokarëv's pioneering work (7) was, of course, comparative-historically oriented and is the basis of the phonological aspects of later works such as Murkelinskij's (67) and, to some extent, Khajdakov's (43). There are phonological sketches in the grammars of individual languages, and in works dealing with language groups such as Gudava's *Consonantism of the Andi Languages* (29) and Bokarëv's *Tsez (Dido) Languages of Dagestan* (6), both in Russian. One of the most valuable works on Dagestan phonetics is Gaprindašvili's *Fonetika darginskogo jazyka* of 1966 (26). Although dealing specifically with the phonetics of Dargi dialects, it contains a great deal of information concerning Dagestanian phonetics in general, and provides some hard data on Dargi in the form of X-ray tracings, kymograms, oscillograms, acoustic spectra, and palatograms. There is a specialized study of the phonetics of the Lezgian language Tsakhur by Ibragimov (33) which is interesting though without instrumental data.

General information on Kartvelian (SC) phonetics and phonology is, of course, contained in comparative-historical works such as those by Schmidt (73), Klimov (49) and Gamkrelidze & Machavariani (24). The structure of the Kartvelian syllable is discussed in Zhghenti's *Comparative Phonetics of the Kartvelian Languages* (89), Part I published in 1960 in Georgian, but with Russian and English summaries. As for Georgian, by far the best described of the SC languages, Zhghenti's *Phonetics of the Georgian Language* (88) (in Georgian) contains X-ray tracings, kymograms, and palatograms of Georgian articulations. More accessible are the shorter descriptions of Georgian phonetics and phonology by Robins & Waterson (71) and Vogt (86).

I now propose to characterize briefly the main features of the consonantal and vocalic systems of Caucasian languages.

Consonants

The consonant systems of all Caucasian languages have certain characteristics in common, namely (i) *stops* articulated at *labial, dentalveolar, velar,* and *uvular* locations (types *p t k q*); (ii) *affricates* at two locations (types *ts tʃ*), *fricatives* at *alveolar, postalveolar,* and *uvular* locations (types *s ʃχ*). Incidentally, it is noteworthy that in Caucasian languages if there is only *one* type of dorsal fricative it is always uvular, not velar. The basic consonant inventory is completed (iii) by two nasals (*m n*), a labial semivowel or fricative (*w / v*), a palatal semivowel (*j*), an apical trill (*r*), and all except the Adyghan languages have a lateral approximant (*l*). In the two Adyghan literary languages all the laterals are fricative: ɮ ɬ ɬ'.

In all Caucasian languages the stop consonants participate in a *voiced, voiceless aspirated,* and *glottalic* triad of the type (*d t t'*). All three types are always represented at the dentalveolar and velar locations, but one or more members of the triad may be absent at the labial or uvular location: thus Avar has *d t t'* and *g k k',* but only *b* and *p* and *q* and *q'*. In just over half the Caucasian languages the triadic series extend to affricates, i.e. we find *dz ts ts', dʒ tʃ tʃ'*. However, in most of the Avar-Andi-Tsez languages and Lak and Dargi the voiced member is absent. Finally, the triadic series extends also to some of the fricatives in the Adyghan languages and in dialects of two Andi languages (Bagwali and Chamali).

What we have outlined here is the universal or common-core Caucasian consonant system. Almost exactly this system is, in fact, realized in the Kartvelian (SC) languages, which have the simplest of all Caucasian consonant systems. The Kartvelian consonant system may be represented thus:

m	n				
b	d		g		
p	t		k	(q)	(ʔ)
p'	t'		k'	q'	
	dz	dʒ			
	ts	tʃ			
	ts'	tʃ'			
v	z	ʒ	ʁ		
	s	ʃ	χ	(h)	
w					
	l	j			
		r			

This is the consonant system of Georgian, Svan, and Zan—the aspirated (*q*) occurs only in Svan, the glottal stop (ʔ) only in Megrelian, and (h) is rare in Georgian.

In all the other Caucasian languages this simple common core system is elaborated in various ways right up to the 80-consonant system of Ubykh. These elaborations for the most part take the following forms. First, there may be an additional term added to triads like *d t t'* or to diadic sets of affricates or fricatives. Additions of this type are usually called *intensive, strong,* or *geminate* with respect to the 18 Dagestanian languages in which they occur, and unaspired or *preruptive* with respect to the two dialects of Adyghe (Shapsugh and Bzhedukh) in which they occur. The term "preruptive" (preruptivnyj) for "strong and unaspirated" was apparently coined in contrast to the commonly used Russian term "abruptive" (abruptivnyj) meaning "glottalic." The result of this type of addition is to produce sets like *b p pp p', g k kk k'* etc in which the fourth, "intensive" term is realized in various ways. Generally in Lak, Dargi, and the Lezgian languages intensive stops *pp tt kk* etc are tense unaspirated, and, when intervocalic, geminate. The corresponding affricates *tts* and *ttʃ* are likewise tense and have a lengthened stop portion and tense unaspirated affrication. In Avar and most of the Andi languages the "intensive" stops are strongly affricated, intensive affricates have lengthened affrication and are unaspirated, and the intensive fricatives are lengthened and unaspirated. In all these languages, the nontense correlates of these phonemes are short and aspirated. Thus in Avar we have the pairs *k-kk, k'-kk', ts-tss, ts'-tss', s-ss, ʃ-ʃʃ*, etc realized as [kʰ-kx, k'-kx', tsʰ-tss, ts'-tss', sʰ-ss, etc]. The tense fricatives in Avar, in addition to being longer, generally have a louder hiss than the corresponding nontense fricatives, which betokens a higher velocity of air flow through the articulatory channel, partly achieved by narrowing the channel, as Gaprindaš-vili's palatograms show for Dargi dialects (26).

The second way in which the consonant system may be augmented is by the addition of more articulatory locations. Thus the stop series is often extended by the addition of a glottal stop. Glottal stop phonemes occur in Abaza and Adyghan, in all three Nakh languages, and in virtually all Dagestanian languages. Indeed a number of languages have more than one glottal stop phoneme. Both of the Adyghan literary languages have plain ʔ and labialized ʔʷ, and the Abdzakh dialect of Adyghe has a slightly palatalized ʔʲ as well. This is the reflex of the Proto-Circassian postalveolar glottalic affricates *tɕ' and *tʃ' which have lost their oral articulation in Abdzakh. The Nakh languages and a few Dagestanian languages, notably the Tsez languages and Dargi, contrast a weak glottal stop ʔ, often realized simply as creak, with a strong glottal stop ʔʔ, which involves tight closure of the ventricular bands (as well as the vocal cords) and some constriction of the pharynx. This is sometimes called a "pharyngal stop" in the literature, but is perhaps better described as a (pharyngalized) ventricular + glottal stop. Incidentally, in reading the literature on Caucasian languages one must note that Georgian linguists generally use the Georgian or Russian equivalent of "pharyngal" to mean what is more commonly (e.g. by Moscow linguists and by the International Phonetic Association) called "uvular."

Additions to the fricative series include a voiceless labial fricative in a few languages—labiodental *f* in the NWC languages and a few Lezgian languages, bilabial *ɸ* in Ingush and Tabasaran. In addition to the uvular fricatives χ and ʁ, most North Caucasian languages except Nakh, Hunzib, and Udi, have at least one *velar* fricative, and many have at least one *pharyngal* fricative or approximant.

Other elaborations involve secondary articulations—*labialization, palatalization, pharyngalization.* The feature of *labialization* is found in all the NWC languages, sporadically elsewhere. In NWC it applies to stops and to apico-laminal, dorsal, and pharyngal fricatives. It takes various forms, which I have described elsewhere (10) including simple lip-rounding, labiodentalization (of the affricats dz ts ts' in Abkhaz, and also in a few Lezgian languages) and, most interesting, complete labial closure. Thus labialized *d t t'* in Abkhaz and Ubykh are in fact *db tp tp'* with simultaneous complete (inner) labial closure. Such "strongly" labialized sounds also occur in some dialects of Lak.

Palatalization is applied to stops and some affricates and fricatives in the NWC languages. Most interestingly, Abkhaz, Abaza, and Ubykh have *plain, labialized,* and *palatalized uvulars* (q qʷ qʲ,χχʷχʲ etc) in which the primary stricture is indeed at the back-velar or uvular location, but the more anterior part of the tongue dorsum is raised up toward the hard palate, forming a longitudinally extended articulation.

Pharyngalization occurs with labials and uvulars in Ubykh, and with uvular fricatives only in the Bzyb dialect of Abkhaz. In both these languages we have the unusual phenomenon of the co-occurrence of the features *labialized* and *pharyngalized* on uvulars.

The features of palatalization and labialization occur with sibilants in NWC (and in Tabasaran, with its labiodentalized sʷ tsʷ etc). The elaboration of sibilant articulation can, however, best be described in terms of the distinct articulatory positions involved. In NWC languages there are four basic sibilant types: s -apico-or lamino-alveolar, ʃ-apico-postalveolar (slightly velarized), ɕ lamino-postalveolar, palatalized, and the peculiar NWC sibilant ŝ, which occurs in slightly varying forms in Bzyb, Ubykh, and the Adyghan languages. The sound ŝ, described in the Russian literature as "hissing-hushing," is indeed acoustically and physiologically between a typical s and a typical ʃ. In its production the tip of the tongue rests against the alveoles of the lower teeth (as for a laminal s), but the main articulatory channel is at the back of the alveolar ridge (as for a lamino-postalveolar ʃ). It is also often slightly pharyngalized. The greatest proliferation of sibilants is found in the Bzhedukh dialect of Adyghe, which, by combining these four basic types with the various initiation-phonation types and the "intensity" opposition, achieves no fewer than 14 sibilants, all phonemically distinct, namely z ʒ ʐ ẑ ẑʷ, ŝ' ŝʷ', s, ʃʰ ʃʃ, ɕʰ ɕɕ, ŝ ŝʷ.

One other characteristic Caucasian extension of the consonant system is a set of lateral fricatives and/or affricates. Nineteen Caucasian languages augment their consonant system in this way. The various types of nonapproximant laterals that occur include glottalic, voiceless, and voiced fricatives (the voiced lateral fricative ɮ occurs in the Adyghan languages, to the exclusion of approximant *l,* which does not occur in these languages), voiceless and glottalic lateral affricates. The intensity opposition is applied to laterals in the Avar and Andi languages, which show the greatest proliferation of laterals, the record being held by Akhwakh which has seven: approximant *l* plus ɬʰ ɬɬ, tɬ tɬɬ, tɬ' tɬɬ'. All are phonemically distinct. Artchi is exceptional among Lezgian languages in having a set of four lateral fricatives and affricates, and even more exceptional in that, according to Mikailov (65) and Kibrik (46), these laterals are all *velar* or slightly palatalized velar with respect to the location of their central obstruction.

In Akhwakh, the duration of the noise-burst and voicing lag of the short lateral affricates is no more than that of an aspirated stop, while the long or "tense" or "geminate" lateral affricates have long and noisy affrication. One might, therefore, speak of an opposition between "lateral stops" (*tɬ̩* and *tɬ'*) and lateral affricates (*tɬɬ* and *tɬɬ'*). For actual durations of the voicing lag of these sounds see Catford (13, p. 214.)

To conclude this section on consonants, here are the consonant systems of Avar and Abkhaz illustrating some of the "elaborations" of the core system.

Avar:

m	n											
b	d			g								
p	t			k	kk			q	ʔ			
p'	t'			k'	kk'			q'				
ts	tss	tʃ	tʃʃ									
ts'	tss'	tʃ'	tʃʃ'	tɬɬ'								
v	z	3						ʁ		ʕ		
s	ss	ʃ	ʃʃ	ɬ	ɬɬ	x	xx	χ	χχ	ħ	h	
	l		r	j								

Abkhaz:

m	n										
b	d	dʷ		gʲ	g	gʷ					
p	t	tʷ		kʲ	k	kʷ					
p'	t'	tʷ'		kʲ'	k'	kʷ'	qʲ'	q'	qʷ'		
	dz	dzʷ	dʒ	dʐ							
	ts	tsʷ	tʃ	tɕ							
	ts'	tsʷ'	tʃ'	tɕ'							
v	z		3	ʐ ʐʷ				ʁʲ	ʁ	ʁ ʷ	
f	s		ʃ	ɕ ɕʷ				χʲ	χ	χʷ	ħ	ħʷ
w			l	r j ɥ							

The symbol ɥ represents a labial plus palatal semivowel, exactly like the initial French sound of *huit*. It is the Abkhaz reflex of the voiced labialized pharyngal approximant of Abaza, ʕ ʷ. The Bzyb dialect of Abkhaz has all the above consonants, plus *dẑ tŝ tŝ' ẑ ŝ ẑʷ ŝʷ* and the pharyngalized uvular fricatives χ χ ʷ, giving a total of 67.

Ubykh lacks six of the Bzyb consonants (g k k' ɥ ħ and ħʷ) but more than makes up for that by adding a set of pharyngalized labials and uvulars, a velar *x* and *γ* (as well as the uvular fricatives), a glottal *h,* and the laterals *tɬ'* and ɬ, to achieve its record total of 80 phonemically distinct consonants.

Consonant Clusters

Caucasian languages have a reputation for permitting enormous intrasyllabic clusters of consonants. This is strictly true only of Kartvelian—above all Georgian, and to some extent NWC. The Nakh languages have a moderate number of consonant clusters, and the Dagestanian languages, with the exception of Lezgi, admit none but the very simplest clusters of consonant + *w*, in initial position at least. The considerable number of initial clusters in Lezgi is no doubt of relatively recent origin; at least the highly varied Lezgi clusters do not conform to what seems to be a Caucasian typological norm.

To return to Kartvelian: in Georgian there are syllable initial clusters of from 2 to 6 terms, and final clusters of from 2 to 5. Such forms as *prtskvna* "to peel," *ts'vrtna* "to train," *brts'q'inva* "to shine," are not at all rare. Vogt (86) lists all the initial clusters that occur in Georgian. They total 740 (cf English with 40 to 50 initial clusters, according to dialect), of which 4 are 6-term clusters, 21 are 5-term, and 148 are 4-term.

The structure of Georgian consonant-clusters though varied is not random, and there is one frequent and highly typical variety of initial cluster which Georgian linguists call "harmonic complexes" of consonants [see Zhghenti (89)]. These clusters are characterized by the following three formation-rules:

1. They consist of *occlusive* (stop or affricate) followed by *occlusive* or *fricative*, i.e. type pk dʁts'q' etc, not *fk *χp etc, except for a limited set of clusters with initial *s* or *ʃ*.
2. They are homogeneous with respect to initiation and phonation, i.e. glottalic, or voiced, or voiceless throughout, i.e. types *p'k' ts'q' bz dʁp*χ *t*χ etc, not *p'b *bs etc.
3. They are "recessive," i.e. in terms of articulation they "recede" back into the mouth, the second term always being posterior to the first term.

There is a relationship of solidarity between the rules such that if any two apply then the third also applies.

Exactly the same rules apply to morpheme-initial clusters in the Adyghan languages, where the only exception is the Adyghe *tf* (which contravenes rule 3). This, however, is clearly of relatively recent origin and results from the change of Proto-Circassian *x^w to *f,* as evidenced by the corresponding cluster in Kabardian, which is *tx^w*. Basically the same initial cluster rules apply to Ubykh, Abkhaz, and Abaza, only in the last two languages more complex clusters have arisen, no doubt through widespread loss of interconsonantal vowel.

In the Nakh languages the numbers of initial consonant clusters are small; excluding clusters of foreign (chiefly Russian) origin, Chechen and Ingush have around 20, Batsbiy a few more. What is interesting, however, is that for the most part the Nakh consonant clusters follow precisely the same formation rules as do the Georgian "harmonic complexes" and the NWC intramorphemic clusters. Of these three rules, the third—that is, the rule that the second term in the cluster must have a more posterior articulation than the first—is particularly interesting. The fact that this rare, if not unique, rule of consonant clustering occurs in three distinct sub-branches of Caucasian—NWC, NCC, SC—is undoubtedly of some significance for general Caucasian typology.

Vowels

We mentioned in the general introduction to Phonology that the five NWC languages have minimal vowel systems. These vowel systems have been the subject of a good deal of discussion and controversy, which I can do little more than suggest here. In a NWC language such as Kabardian we can hear many nuances of vowel quality such as *i ι ɨ ɷ ü u e ë ə ɔ̈ o a ʌ a* etc. It soon becomes apparent to any observer, however, that many of these vowel qualities are environmentally conditioned. Thus *i* or *ι* occur in the neighborhood of *j,* ɷ ü u ɔ̈ o etc in the neighborhood of *w* and labialized consonants, and so on. Apparent minimally contrasting sets such as *bzɨ* "female," *bzi* "ray," *bzu* "sparrow," *bzë* "language," *bi* "enemy," *be*(i) "rich," *bë* "much," *ba* "kiss," etc can be shown by simple morphological tests to be analyzable as containing a vowel + *j* or *w*. Thus, though *bzɨ* "female" + *f'ɨ* "good" yields *bzɨf', bzi* + *f'ɨ* yields *bzijf'* (not *bzi:f'), *bzu* + *f'ɨ* yields *bzuwɷf'* (not *bzu:f'), and so on. In short, one quickly discovers that there seem to be only three distinctive vocalic units: a *close* vowel which one may write, following Jakovlev, *ə* (with allophones i ι ɨ ɷ u etc), a *mid* vowel *e* (with allophones e ɛ ʌ ɔ u etc), and a *third unit,* which we may write *a* (with allophones a α). In 1923 Jakovlev published a remarkably detailed study of Kabardian phonetics-phonology (36) in which he analyzed the vowel system as *ə e a* in which there were two vowel *qualities, ə* and *e, a* being in fact the *long* of e. Trubetskoy, in his 1925 review of Jakovlev (83), distinguished the vowels as *close mid* and *open*. For a long time the Kabardian (and Adyghe) *vertical* vowel system, *ə e a,* was regarded as unique, though we now know that vertical vowel systems of this type occur in some languages of New Guinea, as reported by E. Pike (70).

Having reached a vertical 3-vowel system for Kabardian, it is tempting to reduce it still further. Jakovlev, as we have seen, regarded *a* as the long of *e* (though measurements show that there is little empirical basis for this assessment—in most environments the difference is primarily one of quality), and he further suggested that since *ə* alternated with *zero* in largely predictable ways, it was possible that *at some period in its history* Kabardian had been a *monovocalic* language, the single vowel phoneme *e* contrasting on the one hand with *ə*~*zero* and on the other *ē* (=a). Jakovlev was prepared to posit monovocalism only as appertaining to an earlier stage of Kabardian; at no time in 1923 or his later works did he ever suggest that present-day Kabardian is monovocalic. Others, however, have been less cautious. The present writer about 1948 (before having seen Jakovlev's work) began to write a paper entitled "Kabardian: a Monovocalic language?" but abandoned it for lack of data. In 1960 Kuipers (53) published a book in which, on the basis of complex arguments, he arrives at a monovocalic analysis of Kabardian. Meanwhile Genko (28) and Allen (1) had proposed a monovocalic analysis of another NWC language, Abaza. The hitherto unheard-of possibility of languages with only one vowel phoneme aroused great interest among linguists since it added plausibility to the postulation of a single vowel phoneme for Proto-Indo-European. The monovocalic hypothesis was attacked by Szemerényi in 1964 (81), and strongly defended with reference to the NWC languages by Allen in 1965 (2).

The monovocalic analysis of NWC languages is certainly very attractive. In his 1960 book, however, Kuipers went even further. Pointing out that a syllable-peak with the unique vowel *e* is distinguished from one with *ə~zero* only by its degree of openness, we could, he suggests, call *e* simply a "feature of openness." And since this feature of openness occurs only along with consonants, it can be regarded, along with labialization and palatalization, as simply another feature of "shape of the mouth resonator." Kabardian would thus be not merely a monovocalic language, but a phonologically vowelless language—a language with no opposition consonant-vowel (nonsyllabic-syllabic) in its phonology. This extreme position was criticized by Halle (31) and is not widely accepted.

An important advance in the discussion of NWC monovocalism was the publication of an article by the Soviet Adyghan specialist Kumakhov (61). Reviewing all the previous discussion, Kumakhov adduces evidence, for Adyghan in particular, casting doubt not only on the "vowelless" but also on the monovocalic interpretation. Among other things he draws attention to certain clear cases of linguistically relevant oppositions between the close vowel *ə* and *zero*, which seem to reinstate this vowel as a phoneme. Kumaxov finally posits a three-vowel system *ə~e~a* for Adyghe and Kabardian and a two-vowel system *ə~a* for Abkhaz, Abaza, and Ubykh.

The latest contribution to the discussion is an article by Kuipers in 1976 (56) in which he responds to the criticisms of Halle and Kumakhov and reaffirms his position, and extends the "vowelless" hypothesis to Abkhaz as well as Kabardian. So the problem of the NWC vowel-systems is not yet resolved. At the very least they are certainly all unidimensional "vertical" systems; possibly one or more of them is monovocalic.

The vowel systems of all the other Caucasian languages are more orthodox, though not without features of interest. The Nakh languages have fairly extensive vowel systems. Thus Chechen is said to have a total of 30 vocalic nuclei—15 vowels and 15 diphthongs. The 15 simple vowels, however, break down into 9 basic vowel qualities, roughly *i e æ a ɔ o u ɨ y* of which 6 can be long *i: e: a: o: u: y:*. Batsbiy, like most of the Andi and Tsez languages, augments its vowel systems by a series of nasalized vowels.

The Dagestanian languages have from 5 to 10 basic vowel phonemes, in many cases augmented by a set of *long* and/or *nasalized* vowels. In addition, about 10 Dagestanian languages have some *pharyngalized* vowels. The fullest sets of pharyngalized vowels are found in Tsez and Khwarshi and in the Lezgian languages Artchi, Tsakhur, Rutul, and Udi. In Tsakhur, for example, we have a basic set of six vowels *i e a o u ɨ* (of which some can occur long), all six also occurring pharyngalized. This pharyngalization takes the form of retraction of the tongue-root, and it appears to induce, as a side-effect, a certain degree of *fronting* of back vowels, particularly the closer vowels *u* and *o*. The exact mechanism of this is not clear, but the fact is that in Tsakhur and Udi the pharyngalized *u* and *o* have a distinctly central quality. Formant frequencies for Tsakhur u show a marked rise (implying a forward shift) in passing from u to pharyngalized u^c. The averages for a small sample (3 or 4 examples) are u F1 380 F2 760, u^c F1 400 F2 1050. This "fronting" associated with pharyngalization, or pharyngal articulation, is also found in NWC. As we saw above, the Abkhaz equivalent of Abaza ʕʷ is the labial + palatal semivowel ɥ (not w). In fact, the rounding applied to ʕʷ or ħʷ in Abaza and to ħʷ Abkhaz is precisely of the ɥ-type. This association of pharyngalization and fronting constitutes what Trubetskoy (84) termed "emphatische Mouillure" ("emphatic softening"). Moreover, the fronting effect of pharyngalization accounts for a number of curiously "skewed"-looking vowel systems. Thus the vowel systems of Lak, Lezgi, and Tabasaran may be represented as:

	Lak		Lezgi		Tabasaran

When we realize that the front or central vowels represented by e æ and œ y or ɵ are slightly pharyngalized, we see that we have basically a triangular vowel system in which the additional vowels result from the probable influence of pharyngal or pharyngalized consonants.

Soviet scholars often refer to vowels of the æ y œ ɵ type as "umlauted," but they do not usually result from the particular diachronic process known as "umlaut" in Western Indo-European languages. There are, however, a few Caucasian languages in which a genuine umlaut process—stressed vowel modified by the quality of the unstressed vowel in the following syllable—has occurred. This is the case in some dialects of Chechen, but it is best known in the SC language Svan, on which see Kaldani (41), in Georgian with Russian summary. Apparently in some dialects of Svan the umlaut process has resulted in rounded front vowels, at least the letters ü and ö are used in the literature. However, the only two Svan speakers I have worked with had *wi* or *iw* for *ü* and *we* or *ew* for *ö*. Examples of Svan umlaut are: *pwir* or *pirw* (cf Geo. *puri*) "cow," *twek'* or *tekw'* (Geo. tok'i) "rope," *wep* (Geo. opli) "sweat," *semi* (*sami*) "three," *didæb* or *didab* (Geo. dideba) "glory," etc.

ORTHOGRAPHIES

Only the Georgian language has its own native writing system and a rich literature going back to the fifth century. The Georgian alphabet is traditionally supposed to have been invented around 400 A.D. by that same Armenian cleric, Mesrop Maštots, who is credited with the invention of the Armenian alphabet and probably also the Caucasian Albanian alphabet. Caucasian Albania was an ancient transcaucasian kingdom located to the southeast of ancient Iberia, largely in what is now Azerbaijan. Known about since the end of the nineteenth century, the Albanian alphabet did not become an object of study until after the discovery in 1937 and 1953 of copies of the alphabet in fifteenth and sixteenth century Armenian manuscripts and, more importantly, the discovery in 1948 of a short inscription on a stone slab, and other fragments, at Mingečaur in Azerbaijan. A number of scholars suppose that the language of these fragments in the Albanian alphabet is an older form of Udi, a Lezgian language which is today unwritten and spoken chiefly in two villages in northern Azerbaijan, but more research is required before this can be established with certainty. Klimov (50) outlines the discovery and research on the Albanian alphabet, and other useful sources are by Shanidze (77) and Gukasjan (30).

There are then only two indigenous alphabets for Caucasian languages, and one of them, the Caucasian Albanian alphabet, apparently went out of use very early. During the five or six centuries preceding the Revolution no Caucasian language other than Georgian had an official or widely used orthography. However, that does not mean that these languages were never written. In Dagestan particularly, where there was a long tradition of Islamic culture and of literature in Arabic, various Caucasian languages were written in the Arabic alphabet. The oldest example of this is a group of marginal and interlinear notes in Dargi on an Arabic manuscript of 1243 A.D., believed to be contemporary with the manuscript. There are other early examples from the end of the fifteenth century of Dargi, Lak, and Avar in Arabic script.

By the nineteenth century there was a fairly well established tradition of writing Avar and Lak in the Arabic script, but it was only after the Revolution that the Soviet government created no fewer than *eleven* new literary languages, providing alphabets for Abkhaz, Abaza, Adyghe, Kabardian-Cherkess, Chechen, Ingush, Avar, Lak, Dargi, Tabasaran, and Lezgi. Most of these languages achieved their literary status in 1918, but Ingush in 1920, Abaza and Tabasaran in 1932.

The first official orthography for Adyghe, Kabardian, Chechen, Avar, Lak, Dargi, and Lezgi used the Arabic alphabet, augmented by additional points and other diacritic marks and by slight modifications of some letter shapes; for instance, the glottalic and voiceless lateral fricatives of Adyghe and Kabardian were represented by the Arabic *l* with, respectively, one and two little ticks added to the letter. In 1928 the Arabic orthographies were replaced by augmented Roman (Kabardian, in fact, went through two different augmented Roman alphabets between 1924 and 1936). Three other languages were written from the start in augmented Roman: Ingush in 1920, Abaza and Tabasaran in 1932. In 1938 (1936 in the case of Kabardian) the augmented Roman alphabets were replaced by Cyrillic. This was a very reasonable move because even though the Caucasians learned to read and write first in their own language, most would eventually learn Russian, and they might as well start out knowing the alphabet. The Cyrillic alphabet introduced at that time and still in use is, in fact, simply the Russian alphabet with no new letters with the exception of capital I, which was, in any case, a letter of the old prerevolutionary Russian alphabet. This capital I, which projects above the line of type in a noticeable way, is called the "paločka" or "little stick" by Caucasians. The *paločka* serves three purposes: first, by itself, it represents *glottal stop;* second, following letters representing a voiceless stop, an affricate, and some fricatives it indicates *glottalic initiation;* and third, it is used after one or two letters to represent pharyngal or glottal or uvular articulation according to language. Since I is the only additional letter in the Caucasian Cyrillic alphabets, many Caucasian phonemes have to be represented by digraphs, trigraphs, and in one case (the Kabardian voiceless aspirated and/or affricated labialized q^w) a quadrigraph, кхъу. This convention is not as cumbersome as it sounds; one quickly becomes used to reading digraphs and trigraphs as unit phonemes, and the Kabardian quadrigraph is very rare, occurring, according to Balkarov (4), only once in 8000 words of text.

The history of Abkhaz orthography is different from that of all the other newly written Caucasian languages. Abkhaz had been reduced to writing in the nineteenth century by Uslar (85), and a modified form of Uslar's Cyrillic-based orthography was used up to 1928. Thereafter, till 1938, Abkhaz was written in augmented Roman. At that time, when Cyrillic was introduced for the other languages, Abkhaz, which is spoken within the Georgian SSR, was provided with a Georgian-based orthography—that is Georgian augmented by a few special letters used either independently or as modifiers. The augmented Georgian alphabet was used until 1954, when an entirely new Abkhaz orthography was introduced, this time on a Cyrillic basis, but differing considerably from all other Caucasian alphabets. The augmented Cyrillic used for Abkhaz not only makes use of digraphs but also includes 13 modified or totally new letters, several of which go back to Uslar's (85) alphabet of the 1860s. The Abkhaz alphabet makes no use of the palочka; instead it represents glottalic stops and affricates either by specially invented or modified letters or by the ordinary Cyrillic voiceless stop characters. In Abkhaz modified letters are used to represent the voiceless *aspirated* stops—letters used by Uslar though borrowed by him from Sjögren's Ossetic grammar of 1844.

One of the decisions which had to be made in developing languages in the Caucasus concerned the selection of a particular dialect upon which to base the literary language. In some cases the problem had already been solved by existing sociolinguistic conditions. Thus Avar was already widely used as a *lingua franca* in part of Dagestan, and the variety which performed this function was the northern dialect of the Khunzaq area, so this became the new literary language. Among the NWC languages the choice depended partly on phonology. For Adyghe, the Temirgoi (or Chemgui) dialect was selected partly because it had the simplest sound system—only 50 consonants as against the 60 of Shapsugh or the 64 of Bzhedukh. For Abkhaz, the first choice was the Bzyb dialect, but later the phonologically simpler Abzhui dialect became the basis of the literary language.

Although all Caucasian literary languages, with the exception of Abkhaz, use basically the same alphabet, there are a number of differences in the utilization of particular letters or digraphs. Thus the Russian "soft š" (šč) character indicates lamino-alveolar palatalized ç in Adyghe, the special NWC ŝ in Kabardian, and intensive or geminate ʃʃ in Avar and Lak. The Russian "k + soft sign" stands for glottalic palatalized k in Abkhaz, for aspirated palatalized k in Abaza, the strong glottalic lateral affricate tɬɬ' in Avar, and glottalic uvular stop q' in other Dagestan languages. The student of Caucasian languages must thus always remember which set of conventions he is working with in reading examples from different languages. Moreover, in addition to the official orthographies, publications on Caucasian languages use several different types of phonetic or phonological transcription based on Roman, Cyrillic, and Georgian.

General information on the orthographies of the modern Caucasian literary languages can be found in Musaev (68) and Isaev (35). For Abkhaz, there is the short study by Bgažba (5).

GRAMMAR

Probably every linguist knows that Caucasian languages are characterized by their possession of the *ergative* type of transitive sentence construction. This is indeed a feature of all Caucasian languages, except the Megrelian dialect of Zan, and it is one of the few general Caucasian features. Though there are grammatical characteristics which stretch over several branches of Caucasian, there are also considerable differences. Thus the NWC languages can rightly be described as "polysynthetic" because of the extreme complexity of their verb forms, which incorporate pronominal and relational indices virtually recapitulating the entire syntactic content of the sentence, while at the other extreme we have the Lezgi verb, which is virtually devoid of indications of anything other than the purely verbal categories of tense, mood, etc.

In spite of some major differences from the well-known Indo-European type of language, Caucasian languages are not so exotic that they cannot be described in terms of the traditional grammatical categories. I propose, therefore, to illustrate some features of Caucasian grammar under such headings as "Nouns," "Pronouns," etc.

Nouns

One interesting characteristic of 28 of the 37 Caucasian languages is that nouns are distributed into a number of gender-like classes. In NWC noun classification is minimal; only in Abkhaz-Abaza do we find the distinction human-nonhuman, marked in the form of numerals and in the pronoun system (which also distinguishes masculine and feminine in the second person). Class systems play a larger role in the three Nakh languages and in 23 languages of Dagestan.

Noun classification is for the most part a *covert* category. That is, it is not indicated on the noun itself but only by the presence of class-markers (prefixes, suffixes, or infixes) on words in a concord relationship with the noun, which include adjectives, verbs, pronouns, and adverbs. Avar has three classes: human male, human female, and neither (m., f., n.) marked by *w, j, b*. These distinctions are not made in the plural, which thus in effect forms a fourth class. Examples: "The good father/mother/table is in the house."

ɬik'a-w emen ro$_q$'o-w w-ugo.	Good father in-house is.
ɬik'a-j tʃʃ'u u ro$_q$'o-j j-igo.	Good woman in-house is.
ɬik'a-b t'ut' ro$_q$'o-b b-ugo.	Good table in-house is.

In Nakh and Dagestanian languages the number of noun classes ranges from *none* in Lezgi, Agul, and Udi, through *two* in Tabasaran to *eight* in Batsbiy. In terms of the semantic bases for the classes, there is always a distinction (in the singular, at least) between *human* and *nonhuman,* and this is the only distinction in the two-class system of Tabasaran. The three-class languages (Avar, six of the Andi languages, and Dargi) distinguish *male* and *female* within the *human* class. In the four-class languages (Tsez, Hinukh, Bežti, Lak, and six of the Lezgian languages) the nonhuman class is basically divided into *animals* and *other things,* but the distinction is not carried out with absolute accuracy, e.g. class III may include a few inanimates, and class IV a few animals, particularly insects. There are two five-class languages, Andi and Chamali. In Andi class III is confined to animals, but in Chamali there is no such clear-cut division, animals and all other things being distributed over classes III, IV, and V. In the Nakh languages, Chechen and Ingush each have six classes and Batsbiy eight. All three languages distinguish *human male* and *human female* from everything else, but there is no obvious principle underlying the assignment of nouns to the other classes. The two six-class Dagestanian languages, Khwarshi and Hunzib, make a more systematic distribution of nouns in classes III to VI, more or less clearly distinguishing animals from inanimates, and both have a special residual class containing, in Hunzib, the single word "child" and in Khwarshi "child" and "family." The following table indicates how the classes are constituted for languages with from 2 to 5 classes:

	Human		Nonhuman	
	men	women	animals	others
2 classes	I		II	
3 classes	I	II	III	
4 classes	I	II	III	IV
5 classes, Andi	I	II	III	IV–V
Chamali	I	II	III–IV–V	

In all languages fewer class distinctions are made in the plural, and it is interesting to see how different languages syncretize or amalgamate class distinctions made in the singular. The following table shows the syncretized plural classes of the four-class languages.

	Animate		Inanimate	
	human		nonhuman	
	male	female	animals	others
Tsez, Hinukh	men		all else	
Bež, Tsakh, Kryz		human	nonhuman	
Lak		animate		inanimate
Budukh	men	women	nonhuman	
Rutul, Arči, Khin		no distinctions in plural		

Another major nominal category is *case*. In only two Caucasian languages, Abkhaz and Abaza, are cases not marked on the surface forms of nouns. In all other Caucasian languages there are systems of case-forms, ranging from only two or three in Ubykh, through four in the Adyghan languages, six or so in the Kartvelian languages, to a maximum of 47 cases in literary Tabasaran (possibly 53 in a Tabasaran dialect). Cases are often divided into two categories: *basic* or *grammatical* cases on the one hand, and *local* cases on the other, and the great exuberance of case-systems in the Dagestanian languages mainly reflects the large number of their local cases. The nearly case-less NWC languages handle location and direction quite differently: chiefly by means of locational preverbs. I discuss both methods of expressing spatial relations together, under "locative expressions."

To return to the "grammatical" cases: all Caucasian languages distinguish an absolutive or *nominative* case and an *ergative* case. The nominative, as in IE, is the case of citation, of the complement of a copula, usually of the subject of an intransitive verb, sometimes the subject of a transitive verb, and finally, unlike IE, the usual case of the *object* of a transitive verb. The ergative is most commonly the case of the subject of a transitive verb. We have to hedge these remarks with "usually" and "commonly" because the function of these case-forms in Caucasian languages are more varied than is often supposed.

In about 10 Caucasian languages the ergative case-form has the unique function of marking the subject of a transitive verb. In the other languages it combines the function of another oblique case; thus the ergative case-form also functions as an instrumental in Avar and the Andi languages, as genitive in Lak, as dative in the Adyghan languages, as a locative in others.

The Adyghan languages have a simple case-system, embracing nominative, ergative-oblique, instrumental and a fourth case called translative or adverbial which has several functions including the important one of marking the pivotal noun in relativizations. In the NWC languages there is no genitive case, the attributive possessive relationship being expressed by pronominal prefixes on the noun referring to the possessed, thus "the boy's hat" is expressed as *k'alem ji-paʔʷer*, i.e. "the-boy his-hat." In Adyghe, incidentally, but in no other Caucasian language, a distinction is made between "organic" or "inalienable" possession and "material" or "alienable" possession, the latter being indicated by an extended form of the pronominal prefix, thus *s-pe* "my nose," but *si-paʔʷe* "my hat".

Outside of NWC all Caucasian languages distinguish nominative, ergative, genitive, and dative cases, and often instrumental. A few languages have additional "grammatical" cases, one of these being the *affective* found in six of the Andi languages and in the Lezgian language Tsakhur. The affective case marks the subject of certain transitive verbs of perception—in other languages such verbs usually have their subject in the dative or a locative case. A recent logico-semantic study of case in a Nakh language is Dešerieva's *Structure of the Semantic Fields of Chechen and Russian Cases* (in Russian) (20).

In general, *pronouns* in Caucasian languages present the same system of case distinctions as nouns, with the exception that in NWC, Kartvelian, and 10 Dagestan languages no formal distinction is made between the nominative and ergative of the first and second person pronouns. Incidentally, the pronoun systems of Caucasian languages include the distinction between inclusive and exclusive first person plural in Nakh, Avar, the Andi languages, about half the Lezgian languages, and the Kartvelian language Svan. There are no specific personal pronouns of the third person, demonstratives being used in this function. These usually distinguish three degrees of deixis (type "this-that-yon"). In a number of Dagestanian languages, however, the demonstratives also systematically incorporate elements signifying "higher" or "lower," distinguishing, for instance, "that-on-this-level," "that-higher," "that-lower." This is interesting, though not surprising, in languages spoken in *auls* or mountain villages, where the roof of one house is frequently the verandah of the house above it.

Locative expressions

In Caucasian languages there are three different ways of expressing spatial relations: postpositions, preverbs, and local cases. All Caucasian languages make some use of postpositions, which are often transparently derived from (or merely special uses of) nouns, and this is the chief type of locative expression in Kartvelian. The NWC languages, particularly Adyghan, use preverbs, and the Nakh and Dagestan languages local cases.

The locational preverbs of the Adyghan languages are prefixed either to what are called "static" verbs such as *be, lie, sit, stand,* or to "dynamic" verbs such as *go, take, write,* etc. The preverbs themselves carry exclusively *orientational* meanings; that is to say, they specify whether the relation holds toward the orientating object *as a whole,* to its *exterior,* to its *interior,* to its *underside,* etc. They do not specify whether the relationship is a *static* one (essive), or involves *approach* to the orientator (lative), or *departure* from it (ablative), or *both* (translative). It is the verb which carries these latter meanings. Thus the Kabardian preverb *de,* for instance, means simply "relationship to the interior of a horizontally bounded (empty) space," and can thus be translated *in, into,* or *out of,* according to what verb it is prefixed to, as in these examples: 1. *He is in the courtyard,* 2. *He went into the courtyard,* 3. *He went out of the courtyard.*

1. ar pŝ'ant'em de-t-ŝ.	"He courtyard in-stand-s."
2. ar pŝ'ant'em de-ħa-ŝ.	"He courtyard in-went-to."
3. ar pŝ'ant'em de-k'aŝ.	"He courtyard in-went-from."

Other Kabardian preverbs include *xe,* "in/into/out of a filled space—e.g. water, sand, a forest, the Party"; *tej* "on/onto/off," *ŝ'e* "under/to under/from under," etc.

What NWC performs by preverbs the Dagestanian languages achieve by means of local, or space-relational, case-forms, augmented where necessary (as are the NWC preverbs) by postpositions. The number of local cases ranges from 5 to 6 in one or two of the southernmost Dagestanian languages spoken in northern Azerbaijan to 32 in Lak (which with 8 grammatical cases has a total of 40) and 43 in literary Tabasaran, which with 4 grammatical cases gives a total of 47—though one Tabasaran dialect may still retain an old systematic distinction, raising the total of local cases to 49 and the grand total to 53.

In most Dagestan languages the local cases form an extraordinarily regular system formed by the combination of two sets of case-suffixes. One set, which is always attached directly to the noun stem, carries the *orientational* meanings (*on, in, under,* etc), and in Dagestanian grammars there are said to be as many "series" of local cases as there are different orientational suffixes. The second set of case-suffixes is attached to the preceding ones and specifies the *directional* meanings (static, approach, departure, etc). We can illustrate this from a language with a moderate set of local cases, Tsez, which has 4 directional cases—essive, lative, ablative, and translative—in 7 series, which [following Bokarëv's (6) numbering] are I *on* a horizontal surface, II *in* an empty space, III *in* a filled space, IV *at around*, V *under*, VI *on* a non-horizontal surface, VII *by, with* (e.g. possession).

This gives us a total of 28 cases. Probably no noun takes all 28 of them since there are obvious semantic incompatibilities, but in principle all 28 combined case-forms occur. Here are the forms of only 12 cases, followed by some examples:

	Essive	Lative	Ablative
I. *on* (horizontal)	–(o)	–(o)r	l(a)j
	–tł(o)	–tł'–or	–tł'–aj
VI. *on* (non-horizontal)	–q(o)	–q–or	–q–aj
II. *in* (empty)	–a/æ	–a–r	–a–j
III. *in* (filled)	–ł	–ł–er	–ł–aj

Examples: 4. There's bread on the table. 5. The bread fell off the table. 6. There's a fly on the wall. 7. He picked a leaf off the tree.

4. istoli-t ł' betʃχo magalu.	"table-on lies bread."
5. istoli-t ł'-aj bokys magalu.	"table-on-from fell bread."
6. qido-q jołt'ut'.	"wall-on is fly."
7. Ƙunno-q-aj jet'urno tłeb.	"tree-on-from he-picked leaf"

8. There's water in the jar. 9. Pour the water out of the jar. 10. There's a worm in the apple. 11. Pour salt into the gruel. 12. A bear is going out of the woods.

8. ł i tung-æ joł.	"water jar-in is."
9. etsi ł i tung-æ-j.	"pour water jar-in-from."
10. heneʃjo-ł jo-ł bikori	"apple-in is worm."
11. qiqo-ł-er tsijo tʃat ł o.	"gruel-in-to salt pour."
12. tsiqe-ł-aj baiχ zej.	"woods-in-from goes bear."

It will be observed that although the locative expressions of NWC and Dagestanian appear on the surface to be very different, using preverbs on the one hand and local cases on the other, they nevertheless have certain typologically interesting similarities. In both systems the two components of locational meanings, the *orientator* and the *direction,* are separately expressed; in NWC by preverb and verb, in

Dagestan by first case-suffix and second case-suffix. Second, both incorporate certain conceptual distinctions in the system which are not systematically expressed in more familiar languages. These include the distinction *in an empty space* vs *in a filled space,* found in both Adyghe and Kabardian in NWC, and in 13 Dagestanian languages, and also the distinction between *on a horizontal surface* and *on a nonhorizontal surface,* found in Kabardian, at least, and also in 10 Dagestanian languages. For those who wish to study the locational expressions of Dagestanian languages more closely, there is a valuable article on precisely this topic by Kibrik (45).

Verbs

As we indicated earlier, the Caucasian verb exhibits greater complexity in NWC than anywhere else. To some extent there is a trade-off between verbal complexity and case-systems: the more relational information you pack into the verb-form the less you need to express by means of nominal case-forms. This is far from being absolutely true, however, and, as Khajdakov (44) points out, relational preverbs are found even in some of the multicasal Lezgian languages, including Tabasaran.

The complexity of the NWC verb is well illustrated by the Adyghe and Kabardian languages, in which the verb may carry exponents of its *static* or *dynamic* status, of *transitivity, finiteness/nonfiniteness, polarity* (affirmative-negative), *person* and *number* of related NPs, up to eight *tenses, mood, causative, version* (action performed for or against the will of a person etc) *association, reciprocity, common action, potential, involuntary action,* and a number of other modal nuances. In addition to all of these the verb may carry *locational* and *directional* preverbs and up to four pronominal prefixes referring to NPs which may or may not actually be present in the sentence. Kumakhov describes and exemplifies many of these complexities in his books of 1964 (58) and 1971 (60) and also in a useful short article in a 1965 symposium on typology (59). In this latter article he gives a number of Kabardian examples, of which the following is a moderately simple one. 13. If I made you(sing) go in together with them = *wadɨxezʁeɦame* which can be analyzed as:

13. w - a - dɨ -xe-z- ʁe - ɦ - a- me.
     thee them with in I cause enter past if.

In all the NWC languages there is a single, fairly rigid, surface sequence of NPs in the sentence, namely S O V. There are, however, two distinct sequences for the pronominal prefixes on a verb: O - S - V or S - O - V, the distinction being of great syntactic importance since it distinguishes the *ergative* construction from the *nominative* construction.

Though the Nakh and Dagestanian verbs are less complex than those of NWC, they still exhibit a rich variety of tenses, moods, and other forms. In most of these languages some, but by no means all, finite verbs carry class-indices relating to an associated NP. The NP with which the verb agrees in class is always one in the nominative case, namely, the subject of an intransitive or the object of a transitive verb. In a few Dagestanian languages transitive verbs also agree in *person* with the subject. In two languages, Lezgi and Agul, the verb carries no concord markers whatsoever.

Syntax

I can merely sketch the most striking syntactical feature of Caucasian languages—the ergative construction. Typically, in the ergative construction, the *subject* of a transitive verb is in an oblique case (*ergative*), while the *object* is in the same unmarked or *nominative* case as is the subject of an intransitive verb. The ergative construction may thus be represented as S^E V O^N while the intransitive, nominal construction is S^N V—an example from Avar: 14. The hunter killed the wolf. 15. The wolf died.

> 14. tʃanaqan-as bats' tʃ'wana.
>   hunter^E wolf^N killed.
> 15. bats' χwana.
>   wolf^{N}died.

In Caucasian languages there are many variations on the theme of ergativity. I have described a number of these elsewhere (11, 12) and so will simply outline the most important points here.

Though the configuration S^E V O^N, (by the way, the sequence SVO is purely arbitrary—many Caucasian languages require, or else favor, the sequence SOV, but the sequence SVO is very common) represents the basic or unmarked ergative construction, in most Caucasian languages transitive verbs of perception and feeling have their S in a different oblique case. Nine Dagestan languages have a speical *affective* case for this function. In others the subject of such verbs is in the *dative* or *locative* or *ablative* or some other case.

The second widespread characteristic of the ergative construction is that in those Nakh and Dagestan languages which have a class-marker on some verbs, the class-marker always reflects the noun which is in the *nominative* case, i.e. the *object* of a transitive verb, but the *subject* of an intransitive verb. Thus in Avar: 16. Father loves his son. 17. Father loves his daughter. 18. Father loves his horse.

> 16. insuje was w-otɬ'ula.
>   father^D son^N loves.
> 17. insuje jas j-otɬ'ula.
>   father^D daughter^N loves.
> 18. insuje tʃu b-otɬ'ula.
>   father^D horse^N loves.

but, on the other hand: 19. Father came, mother came, the horse came.

> 19. emen w-atʃ'ana, ebel j-atʃ'ana, tʃu b-atʃ'ana.

In three Dagestan languages—literary Tabasaran, Dargi, and to some extent in Lak—in transitive sentences the verb agrees with the *object* in *class*, but with the ergative *subject* in *person*. In southern Tabasaran dialect and in Udi there are no classes, and the verb agrees only with the ergative subject, in person. Udi, incidentally, is perhaps unique among the world's "ergative languages" in that it has an ergative construction S^E V $O^{D/A}$, that is, with the subject in the ergative case and the object in another oblique case—the "dative-accusative." The most recent descriptions of Udi are in (21a) and (30a). In NWC and Kartvelian the verb agrees in person with both subject and object, both of which are, in principle, marked in the verb form.

In NWC the sequence of pronominal prefixes is crucially related to ergativity. In the *ergative* construction the prefixes are in the sequence O-S-V. In the contrasting *nominative* construction they are in the sequence S-O-V. In Abkhaz and Abaza, where nouns carry no surface case markings, the distinction between the nominative and ergative construction is made solely by the difference in sequence (and a few differences in form) of the pronominal affixes.

The Kartvelian languages Georgian and Svan are anomalous in that in them the ergative transitive construction S^E V O^N occurs only with verbs in the aorist set of tenses. In the present series, the construction of transitive sentences is S^N V $O^{D/A}$, i.e. subject in nominative, object in dative-accusative. In the two Zan dialects, however, the ergative construction has generalized from exclusive use with aorist transitives in two distinct ways. In Laz, *all transitives* (present as well as aorist) have the construction S^E V O^N. In Megrelian, on the other hand, the generalization has gone the other way, so that *all aorists* (transitive or intransitive) have their subject in the ergative, S^E V O^N, S^E V. Megrelian can thus hardly be said to possess an ergative construction any more, since the ergative case-form is completely dissociated from transitivity.

So far, we have referred only to the construction S^N V and S^E V O^N. But most, perhaps all, North Caucasian languages have a second type of transitive, or on both morphological and semantic grounds, a "semitransitive" construction. In the Adyghan languages this nominative semitransitive construction has the configuration S^N V O^E, that is, subject in the nominative case, object in the ergative-oblique case, and pronominal prefixes on the verb in the sequence S-O-V. This opposition of the two transitive constructions, S^E V O^N and S^N V O^E, is not merely formal; it is functional, i.e. meaningful.

A Kabardian example of the opposition between the ergative (transitive) construction S^E V O^N and the nominative (semitransitive) construction S^N V O^E is given in sentences 20 and 21, both of which can be roughly translated as "The boy is reading the book."

20. š'alem txɨɬɨr je-dʒe.
    boy^E book^N reads.
21. s'aler txɨɬɨm jew-dʒe.
    boy^N book^E reads.

Jakovlev has clearly described the semantic distinction between these constructions in both his Adyghe and Kabardian grammars (38, 39) and in an important article published in 1940 (37). In this article he describes the ergative construction as "aim-full," implying the actor's intention to carry the action to completion and "to full penetration into the object," whereas the nominative construction is "aimless"; the action is not necessarily completed, and "the action in this case makes only superficial contact with the object." The construction of example 21 suggests comparison with an English intransitive verb + prepositional phrase: "He's reading in the book," or even better, the Scots expression "He's haein a bit read o' the buik." It would, however, be an error to conclude that example 21 is just an intransitive verb with a locative complement. We know that this is not so since in the S^N V O^E construction the verb is in neither the normal transitive form *jedʒe* nor the intransitive form *madʒe*, but in a special form which I call semitransitive. In a normal sentence with locative complement the verb would be in the intransitive form.

Analogous semitransitive, or "nominative-transitive" constructions occur in all NWC languages, all Nakh languages, and several (perhaps all?) Dagestanian languages. In some they are closely similar to the NWC S^N V O^E construction. Dargi, for instance, contrasts the regular S^E V O^N with S^N V O^E, whereas the oblique case used in the semitransitive construction in Hunzib is instrumental, S^N V O^I. In the Nakh languages and in Avar, Tsakhur, and Khinalug (and probably others) the semitransitive construction is S^N V O^N, i.e. the object, like the subject, is in the nominative case. In all of these examples the opposition between the ergative transitive and the nominative (semi-) transitive is of the same general kind. The ergative construction implies a tight, penetrative association between the verb and its object. The nominative construction, on the other hand, implies a tight relationship between the verb and its subject—it stresses the activity of the subject rather than the effect upon the object.

In the anomalous Kartvelian languages there is no direct opposition between the ergative transitive and the nominative transitive construction. Either, as in Laz, the ergative construction is obligatory with all transitive verbs, or, as in Georgian and Svan, it is excluded from the present tenses. In either case there is no freedom to select the ergative or the nominative construction in order to express different nuances in the relationship between the transitive verb and its associated NPs. The Georgian-Svan restriction of the ergative construction to aorists is comprehensible in light of what was said above. The ergative construction, being effect-oriented, has a certain affinity with pasts and perfectives, whereas the nominative construction, being more action-oriented, has more affinity with presents and imperfectives. In Georgian-Svan the opposition between the ergative and nominative constructions has been absorbed, so to speak, in the tense-aspect opposition and thus has no independent semantic function.

In the Kartvelian languages, the ergative construction is obligatory with transitives, and further restricted in Georgian and Svan to the aorist, and is thus purely *formal* and meaningless. In North Caucasian languages the ergative construction is in meaningful contrast with the nominative construction and is thus *functional.* This distinction is not confined to the Caucasus and, as I have suggested elsewhere (12), one can classify all the world's "ergative" languages as possessing either a formal or a functional ergative construction.

It is not surprising that there is a very considerable literature on ergativity in Russian. This includes two collections of articles. One of these (22) brings together many of the older key works on the topic (all in Russian translation), while the other (23) consists of specially written articles of which 10 are on Caucasian languages. There are also two important books on the subject by leading authorities on ergativity: Mêščaninov's work (64) and Klimov's (52) excellent "General Theory of Ergativity."

I would like to mention one other syntactic characteristic of north Caucasian languages, namely the fact that in them virtually all forms of sentential conjoining and subordination, including relativization, are carried out by verbal means—i.e. by the use of special conjunctive verb forms, participles, verbal nouns ("masdars")—and not by the use of conjunctions, which are few, or relative pronouns and adverbs, which are nonexistent. The Kartvelian languages again are anomalous since they possess, and use, conjunctions and relative pronouns.

The following examples give some indication of how relativization works in Adyghe: 22. The girl who brought the old man said (something). 23. The guest whom the boy brought has gone away again. 24. The village where the guest went is pretty.

22. pšašew   ɬ'ɨzɨr   zɨ-ϛaƘem   ɨʔʷaƘ.
    girl$^{A(E)}$ old man^N (E)-having-brought^E said-something.
23. ħak'ew   k'alem   qɨϛaƘer   kʷ'eƶɨƘe.
    guest$^{A(N)}$ boy^E hither-having-brought^N went-again.
24. tϛilew   ħak'er   zɨdekʷ'aƘer   tϛile   dax.
    village$^{A(E)}$ guest^N (E)-having-gone-to^N village   pretty.

In each of these the pivotal noun is in the so-called "adverbial" case, ending in w and labeled "A" for "adverbial" with a parenthetic indication of the case—ergative-oblique (E) or nominative (N)—it would have had in the underlying sentence. The participal expression carries the prefix zɨ- when the related pivotal noun is underlyingly ergative (whether subject, as in 22, or indirect object, or relational object as in 24, etc). The whole phrase is marked by the case-suffix on its last component (the participle) as ergative, -m in 22, or nominative -r in 23 and 24, according to the transitivity of the sentence in which it is embedded.

Finally, here are two sentences illustrating relativization in Avar: 25. The boy to whom Musa gave the money went away, and 26. The day when Ahmad came we had gone to the Institute.

25. musatsa   ϛarats   tɬ'uraw   was   ana.
    Musa^E money^N given   boy^N went.
26. aħmad   w-atʃ'ara-b   q'ojaɬ   niƶ   institutalde   un   r-uk'ana.
    Ahmad^N having-come   day^E we(excl.)^N inst.-to   gone   were.

Note that in 26 the participle agrees in class, like an intransitive verb, with its subject, w-(m) but also, like an adjective, with the noun it is attributive to, -b (n). The ergative/instrumental case on the word for *day* is used in its time-marking function.

INTERNAL AND EXTERNAL RELATIONS OF CAUCASIAN

Before discussing the question of the relationships among the Caucasian languages themselves, and between them and other language families, it will be well to summarize some of their characteristic features. This can perhaps best be done by tabulating various phonological and grammatical characteristics which have been discussed above, indicating by +, (+) (= an 'attenuated' +), or –, their presence or absence in the various subgroups: Kart(velian), NWC, Nakh, Dag(estanian), and with an additional column for Indo-European (IE) for purposes of comparison.

	Kart	NWC	Nakh	Dag	IE
1. Glottalic consonants	+	+	+	+	very rare
2. Uvulars	+	+	+	+	rare
3. Pharyngals	–	+	–	+	–
4. Labialized consonants	–	+	–	(+)	very rare
5. Non-approximant laterals	–	+	(+)	+	very rare
6. "Harmonic complexes" of CC	+	+	+	–	–
7. Minimal vowel system	–	+	–	–	–
8. Noun classes	–	(+)	+	+	(+)
9. More than 2 or 3 "grammatical cases"	+	–	+	+	+
10. Numerous local cases	–	–	(+)	+	–
11. Directional preverbs	(+)	+	–	(+)	(+)
12. "Orientator" and "direction" separately expressed	–	+	–	+	–
13. Unusual semantic distinctions of *on* and *in*	–	+	–	+	–
14. Ergative construction					
a. funtional	–	+	+	+	–
b. formal	+	–	–	–	(+)
15. Conjoining, Relativization etc by verb	–	+	+	+	(+)

It is clear that there are not many traits common to all Caucasian languages—only 3 out of the 15 listed above. And yet anyone working with these languages receives a strong impression of "family likeness" running through all of them. Whether the 37 Caucasian languages constitute a single "language family" derived from a common Proto-Caucasian, or whether the typological resemblances between them result from the convergence of features in languages of more than one "genetic" origin through millenia of symbiosis, is still an open question. Some Soviet linguists, particularly in Georgia, seem to accept the common-origin hypothesis as self-evident, and merely await definite proof. Others are agnostic and prepared to believe that Caucasian languages constitute a *Sprachbund,* or language union.

The establishment of relationships between languages requires above all the setting up of regular sound-correspondences between the languages constituting a presumptive "family," and this task has proved extremely difficult, particularly within the Dagestanian and NWC subgroups of Caucasian. We can confidently accept Kartvelian as a genetically related group; much of the evidence is available in (24, 49, 73), to which I have referred above. The relationship of the Nakh languages, too, is well established, on which see (18, 78). The Dagestanian languages are more problematic. They obviously fall into a few subgroups: Avaro-Andi, Tsez, Lezgian, and some scholars regard Lak and Dargi as forming a single close-knit Lak-Dargi subgroup. The publication in 1961 of Bokarëv's *Introduction to the Comparative Study of Dagestanian Languages* (in Russian) (7) was an important advance toward the establishment of the sound-correspondences within Dagestanian as a whole, and Bokarëv's reconstruction of a Proto-Dagestanian sound system is still generally accepted by specialists. The relationships of languages within some Dagestanian subgroups were placed on a solid footing by Bokarëv's work on the Tsez languages (6) and Gudava's on the Andi languages (29), and the study of Dagestanian as a whole has been facilitated by comparative Dagestanian word lists, the one edited by Murkelinskij (67), the other compiled by Khajdakov (43). Between them, these works deal with about 1000 Dagestanian words. However, far from all these items are represented in all Dagestanian languages, and the cognate status of some is dubious. And though the 1971 book lists and exemplifies all the consonantal correspondences of Dagestanian, one is struck by the number of apparent irregularities.

The fact is that in dealing with Dagestanian languages we are faced with a state of affairs quite different from what we find in some of the better known language families, particularly in Indo-European. In Indo-European we know that most languages and language groups have developed for centuries, even millenia, in total separation from each other. We can be virtually certain, for instance, that regular correspondences between Sanskrit and Germanic or Celtic are due to common origin and not to borrowing. In Dagestan (and to some extent in the Caucasus generally) we have a totally different situation, namely a group of languages which have been spoken in very much their present location for probably 4000 years or more. The greatest straight-line distance between any two Dagestanian languages is about 150 miles. While the extremely mountainous terrain probably doubles that maximum distance, nevertheless one must assume some degree of contact throughout the millenia. Strabo explained the great number of different Caucasian languages by the fact that their speakers lived in scattered groups without mixing, because of "their stubbornness and ferocity." But at the very least, there must have been intertribal wars and the taking of prisoners, particularly women. So it is possible that one reason for the difficulty in establishing regular sound-correspondences in Dagestanian is that genetic relationship is heavily overlaid by borrowing throughout millenia of symbiosis.

The NWC languages have so many striking common traits that one is easily convinced of their common origin. They clearly fall into two closely related subgroups, Abkhaz-Abaza and Adyghan, with Ubykh as an isolated language. Thanks very largely to the work of such scholars as Jakovlev and Kuipers, the sound-correspondences of Adyghan are well established. Kuiper's 1975 *Dictionary of Proto-Circassian Roots* (57) is an invaluable aid to the further study of NWC. Nevertheless, we are still far from establishing a thoroughly satisfactory "Common NWC." The Abkhaz linguist Shakryl has published what might be called "comparative-descriptive" works on NWC (75, 76) in which he lists about 500 words which seem to be common to all or most of the NWC languages. However, his lists contain inaccuracies, and no attempt is made to identify borrowings (within NWC or from other languages, e.g. Arabic and Persian). More convincing are the lists of NWC cognates given by Shagirov (74) and Klimov (51). Between them these provide us with about 120 very plausible cognates. However, as Kuipers (55) has well explained, the problem of establishing regular sound-correspondences is very great when one is dealing with languages in which most, if not all, roots consist of a single consonant or consonant cluster, particularly when the consonant systems are very rich and there are numerous homonyms. In these conditions it is difficult to find series of correspondences which confirm each other, as one can in, for example, Indo-European.

In spite of these difficulties, there can be little doubt that each group within Caucasian—NWC, Nakh, Dagestanian, and Kartvelian—constitutes a genetically related unit. It is the wider relationships within Caucasian as a whole which are more dubious. The number of pan-Caucasian cognates is very small: Klimov (50) lists only 22 of these, embodying 28 sound-correspondences, only one of which occurs in two items.

It is interesting to note that the general impressions of relative closeness of relationships between Caucasian languages are reflected in what little attempts have been made at lexicostatistical comparisons between Caucasian languages. Klimov (50) reports results obtained by Tovar (82) for comparisons between Georgian and Adyghe, Georgian and Avar, and Adyghe and Avar. Klimov himself (48), using Swadesh's 100-word list, has compared the three Kartvelian languages, and the present writer has carried out some very tentative lexicostatistical comparisons between the NWC languages, and between them and Chechen and Avar, and within Dagestanian, between Avar and Akhwakh, Hunzib, and Lezgi. The last three are very dubious, having been carried out with an incomplete set of 80 to 90 items. For what they are worth, however, I set out the figures for percentage of cognates for these comparisons.

Within Kartvelian (Klimov)

Georgian-Svan 30%, Zan-Svan 30%, Georgian-Zan 44%

Within NWC (JCC)

Abkhaz-Adyghe 27%, Abkhaz-Kabardian 27%, Abaza-Adyghe 31% (average for Abkhaz-Abaza and Adyghan 28%), Ubykh-Abkhaz and Ubykh-Adyghe 36%, Ubykh-Abaza and Ubykh-Kabardian 40%, Abkhaz-Abaza 80%, Adyghe-Kabardian 92%

Within Dagestanian (JCC)

Avar-Akhwakh 48%, Avar-Hunzib 34%, Avar-Lezgi 27%

NWC-Kartvelian (Tovar)

Adyghe-Georgian 7.5–5.14%

NWC-Dagestanian

Adyghe-Avar (Tovar) 12.9–9.75%, (JCC) 14%–10%, Abkhaz-Avar, (JCC) 13–8% (average for NWC-Dag. 13.27–9.25%)

Any attempt to attach absolute time-depths to these lexicostatistical percentages is fraught with great difficulties. The glottochronological standard rate of cognate loss is somewhat dubious in general, and it is likely to be influenced in particular ways in the Caucasus. For instance, if longevity and great respect for elders have been characteristic of Caucasian peoples for many centuries (as they are today), one might expect this to have a slowing effect on language development. Even so, it is interesting to look at some of the time-depths suggested by these cognate retention percentages. Using the conversion table of Swadesh's posthumous book (80, p. 284) we find the following: *Kartvelian*: separation of Svan from Georgian and Zan, about 4000 years ago; separation of Georgian from Zan, about 2700 years ago. Klimov, though critical of the method, finds these figures plausible on linguistic and archeological grounds. *NWC* Abkhazo-Abaza/Adyghan 4220 years, Abkhaz/Abaza 740 years, Adyghe/Kabardian 270 years. The figure for Abkhaz-Abaza/Adyghan puts the date of separation of these branches of NWC at a little before 2000 B.C. Now it is interesting to note that, according to Sulimirski (79), the inception of the North Caucasian Maikop culture is dated at about 2500–2000 B.C., and one theory is that it was brought about by a northward migration from the Black Sea coast. It is at least possible that the major NWC divergence began at this time, the speakers of what became Abkhaz remaining on the coast. Any glottochronological interpretation of the lexicostatistic data in terms of time-depth of separation of the various groups within Caucasian as a whole is meaningless unless one definitely accepts the view of a common origin for all Caucasian languages.

Finally, I must leave the speculative area of glottochronology to consider very briefly another which is equally speculative—the possible external relations of Caucasian. The ergative construction is the Caucasian trait which has, for a century or more, aroused the interest of scholars and has prompted suggestions of relationship with virtually any language that has an ergative construction, notably Basque, Burushaski, Paleo-Siberian, and among ancient "ergative languages" Sumerian and Urartian.

That the Caucasian languages, isolated in the mountains of the extreme east of Europe, and Basque in the extreme western mountains might be remnants of a language or language-family once spoken all over Europe is not in itself implausible. However, during the century or so that this hypothesis has been current no fully convincing evidence has been forthcoming. The French linguist, Lafon, has published more than anyone on this topic (see 63), but the sound-correspondences which he has adduced are not supported by many examples, and necessarily carry less conviction than they might because there is as yet no well-established Proto-Caucasian with which to compare Basque or any other language.

The relationship with Burushaski, the isolated language of the Karakoram, is based on little more than the fact that Burushaski has an ergative construction and a few rather random word-equations. The Caucasian-Burushaski hypothesis put forward by Bleichsteiner was reviewed and criticized by Morgenstierne (66).

Gamkrelidze & Machavariani (24) have clearly shown similarities between Kartvelian and Indo-European, but they regard them as no more than simply typological resemblances. Incidentally, the student of NWC also cannot but be impressed by the resemblance between certain NWC consonant systems, with their triadic series of stops, labialized velars and uvulars, plain and labialized "laryngeals" and so on, and reconstructed Proto–Indo-European.

The most ambitious attempt at a wider synthesis of Caucasian with other language families is that of Illič-Svityč, who, in a posthumous work published in 1971 (34), develops the "Nostratic Theory" first adumbrated in the latter half of the nineteenth century. Illič-Svityč purports to show a relationship between Kartvelian, Indo-European, Altaic, Uralic, Dravidian, and Semito-Hamitic. He sets up sound-correspondences not (as so many other have done) between isolated languages of these different families, but between their respective proto-languages. His results are interesting and indeed suggest some form of relationship but whether of a *"Sprachbund"* or of a "genetic" nature is difficult to say.

It would not be surprising if Caucasian languages were related to one or another of the ancient languages of the Near East, and the most plausible candidate for this relationship is Urartian, the ancient language spoken in the area of Ancient Armenia before the Indo-European speakers of Armenian arrived there. Braun & Klimov (9) have adduced some apparent material correspondences between Urartian and North Caucasian.

The internal and external relations of Caucasian languages are still uncertain, and present an intriguing challenge to linguists—a challenge which is being met by continuous intensive research by Soviet linguists, many of whom are themselves native speakers of Caucasian languages, and by a very small number of scholars in the rest of the world.

Literature Cited

1. Allen, W. S. 1956. Structure and system in the Abaza verbal complex. *Trans. Philol. Soc.* 1956:127–76
2. Allen, W. S. 1965. On one-vowel systems. *Lingua* 13:111–24
3. *Atlas narodov mira.* 1964. Moscow: Akad. Nauk SSSR
4. Balkarov, B. X. 1970 *Fonetika adygskix jazykov.* Nalchik: Elbrus
5. Bgažba, X. S. 1967. *Iz istorii pis'mennosti v Albaxazii.* Tbilisi: Metsniereba
6. Bokarëv, E. A. 1959. *Tsezskie (didojskie) jazyki Dagestana.* Moscow: Akad. Nauk SSSR
7. Bokarëv, E. A. 1961. *Vvedenie v sravnitel'no-istoričeskoe izočenie dagestanskix jazykov.* Makhachkala: Dagestan. Gos. Univ.
8. Bouda, K. 1960. Introducción a la lingüística caucásica. *Acta Salmat. Filos. Let.* 15 (1):5–90
9. Braun, I., Klimov, G. 1954. Ob istoričeskom vzaimootnošenii urartskogo i iberijsko-kavkazskix jazykov. *Tezisy Dokl.* (quoted in Ref. 18)
10. Catford, J. C. 1972. Labialization in Caucasian languages, with special reference to Abkhaz. *Proc. 7th Int. Congr. Phonet. Sci.* The Hague, Paris
11. Catford, J. C. Jan.-June 1976. Ergativity in Caucasian languages. *Resources in Education,* ERIC 112704, Arlington, Va.
12. Catford, J. C. 1976. Ergativity in

Caucasian languages. *Papers 6th Meet. Northeast Ling. Soc.,* Montreal
13. Catford, J. C. 1977. *Fundamental Problems in Phonetics.* Edinburgh Univ. Press, Indiana Univ. Press
14. Črelašvili, K. 1975. *Naxuri enebis tanxmovanta sist'ema* Tbilisi Univ. Press; *Sistema soglasnyx v naxskix jazykax* (avtoreferat). Tbilisi Univ. Press
15. Deeters, G. 1963. Die kaukasischen Sprachen. *Handbuch der Orientalistik* 7(1):1–79
16. Dešeriev, J. D. 1959. *Grammatika xinalugskogo jazyka.* Moscow: Akad. Nauk SSSR
17. Dešeriev, J. D. 1960. *Sovremennyj Čečenskij literaturnyj jazyk: Čast 1 Fonetika.* Grozny: Chechen-Ingush Sci. Res. Inst.
18. Dešeriev, J. D. 1963. *Sravnitel' no-istoričeskaja grammatika naxskix jazykov i problemy proisxoždenija i istoričeskogo razvitija gorskix kavkazskix narodov.* Grozny: Chechen-Ingush Sci. Res. Inst.
19. Dešerieva, T. I. 1963. *Sravnitel'no-tipologičeskaja fonetika čečenskogo i russkogo literaturnyx jazykov.* Grozny: Chechen-Ingush Sci. Res. Inst.
20. Dešerieva, T. I. 1974. *Struktura semantičeskix polej čečeuskix i russkix padežej.* Moscow: Nauka
21. Dirr, A. 1928. *Einführung in das Studium der Kaukasischen Sprachen.* Leipzig: Verlag der Asia Major

21a. Džeiranisvili, E. 1971. *Udiuri ena* (Udi language—in Georgian with Russian summary). Tbilisi Univ. Press

22. *Ergativnaja konstruktsija predloženija* 1950. Moscow: Izd. inostrannoj literatury

23. *Ergativnaja konstruktsija predloženija v jazykax različnyx tipov* 1967. Leningrad: Nauka

24. Gamkrelidze, Th. V., Machavariani, G. I. 1965. *Sonant'ta sist'ema da ablaut'i kartvelur enebši* (The system of sonants and ablaut in Kartvelian languages—in Georgian with Russian summary). Tbilisi: Metsniereba

25. Gamkrelidze, Th. V., Gudava, T. E. 1974. Caucasian languages. *Encyclopaedia Britannica,* pp. 1011–15

26. Gaprindasvili, S. G. 1966. *Fonetika darginskogo jazyka.* Tbilisi: Metsniereba

27. Geiger, B., Halasi-Kun, T., Kuipers, A. N., Menges, K. H. 1959. *Peoples and Languages of the Caucasus.* Janua Linguarum, Series Minor 6. 'S-Gravenhage: Mouton

28. Genko, A. N. 1955. *Abazinskij jazyk.* Moscow-Leningrad: Akad. Nauk SSSR

29. Gudava, T. E. 1964. *Konsonantizm andijskix jazykov.* Tbilisi: Akad. Nauk Gruz. SSSR

30. Gukasjan, V. 1969. Opyt desifrovki albanskix nadpisej Azerbajdžana: *Izv. Akad. Nauk Az. SSR Ser. Lit. Jaz. iskusstva* No. 2, pp. 52–74

30a. Gukasjan, V. 1974. *Udinsko-azerbajdžansko-russkij slovar'* (with grammatical sketch in Russian). Baku: Elm

31. Halle, M. 1970. Is Kabardian a vowelless language? *Found. Lang.* 6:95–103

32. Holmer, N. M. 1947. Ibero-Caucasian as a linguistic type. *Stud. Ling.* 1:11–44

33. Ibragimov, G. X. 1968. *Fonetika tsaxurskogo jazyka.* Makhachkala: Dagestan. Filial Akad. Nauk SSSR

34. Illič-Svityč, V. M. 1971. *Opyt sravnenija nostratičeskix jazykov.* Moscow: Nauka

35. Isaev, M. I. 1970. *Sto tridtsat' ravnopravnyx.* Moscow: Nauka

36. Jakovlev, N. F. 1923. *Tablitsy fonetiki kabardinskogo jazyka,* Moscow: Travaux de la section des langues du Caucase septentrional de l'Institut oriental à Moscou

37. Jakovlev, N. F. 1940. Drevnye jazykovye svjazi Europy, Azii i Ameriki *Izv. Akad. Nauk SSSR Otd. Lit. Jaz.* 5(2): 143–48

38. Jakovlev, N. F. 1948. *Grammatika literaturnogo kabardino-čerkesskogo jazyka.* Moscow-Leningrad: Akad. Nauk SSSR

39. Jakovlev, N. F., Asxamaf, D. A. 1941. *Grammatika adygejskogo Literaturnogo jazyka.* Moscow-Leningrad: Akad. Nauk SSSR

40. *Jazyki narodov SSSR,* Vol. 4. 1967. *Iberijskokavkazskie jazyki.* (Moscow: Nauka

41. Kaldani, M. 1969. *Svanuri enis ponet' ik'a: l umlaut'is sist'ema svanurši* (Phonetics of Svan 1, Umlaut system in Svan —Georgian with Russian summary). Tbilisi: Metsniereba

42. Khajdakov, S. M. 1967. Arčinskij jazyk in *Jazyki narodov SSSR,* pp. 608–26. Moscow: Nauka

43. Khajdakov, S. M. 1973. *Sravnitel'nosopostavitel'nyj slovar dagestanskix jazykov.* Moscow: Nauka

44. Khajdakov, S. M. 1975. *Sistema glagola v dagestanskix jazykaz.* Moscow: Nauka

45. Kibrik, A. E. 1970. K tipologii prostranstvennyx značenii (na materiale padežnyx sistem dagestanskix jazykov). In *Jazyk i čelovek,* ed. V. A. Zveginstev. *MGU Pub. Otd. Strukt. Prikl. Ling.,* Issue 4, pp. 110–56

46. Kibrik, A. E., Kodzasov, S. V. 1970. Printsipy fonetičeskoj transkriptsii i transkriptsionnaja sistema dlja kavkazskix jazykov. *Vopr. Jaz.* 1970 (6):66–78

47. Kibrik, A. E., Kodzasov, S. V., Olovjannikov, I. P. 1972. *Fragmenty Grammatiki Xinalugskogo Jazyka. MGU Publi. Otd. Strukt. Prikl. Ling.: Ser. Monogr.,* Vyp. 9. Moscow

48. Klimov, G. A. 1961. O leksiko-statističeskoj teorii M. Svodeša. *Vopr. Teor. Jaz. Sovrem. Zarubeznoj Ling.,* pp. 239–53. Moscow: Akad. Nauk SSSR

49. Klimov, G. A. 1964. *Etimologičeskij slovar' kartvel'skix jazykov.* Moscow: Akad. Nauk SSSR

50. Klimov, G. A. 1965. *Kavkazskie jazyki.* Moscow. 1969. *Die kaukasischen Sprachen.* Hamburg: Buske Verlag

51. Klimov, G. A. 1967. Abxazskoadygskie etimologii I, Iskonnyj fond. *Etimologija 1965:* 296–306

52. Klimov, G. A. 1973. *Očerk obščej teorii ergativnosti.* Moscow: Nauka

53. Kuipers, A. N. 1960. *Phoneme and Morpheme in Kabardian.* Janua Linguarum Series Minor 8 'S-Gravenhage: Mouton

54. Kuipers, A. N. 1963. Caucasian. In *Current Trends in Linguistics,* ed. T. Sebeok, pp. 315–44

55. Kuipers, A. N. 1963. Proto-Circassian phonology: an essay in reconstruction. *Stud. Caucasica* 1: 56–92

56. Kuipers, A. N. 1976. Typologically salient features of some North-West Caucasian languages. *Stud. Caucasica* 3:101–27.
57. Kuipers, A. N. 1975. *A Dictionary of Proto-Circassian Roots.* Lisse: Ridder
58. Kumakhov, M. A. 1964. *Morfologija adygskix jazykov.* Moscow, Nalchik: Kabardino-Balkar
59. Kumakhov, M. A. 1965. Tipologičeskaja xarakteristika slova v polisintetičeskix jazykax Zapadnogo Kavkaza. *Ling. Tipol. Vost. Jaz.* 159–71
60. Kumakhov, M. A. 1971. *Slovo izmenenie adygskix jazykov.* Moscow: Nauka
61. Kumakhov, M. A. 1973. Teorija monovokalizma i zapadnokavkazskie jazyki. *Vopr. Jaz.* 6:54–67
62. Kumakhov, M. A., ed. 1969. *Očerki Kabardino-čerkesskoj dialektologii.* Nalchik
63. Lafon, R. 1952. Etudes basques et caucasiques. *Acta Salmant. Filos. Letra* 5(2):5–91
64. Meščaninov, I. I. 1967. *Ergativnaja konstruktsija v jazykov različnyx tipov.* Leningrad: Nauka
65. Mikailov, K. S. 1967. *Arčinskij jazyk.* Makhachkala: Dagestan. Filial Akad. Nauk SSSR
66. Morgestierne, G. 1935. Preface to D. L. R. Lorimer, *The Burushaski Language: Introduction and Grammar* 1:7–30. Inst. Samlignende Kulturforskning, Oslo
67. Murkelinskij, G. B., ed. 1971. *Sravnitel'no-istoričeskaja leksika dagestanskix jazykov.* Moscow: Nauka
68. Musaev, K. M. 1965. *Alfavity jazykov narodov SSSR.* Moscow: Nauka
69. Paris, C. 1974. *Système phonologique et phénomènes phonétiques dans le parler Besney de Zennun Köyü (Tcherkesse oriental).* Collect. Ling. Soc. Ling. Paris 69
70. Pike, E. V. 1964. The phonology of New Guinea languages. *Am. Anthropol.* 66 (4), Pt. 2:121–32, 309–22
71. Robins, R. H., Waterson, N. 1952. Notes on the phonetics of the Georgian word. *Bull. Sch. Orient. Afr. Lang.* 14 (Pt. 1): 55–72
72. Rogava, G. V., Keraševa, Z. I. 1966. *Grammatika adygejskogo jazyka,* Maikop, Krasnodar
73. Schmidt, K. H. 1962. *Studien zur Rekonstruktion des Lautstandes der Südkaukasischen Grundsprache.* Wies-

baden: Kommissionsverlag Franz Steiner GMBH
74. Shagirov, A. K. 1962. *Očerki po sravnitel'noj leksikologii adygskix jazykov.* Nalchik: Kabardino-Balkar
75. Shakryl, K. S. 1968. *Nekotorye leksičeskie i zvukovye sootvetstvija v abxazsko-adygskix jazykax.* Sukhumi: Alašara
76. Shakryl, K. S. 1971. *Očerki po abxazsko-adygskam jazykam.* Sukhumi: Alašara
77. Shanidze, A. 1963. Jazyk i pis'mo kavkazskix albantsev. *Trudy dvadtsat' pjatogo meždunarodnogo kongressa vostokovedov,* Vol. 3. Moscow
78. Sommerfelt, A. 1934, 1938, 1947. Etudes comparatives sur le caucasique du nord-est. *Nor. Tidsskr. Sprogvidenskap* 7:178–210, 9:115–43, 14:141–55
79. Sulimirski, T. 1970. *Prehistoric Russia.* New York: Humanities Press
80. Swadesh, M. 1971. *The Origin and Diversification of Language.* Chicago: Aldine, Atherton
81. Szemerényi, O. 1967. The new look of Indo-European: Reconstruction and typology. *Phonetica* 17:65–99
82. Tovar, A. 1961. El metodo lexicoestadistico y su aplicación a las relaciones des vascuence *Bol. R. Soc. Vascongada Amigos País,* Vol 17. San Sebastian
83. Trubetskoy, N. S. 1925. Review of Jakovlev "Tablitsy fonetiki Kabardinskogo jazyka" *Bull. Soc. Ling. Paris* 25 (3):277–81
84. Trubetskoy, N. S. 1931. Die Konsonantensysteme der ostkaukasischen Sprachen. *Caucasica* 11:1–39
85. Uslar, P. K. 1887. *Etnografija Kavkaza: Jazykoznanie I. Abxazskij jazyk.* Tiflis
86. Vogt, H. 1958. Structure phonémique du géorgian. *Nor. Tidsskr. Sprogvidenskap* 18:5–90
87. Vogt, H. 1963. *Dictionnaire de la langue Oubykh.* Oslo: Inst. Sammenlignende Kulturforskning, sér. B52
88. Zhghenti, S. 1956. *Kartuli enis ponet' ik'a* (Georgian Phonetics). Tbilisi Univ. Press
89. Zhghenti, S. 1960. *Kartveluri enuta šedarebiti ponet'ik'a,* I, *martsvlis agebulebis p'roblemi* (Comparative phonetics of Kartvelian languages I, the problem of syllable structure). Tbilisi Univ Press

Ann. Rev. Anthropol. 1977. 6:315–47
Copyright © 1977 by Annual Reviews Inc. All rights reserved

RECENT ANTHROPOLOGICAL STUDIES OF MIDDLE EASTERN COMMUNITIES AND ETHNIC GROUPS

♦9597

Erik Cohen[1]

Department of Sociology and Social Anthropology, The Hebrew University of Jerusalem, Jerusalem, Israel

INTRODUCTION

Change in the contemporary Middle East is ubiquitous and often rapid and pervasive (87, 171, 212). In some countries, such as Israel (73, 159), Lebanon (109, 172), Egypt and some regions of the Maghreb, change started early and has been going on ever since; in others such as the Gulf States and Oman (121, 181), it has only just begun. But as some studies of remote areas indicate, the winds of change have by now penetrated even the more outlying, isolated communities (e.g. 146, 147; see also 34, 79). The process blurs the traditional boundaries between the component pieces of the Middle Eastern "mosaic of people" (50, p. 2); but the mosaic does not disappear; new and larger pieces are formed and imposed upon the older ones as new boundaries are forged and older ones reassert themselves in new disguises (114, p. 308–309). Change is not a unidirectional homogenizing process of "modernization" or "Westernization." There is little doubt that the announcement of the "Passing of Traditional Society" (142) was vastly premature. How deep reaching is that change? Does it actually transform Middle Eastern societies and communities, or are their basic features resilient to the forces of change? Is the process of change essentially the same throughout the region, or can one distinguish different kinds of processes and different types of communal response to them? To what are the differences related? Anthropologists of an older generation were chiefly concerned with the description and analysis of the transmitted, traditional traits of Middle Eastern societies [e.g. 143; 210, Vol. 1; see also Hart's review of French anthropology in Appendix III of Antoun's work (9)]. Among the new generation,

[1]I should like to thank Ms. G. Portnoy and Mr. E. Ben Ari for their assistance in the preparation of this review.

a change in orientation is perceptible. Boissevain's (30, p. 15) observation concerning modern anthropology in general is also appropriate to the study of Middle Eastern communities:

> Up to the 1960's, the dominant question asked by most sociologists and social anthropologists was: What makes social order possible? . . . The accent was on the description of institutions and customs, and the way they were interconnected to form a system. . . . But anthropologists now are no longer concerned with merely describing what exists. . . . They are asking new questions. . . . (A)nthropologists now seek to explain the events of change, to chart the forces influencing the people they study.

The reorientation of Middle Eastern anthropology often involved a change of paradigm in terms of which the data are analyzed. As Antoun (9) pointed out, the homeostatic model is losing its dominant position and a diachronic model is gaining influence. This change of orientation can be seen in the self-criticism of one of the most outstanding Middle Eastern anthropologists, E. L. Peters, who found his own earlier analysis (176) of a Lebanese village in terms of a "system" model invalid (175). To this should be added another point, which also figures prominently in Peters's analysis—and which will be one of the chief foci of this survey—namely, that as part of the process of change, Middle Eastern communities were opened up to external forces and influences, so that their internal processes cannot be understood satisfactorily without taking into account their interface with broader societal frameworks.

Though the topic of change cropped up in the earlier literature (189), it is in the publications of the 1970s (on field work conducted mostly in the 1960s) that change figures most prominently. The studies reported have been carried out in a wide variety of communities, from divergent theoretical perspectives and research interests. The very abundance of their approaches, interests, and findings, however, is often more bewildering than enlightening to the comparatist. Several recent analyses of Middle Eastern studies (e.g. 9, 83, 108) lean more heavily on the earlier rather than on the most recent studies. Moreover, they are not primarily concerned with the analysis, conceptualization, and comparison of processes of change common to communities of different types and in various Middle Eastern countries. The present survey is intended to make a first step in this direction.

THE STUDIES—AN OVERVIEW

The development and present state of Middle Eastern anthropology has been reviewed recently by Fernea & Malarkey (83) and Antoun (9). Gulick's (108) book is the most recent comprehensive survey of all the major aspects of Middle Eastern anthropology. Of the countries in the region, only the anthropology of Israel has been surveyed separately (95, 112, 149).

There are several recent comparative studies or analyses of specific ecological or institutional arrangements: Johnson (125, 126) and Marx (153) on nomad ecology; Bates (21), Barth (18), and Swidler (211) on peasant-nomad relations; Black-Michaud (29) on the feud; Fernea (81) on village types; Rosenfeld (189) on village politics; and Harik (114) on ethnicity under changed political conditions. Several major collections of articles have appeared: on the region as a whole (143, 209, 210); on classes of communities—nomads (166) and villages (12) (but none on cities)— and on subareas—the Maghreb (91) and Israel (96); (Marx is about to publish another collection). There exists no comprehensive bibliography on anthropological research in the region, but there are useful bibliographical summaries by Gulick (108), as well as bibliographical lists attached to the reviews cited above, and to Bonine's (31) general survey of Middle Eastern urban studies.

This review deals with the anthropological and related work on the Middle East (excluding Turkey, Iran, and Afghanistan) for the period from 1970 to early 1976. We have collected more than 200 bibliographical items for that period.[2] We identified 95 distinct anthropological studies of communities and ethnic groups reported on during the period. To be eligible for inclusion, a study had to be based, at least in part, on anthropological fieldwork (primarily intensive, long-term participant observation); it had to be concerned, at least partly, with the contemporary life of its subjects (purely ethnohistoric studies were excluded); and it had to refer, at least implicitly, to a communal or groupal context (e.g. region, tribe, village, town, neighborhood, ethnic group). The distribution of these studies among countries in the region and classes of communities is uneven, as can be seen from Tables 1 and 2.

Close to half the studies have been conducted in Israel (and in the territories occupied by Israel). This is an enormous number considering the fact that Israel represents a tiny fraction of the total Middle Eastern population. Even if we allow for the possibility that the author, being Israeli, had better access to information on studies on Israel than on the other countries in the region, there is no doubt that the anthropological study of Israeli communities is far more comprehensive than that of any other Middle Eastern country.[3] Though anthropologists of various origins and orientations worked in Israel, the major contribution has been that of the group of students of the Department of Social Anthropology at the University of Manchester, who, under the leadership of the late Prof. M. Gluckman, conducted about a dozen separate studies (149). Several less intensive but useful studies have been conducted by the regional sociologists of the Settlement Department of the Jewish Agency (194). The fact that despite this intensive work there nevertheless still exist considerable lacunae in data on Israeli communities and ethnic groups only emphasizes the extent of our ignorance concerning the other countries of the region. Among these, Lebanon and Morocco have been relatively intensively studied. In the former, the major contribution has been made by the staff and students of the American University in Beirut (131, 132); in the latter, the earlier lead of French anthropologists (9, Appendix III by Hart; 83) has been more recently taken over by Americans, particularly the group of researchers drawing their inspiration from Geertz's work (68, 69, 180, 182–185). Tunisia and Egypt are next in line in terms of number of studies, but these were generally less intensive and less compre-

[2]These do not include unpublished German and French doctoral dissertations, on which no information was available.

[3]Antoun (9), in his survey of Middle Eastern anthropology, also found a disproportionately large number of studies on Israel.

Table 1 Distribution of studies by country and type of publication

| | Type of publication | | | |
Country	Book or monograph	Articles only	Unpublished PhD or MA theses	Total
Israel[a]	16	19	10	45
Morocco	3	6	4	13
Lebanon	3	4	4	11
Tunisia	1	6	1	8
Egypt	1	5	1	7
Libya	—	1	2	3
Jordan	2	—	—	2
Iraq	1	1	—	2
Southern Yemen	1	—	—	1
Saudi Arabia	1	—	—	1
Algeria	—	1	—	1
Syria	—	1	—	1
TOTAL	29	44	22	95

[a] Including studies in the territories occupied by Israel.

hensive, as attested by the fact that only one book was published on each [Egypt (78) and Tunisia (66)]. These five countries account for close to 90% of all the studies conducted in the region between 1970 and 1976, leaving only 11 studies for all the other Middle Eastern countries. The latter, however, include some important monographs such as Antoun's (10) and Gubser's (106) work on Jordan, Fernea's (82) on an Iraqi town, Bujra's (34) on a Hadramauthi community, and Cole's (49) on a Saudian tribe; some important work (23, 52, 158) was also done on Libya. There is little or nothing on Syria, Yemen, and the Gulf States. Political circumstances, the remoteness of some of these areas, and the difficulties of foreigners to conduct fieldwork probably account for the scarcity of anthropological studies in these countries.[4]

Foreign researchers predominate in most countries, except for Israel and Lebanon, where local anthropologists—albeit mostly foreign trained—made important contributions; however, judging from the list of recent doctoral dissertations, an increasing number of younger anthropologists native to the countries of the region are entering the field.

Table 2 indicates that, in comparison with an earlier period, there is a shift of interest from tribal studies to villages and towns and, more recently, urban neighborhoods. Villages are still the most extensively studied class of communities (35

[4]Antoun (9), in his questionnaire inquiry among anthropologists, found that whereas Israel ranked first in terms of research interest, not a single respondent stated an interest in Syria, Iraq, Jordan, or the Gulf States.

Table 2 Distribution of studies by class of community and type of publication

Class or community	Type of publication			Total
	Book or monograph	Articles only	Unpublished PhD or MA theses	
Tribe[a]	2	10	5	17
Village[b]	12	17	6	35
Town[c]	8	7	2	17
City[d]	6	9	9	24
Refugee camps	1	—	—	1
Other	—	1	—	1
TOTAL	29	44	22	95

[a] Including tribal villages.
[b] Excluding tribal villages.
[c] Including studies of town and surrounding region.
[d] Mostly studies of urban neighborhoods.

studies); cities, however not only rank second (24 studies), but the large number of doctoral and master's theses on urban subjects hold out a promise for a crop of new books in the next few years.

Though several authors have pointed out the growing interdependence of town and countryside (9; 108, p. 56), students still tend to concentrate on the study of narrow ecological units, e.g. tribes, villages, or towns, rather than of larger ecological complexes in which the intricate interrelationships between cities, towns, villages, and nomads could be discerned [on the lines of English's (75) study of the Kirman basin]. Indeed, only 4 studies (68, 82, 106, 180) could be classified as regional in scope.

Table 3 presents the distribution of the studies by country and class of community.

Three Points are worth noting in Table 3:

(*a*) Half the Israeli studies refer to villages, particularly *moshavim* (cooperative small-holder settlements); only a few are studies of *kibbutzim* (collective settlements) or Arab villages. The moshav is probably the most thoroughly studied type of communities anywhere in the Middle East. The towns studied are mainly development towns, i.e. new towns established in recently settled development areas (46). Studies in Israeli cities were primarily conducted in neighborhoods inhabited by Oriental Jews and Arabs in Jerusalem and Tel Aviv.

(*b*) In both Morocco and Lebanon, urban anthropological studies were more numerous than tribal and rural ones; in the case of Morocco this reflects primarily the recent surge of interest in Moroccan cities among American anthropologists; in the case of Lebanon it reflects the great preoccupation with Beirut, which is probably the anthropologically most extensively studied Middle Eastern city.

Table 3   Distribution of studies by country and class of community[a]

Country	Tribe	Village	Town	City	Refugee camp	Other	Total
Israel	2	22	9	10	1	1	45
Morocco	3	1	2	7			13
Lebanon	1	5	1	4			11
Tunisia	2	3	1	2			8
Egypt	4	2		1			7
Lybia	3						3
Jordan		1	1				2
Iraq	1		1				2
Southern Yemen			1				1
Saudi Arabia	1						1
Algeria		1					1
TOTAL	17	35	17	24	1	1	95

[a] See notes to Tables 1 and 2.

(c) In the other countries, studies of tribes and villages tend to predominate; the scarcity of urban anthropological studies in Egypt is particularly noteworthy [though Cairo has been intensively studied sociologically by Abu-Lughod (2–4)].

What are the major foci of research?[5] Despite the holistic tradition of anthropology, only a minority of the studies are general in character, either standard ethnographic descriptions or analyses of the complex interrelationships between the various constitutive parts of the community. However, most of the major publications, i.e. books and monographs, are still of that nature (17 out of 29).

The more narrowly focused studies deal with a wide variety of institutional aspects of the community, with ecological processes, or with specific social groups. The most frequently studied institutions are the political, to which several books (12, 13, 34, 62, 106) and doctoral theses (e.g. 127, 141, 162, 165, 185, 190) as well as many articles (e.g. 19, 52, 56, 63, 107, 123, 169, 200) have been devoted. Second in importance are studies in economic anthropology [e.g. Abarbanel's (1) book, Auerbach's (15) and Dwyer's (67) theses, as well as several articles]. There is one book-length study on processes of stratification [in the kibbutz (136)] and one on urban religious institutions (68), though several others devote considerable attention to that latter topic (e.g. 13, pp. 149–76; 62; 180).

Ecology is a major preoccupation in many studies, particularly those of nomadic tribes (49, 151, 155, 166), and of villages (e.g. 10, 82). Urban ecological processes were examined more from a geographic perspective (131, 179) than an anthropologi-

[5] The major subjects of interest in Middle Eastern anthropology have been examined by Antoun (9).

cal one, with the notable exception of Khuri's (132, pp. 21–62) analysis of patterns of settlement in two suburbs of Beirut.

Most studies of social groups are concerned with ethnicity and ethnic relations, while only two studies focus on other kinds of groups: al-Khakim on the *zabbaleen* (refuse collectors) of Cairo (22) and Miner (161) on the weavers of Fez.

The bulk of the studies of ethnic groups examines the multifarious aspects of ethnicity in Israel (97), within the Jewish or the Arab sectors of the society as well as between them. The ethnic groups studied within the Jewish sector were primarily those of African and Asian origin: Marx (148, 153, 154) and Shokeid (199, 202) studied Moroccans; Deshen & Shokeid (64) and Deshen (62) studied Moroccans and Tunisians; Deshen & Jaeger (63) and Deshen (54, 57, 59, 60) studied Tunisians; Goldberg (98–102) focused on Tripolitarians; Kushner (139), Shokeid (203), and Weil (216) concentrated on Jews from India, Eilam (70, 71) on the Georgian Jews, Ben Shaul (24) the Bukharan Jews, Shapiro (193), Shai (192), and C. Cohen (37) the Kurds, and Katzir (130) the Yemenites; studies in Oriental Jewish ethnic neighborhoods were conducted by Halper (110), Mendes-Flohr (160), and Aviel (16); on urban Oriental protest movements by Bernstein (26; see also 44). There are few studies of European or American Jews: chiefly, Katz's (129) study on Americans and Kressel's (134) on relations between Eastern and Western European Jews in a kibbutz. Israeli Arabs were studied by Rosenfeld (187, 188), Nakhleh (164, 165), and Shokeid (200, 201); Beduins by Marx (146, 147, 150, 151, 155) and in an urban setting by Kressel (135, 137); Druzes by Oppenheimer (169) and Kasdan (128); Baha'is of Iranian origin by Cohen (43). The general field of ethnic relations in Israel was examined by Weingrod (219) and more recently by Peres (173, 174). Studies on Jewish-Arab ethnic relations were conducted by Rubin (191) and Cohen (42, 45, 47), both in the city of Acre. However, despite this proliferation of studies on Israeli ethnicity, large areas remain uncovered. To facilitate further studies, a survey of Central, South, and East Asian Jewish communities in Israeli settlements (195) and a bibliography and a survey of Israeli minorities (41, 48) have been carried out.

Ethnicity in other Middle Eastern countries has been much less intensively studied: Harik (114) surveys the field and deals in detail with the Lebanese case. Gellner & Micaud's (91) collection examines Arab and Berber ethnicity in Morocco in a variety of contexts. Of the different Middle Eastern minorities, the Jews are the most frequently studied group (9); Goldberg (98, 101, pp. 9–45) worked on the ethnohistory of Tripolitarian Jews, Deshen (55) attempted a reconstruction of the Jewish community of Djerba, while Shokeid (202, pp. 15–33) reconstructed the Jewish community in the Atlas Mountains. Gerber (93) studied the Jews of Fez, and Rosen (182) studied the relations between Jews and Arabs in a small Moroccan city. Studies of other ethnic groups are rare; the situation of the Druzes (225) and Armenians (124) in several Middle Eastern countries has been compared, while Sweet (208) studied a Druze village in Lebanon. Hamalian (111) studied one particular economic institution of urban Armenians in Lebanon, the *shirket;* a useful review of Christian communities in the Middle East has been published recently by Betts (28). Contemporary statistical information on different Middle Eastern minorities is found in *Ethnic and Religious Minorities* (76).

European groups in Middle Eastern countries remained largely outside the scope of traditional Middle Eastern anthropology. Labaied (140) studied the European quarter of Tunis; Khalaf & Kongstad (131) studied a neighborhood of Beirut with a large European population. The author is presently studying the non-Jewish, American, and British expatriate communities in Jerusalem.

Many ethnic studies were conducted in urban settings and concentrated on particular ethnic groups—e.g. Berbers in Moroccan cities (7, 215), and Oriental Jews (e.g. 16, 26, 37, 110, 160, 192) or Arabs (135, 200, 201) in Israeli cities. Most studies of Israeli *moshavim* are in fact studies of ethnic groups, since most were settled by people of common origin. A unique study is Zenner's (223), concerned with stereotypes between different ethnic groups in a rural setting.

The bewildering variety of communities, groups, and topics studied by anthropologists in the region during the 1970s precludes any exhaustive analysis within the scope of a short review. I shall hence limit my remarks to the examination of the most ubiquitous theme in the literature: the process of change.

THE PROCESS OF INCORPORATION

"Eclipse of community" (207), or the gradual incorporation of local communities into broader societal frameworks, resulting often in loss of local autonomy, has been a major theme in the analysis of community studies in modern Western societies [Giner (94, pp. 108–23) and Stein (207) in the United States, Frankenberg (86) and Pahl (170) in Great Britain]. However, despite the mounting evidence of similar processes in developing countries, the theme is much less prominent in the analysis of contemporary anthropological studies in those countries, and the Middle East is no exception. Gulick (108, p. 90) talks about a ". . . decrease of *relative* isolation of villages and pastoral groups from the centers of power and innovation in the cities," and Fernea (81) uses "urban influence" as one variable in his typology of Middle Eastern village communities. There are few theoretical statements on the process of incorporation and increasing regional and national involvement of different types of communities [the kind contained, for example, in Cohen's (40) analysis of the structural change in the Israeli *kibbutz*]. Moreover, the variety of external forces impinging upon the community, abrogating its economic, social, political, and cultural autonomy and permeating ethnic group boundaries has never been comparatively examined. It is through the impact of these forces, and the communities' response to them, that local society is transformed and that previously isolated communities emerge into the modern world through progressive enmeshment into regional, national, and sometimes even transnational frameworks.

The various communities and groups are differentially exposed to forces emanating from the broader frameworks; a few isolates are still preserved in the extreme margins of the region (e.g. 65), while in other cases (34, 82) incorporation has only recently occurred. However, the process of community change cannot be simply understood in terms of "degree of incorporation." Social change in Middle Eastern communities is neither a uniformly linear nor a unidirectional process, but rather a consequence of the differential impact of a variety of forces eliciting different kinds of response in the various component groups of the community. Our first task then is to study the kinds of forces and their impact and the types of responses they elicit in the community.

Few Middle Eastern communities have even in the past been completely autarchic or isolated. Indeed, Coon (50, pp. 3–4) conceived of the Middle Eastern "mosaic" as based on a division of labor among ethnic groups, and many earlier students assumed the existence of an "ecological trilogy" of nomads, peasants, and urbanites. Barth (20) based his analysis of the ecological system on an assumed symbiosis between culturally specialized groups. However, traditional relations between groups were conceived of as more or less permanently fixed, as well as rather narrowly defined. Anthropologists could thus concentrate on one specific group, e.g. a tribe or a village, and analyze its social structure and culture in terms of its "adaptation" to the physical habitat and the other groups in its environment. Recently, however, doubts were cast upon the claim that equilibrium in the ecological system has been simply automatically achieved through an ethnic or cultural division of labor, even in the traditional situation; thus Bates (21) pointed to the role of the state in the regulation of relations between nomads and peasants. Moreover, in the contemporary period, the mesh of interrelationships has widened and increased in variety; the traditional "ecological trilogy" has begun to disappear (74) as the boundaries of the division of labor gradually blur (211, p. 36). The study of individual component pieces of the "mosaic" has become less and less rewarding as the region, embracing a variety of different groups intricately interrelated, becomes the important unit to be studied—as both Gulick (108, p. 56) and Antoun (9) pointed out; but as yet few anthropologists have paid primary attention to the pattern of interrelationships between the different groups in the region [most notably, Fernea (82)].

Under contemporary conditions, the circumstances of the immediate habitat become of progressively decreasing relevance for the analysis of a group's culture and social structure; and though studies of traditional, particularly nomadic societies show the analytic potential of an "ecological" approach (152), most contemporary situations ask for a consideration of a much wider set of circumstances than those inherent in the immediate environment, even for the study of nomads (49, 166).

The ecological significance of "environment" should not, however, be assumed as given. An interesting implication of the new situation is that the significant features of the immediate environment for the group may themselves change as some of its heretofore neglected aspects become "resources," while the importance of traditional resources diminishes (38, p. 52).

Recent ethnohistorical studies (98, 118–120, 214) and local histories (106) of villages and towns have also demonstrated the traditional enmeshment of such communities into wider frameworks; but in the past, only few Middle Eastern anthropologists dealt systematically with such external relations (163). In the contemporary period these relations have vastly expanded, both in terms of content as well as range. This is documented by all recent studies, even those of the more traditional areas in the region, [e.g. Iraq (82), Jordan (10, 106), Hadramauth (34), Lybia (52), Morocco (68, 69, 180), and Southern Tunisia (79)].

Under modern circumstances, groups often change habitats or their old habitats are changed by new forces. Thus where nomadic groups are sedentarized (32, 33, 92, 167, 196–198), the conditions of their habitat are changed even if they are not removed from their traditional area, and their contacts with wider frameworks are broadened. Where groups have migrated within or between countries, their habitats change dramatically and they are exposed to the impact of often unfamiliar wider social forces, e.g. when ruralites migrate to cities (7, 132, 144, 215) or Middle Eastern or Asian Jews migrate to Israel [see (25, 64, 202) for Moroccan Jews; see (99, 100) for Tripolitarian Jews; see (139) for Indian Jews]. However, as most of these studies show, different social and institutional mechanisms often cushion the individual migrant against the full impact of the forces of incorporation.

Middle Eastern communities and ethnic groups of all kinds are, therefore, in the throes of a multifarious and all-encompassing process of incorporation into broader societal frameworks (114). Its importance not withstanding, the process itself has not yet been analyzed theoretically. Most anthropologists discuss concrete changes in their communities which ensue from external forces, but they neither attempt to classify these forces and study their impact comparatively, nor do they conceptualize the interplay between the community and the wider society in more general theoretical terms. I shall attempt to codify the forces of incorporation in terms of a threefold typology, and to propose a conceptual framework for the analysis of the different kinds of *impacts* they have upon communities, and of the varieties of communal or groupal *response* to these impacts.

The literature points to three kinds of forces of incorporation:

1. *Communicative forces:* expansion of communication systems into heretofore relatively isolated communities; the two most important mechanisms of such expansion are (a) the mass media and particularly the radio (114, pp. 303–4; 142) which, through the dissemination of transistors, penetrates even the most outlying communities (e.g. 34, p. 169); and (b) the road and aereal transportation system which increases both the speed and frequency of contact with major urban centers (35; 49, p. 16; 52, p. 269; 121, p. 310).

2. *Economic forces:* expansion of national and international systems of production and exchange into heretofore economically relatively self-sufficient ecological systems. The most important mechanisms here are (a) increased supply of products and services to national or transnational markets (116), e.g. through the commercialization of agricultural production (e.g. 49, p. 158; 78, pp. 30–37), through tourism (8, 45), through new forms of entrepreneurship (e.g. 7, 52, 67, 215), or through the introduction of cooperative or governmentally organized forms of marketing [on Israel (1, 17) and on Syria (123)]; and (b) the increased participation of locals in the national labor market, either through employment in development projects in the region (49, p. 28; 52; 147), through wage labor in urban centers (10,

p. 28–33; 49, pp. 158–62; 106, p. 128; 128; 132, p. 71; 175) or through emigration abroad (175, 222).

3. *Political - administrative forces:* the penetration of national political forces and administrative machinery into the local community. The most important mechanisms here are (*a*) incorporation of local into national politics through political parties (13, 14, 106, 127) or other nation-wide political bodies such as family associations (132, pp. 155–91) or sectarian organizations (132, pp. 201–5; 133) in Lebanon; (*b*) the penetration by the central government of previously self-governing communities—the "Coming of the Government" in Bujra's (34, p. 193) picturesque phrase—and the incorporation of their traditional leaders into the governmental administrative apparatus (e.g. 10, p. 104; 82, p. 109) or the transfer of their authority to local councils, (106, p. 147; 115, p. 297; 164); (*c*) the penetration of local communities by regional and national administrative, regulative, servicing, and planning agencies, e.g. nomadic tribes in the process of sedentarization (92, 166, 196) or traditional villages and sedentary tribal areas (10; 81, pp. 88–90; 82; 106; 115; 123). In Israel in particular this mechanism was of decisive impact in both new rural (139, 194, 220) and new urban Jewish settlement (13, 46); while national agricultural planning has a growing impact even upon mature villages (1, 17).

In concrete situations these kinds of forces and their respective mechanisms usually appear conjointly, or the appearance of one fosters that of the others. However, one kind of force or associated mechanism is often dominant, and one could isolate its impact on the community. Thus Fernea (81) implemented the distinction between economic and political external forces of domination as one basis of his typology of Middle Eastern villages, while Bujra (34, pp. 169–82) emphasizes the importance of communicative processes as a factor in the change of criteria for leadership selection.

The precise interplay between these forces and local communities has never been explicitly conceptualized. I propose to approach this problem in terms of *impact* and *response.* Each type of force of incorporation reconstitutes the *field of opportunities* open to the community or to specific groups within it. It may open up new opportunities, e.g. new markets for local products and labor, new types of political participation etc, as well as encroach upon old ones, particularly in areas where communities enjoyed traditional autonomy, e.g. political organization and control over local economic resources. The forces of incorporation may hence both *expand* and *contract* the field of opportunities facing a community or social group. The available literature does not permit us to draw any simple empirical generalizations about the relationship between the *kinds* of forces and their *impact* upon the field of opportunities; my impression, however, is that all three kinds generally contribute more to an expansion than to a contraction of the field, albeit to different degrees. Communicative processes have the most expanding impact; economic, and even more political, forces often have important contracting consequences.

The extent to which the field of opportunities expands or contracts is here seen "objectively," i.e. as estimated by the researcher or analyst. It is essential to realize that the community, or groups and individual members of it, may take quite a different "subjective" view. Moreover, even if they admit the availability of new opportunities, they may reject them on cultural grounds or because of economic and political vested interests. Whatever the change in the field of opportunities, they may take a variety of attitudes toward it, ranging from positive to negative, i.e. from complete *acceptance* to utter *rejection*. Within that range, a variety of specific configurations of attitudes, accepting some while rejecting other elements in the changed situation, are possible. Disregarding these for the sake of simplicity, and crossing the two main types of attitudes with the two main forms of impact of the forces of incorporation, we obtain a fourfold table of community (or group) *response* (Table 4).

It is important to note that for different groups and segments within the community the field of opportunities may be differentially structured by the forces of incorporation—or they may respond differentially to the same field, according to their attitude. Let me illustrate the use of this conceptual framework by some of the findings in the literature under consideration.

1. *Exploitation:* The community or group actively avails itself of the new opportunities proferred, e.g. by improved communications (e.g. 35, 52), by an upsurge in urban demand creating new openings for enterprising individuals, as e.g. the Swasa Berbers in Casablanca (7, 215), or by disbursement of governmental funds, as e.g. in a Lybian oasis (52, 53).

2. *Submission:* The community or group acquiesces in the contraction of its field of opportunities, particularly through governmental encroachments upon its traditional autonomy or sources of livelihood. Such acquiescence is sometimes forthcoming only after repeated attempts to defy the central authorities fail (e.g. 10, 118). Submission is common among groups such as nomadic tribes who lost their dominant status over against sedentary groups upon incorporation into the wider society (32, 33), or which have been sedentarized by governments eager to curtail their independence (92). Minorities also might be forced to submit to pressure, e.g. the Israeli Arabs to the expropriation of their land (164, p. 501) or the Armenians (124) to the loss of economic or political privileges.

3. *Insulation:* The community or group rejects or does not exploit the new opportunities, either through subjective miscalculation or a distrust of the new and preference for the old, and retreats upon itself. The traditional elites are most likely

Table 4   Types of responses to impact of forces of incorporation

		Impact of forces of incorporation	
		Expanding field of opportunities	Contracting field of opportunities
Community or group attitude	Acceptance	1. Exploitation	2. Submission
	Rejection	3. Insulation	4. Defiance

to initiate such a rejection and steer the community into self-insulation as was the case in an extreme form with the Bengi-Isguen (79). The descendants of Sidi Lahcen (180) similarly strove to preserve their "symbolic domination" at the price of steering their community away from the opportunities which the development of the region offered.

4. *Defiance:* The community or group actively defy the encroachment upon traditional rights and liberties or sources of livelihood by political or in extreme cases armed struggle. Defiance of the central government was common in the past before outlying areas were "pacified" (10, 118). Duvignaud's (66) action research on Shebika in Tunisia shows how an expectant attitude towards socialism in the 1960s eventually turned into defiance of governmental coercion. Marx (148, 153, 154) shows how personal violence develops out a sense of helplessness (i.e. of the foreclosure of opportunities). On a much larger scale the struggle of the Kurds and the struggle of Palestinian Arabs are perhaps the most outstanding examples of a defiant response. It is regretable that we do not possess any good ethnographies of "communities in revolt."[6] The study of a Palestinian refugee camp (205) is rather tendentious, and a more systematic study of a camp in the occupied West Bank (156, 157) is not directly concerned with this problem. Nakhleh (164, p. 511), in his study of Israeli Arab villages, alludes to a future change from submission to defiance in the political arena but does not enlarge upon that contingency. More studies of defiance, of political as well as of economic forces encroaching upon the community, are called for.

The various types of community (or group) response to the forces of incorporation may of course appear in conjunction in different spheres. The Arabs in Israel are a case in point: while they generally submitted to (or only mildly defied) political and economic encroachments, such as a prohibition to give political expression to their national aspirations or to the confiscation of their land, they availed themselves eagerly of the new opportunities provided by Israel's expanding economy. Moreover, even these members of the younger intelligentsia who defy political and economic encroachments nevertheless strive to exploit the economic opportunities.

Different groups in the same community may respond differently to changes in the field of opportunities. Thus the male Yemeni Jewish settlers in the *moshav* studied by Katzir (130) were more insulative and their wives more exploitative in their response to the new opportunities which they faced in Israel. Moreover, individual "subjective" estimates of the field of opportunities may vary, so that some may fail to attempt to exploit new opportunities for lack of trust that they are indeed open to them. Mendes-Flohr's (160) recent detailed examination of the occupational choices of individual Oriental youths in a handicapped urban neighborhood in Jerusalem relates to this problem.

[6]This is a general deficiency in anthropology; Gough's (104, p. 407) advice that revolutionary and proto-revolutionary movements should be studied has been little heeded in the Middle East or elsewhere.

Our typology of attitudes and responses is somewhat simplistic; more sophisticated but nevertheless generally applicable typologies of responses of the kind developed by Deshen (60) for the analysis of *symbolic change,* are called for.

The thrust of my argument is that the process of incorporation strikes different communities and groups in different ways; moreover, similar kinds of change in the field of opportunities may elicit different types of responses among otherwise similarly placed social groups or individuals, thus leading to highly varied outcomes in the process of change. Hence a crucial theoretical problem: given certain changes in the field of opportunities, what factors shape the response? How can we explain, for example, that the traditional elite of Hureidah (34) availed itself of the new economic opportunities while a similar group in Sidi Lahcen (180) rejected them? A broad symbolic interactionist approach to such questions may help much to resolve them: namely, an examination of the processes through which the *meaning* for the group of the changes in the field of opportunities is negotiated; the extent to which the group adheres to its traditional values and symbols, and even more the inventive capacity of its members in the reinterpretation and reformulation of those values and symbols appear to be the crucial factors for an explanation of their response. Unfortunately, only a few students have dealt explicitly with this problem (e.g. 56, 60, 180). The problem touches upon some complex general issues concerning the relationship between social stability and change and the "dynamics of tradition" (72) which will not be discussed here. As far as community studies are concerned, this problem could be most effectively examined in a comparative manner in the Israeli *moshav,* where a large number of studies of different groups of settlers facing roughly similar conditions is already available.

Incorporation typically proceeds on three distinct levels: the regional, the national, and the transnational. Development sociologists are mainly interested in the second level: incorporation of communities and groups into the new national societies (e.g. 88). Though anthropologists are also concerned with this level, their more detailed studies often unravel the importance of the intermediary, regional level (e.g. 180).

Little attention has been paid by both sociologists and anthropologists to the impact of transnational forces, though communities, particularly in the Middle East, are often harshly affected by them. Thus changes in international political relations —e.g. between Israel and the Arab states—affect group relations in mixed Israeli communities, as I myself observed in the mixed city of Acre; they may even affect Jewish-Arab relations in countries remote from the conflict (186); war and its aftermath, particularly occupation, has far-reaching effects, but such factors seldom figure explicitly in the studies. Economic factors, particularly oil and tourism, often bring remote and heretofore secluded communities into sudden contact with the outside world. Such a confrontation is particularly sharp in the oil-producing Gulf states (113, 121, 122), where the modern oil industry and the sudden availability of modern Western products, impinging upon an orthodox Islamic society, produce a situation in which traditional villagers live in a deeply split world (113); the ways in which they cope with their predicament have yet to be thoroughly examined.

Though tourism is an important economic factor in several Middle Eastern countries—the Maghreb, Egypt, Israel, and Lebanon—its transnational impact has not yet been studied extensively. Alouche's (8) study deals with the evolution of a Lebanese village serving primarily internal tourism. My own work on Arab boys and tourist girls (45) deals with a very limited problem within the vast area of interplay between international tourism and local groups and communities. This field deserves more systematic attention.

PATTERNS OF SOCIAL CHANGE IN MIDDLE EASTERN COMMUNITIES

Social change on the communal level has been studied in the 1970s in a wide spectrum of Middle Eastern communities, ranging from nomadic tribes (49, 135, 151, 155, 166), oases (52, 158), sedentary tribal people (35, 117, 118, 180, 213), peasant villages (8, 10, 66, 67, 78, 82, 100, 130, 139, 141, 164, 165, 168, 169, 175, 183, 188, 194, 202, 218, 221), towns (13, 34, 51, 68, 79, 106, 148, 182, 184, 185, 191), and neighborhoods (69, 75, 85, 127, 131, 192). Despite this proliferation of studies, little has been done to examine on a more general theoretical or comparative level the patterns of change within the region as a whole or even within given classes of communities. The general works, such as Patai (171), van Nieuwenhuijze (212), Gulick (108), and Antoun (9), mostly review the earlier literature without attempting major theoretical generalizations. The general process of change among nomadic and tribal groups has received little attention [but see Swidler (211)]. Processes of change in villages as related to community politics have been analyzed comparatively in (12), particularly in articles by Rosenfeld (189) and Antoun (11); urban change has been reviewed recently by Bonine (31), but his article pays little attention to the work of urban anthropologists.

Our picture of traditional Middle Eastern society, the baseline against which any analysis of processes of change has to be set, is far from uniform. The image of the "mosaic" indicates that traditional society was composed of closed, often corporate groups. This generalization has to be qualified in the light of recent findings. Tribal, particularly nomadic groups, tend indeed to be corporate (49, 151, 155, 178); but in some peasant areas such as Egypt, lineages in village communities do not belong to wider corporate groups (82, p. 87). Moreover, Evans-Pritchard's (77, pp. 192–95) model of segmentary opposition between corporate groups is not simply applicable in all Middle Eastern areas. Thus Hart (119, 120) has demonstrated that although the tribes of the Moroccan Rif possessed characteristics of corporate groups, feuds between close agnates were common, feuds often involving alliances such as between "neighboring clans of bordering tribes" (119, p. 43), which followed the principles of the *liff*-system rather than that of segmentary opposition. Finally, Rosen (182) and Eickelman (69) have conceived a model of the traditional Moroccan society, based on individuals in "dyadic" relationships rather than corporate groups, as the fundamental units of Moroccan social structure. However, Rosen concedes that even though traditionally in Morocco "groupings were only minimally corporate"

(182, p. 437), there was still "a clumping up, an overlapping of affiliations of certain groups of persons" (182, p. 442).

Whatever the degree of internal corporateness and external closure of traditional Middle Eastern society might have been, the different forces of incorporation discussed above may be assumed to weaken and even to destroy the corporate nature of local communities or groups as these are "opened up" socially and as their members link up with ever wider social circles in regional, national or even transnational frameworks. There is indeed considerable evidence to support such an expectation. Historical studies such as Antoun's (10) of a Jordanian village abundantly document the processes of gradual decorporation. Even in areas where "dyadic" relationships rather than corporate groups are said to have traditionally prevailed, the "clumping up" and "overlapping of affiliations" has been loosened as the pace of modernization increased (182, p. 442).

A great number of studies illustrates the "opening up" of tribal and village communities to the wider world. Thus Gubser (106, p. 46), in a study of a Jordanian town, points out that ". . . in former days, the district of Al-Karak was the largest meaningful political entity . . . over the last seventy-five years, and especially the last two decades, there has been a growing identity with Jordan as the larger political identity." Hart (118) documented the gradual incorporation of two Moroccan Berber tribes with originally narrow "terminal loyalties" into the broader national framework. Myriad social links criss-cross the boundaries of once fairly closed communities: improved travel facilities bring once remote people in contact with cities and increase the scope of social relations between countryside and villages; ruralites entertain close relations with their covillagers who emigrated to the towns, while the latter remain continuously involved in the affairs of their villages of origin (132, 215). Businessmen enter into relations with partners in remote modern capitals (121, p. 313). Village women establish ties with urban housewives whom they supply with produce (130). Bedouin establish linkages along smuggling routes (147, 151, 155). Regional towns and cities rather than individual communities thus increasingly become the foci of social integration (180, p. 56).

Though our hypothesis seems to find abundant confirmation in the recent literature, it does so only at a very general level. Closer scrutiny of the studies reveals that the relationship between the forces of incorporation and social change in the community is neither simple nor easily understood; change is not even necessarily unidirectional. On the basis of the data at hand several generalizations can be proposed which substantially qualify the above hypothesis.

First, the processes of decorporation of local communities on the one hand and their "opening up" to broader frameworks on the other are not necessarily obversely related. Indeed, a community may open up without necessarily changing internally, as Goldberg's (100) and to a lesser extent, Shokeid's (202) studies of North African Jewish immigrants in Israeli *moshavim* have demonstrated. The relationship seems to depend on the communities' response to the forces of incorporation and on the mechanisms which mediate between the community and the wider frameworks.

Secondly, the kind of impact which the forces of incorporation have on the community, namely whether they expand or contract the field of opportunities, and the type of response of the community are important intervening variables in a comparative examination of the relationship between the forces of incorporation and community change. I am not yet in a position to construct a series of theoretical propositions on the influence of variables, but several empirical generalizations can be extracted from the studies under consideration:

(*a*) An expansion in the field of opportunities is more likely to increase the linkage between the community and the broader frameworks than a contraction in the field, since many of the new opportunities (e.g. employment, business, etc) will be found outside the traditional tribal or village frameworks. A contraction in the field of opportunities, insofar as it involves an encroachment upon spheres of life in which the community was traditionally self-regulating, leads primarily to a reduction or break up of its corporateness (10).

(*b*) An acceptive attitude on the part of the community seems to promote both external linkages and decorporation, while a rejective attitude seems to block both these processes. Assuming that the changes in the field of opportunities are of primary influence and the response of the community of only secondary influence, we may formulate the following tentative generalizations concerning the relationship between types of community responses and the processes of decorporation and opening up of the community: an *exploitative* response leads primarily to increased linkages and only secondarily to decorporation; indeed, in some cases communities remained largely intact despite their exploitation of new opportunities (100, 215); a *submissive* response leads primarily to decorporation and only secondarily to increased linkages (10); an *insulative* response obstructs linkages and conserves corporateness (79); while a *defiant* response may even cut linkages and reinforce corporateness (e.g. 66).

(*c*) The extent to which the impact of the forces of incorporation is uniform for all the constituent groups of the community and the degree to which the community responds as a collective to this impact appear to be crucial factors for an understanding of the process of change. If the external forces have a differential impact upon the various groups, as they did in the case of the El Shabana, where they favored the shaykhly lineages to the detriment of the other tribesmen (80), or in the Israeli moshav, where they favored some types of farmers to the disadvantage of others (1, 17), or if the groups respond differentially to the same impact, the corporateness or unity of the group will be impaired. Insofar as a community or a group responds collectively, it preserves or even reinforces its corporateness, whatever the nature of its response may be. Here seems to lie part of the explanation for the relative lack of internal social change reported by Goldberg (100).

Thirdly, the relationship between the forces of incorporation and social change is not necessarily unidirectional. As communities or groups turn against the external forces they may "reincorporate," as happened in Shebika (66) or in the case of various ethnic groups.

Finally, the specific mechanisms which mediate the impact of the forces of incorporation upon the community or link it to the wider society play an important role in the conservation, namely the accelerated change, of the community's social structure. Thus the *mazkir* (secretary) (102), the social instructor (145), or other administrators (139) in the Israeli moshav play a "conservational" role, in that they cushion off the immigrants from the full impact of the wider societal forces.

Heretofore we have discussed social change in general, without taking account of differences in the various spheres of life. However, the study of migrants in cities has taught us that urbanization may lead to the selective decorporation and "opening up" of a group in one sphere while preserving its corporateness in another (e.g. 105). The forces of incorporation impinging upon nonurban communities may lead to similar consequences: some spheres in the community may be decorporated or opened up while others remain static or become even more closed; and though one would expect lateral influences between the spheres, these may be blocked by some features of the culture or of the social structure. For example, Mason (158) reports that work in the oil companies *reinforced* the fraternal joint family among Arabized Berbers on a Lybian oasis. The Druzes in Israel, though generally responding exploitatively to new opportunities, remain socially and religiously tightly bounded (168). In the Israeli Arab village, despite the growing integration of its members in the national labor market, endogamy is on the increase (187), and the joint family group continues to be the chief building block of social life and of local politics (36, 164).

A detailed comparative analysis of social change in different spheres of community life would uncover both the configurations of change and the mechanisms which promote or impede it in different spheres.

As communities become decorporated and linked up with wider frameworks, the values, interests, allegiances, and powers of groups and individuals within them alter constantly. New and often permanent types of relationships are forged with comembers of the community as well as with outsiders, and novel, shifting cleavages and conflicts emerge in the community as well as in the wider social frameworks. Old prestigious groups find themselves in new circumstances; new social groups, particularly classes, emerge (82). I have chosen for consideration three specific processes of change which are among the most important, as well as most commonly reported of the studies under consideration.

1. *Factionalism:* At the risk of some oversimplification, one could characterize the change in patterns of conflict between structurally parallel units in Middle Eastern communities as a shift from *feud* to *factionalism*. Traditional communities were often split into moieties (171, pp. 177–250); conflict between these typically took the form of a feud (29).

The distinguishing characteristic of the recent changes is that as traditional allegiances and alliances loose force, factions based on immediate and often shifting interests tend to emerge. Though often centered on a core group, the factions tend to realign according to circumstances (132, pp. 192–201; 164, 165, 194, 202, 217). The distinction between feud and factional strife is sometimes clearly drawn by the people themselves; e.g. in the two suburban communities of Beirut studied by Khuri, *ḥazāzah* (conflict, i.e. feud) was distinguished from *ḥizbiyyah* (faction or alliance).

"*Ḥazāzah*" creates a cleavage between two families or branches of families that may take a long time to heal and may continue for several generations. By contrast, *ḥizbiyyah* changes rapidly, following political and economic interests as well as social mobility (132, p. 196). It is the latter which appears to have become the dominant form of local strife, not only in the Lebanon, but also in Israeli Arab villages (164), development towns (13), and new immigrant *moshavim* (194, 202) [though not in all (100)].

2. *Patron-Client relationships:* As the feud precedes the faction, so the traditional "vassalage" or clientship of subordinate corporate groups or individuals to "noble" or dominant groups or individuals (34, pp. 49–51; 49, pp. 105–8; 106, pp. 52–54, 69–70; 171, pp. 251–66; 177; 213, pp. 213–14) precedes the contemporary individualized patron-client and faction-client (132, pp. 169–70) relationships. Modern forms of patronage differ from the traditional ones in several respects; as the individual becomes exposed to ever wider social forces, while traditional protective arrangements (such as corporate groups) break down, he needs help in ever more remote, central places. Hence the links of patronage tend to extend farther and farther, reaching eventually into national capitals (107; 132, pp. 198–99). In the past, patron-client relationships tended to be fairly permanent. However, under the impact of the forces of incorporation, these tend to break down (34, pp. 51–52). Contemporary patron-client relationships tend to shift according to circumstances, as new patrons, providing new types of services, compete with traditional leaders (52). The contents of patronage relationships become more varied. Whereas in the past the dominant or "noble" group or individual would mostly provide security or protection against provision of fighters in warfare, economic services, or payments (34, p. 51; 49, pp. 105–8; 106, pp. 69–70), modern patron-client relationships are much richer in content. The patrons may "exchange economic, social and administrative aid for the political support and loyalty of their followers and clientele" (107, p. 173), disburse economic incentives for political support (13, p. 270), etc; in the case of faction-client relationships, the leading group in the faction provides the customers for the practitioners of a variety of occupations in exchange for the latter's political support (132, pp. 169–70). Though much detailed information is contained in the studies, a comparative examination of contemporary forms of patronage in Middle Eastern communities has yet to be conducted.

3. *Elites:* A common feature of traditional Middle Eastern communities is their division into ordinary and "noble," often "holy," constituent groups. In the Maghreb, such groups usually *trace* direct descent to a charismatic religious personality, a "saint" or *marabout* possessing *baraka* (5, pp. 120–21; 69, p. 278; 89, 90; 118, p. 38; 119, pp. 28–34; 180, pp. 7–8), but they *claim* descent from the descendants or family of the Prophet; thus e.g. Sidi Mhammed Sharki, and his descendants, the Sharkawa, "claimed descent from 'Umar, the second caliph in Islam" (69, p. 278). Among the Shi'a Moslems, "holy" familes also exist, but they trace their descent specifically to 'Ali and his wife Fatima (213, p. 208).

Such "holy" groups commonly bear the designation *Sada* (sing. *Sayyid*), i.e. descendants of the Prophet. Traditionally they performed the most prestigious function of leadership, that of mediation between feuding corporate groups (29, pp. 93–95; 82, p. 96; 89, 90; 118, p. 38; 180, pp. 34–41; 213, p. 213). In the past the elevated religious status of the *Sada* facilitated their accumulation of considerable power and wealth converting them into a diffuse, religious, social, economic, and political elite (6, p. 270; 34; 68; 69, pp. 281–82; 213). Thus, e.g. in Boujad, a pilgrimage center in Morocco, "until 1912 all significant economic, political and religious activities . . . were dominated by Sharkawa marabouts, who acquired vast wealth and influence from those who sought their aid and intercession" (69, pp. 281–82). Owing to its value, *Sada* status was often a matter of fierce competition (69, p. 282) and even usurpation (69, p. 288).

How did social change affect these groups? This problem can be fruitfully approached in terms of the conceptual framework developed above by asking (*a*) what was the impact of the forces of incorporation upon such groups, and particularly, did they expand or contract the field of opportunities facing the groups? and (*b*) how did the groups respond to expanded opportunities?

Though the data do not permit a systematic answer, some major trends can be discerned. In Boujad after 1913, the French, distinguishing sharply between religious and nonreligious activities, effectively contracted the field of opportunities for the Sharkawa; consequently, "Like other bases of status and prestige (maraboutic) attributes have been revalorized significantly with the social and economic transformations which have affected Boujad over the last sixty years" (69, p. 281). The Sharkawa have here clearly lost status. Elsewhere, however, particularly if moderate change came at a slow pace, the opportunities facing the *Sada* seem to have been expanded rather than contracted. However, they did not always readily avail themselves of the new opportunities. Rigid adherence to traditional symbols of status engendered an insulative response among the descendents of Sidi Lahcen, who strove to preserve their "symbolic domination" at the price of isolating their community from the developments in the region, but eventually lost their own *baraka* (180, p. 96). In several cases, however, by judiciously using their traditional positions of status and power, the *Sada* succeeded in exploiting the new opportunities, thereby preserving, and even reinforcing, their position in the community or wider society. Thus, e.g. in Ḥureiḍah, the penetration of the community by the new political forces of incorporation, what Bujra calls the "Coming of the Government," saw the ". . . collaboration between the traditional ruling groups and the new government and, therefore, the immediate return to power of the group" (34, p. 193). The wealth of the group and its links with the new administrators helped to ensure that ". . . the highest group in the stratified society acquires immediate power under the new political system" (34, p. 193). Only further studies will show to what extent Bujra's conclusion applies to communities in the region.

The comparative study of the dynamics of stratification in Middle Eastern communities under conditions of change is only commencing. The examination of the changes which "holy" groups have gone through should be supplemented by a study of the changes in status of other traditionally elevated groups, not only in the

Moslem but also in Jewish and Christian communities, and of the gradual appearance of social classes [as e.g. in (82)]. A careful comparative examination of such changes among Afro-Asian Jewish immigrant groups in Israel would be most enlightening.

THE CHANGING WORLD OF ETHNICITY

The proverbial ethnic and religious diversity of Middle Eastern societies has been the major constitutive factor of the traditional Middle Eastern social "mosaic" (50, 114). It is doubtful, however, that "ethnicity" as such played a very significant role in people's consciousness in the traditional period. For traditional life was largely segregated; in the countryside ethnic and religious groups were secluded in their villages and regions (114, p. 306), while the "cellular" ecological structure of the towns (31, p. 6; 69, pp. 277–78) separated groups living in close spatial proximity. The boundaries of ethnic groups (19) were permanent and objectively defined.

The division of labor between the ethnic groups entailed interaction between them, but relations were specific in nature and bounded by well-defined rules of conduct. Diffuse, informal socializing was rare. Even where dyadic relations are said to have prevailed in society, such relations between members of different ethnic groups were impersonal and specific in content (182, p. 444). Though persecution of minorities and pogroms (103) have occurred, there were few "ethnic problems" in the modern sense of the term. Indeed, though one can speak of "ethnic groups" in the traditional Middle East, "ethnicity" in the sense of a conscious, subjective ethnic identity distinguishing an individual or group within wider social entities is a modern phenomenon, a consequence of the widening horizons and the proliferation of external linkages which came about under the impact of the forces of incorporation.

Ethnicity is also an "emergent phenomenon" (222) in the Middle East as it is elsewhere. Groups without a distinct ethnic identity, such as tribes, territorial groups (e.g. the Palestinians), or religious groups (e.g. the Druzes) acquire the character of an ethnic or national group under changing economic, political, and cultural circumstances (114, p. 308). This process has been studied but little by anthropologists in the region, the only exception being the Druzes (168, 225).

The forces of incorporation had a differential and often contrary impact on ethnic groups. While they expanded the field of economic and cultural or even political opportunities to heretofore isolated or segregated ethnic groups, they also dislodged them from their traditional ecological niche and exposed them to new external influences which threatened their integrity and identity. The new national states often limited or foreclosed economic or political opportunities for some of the established minorities such as the Armenians (124), and encroached upon their opportunities for cultural self-expression or internal self-regulation. The separate identities of ethnic groups often became questionable or outrightly illegitimate, and they were put under pressure to integrate (114, p. 310) or, in Arab states, to "Arabize" [for a recent review of these problems, see (204)]. Policies, however, are not uniform. The Middle Eastern governments permit different degrees of pluralism, often discriminating between different ethnic groups or spheres of life. Lebanon, for example, has been based on a recognition of the legitimate distinctiveness of different ethnic and religious groups (114). In Israel, while Arabs enjoy considerable cultural and religious (but *not* political) autonomy, the policy of "blending the exiles" was intended to amalgamate the Jews of different backgrounds into a single nation and thus to obliterate their cultural differences in most spheres of life, except in ritual (60, 216). Only lately has reluctant recognition been given to the cultural differences between ethnic groups of Jews; but these are tolerated rather than encouraged. The different approaches to Jews and Arabs can be seen concretely in governmental planning decisions (e.g. 42).

Ethnic groups throughout the region lost in the contemporary period much of their separateness, compactness, and internal homogeneity. As their traditional boundaries have been penetrated by the forces of incorporation, they have suffered crises of identity. However, the evidence of recent research indicates that although they often exploited the new opportunities, particularly in the economic sphere, if these were offered them, they did not meekly submit to encroachments upon their identity and cultural distinctiveness; neither can we speak of a simple, monotonous process of absorption of ethnic groups into national societies which will eventually make them into indistinguishable members of the new "nations." If we said before that traditional society is not simply "passing," then "the business of ethnicity," in Deshen's (61) phrase, is also far from "finished" in the Middle East, as indeed it is not anywhere else (222). Though ethnic groups responded differently to encroachments upon their identity, the literature indicates that the ethnic factor, increased if anything, in saliency in the contemporary period (114); "ethnicity" in the Middle East as elsewhere is a modern phenomenon. The very confrontation of ethnic groups raised ethnic awareness and self-consciousness, particularly in the urban environment, as indeed recent urban theory would lead us to expect (84). The increased salience of the ethnic factor has been particularly well documented in studies of Jewish ethnic groups in new Israeli towns and urban neighborhoods (26, 44, 46, 58, 62, 70, 110, 191, 192). Though smaller groups of origin—e.g. joint families or immigrants hailing from adjoining communities of origin—tend to become fused into a simple entity in most situations of urban living, the newly emergent ethnic groups, encompassing members from an area or country of origin, are often fairly strongly bounded. The salience of ethnicity, however, and consequently the strength of the boundaries, may oscillate from issue to issue and from one historical period to another (58, p. 306; 61). In Israel, the degree of international tension is a major factor which influences the salience of ethnic differences between Jews—the lower the tensions, the higher generally the salience of internal differences (39, 44).

An important problem of research is the relationship between particular ethnic and wider national identities. Ethnic self-awareness does not automatically involve a denial of a common national identity; one can be "embedded" in the other. This may be easier for some groups, e.g. Jewish ethnic groups in Israel, and more problematic for others, e.g. the Arabs in Israel. Outright denial of the legitimacy of the claims of allegiance of the nation state, and consequent attempts at secession, are rare; the most outstanding example in the region being the Kurds (80). However, most groups face the problem of negotiating the boundaries between their narrower ethnic and the broader national identity—a process studied in detail by Deshen (54, 60) for South Tunisian Jews in Israel, but little for any other group. Hence we are quite ignorant about the conditions in which a group negotiates harmoniously the boundaries between itself and the national entity and thus becomes "embedded," or conversely, when does such a negotiation falter and ethnic tensions of the type exemplified in Israel by the Black Panther movement (26, 44) evolve. The studies indicate, however, that ethnic boundaries, whatever the manner of their negotiation, are neither permanently fixed nor equally tight on all fronts. Rather, as boundaries break up on one front (e.g. the economic or political) under the impact of the forces of incorporation, new symbolic ways are invented to reinforce them on another front, e.g. the religious or cultural (57, 58). Moreover, ethnic groups open up selectively to kindred groups in society while preserving tight boundaries toward other groups, as Zenner's (224) comparative study of Syrian Jewish in three different settings has shown.

The concept of "situational ethnicity," which specifies that the various identities of an individual or member of a community of origin, ethnic group, nationality, etc vary in salience from one situation to another (27), has as yet been little applied in Middle Eastern anthropology to elucidate the dynamics of ethnicity. Neither has the concept of pluralism (138, 206) been given much attention in anthropological studies of Middle Eastern ethnic groups [except in (213)].

As the conditions of life for Middle Eastern ethnic groups change, the meaning of their ethnic identity and the symbols of their expression alter inevitably; this problem has gained increasing attention among Israeli anthropologists (58, 95, 96), but little among students of other Middle Eastern societies. The changing cultural content of the domain of ethnicity, as well as its significance for and interrelations with economic and political processes in Middle Eastern communities and societies, is hence a most important topic for future comparative examination.

CONCLUSIONS

Fernea & Malarkey (83, p. 183) complained recently that "... contributions to anthropological literature based on Middle Eastern research failed to have an important impact upon theoretical concerns in the field of ethnology." In this survey of recent anthropological studies of communities and ethnic groups in the region, an attempt was made to formulate a conceptual framework for the analysis of change in communities which will not only facilitate the study of the diversity of processes of change in the Middle East, but will also have an impact upon some broader "theoretical concerns." Realizing that social change in Middle Eastern communities is neither a uniformly unilinear nor a unidirectional process, I attempted to develop a model which will make the processes of change comprehensible as a consequence of the different *types of responses* in terms of which communities or groups within them react to the differential impact of the various *forces of incorporation* upon the *field of opportunities* which they face. That my success in the application of this model to the body of studies under examination or the extrapolation of specific generalizations has been far from complete may be partly due to the shortcomings of my analysis. But it is also a reflection of the inadequacy of the available data for purposes of comparative analysis. In conclusion, I hence raise several problems, theoretical as well as methodological, and make a few suggestions concerning the future trend in field studies in order to enhance the theoretical significance and the comparability of the findings.

(a) *The distribution of the studies:* Though we identified close to 100 field studies on which reports were published in the 1970s, the gaps in the coverage of different areas and classes of communities in the region make any systematic comparative analysis almost impossible. The studies are unevenly distributed; while almost half have been conducted in Israel, no recent work is available on some countries. Moreover, the dearth of studies of communities and groups which respond rejectively to the forces of incorporation, e.g. defiant, and particularly revolting, communities, is likely to create the impression that communities and groups are more acceptively oriented to such forces than is actually the case.

(b) *Research focus and orientation:* The studies reveal a great diversity of research interests, conceptual approaches, and methods; though this is unavoidable and in fact desirable, it also makes comparison enormously difficult. A good case in point is the problem of deciding whether the conceptualization of social relationships in Moroccan society in "dyadic" terms (182, 184) points to an empirical difference between the Maghreb and the rest of the region, or introduces a new conceptual approach which, when applied to other areas of the region, will lead to a reconceptualization of the prevailing "corporate" image of their traditional social structure. Moreover, many studies are still plainly descriptive or lack an explicit theoretical focus or well-defined empirical problem. Though the strength of anthropology lies in a holistic approach, significant advances in anthropology depend on the explicit statement of theoretical concerns and the formulation of a clear empirical focus even prior to the commencement of fieldwork. Indeed, concern with such issues is likely to lead to a reorientation of present tendencies in research, as suggested below.

(c) *Definition of the unit of study:* Antoun (9) pointed out that anthropologists tend traditionally to concentrate upon one type of community (e.g. a nomadic tribe or a village) and thereby disregard the linkages between the different groups in the ecological system of the region. Under contemporary conditions, the scope and importance of these linkages increase tremendously. Hence the study of larger units, particularly of the region surrounding a central place and including different types of communities is called for, along the lines of English's (75) study of Kirman and its region. Some work of this nature has already been conducted (e.g. 68, 82, 106, 180), but much more is called for.

(d) *Study of wider societal interdependencies:* Under conditions of progressive incorporation of local communities into wider frameworks, the processes of incorporation themselves and the responses of communities to them ought to be explicitly studied; this might necessitate the conduct of research in more than one locality, e.g. on the lines of Kushner's (139) study of the bureaucratic framework within which his *moshav* of Kochin Jews was set. Such an approach may lead to studies which are not necessarily encompassed by a single research site, but range throughout the country in pursuit of the ramifications of an institution or of a network of social relationships.

(*e*) *Focus on "topical" or neglected problems:* Some problems are traditional or fashionable in anthropological research. In the past these were, for example, FBD marriage (83) or the feud (29). Today it is often factionalism or urban ethnicity. Conceding the importance of these topics, we should not lose sight of several important but neglected ones; such topics abound particularly in the urban environment. Thus, except for political and to a smaller extent economic institutions, particularly markets, little work on institutional arrangements in the other fields of urban life (e.g. religion, education) has been conducted. And except for migrant ethnic groups, few other urban groups, such as occupational, have been given much attention—the notable exceptions are Miner's (161) study of the weavers in Fez and Khuri's (132, pp. 63–101) interesting description of several urban occupations. Even fewer studies are concerned with that most topical question, the effect of development plans on different groups (here the major exceptions are the studies of Israeli *moshavim* and new towns and some of the studies on the sedentarization of nomads). Nor have anthropologists participated much in guiding planned change or in action research [the exceptions are again the Israeli anthropologists employed by the Settlement Department of the Jewish Agency (194) and the notable work of Duvignaud (66)].

(*f*) *Diachronic studies:* Although the study of change is a growing concern of anthropologists in the region, few genuinely diachronic anthropological studies are available in the sense that the same community had been studied in similar terms at different points in time—the major example being Peters's (175, 176) repeated study of a Lebanese *shià* village. The many in-depth studies of change, e.g. those by Gellner & Micaud (91) and those by Hart (117, 119, 120), Vinogradov (213, 214), Gubser (106), Goldberg (100), and Shokeid (202), contain either historical or ethnohistorical reconstructions. Comparative longitudinal studies of change in several communities or groups under the impact of similar forces of incorporation are much needed and could be a highly rewarding enterprise.

(*g*) *Explicit comparative orientation:* With very few exceptions (e.g. 123, 164, 165), the studies under review are case studies of one specific community or group; the reports often disregard the broader comparative implications of the findings. As the problems we encountered in the substantive sections of this survey clearly indicate, the absence of an explicit comparative perspective make any attempt at a codification of findings or the extraction of generalizations both a difficult and a risky enterprise. Hence more specifically designed comparative studies of groups within a given community, of different communities within the same area, or of similar communities in different areas are called for. And even students of single cases would do well to make explicit the implications of the contextual parameters of their case study for their findings. Such an explication becomes the more important as anthropologists move away from isolated communities and expand into an ever more varied range of situations, many of which are located in complex regional and urban contexts.

Anthropology provides a unique opportunity to view the processes of change in Middle Eastern societies from a grass-roots level; but in order to contribute toward an understanding of these processes, the links between the grass-roots and the wider frameworks have to be made explicit. Some ideas to that end have been proposed in this survey. But the main challenge is still ahead; we need more, and more varied, studies of communities and groups. We also need studies which would help us put together a wider picture of the changing Middle Eastern scene.

Literature Cited

1. Abarbanel, J. S. 1974. *The Co-operative Farmer and the Welfare State: Economic Change in an Israeli Moshav.* Manchester, England: Manchester Univ. Press. 236 pp.
2. Abu-Lughod, J. 1973. Cairo: perspective and prospectus. In *From Madina to Metropolis,* ed. L. C. Brown, pp. 95–116. Princeton: Darwin
3. Abu-Lughod, J. 1971. *Cairo: 1001 Years of the City Victorious.* Princeton Univ. Press
4. Abu-Lughod, J. 1970. Migrant adjustment to city life: the Egyptian case. See Ref. 143, pp. 664–78
5. Abu-Zahra, N. M. 1974. Material power, honour, friendship and the etiquette of visiting. *Anthropol. Q.* 47(1):120–38
6. Abu-Zahra, N. M. 1972. Inequality of descent and egalitarianism of the new national organizations in a Tunisian village. See Ref. 12, pp. 267–86
7. Adam, A. 1972. Berber migrants in Casablanca. See Ref. 91, pp. 325–45
8. Alouche, R. 1970. *Evolution d'un Centre de Villlégiature au Liban (Broummana).* Beirut: Dar El-Machreq
9. Antoun, R. T. 1976. Anthropology. In *The Study of the Middle East,* ed. L. Binder, pp. 137–228. New York: Wiley
10. Antoun, R. T. 1972. *Arab Village: A Social Structural Study of a Trans-Jordanian Peasant Community.* Bloomington: Indiana Univ. Press. 182 pp.
11. Antoun, R. T. 1972. Pertinent variables in the environment of Middle Eastern village politics: a comparative analysis. See Ref. 12, pp. 118–62
12. Antoun, R. T., Harik, I., eds. 1972. *Rural Politics and Social Change In the Middle East.* Bloomington: Indiana Univ. Press. 498 pp.
13. Aronoff, M. J. 1974. *Frontiertown: The Politics of Community Building in Israel.* Manchester Univ. Press and Jerusalem Academic Press

14. Aronoff, M. J. 1974. Political change in Israel: the case of a new town. *Polit. Sci. Q.* 89(3):613–26
15. Auerbach, S. D. 1975. *Occupational Options and Adaptive Strategies in a Tunisian Town: The Effects of the Tunisian Government's Ideology of Modernization.* PhD thesis. Univ. Illinois, Chicago, Ill.
16. Aviel, A. 1976. *Ne'arim Ba-Shekhuna, Ha'yéy Yom Yom Be-Shkhunat Ha-tiqwa (Boys in the Neighborhood: Everyday Life in the Ha-Tiqwa Quarter.)* PhD thesis. Hebrew Univ. Jerusalem, Israel
17. Baldwin, E. 1972. *Differentiation and Cooperation in an Israeli Veteran Moshav.* Manchester Univ. Press. 240 pp.
18. Barth, F. 1973. A general perspective on nomad-sedentary relations in the Middle East. See Ref. 166, pp. 11–22
19. Barth, F. 1969. Introduction. In *Ethnic Groups and Boundaries,* ed. F. Barth, pp. 9–38. Boston: Little Brown
20. Barth, F. 1956. Ecological relationships of ethnic groups in Swat, West-Pakistan. *Am. Anthropol.* 58:1079–89
21. Bates, D. G. 1971. The role of the state in peasant-nomad mutualism. *Anthropol. Q.* 44(3):109–31
22. Beeson, I. 1976. Cairo's Refuse Collectors: Rich and Untouchable. *Jerusalem Post* 7/11/76
23. Behnke, R. H. 1975. *Ecology, Economy and Kinship Among the Bedouin of Cyrenaica, Libya.* PhD thesis. Univ. California, Los Angeles, Calif.
24. Ben Shaul, R. 1975. *Olei Bukhara - Beit Shemesh (Immigrants from Bukhara— in Beit Shemesh).* Jerusalem: Minist. Immigr. Div. Plann. Res. and Sociol. and Soc. Anthropol., Hebrew Univ. Jerusalem
25. Bensimon-Donath, D. 1970. *Immigrants d'Afrique du Nord en Israel.* Paris: Ed. Anthropos
26. Bernstein, D. 1976. *The Black Panthers of Israel 1971–1972: Contradictions and*

Protest in the Process of Nation Building. PhD thesis. Univ. Sussex, Brighton, England

27. Berreman, G. D. 1972. Social categories and social interaction in urban India. *Am. Anthropol.* 74:567–86

28. Betts, R. B. 1975. *Christians in the Arab East.* Athens: Ly Caluttus Press. 293 pp.

29. Black-Michaud, J. 1975. *Cohesive Force: Feud in the Middle East.* New York: St. Martin

30. Boissevain, J. 1975. Introduction: towards a social anthropology of Europe. In *Beyond the Community: Social Process in Europe,* ed. J. Boissevain, J. Friedl, pp. 9–17. The Hague: Dep. Educ. Sci. Netherlands

31. Bonine, M. E. 1976. Urban studies in the Middle East. *Middle East Stud. Assoc. Bull.* 10(3):1–37

32. Bourgeot, A. 1972. Nomadisme et sédentarisation. Le processus d'integration chez les Kel Ahaggar. *R. Occident. Musulman Mediterr.* 11:85–92

33. Bujra, A. S. 1973. The social implications of developmental policies: A case study from Egypt. See Ref. 166, pp. 143–58

34. Bujra, A. S. 1971. *The Politics of Stratification. A Study of Political Change in a South Arabian Town.* Oxford: Clarendon. 201 pp.

35. Chatty, D. 1974. *From Camel to Truck: A study of the Pastoral Economy of the Al-Fadl and the Al-Hassanna in the Beqaa Valley of Lebanon.* PhD thesis. Univ. California, Los Angeles, Calif.

36. Cohen, A. 1965. *Arab Border Villages in Israel.* Manchester Univ. Press

37. Cohen, C. 1975. *Grandir au Quartier Kurde: Rapports de Generations et Modeles Culturels d'un Group d'Adolescents Israeliéns D'Origine Kurde.* Paris: Inst. Ethnol., Mus. De L'Homme. 184 pp.

38. Cohen, E. 1976. Environmental orientations: A multidimensional approach to social ecology. *Curr. Anthropol.* 17(1):49–70

39. Cohen, E. 1976. Jewish marginal youth in a mixed city. In *Youth Unrest,* ed. S. G. Shoham, pp. 219–33. Jerusalem Academic Press

40. Cohen, E. 1976. The structural transformation of the Kibbutz. In *Social Change: Explorations, Diagnoses and Conjectures,* eds. G. K. Zollschan, W. Hirsch, pp. 703–42. New York: Wiley

41. Cohen, E. 1974. *Bibliography of Arabs and Other Minorities in Israel.* Givat Haviva Center for Arab and Afro-Asian Stud. and Univ. Publ. Proj.

42. Cohen, E. 1973. *Integration vs. Separation in the Planning of a Mixed Jewish-Arab City in Israel.* Jerusalem: Levi Eshkol Inst. Econ., Soc., Pol. Res., Hebrew Univ.

43. Cohen, E. 1972. The Bahá'í community of Acre. *Folklore Res. Cent. Stud.* (Jerusalem) 3:119–41

44. Cohen, E. 1972. The Black Panthers and Israeli Society. *Jewish J. Sociol.* 14(1):93–109

45. Cohen, E. 1971. Arab boys and tourist girls in a mixed Jewish-Arab community. *Int. J. Comp. Sociol.* 12(4):217–33

46. Cohen, E. 1970. Development towns—the social dynamics of "planted" urban communities in Israel. In *Integration and Development in Israel,* ed. S. N. Eisenstadt, R. Bar Yosef, Ch. Adler, pp. 587–617. Jerusalem: Israel Univ. Press

47. Cohen, E. 1969. Mixed marriage in an Israeli town. *Jewish J. Sociol.* 11(1): 41–50

48. Cohen, E., Gronau, H. 1972. *Seqer Hamiutim Be-Yisrael (A Survey of Israel Minorities).* Jerusalem: Res. Cent. for Israeli Arabs

49. Cole, D. P. 1975. *Nomads of the Nomads: The Al Murrah Bedouin of the Empty Quarter.* Chicago: Aldine

50. Coon, C. S. 1951. *Caravan: The Story of the Middle East.* New York: Holt. 376 pp.

51. Cooper, S. 1976. *New Gate: An Old-New Town in the Negev.* PhD thesis. Catholic Univ. America, Washington DC

52. Dalton, W. G. 1973. Economic change and political continuity in a Saharan oasis community. *Man* 8(2):266–84

53. Dalton, W. G. 1971. *The Social Structure of an Oasis Community in Lybia.* PhD thesis. Manchester Univ., Manchester, England

54. Deshen, S. A. 1977. Ethnic boundaries and cultural paradigms: the case of southern Tunisian immigrants in Israel. *Ethos.* In press

55. Deshen, S. A. 1976. Kavim la-mivneh ha-hevrati shel kehilot yehudei Djerba ve-derom Tunisia be-sof ha-me'ah ha-yod-tet (An outline of the social structure of the Jewish communities in Djerba and southern Tunisia from the end of the 19th century until the 1950's). *Zion* 41:97–108

56. Deshen, S. A. 1976. Of signs and symbols: the transformation of designations in Israeli electioneering. *Polit. Anthropol.* 1(3/4):83–100

57. Deshen, S. A. 1975. Ritualization of literacy: the works of Tunisian scholars in Israel. *Am. Ethnol.* 2:251–59
58. Deshen, S. A. 1974. Political ethnicity and cultural ethnicity in Israel during the 1960's. In *Urban Ethnicity*, ed. A. Cohen, pp. 281–309. London: Tavistock
59. Deshen, S. A. 1973. Ha-hilulot shel yozei Tunisia—behinatan hadatit (The *hilulot* of Tunisian immigrants—their religious aspects). *Megamot* 19(4): 374–82
60. Deshen, S. A. 1972. Ethnicity and citizenship in the ritual of an Israeli synagogue. *Southwest. J. Anthropol.* 28(1): 69–82
61. Deshen, S. A. 1972. "The business of ethnicity is finished?": The ethnic factor in a local election campaign. In *The Elections in Israel—1969*, ed. A. Arian, pp. 278–302. Jerusalem Academic Press
62. Deshen, S. A. 1970. *Immigrant Voters in Israel*. Manchester Univ. Press. 239 pp.
63. Deshen, S. A., Jaeger, D. 1971. Culture and politics in a village of immigrants from Djerba. See Ref. 194, pp. 125–38
64. Deshen, S. A., Shokeid, M. 1974. *The Predicament of Homecoming: Cultural and Social Life of North African Immigrants in Israel.* Ithaca: Cornell Univ. Press
65. Dostal, W. 1972. The Shihuh of Northern Oman: a contribution to cultural ecology. *Geogr. J.* 138(1):1–7
66. Duvignaud, J. 1970. *Change at Shebika: Report from a North African Village.* New York: Pantheon. 303 pp.
67. Dwyer, K. T. 1974. *The Cultural Bases of Entrepreneurial Activity: A Study of a Moroccan Peasant Community.* PhD thesis. Yale Univ., New Haven, Conn.
68. Eickelman, D. F. 1976. *Moroccan Islam.* Austin: Univ. Texas Press
69. Eickelman, D. F. 1974. Is there an Islamic city? the making of a quarter in a Moroccan town. *Int. J. Middle East Stud.* 5(3):274–94
70. Eilam, Y. 1975. Defusei hit'argenut shel olim me-Gruzia: shimush be-koah ke-emzai shel gibui kehilati (Patterns of social organization of Georgian immigrants: the use of power as a means for community support). *Megamot* 21(4): 377–93
71. Eilam, Y. 1975. *H*atuna yehudit Gruzinit ke-bitui le-hitgashrut *h*evratit re*h*avat meimadim (The Georgian Jewish wedding ceremony—as an expression of

wide-ranging social integration). *Megamot* 22(1):20–35
72. Eisenstadt, S. N. 1973. Post-traditional societies and the continuity and reconstruction of tradition. *Daedalus* 102(Winter):1–28
73. Eisenstadt, S. N. 1967. *Israeli Society.* New York: Basic Books. 451 pp.
74. English, P.W. 1973. *Geographical Perspectives on the Middle East: The Passing of the Ecological Trilogy.* Univ. Chicago, Dep. Geogr. Res. Pap.
75. English, P. W. 1966. *City and Village in Iran: Settlement and Economy in the Kirman Basin.* Madison: Univ. Wisconsin Press
76. Ethnic and Religious Minorities in Egypt, Iraq, Jordan, Lebanon, Syria: A Table. *Middle East Rev.* 9(1):60–9 (Appendix, Spec. Issue)
77. Evans-Pritchard, E. E. 1971. [1940]. *The Nuer.* Oxford: Clarendon. 271 pp.
78. Fakhouri, H. 1972. *Kafr-el-Elow: An Egyptian Village in Transition.* New York: Holt, Rinehart & Winston
79. Farrag, A. 1971. Social control amongst the Mzabite women of Beni-Isguen. *Middle East. Stud.* 7(3):317–27
80. Feili, O. Y., Fromchuck, A. R. 1976. The Kurdish struggle for independence. *Middle East Rev.* 9(1):47–58
81. Fernea, R. A. 1972. Gaps in the ethnographic literature on the Middle Eastern village: a classificatory exploration. See Ref. 12, pp. 75–102
82. Fernea, R. A. 1970. *Shaykh and Effendi: Changing Patterns of Authority Among the El Shabana of Southern Iraq.* Cambridge: Harvard Univ. Press
83. Fernea, R. A., Malarkey, J. M. 1975. Anthropology of the Middle East and North Africa: a critical assessment. *Ann. Rev. Anthropol.* 4:183–206
84. Fischer, C. S. 1975. Toward a subcultural theory of urbanism. *Am. J. Sociol.* 80(6):1319–41
85. Foster, B. G. 1974. *The Moroccan Power Structure as Seen from Below: Political Participation in a Casablanca Shanty-town.* PhD thesis. Princeton Univ., Princeton, NJ
86. Frankenberg, R. 1969. *Communities in Britain: Social Life in Town and Country.* Middlesex: Harmondswerth
87. Freund, W. S. 1974. *Das arabische Mittelmer-Entwicklungsprobleme.* München: Goldmann
88. Geertz, C., ed. 1963. *Old Societies and New States: The Quest for Modernity in Asia and Africa.* New York: Free Press

89. Gellner, E. 1969. *Saints of the Atlas.* Chicago: Univ. Chicago Press; London: Weidenfeld & Nicolson
90. Gellner, E. 1970. Saints of the Atlas. See Ref. 210, pp. 204–19
91. Gellner, E., Micaud, C., eds. 1972. *Arabs and Berbers: From Tribe to Nation in North Africa.* Lexington, Ky: Lexington Books
92. George, A. R. 1973. Processes of sedentarization of nomads in Egypt, Israel and Syria: a comparison. *Geography* 58(2):167–69
93. Gerber, J. S. 1972. *Jewish Society in Fez: Studies in Communal and Economic Life.* PhD thesis. Columbia Univ., New York, NY
94. Giner, S. 1976. *Mass Society.* London: Robertson
95. Goldberg, H. E. 1976. Anthropology in Israel. *Curr. Anthropol.* 17(1):119–21
96. Goldberg, H. E., ed. 1977. Ethnic Groups in Israeli Society. *Ethnic Groups* 1(3):163–262 (Spec. Issue)
97. Goldberg, H. E. 1977. Introduction: culture and ethnicity in the study of Israeli society. See Ref. 96, pp. 163–86
98. Goldberg, H. E. 1974. Tripolitanian Jewish communities: cultural boundaries and hypothesis testing. *Am. Ethnol.* 1(4):619–34
99. Goldberg, H. E. 1973. Cultural change in an Israeli immigrant village: the twist in Even Yosef. *Middle East. Stud.* 9(1): 73–80
100. Goldberg, H. E. 1972. *Cave Dwellers and Citrus Growers: A Jewish Community in Libya and Israel.* Cambridge Univ. Press
101. Goldberg, H. E. 1971. Ecological and demographic aspects of rural Tripolitanian Jewry, 1853–1949. *Int. J. Middle East Stud.* 2(3):245–65
102. Goldberg, H. E. 1970. From Sheikh to Mazkir: structural continuity and organizational change in the leadership of a Tripolitanian Jewish community. *Folklore Res. Cent. Stud.* 1:29–41
103. Goldberg, H. E. (typescript) Rites and Riots: The Tripolitanian Pogrom of 1945
104. Gough, K. 1968. New proposals for anthropologists. *Curr. Anthropol.* 9(5): 403–7
105. Gould, H. A. 1970. Some preliminary observations concerning the anthropology of industrialization. In *Peasants in Cities,* ed. W. Mangin, pp. 137–49. Boston: Houghton Mifflin
106. Gubser, P. 1973. *Politics and Change in Al-Karak, Jordan. Study of a Small Arab Town and its District.* New York: Oxford Univ. Press
107. Gubser, P. 1973. The Zu'ama' of Zahlah: the current situation in a Lebanese town. *Middle East J.* 27(2):173–89
108. Gulick, J. 1976. *The Middle East: An Anthropological Perspective.* Pacific Palisades, Calif: Goodyear. 244 pp.
109. Hachem, N. 1969. *Libanon: Sozioökenimische Grundlagen.* Opladen: Leske
110. Halper, J. 1976. *Ethnicity and Education: The Schooling of Afro-Asian Jewish Children in a Jerusalem Neighborhood.* PhD thesis. Univ. Wisconsin, Milwaukee, Wis.
111. Hamalian, A. 1974. Shirkets—visiting pattern of Armenians in Lebanon. *Anthropol.* 47(1):71–92
112. Handelman, D., Deshen, S. 1975. *Social Anthropology of Israel: A Bibliographical Essay with Primary Reference to Loci of Social Stress.* Inst. Soc. Res., Dep. Sociol. Anthropol., Tel Aviv Univ.
113. Hansen, H. H. 1968. *Investigations in a Shi'a Village in Bahrain.* Copenhagen: Natl. Museum Denmark
114. Harik, I. F. 1972. The ethnic revolution and political integration in the Middle East. *Int. J. Middle East Stud.* 3(3): 303–23
115. Harik, I. F. 1972. Mobilization policy and political change in rural Egypt. See Ref. 12, pp. 287–334
116. Harik, I. F. 1972. The impact of the domestic market on rural-urban relations in the Middle East. See Ref. 12, pp. 337–63
117. Hart, D. M. *The Aith Waryaghar of the Moroccan Rif: An Ethnography and History.* Viking Fund Publ. Anthropol. No. 55. Univ. Arizona Press. In press
118. Hart, D. M. 1972. The tribe in modern Morocco: two case studies. See ref. 91, pp. 25–59
119. Hart, D. M. 1970. Clan, lineage, local community and the feud in a Rifian tribe (Aith Waryaghar, Morocco). See ref. 210, 2:3–75
120. Hart, D. M. 1970. Conflicting models of a Berber tribal structure in the Moroccan Rif: the segmentary and alliance system of the Aith Waryaghar. *Rev. Occident. Musulman Mediterr.* 7:93–100
121. Heard-Bey, F. 1972. Social changes in the Gulf states and Oman. *Asian Affairs* 59(3):309–16
122. Hill, A. G. 1973. Segregation in Kuwait. In *Social Patterns in Cities,* ed. B. D. Clark, M. B. Gleave. Spec. Publ. No.

5, pp. 123–42. London: Inst. Br. Geogr.
123. Hinnebusch, R. A. 1976. Local politics in Syria: organization and mobilization in four villages. *Middle East J.* 30(1): 1–24
124. Hovannisian, R. G. 1974. The ebb and flow of the Armenian minority in the Arab Middle East. *Middle East J.* 28(1)19–32
125. Johnson, D. L. 1975. Cultural ecology of pastoral nomadism. *Geogr. Rev.* 65(1):118–20
126. Johnson, D. L. 1969. *The Nature of Nomadism.* Univ. Chicago, Dep. Geogr. Res. Pap. No. 118
127. Joseph, S. 1975. *The Politization of Religious Sects in Burj-Hammoud, Lebanon.* PhD thesis. Columbia Univ., New York, NY
128. Kasdan, L. 1970. Short term migration in a Middle Eastern religio-ethnic community: commuters and the changing broker role in Banu Mawruf. In *Migration and Anthropology.* Proc. Ann. Spring Meet. Am. Ethnol. Soc., ed. R. F. Spencer, pp. 120–32. Seattle: Univ. Washington Press
129. Katz, P. 1974. *Acculturation and Social Networks of American Immigrants in Israel.* PhD thesis. State Univ. New York, Buffalo, NY
130. Katzir, Y. 1976. *The Effects of Resettlement on the Status and Role of Yemeni Jewish Women: The Case of Ramat Oranim, Israel.* PhD thesis. Univ. California, Berkeley, Calif.
131. Khalaf, S., Kongstad, P. 1973. *Hamra of Beirut: A Case of Rapid Urbanization.* Leiden: Brill. 152 pp.
132. Khuri, F. I. 1975. *From Village to Suburb: Order and Change in Greater Beirut.* Chicago: Univ. Chicago Press. 272 pp.
133. Khuri, F. I. 1972. Sectarian loyalty among rural migrants in two Lebanese suburbs: a stage between family and national allegiance. See Ref. 12, pp. 198–213
134. Kressel, G. 1977. Ethnic duality in a Kibbutz. See Ref. 96, pp. 241–62
135. Kressel, G. 1975. *Pratiyut Le'umat Shivtiyut: Dinamiqa Shel Qehilat Beduim Be-Tahalikh Hit'ayrut. (Individualism versus Tribalism: The Social Dynamics of a Bedouin Community in the Process of Urbanization.* Tel Aviv: Kibbutz Ha-meuḥad and Hebrew Univ., Harry S. Truman Inst. Res.
136. Kressel, G. 1974. *"Mikol Eḥad Lefi Ykholto": Ribud Mul Shiwyon Ba-Kibbutz (From Each According to his Ability:*

Stratification vs. Equality in a Kibbutz). Tel Aviv: Gome
137. Kressel, G. 1970. Nisue Walad im Jawārīsh—Aspectim shel iyur vemasoret (Endogamous marriage among the Jawārīsh—aspects of urbanization and tradition). *Ha-mizrah He-hadash* 20(1): 20–54
138. Kuper, L., Smith, M. G. 1969. *Pluralism in Africa.* Berkeley: Univ. California Press
139. Kushner, G. 1973. *Immigrants From India in Israel: Planned Change in an Administered Community.* Tucson: Univ. Arizona Press
140. Labaied, H. 1972. Etude du quartier Europeen de la ville de Tunia. *Rev. Tunis. Sci.* 9(28–29):153–84
141. Larson, B. K. 1975. *The Impact of National Government on Local Life and Politics in a Tunisian Village.* PhD thesis. Columbia Univ., New York, NY
142. Lerner, D. 1958. *The Passing of Traditional Society: Modernizing in the Middle East.* Glencoe, Ill. Free Press. 466 pp.
143. Lutfiyya, A. M., Churchill, C. W., eds. 1970. *Readings in Arab Middle Eastern Societies and Cultures.* The Hague: Mouton: New York: Humanities Press
144. Malik, S. A. 1973. *Rural Migration and Urban Growth in Riyadh, Saudi Arabia.* PhD thesis Univ. Michigan, Ann-Arbor, Mich.
145. Mars, L. 1976. The position of the administrator in an Israeli cooperative village. *Sociol. Ruralis* 16(1–2):41–55
146. Marx, E. 1977. Political environment vs. natural environment: the economy of the Bedouin of South Sinai. *Polit. Anthropol.* 2. In press
147. Marx, E. 1977. Pilgrimages to saint tombs in South Sinai. In *Regional Cults,* ed. R. Werbner. London: Academic. In press
148. Marx, E. 1976. *The Social Context of Violent Behavior.* London: Routledge & Kegan Paul.
149. Marx, E. 1975. Anthropological studies in a centralized state: the Bernstein research project in Israel. *Jewish J. Sociol.* 22(2):131–50
150. Marx, E. 1975. Changing employment patterns among Bedouin of South Sinai. In *An Anthropological View of Labor,* ed. A. Palerm, R. Owen. Mexico City: INAH
151. Marx, E. 1974. *Ha-ḥevra Ha-bedwit Ba-Negev (Bedouins of the Negev).* Tel Aviv: Reshafim

152. Marx, E. 1973. The organization of nomadic groups in the Middle East. In *Society and Political Structure in the Arab World*, ed. M. Milson, pp. 305–36. New York: Humanities Press

153. Marx, E. 1972. Coercive violence of official-client relationships. *Israel Stud. Criminol.* 2:33–68

154. Marx, E. 1972. Some social contexts of personal violence. In *The Allocation of Responsibility*, ed. M. Gluckman, pp. 281–321. Manchester Univ. Press

155. Marx, E. 1967. *Bedouin of the Negev.* Manchester Univ. Press

156. Marx, E., Ben-Porath, Y. 1971. *Some Sociological and Economic Aspects of Refugee Camps on the West Bank.* Santa Monica, Calif.: Rand Corp. Rep. R-835-FF

157. Marx, E., Ben-Porath, Y., Shamir, S. 1974. *Mahane Plitim Be-harim (A Refugee Camp in the Hills).* Tel Aviv Univ., Shiloah Inst.

158. Mason, J. P. 1971. *The Social History and Anthropology of the Arabized Berbers of Augila Oasis in the Lybian Sahara Desert.* PhD thesis. Boston Univ. Grad. Sch., Boston, Mass.

159. Matras, J. 1965. *Social Change in Israel.* Chicago: Aldine. 211 pp.

160. Mendes-Flohr, R. 1976. *The Courtyard Youth: A Study of Adaptation Strategies in a Market Environment.* MA thesis. Dep. Sociol. Soc. Anthropol., Hebrew Univ., Jerusalem, Israel

161. Miner, H. M. 1973. Traditional mobility among the weavers of Fez. *Proc. Am. Philos. Soc.* 117(1):17–36

162. Mohsen, S. K. 1971. *Quest for Order Among Awlad Ali of the Western Desert of Egypt.* PhD thesis. Michigan State Univ., East Lansing, Mich.

163. Nader, L. 1965. Communication between village and city in the modern Middle East. *Hum. Organ.* 24:18–24

164. Nakhleh, K. 1975. The direction of local level conflict in two Arab villages in Israel. *Am Ethnol.* 2(3):497–516

165. Nakhleh, K. 1973. *Shifting Patterns of Conflict in Selected Arab Villages in Israel.* PhD thesis. Indiana Univ., Bloomington, Ind.

166. Nelson, C., ed. 1973. *The Desert and the Sown: Nomads in the Wider Society.* Berkeley: Univ. Calif. Res. Ser. No. 21, Inst. Int. Stud. 173 pp.

167. Obermeyer, G. J. 1973. Leadership and transition in Bedouin society: a case study. See Ref. 166, pp. 159–73

168. Oppenheimer, J. 1977. Culture and politics in Druze ethnicity. See Ref. 96, pp. 221–40

169. Oppenheimer, J. 1976. *The Social Organization of a Druze Village in Israel.* PhD thesis. Univ. London, London, England

170. Pahl, R. 1970. *Patterns of Urban Life.* London: Longman's

171. Patai, R. 1971. *Society, Culture and Change in the Middle East.* Philadelphia: Univ. Pennsylvania Press

172. Patai, R., ed. 1956. The Republic of Lebanon. New Haven: Human Relat. Area Files

173. Peres, Y. 1976. *Yahasei Eidot Be-Yisrael (Ethnic Relations in Israel).* Tel Aviv: Sifriat Ha-Poalim and Tel-Aviv Univ.

174. Peres, Y. 1971. Ethnic relations in Israel. *Am. J. Sociol.* 76(6):1021–47

175. Peters, E. L. 1972. Shifts in power in a Lebanese village. See Ref. 12, pp. 165–97

176. Peters, E. L. 1970[1963]. Aspects of rank and status among Muslims in a Lebanese village. See Ref. 210, 2:76–123

177. Peters, E. L. 1968. The tied and the free (Libya). In *Contributions to Mediterranean Sociology*, ed. J. G. Peristiany, pp. 167–91. Paris, The Hague: Mouton

178. Peters, E. L. 1960. The proliferation of segments in the lineage of the Bedouin in Cyrenaica. *J. R. Anthropol. Inst. G. B. Irel.* 90:29–53

179. Petonnet, C. 1972. Espace, distance, et dimension dans une société Musulmene: a propos du bidionville Marocain de Douar Doum a Rabat. *L'homme* 12(2):47–84

180. Rabinow, P. 1975. *Symbolic Domination: Cultural Form and Historical Change in Morocco.* Chicago, London: Univ. Chicago Press. 107 pp.

181. Rentz, G. 1974. A Sultanate assunder. *Nat. Hist.* 83(3):57–68

182. Rosen, L. 1972. Muslim-Jewish relations in a Moroccan city. *Int. J. Middle East Stud.* 3(4):435–49

183. Rosen, L. 1972. Rural political process and national political structure in Morocco. See Ref. 12, pp. 214–36

184. Rosen, L. 1972. The social and conceptual framework of Arab-Berber relations in Central Morocco. See Ref. 91, pp. 155–75

185. Rosen, L. 1969. *The Structure of Social Groups in a Moroccan City.* PhD thesis. Univ. Chicago, Chicago, Ill.

186. Rosen, L. 1968. A Moroccan Jewish community during the Middle East crisis. *Am. Scholar* 37(3):435–51

187. Rosenfeld, H. 1976. Social and economic factors in explanation of increased rate of patrilineal endogamy in the Arab village. In *Mediterranean Family Structures*, ed. J. G. Peristiany. Cambridge Univ. Press

188. Rosenfeld, H. 1974. Non-hierarchical, hierarchical and masked reciprocity in an Arab Village. *Anthropol. Q.* 47(1): 139–66

189. Rosenfeld, H. 1972. An overview and critique of the literature on rural politics and social change. See Ref. 12, pp. 45–74

190. Rothenberger, J. E. 1970. *Law and Conflict Resolution: Politics and Change in a Sunni Muslim Village in Lebanon*. PhD thesis. Univ. California, Berkeley, Calif.

191. Rubin, M. 1974. *The Walls of Acre: Intergroup Relations and Urban Development in Israel*. New York: Holt, Rinehart & Winston

192. Shai, D. 1970. *Neighborhood Relations in an Immigrant Quarter*. Jerusalem: Szold Inst.

193. Shapiro, O. 1971. Nissim: a hill village settled by "Kurds". See Ref. 194, pp. 37–60

194. Shapiro, O., ed. 1971. *Rural Settlements of New Immigrants in Israel*. Rehovot: Settlement Study Center

195. Shiloah, A., Cohen, E., Ben-Ami, I. 1976. *Ha-Kehilot Ha-Yehudiot Me-Assia Ha-Tikhona, Ha-Dromit, VeHa-Mizrahit Be-Yisrael - Rikuz Netunim (Jewish Communities from Central, Southern and Eastern Asia in Israel - A Compilation of Data)*. Jerusalem: Hebrew Univ. Folklore Res. Cent.

196. Shmueli, A. 1976. *Bedouin Rural Settlement in Eretz-Israel*. Geography of Israel: Papers presented at 23rd Int. Geogr. Congr., USSR, July-August, 1976, pp. 308–26

197. Shmueli, A. 1973. *Hitnahalut Nawadim Be-Merhav Yerushalaim Be-mea Haesrim (Sedenterization of Nomads in the Region of Jerusalem During the Twentieth Century)*. PhD thesis. Hebrew Univ., Jerusalem, Israel

198. Shmueli, A. 1970. *Hitnahalut Ha-bedwim shel Midbar Yehuda (Sedentarization of Bedouins in the Judean Desert)*. Jerusalem: Ministry of Housing, Dep. Geogr. Hebrew Univ.; Tel Aviv: Gome

199. Shokeid, M. 1976. Conviviality versus strife: peacemaking at parties among Atlas Mountain immigrants in Israel. *Polit. Anthropol.* 1(3/4):101–21

200. Shokeid, M. 1975. Strategy and change in the Arab vote: observations in a mixed town. In *The Elections in Israel – 1973*, ed. A. Arian. Jerusalem: Academic

201. Shokeid, M. 1973. *Uses of Drugs among Arabs in Israel*. Presented at 9th Int. Congr. Anthropol. Ethnol. Sci., Chicago

202. Shokeid, M. 1971. *The Dual Heritage: Immigrants from the Atlas Mountains in an Israeli Village*. Manchester Univ. Press

203. Shokeid, M. 1971. Moshav Sela: frustration and crisis in the process of absorption. See Ref. 194, pp. 103–24

204. Sinai, A. S., Waxman, Ch. I., eds. 1976–77. Ethnic and religious minorities in the Middle East. *Middle East Rev.* 9(1); 9(2) (Spec. Issues)

205. Sirhan, B. 1975. Palestinian refugee camp life in Lebanon. *J. Palastine Stud.* 4(2):91–107

206. Smith, M. G. 1960. Social and cultural pluralism. *Ann. Am. Acad. Sci.* 83: 763–77

207. Stein, M. R. 1960. *The Eclipse of Community*. New York: Harper

208. Sweet, L. E. 1974. Visiting patterns and social dynamics in a Lebanese Druze Village. *Anthropol. Q.* 47(1):112–19

209. Sweet, L. E., ed. 1971. *The Central Middle East: A Handbook of Anthropology and Published Research on the Nile Valley, the Arab Levant, Southern Mesopotamia, the Arabian Peninsula and Israel*. New Haven, Conn.: HRAF Press

210. Sweet, L. E., ed. 1970. *Peoples and Cultures of the Middle East: An Anthropological Reader*. Garden City, NY: Am. Mus. Nat. Hist., Nat. Hist. Press

211. Swidler, W. W. 1973. Adaptive processes regulating nomad-sedentary interaction in the Middle East. See Ref. 166, pp. 23–42

212. Van Nieuwenhuijze, C. A. O. 1971. *Sociology of the Middle East*. Leiden: Brill

213. Vinogradov, A. R. 1974. Ethnicity, cultural discontinuity and power brokers in Northern Iraq: the case of the Shabak. *Am. Ethnol.* 1(1):207–18

214. Vinogradov, A. R. 1972. To sociopolitical organization of a Berber Taraf tribe: pre-protectorate Morocco. See Ref. 91, pp. 67–85

215. Waterbury, J. 1972. Tribalism, trade and politics: the transformation of the Swasa of Morocco. See Ref. 91, pp. 231–59

216. Weil, S. 1977. Names and identity

among the Bene Israel. See Ref. 96, pp. 201–19

217. Weingrod, A. 1970. Change and stability in administrated villages: The Israeli experience. See Ref. 210, 2:124–42

218. Weingrod, A. 1966. *Reluctant Pioneers: Village Development in Israel.* Ithaca: Cornell Univ. Press

219. Weingrod, A. 1965. *Israel: Group Relations in a New Society.* Inst. Race Relat.; London: Pall Mall Press

220. Weintraub, D., et al 1971. *Immigration and Social Change: Agricultural Settlement of New Immigrants in Israel.* New York: Humanities Press

221. Wigle, L. D. 1974. *The Effects of International Migration on a Northern Lebanese Village.* PhD thesis. Wayne State Univ., Detroit, Mich.

222. Yancey, W. L., Eriksen, E. P., Juliani, R. N. 1976. Emergent ethnicity: a review and reformulation. *Am. Sociol. Rev.* 41(3):391–403

223. Zenner, W. P. 1972. Some aspects of ethnic stereotype content in the Galilee: a trial formulation. *Middle Eastern Stud.* 8(3):405–16

224. Zenner, W. P. 1968. Syrian Jews in three social settings. *Jewish J. Sociol.* 10(1):101–20

225. Zenner, W. P., Richter, M. N. Jr. 1972. The Druzes as a divided minority group. *J. Asian Afr. Stud.* 7(3–4):193–203

Ann. Rev. Anthropol. 1977. 6:349–78
Copyright © 1977 by Annual Reviews Inc. All rights reserved

ANTHROPOLOGY COMES   ❖9598
PART-WAY HOME: COMMUNITY
STUDIES IN EUROPE

John W. Cole

Department of Anthropology, University of Massachusetts, Amherst, Massachusetts 01003

INTRODUCTION

Robert Redfield's research in the Mexican village of Tepoztlan in the late 1920s marks the expansion of field research in social anthropology into complex societies. Certainly in the decades which followed this work there was a proliferation of research among peasants, pastoralists and fishermen. Anthropologists conducted field work not only in Latin America, but in the civilizations of Asia and Africa as well. In this general expansion, a few studies were conducted in Europe in the late 1920s and 1930s, notably by Arensberg in Western Ireland (5, 6), by Chapman in Sicily (30), and by Sanders (97) in the Balkans. But the cultures of contemporary Europe held little interest for the profession at large.[1] As a number of writers have noted, little social anthropological research was carried out in Europe until the 1950s (2, pp. 2–3; 5, pp. 9–13; 56, p. 743).

This was certainly not because of a lack of familiarity with the continent. The study of historical sources on the ancient civilizations of the Mediterranean and on the Celtic and Germanic "tribes" of antiquity played a prominent role in the formation of nineteenth century anthropological ideas. As John Davis (38, pp. 1–4; see also 76) has pointed out, Maine, Fustel de Coulanges, Robertson-Smith, Fraser, Durkheim, and Westermark all drew on Mediterranean sources in formulating their comparative and theoretical schemes, and Maine especially made much use of material on the Irish Celts. Morgan drew on all of these societies in his evolutionary formulations, and anchored his work in classic Greece and Rome. Marx and Engels used the ancient civilizations as a kind of watershed. Writings which focus on the processes that led to the formation of capitalism began with these slave-based

---

[1] Of these three studies, only Arensberg's found its way into print with relatively little delay. Sanders' work was not published until after World War II, and Chapman's was not published until the manuscript was "rediscovered" in 1970, more than 40 years after the original research.

societies, while those writings which deal with primitives end there. Thus the advancement of nineteenth century European and American understanding of civilizations elsewhere in the world, and of primitive cultures as well, was in comparison to historical materials on ancient Europe. However, this interest in historical Europe was not translated into an impulse to gather information in European communities. Nor did personal experience on the continent lead to field research in Europe. Many, if not most, anthropologists in both the nineteenth and twentieth centuries had personal familiarity with contemporary Europe. Morgan, the founding father of American anthropology, spent an extended period traveling in Europe, but left his impressions only in private journals (116). British anthropologists regularly included the grand tour as a part of their education, and many of the leading figures in anthropology were of continental origin. Franz Boas, Robert Lowie, Bronislaw Malinowski, and Siegfried Nadel, to name a few, were all born and at least partly educated on the continent.

Malinowski even maintained a villa at Oberbozen in the South Tyrol where he and his students regularly vacationed. An entire generation of British anthropologists experienced invigorating walks in the mountains and enjoyed what Malinowski is said to have regarded as the finest scenery in all of Europe (50, pp. 4, 10; 78, p.34). But the discussions on these vacations were of research conducted far afield, and while all enjoyed the scenery, their professional gaze was across the seas, among the black and brown inhabitants of the dominions and colonies of the British Empire.

The beginnings of a more concerted effort on contemporary Europe are to be found in the enlistment of anthropology in the war effort of World War II and in the so-called cold war which followed. In the United States, anthropologists attempted to provide characterizations of "cultures of various societies which were inaccessible to direct observation" (88, p. xx). This effort resulted in a series of studies, both published and unpublished, and included a number on allies and enemies in Europe. Anthropologists from Columbia University had been prominent in the wartime studies, and it was Columbia University which fielded the largest contingent of researchers in Europe during the 1950s.[2] Others came from Harvard,

[2] The Columbia University group, founded by Ruth Benedict and later led by Margaret Mead, was interdisciplinary in nature and had strong psychological leanings. Its intent was to formulate statements about national character and its method was the study of "culture at a distance." This method was to compensate for the absence of direct field observation by interviewing people who originated in an inaccessible society and were living in or visiting in the New York area. Additional data were gleaned from movies, published sources, and other available cultural materials. The method and some of its results were published by Mead & Metraux (89) in 1953. Other findings were published in a series of monographs which appeared in the decade following World War II (e.g. 16, 95). Mead suggested that the method would continue to be valuable when the inaccessible societies were again opened up, and could be combined with direct observation. Except for several studies published by Rodnick over the years (57, p. 27), her advice has been ignored by Europeanists, even by those who received their introduction to an anthropology of Europe as members of the group.

Robert Lowie, working at the University of California, also contributed a volume on Germany based on war-time library research and a postwar visit. Although California has contributed its share of Europeanists, Lowie's work on Europe has not been influential.

Yale, and the University of California. Since that time the number of anthropologi-cal studies in Europe has increased at a geometric rate, and Europeanists are now being trained at many different universities. By 1975 the number of researchers was large enough that the American Anthropological Association determined to publish a directory of North American Europeanists (57).

During the same time period, field research in Europe by British anthropologists underwent a parallel expansion. Led by students from Oxford, field research in Mediterranean Europe got under way (38, pp. 237–46), and students from the London School of Economics and Manchester University conducted studies in Britain itself (53, 62). Moreover, a number of European scholars, especially on the western rim of the continent, have also worked in Europe. Norwegian and Dutch social anthropologists have been particularly active. Some of these scholars were trained in British or American universities, and they regularly report at least a portion of their findings in English-language publications.

All of these scholars, whether living in North America, Britain, or on the conti-nent, regularly read one another's publications, review one another's books and exchange manuscripts and personal communications. They interact at national and international professional meetings. Moreover, it is *de rigueur* for North American anthropologists to visit colleagues in Holland or Britain on the way to and from field locations in Europe, and British and continental colleagues have lectured or taught for varying periods of time at American universities.

For better or worse, these interactions define an international intellectual commu-nity, an "Anglophone Anthropology" of Europe. It is by no means a closed commu-nity, since its participants are active in other intellectual pursuits as well, and some publish in other languages in addition to English. But the social anthropology of Europe has come to constitute an academic tradition with shared concerns and a distinctive literature. Not only have members of this community themselves pro-duced a respectable volume of published material, but they have also marked out writings by demographers, European ethnologists, geographers, historians, political scientists, and rural sociologists for incorporation into an "essential literature." At this writing the total literature has reached formidable proportions.

The intention of this article is to discuss the directions that anglophone an-thropology is taking, to outline its theoretical thrust, and to discuss some of its more important contributions and shortcomings. To do this, I believe it is necessary first to understand its relationship to the field of anthropology as a whole. In particular, I wish to raise the question of why anthropological interest was not fastened on contemporary Europe sooner and why it has become so vigorous in the 1960s and 1970s.

ANTHROPOLOGY: THE STUDY OF OTHERS

The origins of anthropology as a scholarly discipline in the nineteenth century in western Europe and North America revolved around two general sets of problems. One was an attempt to come to grips with the biological, linguistic, social, and cultural characteristics of the populations on other continents. Europeans had been in direct contact with these people for several centuries and during the nineteenth century were in the process of consolidating colonial empires. Western European anthropologists directed their efforts primarily toward the populations of their overseas colonies, while American anthropologists were generally concerned with the indigenous populations of the Americas. The second set of problems had to do with attempts to understand the European past. The archaeologist's spade had proved that man's antiquity in Europe was far greater than recorded in historical sources, and intellectuals wished to explicate this long prehistory. If the bones and artifacts that the archaeologists found could not speak for themselves, then perhaps those populations elsewhere in the world who still used such ancient implements might speak for them. The expectation was that what the ethnographer learned from his studies of contemporary "savage" and "barbarian" cultures could contribute to an understanding of early stages in the evolution of European civilization.

Anthropology thus secured itself a place and a mission in the division of labor in nineteenth century social science. It developed a comparative approach in which the institutions of the peoples of other continents were compared to one another and to those of the European past. Society in modern Europe and North America was the province of a bevy of other social sciences which dissected it into various parts, each staking out its own exclusive subject matter. The institutions of Europe were regarded as unique, the distinctive product of an evolutionary process which had raised them to a stage unmatched anywhere else in the world. Therefore, while anthropology could contribute to an understanding of the antecedents of these institutions, it was not relevant to an understanding of their present forms.

During the first half of the twentieth century, anthropologists became skeptical of many of the evolutionists' claims, but they continued to focus on the exotic and the primitive. They were less interested in studying other cultures as representatives of past stages of European civilization, but continued to study primitive and peasant cultures in the purest state possible. Ethnographers were bent on describing these societies as they were believed to have been before they felt the impact of the European presence.

Even when the intent of research has been deliberately cross-cultural, the cultures of Europe were for the most part excluded. While A. L. Kroeber (77) may have claimed the peasants of Europe for anthropology in 1948, his claim is not substantiated by any body of monographs or comparative works extant at the time. Anthropologists, with the few exceptions mentioned above, did not do field work in Europe, and they rarely made use of materials on European society published by other scholars. Only those peoples who appeared to be most marginal to the mainstream of European civilization, and thus not fully European at all, were recognized as fit subjects for anthropological comparison. As recently as 1962, the culture area and ethnic group map of Europe in Spencer & Johnson's ethnographic atlas (108) included only non–Indo-European speakers (Basques, Finns, Lapps, Magyars), and those Indo-European speakers who were proving the most intractable in the face of modernization—the Albanians, Bretons, Irish, Latvians, and Welch. A perusal of other comparative compilations and of introductory textbooks in both general and social anthropology yields similar results.

The same separation between the study of Europeans and others also took place on the continent. Each of the European countries has a well-developed program for the study of their own "folk culture" and rural, social, and economic problems. But, as the Hungarian ethnologist Tamás Hofer (70, p. 6) has pointed out, ". . . ethnographers studying their own peoples form a separate body from those studying other, non-European peoples. They have their own chairs at the Universities and their own museums." In most instances, professors of European ethnology are in the humanities faculty while overseas ethnologists are in the social science faculty. Students in the two disciplines have entirely separate training.

Moreover, the incorporation of an anthropology of Europe into general anthropology has met with substantial resistance from within the anthropological ranks and continues to face accusations of illegitimacy. Consider a letter which appeared in the *Anthropological Newsletter* in 1972 (51). Entitled "Peasants' Revolt," the letter purports to express the gratitude of those European peasants only recently discovered by American anthropologists. It has two main themes. One of these is the absence of privation experienced by European researchers: "Situated in countries where neither cobras, nor poisoned arrows, nor temperatures in the range of -40°F make daily life miserable, the American discoverers of new frontiers can safely engage in skiing, lake swimming and occasional opera visits while studying us natives." The second theme is a suggestion of triviality. After mentioning the "milliards of volumes" produced by European scholars about their own cultures, the letter goes on to ask, "What is that compared with the abysmal insight gained by an American undergraduate who, under the paternal supervision of the Peasantry Guru of his department, finds out how the Swiss plant potatoes and what brand of transistor radio is preferred in a Serbian village."

The letter is signed by five names which pretend to be those of European peasants. To my knowledge, this is the only pseudonymous letter ever published in the *Newsletter:* it is accompanied by an editor's statement that "The *Newsletter* will not make a practice of publishing pseudonymous letters." The publication of this letter in an official organ of the American Anthropological Association is a symptom of widespread *sub-rosa* resistance to European anthropology in the discipline.

Such resistance is apparently not confined to the United States. Commenting on the British scene, John Davis reports that, "It is not uncommon, at any rate in England, to meet backwoods anthropologists who clearly convey their sense of superiority" (over those who study in the Mediterranean). According to Davis, they hold that "Anthropology is only anthropology if it is done very much abroad, in unpleasant conditions, in societies very different from the ethnographer's habitat, very different indeed from the sort of place where he might go on holiday" (38, p. 7). In the United States one hears Europeanists complain of tenure refused, of articles rejected, and of grant requests denied because of their area of interest. While such complaints may well be rationalizations for actions which were in reality based on relative merit, it is significant that Africanists, Oceanists, and Americanists do not rationalize their failures in similar ways.

On the surface such attitudes apparently refer to the role of field work as a rite of passage which is necessary for full acceptance into the anthropological clan. The suggestion is that the field experience in Europe is not sufficiently traumatic or physically demanding to serve this initiation function. Research in Europe is really not anthropology at all, but sociology, and that is better left to those with formal training as sociologists. Such attitudes may appear trivial, little more than expressions of private insecurity, professional jealousy, or barroom and hallway banter. However, I believe that they are a surface expression of a more deep-seated and significant phenomenon. Focus on the conditions under which anthropology is conducted in Europe draws attention away from the content of this research. It is a way of attempting to discredit it without considering what it has to say. It masks the uneasiness that some anthropologists continue to feel at the application of the same methods and theories used in the study of "primitives" to the study of "civilized" Europe.

Resistance within the profession is paralleled by the resentment that many European intellectuals feel when they learn that their countrymen are to be the subject of social anthropological enquiry. Anthropologists regularly experience confrontations with educated Europeans who, more or less politely, voice their objections to the research. I am not referring here to the sophisticated objections which are sometimes raised to research in Europe by any North Americans on the grounds that it is an aspect of American imperialism. Rather, I am referring to the objections to anthropological research by individuals who know anthropology (or ethnology) as the study of noncivilized peoples of other races. To be studied by an anthropologist is therefore to be put into the same category as "primitives." It is taken as an insult by these individuals, to be put into the same category as people whom they regard as fundamentally different from and inferior to themselves and their civilization. Their resentment is compounded because they assume the same attitudes are held by the anthropologist.

In the words of Del Hymes (73, p. 5), anthropology has developed as "an autonomous discipline that specializes in the study of others." As such, an anthropology of Europe (or America) is a contradiction in terms. Until the post-World War II period such a contradiction did not exist. One set of social sciences developed to explain human society and behavior in Europe and America, and anthropology developed to explain it in the rest of the world. Whether Europeans and Americans regarded the social forms of a non-European society as worthy or not, these forms were seen as the products of the society's own past. Poverty and misery might even be their lot, but that too could be laid to their traditions and customs. Research into the traditions and customs of primitives could illuminate the nature of *their* problems, but it could have little meaning for the citizens of modern Europe or America. Organized into modern, industrial nation states, the social forms of Europe and America were of a different order from those in the rest of the world.

Such an intellectual division of labor was congenial to the division of economic and political power in the world. It served to mask the nature of the relationships which bound all of the societies of the world into a single political-economic system where wealth and power in one corner of the globe were gained at a cost of poverty and underdevelopment elsewhere (65, 74). To focus on the nature of these relationships and their role in producing and maintaining the conditions which had once been attributed to the survival of traditional social forms was to attack the ideological underpinnings of the world system. To scrutinize European communities and social institutions with an anthropological lens polished in the villages of Africa and Asia and the barrios of South America further threatened this ideology. It held out the potential of debunking the myth of the innate uniqueness and superiority of European society.

BEGINNINGS IN EUROPE

Since an anthropology of Europe was not a viable possibility in the nineteenth and the first half of the twentieth centuries, and since substantial objections to it persist in the present, the question remains of why it has become well established now. It is not enough to note that there was an expansion of anthropological concern to include complex societies, including those in Europe. The question is why this expansion took place when it did. I would like to suggest that the rise of an anthropology of Europe was related to changes which took place in the world political economy in the period following World War II and to the new intellectual problems which this raised for social science research.

One aspect of this altered world situation is that anthropologists are finding it more difficult to conduct research in the places where they used to work, either because the groups they once studied as isolated tribesmen or rural folk have been transformed into something else, or because they are no longer allowed access to the areas where they live. Before World War II anthropologists could carry out research in European colonies or client states with impunity, and in the euphoria of the early days following liberation, when it was assumed that political independence would automatically be followed by modernization and development, anthropologists and other scholars were also welcome. Western scholars and technicians would contribute to the process of modernization through studies which pinpointed problems to be overcome and would help to outline methods to overcome them. But when this did not happen, suspicions arose that the development projects and the scholarly studies which underlay them might be a part of the problem. As Eric Wolf has put it:

> Gone is the halcyon feeling that knowledge alone, including anthropological knowledge, will set men free.... the pacific or pacified objects of our investigation, primitives and peasants alike, are ever more prone to define our field situation gun in hand. A new vocabulary is abroad in the world. It speaks of "imperialism," "colonialism," "neocolonialism," and "internal colonialism," rather than just of primitives and peasants, or even of developed and underdeveloped. Yet anthropology has in the past operated among pacified or pacific natives; when the native "hits back" we are in a very different situation from that in which we found ourselves only yesterday (119, pp. 257–58).

As the borders were shut in Africa, Asia, and South America, and as even reservation Indians in North America became hostile to anthropology, some anthropologists, needing field research to support their professional careers, turned to one of the few areas still open to them, the nations of Europe.

Certainly substantial numbers of anthropologists with experiences in many different corners of the globe expanded their interest in the 1960s to include research in Europe. This involved some of the most respected members of the profession. A few of this distinguished group, and their areas of former research, are Bailey (India), Barth (Middle East), E. Friedl (North America), Hammel (South America), Honigmann (North America), Meggit (Oceania), Netting (Africa), Peristiany (Africa), Pospisil (Oceania), Pelto (Mexico), Reining (Africa), and Wolf (Latin America). Without speculating on the particular reasons which motivated any individual anthropologist to come to Europe after beginnings elsewhere, it is more than a coincidence that so many members of the profession have established a European research interest during a single decade which coincides with constricting opportunities for research elsewhere. Joining those anthropologists who had made a beginning in the fifties, these professors formed a cadre available for the training of Europeanist anthropologists.

While the closing of traditional research areas was providing a push, the establishment of resources for European research exercised a pull. The Council for European Studies, the Ford Foundation, and the International Research Exchanges Board (IREX) all made an effort to increase funds or create new funds for the express purpose of supporting European research. At the same time they announced that anthropologists were welcome to apply for these grants and in some cases singled out anthropology for special encouragement.[3]

Younger students who conducted doctoral research in Europe in the sixties and seventies were well aware that European anthropology was an expanding field, but their interest in the continent did not involve a shift in commitment as it had for their teachers. Rather, with an experienced staff available and foundations willing to fund their research, Europe was but one alternative out of a number which were available. In spite of the considerable resistance I have noted above, countervailing forces carried the day and an anthropology of Europe was established and "normalized" in a single intellectual generation.

[3]The reason for the increase in funds available for European research in the 1960s and 1970s is a matter for further research. The expansion of funds for European research accompanied the rapidly changing nature of the international climate in Europe in the 1960s. Whereas throughout the Cold War period Europe appeared to be divided into two well-integrated camps, one led by the United States and the other by the Soviet Union, dissensions appeared in the late fifties and sixties, and some states within both camps began to assume more independent international stances. As long as they had remained unwavering allies (Western Europe) or puppet satellites (Eastern Europe) there was little point to research. But once they began to become independent actors on the European scene information was required by power brokers in order to be able to predict and influence their course of action. This meant, among other things, more money for social science research.

In Britain interest in Europe may very well be tied to the loss of colonies and the reluctant reorientation of Britain to the continent. It parallels in time the switch from Britain's status as a world colonial power to a relatively underdeveloped member of the European common market.

The transformation of the world political economy affected anthropology in a second way which contributed to the establishment of an anthropology of Europe and provided it with an intellectual rationale. Into the 1950s anthropology had regularly regarded the communities and societies it studied as relatively autonomous and as variations on the theme of "traditional" and "primitive" societies which coexisted in the world with modern industrial nation states. While well aware of the inroads which had been and continued to be made by institutions such as Christian missions, slave raiding, the fur trade, the development of plantation economies, the introduction of cash crops, and the imposition of colonial or reservation administration, the impact of such institutions on the social organization of the communities which were being studied was rarely taken as a matter of anthropological interest. Where there was an interest in change, as in some personality and culture studies, the focus was on enculturation of individuals and their personal adjustments to new situations (as in the Harvard value studies in the American Southwest).

But studies of society were overwhelmingly dominated by a concern with stability. Not only in anthropology, but throughout Western social science structural-functionalist analysis of society held sway (65). This mode of analysis—paradigm —consistently emphasizes social order. Society is seen as a static entity made up of a variety of institutions. The behavior of individuals is explained in terms of rights and duties determined by the formal positions they hold in these institutions. The institutions serve both to maintain the society as a whole and to fulfill the social, psychological, and biological needs of the members of the society. Change is seen as coming from outside of the system and social process works to resist these pressures and to return the society to the status quo.

As indigenous movements led to political independence throughout the world and to a universal commitment to programs of economic, social, and political development, the focus of social science research began to shift from the study of social equilibrium to the factors which promote and retard social change. The theoretical systems which were erected to handle these new interests were initially Eurocentric and incorporated a duality between a traditional past and a modern present or future. Modernization for the Third World was seen as the emulation of the program for development which had been undergone in western Europe. This resulted in a proliferation of theoretical works which attempted to clarify this process and to explain its applicability for the new nations (15, 45, 60, 72, 82, 96, 113). In this view the underdevelopment and poverty which was the lot of most communities throughout the world was equated with the characteristics of traditional societies, whether primitive or peasant. These conditions could be alleviated through the shedding of traditional characteristics and the acceptance of modern technology, social organization, politics, and values. Community studies were then structured to take this transformation into consideration.

The monographs which result from such research are all variations on a single format. There is a chapter on "the setting" which contains statements about the community's location and history. This is "background" which figures little if at all into the analysis. The remainder of the book consists of a presentation of the traditional characteristics of the community and of the changes which have taken place. The traditional character of the community is examined for aspects which either inhibit or promote change. There may or may not be a discussion of a few of the external influences which are seen as agents for change. Concepts such as "Culture of Poverty" and "the limited good" were attempts to develop generalizations about those aspects of traditional societies which inhibited beneficial change.

FROM TRADITIONAL TO MODERN

The anthropology of Europe drew its rationale from this developmentalist perspective. Studies of communities located in developed countries could serve as models of what the new nations were attempting to achieve. At the same time, studies conducted in European countries which still had traditional communities could also be informative. Although traditional, they *were* European and therefore they were generally farther along the path of modernization. They could be taken as representative of stages through which Third World communities would have to pass on their way to full modernization. Moreover, since these European nations already had considerable experience with modernization programs and the problems associated with them, non-European states could benefit from an understanding of their successes and failures.

In putting European communities together with those in other parts of the world into a framework of modernization, anthropologists follow two different lines of reasoning. One is to banish the traditional communities from Europe and the other is to continue to insist on the integrity of Europe in contrast to the rest of the world.

The first is represented by Banfield's well-known study of Montegrano in southern Italy. He puts southern Italy into the non-Western world, maintaining the dichotomy between us and others, by expanding the other now to include the parts of Europe left behind by modernization. He maintains that people in such areas are different from ourselves and even argues that "There is some reason to doubt that the non-Western cultures of the world will prove capable of creating and maintaining the high degree of organization without which a modern economy and a democratic political order are possible" (11, p. 8). It is their traditions which hold them back, but "While it is easy to see that culture may be the limiting factor which determines the amount and character of organization and therefore of progress in the less developed parts of the world, it is not obvious what are the precise incompatibilities between particular cultures, or aspects of culture, and particular forms or levels of organization" (11, p. 9). The purpose of the community study thus becomes evident: it is to discern those characteristics which inhibit progress. Thus Banfield discovered among the Montegranesi an "amoral familism" in which individuals act to "maximize the material, short run advantage of the nuclear family; assume that others will do likewise" (11, p. 83). The result of such behavior is that "In a society of amoral familists, no one will further the interest of the group or community except as it is to his private advantage to do so" (11, pp. 83–84). Such a traditional ethos, inherited from the past, prevents modernization and explains Montegrano's backwardness.

The emphasis on tradition preserved has not been a mere passing phase in European research. This is demonstrated by its domination of numbers of recent studies (1, 2, 27, 36, 54, 85). One example is Golde's (64) recent monograph on villages in Baden-Württemberg. He describes a transition from a traditional type of family farm into a modernized and highly rationalized family farm. However, the two villages he studied do not change in exactly the same way or at exactly the same speed. The differences are attributed to contrasting religious traditions; one community is Protestant, the other Catholic. Another example is provided in du Boulay's sophisticated structural analysis of domestic relations in a Greek village. In her epilogue she offers the observation that, "The structure which has been examined in this book represents on the whole a static pattern which is based on respect for traditional knowledge and an unquestioning acceptance of the social forms in which this knowledge was preserved" (41, p. 257). She goes on to speculate about what happens when the stability of such a society is threatened by modernization and the rationale for this knowledge is lost:

... preservation without understanding produces a precarious equilibrium which is easily upset when violently challenged by an opposing system, and is liable to two dangers. One is that an inflexibility, leading to ignorance and even to barbarism, should develop through a lack of enlightenment from within; the other that the inherited conviction of the validity of these forms should succumb easily to a philosophy with a more readily comprehensible rationale (41, p. 257).

Although the three authors cited here agree in that each has presented an analysis of tradition preserved, the fates of the three communities are widely divergent. While the Italian village clings tenaciously to its traditional ways, the German communities are rapidly evolving into modern mechanized farming villages and the Greek villagers are just as rapidly abandoning their village for an urban life.

These authors share Banfield's view of some European communities as bastions of ongoing traditions which impinge on the forces of modernization, but neither accepts the banishment of their communities from Europe nor Banfield's moral judgment. While Banfield regrets the tenacity of tradition, Golde is objectively indifferent and du Boulay regrets the passing of traditional values. The latter two also diverge from Banfield in seeing their communities as integral parts of European civilization, implicitly accepting the time-honored dichotomy between Europeans and others [although du Boulay expresses her fears about a lapse into "barbarism" and "savagery" and detects such a lapse in some Greek communities (41, pp. 257–58)].

The few attempts to survey the results of community studies in Europe are anchored to the concept of a traditional modern dichotomy and have at the same time labored to set forth the characteristics which define a European civilization and differentiate it from other cultures of the world. One of the first modern anthropological attempts was by Arensberg in 1963 (4). Europe, together with other civilizations, is set off from all others as being "Peoples of the Book"; within this grouping it is combined with the Middle East and contrasted with other civilizations on the basis of a distinctive bread-milk-meat subsistence base; finally, it stands unique even in contrast with the Middle East on the grounds of distinctive social organization. In this way a *European Culture Area* can be defined, based on a unique constellation of enduring culture traits. It is a matter of identifying persistent traditions great and small, which are common to all parts of Europe, and which are of great antiquity. He explains that there are both practical and theoretical reasons to understand Europe's uniqueness even today, as these traditions continue to act in the face of modernization. By identifying the way in which traditional elements have influenced European development, we can then also identify more clearly what the essence of development is. This knowledge will be useful to countries where development is now diffusing. In fact, this understanding "is essential if nativistic reaction is to be weathered and viable amalgamations of native culture and imported institutitions are to be evolved for the developing nations of the globe" (4, p. 77).

In the early seventies Anderson came out with a pair of studies (1, 2) which further developed these ideas. He explains traditional or feudal Europe as made up of three cultures or classes—aristocrats, burghers, and peasants. These are functionally integrated in any given locale through patron-client ties. Aristocrats and burghers are tied to other members of their class in different locations through networks which they use to transmit culture. This serves to maintain a single shared cultural tradition or civilization throughout the continent. Centers of cultural innovation rise and fall in different places, but members of these classes, regardless of where they live, keep up with the times as a result of their active networks. Peasants, on the other hand, do not move much from place to place and so regional differences among them are more pronounced. Similarities among peasants are mostly the result of shared patterns of dominance which have been diffused among the aristocracy. This civilization began in western Europe and diffused outward so that it was expanding into eastern Europe at a time when it was already declining in the west.

The two volumes go on to speak of the modernization of Europe in terms of the development of an urban-industrial order in northwestern Europe which created a middle class, a working class, and converted subsistence-oriented peasants into market-oriented farmers. This new order then proceeds to spread from the northwest across all of Europe, wiping out tradition as it goes. Thus:

> The end of the traditional way of life and the beginning of the modern may be dated as the time of urban-industrial growth. For Europe, this means the nineteenth century in the low valleys and great plains of the northwest, including Great Britain. It means the twentieth century for isolated areas in the west and for most of the east, far north and Mediterranean south. For certain parts of England it means the last part of the eighteenth century. For convenience we take the eighteenth century as the last century of Traditional Europe (1, p. 72).

Arensberg's contribution was an attempt to identify the characteristic traditions which establish the uniqueness of Europe. Anderson has taken this lead, elaborated on it, and added a focus on the transformation from traditional to modern. Implicit in their writings is a view that the transformation of Europe carries a message for the rest of the world. It is this theme that George Dalton has picked for elaboration. In the process he has provided an explicit rationale for anthropological research in

Europe. He suggests "that to understand today's peasantries in India or Peru it is useful to study European serfs in the tenth century and European farmers in the twentieth century because we must know what Third World peasantries changed from and what they are changing into. Looking at a thousand years of European peasantry shows us what peasants were before, during and after modernization seriously began" (36, pp. 385–86). For Dalton then the study of European peasant communities can provide an agenda for the transformation of the rest of the world.

We thus stand, in the mid-seventies, with a collection of monographs analyzing "traditional" communities undergoing "modernization" as a result of external pressures for change which are diffusing across the European culture area. A few survey and theoretical works support this perspective, and all tie in to the general literature on modernization cited earlier. As a whole, this literature both supports the division of the world into Europeans and others, and sets up the transformation of Europe as a model for others to emulate.

ENTREPRENEURS, NETWORKS, PROCESSES

While many anthropologists continue to think in terms of a traditional/modern dichotomy, culture areas, and diffusion, serious questions about the validity of this paradigm have been raised and alternative perspectives have been advanced. One of these alternatives has developed as a critique of structural-functionalism and can be referred to as either the "social process" or the "entrepreneurial" approach. It has two major objections to structural-functionalism. The first is that it is a static model which is not only incapable of analyzing social change, but supports stability as normal and opposes change as abnormal. The second is that it was developed as a mode of analyzing traditional societies in which social relations are attributed to roles which are based on membership in a small number of corporate groups. In these analyses people appear to passively play out the roles that are assigned to them.

If this view is accepted, social process analysts argue, then it follows that social organization is determined differently in small scale societies than in large scale modern ones, since people in modern societies actively determine their social roles. In the social process view, people, whether in simple or complex societies, are active determiners of social relations, and society is not static. As Boissevain has put it, "Instead of looking at man as a member of groups and institutional complexes passively obedient to their norms and pressures, it is important to see him as an entrepreneur who tries to manipulate norms and relationships for his own social and psychological benefit" (23, p. 7). The interaction of these manipulating human beings gives society a dynamic which is the basis for all social process, including change (14, 22, 23). This method is used in the analysis of social process in particular places, but it is also used to generalize about the nature of social process in all societies. In its generalizing aspect the particulars of tradition and history are stripped away to lay bare the essence of social process and of the human behavior which underlies it.

The concept of social networks has been an important aspect of the entrepreneurial approach, and has developed in the study of complex societies. Here social relations are developed on an expedient basis from among a large number of possible alternatives, so students of these societies needed a method which could be used to describe the formation, maintenance, and function of social ties. The concept was first used explicitly over 20 years ago and has been vigorously developed in the intervening years. This literature has been subjected to several thorough reviews in recent years (13, 91), so here I simply want to call attention to its use both in Europe and in other areas of the world. While some of the earliest formulations of the network concept came out of research in Norway (12) and England (26) beginnings were being made in Africa and Latin America at about the same time. A number of monographs using network analysis in specific societies have appeared as well as collections which bring together under one cover case studies from different world areas (25). In these, in Boissevain's (23) theoretical volume, and in the volumes mentioned above, network analysis is presented as an abstract, generalized method which is equally applicable in a British or an African city, in a Norwegian parish or in rural Tanzania.

Bailey has developed a variant of the entrepreneurial approach in the study of politics which is relevant here because much of its application has been in Europe. His theory is set forth in *Strategems and Spoils* (8) and is predicated on the assumption that in any given society the political actors are agreed on the parameters of political behavior such as the nature of political goals and how one competes to obtain them. Generally people play by the rules, but sometimes individuals will try to establish new rules so that the going gets nasty and the political system may change as a result. In the chapters of this book he lays out what he regards as universals about the ways in which politics are conducted, whether these be in an Indian village in Orissa or in the halls of Whitehall. Case studies applying the method, mostly by his students, are presented in two additional volumes which cover different aspects of political behavior, broadly defined (9, 10). All of the case material here comes from European communities, but the referent is the theoretical model with its claims to universal applicability. Indeed, entrepreneurial analysis has much in common with the "processual" approach worked out by Marc Swartz and his colleagues (111) with its case studies drawn from all parts of the world.

The incorporation of European data into these schemes has done much to break down the arbitrary distinctions between the nature of the European and the inhabitants of other continents. To attribute differences between populations to age-old but unexplained traditions is both arbitrary and mystifying. It is arbitrary because whether a society is to be included or excluded from a particular culture area is decided first and only then is the rationale for the classification developed. It is mystifying because the grounds for selecting the identifying traditions are not specified. There is no method that one can learn which can be applied in any situation to determine culture area affiliation. The entrepreneurial approach is demystifying because it strips away the differences and discovers modes of behavior which are common to all societies.

The entrepreneurial approach has made a second major contribution in its focus on process. When social analysis is based on the study of structure the social analysis of change is difficult if not impossible. Structure implies stability, or equilibrium, and while structural-functionalists can analyze one set of institutions and compare them to another set which develops in the same society after a period of change, they cannot analyze the change itself. The logical result, which Gluckman has advocated, is that change is banished from social inquiry and assigned to history while the social anthropologist confines himself to the analysis of equilibrium situations (33, pp. 783–85; 63). But when society is seen as consisting of processes rather than structures, social analysis becomes the study of motion. Processes may remain repetitive —in equilibrium, if you will. But processes may also alter their direction either as the result of an internal dynamic or because of a change in the biophysical or cultural environment. In this paradigm the absence of change is as problematic as change.

The implications of this for social analysis are profound. We can no longer accept a traditional, unchanging society as the base of our analysis and seek only to explain what changes while assuming that what does not change requires no explanation. Indeed, we cannot assume that any given society has been static—that it has been tenaciously clinging to traditional forms perhaps because of a peasant ethos of conservatism. Whether the social processes we are investigating are repetitive or changing, we must explain what is happening.

However, in spite of its very substantial contributions, the entrepreneurial analysis alone is ultimately incomplete. While concentrating on the underlying similarities in the social processes of different societies does serve to break down the credibility of assumptions of innate differences between societies or culture areas, it begs the question of why they are different in the first place. It offers nothing to replace the use of tradition as an explanation for why differences occur. It would not, for example, offer us insights into why the south German villages I mentioned above are modernizing production while Banfield's south Italian villagers are resisting change and the Greek village du Boulay analyzed is being abandoned. As Sydel Silverman has pointed out in her review of the work of Bailey and his students (104, p. 120), the study of social process is ultimately subject to the same criticism that has been leveled at structural-functionalism, namely that "it directs attention away from the critical analysis of the social order." The question of how particular social processes are initiated, perpetuated, or changed remains.

COMMUNITY, REGION, WORLD SYSTEM

Concomitant with the development of anglophone anthropology of Europe, anthropology as a whole has been undergoing a radical reappraisal. This has been developed in such books as *The Culture of Poverty, a Critique* (80), and *Reinventing Anthropology* (74), and in the journals *Critique of Anthropology,* founded in London in 1974, and *Dialectical Anthropology,* founded in New York in 1975, as well as in articles in the older anthropological journals and elsewhere. This reappraisal has been brought about by the same political economic developments discussed above that have led to the expansion of European research. At the heart of this critique is a rejection of the idea that the societies which anthropologists have studied are traditional peasant or primitive communities which have survived into the present and are now undergoing modernization. Instead it points out that these societies have for centuries been integrated into large scale political and economic processes. Most have been subject peoples, and the nature of their subjugation has played a leading role in determining the nature of their social organization. Embedded in this perspective is an understanding of poverty and underdevelopment, not as aspects of conservative tradition, but as results of inclusion in the overseas and internal hinterlands of industrial states. In addition, many regions had previously been subjected to the political and economic control of tribute-collecting empires. Being subjected to such political and economic domains has an impact on all aspects of community life: it affects how the people use their environment and make a living, how their social relations are structured, and what they think about the universe and their place in it.

This perspective necessarily calls into question the concept of tradition. It rejects the assumption that social and cultural patterns, once laid down, will persist tenaciously and questions research based on this assumption. Instead, it insists on knowing what produces social processes and what acts to maintain or change them. In this view the concept of tradition and the attribution of the persistence of tradition to a peasant ethos of conservatism is a substitute for analysis.

Once capitalism was established in the sixteenth century, a geographical division of labor and capital developed. Involved in this division are *cores* or *metropolises*, which import primary products and export manufacturers, and *peripheries* or *hinterlands*, where the primary products originate and which receive some of the manufactured goods (114, 115). The result of these interactions was to modernize both kinds of regions. Modernization in the core areas, in western Europe, and North America, and later in Japan and Soviet Russia, resulted in urbanization, industrialization, capital accumulation, and in the formation of nation states which were either parlimentary democracies, as in Holland, Britain, France, and the United States; authoritarian, totalitarian as in Germany and Japan; or state socialist as in Stalinist Russia (68, 92). But in the hinterlands modernization resulted in what Wolf has called the "triple crisis" (118). This consists of structural overpopulation, modes of production which gear hinterland production to the demands of the core and the erosion of power of precapitalist elites. Thus what we have been used to calling "traditional" or "underdeveloped societies" turn out to derive their characteristics not from tenacious social forms transmitted from the remote past, but from constellations of characteristics developed within the past few hundred years. Moreover, while some hinterlands have managed to resist or overthrow the hegemony of the industrial core and have undertaken genuine development, most have remained in this peripheral relationship for a long period of time. The nature of this ongoing relationship is a principal factor in the maintenance of social organization in both core and periphery.

Armed with the insights provided by this perspective, new methods of community research have been developed. These involve an understanding that the communities we study are a setting for the interplay of a variety of forces. Some of these stem from the nature of the community's environment and the methods it uses to exploit it. Others are derived from patterns of social and economic interaction between communities. Still others originate in processes of national integration and the place of the communities we are studying in these processes. As a result of this understanding we have learned to appreciate the region as a unit of analysis (107).

As Schneider, Schneider & Hansen (100) have pointed out, a region is not just an expression of geography, nor is it a culture area in the sense of a collection of communities with a shared cultural tradition. Rather it is a unit of *political ecology,* where local resources and people are organized by an elite which is interposed between community and nation—and which may even bypass the nation in its relations with the world system. While the relative autonomy of such regions may be broken down in the process of national integration, regions have in the past played, and continue in the present to play, major roles in shaping the fortunes of both nation and community. In the villages and towns, people must reconcile ecological and social forces generated on the local scene with pressures which emanate from the political goals and strategies of elites. A more rewarding approach to the study of the community has come out of understanding it as a stage in the playing out of these forces. By coming to grips with the region, the researcher can approach an understanding of what goes on in the village. Conversely, when informed by this perspective, community research can contribute to an understanding of the region (55, pp. xiii–xviii).

CONTEMPORARY RESEARCH IN EUROPE

A few anglophone anthropologists have carried out research in urban areas in the more industrialized parts of Europe, mostly in Britain (47, 53), but by and large they have chosen town or country for their research sites, and these mostly in the parts of Europe which are the least industrialized. A case can certainly be made for the use of anthropology in urban research, but in Europe at least this assumption is supported by very few monographs and articles. While these studies individually present some useful insights into urban life, the number of studies is too few to generate any substantial trend which could serve as the basis for the characterization of an urban anthropology of Europe. Thus the anglophone anthropology of Europe is overwhelmingly the study of rural Europe. I note this with neither regrets nor apologies. In the total of social science and historical writings on Europe, peasants and other country folk have been rather badly neglected in comparison to other segments of society. But we know enough to be able to say that the ignorance of social forces generated in the countryside is at the peril of both intellectual understanding and political process in the modern world (66, 69, 79, 118).

In entering into research on rural Europe, investigators armed with anthropological training bring certain positive elements. They are trained in making close observations of behavior within a community over an extended period of time and they have techniques to record and organize their data based on an understanding of the genealogical method, of networks and coalitions, and of ecological relations. They know how to interview people and are alert to discrepancies between what people say they do and what they do. Increasing numbers of investigators also know how to talk to a computer and have an appreciation for the results which can be obtained from gathering data in quantities, however arduous that may at times be. Without too much straining of their anthropological "tradition," the investigators can also be taught to use documents and other archival material. And, of course, they have at hand the theoretical awareness of the community as a product of its past and present integration into both its local setting and regional and national processes.

While thus methodologically and theoretically equipped to gather data in European communities, anthropologists initially were handicapped by a real ignorance about Europe itself. I have already discussed the virtual absence of writings on Europe in the anthropological literature. American and British anthropologists had some familiarity with European ethnology (112), but little of this focused on the questions of power, economy, and social organization which form the central concerns of anglophone anthropology. While there was a vast literature on different aspects of European history and society, the amount which dealt with rural European societies was relatively small. The study of rural communities in Europe was probably most advanced in Eastern and Central Europe, where it dated well back into the nineteenth century. But this was written in languages which were not widely read in the West and remained virtually unknown until quite recently. As a result of this ignorance, their research reports often included "some rediscoveries of truths long known outside the autarky of the English-speaking world" (102, p. 12). But most English-speaking anthropologists did consult with peasant specialists in the countries where they conducted their research and began to incorporate the insights of these scholars into their interpretations. A few European scholars, such as Hofer (49, 70) and Shanin (102, 103), took the trouble to draw our attention to this literature. They were joined by others with the necessary linguistic abilities who began to translate some of this material into English, or to write books which drew on the national literature of one or another European country.

As a result of these efforts a number of the most important works by Russian and Polish scholars are now available. Both Lenin's (81) and Marx's (87) interpretations of peasants and their relationship to capitalist development are available, as well as Preobrazhensky's formulations (94) from the pre-Stalinist period on how to strengthen peasant production and use it to finance industrial growth. While these works are largely programmatic, Chayanov's (31) researches provided much data on the nature of the peasant village and family economics. More recently, Shanin has drawn on Russian sources to analyze the transformations of life in European Russia from the turn of the century up until 1925 (101). While providing his own insights into the permutations of rural life during this period, he also carefully sets forth what contemporary Russian scholars saw as problems and how they analyzed them at the time. The remarkable *Smolensk under Soviet Rule* (48) details the transformations of one *oblast* (region) under the Soviets by analyzing extensive documents captured by the German army during World War II. Additional contributions have been made by Stephen and Ethel Dunn (44) in translating into English material by contemporary Russian ethnologists and in Benet's (17) translation of the study of the Russian village of Viriatino, where Russian scholars conducted research both before and after the 1918 revolution. Also see the evaluation of this work by the Russian emigré ethnologist, Zil'berman (120), and replies by the Dunns (42, 43).

There has also been a substantial development of historical and sociological studies of rural society in Poland. This has been informed not only by research on the Polish rural population, but by Marxist theory and anglo-American anthropology as well. The historian Kieniewicz's study (75) of the effects of modern capitalist penetration into the Polish countryside in the nineteenth century is an excellent example of the nature of capitalism in a hinterland area, and Galeski's *Basic Concepts of Rural Sociology* (59) must be regarded as a major theoretical work on rural social organization and its permutations in the modern world.

Work by scholars in western Europe were better known and more accessible since German and French are more widely read in English-speaking countries. Nevertheless, translations of works such as Bloch's (20) on feudal Europe, Slicher van Bath's (106) on agrarian history, Braudel's (28) on Mediterranean Europe, Dovring's (40) on peasant farming, Mendras's (83, 90) on French peasants, and Elias's (46) work in English on state formation have done much to advance our understanding of social and economic aspects of rural life in Europe in the past and present.

Familiarity with these and related works by European scholars has had a threefold impact on anglophone anthropology. First, it has been useful in the very specific way of providing information about particular places in Europe at particular times. Second, because these scholars deal with larger areas and longer time spans than anthropologists usually deal with in their field research, their publications have served to help the anthropologist put his work into a wider perspective. Anthropologists have become more aware of the relationship of their communities and regions to long-term historical processes of national and international scope. This is reflected in many of the studies which have been conducted in Europe over the past 10 years (24, 35, 71, 93). Of course, this relationship has not been all one way. While rural sociologists and social historians are often interested in the same sort of interplay between social, political, economic, and ideological phenomena as anthropologists, they habitually look at these relationships in terms of regional or national aggregates and statistically determined trends. These often mask substantial variation both within communities or regions and between them. Detailed local studies help to make clear the rich variation in rural life which these aggregate approaches overlook.

Finally, the theoretical thrust of the European social science I have discussed above is to see rural communities and regions as integral parts of larger social entities. These investigations seek not only to describe the conditions of rural life, but to explain why they are the way they are. While they, too, sometimes speak of tenacious tradition as a deterrent to "progress," they are more likely to look to the nature of relations between rural communities and other social categories to explain rural life. These views developing in Europe have been congenial to those which have developed in America and Britain; in recent years there has been a growing dialogue between them.

The result has been that increasing numbers of Europeanist anthropologists and other social scientists working in Europe have found the boundaries of their academic disciplines confining. While continuing to publish in standard professional journals, these have not reached this growing international "antidisciplinary" audience. One result of this dissatisfection has been the formation of a series of new journals which focus on interests common to several established disciplines. The European Society for Rural Sociology was founded in 1957, and in 1960 it began publishing an international journal, *Sociologia Ruralis*. Today social scientists from many different disciplines, including anglophone anthropology, use its pages to communicate with one another. Other journals such as *Comparative Studies in Society and History, The Journal of Peasant Studies, Economy and Society,* the *Peasant Studies Newsletter,* and *Review,* while by no means exclusively concerned with European rural society, carry the kind of antidisciplinary and critical scholarship which is beginning to characterize the study of rural Europe.

The development of a world system divided into urban-industrial nation states and agrarian hinterlands is not simply a division between Europe and the rest of the world. Europe itself was divided into cores and peripheries. As capitalist nation states emerged in northwestern Europe they established economic dominance over southern Europe and contested eastern Europe with the Moscovite, Polish, and Ottoman empires that were already present. Capitalist penetration into these areas did not result in capital accumulation, industrialization, and mechanized agriculture there. But it did transform southern and eastern Europe as they became geared to production for export to the West. The peasantry did not become workers and farmers, but they were transformed into new types of peasantry, and new forms of elites arose to exploit the opportunities which the new economic relations presented. Accompanying these emerging forms of political economy were new ideologies. Conservatives glorified an idealized version of the past while liberals extolled the potential of capitalism to improve the human conditions and leftists of various sorts saw an unjust present giving way to a more human future through a radical transformation of society.

Moreover, relationships both within and between core and periphery were not static. The entire system was dynamic with changes in the core being matched by those in the peripheries. As mines and soils were depleted in one area, new resources were developed in another; peasant revolts in peripheries were matched by worker unrest in the cores; elites of different colors succeeded one another, changing internal policies and international allies; wars were fought; nationalist movements succeeded or failed; ethnic and regional minorities strived for rights, recognition, and special status; regions were transferred from one political system to another; new nations arose and old ones disappeared. It can hardly be assumed with conviction that rural communities anywhere in Europe have escaped with their social processes unchanged from the turbulence of the past few centuries. However, since few of the research reports which have been written about Europe have explicitly considered the relationship of local processes to large scale ones, much reevaluation is in order. Moreover, future research can expect to be examined for its effectiveness in analyzing such relationships.

CURRENT DIRECTIONS

Not all research being conducted in Europe today demonstrates all of the characteristics which I am suggesting here. But there has been a substantial increase in the awareness of the importance of looking at how village social processes have developed through time. A number of recent monographs and articles have explicitly advocated this and have quite successfully demonstrated how it can be done, and Davis, in his review of Mediterranean research, has fashioned an explicit argument for the necessity of incorporating historical perspectives into social anthropological analysis (38, pp. 239–58). At the same time, there are increasing numbers of studies which show an appreciation for the importance of understanding the nature of village integration into its regional setting. The best of the recent studies have shown an appreciation for both regional integration and for the way in which this has developed through time. Moreover, anthropological understanding of the large scale social processes in Europe has been expanding so that community and regional studies show more sophistication in investigating the interplay between local, regional, and national processes. In the final section of this paper I want to discuss briefly some of the specific works which seem to me to best exemplify these trends.

Northwestern Europe might be expected to bear the closest resemblance to the developmentalist perspective since it served as the model on which it was based. Amazingly enough, we find research in the twentieth century which reports on areas in Ireland, or in Britain itself, as if they were traditional and which have little or nothing to say about the relationship of community to nation, except to report changes going on in the present. There are exceptions. Frankenberg's (52) short yet detailed account of relations between classes and between locals and outsiders in a Welsh border village, in spite of its overall structural-functionalist tone and an absence of historical depth, shows a keen awareness of the integration of the community into British society. He does not use its remote location as a justification for regarding it as a traditional village, but instead looks at the nature of its linkages to the outside and how these are related to its internal processes. In similar fashion, in his later review of community studies in Britain, he does not accept researchers' assertions about the traditional state of their villages, but instead notes that each has in one way or another been integrated into the British polity and economy (53).

For Ireland, we now have Hecter's (67) detailed analysis of how that island has been tied to Britain since at least the sixteenth century in such a way as to siphon off capital and labor to benefit British development while simultaneously creating and perpetuating Irish poverty. Since for much of its history Ireland was directly under British rule, Hecter calls this relationship *internal colonialism.* Writing earlier than Hecter, but clearly thinking along the same lines, Gibbon (61) has used the occasion of the publication of several new Irish community studies to review the state of anthropological research on Ireland. Using information about agriculture, land holdings, and mental illness available from several statistical sources (including some available when the first research was conducted in the 1930s), he questions the assumption that *any* community in Ireland could have been traditional (the "real Ireland") in the twentieth century. Other investigators have seen harmonious, parochial communities, characterized by internal egalitarian relations and insulation from outside influences, still existing in the 1930s. But Gibbon finds cash cropping, high incidence of mental illness, and internal differentiation, all of which he attributes to the nature of their integration into the national political economy. On the basis of data he has assembled, he suggests that these conditions date *at least* to the turn of the century. This is in contrast to the modern studies he reviews, which see these as happening only in the present.

Gibbon's treatment of "cooring," usually presented as a traditional system of mutual aid between equals, is an example of the kind of rethinking of past analyses that needs to be carried out. He notes that farmers with larger holdings also participated in this system, and that there is some evidence that they exchanged mechanized labor for hand labor. Since farm machinery was in short supply, the farmers who owned it could control the timing of the exchange. Moreover, while the owner could carry out his end of the exchange by working alone with his machine, thus keeping his family at work at home, his partner in the exchange would have to reciprocate by turning out with his entire family. The exchange thus worked to the advantage of the big farmer since he could get all the labor he needed without having to hire it. ". . . in many respects the participation of the larger farmer in the cooring system seems to have represented for him a rational adjustment to the post-famine problem of maintaining plentiful supplies of labour for relatively undercapitalized holdings" (61, p. 487). He also suggests that its impact on the smaller farmers was demoralizing since it deflected their labor away from their own holdings. This may well have contributed to the well-documented decline of small scale agriculture and the high frequency of mental illness in Ireland.

While the evidence for Gibbon's interpretation is only suggestive, his analysis is plausible. This particular analysis will have to be tested by further research, but Hecter's detailed account of the transformations of Irish society, coupled with the questions Gibbon has raised about the validity of many of the conclusions presented in existing Irish community studies, should alert future research to the problems of community integration into the Irish political economy.

Developmentalist perspectives see modernization in the Mediterranean, the Alps, East Central Europe, and the Balkans as the result of diffusion. This process, developmentalists feel, is not yet complete because of culture lag and traditions which differ from those of northwestern Europe and which are more tenaciously resistant to change (e.g. 27, pp. 8–13). But instead we now see that these areas were in fact modernized beginning in the sixteenth century as their agriculture began to be redirected toward the requirements of capitalist core that was beginning to emerge in Western Europe. While Italy and the Iberian states were themselves core areas as capitalism began to emerge, they were reduced to peripheries by the seventeenth century. Since that time, as the Steins (110), among others (28), have pointed out, they became economic colonies of the industrializing northwestern core.

Alpine research, since its inception in the early 1960s, has had an ecological orientation. It has in the main been directed toward explaining the relationship between village social organization and patterns of exploitation of the Alpine environment. Thus it has not simply accepted local social processes as given, but has attempted to explain why they persist through time by examining them in relationship to local circumstances. Most of these studies are also concerned with the changes which are now taking place in the economic and political relations of these communities with the outside and have examined how both the use of local resources and local social organization have responded to these changing circumstances. While the idiom of tradition is sometimes used in these studies, it is in reference to these patterns of adaptation; that is, traditions here are explained rather than simply accepted as given (3, 58).

Research in the Alps has also been characterized by a concern with local history, and many of the studies have a time depth in their analysis which is not found in most community studies. However, past integration of these communities into large scale political and economic processes has been underplayed in most analysis. Instead of following Frankenberg's lead and showing how these communities, although remote, are integrated into the region, they rely on the concept of marginal location and isolation as a justification for concentrating almost exclusively on adaptation to local circumstances.

This does not seem to be warranted. Many upland communities were initially settled under the sponsorship of lowland elites, and in any case, the nature of their ongoing relationship with elites, with lowland communities, and with processes of regional and national integration have been major forces in shaping their social, economic, and political organization. Throughout the Alps, upland villages have relied on out-migration of up to 50 percent of each generation as a means of removing excess population from the villages and maintaining the viability of their social organization. Moreover, in most Alpine areas, substantial numbers of households depend on wage labor as a supplement to farm income. Some members of these households are regularly dispatched to the lowlands as workers to earn these wages. This suggests that upland communities are in fact serving as a labor reserve for the relatively urban and market oriented lowlands.

Such patterns are not new, but have been developing over the past several hundred years. Moreover, the nature of upland family organization, patterns of land tenure and inheritance, village political organization, and virtually every other aspect of upland life have developed not just in response to local conditions, but have grown out of the way in which environmental requirements have been balanced by villagers against pressures which emanate from the regional political economy (35).

Without a doubt, the Mediterranean region has attracted more anthropological attention than any part of Europe to its north, and this attention has resulted in some of the most successful recent community and regional studies. Davis's *Peoples of the Mediterranean* (38) evaluates the bulk of the research produced up to 1975. He thoroughly discusses each of the topics and issues that have concerned Mediterranean anthropologists, accurately presenting the work of others and adding his own penetrating insights. The work is intended not only to report on what has been done, but also draws attentions to problems and failures, and includes recommendations about what he feels are the most promising directions for future research. What he advocates is in accord with the thrust of this essay; in his words, this is the study "of the creation of history locally, of its reciprocal relation to national events and processes, of concomitant variation among a number of communities . . ." (38, pp. 256–57).

In this work, Davis specifically rejects the concept of tradition:

> Mediterranean social order does not therefore refer to an aboriginal society, the institutional equivalent to the grunts and glottal stops of some primordial language. Nor was it ever a complete social order, in the sense that there was a complete and uniform range of social institutions . . . It is, rather, those institutions, customs and practices which result from the conversation and commerce of thousands of years, the creation of the very different peoples who have come into contact around the Mediterranean shores (38, p. 13).

To this one can add that the populations of the Mediterranean on both the northern and southern shore have been drawn into economic and political relations with the northwestern European industrial core as markets and sources of raw materials (28, 114), as areas for colonization (18), and as sources of unskilled labor (29). The way in which peripheral status has developed in the Mediterranean has much to do with the characteristics of local and regional social processes there (100) and is what justifies it as a unit of study. In this light, the north shore has more in common with the south shore than it does with the industrial states across the Alps.

In the past three years a number of monographs have appeared which in varying degrees practice the kind of analysis that Davis and I are advocating. Davis's own analysis of social and economic relations in the south Italian town of Pisticci shows how these have grown largely out of the integration of the south into the Italian market economy (37). Blok's volume (21) and that of the Schneiders (98, 99) focus on the relationship between the growth of mafia and related social and economic institutions and the nature of western Sicily's past and present integration into the Italian and world political economy, and Silverman (105) has analyzed the development of the political economy of a central Italian hill town as a manifestation of its integration into the Italian state.

Other recent research has been directed toward the characterization of regional processes. Aya (7) has contributed a study of the failure of rural revolts in southern Spain and Sicily. He notes that these areas have experienced the same depredations from capitalist penetration as other areas where revolutions have succeeded, but here uprisings were suppressed. His comparison of success with failures stresses the relationship of the peasantry to public and private power holders and calls attention to variations in the political economy of different hinterland areas. At the other end of the Mediterranean, Markides (86) has documented the interplay between internal and external political and economic pressures which have molded life on the island of Cyprus. He focuses especially on political processes and skillfully traces how the movement for union with Greece during the British colonial period was diverted into an independence movement, and how Greek and Turkish interference in Cypriot affairs is related to the nature of local politics within the island. Finally, there is the encyclopedic assault on the regional variations within Greece edited by Dimen & Friedl (39). This contains over 40 contributions including reports of research on modern communities and regions, various topical essays, and some historical and prehistoric analyses. Although the contributions are uneven and there is no attempt at formulating an overview which would systematically account for the similarities and differences between areas and within areas through time, the possibility of developing such an analysis is implicit in the organization of the material into sections and in the content of many of the articles.

Eastern Europe, like the Mediterranean, has long been integrated into the economic sphere of western Europe. The Steins note that, "Paradoxically, as west European economic development brought social differentiation, mobility and greater personal freedom to peasant proprietors and urban and rural wage laborers, in peripheral areas of the west European economy, labor became more 'unfree.' In Central and eastern Europe it became the 'second serfdom.' In America it took various forms: encomienda, repartimento, mita, and ultimately debt peonage and slavery" (110, pp. 33–34). This insight, made in passing by the Steins, has been carefully documented in detailed studies of eastern Europe. For example, the Hungarian economists Berend & Ranki (19) have traced the penetration of capitalist economic relations in these areas, concentrating especially on the nineteenth and twentieth centuries. Their study details the way in which this penetration tied agricultural production in the East to the requirements of the West, inhibited the development of industry, and served to perpetuate the agrarian nature of these societies. These ties became especially intense as Eastern Europe was integrated into the German war economy during the decade before World War II.

Following the war, ties to the West were abruptly severed as Communist parties came to power in the various countries. While in the early years of Communist rule it appeared as if Eastern European states were carefully controlled "satellites" of the Soviet Union, it is now clear that each has its own distinctive brand of "socialism." This is theoretically expected and empirically demonstrable; the present social processes in these Eastern European states are the result of interaction of their distinctive pasts and geographical circumstances with their present Marxist-Leninist political economic organization and ideologies.

Because these societies explicitly promote the development of planned societies and reject Western models of development, and since they have in the past shared hinterland status with Third World areas such as Latin America, the potential rewards for Eastern European research are high. Moreover, opportunities for research there have expanded markedly in recent years although few full scale studies have yet appeared.

A recent monograph by the sociologist Daniel Chirot (32) traces the development of ties of dependency with the West in Wallachia, one of the regions which make up present-day Romania. Drawing on the theoretical model of Wallerstein (114) and the brilliant analyses of the Romanian sociologist Henri Stahl (109), Chirot explains that the so-called "traditional" or "feudal" social processes in Wallachia are in reality the product of its colonial status. While Chirot's analysis ends with World War I, his examination of the interplay of local and international processes is precisely the kind of analysis required if we are to come to grips with the way in which social processes have been formed, maintained, and transformed in Eastern

Europe. Other recent studies in Eastern Europe have been concerned with the integration of communities and regions into large scale processes, but have been less theoretically explicit on this point than Chirot. These include research on social transformation since the advent of communism in a county in the south of Romanian Transylvania (34); a study of contrasts in the kinds of social integration within Bosnian villages and between villages in the marketplace (84); and a study of social and economic transformations in a Slovenian village (117).

CONCLUSIONS

In this essay I have offered an explanation for the establishment of an "anglophone anthropology" of Europe and have traced its theoretical and methodological development. I have not attempted to provide complete coverage of Europeanist literature, or of the topics which interest Europeanists. My contention is that whether one is interested in household demography, inheritance patterns, peasant revolts, marriage customs, or anything else, the goal of research is to explain how phenomena come into being, how they have been perpetuated, or how they have been transformed. A reliance on the concepts of tradition and modernization will not provide this understanding since it is clear that what we have been calling "tradition" is a product of social forces, mostly of relatively modern origin. While much research in Europe continues to rely on these outmoded concepts, there has been an upswing in the number of studies which are informed by a more promising perspective. In this perspective the integration of community into regional and national processes is as decisive for community and region as local ecological and social relations. Regional processes, moreover, can be understood only in reference to the position of the region in the world political economy. Future research reports can expect to be evaluated in terms of how well they are able to explain local social phenomena in terms of the interrelationship of local, regional, national, and international pressures.

Acknowledgments

I wish to thank my colleagues in the Romanian Research Project at the University of Massachusetts—Sam Beck, David Kideckel, Marilyn McArthur, Marin Popescu, Steve Randall, and Steve Sampson—not only for their constructive criticism, but for allowing me to temporarily set aside our joint undertaking in order to complete this manuscript. I also want to thank Dick Woodbury for taking the trouble to ferret out the "Peasants' Revolt" letter for me from his file of *Newsletters.* Finally, I want to thank Ellan Cole, Sydel Silverman, and Eric Wolf for critical reading of the manuscript.

Literature Cited

1. Anderson, R. T. 1971. *Traditional Europe: A Study in Anthropology and History.* Belmont: Wadsworth. 195 pp.
2. Anderson, R. T. 1973. *Modern Europe: An Anthropological Perspective.* Pacific Palisades: Goodyear. 163 pp.
3. *Anthropological Quarterly* 1972. Dynamics of ownership in the circum-Alpine area. *Anthropol. Q.* (special issue) 45:117–205
4. Arensberg, C. M. 1963. The old world peoples: the place of European cultures in world ethnography. *Anthropol. Q.* 36:75–99
5. Arensberg, C. M. 1968. *The Irish Countryman.* Garden City: Natural History Press. 197 pp.
6. Arensberg, C. M., Kimball, S. T. 1968. *Family and Community in Ireland.* Cambridge: Harvard Press. 417 pp. Rev. ed.
7. Aya, R. 1975. *The missed revolution: The fate of rural rebels in Sicily and southern Spain.* Papers on European and Mediterranean Societies No. 3. Antropol.-Sociol. Centrum, Univ. Amsterdam. 159 pp.
8. Bailey, F. G. 1970. *Stratagems and Spoils: A Social Anthropology of Politics.* Oxford: Blackwell. 240 pp.
9. Bailey, F. G., 1971. *Gifts and Poison: The Politics of Reputation.* Oxford: Blackwell. 318 pp.
10. Bailey, F. G., ed. 1973. *Debate and Compromise: The Politics of Innovation.* Oxford: Blackwell. 343 pp.
11. Banfield, E. C. 1958. *The Moral Basis of a Backward Society.* New York: Free Press. 188 pp.
12. Barnes, J. A. 1954. Class and committees in a Norwegian island parish. *Hum. Relat.* 7:39–58
13. Barnes, J. A. 1972. *Social Networks.* Modular Publ. Anthropol. 26. Reading: Addison-Wesley. 29 pp.
14. Barth, F. 1966. *Models of Social Organization.* Occas. Pap. No. 23, R. Anthropol. Inst. 33 pp.
15. Bendix, R. 1967. Tradition and modernity reconsidered. *Comp. Stud. in Soc. Hist.* 9:292–347
16. Benedict, R. 1972. *Rumanian Culture and Behavior.* Occas. Pap. Anthropol. No. 1, Colorado State Univ. 55 pp.
17. Benet, S., ed. 1970. *The Village of Viriatino: An Ethnographic Study of a Russian Village from Before the Revolution to the Present.* Garden City: Doubleday. 300 pp.
18. Bennoune, M. 1976. The origin of the Algerian proletariat. *Dialectical Anthropol.* 1:201–24
19. Berend, I., Ranki, G. 1974. *Economic Development in East-Central Europe in the 19th and 20th Centuries.* New York, London: Columbia. 402 pp.
20. Bloch, M. 1961. *Feudal Society.* Chicago: Univ. Chicago Press. 2 vols. 498 pp.
21. Blok, A. 1975. *The Mafia of a Sicilian Village.* New York: Harper & Row. 293 pp.
22. Boissevain, J. 1973. Preface. See Ref. 25, pp. VII–XIII
23. Boissevain, J. 1974. *Friends of Friends: Networks, Manipulators and Coalitions.* Oxford: Blackwell. 285 pp.
24. Boissevain, J., Friedl, J., eds. 1975. *Beyond the Community: Social Process in Europe.* The Hague: Dep. Educ. Sci. The Netherlands. 184 pp.
25. Boissevain, J., Mitchell, J. C., eds. 1973. *Network Analysis: Studies in Human Interaction.* The Hague, Paris: Mouton. 271 pp.
26. Bott, E. 1971. *Family and Social Networks.* New York: Free Press. 363 pp.
27. Brandes, S. H. 1975. *Migration, Kinship, and Community: Tradition and Transition in a Spanish Village.* New York, London: Academic. 220 pp.
28. Braudel, F. 1972. *The Mediterranean and the Mediterranean World in the Age of Phillip II.* New York: Harper & Row. 1375 pp.
29. Castles, S., Kosack, G. 1973. *Immigrant Workers and Class Structure in Western Europe.* London: Oxford. 514 pp.
30. Chapman, C. G. 1971. *Milocca: a Sicilian Village.* Cambridge, London: Schenkman. 253 pp.
31. Chayanov, A. V. 1966. *The Theory of Peasant Economy.* Homewood, Ill: Irwin. 317 pp.
32. Chirot, D. 1976. *Social Change in a Peripheral Society: The Creation of a Balkan Colony.* New York, London: Academic. 179 pp.
33. Cole, J. W. 1973. Social process in the Italian Alps. *Am. Anthropol.* 75:765–86
34. Cole, J. W., Kideckel, D., Randall, S., Sampson, S., McArthur, M., Beck, S. 1976. Field work in Romania. *Dialectical Anthropol.* 1:239–85, 321–75
35. Cole, J. W., Wolf, E. R. 1974. *The Hidden Frontier: Ecology and Ethnicity in*

an *Alpine Valley.* New York: Academic. 348 pp.
36. Dalton, G. 1972. Peasantries in anthropology and history. *Curr. Anthropol.* 13:385–407
37. Davis, J. 1973. *Land and Family in a South Italian Town.* London: Athlone. 200 pp.
38. Davis, J. 1977. *People of the Mediterranean: An Essay in Comparative Anthropology.* London: Henley; Boston: Routledge & Kegan Paul. 288 pp.
39. Dimen, M., Friedl, E. 1976. *Regional variation in modern Greece and Cyprus: Toward a perspective on the ethnography of Greece.* Ann. NY Acad. Sci., Vol. 268. 465 pp.
40. Dovring, F. 1965. *Land and Labor in Europe in the Twentieth Century.* The Hague: Nijhoff. 511 pp.
41. du Boulay, J. 1974. *Portrait of a Greek Mountain Village.* Oxford: Clarendon. 296 pp.
42. Dunn, E. 1976. Reply to Zil'berman. *Dialectical Anthropol.* 1:157–60
43. Dunn, S. 1976. Reply to Zil'berman. *Dialectical Anthropol.* 1:155–56
44. Dunn, S., Dunn, E. 1974. *Introduction to Soviet Ethnography.* Berkeley: Highgate Road Soc. Sci. Res. Stn. 2 vols. 708 pp.
45. Eisenstadt, S. N. 1968. *Modernization: Protest and Change.* Englewood Cliffs: Prentice-Hall. 166 pp.
46. Elias, N. 1972. Processes of state formation and nation building. *Trans. 7th World Congr. Sociol.* Geneva: Int. Sociol. Assoc.
47. Elias, N., Scotson, J. L. 1965. *The Established and the Outsiders. A Sociological Inquiry into Community Problems.* London: Case. 199 pp.
48. Fainsod, M. 1958. *Smolensk under Soviet rule.* New York: Random House. 484 pp.
49. Fél, E., Hofer, T. 1969. *Proper Peasants: Traditional Life in a Hungarian Village.* Chicago: Aldine. 440 pp.
50. Firth, R. 1957. Introduction: Malinowski as scientist and as man. In *Man and Culture,* ed. R. Firth, pp. 1–14. London: Routledge & Kegan Paul. 292 pp.
51. Flannigan, P., Dupont, J., Valdez, J., Untermayer, H., Ivanovitc I. etc. etc. (sic) [pseudonyms]. 1972. Peasants' revolt. *Anthropol. Newsl.* 13 (1):4
52. Frankenberg, R. 1957. *Village on the Border: A Social Study of Religion, Politics and Football in a North Wales Community.* London: Cohen & West. 163 pp.

53. Frankenberg, R. 1966. *Communities in Britain: Social Life in Town and Country.* Baltimore: Penguin. 313 pp.
54. Franklin, S. H. 1969. *The European Peasantry: The Final Phase.* London: Methuen. 256 pp.
55. Freeman, S. T. 1970. *Neighbors: The Social Contract in a Castilian Hamlet.* Chicago, London: Univ. Chicago Press. 233 pp.
56. Freeman, S. T. 1973. Introduction. In *Studies in European Social Organization,* ed. S. T. Freeman. *Am. Anthropol.* 75:743–50
57. Freeman, S. T., Walters, L. W., compilers 1975. Europeanist social anthropologists in North America. *Am. Anthropol. Assoc. Spec. Publ. 13.* 34 pp.
58. Friedl, J. 1974. *Kippel: A Changing Village in the Alps.* New York: Holt, Rinehart & Winston. 129 pp.
59. Galeski, B. 1971. *Basic Concepts of Rural Sociology.* Manchester: Manchester Press. 209 pp.
60. Gellner, E. 1964. *Thought and Change.* London: Weidenfeld & Nicolson. 224 pp.
61. Gibbon, P. 1973. Arensberg and Kimball revisited. *Econ. Soc.* 2:479–98
62. Gluckman, M., ed. 1964. *Closed Systems and Open Minds: The Limits of Naïvete in Anthropology.* Chicago: Aldine. 274 pp.
63. Gluckman, M. 1968. The utility of equilibrium models in the study of social change. *Am. Anthropol.* 70:219–37
64. Golde, G. 1975. *Catholics and Protestants: Agricultural Modernization in Two German Villages.* New York, London: Academic. 198 pp.
65. Gouldner, A. W. 1970. *The Coming Crisis in Western Sociology.* New York: Avon. 528 pp.
66. Halpern, J. 1967. *The Changing Village Community.* Englewood Cliffs: Prentice Hall. 136 pp.
67. Hecter, M. 1975. *Internal Colonialism: The Celtic Fringe in British National Development 1536–1966.* Berkeley, Los Angeles: Univ. California Press. 361 pp.
68. Hobsbawm, E. J. 1969. *Industry and Empire.* Baltimore: Penguin. 384 pp.
69. Hobsbawm, E. J. 1973. Peasants and politics. *J. Peasant Stud.* 1:3–22
70. Hofer, T. 1970. Anthropologists and native ethnographers at work in central European villages. See Ref. 71, pp. 5–22
71. Honigmann, J. J., ed. 1970. Modernization and tradition in Central European rural cultures. *Anthropologica* (Ottawa) n.s. 12 (1). 148 pp.

72. Hunter, G. 1969. *Modernizing Peasant Societies: A Comparative Study in Asia and Africa.* New York, London: Oxford Press. 324 pp.
73. Hymes, D. 1974. The use of anthropology: critical, political, personal. See Ref. 74, pp. 3–82
74. Hymes, D., ed. 1974. *Reinventing Anthropology.* New York: Vintage. 470 pp.
75. Kieniewicz, S. 1969. *The Emancipation of the Polish Peasantry.* Chicago, London: Univ. Chicago Press. 285 pp.
76. Kluckhohn, C. 1961. *Anthropology and the Classics.* Providence: Brown Univ. Press. 76 pp.
77. Kroeber, A. L. 1948. *Anthropology.* New York, Burlingame: Harcourt, Brace & World. 856 pp.
78. Kuper, A. 1973. *Anthropologists and Anthropology: The British School 1922–72.* Baltimore: Penguin. 256 pp.
79. Landsberger, H., ed. 1973. *Rural Protest: Peasant Movements and Social Change.* New York: Barnes & Noble. 430 pp.
80. Leacock, E. B., ed. 1971. *The Culture of Poverty: A Critique.* New York: Simon & Schuster. 382 pp.
81. Lenin, V. I. 1972. *The Development of Capitalism in Russia.* Vol. 3 of *Lenin's Collected Works.* London: Wishart. 607 pp.
82. Lerner, D. 1958. *The Passing of Traditional Society.* New York: Free Press. 466 pp.
83. Lévi-Straus, L., Mendras, H. 1974. Survey of peasant studies: rural studies in France. *J. Peasant Stud.* 1:363–79
84. Lockwood, W. 1975. *European Moslems: Economy and Ethnicity in Western Bosnia.* New York, London: Academic. 241 pp.
85. Lopreato, J. 1967. *Peasants No More: Social Class and Social Change in an Underdeveloped Society.* San Francisco: Chandler. 281 pp.
86. Markides, K. C. 1977. *The Rise and Fall of the Cyprus Republic.* New Haven: Yale Univ. Press. 224 pp.
87. Marx, K. 1965. *Pre-Capitalist Economic Formations.* New York: International. 153 pp.
88. Mead, M. 1976. Introduction. In *Communal Families in the Balkans: The Zadruga,* ed. R. F. Byrnes, pp. xvii–xxvii. Notre Dame, London: Univ. Notre Dame Press. 285 pp.
89. Mead, M., Metraux, R., eds. 1953. *The Study of Culture at a Distance.* Chicago, London: Univ. Chicago Press. 480 pp.

90. Mendras, H. 1970. *The Vanishing Peasantry: Innovation and Change in French Agriculture.* Cambridge: MIT Press. 289 pp.
91. Mitchell, J. C. 1974. Social networks. *Ann. Rev. Anthropol.* 3:279–99
92. Moore, B. Jr. 1966. *The Social Origins of Dictatorship and Democracy: Lord and Peasant in the Making of the Modern World.* Boston: Beacon. 559 pp.
93. Pi Sunyer, O., ed. 1971. *The limits of integration: ethnicity and nationalism in modern Europe. Univ. Mass. Dep. Res. Rep. 9.* 186 pp.
94. Preobrazhensky, E. 1965. *The New Economics.* Oxford: Clarendon. 310 pp.
95. Rodnick, D. 1948. *Postwar Germans.* New Haven: Yale Univ. Press. 233 pp.
96. Rostow, W. W. 1960. *The Stages of Economic Growth: A Non-Communist Manifesto.* Cambridge: Cambridge Univ. Press. 179 pp.
97. Sanders, I. 1949. *Balkan Village.* Lexington: Univ. Kentucky Press. 291 pp.
98. Schneider, J. 1971. Of vigilance and virgins: honor, shame and access to resources in Mediterranean societies. *Ethnology* 10:1–24
99. Schneider, J., Schneider, P. 1976. *Culture and Political Economy in Western Sicily.* New York, London: Academic. 256 pp.
100. Schneider, P., Schneider, J., Hansen, E. 1972. Modernization and development: the role of regional elites and noncorporate groups in the European Mediterranean. *Comp. Stud. Soc. Hist.* 14:328–50
101. Shanin, T. 1972. *The Awkward Class.* Oxford: Clarendon. 253 pp.
102. Shanin, T., ed. 1971. *Peasants and Peasant Societies.* Harmondsworth: Penguin. 448 pp.
103. Shanin, T., Worsley, P. 1972. Editors' preface. See Ref. 59, pp. vii–xvi
104. Silverman, S. 1974. Bailey's politics: review article. *J. Peasant Stud.* 2:111–20
105. Silverman, S. 1975. *Three Bells of Civilization: The Life of an Italian Hill Town.* New York, London: Columbia Univ. Press. 263 pp.
106. Slicher van Bath, B. H. 1963. *The Agrarian History of Western Europe, A.D. 500–1850.* New York: St. Martin's. 364 pp.
107. Smith, C. A., ed. 1976. *Regional Analysis.* Vol. 1, *Economic Systems,* 370 pp.; Vol. 2, *Social Systems,* 381 pp. New York, London: Academic
108. Spencer, R. F., Johnson, E. 1968. *Atlas*

for Anthropology. Dubuque: Brown. 61 pp. 2nd ed.

109. Stahl, H. H. 1969. *Les anciennes communautés villageoises roumaines.* Bucharest, Paris: Académie Roumaine and C.N.R.S.

110. Stein, S., Stein, B. 1970. *The Colonial Heritage of Latin America.* New York: Oxford. 222 pp.

111. Swartz, M., ed. 1968. *Local Level Politics.* Chicago: Aldine. 437 pp.

112. Theodoratus, R. J. 1969. *Europe: A Selected Ethnographic Bibliography.* New Haven: HRAF. 544 pp.

113. Tipps, D. C. 1973. Modernization theory and the study of national societies: a critical perspective. *Comp. Stud. Soc. Hist.* 15:199–226

114. Wallerstein, I. 1974. *The Modern World System: Capitalist Agriculture and the Origins of the European World-Economy in the Sixteenth Century.* New York, London: Academic. 410 pp.

115. Wallerstein, I. 1974. The rise and future demise of the world capitalist system: concepts for comparative analysis. *Comp. Stud. Soc. Hist.* 16:387–415

116. White, L. A., ed. 1937. Extracts from the European travel journals of Lewis H. Morgan. *Rochester Hist. Soc. Publ.* 16:219–289

117. Winner, I. 1971. *A Slovenian Village: Zerovnica.* Providence: Brown Univ. Press. 267 pp.

118. Wolf, E. R. 1969. *Peasant Wars of the Twentieth Century.* New York: Harper & Row. 328 pp.

119. Wolf, E. R. 1974. American anthropologists and American society. See ref. 74, pp. 251–263

120. Zil'berman, D. 1976. Ethnography in Soviet Russia. *Dialectal Anthropol.* 1:135–53

Ann. Rev. Anthropol. 1977. 6:379–97
Copyright © 1977 by Annual Reviews Inc. All rights reserved

RECENT RESEARCH ON THE ORIGIN OF THE STATE

❖9599

Henry T. Wright

Museum of Anthropology, University of Michigan, Ann Arbor, Michigan 48109

To explain the origin of primary states—those which arise in a context of interacting prestate societies—has remained an objective of anthropologists since the publication of Morgan's *Ancient Society* (35) 100 years ago. It is a fundamental problem which, though it cannot have an ultimate solution, serves as a measure against which to evaluate the effectiveness of new perspectives and new methods. The centennial of Morgan's publication has not inspired comprehensive new explanatory theories or research insights, but it has been marked by a synthesis of past work, by provocative restatements of extant theoretical approaches, and by the testing of proposed explanations derived from these approaches utilizing new methods. This review begins with a commentary on a recent synthesis, discusses definitional problems, and assesses recent research on several cases of state development. In conclusion, it is argued that recent research has already obviated some of the positions taken in the synthesis and has clarified the directions which future theory-building and research must take.

A RECENT SYNTHESIS OF STATE ORIGINS

Let us begin with a consideration of *The Origins of the State and Civilization* by Service (44), not simply because it is the culmination of 40 years of a scholar's thought or because I consider it conceptually or methodologically successful. It is most important because its conclusions both summarize some conditions of early state emergence which all explanations must take into account, and exemplify some possible weaknesses of existing positions. Service focuses on the origins of "government." A government is defined as "a bureaucracy instituted to rule a populace by right of authority" (44, p. 10), a bureaucracy being a hierarchy of offices (44, p. 72). Government begins with the first institutionalization of centralized leadership in "chiefdoms." Societies in this evolutionary stage "have centralized direction, hierarchical status arrangements with an aristocratic ethos, but no formal legal apparatus of forceful repression" (44, p. 16). "This political power organized the economy . . .

379

and it was a redistributive, an allocative system, not an acquisitive system . . ." (44, p. xiii). For Service, the origin of the state turns on the question of the use of force as an institutionalized sanction. However, "good government is not necessarily or evidently a repressive body since a responsible control of violence equals peace" (44, p. 307). Indeed, in his consideration of the archaeologically attested archaic civilizations, Service finds that state origin defined in terms of forceful repression is not evidenced in the existing data.

After considering many cases of the development of institutionalized government, both ethnohistoric and archaeological, Service presents a series of conclusions which he divides into positive and negative. His "negative conclusions" usefully emphasize some general conditions which all efforts to explain state origins must take into account (44, pp. 266–89).

1. Warfare as a motivation for cooperation and an eliminator or subjugator of less effective organizations is universal in human development and cannot by itself explain state emergence.
2. Intensification of production, and in particular irrigation agriculture, long precedes state emergence as a technique of local production units and only becomes a major focus of societal investment and higher political concern after state emergence.
3. Growth, particularly population growth, is an enabling or necessary condition of state emergence, but not a causative condition. (However, Service provides little argument or evidence in defense of this as a general point.)
4. Urbanism, considered as population nucleation, evidently follows state origin and is correlated with the pattern and intensity of warfare between existing states.
5. Class stratification and consequent repression to protect the privileged class is a construct not useful in consideration of state origins since the classes of early civilizations are governmentally rather than economically based and repression by a government to protect itself cannot be an explanation of that government's development.

Service's "positive conclusions" are a logical chain (44, pp. 290–308) beginning with the point that inequality is basic and even the simplest society periodically requires its more esteemed members to act as leaders. Leadership becomes a regular activity when it is linked to the pooling and redistribution of commodities. When the office of leader comes to be regularly filled, typically by inheritance, a chiefdom has emerged. If a state is anything more than this, it is a society in which coercion is used to correct chiefly failures. In the gradually developing archaic civilizations, the point of actual state emergence is not easily definable, as befits its relative unimportance.

It would be fair to infer that, for Service, the origin of chiefdoms is the key problem. Indeed, many of the recently published or circulated short papers seem more relevant to this problem than to that of state emergence itself. While this is not a review of chiefly origins, one must commence with a consideration of some recent work on "complex" or developed chiefdoms and their operation. In contrast, we must also consider what minimally constitutes a state and how these operate. This contrast will show that states can be recognized by many characteristics in addition to those related to coercion. Definitions based upon such other characteristics may be more useful in guiding research on state origins than is the classical definition adopted by Service. Only after such taxonomic discussions can we focus on ongoing research on evolutionary developments.

CHIEFDOMS AND STATES

In the static conceptualization of traditional anthropology, a complex chiefdom is recognized as a society with ranked classes in which membership is ascriptive. High offices are filled from the most prestigious class. However, if one is interested in change, he must define his phenomena in terms of processes through time. As our interest is in political evolution, we must look at that process which controls other processes: at the central decision-making or regulatory activity of the system of activities, rather than at groups, institutions, or roles. In this perspective a chiefdom can be recognized as a cultural development whose central decision-making activity is differentiated from, though it ultimately regulates, decision-making regarding local production and local social process; but is not itself internally differentiated. It is thus externally but not internally specialized (54, p. 267). Lacking internal specialization, any delegation of decision-making prerogatives is a complete delegation, and the subordinate decision-maker would be capable of independent action. The dominant strategy of decision-making with regard to lower level organization is that there should be only two levels of actual decision-making hierarchy—local and central—and that local units should handle as many of their own operations as possible, each placing few demands on the central regulator and thus allowing it to control a larger number of local units given its limited capacity or span of control. One way to do this is to adjust local unit territories so that all of them have access to most resources and there is little exchange between units (20). In practice, as a successful paramount consolidates broader control or as a declining paramount approaches his death, intermediate levels of hierarchy do operate. Through time one would expect cycling from two to three levels of actual hierarchy. The symbolized hierarchy of chiefly offices may recognize three or more levels of hierarchy; however, such should not be confused with the actual hierarchy of decision-making.

How might higher level decision-making regulate those local unit problems beyond the capacities of the local regulators? No general study either theoretical or empirical has been done, but there are some provocative case studies. In one case in Hawaii, Peebles & Kus (38) have argued that the general condition of local production is signaled by the flow from local units of materials and craft goods useful for elite display (Figure 1). As food production is intensified, as in response to increased population, fewer craft materials and goods can be produced and the decreased flow will signal the difficulties before they become critical for the sphere of subsistence production. The goods are redistributed by the paramount to other members of the ranking class. If the amount redistributed is seen to decrease, either

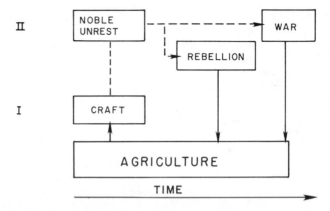

Figure 1 A diagram of an aspect of regulation in a Hawaiian chiefdom. The dotted lines represent the movement of information between spatially discrete activities, while the solid lines represent movement of material or labor.

the members of this class may foment a rebellion to replace the paramount or he may pursue a war in order to acquire more resources. Thus in this analysis goods redistribution is an element in second-level regulation. Regardless of the action pursued and of its success or failure, the indirect result will be similar: a reduction of population of both commoners and of troublesome nobility and some adjustment of the relation between consumers and production.

This analysis has several interesting features. First, the participants in this regulatory system probably did not cognize that chiefly political activity was ultimately triggered, via the flow of certain goods, by problems at the local level, and that this activity would result in a solution for these problems. Insofar as the regulatory system is thus hidden, the participants cannot falsify information or otherwise tamper with it (40). Second, the flow of goods is a result of production secondary to sustenance production for local needs. As such it transmits information in simplified form derived from the local or primary regulatory process. However, the impact of chiefly activity, insofar as population is lost or resources are increased, is directly on local unit production, rather than first on the local decision-making process and then on production. Third and parenthetically, note that the central decision-maker does not regulate a "redistributional economy" in the strict sense, pooling sustenance resources and provisioning local units. Whatever the importance of such redistribution in simple chiefdoms and in more complex states, what is termed "redistribution" in complex chiefdoms is extraction or mobilization of sustaining resources involving minimal central decision-making (21).

To this point, the complex chiefdom has been presented in isolation. Such may exist on favored islands, but they do not seem to develop into states until they are drawn into a larger system. Our concern is with networks of chiefdoms regulated by warfare and alliance. Most ethnographically reported chiefdoms seem to be involved in constant warfare. In contrast, archaeologically documented cases—

traditionally termed "cults" (8) but more recently viewed as "interaction spheres" (13)—may represent networks with more emphasis on alliance than on warfare.

Now let us turn to states. If in examining the traditional definitions of states one looks beyond ephemeral corrective mechanisms such as institutionalized coercion or law, one finds frequent reference to "specialized government." This static conceptualization can be phrased in terms of processes through time. In contrast to a developed chiefdom, a state can be recognized as a cultural development with a centralized decision-making process which is both externally specialized with regard to the local processes which it regulates, and internally specialized in that the central process is divisible into separate activities which can be performed in different places at different times. Aspects of decision-making can be delegated with minimal fear that subordinate elements in the hierarchy will engage in effective independent action. Indeed, the dominant political strategy in higher-order decision-making is to encourage as much hierarchy and segmentation as possible in order to create contexts of organic solidarity. This organizational strategy is reinforced by a complementary lower-order decision-making strategy of insuring supporting resources by attacking or undermining equivalent, or if possible higher-order, decision-makers. With the wealth of regulatory capacity in a state development, the control of many local units and the administration of exchange economies or redistribution from pools of sustenance products is not difficult. Indeed, the specialization of production activities, in essence "urbanism" (52, pp. 1–6), is merely an expected extension of the specialization of the strategy of central decision-making to local processes. Given the pervasiveness of state regulatory structures, one would expect the short-term fluctuation in the number of levels of hierarchy characteristic of chiefdoms to be less pronounced. In any development's history, as the opposed strategies of lower- and higher-order relation interact, an almost continual increase in hierarchical complexity would be expected.

Does higher-order decision-making in states regulate local processes in a different way than in chiefdoms? There are, as before, no general studies either theoretical or otherwise and few case studies in the world of primitive states. Most anthropological studies focus on roles and their relationships rather than actual activities, regulatory or otherwise. Let us take as an example a single activity—irrigation canal construction—in the state of Larsa on a branch of the Euphrates River in the reign of King Sumuel, about 1880 B.C. This regulatory system is known to us through the study of a fragmentary archive by Walters (48). These cuneiform documents detail the relations between one Nur-Sin, an administrator close to the king, and Lu-igisa, one of his several assistants in charge of canal construction and maintenance, as well as letters to the latter from one Išar-Kubi, a higher level inspector of canal work. Such a study of the "waste paper" of administration directly documents actual activities, though interpretation is fraught with philological and historical difficulties. While Walters' study has such difficulties, it may be more interesting to anthropologists than other examples of administration because of its focus on irrigation. Canal construction—or reconstruction—begins with a survey and estimate of the amount of earth to be moved by the Inspector (Figure 2). Using set formulae, information condensed from centuries of experience with canals in

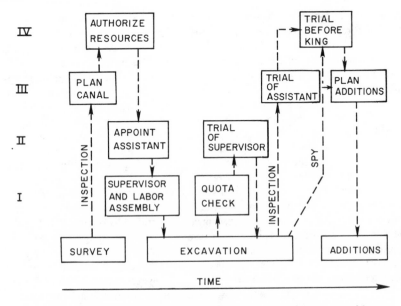

Figure 2   A diagram of the regulation of canal construction in the state of Larsa.

Mesopotamia, he estimates the man-days required and the resources, either grain or silver to buy grain, needed to sustain the workers. The Inspector then authorizes the Administrator to draw the resources and appoint one of the assistants to organize the job. The Assistant assembles the laborers, sometimes with the help of what seems to be an outside labor broker, and the actual work supervisors, the agents of first level regulation. Work quotas are assigned and actual progress is monitored frequently. If necessary, the Assistant requests that the Administrator use his police powers to bring supervisors before the Assistant for trial, an aspect of second level regulation. As work nears completion, the Assistant reports progress to the Inspector. The Inspector checks the actual work and either approves, asks that more be done, or asks the Administrator that the Assistant be brought to trial, these all being elements in third level regulation. After checking for himself, the Administrator can hear the case or carry the dispute before the King for fourth level regulation. The King seems to receive private information on actual work of this sort from a traveling judge. If the schedule has not been met, one of these trials will specify who must provide further support for more workers to finish the job.

This single area of state operation is different in a number of striking ways from the chiefly example previously outlined. First, the information on the activity from planning to completion and at all levels of regulation is public between two or more of the participants, and falsification is advantageous to some participants. Higher-order regulators attempted to detect falsification and distortion by taking information from both lower-order regulators and from independent sources and cross-checking the two. Second, except in the case of the initial survey, higher-order regulators use summary information from both lower-order regulators and their own brief inspections. Their decisions take the form of changing the actual assistant-in-charge, or of alloting fines which are to be used as resources to do more work, or both. Thus summary information is handed down to lower-order regulators, but there is no evidence of direct control of the basic work of canal construction. Third, regulation three steps removed from the work seems to involve the complementary activities of two figures: the Administrator does not officially inspect the assistants and canal work supervisors, and the Inspector does not have police powers to bring people to trial. Neither can work without the other, and either would find it difficult to abuse canal work for personal ends. The two figures can be thought of as the victims of the dominant political strategy of creating specialization in order to minimize the autonomy of subordinates. In opposition to this higher strategy, these figures and their subordinates follow the complementary strategy of attacking equivalent figures in related segments, as illustrated by the bad personal relations between Nur-Sin, the Administrator, and Išar-Kubi, the Inspector. The fact that the former seems to control the specialized police apparatus which the latter must request casts some light on the "monopoly of force". Both chiefdom and state ruling apparatuses can bring coercive force, though by no means a monopoly thereof, to bear on activities; however, in states there are specific types of force which can be used only by certain officials.

To this point we have talked about states in isolation, but they, like chiefdoms, usually exist in networks of states. Among simple states these networks seem to be regulated by competition and alliance, as was briefly noted for chiefdoms. A difference is that developing state networks are periodically centralized into a single political unit incorporating most previously existing polities. Such polities, which may be termed "empires," have many interesting features, but they are not of direct concern in this review.

Finally, this definitional discussion raises several points relevant to Service's work and to any future attempt to explain state origins. First, networks of both complex chiefdoms and simple states can be viewed as systems with several levels of self-regulation theoretically capable of oscillating endlessly without increase in complexity. One cannot merely assume that chiefdoms will develop inevitably into states; one must isolate the conditions which destroy or transform chiefly mechanisms of regulation and generate new ones. Second, states differ from chiefdoms in many ways, among which I have noted regulatory pattern, regulatory strategy, hierarchical structure, and oscillation of hierarchical pattern in time. Many of these differences are archaeologically detectable, and there is no reason why the period of state origin in any particular historical sequence cannot be specified. Such is not an idle taxonomic exercise since if one cannot specify when the state begins, one cannot begin to reject explanatory hypotheses. Third, any proposed explanation of state emergence must account for not only a single change in coercive mechanism, but for a whole series of changes in a subsystem of variables, each differently related to changing variables in the large "environmental" context. The review of selected recent research on state origins will show that work has focused almost exclusively on these variables of the larger systemic context.

SOME RECENT RESEARCH

How many cases of the emergence of primary states—states which evolve in a context of interacting chiefdoms—occurred on this planet? The question is unanswerable, not because there are evidences of "lost civilizations" waiting to be discovered in unknown corners of the world, but because some of the familiar cases of state origin are not yet understood, even in the most minimal sense. For example, we do not know whether there were one, two, or more essentially independent centers of primary states emerging in Andean America; we know virtually nothing about the history of primary state emergence in West Africa, etc. Even were present understanding extended beyond the more intensively studied areas, comprehensive review would be beyond both the capacities of any one research worker and beyond the limitations of this short review.

Greater Mesopotamia is archaeologically unusual in that the administration of the economy is directly attested in the occurrence of unbaked clay sealings, counting devices, and (later in the development) of clay tablets with written information. Each such discarded item represents an administrative act. However, research has not focused on administration. Most workers have chosen the more general topics such as "urbanism" or "civilization" as an object of research. The origin of the state has been a neglected topic.

The state as I have defined it emerged in Greater Mesopotamia—the watersheds of the Tigris, Euphrates, and Karun Rivers—at the beginning of the Uruk Period approximately 3700 B.C., almost two millennia before the reign of Sumuel of Larsa. Mesopotamianists have long known that the Uruk or Early Protoliterate Period was one of fundamental change in art and architecture (27), but the political institutions were thought to be small-scale and theocratic, rather like those of chiefdoms (1, pp. ix–130; also 46, 50). State government was thought to have arisen about 2500 B.C. when recognizable dynasties of kings are recorded. This documentation, and the parallel archaeological documentation of palaces and tombs, is deceptive. It reflects the increasing versatility and political use of writing in the later Third Millennium B.C. and the widespread exposure of Third Millennium layers near the surfaces of town sites in southern Iraq. In fact, the study of the distribution of seals and sealed items on sites of both the Middle and Late Uruk in both northern Iraq, ancient Assyria (45), and southwestern Iran, ancient Elam (54, pp. 270–72), indicates that an administration controlled the movement of goods from production points to assembly points and thence to central points for aggregation and subsequent redistribution. In southwestern Iran where Middle Uruk Susa, a center of about 5000, dominated a population of 20,000 or more, we know that invoice records were sent to centers for checking and if necessary adjudication, and that some form of summary records were kept, presumably for the use of yet higher authorities. Thus above production there was regulation at least at the level of assembly, aggregation and adjudication, and planning by a higher authority, each step using summary information from that below. Conversely, there was redistribution of goods from these centers down to the level of production units through various channels (54, p. 272).

What social units did Uruk administrative networks control? Each had a major center in an agriculturally rich area, within which was a network of smaller administrative centers and production centers. Production in these networks was differently organized. For example, while some settlements seemed to be primarily concerned with agriculture and moved their products through central pools into redistribution networks, parts of central settlements were concerned with ceramics production and moved their products to agricultural settlements by nonredistributional means (28, pp. 107–29). The major centers, furthermore, controlled small centers in distant areas, some of which had special resources (53) and some of which were on important travel routes (51).

From what did Middle Uruk states arise? No more than four centuries earlier, Mesopotamia proper was occupied by communities of the later 'Ubaid Period. In southwestern Iran, during one of the most complex florescences of this period, the Susa A Phase of the Susiana Plain, a center of about 2000 people dominated an area with more than 10,000 inhabitants. The center was dominated by a solid brick platform on whose summit, 10 meters above the other surrounding residences, were a large and elaborate residence, a storage area, and a possible temple. Smaller versions of such residences on platforms are attested at a number of earlier and contemporary small sites. This pattern probably indicates a discrete class of ranking families. There were few if any settlements in the nearby valleys, and it is unlikely that Susa controlled areas beyond the limits of its plain. Within the plain we find evidence of the regulation of goods movement at both the large center and the smaller settlements; however, the same seals and seal impressions are found in both types of settlement, indicating only that goods storage and redistribution were locally authorized and carried out. At present there is no evidence of the administered movement of goods from smaller settlements to the center. At most there is one level of regulatory hierarchy above the level of production regulation itself. Since all excavated settlements exhibit evidence of agriculture, stone blade working, and fabric production, and most have evidence of pottery manufacture, there would be minimum need for movement of goods and minimum need for administration (54, p. 273).

The evidence from both repeated intensive archaeological survey and limited excavation, upon which these contrasting presentations of state and prestate organization are based, was recovered by 1971 and was publicly available by 1973. These data allowed the rejection of "prime mover" explanations involving population growth and long range trade (54), though it must be emphasized that further investigation of such factors with new methods and new data sets is necessary. Research since that date has focused primarily on the further study of Middle and Late Uruk organization and secondarily upon hypotheses designed to explain the development of Uruk states. In southwestern Iran, more has been learned about the later Uruk as a result of continuing excavations at Susa by the Delégation Archéologique Française en Iran and of nearby sites by H. J. Kantor and P. Delougaz of the University of Chicago and UCLA, E. O. Negahban of the University of Tehran, and G. A. Johnson of the City University of New York (4–6). The preliminary announcements show that the types of sites, the internal arrangements of activities on sites, and the economic and political relations between sites are even more complex than outlined above. In southern Iraq, recent survey by Adams of the University of Chicago has revealed an Uruk development on a short-lived channel of the Tigris. Documentation of this settlement system and the large late Uruk system around the city of Uruk itself (2) with the evidence of excavations is vital to our understanding of the first Mesopotamia state network, but it is likely that key sites will be destroyed by agro-industrial development before such work can be undertaken. In northern Iraq there has been no recently reported work. This remains the only region not covered by comparably intensive archaeological survey techniques, a sad fact which severely limits the uses to which the unparalleled excavation data from the area (45) may be put.

The systems evident during Middle and Late Uruk times must have arisen during the preceding Early Uruk Period, and the data needed to test hypotheses explaining their rise must be recovered from Early Uruk sites and preceding Terminal 'Ubaid or Terminal Susa A sites of the first half of the Fourth Millennium B.C. There is evidence that, at the beginning of this time, throughout the lowlands there was abandonment of the smaller valleys and decline in the total amount of settled population, and there is also widespread evidence of minor conflict (55). On the Susiana Plain only a few isolated centers including Susa survive, each with a few surrounding smaller settlements, the whole plain having a population of about 6000 people. Recent research indicates that during the Early Uruk Period Susa itself shrank and several small centers on the southern plain grew. The result is a closely spaced pattern of small centers and villages. Unfortunately, our evidence for administration consists of a few sealings and counters from a small settlement. The question of what factors operated during this period of disorganization and subsequent growth such that there was a transformation in the organization of regulatory activities cannot be answered with one tiny sample.

However, work has been undertaken on two possible factors. First the question of what happened to the people who abandoned the Late 'Ubaid and Late Susiana communities raises the possibility that they became transhumant pastoralists. Could an increase in the number of pastoralists appearing every winter in the lowlands put pressure on the regulatory institutions of the settled enclaves? Several archaeological programs directed at the early history of pastoralism are now being undertaken in the Zagros Mountains (36, 56) and the deserts to the south of the Euphrates (34). While no one has completely overcome the formidable problems of locating nomad sites and assessing their relative density, and while none of these programs are finished, no researcher has claimed increased evidence of pastoralists early in the Fourth Millennium. While pastoralists may be present, it is difficult to conceive of them as a major factor. Second, the change to more standardized and usually undecorated ceramics at the beginning of the Uruk raises the possibility that the centralization of craft production, whatever its stimulus, led to complementary specialization in other areas of production, and concomitant patterns of exchange created pressures for a transformation in the regulatory system. However, it is undeniable that we cannot comprehensively document one Early Uruk craft, from workshop evidence or otherwise, and we are not certain when the state emerged during the Early Uruk Period, so the relations between these productive and regulatory subsystems remain unclear. There is a need for data from excavations on Early Uruk communities; without them one cannot even properly define the problem.

In summary, research has defined—though not as accurately as it could and must be defined—the period of state emergence in Greater Mesopotamia. Several simple propositions about one or a few variables acting upon the regulatory system have been tested; others are in the process of being investigated. Workers in this area now face the problem of constructing and testing possible explanations in which it is not the variables themselves but the interaction between a number of variables and their interaction with various elements of regulatory systems which are important. Progress in this area will require both more sophisticated theoretical constructs and more research, both in-depth research on Early Uruk systems and broader research to bring understanding of the different developing societies of the interregional network to an equivalent level throughout greater Mesopotamia.

In Mesoamerica, much useful evidence of political organization comes from carved stone monuments, many of which record events in the lives of rulers and the histories of politics. However, these are common only in a few areas and, since the administration of production is not directly attested by an administrative technology, the understanding of regulatory systems will require the patient application of standard archaeological techniques. This work will be facilitated by the fact that there is a direct historical continuity from Formative times until the Spanish conquest in much of Mesoamerica, and the ethnohistoric record provides useful hypotheses as to the uses of artifacts and the meaning of symbols.

Most recent research in Mesoamerica has focused on Early and earlier Middle Formative societies, which are widely recognized to have been chiefdoms (43), and on the developed states of the Classic Period, rather than on the interesting developments of the Late and Terminal Formative Periods. State emergence is indicated in the area by the rise everywhere of large centers dominating three or more subsidiary levels of settlement hierarchy. These centers characteristically have major secular architecture, and some have monuments indicating new and expansive forms of territorial control. For example, state emergence thus defined probably emerged in Oaxaca (26, pp. 215–19) about 300 B.C., during Late Formative times in the Valley of Mexico (19, 37), and highland Guatemala (42) about 100 B.C. during Terminal Formative times, and elsewhere during the early Classic Period after A.D. 200. In this review, I want to consider central Oaxaca for two reasons. First, there are a number of classes of evidence relating to administration. Second, much new analysis of this evidence, particularly of that relating to prestate societies, is assembled in a recent work edited by Flannery (23).

In central Oaxaca, by 100 B.C., the end of the Monte Alban I Period and the beginning of the Monte Alban II Period, the great center of Monte Alban on a high mountain top overlooking the three arms of the Valley of Oaxaca is well established (9, 16). The central ceremonial area and the various wards of the city are clearly differentiated. The overthrow of centers, some of which appear to be outside the Valley of Oaxaca (33), was commemorated by the erection of monuments in the central area. The city itself has massive defensive walls. Within each arm of the valley there are large subsidiary centers with differentiated palaces, temples, and other buildings (26), smaller centers, and hamlets. Is this type of settlement hierarchy, architectural pattern, and pattern of monument construction definitive evidence that the Monte Alban II polity was a state? Insofar as three levels of hierarchy above the level of hamlets implies that paramount rulers were making decisions about other decision-makers, probably using summary information for both assessment and decision implementation, we can say that there must have been both internal and external specialization of the central regulatory subsystem by this time. However, one would prefer evidence of the actual hierarchy of regulation. Such will probably become available only when intermediate centers are excavated and the path of products from center to center are traced and associated with elite households and public buildings in the centers. In addition, the identification of particular elite families and the tracing of their members from place to place through the study of tombs may prove to be useful. At present, with data only on Monte Alban itself (9, 16) and from various small settlements (18, 23), it is not possible to pursue these types of study.

What did the Terminal Formative state control? Intensive archaeological survey of the valley is not yet complete, but from extrapolation of the completed surveys, the population of the whole valley by 100 B.C. must have been around 50,000 people (31, 47). For the first time in more than a millennium of village life in the valley, much of the population lived on the upper piedmont near streams useful for small scale canal irrigation, as opposed to the well irrigation of the main river alluvium (25). Whether or not there was some specialization in crops between these two parts of the valley, with more maize in the piedmont and other crops in the alluvium, is not certain. However, it is clear that the large population of Monte Alban itself, high on its rocky and poorly watered mountain, must have received food from the smaller valley settlements. Village craft specialization is revealed most outstandingly in the villages close to localized sources of clay and chert in the various arms of the valley. There is little evidence for craft specialists on Monte Alban itself. The degree to which such specialization in agriculture and craft would compromise the autonomy of the smaller settlements and the arms of the valley is not certain. Indeed, the positive evidence of Monte Alban's location and the iconography of its monuments could be taken to indicate that its rulers were far more concerned with conflict and conquest than with the administration of their state's economy.

From what did the early Oaxacan state arise? The recently defined Rosario Phase, which began a century or so before the founding of Monte Alban and 450 years before state florescence during the Monte Alban II Period, is not yet as well documented as the earlier and simpler chiefdom of the San José Phase. In comparison with Middle Formative chiefdoms elsewhere in Mesoamerica, for example in Veracruz, polities were small, incorporating perhaps 4000 people in one arm of the valley. There were two classes of settlements—hamlets and large nucleated villages in the standard Mesoamerican terminology, equivalent to the small villages and centers in Mesopotamia—in all of which there is evidence of elite residences and ritual activity. In the smallest hamlets there may be only a single elite household and limited evidence of household ritual (18). In others there may be a specially constructed plaza with evidence of public ritual as well (26, pp. 211–13). In the largest center, there are large buildings on a massive platform in the center of the settlement, a precursor of Monte Alban itself (26, pp. 214–15). There are indications of the distribution of commodities such as obsidian from central pools to households, particularly elite households. If such distribution served regulatory functions, one would expect more obsidian available during stable periods and less during unstable periods. For example, slightly pre-Rosario Household Cluster LG-1, an elite household at the subsidiary hamlet of Fábrica San José, shows high obsidian to chert ratios during the earlier and later use phases; but during the middle use phase when the house was burned there was no obsidian (18, pp. 89, 206). While one burned house does not conclusively demonstrate a period of instability, the example does show that evidence of this sort can be recovered with careful excavation. If the distribution of obsidian obtained in interregional exchange rather than locally produced does provide regulatory information, then in contrast to the locally produced redistributed goods of Hawaii, obsidian conveyed information about conditions in the broader network of polities rather than in the local polity. Given that the Rosario Phase polities—there were perhaps three of them in the valley, one in each arm—had two or at most three levels of settlement hierarchy, that residential differentiation suggests elementary class stratification, and that there is minimal evidence of regulation in rituals and distributional networks, it is likely that this is a period of developed chiefdoms very much like the Susa A example presented in the discussion of Greater Mesopotamia. While the details of Rosario agriculture and craft have not been synthesized, several points indicate that there was little movement of goods from center to center. For example, settlements were focused on the rich alluvial terraces, and even if the center had 200 households, there was still enough alluvial land nearby to support more than twice the number of households (24). Direct mobilization of food for the center would not ordinarily have been necessary, and movements of goods to the center would probably have been restricted to certain clays (31) and stones (18) of local occurrence.

The contrasting presentations of prestate Rosario organization and developed state organization in Monte Alban II are drawn from the results of the ongoing research program of Flannery and his colleagues. While the scope and caliber of excavation data and analysis are unparalleled, any attempt to outline the processes critical in state emergence are hampered by the facts that most of the excavation has been concentrated on Rosario and earlier layers and features, and that the intensive archaeological survey of the Valley of Oaxaca is still in progress, while surveys of surrounding valleys are few. Thus estimates of population change must be imprecise and assessments of conflict based on settlement pattern configuration are not yet possible. In spite of these problems some changes can be outlined. With the end of the Rosario Phase, the one well-studied center was abandoned and the new valley-wide center of Monte Alban was founded. In spite of this political disjunction, the one portion of the valley in which Rosario sites were differentiated from preceding Guadalupe Phase sites shows that after a period of stability during these two phases, there was a population rise of about 400% during the early Monte Alban I Phase (31, pp. 38, 81–82). The new center is far above good soil and water, its primary locational advantages being political rather than productive. From its inception the elite of the new center were raising monuments with portrayals of slain or sacrificed captives, presumably their enemies and probably an indication that they were involved in repeated conflicts (33). During this time there are abandonments at a number of the excavated sites in the valley, perhaps as a result of such disturbances. During Late Monte Alban I times there is a further 700% increase in estimated population, with expansion of the regional center itself and the founding of many surrounding small sites in what appears to be a planned settlement program (31, pp. 221–25). New elite funerary patterns became established (16), and future work will probably demonstrate that the elite residential patterns of the Monte Alban II Phase were becoming established at this time. All the Late Monte Alban I communities used a more standardized series of ceramics, suggesting that changes in craft specialization were occurring, but the necessary statistical and technical studies needed to demonstrate this have not yet been undertaken. All these demographic, social, and economic changes follow the disruption preceding the founding of Monte Alban, but none of the presently available data allows us to define the associated changes in regulatory process.

Even greater difficulties cloud the understanding of regulation in other cases of early state emergence in Mesoamerica such as the Valley of Mexico, Chiapas, and Highland Guatemala, where the exacting excavation techniques of the Oaxaca project have not yet been applied. Only in the relatively late but richly literate Petén Maya development is regulatory structure clearly evidenced and to some extent understood (32). Here, however, both the environment of the Petén and the type of archaeology that has been pursued conspire to cloud our understanding of exactly what is being regulated.

The lack of evidence has not deterred Mesoamericanists from making propositions about state origins. Mention of a few of these will suffice to illustrate the current state of progress. In a number of papers, Sanders (141), developing Wittfogel's ideas, suggests that military competition for limited agricultural resources impelled some elites to control, reorganize, and extend canal irrigation. Increased and more reliable production and more effective administration would give these elites competitive success which would promote further growth of irrigation and administration. However, the development of irrigation in Formative Mesoamerica is limited in extent and could have served this amplifying function in only a few cases. In a recent paper, Webster (49) raises the question of how a chief could escape the checks and balances inherent in chiefly redistribution, which he must do if he is to support a specialized administration. Building on ideas presented by Carneiro (15), he suggests that with competition under conditions of social circumscription, successful rulers who took control of local units outside their own kin networks would be able to extract resources from these marginal units while redistributing nothing in return. These resources could be used to build military and administrative forces and to further increase competitive advantages. While the importance of balanced redistribution in complex chiefdoms is arguable (21, 38), as previously noted, both this construct and that of Sanders usefully emphasize the importance of exogenous or uncontrolled resources in administrative transformations. Such propositions are at present difficult to test; however, Brumfiel (11) has developed a method of estimating relative demands on a community's resources which may allow direct consideration of such problems.

In summary, as in Mesopotamia, the period of state emergence is well bracketed. However, in the two most intensely studied areas—the Valleys of Oaxaca and Mexico—the presently available evidence is not comparable. In the former, there is much community data derived from excavation, particularly on prestate communities, but regional surveys are still incomplete. In the latter area, regional data derived from surveys are superb, but there are very few detailed excavations on Late and Terminal Formative sites. Only when these and other areas of early Mesoamerican state formation are brought to equivalent levels of documentation will it be possible to use the data of the development of the network of Formative societies to test the forthcoming generation of theoretical constructs involving the interaction of many variables.

Some aspects of the two research cases upon which this review has focused are presented in Figure 3. There are a number of notable similarities between the two developments. In both, complex chiefdoms collapse and fragment, though only in the Mesopotamian case does this phase of collapse last long enough to appear as a demographic disturbance in the archaeological record. In both cases there is a close relationship between the changes in regulatory organization that mark the origin of the state and in the reorganization of certain crafts, though in neither is it conclusively demonstrable which has primacy. In both cases, within 200 years after state foundation there is territorial expansion of control into surrounding border regions. In both cases the political and economic organization of the initial complex chiefdom and the developed primary state seem broadly similar. Furthermore, other archaeologically known cases, such as the North Coast of Peru in the First Intermediate Period and most of the ethnohistorically known cases of actual state formation such as the Zulu of Southern Africa (12), the Baganda of East Africa (30), and the Merina of Central Madagascar (14, 17), none of which we are able to detail in this review, show very similar patterns of development. I cannot detect any consistent qualitative difference between the archaeologically known cases of primary state formation and the ethnohistorically known cases of the past few centuries. Thus the marked differences which Service sees between the "archaic civilizations" and the "modern primitive states" seem to me to result from the use in his study of an inadequate archaeological record (44, pp. 303–4). Any proposed explanation of primary state origins must account for the common elements in all known cases.

NEW DIRECTIONS IN THE CONSTRUCTION OF EXPLANATIONS

The review of definitional issues and of the two cases of ongoing research has raised repeatedly the need for better theoretical structures with which to guide future research. It would be gratifying to be able to close this essay with a synthesis of recent contributions toward a formal theory of state origins; unfortunately, progress has been fragmented at best. Most anthropologists involved in field research on state

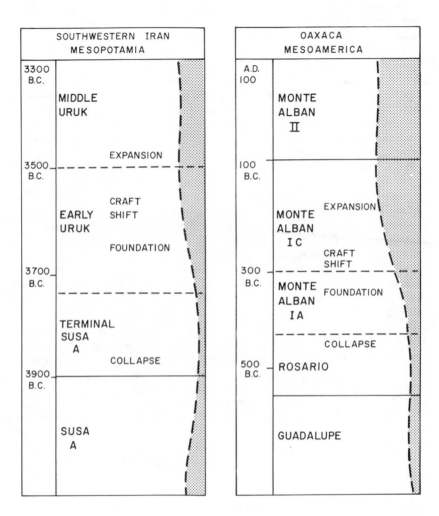

Figure 3 Comparative chronologies of Southwestern Iran and Oaxaca. The shaded area on the right side of each column provides a relative indication of population for the two areas. The indicated placement of the periods of the collapse of chiefdoms, the foundation of states, the shift in the organization of crafts, and the territorial expansion of the state is in both cases suggestive, not exact.

developments are aware of the complexities of the interacting processes. Many of those who are working with archaeologically documented cases attempt to utilize an explicitly systemic frame of reference following the outline proposed by Flannery (22) in his seminal review of early civilizations based on a paper by Rappaport (40). Many of the papers mentioned previously deal with innovative ways to estimate and understand changes in human population and thus in demand and available labor, with techniques for monitoring interregional movement of materials and explicating these movements as systems of exchange, and with approaches to other basic system flows. However, the problems of information flow and regulatory decision-making in networks of chiefdoms and states have received little attention.

There are innovative approaches both within and outside anthropology that deal with various aspects of these problems of which a few examples will suffice. The symbolic context of regulatory information and how this context could be transformed has been considered by several anthropologists (10). Aspects of regulatory pattern—how and in what form information on flows is obtained and how decisions are passed down and implemented—have been considered by cyberneticists and management analysts (7). Strategies for grouping or segmenting regulatory operation and resources are seemingly within the province of game theorists, though its most interesting aspect—n-person game theory—has been developed as a theory of collusion and alliance relevant to only a few aspects of our problem, and even it has been developed to the point where it elucidates conflict definition more than conflict strategies themselves (39). Mechanisms by which hierarchies of regulators can be built up have also been considered by cyberneticists. Studies by anthropologists have tested the proposition that the rate at which decisions must be made determines the number of levels of hierarchy (52), and they have developed the proposition, based upon Ashby's principle of requisite variety (3), that there is an optimally efficient number of subsidiaries under each higher-order regulator (29). Each such study provides another element which may in time be subsumed under a formal theory of the evolution of regulatory hierarchies. However, better understanding of decision-making subsystems to match our increasingly sophisticated understanding of demographic and productive subsystems will not in itself result in new or improved explanations of state origins. Such explanations will probably involve the interaction of these subsystems and the interaction of systems in networks of chiefdoms and states. Let us hope that such formulations, necessary as both a guide and a target for ongoing research, will soon be developed.

ACKNOWLEDGMENTS

I wish to thank Richard I. Ford, Kent V. Flannery, and Joyce Marcus, who read and offered valuable suggestions on early drafts of this review, and to Jane Mariouw, who prepared the art work. The chapter has also benefited from discussions with members of my seminar on Origin of the State: Charles Hastings, William Mac-Donald, Eve Pinsker, Elsa Redmond, Douglas Roblin, Charles Spencer, and Vincas Steponaitis. All have contributed to the clarity of the article, but its failures are my own.

Literature Cited

1. Adams, R. McC. 1966. *The Evolution of Urban Society.* Chicago: Aldine
2. Adams, R. McC., Nissen, H. J. 1972. *The Uruk Countryside.* Chicago: Univ. Chicago Press
3. Ashby, W. R. 1956. *Introduction to Cybernetics.* London: Chapman & Hall
4. Bagherzadeh, F., ed. 1975. *Proc. 2nd Ann. Symp. Archaeol. Res. Iran.* Teheran: Iranian Cent. Archaeol. Res.
5. Bagherzadeh, F., ed. 1976. *Proc. 3rd Ann. Symp. Archaeol. Res. Iran.* Teheran: Iranian Cent. Archaeol. Res.
6. Bagherzadeh, F., ed. 1977. *Proc. 4th Ann. Symp. Archaeol. Res. Iran.* Teheran: Iranian Cent. Archaeol. Res.
7. Beer, S. 1972. *The Brain of the Firm.* London: Herder & Herder
8. Benson, E., ed. 1972. *The Cult of the Feline.* Washington: Dumbarton Oaks
9. Blanton, R. E. 1976. The origins of Monte Alban. In *Cultural Change and Continuity,* ed. C. Cleland, pp. 223–32. New York: Academic
10. Block, M., ed. 1975. *Marxist Analyses and Social Anthropology. Assoc. Soc. Anthropol. Stud. No. 3.* London: Malaby
11. Brumfiel, E. 1976. Regional growth in the eastern valley of Mexico: A test of the population pressure hypothesis. See Ref. 23, pp. 234–47
12. Bryant, A. T. 1919. *Olden Times in Zululand and Natal.* London: Longman's, Green
13. Caldwell, J. R. n.d. Interaction spheres in prehistory. *Hopewellian Studies, Sci. Pap. Vol. 12,* ed. J. R. Caldwell, R. Hall. Springfield: Ill. State Mus.
14. Callet, R. P. 1953. *Tantaran'ny Andriana: Histoire de Rois.* transl. G. Chapus, E. Ratsimba. Antananarivo: Academie Malgashe
15. Carneiro, R. L. 1970. A theory of the origin of the state. *Science* 169:733–38
16. Caso, A., Bernal, I., Acosta, J. 1967. *La Ceramica de Monte Alban, Memorias No. 13.* Mexico D.F.: Inst. Nac. Antropol. Hist.
17. Deschamps, H. 1965. *Histoire de Madagascar.* Paris: Guethner
18. Drennan, R. D. 1976. *Fabrica San Jose and Middle Formative Society in the Valley of Oaxaca, Memoirs 8.* Univ. Michigan Mus. Anthropol.
19. Earle, T. K. 1976. Nearest neighbor analysis of two formative settlement systems. See Ref. 23, pp. 196–222
20. Earle, T. K. 1977. *Economic and Social Organization of a Complex Chiefdom:*

The Halelea District, Kaua'i, Hawaii, Anthropol. Pap. 64. Univ. Michigan Mus. Anthropol.
21. Earle, T. K. 1977. A reappraisal of redistribution: Complex Hawaiian chiefdoms. In *Exchange Systems in Prehistory,* ed. T. K. Earle, J. E. Ericson, pp. 213–29. New York: Academic
22. Flannery, K. V. 1972. The cultural evolution of civilization. *Ann. Rev. Ecol. Syst.* 3:399–426
23. Flannery, K. V., ed. 1976. *The Early Mesoamerican Village.* New York: Academic
24. Flannery, K. V. 1976. Linear stream patterns and riverside settlement rules. See Ref. 23, pp. 173–80
25. Flannery, K. V., Kirkby, A. V. T., Kirkby, M. J., Williams, A. W. 1967. Farming systems and political growth in ancient Oaxaca. *Science* 158:445–54
26. Flannery, K. V., Marcus, J. 1976. The evolution of the public building in formative Oaxaca. See Ref. 9, pp. 205–22
27. Frankfort, H. 1955. *Art and Architecture of the Ancient Near East.* Baltimore: Penguin
28. Johnson, G. A. 1973. *Local Exchange and Early State Development in Southwestern Iran. Anthropol. Pap. 51.* Univ. Michigan Mus. Anthropol.
29. Johnson, G. A. 1978. Information sources and the development of decision-making organizations. In *Anthropology as a Social Science,* ed. C. L. Redman. New York: Academic
30. Kiwanuka, M. S. 1971. *A History of Baganda.* London: Longman's
31. Kowalewski, S. A. 1976. *Prehispanic Settlement Patterns of the Central Part of the Valley of Oaxaca.* PhD thesis. Univ. Arizona, Tucson, Ariz.
32. Marcus, J. 1976. *Emblem and State in the Classic Maya Lowlands.* Washington: Dumbarton Oaks
33. Marcus, J. 1976. The iconography of militarism at Monte Alban and neighboring sites in the Valley of Oaxaca. In *The Origins of Religious Art and Iconography,* ed. H. B. Nicholson. Los Angeles: UCLA Latin American Res. Cent.
34. Masry, A. H. 1974. *Prehistory in Northeastern Arabia: The Problem of Interregional Interaction.* Coral Gables: Field Res. Proj.
35. Morgan, L. H. 1964 (1877). *Ancient Society.* Cambridge: Harvard Univ. Press
36. Mortensen, P. 1974. A survey of prehis-

toric sites in Northern Luristan. *Acta Archeol.* 45:1–47

37. Parsons, J. R. 1974. The development of a prehistoric complex society: A regional perspective from the Valley of Mexico. *J. Field Archaeol.* 1:81–108

38. Peebles, C. S., Kus, S. M. 1977. Some archaeological correlates of rank societies. *Am. Antiq.* 42

39. Rapoport, A. 1970. *N-Person Game Theory.* Ann Arbor: Univ. Michigan Press

40. Rappaport, R. A. 1970. Systems and sanctity. *Io* 7:46–71

41. Sanders, W. T. 1968. Hydraulic agriculture, economic symbiosis and the evolution of states in Central Mexico. In *Anthropological Archaeology in the Americas,* ed. B. J. Meggers. Washington DC: Anthropol. Soc. Washington

42. Sanders, W. T. 1974. Chiefdom to state: Political evolution at Kaminaljuyu, Guatemala. In *Reconstructing Complex Societies,* ed. C. Moore. Cambridge: Sawyer

43. Sanders, W. T., Price, B. J. 1969. *Mesoamerica: Evolution of a Civilization.* New York: Random House

44. Service, E. 1975. *Origins of the State and Civilization.* New York: Norton

45. Tobler, A. J. 1950. *Tepe Gawra II.* Philadelphia: Univ. Pennsylvania

46. Tumenyev, A. I. 1969. The state economy in ancient Sumer. In *Ancient Mesopotamia,* ed. I. Diakonov. Moscow: Nauka

47. Varner, D. M. 1974. *Prehispanic Settlement Patterns in the Valley of Oaxaca, Mexico: The Etla Arm.* PhD thesis. Univ. Arizona, Tucson, Ariz.

48. Walters, S. J. 1970. *Water For Larsa.* New Haven: Yale Univ. Press

49. Webster, D. 1975. Warfare and the evolution of the state: A reconsideration. *Am. Antiq.* 40:464–70

50. Webster, D. 1977. On theocracies. *Am. Anthropol.* 78:812–28

51. Weiss, H., Young, T. C. Jr. 1976. The merchants of Susa. *Iran* 14

52. Wright, H. T. 1969. *The Administration of Rural Production in an Early Mesopotamian Town. Anthropol. Pap. No. 38.* Univ. Michigan Mus. Anthropol.

53. Wright, H. T. 1969. Tepe Farukhabad. *Iran* 7

54. Wright, H. T., Johnson, G. A. 1975. Population, exchange, and early state formation in southwestern Iran. *Am. Anthropol.* 77:267–89

55. Wright, H. T., Neely, J. A., Johnson, G. A., Speth, J. D. 1975. Early Fourth Millennium developments in Southwestern Iran. *Iran* 13

56. Zagarell, A. 1975. Archaeological survey in the northwestern Baxtiari Mountains. See Ref. 4, pp. 145–56

Ann. Rev. Anthropol. 1977. 6:399–417
Copyright © 1977 by Annual Reviews Inc. All rights reserved

HISTORY OF ANTHROPOLOGY   ❖9600
IN HISTORICAL PERSPECTIVE

Regna Darnell

Department of Anthropology, University of Alberta, Edmonton, Alberta, Canada

INTRODUCTION

History of anthropology has a long-established history within the discipline. Virtually every major graduate program requires of its students a course in the history, sometimes combined with the theory, of anthropology. It is not obvious, however, that this has caused history of anthropology to fill a significant or integral role in the teaching and practice of the discipline. Indeed, the opposite has traditionally been true. The required course is frequently taught by the eldest member of the department, who is presumably qualified to teach the history because he has lived through more of it than anyone else. At best such a course provides the fledgling anthropologist with a collection of anecdotes, later to prove useful in socializing his own students within the profession. At worst such a course convinces the student that there is no intelligent reason to consider research done more than a decade previously.

All along, however, there have been a few anthropologists who have insisted that the history of the discipline is of relevance to its current practice. As a result of such convictions, coupled with the increasing interest of historians and historians of science in anthropology, the legitimacy of this subfield has been relatively clearly established. The starting point for what one might call the professionalization of history of anthropology is perhaps the 1962 conference sponsored by the Social Science Research Council. As Hymes (32) suggests, the importance of this conference is that it was held, the particular papers and topics being of less concern. It is notable primarily that most of the authors and participants were anthropologists, with a smattering of historians. Hymes (32) suggests further that a parable describes the ambiguous situation in which anthropological historians of their discipline found themselves at that time. Anthropologists, the members of a professional tribe, were simultaneously flattered by the attention of historians of science and disturbed by differences between their presumably objective accounts and the oral history of anthropology handed down by the elders of the discipline. The dilemma, and it is one which persists in the history of anthropology, is who shall write the history, anthropologists or historians?

The literature since 1962 reflects the dichotomy. Professionalization of the history of anthropology has largely involved the imposition of historical standards on scholarship considered to be a contribution to the disciplinary history. The first issue of the *Journal of the History of the Behavioral Sciences* in 1965 posed the issue clearly with reference to anthropology. Stocking [reprinted in (71)] drew a dichotomy between historicism as understood by historians and presentism, the use of history to justify or rationalize present-day concerns. His own credentials as a historian gave him the dubious honor of becoming the methodological mentor of the emerging subfield of history of anthropology. Although Stocking himself was concerned to point out that interests other than those of history per se permeated the existing literature on anthropological history written by practitioners of the discipline, and not necessarily to argue that such works did not contribute to anthropology in the large sense, anthropologists adapted the critique to invalidate quasi-historical scholarship which attempted to find roots in the past for current theoretical and methodological questions. As a result of editorially clarifying the issues, Stocking found himself in the potentially awkward position of appearing to have criticized the historical efforts of a variety of anthropologists. His own substantive scholarship simply practices what he preaches and avoids the polemics common in the historical writings of anthropologists themselves. Interestingly enough, the audience for Stocking's work has been an anthropological one, and his own focus has become increasingly anthropological.

Hallowell (24) wrote in the same 1964 volume of *JHBS* about the history of anthropology as an anthropological problem. There he argued that anthropologists writing their disciplinary history legitimately used the same standards of scholarship which they applied to their fieldwork among "primitive" people. In his view, the dichotomy between the methods of anthropologists and historians was an artificial one, and anthropologists had always known how to write history, including disciplinary history. His contention was that anthropologists who mixed current and historical concerns were doing bad anthropology as well as bad history.

By this point the alternatives had been clearly posed. A small but vocal group of anthropologists, with some support from historians, were arguing that the history of the discipline was not appropriately a haphazard matter, but an integral part of the ongoing practice of anthropology. This constituted a self-conscious recognition of the need for a new status for history of anthropology within the discipline as a whole. The working out of these dichotomies is still an ongoing process. The significant questions are not so much those of content of the history of anthropology but of how it should be written. Indeed, it would be virtually impossible to define the history of anthropology as a coherent subfield on the basis of substance or content. There is, of course, a historical dimension to any topic within the broadly defined discipline of anthropology. And it is unquestionable that the scope of anthropology is difficult to unify. To collect a bibliography of peripherally historical articles and books would, therefore, be an impossible task.

There are thus clear biases in the organization of this review. These biases are, however, a result of the emphases within the anthropological literature and the way in which history of anthropology has become a legitimate subfield of the discipline as a whole. The stress is on developments in the North American tradition, because this is where the concern with the methodological and theoretical bases of disciplinary history have arisen. Cultural anthropology, perhaps because it has been most explicitly concerned with the theoretical bases of the study of man in all his temporal and spatial diversity, has been the major focus of history of anthropology scholarship. And, finally, the focus will remain on literature which addresses the scope of history of anthropology within the discipline and/or the manner in which such history should be written.

The review will proceed in the following manner: First, the traditional literature of history of anthropology will be briefly noted, largely to provide a context for the more recent trends in the subfield. Then recent efforts to provide a general treatment of the history of the discipline will be discussed in light of the kinds of issues presented above. We will then turn to source materials for the general history of anthropology, their proliferation in recent years indicating the increasing concern of anthropologists with their own past. The problem of diverse development of national traditions within anthropology will be dealt with briefly, using the British and Canadian traditions as examples. Finally, historical work within the subdisciplines of archaeology, physical anthropology, and linguistics will be discussed cursively. The conclusion will summarize major trends in the historically constituted emergence of the history of anthropology within the discipline.

NOT-SO-RECENT LITERATURE

The first crop of histories of anthropology appeared in the 1930s. This timing is significant since it effectively delineates the closing of the period of professionalization of the discipline both in North America and elsewhere. Darnell (10, 11) has argued that the process of professionalization, producing what we label today as Boasian anthropology, was essentially complete in North America by 1920. As the discipline grew in size and diversity of focus, it became imperative to demonstrate its unity in historical perspective. The first effort at synthesis was a history of American anthropology by an Indian student of Wissler, himself a significant figure in the Boasian tradition; Mitra (51) was naively uncritical of the individuals and events he described, and his volume is interesting largely for the limited factual data it presents. Mitra's work was received without enthusiasm at the time, and indeed was published in India. In this context, his dedicated devotion to Boas-inspired truths cannot be taken as typical of Boasians in that period; it is notable that Mitra was an outsider.

The next Boasian effort was prepared by a member of the core group of American anthropologists. Lowie (43) discussed the intellectual roots of the discipline from his own point of view, with an unsurprising stress on early German sources. His treatment ended with the Boasian school and some effort at prognosis for the future. The book is informative but unexciting, in spite of Lowie's participation in the tradition he describes.

Penniman's 1935 review of the previous century (60) is a catalog of facts. British anthropologist Haddon's 1934 effort (22) also stresses facts (the first edition appeared in 1910). But it follows the continental terminology and definition of the scope of anthropology, and is consequently somewhat more informative to North American readers.

Several works appeared in the 1960s which provided additional materials for the history of anthropology. Mead & Bunzel (50) edited a collection of papers in a series about the "golden age of X" which reviewed many of the contributions of the Boasian tradition. Commentaries were minimal. Kardiner & Preble (37) produced a collection of essays on major anthropologists; the historical contribution is biographical rather than analytical. Slotkin's (67) major collection of readings in the intellectual background of anthropology appeared in 1965. The editor was an anthropologist whose commentaries on his own wide reading in history, philosophy, and classics helped many anthropologists to expand their notions of the scope of the history of the discipline. Moreover, Slotkin provided a certain amount of basic commentary which at least began the task of tying together the immense range of material covered. Brew (5) edited a collection of papers designed to chronicle the past century of anthropological history, but which were in fact much more limited in their scope. Virtually all of the papers define their topics quite narrowly and evade larger interpretation.

These materials, taken in sum, made it quite possible for anthropologists to teach the history of their discipline and to require basic facts about its development to be known by all students as a rite of passage. History of anthropology in the more theoretical sense, however, had not yet emerged. The year 1968 provides a watershed: in that year, two volumes were published which provided models for the polar extremes of anthropological historical writing and research styles (25, 71).

Stocking's book, republishing a number of previous essays and presenting considerable new material as well, deals with three concepts—race, evolution, and culture—as they changed through time. He begins with Tylor, although most of the papers deal with aspects of the American Boasian tradition. The emphasis is on the context of ideas at the time they were propounded. Stocking's concerns are those of a historian, and he expresses considerable ambivalence about the relation of his work to the anthropological task of self-examination in the context of which readers had received the original essays. Several of the essays, and many of the introductory comments, deal specifically with problems of methodology in writing the history of anthropology. This book remains the model for those anthropologists who espouse standards of historical scholarship in the pursuit of disciplinary history. In contrast to much of the historical writing of anthropologists, Stocking's papers are organized around clearly isolated problems of intellectual history; archival documentation replaces published and easily available sources as central to the analysis; individual anthropologists are placed within a general social context as well as that of their discipline itself; judgments of merit are subordinated to clarifying the nature of changes in ideas and their form of embodiment through time; generalizations are not made unless supported by evidence, and the nature of that evidence is clearly stated.

Also in 1968, Harris's discussion of anthropological theory appeared. This book is quite different, primarily in that it attempts to deal with the full scope of the history of anthropology from the Enlightenment to what Harris calls "techno-environmental determinism," described as the culmination of anthropological theory. There is no denying that Harris's book was, and is, important. Its very scope made it the most obvious textbook for courses in history of anthropology; those courses which combined history and theory received the additional benefit that current theory was clearly present, this being particularly welcome to those who subscribed to Harris's brand of theory.

Simultaneously with the publication of Harris's book, *Current Anthropology* presented a group book review (26) based on prepublication copies and a brief summary of the theoretical argument by Harris. The reviewers' comments ranged from eulogy to depreciation. The correlation with theoretical persuasion of respondent was notable, with those who favored nomothetic theory, techno-environmental determinism, and dialectical materialism being most enthusiastic. Others, particularly those interested in cognitive or ideational anthropology and those who preferred to think of theory as problematical rather than deterministic, objected strongly to what they considered subordination of historical presentation to polemical argument.

Given the enormous scope of the volume, a remarkable amount of attention is devoted to a critique of Boasian anthropology, described as buried in a morass of "historical particularism." Boas and his major students are dissected, not in terms of their own reasons for propounding the arguments they did, but in terms of holding back the progress of the theory as understood by Harris. In the process, a great deal of fascinating information about the Boasians is presented. But the reader who wishes to separate Harris from his subject matter must constantly evaluate the basis of generalizations made. Partially because of its commitment to a current and popular anthropological theory, Harris's book has attained a circulation unequaled in the literature of history of anthropology. Unfortunately, many of those who extolled its virtues were, by their own admission, not interested in the history of anthropology. The surface paradox is one which precisely delineates the dichotomy still present in the history of anthropology. Harris's book is an explicit model for much of the current literature, and the majority of that takes exception either to his intermingling of history and current theory or to the particular current theory to which Harris subscribes. Many of the critiques are along lines advocated by Stocking, and most are presented by anthropologists with a clear commitment to the need for a currently relevant *and* historically valid history of the discipline. There are clearly issues which at least a substantial number of anthropologists feel need to be resolved, resulting in a considerable upsurge in the amount of interest shown in the history of anthropology. With these general concerns, we may suggest that the subfield is coming, or perhaps even has come, of age.

RECENT EFFORTS AT SYNTHESIS

Expansion of interest in the history of anthropology has given rise to a feeling of self-conscious identity among the small group of anthropological historians, which to a certain extent transcends their variable disciplinary roots. Increasingly there are historians among them. There are at least two journals that specifically seek articles in the history of anthropology, *ISIS* and the *Journal of the History of the Behavioral Sciences*. It is, however, questionable how frequently these journals are read by anthropologists, indicating that while historians of the discipline may feel they have attained some professional maturity, other anthropologists may be little affected by their conviction.

Moreover, there is now a *History of Anthropology Newsletter,* published twice a year and now collecting material for Volume 4. The general editor is George Stocking, Department of Anthropology, University of Chicago. Subscribers and contributors represent a fair cross-section of anthropologists and some historians. There is a substantial group of young scholars who are defining history of anthropology as their major area of specialization. There is also a notable group of senior anthropologists who see history of anthropology as crucial to the practice of the discipline as they understand it. *History of Anthropology Newsletter* presents bibliography, notes on work in progress, brief articles, obscure items of interest, and reports of thesis work of relevance.

A number of dissertations have appeared in the last few years which are specifically concerned with topics in the history of anthropology: Late nineteenth century anthropology in Washington, D.C., centered in the Bureau of American Ethnology, is the focus of Hinsley (29a) and Noelke (56), as well as a partial concern of Darnell (10). Tax (74) deals with nineteenth century American archaeology and Quade (61) with American physical anthropology. Thoresen (75) combines history and theoretical analysis of Kroeber's early work. And Bieder (2) explores the influence of the American Indian on the development of American anthropology. Considerable additional work is in progress.

There is no definitive bibliography of the history of anthropology, perhaps because the scope and content of the subfield are still in question to many of the contributors. At least four individuals, however, have collected extensive bibliographies, with varying degrees of annotation, which can be obtained from the collators by interested parties. These are D. Fowler, D. H. Hymes, R. V. Kemper, and W. Sturtevant.

In addition to these indications of burgeoning interest in the history of anthropology, there are now available a substantial number of potential textbooks, all differing somewhat in focus and purpose.

In 1973 a collection of readings (4) and a treatment of major thinkers and their ideas (27) posed a contrast in styles of approaching the history of anthropology (13). The Bohannan & Glazer reader (4) precedes primary sources with biographical and career information about the authors. Considerable anecdotal or personalized material is included, providing some sense of the oral history of the discipline. The editors argue that history of anthropology should be concerned with current theoretical interests but not committed to particular theories. Interest in the history is justified by the continuous need for disciplinary self-examination. Professional anthropology up to 1960 is presented through the major ideas dominating the discipline—evolution, culture, and structure. In spite of the brevity of the commentaries, there are a number of interesting historical connections suggested, e.g. a comparison between Durkheim's collective consciousness and Kroeber's superorganic, and a number of myths from the oral history of anthropology are exploded, e.g. Radcliffe-Brown's presumed objection to history in any form. The volume is therefore useful both for the primary sources it makes easily available and for its matter-of-fact, informative approach to the notion of anthropological history.

Hatch (27) proceeds in quite a different manner, being concerned with the theories of ten significant anthropologists. Tylor alone represents the nineteenth century. Boas is placed in antithesis to Tylor, being anti-intellectual, idealist, relativist, subjectivist, deductive, ethnographically particularist (shades of Harris), and modern; Tylor is presented as intellectualist, positivist, rationalist, reductionist (culture to individual), utilitarian, inductive, comparative, and premodern. Hatch does not discuss the nineteenth century basis of Boas's ideas.

Benedict, Kroeber, Steward, and White are discussed as students of Boas. Little attention is given to relative chronology and to connections among the individuals. Hatch's concern with the connections of a logical nature between the theories of Kroeber and Steward, for example, leads him to ignore the chronological intervention of psychological anthropology as represented by Benedict between the theories of Kroeber and his pupil. Further, to consider White a Boasian is somewhat inaccurate at best.

Durkheim, Radcliffe-Brown, Evans-Pritchard, and Malinowski represent British and continental anthropology. The same kinds of criticisms apply here. Hatch appears unaware of scholarship in history of science which might be considered relevant to his analysis. The book was written for a course in history and theory, and the two are not clearly distinguished. Analyses of theoretical premises are certainly necessary in anthropology, but not at the expense of historical distortion. Hatch is presumably not presenting his own synthesis of the useful ideas of these ten great men, but reviewing their theoretical positions. These, in terms of history of anthropology in historical terms, should be presented in their own appropriate historical context. Hatch appears unduly concerned with what would have happened if history had happened differently. This is feasible when juggling ideas on paper, but has little relation to the realities of historical events.

Another reader in history of anthropology appeared in 1974 (12). The book is organized in four sections, none intended to provide exhaustive primary sources, but each making a claim about the importance of certain kinds of material for the history of anthropology. The first section takes the view that anthropology, broadly conceived as the study of man, is not unique to the anthropological tradition which developed in the western world. First, there is some kind of anthropological folk knowledge in every human culture. Moreover, such knowledge has been formalized at least by the Greeks, Romans, Arabs, and Chinese (not represented), as well as during the European Renaissance. The anthropological method of cross-cultural comparison is applied to defining the discipline itself.

The second section, the most obviously arbitrary and incomplete, deals with reports of voyages of exploration and with the philosophical incorporation of information from them as the Renaissance world found itself expanded in time and space.

The third section is concerned with the professionalization of anthropology as a scientific discipline, correlated with the rise of other scientific disciplines. The emphasis is on the North American tradition, including, for example, British anthropologist Tylor's comments on American anthropology. A number of figures are represented whose reputations in anthropology have been considerably eclipsed by time, e.g. McGee, Brinton, Gibbs, and Haven. Boas and Malinowski (represented in a review by Stocking) are anthropologists whose notions of professionalism in anthropology have persisted to the present day.

The final section deals with the history of anthropology as perceived by disciplinary practitioners. It is the longest and potentially the most interesting portion of the volume. There is a considerable range of topics and approaches: anthropologists are disturbed by historical probings into their traditions; anthropologists are historians anyway; the discipline may be conceived as having a personality; controversies in anthropology point out the essential nature of the discipline: ideas of man, culture, and evolution have changed through time; anthropologists repeat the same mistakes in virtual ignorance of disciplinary history; ideas about the nature and antiquity of man are conditioned by general scholarly and intellectual climate. A previously unpublished essay on nineteenth century cultural evolution by Stocking is included as well as a long address on British social anthropology by Fortes which sharply contrasts with the American material.

Each section is preceded by a discussion, partially bibliographical, by the editor. Darnell is an anthropologist with a specialization in history of anthropology, who argues that disciplinary history should be part of the training and self-image of every anthropologist. The volume clearly demonstrates that there is a considerable literature about the history of anthropology written by anthropologists and that at least some of it is concerned with these sorts of issues.

Two potential textbooks have recently appeared which are an answer to Harris (25), preserving something resembling the scope of his treatment of anthropological theory but with explicit lack of commitment to any particular theory. The first of these (79) claims to be a history of ethnology, rather than of anthropology in total. Previous to this book, Voget has written a number of papers on the intellectual roots of anthropology. In this volume, he deals very briefly with Graeco-Roman, Renaissance, and Arabic ideas about man and culture, concluding that no new discipline emerged from these inquiries. Somewhat more attention is given to the eighteenth century, characterized by the emergence of a generalized social science out of history. But the existence of anthropology itself is not recognized until it emerges in the nineteenth century with a unique theory, methodology, subject matter, and set of facts for its basis.

Voget defines a period of structuralism from 1890 to 1940 which he associates with professionalization of the discipline and divides into social anthropology, functionalism, and culture historicism, the latter again divided according to its three national branches, American, British and German. He suggests that all the schools of structuralism share certain essential features: all react negatively to developmentalism; causality is attributed to structure within the sociocultural realm; form and order are stressed; the aim is an inductive natural science which is value-free; questions of ultimate origin are avoided; explanations at the individual level are rejected. It is interesting to note that these are all features which have been associated with the discipline of anthropology, rather than with specific schools within it. Because this was the period of professionalization, its long-term influence has been extreme. In fact, this observation may provide the context for the frustration of Harris and others with the accepted definition of the scope of anthropology, forcing a rewriting of disciplinary history to justify their current theoretical concerns.

Voget's fourth period is one of specialization which began in the 1930s and has continued to the present. This period is characterized by recognition of variations from structure and by greater emphasis on the active role of the individual in culture. Voget sees the immediate future as involving synthesis and reorientation in these directions, rather than a disintegration of anthropology itself. He stresses the "scientific mission" of anthropology within the Western world as a science of non-Western peoples which should remain independent of political ideologies.

The development of anthropology is recognized as an evolutionary process largely involving substitution or replacement of increasingly complex explanatory models. Voget envisions a series of specializations leading to convergence in theory within a dominant paradigm, presumably yet to come. The notion of paradigm is taken from Kuhn (39), where it is applied to the natural sciences. Although Kuhn himself believed that the social sciences were essentially preparadigmatic, lacking a single theory which organized research during a given period or cycle, historians of anthropology have found the notion useful, albeit sometimes as a metaphor. Voget claims that the social and natural sciences are parallel in that they aim for reality control and that the paradigmatic status of theories and models is therefore also parallel.

Voget is careful to avoid the explicit commitment to a particular theory which characterizes Harris (25). It is, however, abundantly clear that he has considerable sympathy with the Boasian position. Indeed, the frontispiece of the volume is a portrait of Boas, who is thereby labeled as the most significant figure in the history of ethnology. Voget concludes, however, that the Boasians did not constitute a "school," since they did not endlessly replicate the same results. This is perhaps more the view of an insider, who will stress productive divergence among colleagues, although the same group may appear quite similar to the outsider. Voget implies that the existence of a school would be a negative thing, again perhaps responding to Harris's (25) critique of the Boasians as a school. From Kuhn's point of view, however, a school is an efficient and productive way to organize scholarship as long as its paradigm allows for meaningful research within the shared framework.

The most recent contribution to the potential textbook collection focuses on what are called anthropological ideas (31). Honigmann's focus on cultural anthropology involves in practice ethnology, social anthropology, and the theoretical foundations of archaeology. Stress is on ideas general to man and culture rather than on the culture-specific. Supernatural explanations are excluded. The basic criterion for inclusion is resemblance to current anthropological ideas. Honigmann intentionally minimizes historical context in order to demonstrate ideational continuities. The treatment is organized according to ideas rather than individuals, although basic biographical information is accurately given.

Honigmann is himself theoretically eclectic and believes that the discipline of anthropology draws its strength from a similar eclecticism. In practice, there is considerably more attention to British social anthropology and its influence on the American tradition than by either Harris or Voget. The treatment of the Boasians is nonpolemic.

Honigmann suggests that the ideas of anthropology have developed more by substitution than by cumulation (Kuhn's point is that scientific development proceeds in cycles or paradigms, not in straight lines). Anthropological ideas are divided into orienting concepts which specify subjects of inquiry, theories which are compounded out of orienting concepts, and methodological propositions which are comparable to theories. The very abstract and deterministic notion of theory propounded by Harris (25) is implicitly rejected. Honigmann notes that ideas are always applied from a point of view and identifies eight in anthropology: historical, developmental, integrational, instrumental, configurational, biological, psychological, and geographical. It is these which are combined in various ways to produce theories and schools. Honigmann also deals with controversies in the discipline over recurrent themes and issues, e.g. the notion of cultural relativism, society versus the individual, nature versus culture. Because he focuses on ideas rather then disciplinary affiliation, Honigmann is easily able to deal with such figures as Freud and Marx, whose appearance in many histories of anthropology is somewhat strained.

Honigmann explicitly deals with the professionalization of anthropology around 1900 in terms of Kuhn's notion of paradigm shift or scientific revolution (39). After 200 years without challenge, the evolutionary paradigm was replaced at this time. As concomitants of this shift, Honigmann notes separation of anthropology from sociology, emergence of professional societies, emphasis on being value-free, and the establishment of competing theories and schools, especially along national lines.

Honigmann explicitly avoids dealing with the Boasians as a school, referring to them instead as "members of the American historical tradition." He notes that they shared a common frame of meaning and that their brand of historical ethnology was clearly distinguishable from the German and British versions thereof.

After World War II, with the decline of structural-functional analysis, new trends included the cognitive definition of culture, renewed interest in culture history and evolution, increased attention to formalism, phenomenological concern with decision-making and social behavior, and increased specialization. Recent trends in social structure and cognitive anthropology are better represented in this volume than in the others reviewed, although Honigmann may also have the most balanced treatment overall.

Indeed, given the obvious specialization and diversification of anthropology over the past three decades, we may perhaps look forward to a whole series of histories of anthropology, each reflecting the historical roots understood by a particular scholar in coming to his own, perhaps even idiosyncratic, definition of the discipline. Put in other terms, to what extent is it possible for a single individual to accurately reflect the diversity of the recent history of anthropology? This question will likely be answered not by historians of anthropology but by anthropologists dealing with the increasing specialization of their own discipline. The exercise of writing disciplinary history merely pinpoints the issues.

Several other works should be mentioned as rather general in their reference, particularly those by Malefijt (45) and Palerm (57, 58). The latter is a series of which the third volume, dealing with the professionals, is yet to appear. These works, published in Spanish, present primary source extracts with comments providing context.

In addition, there are two collections of papers in history of anthropology which deserve consideration here. The volume edited by Murra (55) results from a symposium of the American Ethnological Society (AES). Topics are variable but the volume retains a certain coherence, both in terms of time period and focus on the American tradition. Two papers deal with the history of the AES itself, one by a historian and one by an anthropological participant. There are three biographical papers dealing with turn of the century figures and a general treatment of Washington anthropology. Three papers discuss the career of Redfield, providing an interesting contrast among them. One paper deals with fieldwork, the museum, and archaeology.

In contrast, the volume edited by Thoresen (76), resulting from the 9th International Congress of Anthropological and Ethnological Sciences, fails to maintain a unity which would permit the general anthropological reader to profit from it as a whole. Several papers deal with the development of anthropology in particular countries (India, Hungary, Yugoslavia); these are basically catalogs of facts. Bibliography, ethnographic film, the Enlightenment, mound builders, and matrilineality all appear in the contents. Two papers are modern, dealing with Kroeber and Benedict. Many of these contributions are useful, but their juxtaposition is frequently confusing, and there is no general introduction which attempts to delineate the scope and purpose of history of anthropology.

In sum the literature of history of anthropology now includes a number of works which seriously attempt to synthesize the history of discipline and to relate that history to current practice. There is a choice of perspectives, both toward history of anthropology and toward the discipline itself. This diversity reflects increased interest in the area by anthropologists and perhaps increasing professionalization of history of anthropology itself. It is now clear that there is not likely to be a single history of the discipline, just as there is unlikely to be a totally complete and adequate description of a culture. The matter is both more complex and more interesting than it was in the not-so-far-distant days when history of anthropology meant a catalog of facts about the past.

SOURCE MATERIALS

Considerable source material for the history of anthropology, particularly in North America, has appeared in recent years, reflecting increased concern of anthropologists about the nature of their own history. In many cases, this has involved republication of materials which previously were scattered or out of print. For example, it is unquestionable that Boas is the most significant figure of twentieth century American anthropology. Coming to terms with Boas is the primary task of many anthropologists in their own professional socialization, and this fact is reflected in the literature of history of anthropology. Boas prepared a collection of his own papers in 1940 which has now been reprinted in a paperback edition (3). The literature includes, in addition to numerous articles, a biography by a former student (29) and two memoirs of the American Anthropological Association (20a, 42). The most outspoken, and historically inaccurate, accounts are probably to be found in the critiques of White (80, 81), who felt the need to justify his own interest in evolution by attacking the essentially nonevolutionary assumptions of Boasian anthropology. This critique is carried on, although in a much more judicious tone, by Harris (25). There are now two Boas readers: Rohner (62) has presented letters and diaries from Boas's northwest coast fieldwork, giving an idea of the standards which guided fieldwork in the early days. The volume includes an introduction which provides context for the primary source material. Stocking (72) has prepared a reader which selects from Boas's writings up to 1911 and thereby balances the picture of his career and of the development of American anthropology which Boas himself encouraged by the emphasis in his own selection of his writings on the later years. As Stocking cogently stresses, by 1911 Boas had already established himself as the leading figure in American anthropology, and his students were beginning to hold important positions in the discipline. The fact that he lived so long and did so much more after 1911 does not diminish the importance of his position in the early period. To ignore the full career of Boas is to accept the rewriting of history by Boasians which obscures both continuity with the earlier American tradition and controversy in the establishment of the Boasian tradition. The paradigm shift which produced Boasian anthropology is discussed by Stocking (71) and Darnell (10, 11), both dealing explicitly with the extent to which Boasian anthropology constituted a paradigm.

It is, of course, also obvious that the role of Boas in the current structure of anthropology as a discipline is of concern in virtually all the efforts to provide general histories. For the history of anthropology, the significant issue is not whether Boas's influence was positive or negative, but whether discussion of Boas and his influence is carried on within scholarly standards, historical or anthropological. Certainly, if the role of Boas is a historical topic of concern to anthropologists, then its salient place in the literature of history of anthropology is fully justified.

Selected papers of various anthropologists have appeared, usually at the instigation of colleagues or former students. Mead has prepared the papers of Benedict (47) for a paperback edition with her comments. Although the historicism of Mead's treatment is somewhat limited, her own participation in the events described contributes to a fascinating document. Fogelson (18) edited a collection of Hallowell papers, including a number on the history of anthropology (with an introduction by Stocking). These range from autobiographical to research scholarship.

Three collected volumes of papers from the *American Anthropologist* have been issued by the American Anthropological Association. The first, edited by de Laguna (14) is a reprint of the 1960 edition and includes Hallowell's still classic paper on early anthropology in North America (23). The volume has some commentary by the editor and considerable bibliography; selections go through 1920. The second volume in the series covers the period from 1921 to 1945 (73). Stocking's long introduction is the most serious attempt to date to deal with the nature and long-range contribution of the interwar period. As he notes, the period is not an inspired one, yet it set the groundwork for the present specialization and growth of the discipline. Stocking discusses extensively the institutional changes which took place during these years, and seeks context both in terms of earlier and later periods. The third volume, edited by Murphy (54), covers the period from 1946 to 1970. As is always the case with the recent period in which specialization and diversification are rampant, the selection often seems rather arbitrary. In general, it is fairly judicious, and a number of important papers are made easily available. All three volumes include photographs of contributors, certainly an important attraction of the volumes, particularly for students. The set provides an important record of the Association during its entire existence and permits professional self-examination by returning these materials to the current literature, complete with commentary on the historical context (although quite limited, and perhaps less necessary, for the third volume).

There is also a good deal of biographical or autobiographical material. The most extensive effort is the Columbia University Press *Leaders in Modern Anthropology* series. These volumes involve a brief biographical sketch by a leading anthropologist who is qualified to evaluate the career of the subject, followed by a selection from the subject's writings. Treatments are nonpolemical, generally stressing positive contributions, and personal reminiscences and asides are kept to a minimum. Volumes currently available deal with Linton (41), Kidder (83), Kroeber (70), Lowie (53), Herskovits (66), and Benedict (49). Forthcoming volumes are expected to include Boas, Hooton, Malinowski, Redfield, Rivers, Sapir, and Whorf. In spite of the brief format and extensive emphasis on the American tradition, these volumes make a real contribution to describing and distinguishing the careers of a number of the major anthropologists of the Boasian camp.

Many miscellaneous biographical works are available. Historians have contributed, e.g. Stegner (69), but the recent work is largely from within anthropology. Helm edited a volume for the American Ethnological Society (28) which raised the general question of the uses of biography in the history of anthropology, as well as presenting a number of biographical papers. A biography of Kroeber was written by his widow (38) and combines objective commentary with personal reminiscence and delightful reading style; Kroeber's anthropological notions of configuration are applied to the problem of conveying his personality. Kroeber is also discussed by Thoresen (75). Lowie's autobiography (44) has long been a major source of information about the tone of Boasian anthropology, and is a fascinating source of information about the conditions of early fieldwork. Lowie's own judicious temperament effectively avoids polemics. More recently, Mead's autobiography (48) has set forth her very personal reactions to being an anthropologist and a professional female during the past half century. This feminist current is followed up in the more historically oriented scholarship of Modell (51a) on Benedict, but dealing also with

Mead. Material comparable to that on Boas's early fieldwork (62) is provided by the publication of Malinowski's field diaries from the Trobriand Islands (46). In both cases, the current standards of fieldwork with which the two men are so intimately associated in the history of the discipline simply do not apply. Finally, there are a few biographical efforts dealing with nineteenth century anthropologists and their relationship to the professionalization of the discipline, e.g. Brinton and Hale (11a, 21).

NATIONAL TRADITIONS

Most of the literature in history of anthropology concedes that anthropology as we know it is uniquely a product of Western civilization. The question of how many anthropologies there might be within that western tradition remains obscure. In English, the literature deals largely with the American and British traditions, with less detailed treatments of French and German anthropology. The specific relationship of anthropology in other parts of the world to these major developments is not explored in comparative terms. The literature which does exist is widely scattered and tends to present dates, names, and facts in the restricted context of a single country.

In the case of British anthropology, however, quite a considerable literature has developed. There are, of course, historians' treatments of evolution (6, 7, 52), at least one anthropologist who has written on evolution (15), medieval and Renaissance foundations of anthropology (30) from the viewpoint of a historian, and an anthropologist writing on the influence of the voyages of discovery (63). Professional anthropology in Britain is described in several places: Firth (16) edited a collection of papers dedicated to Malinowski by his former students which set out much of the history of the group. Malinowski's field diaries provide an additional source of information (46). Fortes's inaugural address at the University of Cambridge dealt with the development of professional anthropology at that university (19). In line with the synchronic emphasis of the British tradition, however, Fortes is not convinced that the history of anthropology, particularly in the preprofessional period, is of relevance to current practice. It is perhaps not surprising that history of anthropology as a self-conscious subfield should have emerged in America where the historical tradition has been strong. Finally, a recent treatment of British anthropology virtually to the present time (40) is written in an essentially historicist mode. A number of oral history myths about the social anthropologists are exploded, e.g. the accidental nature of Malinowski's internment in the Pacific during World War I; the degree to which the British social anthropologists constitute a "school" is addressed at length. The work of G.W. Stocking now in preparation will further extend our information about British anthropology and may be expected to deal both with forerunners of professional anthropology and the growth of the professional discipline.

A concern with the history of anthropology in Canada has developed quite recently, probably to establish a contrast with the American tradition which was receiving so much attention to the south. The early literature was somewhat limited and sporadic, e.g. the biographical work of Trigger (77, 78). Over the last few years, however, Canadian learned societies have given some attention to problems of disciplinary history. Two symposia of the Canadian Sociology and Anthropology Association have been published in its journal (1), although these papers largely present bibliography for the study of various culture areas of native Canada. Nonetheless, the label of history of anthropology is attached to this effort. Other papers presented at the symposia were not included, to the detriment of the volume.

The most interesting Canadian production to date is a published plenary session of the Canadian Ethnology Society (20). Two papers deal with the National Museum of Man program in anthropology, one by a former ethnologist there and the other dealing historically with the years of Sapir's administration. A further paper along the same lines deals with Barbeau. Quebec anthropology is discussed both from the Francophone and Anglophone perspectives by established participants. And finally, the anthropological contribution to Canadian Indian policy is reviewed from a historical point of view. The published version incorporates considerable discussion at the conference in which the principals, Hawthorn and Tremblay, saw the matter somewhat differently from the uninvolved analyst. It is this interaction between historical scholarship and oral history which needs to strike a balance in the history of anthropology, not only in Canada.

SUBDISCIPLINES

The question of historical research in the subdisciplines of anthropology is one which arises largely in relation to the American tradition, in which archaeology, physical anthropology, and linguistics have long been combined with ethnology. The omnipresent fact of the American Indian has generally been blamed for the holistic scope in the oral history of the discipline. And historians have contributed to a picture of American history consistent with such an analysis (e.g. 59, 68).

Archaeologists have recently become somewhat more interested in their own history, a phenomenon which may be correlated with the increasingly theoretical nature of archaeology. The traditional sources are European in focus (8, 9) and of no aid in self-examination of American archaeologists. Fitting's edited collection (17), in spite of a promising title, catalogs history of archaeological work in various culture areas. Schuyler (64) is largely devoted to current methodological concerns. The work of Willey & Sabloff (82) is an extensive and carefully documented treatment of the facts of the development of American archaeology. It is full of interesting detail, although it does not directly address issues of the appropriate theoretical basis for writing the history of anthropology. Tax (74), a historian, has also worked in this area.

Physical anthropology has received less historical attention, although this is beginning to change. The Columbia *Leaders in Anthropology* series includes Hooton. Discussions of Washington anthropology (e.g. 29a, 56) also deal extensively with physical anthropologists. Quade (61) is also useful. In addition, there is considerable work in progress, particularly in dissertations, e.g. by P. Erickson and F. Spencer.

There is a whole separate literature dealing with the history of linguistics. Insofar as that history relates to anthropology, the major figure is Hymes, who first raised these issues in the early 1960s (33). He has discussed application of linguistic methods in ethnography within the Boasian tradition (34) and the development of American structural linguistics (36) in partial connection to anthropology. His edited book on paradigms and traditions in linguistics (35) contains a number of articles of interest to anthropologists, although the emphasis remains on the intellectual underpinnings of linguistics, particularly Indo-European. A further source which should be mentioned, however, is a collection of obituaries of linguists (65) which provides biography, commentary, and professional evaluation. A number of anthropological linguists are included.

In general, it appears that history of anthropology, insofar as it is a theoretical enterprise, is likely to retain its focus on cultural anthropology. However, in cases where the anthropological historian himself works in more than one subdiscipline, connections which rationalize or motivate the subdisciplinary scope may emerge. Again this is part of the perceived need for disciplinary self-examination which seems to motivate interest in history of anthropology itself.

CONCLUSION

No attempt has been made to exhaustively catalog the literature of history of anthropology, even for the last 5 to 10 years. Rather, an effort has been made to describe the growth and increasingly theoretical development of history of anthropology. Greater attention has been given to works which raise issues of the role of history of anthropology within the discipline and its practice. Collections of historical facts are considered less significant, whatever their intrinsic interest, than treatments which discuss how the history of anthropology should be written. As a result of this examination, it is clear that there is a considerable literature, much of it of excellent quality, in the history of anthropology, most of it very recent. This literature provides an interesting balance between historians, who tend to set the scholarly standards, and anthropologists, who tend to define the topics of interest. It appears certain that the field will continue to grow, both in quantity and sophistication of its productions. Out of this interdisciplinary collaboration a new paradigm for the history of anthropology is emerging.

Literature Cited

1. Ames, M., Preston, R. J. 1975. Symposium on the history of Canadian anthropology—Introduction. *Can. Rev. Sociol. Anthropol.* 12:243
2. Bieder, R. 1972. *The American Indian and the development of anthropological thought in the United States, 1780–1851.* PhD thesis. Univ. Minnesota, Minneapolis, Minn.
3. Boas, F. 1940. *Race, Language and Culture.* New York: Macmillan. 647 pp.
4. Bohannan, P., Glazer, M., eds. 1973. *High Points in Anthropology.* New York: Knopf. 449 pp.
5. Brew, J. O., ed. 1968. *A Hundred Years of Anthropology.* Cambridge, Mass: Harvard Univ. Press. 276 pp.
6. Bryson, G. 1945. *Man and Society: The Scottish Inquiry of the Eighteenth Century.* Princeton, NJ: Princeton Univ. Press. 287 pp.
7. Burrow, J. W. 1966. *Evolution and Society: A Study in Victorian Social Theory.* Cambridge, England: Cambridge Univ. Press. 295 pp.
8. Daniel, G. E. 1950. *A Hundred Years of Archaeology.* London: Duckworth. 343 pp.
9. Daniel, G. E. 1962. *The Idea of Prehistory.* London: Watts. 186 pp.
10. Darnell, R. D. 1969. *The development of American anthropology 1880–1920: From the Bureau of American Ethnology to Franz Boas.* PhD thesis. Univ. Pennsylvania, Philadelphia, Pa.
11. Darnell, R. D. 1971. The professionalization of American anthropology: A case study in the sociology of knowledge. *Soc. Sci. Inform.* 10:83–103
11a. Darnell, R. D. 1974. Daniel Brinton and the professionalization of American anthropology. See Ref. 55, pp. 69–98
12. Darnell, R. D., ed. 1974. *Readings in the History of Anthropology.* New York: Harper & Row. 479 pp.
13. Darnell, R. D. 1975. The history of cultural anthropology: Two views. *Rev. Anthropol.* 2:118–25
14. de Laguna, F., ed. 1960. *Selected Papers from the American Anthropologist 1888–1920.* Evanston, Ill: Row Peterson. 960 pp.
15. Eiseley, L. C. 1958. *Darwin's Century.* New York: Doubleday. 378 pp.
16. Firth, R., ed. 1957. *Man and Culture.* London: Routledge & Kegan Paul, 292 pp.

17. Fitting, J. E., ed. 1973. *The Development of North American Archaeology.* Garden City, NY: Anchor. 309 pp.
18. Figelson, R., ed. 1976. *Contributions to Anthropology: Selected Papers of A. Irving Hallowell.* Chicago: Univ. Chicago Press. 552 pp.
19. Fortes, M. 1953. *Social Anthropology at Cambridge Since 1900: An Inaugural Lecture.* Cambridge, England: Cambridge Univ. Press. 47 pp.
20. Freedman, J., ed. 1976. *The History of Canadian Anthropology. Proc. Can. Ethnol. Soc.* 3. 200 pp.
20a. Goldschmidt, M., ed. 1959. *The Anthropology of Franz Boas.* San Francisco: Chandler. 165 pp.
21. Gruber, J. W. 1967. Horatio Hale and the development of American anthropology. *Proc. Am. Philos. Soc.* 3:5–37
22. Haddon, A. C. 1934. *History of Anthropology.* London: Watts. 206 pp.
23. Hallowell, A. I. 1960. The beginnings of anthropology in America. See Ref. 14, pp. 1–90
24. Hallowell, A. I. 1965. The history of anthropology as an anthropological problem. *J. Hist. Behav. Sci.* 1:24–38
25. Harris, M. 1968. *The Rise of Anthropological Theory: A History of Theories of Culture.* New York: Crowell. 806 pp.
26. Harris, M. et al 1968. CA* book review of *Rise of Anthropological Theory. Curr. Anthropol.* 9:519–33
27. Hatch, E. 1973. *Theories of Man and Culture.* New York: Columbia Univ. Press. 384 pp.
28. Helm, J., ed. 1966. *Pioneers in American Anthropology: The Uses of Biography.* Seattle: Univ. Washington Press. 247 pp.
29. Herskovits, M. J. 1953. *Franz Boas: The Science of Man in the Making.* New York: Scribner's. 131 pp.
29a. Hinsley, C. M. 1976. *The development of a profession: Anthropology in Washington D.C. 1846–1903.* PhD thesis. Univ. Wisconsin, Madison, Wis. 539 pp.
30. Hodgen, M. T. 1964. *Early Anthropology in the Sixteenth and Seventeenth Centuries.* Philadelphia: Univ. Pennsylvania Press. 523 pp.
31. Honigmann, J. J. 1976. *The Development of Anthropological Ideas.* Homewood, Ill: Dorsey. 434 pp.
32. Hymes, D. H. 1962. On studying the

history of anthropology. *Kroeber Anthropol. Soc. Pap.* 26:81–86

33. Hymes, D. H. 1963. Notes toward a history of linguistic anthropology. *Anthropol. Ling.* 5:59–103

34. Hymes, D. H. 1970. Linguistic method in ethnography: Its development in the United States. In *Method and Theory in Linguistics,* ed. P. Garvin, pp. 249–325. The Hague: Mouton

35. Hymes, D. H., ed. 1974. *Studies in the History of Linguistics: Traditions and Paradigms.* Bloomington: Indiana Univ. Press. 519 pp.

36. Hymes, D. H., Fought, J. 1975. American structuralism. In *Historiography of Linguistics, Current Trends in Linguistics,* ed. T. A. Sebeok, 10:903–1176. The Hague: Mouton

37. Kardiner, A., Preble, E. 1961. *They Studied Man.* New York: Mentor. 255 pp.

38. Kroeber, T. 1970. *Alfred Kroeber: A Personal Configuration.* Berkeley: Univ. California Press. 292 pp.

39. Kuhn, T. 1962. *The Structure of Scientific Revolutions.* Chicago: Phoenix. 172 pp.

40. Kuper, A. 1973. *Anthropologists and Anthropology: The British School 1922–72.* Baltimore: Penguin. 256 pp.

41. Linton, A., Wagley, C. 1971. *Ralph Linton.* New York: Columbia Univ. Press. 196 pp.

42. Linton, R., ed. 1943. *Franz Boas 1858–1943.* Am. Anthropol. Assoc. Mem. 61. Menasha, Wis.: Banta

43. Lowie, R. H. 1937. *The History of Ethnological Theory.* New York: Rinehart. 296 pp.

44. Lowie, R. H. 1959. *Robert H. Lowie Ethnologist: A Personal Record.* Berkeley: Univ. California Press. 198 pp.

45. Malefijt, A. 1974. *Images of Man.* New York: Knopf. 383 pp.

46. Malinowski, B. 1967. *A Diary in the Strict Sense of the Word.* New York: Harcourt, Brace & World. 315 pp.

47. Mead, M. 1966. *An Anthropologist at Work: The Writings of Ruth Benedict.* New York: Atherton. 583 pp.

48. Mead, M. 1972. *Blackberry Winter: My Early Years.* New York: Morrow. 305 pp.

49. Mead, M. 1974. *Ruth Benedict.* New York: Columbia Univ Press. 180 pp.

50. Mead, M., Bunzel, R. 1960. *The Golden Age of Anthropology.* New York: Braziller. 630 pp.

51. Mitra, P. 1933. *A History of American Anthropology.* Calcutta: Univ. Calcutta Press. 239 pp.

51a. Modell, J. 1975. Ruth Benedict, anthropologist. See Ref. 76, pp. 183–204

52. Murphree, I. 1961. The evolutionary anthropologists. *Proc. Am. Philos. Soc.* 105:265–300

53. Murphy, R. 1972. *Robert H. Lowie.* New York: Columbia Univ. Press. 179 pp.

54. Murphy, R., ed. 1976. *Selected Papers from the American Anthropologist 1946–1970.* Am. Anthropol. Assoc. 485 pp.

55. Murra, J. V., ed. 1974. *American Anthropology: The Early Years.* St. Paul: West. 260 pp.

56. Noelke, V. H. 1975. *The origin and early history of the Bureau of American Ethnology 1879–1910.* PhD thesis. Univ. Texas, Austin, Tex.

57. Palerm, A. 1974. *Historia de la Etnología: Los Precursores.* Mexico: Centro de Investigaciones Superiores, Instituto Nacional de Antropología e Historia.

58. Palerm, A. 1976. *Historia de la Etnología: los Evolucionistas.* Mexico: Centro de Investigaciones Superiores, Instituto Nacional de Antropolgía e Historia. 196 pp.

59. Pearce, R. H. 1953. *Savages of America: A Study of the Indian and the Idea of Civilization.* Baltimore: Johns Hopkins Univ. Press. 260 pp.

60. Penniman, T. K. 1935. *A Hundred Years of Anthropology.* London: Duckworth. 397 pp.

61. Quade, L. G. 1971. *American physical anthropology: A historical perspective.* PhD thesis. Univ. Kansas, Lawrence, Kans.

62. Rohner, R. P., ed. 1969. *The Ethnography of Franz Boas.* Chicago: Univ. Chicago Press. 331 pp.

63. Rowe, J. H. 1965. The renaissance foundations of anthropology. *Am. Anthropol.* 67:1–20

64. Schuyler, R. L. 1971. The history of American archaeology: An examination of procedures. *Am. Antiq.* 36:383–409

65. Sebeok, T. A., ed. 1967. *Portraits of Linguists: A Biographical Sourcebook for the History of Western Linguistics, 1746–1963.* Bloomington: Univ. Indiana Press. Vols. 1,2. 580 pp., 605 pp.

66. Simpson, G. E. 1973. *Melville Herskovits.* New York: Columbia Univ. Press. 200 pp.

67. Slotkin, J. S., ed. 1965. *Readings in Early Anthropology.* Viking Fund Publ. Anthropol. 40. 530 pp.
68. Smith, H. N. 1950. *Virgin Land: The American West as Symbol and Myth.* New York: Vintage. 305 pp.
69. Stegner, W. 1954. *Beyond the Hundredth Meridian: John Wesley Powell and the Second Opening of the West.* Boston: Houghton Mifflin. 438 pp.
70. Steward, J. H. 1973. *Alfred Kroeber.* New York: Columbia Univ. Press. 137 pp.
71. Stocking, G. W. 1968. *Race, Culture and Evolution: Essays in the History of Anthropology.* New York: Basic Books. 380 pp.
72. Stocking, G. W. 1974. *The Shaping of American Anthropology 1883–1911: A Franz Boas Reader.* New York: Basic Books. 354 pp.
73. Stocking, G. W., ed. 1976. *Selected Papers from the American Anthropologist 1921–1945.* Am. Anthropol. Assoc. 485 pp.
74. Tax, T. 1973. *The development of American archaeology 1800–1879.* PhD thesis. Univ. Chicago, Chicago, Ill.

75. Thoresen, T. H. 1971. *A. L. Kroeber's theory of culture: The early years.* PhD thesis. Univ. Iowa, Iowa City, Ia.
76. Thoresen, T. H., ed. 1975. *Toward a Science of Man: Essays in the History of Anthropology.* The Hague: Mouton 232 pp.
77. Trigger, B. G. 1966. Sir Daniel Wilson: Canada's First Anthropologist. *Anthropologica* 8:3–28
78. Trigger, B. G. 1966. Sir John William Dawson: A faithful anthropologist. *Anthropologica* 8:351–59
79. Voget, F. W. 1975. *A History of Ethnology.* New York: Holt, Rinehart & Winston. 879 pp.
80. White, L. 1963. *The Ethnography and Ethnology of Franz Boas.* Austin: Texas Mem. Mus. Bull. 6. 76 pp.
81. White, L. 1968. *The Social Organization of Ethnological Theory.* Rice Univ. Stud. 52
82. Willey, G. R., Sabloff, J. A. 1973. *A History of American Archaeology.* San Francisco: Freeman. 252 pp.
83. Woodbury, R. B. 1973. *Alfred V. Kidder.* New York: Columbia Univ. Press. 200 pp.

Ann. Rev. Anthropol. 1977. 6:419–55
Copyright 1977 by Annual Reviews Inc. All rights reserved

CULTURE, BEHAVIOR, AND THE NERVOUS SYSTEM

Horacio Fabrega, Jr.[1]
Department of Psychiatry, University of Pittsburgh,
Pittsburgh, Pennsylvania 15261

INTRODUCTION

This chapter offers an analysis of the problem of behavioral differences in terms of nervous system organization and function. Emphasis is placed on issues which have relevance to traditional anthropological pursuits. This bias needs to be underscored since the material which will be discussed could be given a different emphasis and interpretation. Several assumptions guide this presentation: (*a*) learning experiences modify behavior; (*b*) members of different groupings of man show "culturally" specific behavioral regularities; and (*c*) the behavior of man is regulated and controlled by the nervous system. It follows that man's nervous system is subject to learning (that it is somehow "plastic") and that any group regularities in behavior traced to cultural influences are in some way correlated with regularities in nervous system functioning.

In this presentation "culture" signifies the symbolic systems of a people. Such symbols are observed and reflected in the style of their social and cognitive behavior. Culture then is viewed as a system which one infers or abstracts from the distinctive mode of life of a group. The following categories of behavior are identified. By *social behaviors* we will refer to activities such as gestures, demeanor, facial displays, and simple or coordinated actions, including the social (i.e. performance) aspects of language and speech, which are viewed from an interpersonal and situational standpoint. The appropriate performance of social roles belongs in this category of behavior as does the "natural" participation in activities which are imbued with shared meanings and which reflect norms in the group. The individualistic correlates of the observable social behaviors of a people are termed *cognitive*. This implies that

[1]Work on this chapter was begun while the author was on sabbatical leave from Michigan State University as visiting professor at the Institute of Neurology (Queen Square) and Institute of Psychiatry (Maudsley Hospital) in London, England. I greatly appreciate the help of members of both these institutions who offered suggestions and provided access to important literature. Support from the Fogarty International Scholarship Program of the National Institute of Health made possible an extended stay at both institutions.

learning has somehow led to the internalization of symbols which members share, it being clearly understood that each category of behavior (i.e. social and cognitive) implies logically the other. Cognitive behaviors embrace phenomena such as thinking, rules for emotional expression, perceiving, remembering, and problem solving. An individual's capacity for and creative use of language will be viewed as a component of this type of behavior. Thus cognitive behaviors embrace the plans, rules, and means-ends strategems which the individual internalizes during the socialization process. A third category of behavior will be singled out analytically and will be termed *motor behavior*. This category includes overt and covert ("hidden") responses viewed purely as physical phenomena. The knee jerk, the pupillary contraction to light stimuli, and the salivation produced by the odor of food constitute visible motor "behaviors," as do the physical movements of overlearned complex and "social" activities (hunting, piano playing, etiquette, etc). In addition, much motor behavior cannot be directly observed—for example, the relaxation or contractions of viscera when stimulated and the constrictions of blood vessels when the surrounding temperature decreases. Motor behaviors underlie those discussed above and are correlated with them.

EVOLUTIONARY CONSTRAINTS ON CULTURAL DIFFERENCES

Despite the seeming uniqueness of human behavior, when its various forms are viewed abstractly and assessed formally by means of comparable procedures of testing, their similarity across peoples and their continuity with the behaviors of the nonhuman primates is striking. Any evaluation of the role of culture in brain-behavior relations must take into account evolutionary factors and work in comparative neuropsychology. Some of the guiding questions in this field include: 1. What anatomical differences are noted between the brain of man and that of the higher primates, and are these differences sufficiently explained by taking into account general evolutionary trends. The latter include body size differences, progressive brain/body ratio increases, and additional predicted ratio increases or "residuals". 2. What are the behavioral correlates or consequences of these trends, usually termed encephalization quotients? 3. What is the range of variation in social and cognitive behavior within and between graded series of primate species? 4. Under carefully controlled circumstances, what are the cognitive behavior capacities of higher primates, and how do these differ from those of man when analogous modes of evaluation are followed? The latter caveat forces the scientist to employ a testing procedure that does not easily lend itself to verbal coding since this obviously places primates at a relative disadvantage. 5. What social and/or cognitive behavior differences are noted between apes and man when homologous brain areas are injured? This question is deceptively simple; establishing brain-area homologies is problematic regardless of whether gross structural, cytoarchitectural, or patterns of anatomical connections are used. Furthermore, establishing comparability of extent of injury in brains of the same (not to say different) species presents no less of a formidable problem. [For a critical review of this see (151; also 35, 58, 150, 204).]

A comparative analysis of the anatomy of the brain of the higher primates and of man points to an evolutionary trend "producing" a proportionate increase in brain size/body size ratio. Many of the unique gross anatomical properties of the brain of man can thus be "predicted" mathematically by taking into account his body size. The relative sizes of different sectors of the human brain can also be predicted by controlling for its overall size. While acknowledging that "reorganization" in and between cortical and subcortical structures has undoubtedly occurred, and that the importance of brain size *does not* imply mass action (because functionally important and specialized sub-areas of the brain show proportionate increases), the continuity between man and primates in brain/body ratios has led many to the parsimonious explanation that brain size alone (selection for this basic trait) can serve to explain a great deal of the bases for man's "higher" behaviors. [For a critical exposition of this theme turn to (77, 87, 90–92, 151, 165, 183, 199, 202).]

The search continues for delimiting structural differences between the brains of man and the higher primates. Thus the human striate cortex (primary visual receiving area) is said to be proportionately smaller than that of a primate's neocortex. The structural asymmetry demonstrated in the human adult and newborn brains in the temporal areas (and possibly also in adults in the right posterior areas) which are held to subserve language (and spatial abilities) suggest a striking contrast to that of the nonhuman primates; yet it is well established that structural asymmetries exist in nonhuman primate brains as well (32, 107, 220). Despite the alleged "unique" importance of certain areas of the human brain (e.g. the angular gyrus, which is believed to subserve abilities requiring intermodal integration, the hippocampus, the association areas, and the frontal lobes), establishing the structural uniqueness compared to brains of higher primates has proved difficult (69).

Studies in ethology and in comparative psychology have amply documented the communicative richness of the social behaviors of nonhuman primates. Indeed, a theme and continuing aim in the field of behavioral biology is to work out the patterns of evolution of the various displays (and their meanings) in mammalian animal forms (18). In this body of research, a vexing problem is the development of useful categories of behaviors and the assignment of meaning to them (1). Most biologists would acknowledge that such displays and communicative behavior patterns are the outcome of genetic programs which unfold in (and require sensitization to) social situations. Because of this the behaviors may be said to be both genetic and learned (39). The dramatic consequences of socially isolating newborn and infant monkeys are testimony to the importance of rearing influences in higher mammalian forms (80). Observations of rhesus isolates indicate that many social behaviors among them are thwarted and grossly altered if not pathologically disturbed. More controlled research has shown that rhesus monkey isolates perform poorly when constrained to send or receive facial displays to other isolates as well as normal conspecifics (135, 136). Thus, although able to learn ("cognitive") discriminations in an instrumental conditioning situation, in the process responding physiologically (showing "motor behaviors") as did normal monkeys, it was the ability to communicate socially through facial displays that was impaired. Such experiments, in verifying the criticalness of social learning for the development of communicative ability in nonhuman primates, support the appropriateness of handling social behavior as a separate (analytic) category of behavior and suggest that relatively independent neurological systems may underlie them. Clearly this body of research, especially when viewed from a neurobiological standpoint, is pertinent to a full understanding of human, social, and cognitive behavior (see subsequent sections). Specifically, this body of research is similar in rationale and aims to that involving the communication of emotion. As is well known, facial expressions of certain emotions are currently viewed as universally characteristic of the human species (41, 42). These, moreover, are judged as similar (in a structural and contextual sense) to those of nonhuman primates (18). Elicitors of human facial expressions vary across human groupings as do the display rules by means of which an individual can mask the expressions, simulate them, and otherwise emblematically use them in discourse (2). Here then one notes universal human patterns (felt to be involuntary, subcortical) which humans can (voluntarily, cortically) use in order to render social behavior creative and symbolically relevant. (Neurologic substrates of social behaviors are dealt with in a later section.)

Regarding social and cognitive behaviors, the unique functions and consequences of human language are acknowledged though the exact specificities of these and their differences from that of apes is controversial and dealt with elsewhere (79, 155, 156). There seems to be agreement that in sensory processes alone, especially audition and vision (including threshold, color, acuity, and movement), few differences exist between man and the higher primates (126). Evidence for other sensory modalities is less substantial and in many instances anecdotal and provocative. For example, it is claimed that chimpanzees may be less sensitive to pain. Nonetheless, the strong commonalities between man and higher primates suggest that their nervous systems retrieve comparable amounts, levels, and units of information from the ambient physical energy of the environment. The apes also appear to be able to respond to the *relations* among sensory units and to discriminate stimulus arrays on the basis of various "cognitive" criteria (e.g. sameness–difference) which suggests a capability to order sensory phenomena by imposing patterns or creating structures (26, 44–46, 66, 79, 126, 131, 132, 151). Rudimentary forms of classification and sorting have been shown to exist among primates, and in some species there are actual instances of intermodal integration. All of this suggests some capacity for "abstraction" and "concept formation." Similarly, although the data here seem less controlled and more informally derived, it appears that apes can remember selectively; can anticipate the consequence of their actions; and can show instances of insight, planning, and foresight in the solution of problems, in the process constructively applying information about their immediate environment. The apes have been shown to possess the capacity for a concept of self, a qualitative difference which (together with man) apparently sets them apart from other primates. The spatial memory organization of apes (their ability to remember the location of objects hidden in a spatial territory) is such that it has drawn emphasis to the importance of considering representational processes in any assessment of their memory and learning abilities. Such a representational ability may thus be independent (in an evolutionary sense) from verbal language abilities. It is when projecting actions into the more distant future or recalling long past "creative" efforts that their cognitive abilities show a clear discontinuity from those of man. Nonetheless the existence of such cognitive behaviors among the higher primates, the obvious preadaptations for a form of language and communication, and indeed the stylistic attributes of their group behavior is what has led to the claim of their possessing "culture" (101, 149).

In short, in the areas of stimulus classification, problem solving, and associative learning (areas of behavior acknowledged as being more evolved and complex) there exist differences among primates of a quantitative (and in some cases qualitative) sort (151). Primate behavioral differences, of course, are magnified when man is considered, but the unique advantages devolving from the use of human verbal language in intermodal associations and in rehearsal of simple and complex actions needs to be stressed. At the very least, the verbal language system includes a phonologic, syntactic, and semantic component, and there is evidence that each has a more or less dissociable neural representation. However, exactly how these mechanisms and neural organizations function during cognition and to what extent they account for differences in behavior between man and the higher primates is not known with any degree of specificity. As an example, despite certain similarities, a prominent behavior difference is reported to exist between man and the primates in the amnestic syndrome, a behavior configuration often associated with hippocampus malfunctioning (202, 208, 209). Nothing fully analogous to the amnestic syndrome, has been observed in the higher primates, and yet the mechanism and/or neural organization which explains this is not known; perhaps size variation alone is responsible.

A clear-cut neural-behavior difference between man and the higher primates appears to be the degree of cerebral lateralization in man; that is, differences in function between the left and right sides of the brain. Few primate species show such preferences for the use of the same hand, nor are there differential behavioral deficits when segments of only one side of the brain are injured (151). Indeed, although there are some exceptions (157), the left and right hemispheres among nonhuman primates appear on the whole to be functionally similar. In man, unilateral cerebral lesions suffice to produce highly specific and differential behavior defects, whereas in nonhuman primates bilateral lesions seem to be required. Among nonprimates a normal rate and level of learning seems to require two interconnected hemispheres, whereas man and apparently nonhuman primates can learn a particular ability with only one hemisphere even if the neural system subserving the ability functions optimally with both hemispheres.

The special language capacities of man are held by many to be the principal sources of and bases for lateralization of function and asymmetries in brain organization. Language functioning also presents the best evidence of the operation of the principle of mass action in the human brain. Despite the structural differentiation between left and right temporal areas, either hemisphere can subserve language capacities, both seem to be required for optimal language and cognitive development, and a deficiency of cerebral tissue in the corresponding areas during development (in either hemisphere) is associated with cognitive behavior deficits (in language and in other abilities) in adult life. The acquisition and mastery of language may have a priority in the development of adult neural organization and function, and the capacity in question appears quite specific in its neuronal requirements (57, 95–97, 114, 115, 151, 176, 190). There is evidence to suggest that the right posterior temporal lobe in man, besides subserving spatial orientation, seems to be uniquely involved in the recognition of faces, and in this regard this capacity is also specific in its neuronal requirements (190). Lateralization of function of this degree is not at present known to be a feature of the brains of other higher primates though instances of functional assymetries have been reported (151, 157). Development of the cognitive capacity of apes to somehow "remove" themselves from the here and now, to represent a spatiotemporal model of the world, and to creatively plan, look ahead, and use previous experience as a basis for action is felt to be associated with the trend toward laterization of cerebral functions, the full realization of which involves the special verbal and visual spatial abilities of man (111, 112).

The reasons for giving attention to nonhuman primate material here seem obvious enough. There is an intrinsic interest in knowing what their behavioral capacities are; and what they are unable to do throws into sharp relief the elemental ingredients behind the human mode of adaptation or maladaptation. Stated succinctly, similarities in primate (human and nonhuman) modes of neural functioning provide the anchoring points of any physicalistic view of "higher" nervous system function and of behaviors thereby regulated. As pertains to the theme of this chapter, common properties in the behavior and neural functioning of man and the higher primates constitute possible boundaries in any examination of cultural influences in brain-behavior relations, regardless of whether such influences involve the organization of neurobehavior routines or their biological significance. Thus if the primates, including man (more specifically, the laboratory versions of captive primates and Western man), are shown to have identical sensory thresholds to X modality of stimulation, to show identical functional effects when homologous brain areas Y are injured, or demonstate similar behavioral stereotypies when toxic amounts of pharmacologic agent Z are administered, then primate brain-behavior functions subserving X modality, attributable to areas Y, or underlying stereotypies produced by Z are obviously similar. Given this state of affairs, it is unlikely that one will find cultural differences when similar means of evaluation are employed. Conversely, if man differs from the rest of the primates and especially from the apes in brain-behavior feature M, then the functioning of this area does not possess the same degree of phylogenetic fixity (e.g. genetic canalization). It is thus more likely that one might find cultural differences when such a neural domain is evaluated, but obviously there is no guarantee that cultural differences will be found either in behavior or brain organization.

The assumptions lying behind these generalizations are well known and indeed axiomatic in general biology and should be operative in the minds of all anthropologists regardless of their preferred emphases. At different points in the evolutionary time scale, prevailing social conditions served as factors that helped select neuroanatomical and neurophysiological changes; behaviors made possible by these in turn led to a modification of the social conditions of man, yielding a necessary "feedback" loop between the social and the neurological. This feedback is the reason why there is continuity in the social and cognitive behaviors of man and other primates and also why the precise origins and meanings of culture are somewhat problematic. Since the process of evolution is by definition cumulative, this means that any gains in adaptation produced by specific changes in the organization of the nervous system and mirrored in "cultural" developments were incorporated in the evolving genome of the hominid line. It also means that specifically human brain-behavior traits are built out of a genetic structure which is shared with the nonhuman primates (25, 67, 143, 203, 205, 221). In examining the question of cultural differences in brain organization and behavior then, one necessarily confronts fundamental aspects involving the meaning of species. There is the obvious fact that verbal language and other cultural traits have been and continue to be all-important in the way brain organization in the human species is realized or expressed in behavior. Developments in brain organization conditioned by culture become part of the human species as a whole. It is thus most unlikely that highly unique modes of brain organization and function will depend on specialized attributes devolving from a group's language, culture, or any other social attribute. Rather, since it is a set of general properties of culture, language, etc which the organization of the human brain necessarily requires for its expression, the properties making up the "average expectable environment," human brain organization will show profound commonalities among cultures. Nonetheless, all anatomists, physiologists, and psychologists acknowledge human variations in their domain of interest; thus one asks if these might offer clues that group differences exist.

The preceding generalizations can be rephrased by stating that evolution equips a member of the human species with the capacity for thought, visuo-spatial orientation, verbal language competence, linear codification of time, musical skills, facial recognition, problem solving, etc. Any differences in their mode of function are best interpreted as involving quantitative and not qualitative differences in brain organization. In short, symbolic systems, culture viewed in the abstract, are more likely to preferentially enhance or de-emphasize brain-behavior capacities rather than to generate entirely novel ones. When one inquires about how a group's prevailing culture might come to affect brain organization and behavior, one is inquiring about different regions of a general human continuum. On the one hand, the continuum itself is dependent on the basic sociality of man. On the other, different regions of the continuum of human functioning need to be seen as wrought out of a species-wide capability which varies continuously (61).

CULTURE AND BRAIN-BEHAVIOR RELATIONS: PUTATIVE MECHANISMS

Since "culture" refers to distinctive attributes of cognitive and social behaviors, one is faced with the need to explain how these may come about. Three explanations will be suggested and because these are speculative they are viewed as models. First, cultural rules involving behavior and child rearing may, in a purely mechanical sense, regulate which physical environmental stimuli (and to what degree) impinge on the newborn and the developing infant (120, 121, 140). In this model, any cultural meaning which the stimulations may have is not considered important. Physical environmental agents typically are studied by neural scientists, and to varying degrees each (given sufficient under or overload conditions) can be expected to affect neural development and function and, by implication, behavior. The extent to which such stimuli have to be controlled in order to produce discernible effects on adult animal behavior is variable. Whether human infants are ordinarily subject to analogous levels of "under" or "over" stimulation is questionable, and the possibility that culture (which is viewed by many as an *adaptive system*) could adversely (i.e. "maladaptively") program physical stimuli which are required for "normal" brain maturation raises obvious philosophical questions. Nonetheless, on logical grounds alone, one should allow for this possibility.

Complementing this more or less "mechanical" model, one may propose a "dynamic" one in which the rationale behind cultural conventions in child rearing practices would play an influential role. Parental influences would be judged to reflect a code that is internalized by the infant and then helps regulate which level and/or pattern of stimuli are attended to, selected, processed, and integrated in the higher levels of the nervous system. This influence might take place not in primary sensory areas, but rather in secondary association areas wherein intermodal integrations and transformations are believed to take place (141). Initially nonverbally (i.e. "emotively," through cooing, touch, fondling, directing, etc) and later through actual language and speech, stimuli from the environment may be viewed as "packaged" or ordered in a meaningful way for the infant. Clearly, a great deal of brain maturation takes place under the influence of social stimulations, the cultural meanings of which are not yet evident to the infant. Moreover, there are obvious limits to the extent to which neural representations of social symbols can "filter" physical stimuli and "tune" the nervous system. This effect of culture on brain functioning is clearly evident in the language which the infant learns. Moreover, culture and language together influence the way a person comes to recognize and like music, the way he shows emotion, and, to some extent, the way he orients spatially. It may be that in an analogous way language and cultural conventions may regulate the way other brain capacities come to be realized, such as those for facial recognition and pain behavior. Clearly so-called "higher" cortical capacities (such as those underlying language) govern not only abstract (semantic) meanings but also hedonic ones (i.e. affective, emotional) which implicate subcortical structures. In contemporary interpretations of human brain organization, emphasis is given to the various "brains" (e.g. protomammalian, limbic, etc) which are seen as somehow fused together. In these accounts, emphasis is given to the role which language and therefore culture play in modifying the functions of the "ancestral" brain.

A final model of how cultural influences might affect the organization of behavior is suggested by considering an adult who migrates to a new social group and comes to adopt its social practices. Such an individual will no doubt learn a great deal (nonverbally) simply by observation and imitation, though his native language system would obviously play an influential role in this process (e.g. through verbal introspection, rehearsal, and training). A better understanding of the conventions of the group would follow from learning its language. In both instances, neurolinguistic substrates play a critical mediating role (69, 122). Second languages seem to be represented in the same cortical centers as the original one, although there are interesting exceptions to this tendency (147). How and to what extent other structures and levels of the nervous system participate in this type of "enculturation" is not known. The literature on aphasia in bilinguals points to patterns of recovery of linguistic function, but the lack of control inherent in these studies does not allow one to draw clear-cut generalizations. Whether deficits in one language influence other facets of communication and behavior "natural" to the language community (i.e. social and cognitive behaviors) cannot be inferred.

SOCIAL BEHAVIOR AND THE FRONTAL SYSTEMS OF THE CEREBRAL CORTEX

Experiments with free-ranging monkeys have underlined the important contributions which the frontal systems of the brain (the cortex of the tip of the temporal lobe and the prefrontal-orbitofrontal cortex) make in social behaviors and affect. Bilateral destruction of this system was associated with decreased frequencies and critical alterations of a number of behavior sequences classically termed social; for example, allogromming, facial expressions, and maternal and sexual behavior (59). In another experiment, similar procedures were found to inhibit the sociality of monkeys, these failing to rejoin their social group on release and remaining solitary until their death. Increased levels of what were viewed as aimless pacing were also documented (142). However, these deficits were not observed after prolonged observations of yearling and infant rhesus monkeys whose frontal systems were destroyed. The behavioral deficits appeared with increasing severity among 2 and 3-year-old juveniles. Thus it appears that a certain degree of maturation is required for social experiences to become neurally represented and for destruction to produce discernible consequences (60). Related to these experiments are the findings that this same neural system appears to regulate the social preferences of monkeys (185). Thus differences in gender-related social preference patterns were noted between (frontal system) operated and control monkeys. The experimenters were unable to detect gross differences in behavior which might underlie the social discriminations of the monkeys. Insofar as discriminations are involved, one must acknowledge that cognitive behaviors were also affected. Observations noted by these researchers on 11 monkeys with bilateral lesions of the frontal system paralleled those reported above, with operates being more withdrawn and showing less proximity and contact with stimulus animals (29). Many other behavioral alterations which were noted can be brought under the rubric "social." At the same time these animals also show distress, "disturbance" behaviors, and differences in aggression that implicate the functioning of the amygdaloid system, with which this frontal system is known to be connected (144). Here one observes a clear illustration of the question of globality-specificity (40, 70, 123, 182). Any one neural system subserves many so-called categories of behavior which cannot be viewed as mutually exclusive; moreover, destruction of this system influences behaviors importantly regulated by other systems to which the original one connects. In other words, emotional expression differences could be said to characterize these operates; clearly, emotion is mirrored in social, cognitive, and motor behaviors (99).

Despite the presence of disturbances in various neural and behavioral spheres, one can view the above animal studies as affirming the value of the analytic category "social behavior." Though operates show some cognitive impairments—which require special methods of procedure for their documentation—many other cognitive capacities are not affected. It is the relative asociality of the operatives which is compelling. A similar relative preservation of cognitive abilities but with deficiencies in the social sphere (perhaps in the ability to judiciously apply such abilities to real-life social situations) characterizes humans with the frontal lobe syndrome. Such persons can reason "logically," can remember appropriately, and use language competently. Elementary sensory functions are likewise "normal." Despite their normality in these spheres, they are in certain ways socially compromised. These observations thus suggest that an important component of social behavior is related to the frontal systems of the cerebral cortex (83).

Although the function of the frontal lobes in man has posed a long-standing puzzle to clinicians and researchers alike, there seems to be consensus now that this part of the brain is important for the overall regulation of action. The accomplishment of complex tasks requires an active state of the cortex, which is believed to be controlled by the frontal lobes. It seems that maintenance of complex programs of activity and the matching of effects with intentions are aspects of this overall regulation. As suggested above, the frontal system cannot be treated as a homogeneous unit and many researchers have emphasized this (8, 33, 124, 144, 164, 192). Teuber (190), for example, points to a mnemonic, spatial, and an affective component of functions disturbed by frontal lobe injury and relates these to more or less distinctive regions (each of which is known to connect with other brain regions believed to subserve the functions in question). Luria (124) distinguishes between the polar, medial, and mediobasal parts (important for the regulation of the state of overall cortical activation and selective functioning) and the convexal parts (more relevant to the complex organization of motor movements). Blumer & Benson (8) indicate that prefrontal convexity lesions in humans produce a "pseudodepression" (indifference and slow, apathetic and automatic-like responses which, however, are proper and intelligible), whereas orbital area lesions seem to produce "pseudopsychopathic" behaviors (with loss of tact and social restraints, coarseness, impulsiveness, antisocial activity, etc). Teuber (193) has offered a general and theoretical account of how frontal lobe functioning might be explained physiologically, suggesting that behavioral regulation always involves two streams of neural impulses: a set of command impulses (to motor and effector systems) and a "corollary discharge" to sensory systems (which preset these for inputs generated by the expected actions and movements that will follow motor discharges).

How might attention to cultural factors broaden our understanding of this area of brain-behavior relations? As traditionally conceptualized by social scientists, social behaviors would seem to encompass at least the following: (*a*) subtle nonverbal facial cues, display mannerisms, and "maskings," all of which enunciate cultural norms of social intercourse; (*b*) mode of locomotion, gesturing, and spatial distancing; (*c*) intonation and paralinguistic features involving communication; (*d*) patterns of execution and restraints involving vegetative functions such as alimentary, excretory, and sexual; (e) patterned forms of interactions with age, sex and status —specific members of the group at large; (f) forms of emotional expression. Many other aspects of social behavior can no doubt be offered, such as the elicitors of and ways of appreciating and showing humor appropriately. The stylistic realization of each of these components of social behavior varies across cultural groups. Moreover, each component is "fully" understood only by cultural comembers. Perfect execution and understanding of styles of social behaviors could be hypothethized as one basic ingredient of culturally appropriate behavior, all peoples being able, as it were, to speak a "social language" of some sort. Anthropologists tend to view style of social behavior as involving a whole—it is the system which makes sense. This system is learned and no doubt programmed into the brain through the mediation of language. Yet whether this system can be defective in an adult even when he or she retains linguistic and cognitive competencies is not ordinarily explored. In other words, anthropologists are keenly interested in social behavior, but its neural basis, which raises the matter of the connectedness of these behaviors and their relationship to others (e.g. linguistic), is totally neglected. To sharpen the relevance of giving attention to neural factors, one may pose other questions. To what extent are *culturally appropriate* social behaviors dependent on the integrity of the frontal lobes? Which cues and facets of each component of social behavior are necessary for the preservation of style, and how are the components themselves tied to the frontal system? Can persons with "frontal lobe pathology" recognize appropriately the subtle social cues of comembers? Is there a species-wide reservoir or style of social behavior to which cultures merely add trivial refinements, or is all of social behavior only realized in a matrix of a distinctive style? Is verbal behavior, memory, thought, and sensory-motor behavior enough for adaptation, or is style a necessary "glue" which holds people together and has unique adaptive value?

Questions such as these immediately raise the issue of coherence, integration, neural representation, and function of social behaviors and of their independence from behaviors represented in other cortical centers. It would seem that answers to questions such as these can only be offered when this category of behavior is analyzed comparatively and also when explicit knowledge is available about the integrity of an individual's nervous system. There exists an obvious need for thick and sharp ethnographies focused on various aspects of social behavior touched on in this section; in particular, those behaviors dealing with social styles and those which reflect general visceral activities and functions. Another need is for careful descriptions of persons showing global disruptions in social behavior. These would include ordinary persons (viewed by co-members as normal or sick) or acutal hospitalized patients with brain pathology, toxic metabolic states, or organ-system diseases.

COGNITIVE BEHAVIORS

In this section we discuss cultural aspects of those brain-behavior problems which are ordinarily studied by neurolinguists, neuropsychologists, and some neurologists. The area of functioning that ties together these investigators involves what has been termed here "cognitive behavior." In the last few decades there has been a great deal of work aimed at specifying the location and mode of operation of neural mechanisms which influence these behaviors (for reviews see 34, 68, 69, 122, 127, 129, 137–139, 145, 153, 154, 177, 191, 194, 197).

Language and Lateralization

Man, like all other higher forms of life, possesses a nervous system that allows him to take in information from the external environment and from the body and act upon it in ways that bear on his level of adaptation. Sensory receptors feed information into the nervous system and some of this reaches its higher levels in the analyzer zones. Adaptive behavior requires that sensory information in any modality be constructively linked to motor effector units. Physical and animate objects to which organisms relate are comprised of features that the nervous system receptors retrieve through different sensory modalities. When all the features of an object are equally available, the nervous system is obviously "informed" about that object. Clearly, efficiency of recognition is gained if one type of feature (processed in one sensory modality) suffices to signal the object or furnishes information which can be related internally to other types of (remembered) features of the object (color related to texture related to consistency related to taste, etc) which in turn signal its recognition. Moreover, adaptation is enhanced to the extent that information in one modality can be equated with that in another and there is transfer across modalities. The capacity for cross-modal equivalence can be structurally determined or it can be acquired (45). Among nonhuman groups and in humans who have not yet acquired language, sensory information in one modality can in fact be related to sensory information in another (26, 44, 45). Strictly speaking human language is not necessary for all forms of cross-modal equivalence. In general this is an active field of research, and it is difficult at this time to draw firm generalization about human and nonhuman primate differences (45).

There exists controversy about how language developed and what its basic neural properties and requirements are. These issues are dealt with elsewhere in this volume (see also 33, 34, 85, 109, 116, 211). Regardless of whether one judges that the preadaptive requirements for, and elemental properties of, language involve the efficient sequencing of motor responses (76, 119, 128, 176), it appears that the realization of such neural capacities in speech and language symbols has changed the character of man's adaptation compared to that of higher primates. Such a verbal language system (VLS), a neuroanatomic and neurophysiologic structure which separates man from the primates, plays a special role in brain organization and function. Research data from any number of sources all seem to indicate that the neuronal requirements for VLS and changes brought about during the realization of VLS have a priority in brain organization, affecting how different brain regions or lobes come to function. The realization of VLS may be viewed as a genetically determined axis which influences if not regulates cerebral lateralization of function, specifically where speech and language are subserved and where other (nonspeech related) cognitive (or perceptual) capacities are involved.

It is not appropriate to summarize here the vast literature which exists on the topic of cerebral asymmetry and lateralization of function. Moreover, many issues in this area of study are controversial and far from being fully understood. The reader wishing details should consult recent reviews. There seems to be a reasonable consensus about the following points:

1. Even for sensorimotor functions, the two hemispheres of man are organized differently and are not "mirror" images of each other as was once believed (73, 108, 109, 176). Representation of these functions in the left hemisphere is said to be more focal, dense, and differentiated; in the right it is more diffuse and general. The left and right hemispheres of the human adult also differ in terms of which cognitive behaviors they influence, and some of these seem to require different modes of neural representations (81, 82, 190).

2. Language is a highly lateralized function, with left hemisphere representation in over 95% of "natural" righthanders and around 60% of lefthanders. Many lefthanders show bilateral language representations, a small percentage show true or complete right hemisphere dominance.

3. There is evidence that in humans at birth the two hemispheres show a size asymmetry in the language area (165, 199, 220). Although the language area on the left is larger (and perhaps more specialized for this ability), it is generally well known that the right hemisphere can represent language functioning. Left-sided lesions early in life produce fewer language deficits than those in adulthood, and with time many of these are overcome. The relation between age of lesion, extent of damage, and degree of disability is controversial (108, 138). Presumably the right hemisphere retains the capacity to influence language and when "forced" to, does so. A hemisphere involved with language tends to show reduced capacity for other nonlinguistic functions.

4. Within a hemisphere wherein language is represented, it appears there are centers which subserve different facets of language competence and performance, and indeed many subscribe to the view that a specific anatomical circuit connects these centers, it being possible to identify sites where lesions produce reasonably well-defined clinical syndromes of language impairment (72). Components of the VLS are represented in the brain such that the modalities of performance (hearing, speaking, reading, writing) and the linguistic functions themselves (syntactic, semantic, phonologic, lexical) show a degree of neurologic independence or separation. Data suggest that lexical and grammatical formatives may be represented differently, and the lexicon itself may be represented both phonologically and semantically (159, 219). In Japanese subjects it appears that the syllabic writing system has a separate representation from the logographic writing system (170–172, 217, 218).

5. The perception of speech involves an "encoding" process that is importantly governed by the actual anatomical and articulatory constraints imposed on speech production (114, 115). This process, which involves the simultaneous encoding of

meaningful sound units, is what permits the inordinately high rate of information that is conveyed through human speech. This distinguishes the language capacity of homo sapiens from that of nonhuman primates and perhaps earlier humanoid forms (116). The speech encoding process resides in the left hemisphere, as experiments in phonetic perception and neuropsychologic case studies indicate. This exposition of the motoric aspects of man's language-speech competence tends to support hypotheses about the gestural origins of language in man (85). The motor speech perception theory is also consistent with the inference that the neural organization of the left hemisphere is more focally represented and favors the integration of similar units (176). This form representation is felt to favor the performance of behaviors requiring fine, descriminative, and highly integrated sensory-motor sequences which some believe are at the core of human language and speech. A number of differences in the functions of the left vs the right cerebral hemispheres have been proposed (9–11, 81, 82, 146).

6. Through the study of aphasia in bilingual subjects, patterns of recovery of language functioning have been identified, and there are indications that in some instances there is a selective recovery of one or some languages (23, 24, 147). This selectivity is thought to be due to emotional, proficiency, and perhaps laterality factors.

7. Spatial abilities are held to be principally represented in the posterior aspects of the *right* hemisphere. In contrast to the "dense" or "focal" representations of function which promote the integrative actions of similar units of behavior, a feature of language performance and of the left hemisphere, function in the right hemisphere is held to be represented more diffusely and to involve the coordination of different units of behavior (214). Spatial abilities are thought to be optimized by the convergence of different modalities of perception—e.g. visual, vestibular, kinesthetic —and a neuroanatomically more diffuse mode of representation would be more likely to promote this. Because language functioning in lefthanders is often represented bilaterally (compared to righthanders), this is held by some to diminish their performance on spatial tests (111).

8. Research findings among people of Western cultures indicate that males outperform females in many spatial ability tests. This intersex difference is manifest early in development and persists and increases as children mature. It is conjectured that the sexes differ in their degrees of laterality and mode of cerebral representations. Specifically, females are held to be less lateralized, with language ability bilaterally represented, a form of cerebral representation which explains their underperformance on spatial tests (81, 82, 111).

9. In general, it appears that comparatively less is known about the organization and mode of functioning of the (right temporo parietal) portion of the brain involved in the integration and analysis of visual-spatial abilities. Not as much is known about the specific location of centers, let alone circuits, controlling this ability as is the case with language. Nor has it been possible to break down visual-spatial abilities into component units of functions, each of which accomplishes separate facets of this admittedly very complex ability. Finally, although lesions in the right side of the brain variously alter spatial orientation and (nonverbal) memory, deficits do not

clearly group together to form clinical syndromes as was the case with language functions (206).

10. Hand preference, though obviously not a cognitive behavior, appears to be a distinctive feature of humans nonetheless and is a salient example of cerebral lateralization. Genetic models of handedness in human populations have been developed (110, 113). The literature dealing with cultural pressures toward conformity in hand use has recently been reviewed (28). The reader is referred to Teng's report (187) for an empirical study involving cultural and genetic influences in hand preferences in a Chinese population.

A basic assumption in neurolinguistics and in the neurosciences generally is that the brain of Homo sapiens reflects localization of function, the general outlines of which have been mentioned. Here one can only point to a few aspects of cerebral lateralization of function which have significance for cultural anthropology. Thus the VLS of members of all human groups no doubt share elemental neural properties and show equally basic constraints in neural functioning. Yet it appears that the VLS of peoples are somehow realized differently. In speaking different languages, people draw on and classify phenomena in different ways and also associate these classifications differently. How is the fact of differences in spoken language reflected in the way the VLS works? Do the set of language universals, whatever these consist of, fully account for the neural schemas which subserve VLS functions? Are natural language differences reflected in a nontrivial way in how VLS processes and associates neural information? For example, people are held to classify and name objects in diverse ways. There is evidence suggesting that among Western people, semantic groupings may have a separate neural representation in VLS (34, 159, 211, 219). One may ask: Are the semantic categories that enable a people to classify phenomena drawn from a neurologically determined common set whose defining properties apply to all groups?—for example, such semantic groupings as me vs not me, body parts, colors, before-after, animate vs inanimate, etc. Alternatively, are there fundamentally different forms of semantic groupings and are these neurally encoded in a unique way?

For example, one could propose that each human language makes special use of a set of phonologically related root-forms which, in light of the cultural history of its speakers possess special core meanings. Such "phono-semes" are integral to many lexical units of the language, and as the social group evolves they can enter into the formation of new lexical units which reflect the changing interpretations that speakers have of the root forms themselves and of the world, given the "cultural path" which the group has taken. Different domains of the experiences of a people are linked in this way, there being little correspondence across different peoples. If this is so, and if the root forms have a neurologic representation, then brain lesions would give rise to patterns of dysphasic or paraphasic errors which reflect the (culturally unique) meaning of the root forms in a language (which tie together lexical units differently in each language) rather than universal semantic distinctions. A competition between culturally linked "phonosemantic" vs broad universal semantic distinctions may be set in motion in certain forms of aphasia. In brief, if there exists a basic and common set of semantic groupings which are a part of all VLS, one anticipates a common neural organization and mode of breakdown of VLS. However, if the capacity for making semantic groupings is more plastic such that it enables VLS to neurally encode words (and by extension, phenomena) along (culturally) unique axes, then one might expect to find different forms of "confusion" and "misnaming' to be manifest among peoples as a result of damage to VLS. Questions similar to those asked about the neural correlates of the semantic aspect of VLS could be developed which pertained to the syntactic and phonological aspects of VLS. The embracing question concerns the universality vs. uniqueness of the basic neural units which go into making up the different components of VLS. One implication of this can be surmised. Thus, if (a) the VLS (which includes semantic units and rules) of peoples do vary in a nontrivial way, and (b) if neural information which is represented or encoded here, in being "associated" with neural information drawn from other sensory regions of the brain, somehow affects its organization, then (c) actions (social, cognitive, or motor) subserved by these latter regions may be judged as importantly influenced by the language and culture of a people. However, even if one holds that neural encodings of nonlanguage information take place in a way that is fully independent of VLS, it still appears that such encodings partially filter through VLS during awareness of self and the regulation of (social, cognitive, and motor) behavior. Here again the features of culture which are represented in VLS somehow influence attention, thought, consciousness of self, and behaviors of all sorts.

Space prohibits pursuing additional implications devolving from the fact of cerebral lateralization in function (e.g. language vs visual-spatial). Obviously, the existence of such differences and the notion that as a consequence man can be described as "having" two brains bears importantly on how one construes the process of human evolution (71). This has been discussed amply in the literature (see also 189, 222). Similarly, the notion of lateralization of function has raised the question of whether there exists "competition" between the hemispheres. It has seemed to some as though during the performance of certain tasks active inhibition of one hemisphere by the other took place. Language-related modes of analysis involving the left hemisphere appear disadvantageous for optimal solution of visual-spatial problems best handled through right-sided neural routines; conversely, visual-spatial modes of analyzing seem less efficient for the solution of problems requiring fine discriminative control of motor sequences [which appear to be undertaken by the language hemisphere (111)]. The idea of hemisphere competition has been discussed in relation to brain maturation and applied in a preliminary way to cultural influences (12, 94, 148, 188). Here it is postulated that developmental, linguistic, sensory-motor, perceptual, and "intellectual" tasks of different sorts are carried out in and come to influence the two halves of the brain in different ways. Cultures, now viewed as collections of tasks and learning routines requiring different mixes of left and right-sided functions, may differentially draw on or more strongly impose requirements on modes of neural function. In this sense, cultures could be described by their relative mixes of left versus right brain emphasis. In emphasizing and explicating the neurologic correlates associated with differences in linguistic versus nonlinguistic abilities, in relating these to diachronic and synchronic issues of brain function which underlie styles of behaving, thinking, and feeling, and in seeing all of the above as realized in socioculturally diverse and changing settings, such investigators appear to be formulating a modern version of the Sapir-Whorf hypothesis.

Perception

Cultural influences in perception and cognition have generated a great deal of interest and controversy among anthropologists and psychologists. Several reviews in this general area have appeared recently, written from the standpoint of behavioral differences (5, 21, 27, 75, 118, 196). It is thus not necessary to summarize empirical findings. Instead, the neural aspects of this body of work will be discussed. Given the nature of this problem area, its state of development, and the relative neglect of neurologic factors, a theoretical and exploratory discussion seems justified.

Because people differ in the way they talk about, orient to, and behave toward physical aspects of the environment, it has been conjectured that they may actually neurally register and process physical stimuli from them differently. Similarly, because people often behave differently when traumatized or during episodes of illness and disease, it has seemed natural to question whether they perceived noxious and/or other internal (bodily centered) stimuli differently. It has never been claimed that people *lacked* certain sensory-perceptual capacities, merely that these capacities might be realized ("programmed") differently as a result of cultural and linguistic influences.

An exemplary problem has involved the perception of color (16). The historical aspects of this problem, the competing positions about it, and recent experimental data bearing on its interpretation have been reviewed (13–15). From a position which ascribed to culture-language factors (e.g. color words, classifications) an important and influential role in perception (i.e. linguistic relativity), opinion has shifted to that which ascribes to perception an influential role on culture and language (i.e. phenomenal absolutism). Specifically, the position now is that basic neuroanatomic structures and physiochemical processes underlie color vision and that these have a determining influence on how humans respond to color, code it through language, and retrieve it in memory. Related but not identical uniformities in neurologic structures and functions characterize infrahuman species so that one can say that among them also "organic" factors serve to categorize or impose color boundaries. Certain culture-linguistic differences in the area of color naming which have been reported among certain peoples are held to stem from differences in retinal pigmentation. The latter influence the visual processing of light in certain areas of the color spectrum and account for color confusions in the blue-green region. Recently, Sahlins (167) has argued that "culture" has always entailed the creative —and therefore unique—use of basic neurophysiologic distinctions that evolution has provided man.

How might this whole problem be conceptualized neurologically? Recall that the cultural-linguistic relativist position ascribes to color words a determining influence on perception. Such native words label native color categories and these somehow are felt to guide the processing of (and the responding to) visual stimuli. In terms of considerations discussed earlier, one can diagram the putative mechanisms and processes (see Figure 1) with a chain believed to eventuate in color-related behaviors (CRB). This diagram summarizes the course of neural impulses through the nervous system, depicting how such impulses might flow both during development (when brain organization is being realized) and during actual perceptual tasks (when impulses generate specific behavioral responses). The string, beginning with color stimuli and ending in CRB, which includes only unbroken links, diagrams the putative relativist's chain. As will be noted, the VLC is shown to be reached early after sensory registration. In this instance CRBs reflect in an important way neural processes (e.g. categorizations, transformations, etc) taking place in the VLC station. Either motor behaviors (reflecting sensori-motor linkages) or cognitive ones (e.g. memory) bear the stamp of color categories which are somehow "encoded" in VLC. The string, which includes the broken chain and bypasses the VLC, would seem to represent a weak version of the universalist's claim. In other words, here CRBs reflect the pure physiological registration of vision, together with linkages with other sensory, association, and motor systems. When nonhuman primates or prelanguage infants are tested, it is essentially this latter chain which seems to be operative. A strong version of the universalist's claim (also termed the phenomenal absolutist) would hold that the relativist string might in fact also be appropriate (though perhaps VLC is reached later, after the "association" areas); but that processes taking place in the VLC station are either analogous across linguistic groupings or trivial, and that the portion of the chain beyond VLC is by and large similar for all peoples.

The preceding analysis has dealt with a linguistically salient model of perception involving color. We can only mention here several additional models which seem to be implicated in the analyses of other types of results of cross-cultural studies of perception. The work dealing with socialization influences on cognitive style, including field dependence-independence and perceptual differentiation, would seem to implicate limbic structures insofar as affective reinforcements (permissiveness-restrictiveness) are viewed as salient (215). The influence which ecological conditions [e.g. carpenteredness (174)] are alleged to have on visual illusions implicate exposure to visual stimuli so that connections between occipital cortex and the rest of the cortex would be striking.

Finally, in the problem involving the two-dimensional representations of three-dimensional objects, complex unimodal (visual) stimuli, presented in flat pictures,

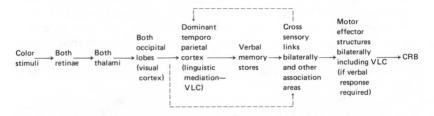

Figure 1   Language influences in perception of color (see text).

appear (conventionally) to represent a three-dimensional object or situation which the subject is required to name (30, 31). In this instance, cultural conventions which are represented pictorially and which the person internalizes come to affect how the rest of the cortex functions (i.e. how such visual cues are used). It is obvious that such pictures acquire their full impact through language. The importance of language would mean that visual stimuli should be "channeled" through VLC early in the neural chain.

Thus far anthropologists have given principal attention to the perception of color and spatial factors. This is not surprising since the operation of these perceptual systems can be brought to bear on items (color chips, figures, etc) which lend themselves nicely to evaluation in field settings and moreover are operative constantly and in public settings. It is now evident that to study even these systems in a rigorous manner, increasingly sophisticated equipment and laboratory facilities are needed. The need for controlled "rigorous" study of the mode of operation of a perceptual system, of course, in no way is meant to imply that traditional approaches to perceptual domains are eschewed. The perception of pain constitutes an additional area which should be studied by anthropologists. There are now available increasingly sophisticated means for the controlled study of pain, and with time it should be possible to compare the pain thresholds of various people. Such information may be viewed as corresponding to the proximal portions of the connected neural chain which subserves pain. Social and psychological influences are already known to influence an individual's tolerance for pain, and it would be unlikely if cultural differences were not shown to exist (133, 207). The range of variation and indeed the modifiability of the level of pain tolerance may well vary, however, and it is important to document this in the event it is so. Similarly, stimuli classed as painful are "arousing," which means that their registration activates wide portions of the nervous system. What were termed an individual's motor behavior (which included external visible and internal vegatative physical responses—see next section) are consequently brought into play, and it is not unreasonable to suppose that cultural differences will be demonstrated here. All of the preceding relate more directly to the neurologically oriented scientist (177) but can be related to interests of cultural anthropologists (55).

Memory

There are at least three aspects to the neural basis of memory and learning. These are: anatomical [i.e. where in the nervous system are memories and learned routines stored? (195)]; physiological [i.e. what are the functional changes that take place in cells, in intercellular junctions, and/or among cellular assemblies which mediate learning and memory-related processes? (93)]; and biochemical (i.e. what are the chemical-molecular changes which underlie the physiological changes?) Learning and memory, when viewed from a developmental standpoint, are central to the question of the degree of plasticity and modifiability of the nervous system.

In light of the interests of psychological anthropologists, the neural correlates of memory and learning raise interesting questions about enculturation. Thus much of an individual's behavior (e.g. in face-to-face interactions, in practical and/or subsistence activities, in ritual enactments, etc) reflects learning and memory so that the whole process of enculturation is somehow embodied in these neuropsychological processes. It is a truism that members of all groups learn, remember, recall, recognize, and perform learned routines. Moreover, there are obvious differences in what is learned and remembered and there is even data to suggest that from a behavioral standpoint how this is accomplished varies across groups (20). Nonetheless, the basic processes are defining properties of man and of living organisms generally. With regards to human beings, one may pose the following questions: In what special ways can participation in cultural activities be reduced to the problem of memory? More specifically, can individuals become so impaired in their memorial capacities that their behavior may approximate that of a "deculturalized" individual? From a general point of view, one can ask what neural impairments which affect memory (and through this, the performance of other cognitive behaviors) are required in order to deprive an individual of his capacity to participate in culture?

An analysis of the neural basis of culturally distinctive behaviors raises the question of holism vs locationism which has been hinted at previously. Can adaptive behavior, which appears so integrated, be an outcome of a mere collection of relatively isolated and antonomous centers that are simply connected together? One needs to recall the obvious fact that an individual's language ability (a "learned" trait that one somehow "remembers") is critical to his participation in culture. In this sense, his ability to speak and comprehend spoken language in a culturally appropriate way obviously requires the centers and circuits described earlier. The destruction of these regions of the brain can render an individual severely impaired in his ability to communicate through speech and/or to comprehend spoken or written language. Aphasia is the name given to this class of disturbances. However, in a number of respects, the aphasic individual's capacity to participate in culture is retained. For example, such individuals very often recognize persons known to them; they retain the capacity to perceive the environment; they judge the social requirements of situations; they indicate likes, dislikes, pain, pleasure, hunger, thirst, etc; they enact learned motor routines; they can bathe and clothe themselves appropriately; they use environmental objects (e.g. furniture, tools, instruments, utensils); and most importantly, their social behavior clearly reflects the sanctions and rules of the group. It is obvious that despite having communicative problems, such individuals know a great deal about their culture.

Brief mention should be made of the syndrome termed "isolation of the speech center" (74). In this instance, the whole speech circuit appears relatively intact but its connections to the rest of the brain are destroyed. The individual studied with this lesion lacked propositional speech and comprehension (except for special verbal responses), seemed not to recognize others or respond to social demands, nor was she able to look after herself properly. Interestingly, when carefully evaluated, she gave evidence that she retained the capacity to repeat spoken words, to complete common sayings after being primed, appeared to correct ungrammatical constructions, and even showed the capacity to learn the words of new songs. Thus this individual, though in many ways asocial and "deculturalized," nonetheless "remembered" information, showed that she recalled her grammar, and could learn new verbal expressions. Rudiments of language were retained and with this rudiments of culture; however, it is clear that this was insufficient to allow the individual to function. This syndrome is in certain ways the complement of the aphasias, where individuals though severely impaired in language can nonetheless function appropriately socially.

Individuals showing disturbances in language ability then constitute one group which though compromised retain certain capacities for culture. Discussion earlier involving frontal lobe lesions involved the question of the neural mechanisms subserving culturally distinctive social behaviors. Individuals so afflicted sometimes lack the capacity for carrying out planned and regularized behaviors and engage in actions which reflect the violation of agreed upon conventions. These features are implicit in the clinical dictum that persons with frontal lobe pathology "lack good judgement"; yet they somehow know how to violate norms and reflect reasonable priorities in which ones they violate! Thus, in certain ways, the grasp of situations is retained. It is their behavior in them which can be changed, though in ways which "make sense." Here at the very least memory is operating so as to promote an understanding of culture. And although "frontal lobe individuals" may reflect an emotional flatness, distance, and detachment, there are very good indications that these individuals retain a capacity for culture. They speak and comprehend appropriately; they recognize others; they show like-dislike preferences that reflect cultural values; and they can use physical objects appropriately. Finally, their retention of accumulated knowledge about the world provided to them by culture is usually intact, which serves to ground their social and language behavior with credibility and naturalness. The capacity for culture thus seems relatively well preserved in these individuals. By a similar mode of analysis one can show that individuals deprived of the capacity for motor performance (i.e. paralyzed or weak) and unable to perceive and discriminate sensory information (i.e. blind, deaf, impaired in touch, temperature, or pain) nonetheless retain enormous amounts of knowledge and abilities which render their behavior in many ways culturally appropriate.

The preceding discussions lead one to a consideration of the neural basis of memory and learning and to the potential "criticalness" of these for the preservation of an individual's capacity to participate in cultural activities in an appropriate manner. It is tautologically true that an individual neurologically deprived of neural tissue and neural organizations which serve to store learned information and programs for behavior is "deculturalized," for such an individual may be viewed as functionally mute and, in a social sense, unconscious. An individual neurologically deprived of all memory would also be unable to learn; he would lack a neural and behavioral context with which to assimilate new experiences. Moreover, if it is the case (as some believe) that acquired experiences are neurologically assimilated through the same processes and cellular assemblies which mediate genetic or "innate memories" of the species, such an individual is indeed unlikely to attend to, let alone carry out, elemental survival functions. The prospect of analyzing the relation between memory and cultural participation is thus best dealt with more narrowly; specifically by analysis of recognizable syndromes, the components of which reflect clear-cut types of memorial alterations.

Brain disturbances that are an outcome of toxic or metabolic factors can produce an interference in immediate recall, sometimes referred to as short-term memory. Such individuals frequently are said to be distractible and unable to concentrate on information. Moreover, they very often misperceive and distort stimuli which are presented through various sensory modalities. Their memorial difficulty is easily demonstrated by having them attempt to repeat a series of digits or names, a task which they often cannot perform. Delirium tremens, which can result upon withdrawal from long-term alcohol use, is perhaps the best recognized of these syndromes. Such delirious individuals, who are usually excited, agitated, grossly "confused" and unable to respond appropriately to stimuli from the environment, are somehow unable to effectively use their stored information so as to participate appropriately in social activities despite the fact that their syntax and lexicon reflect knowledge of their native language and they can recognize and identify objects and persons. Although social functioning is grossly impaired, much culturally appropriate behavior remains. Other behavioral manifestations of delirium tremens raise interesting questions about the role of cultural symbols in brain-behavior relations. A "paranoid"—terror stricken and agitated—demeanor, for example, is said to be very common. What is feared—and its significance—is obviously culturally determined. However, are formal attributes of the condition (e.g. suspicion, fear, destructiveness) inevitable or are they somehow dependent on the symbols and paradigms people use in constructing realities? A basic question then is whether the disturbance is structurally universal or whether it depends on the kind of "reading" which the brain makes of the alteration—a reading which takes into account the meanings of cultural symbols. The whole problem of the "preparedness" of learning and of the universality vs cultural specificity of phobias is pertinent here (175). Similar questions can be raised about the Lilliputian hallucinations which are said to delight the patient and are not associated with terror. Do objects always appear changed in size, and are all classes of animate beings always altered or merely those which carry a particular meaning in the group? Another common feature of the syndrome is said to be work-related hallucinations in various modalities, with the patient enacting his or her work tasks and relationships in a detailed and explicit way. At present we have no way of explaining in a compelling way the reasons for these types of behavioral symptoms of delirium tremens. There is an obvious need to clarify whether the behavioral symptoms retain anything near their form and general meaning in other cultures. From the standpoint of the argument developed here, it is obvious that individuals so afflicted, who in many respects may be said to show an asociality and an inability to participate appropriately in cultural activities, nonetheless reflect (behaviorally and in a very compelling way) a neural representation of their culture.

The next neurological memory-learning disturbance to be considered is the amnestic syndrome. This has a number of interesting anatomical and behavioral properties that are reasonably well understood, though an interpretation (186, 198, 200) of the mechanisms of the syndrome are far from being established (202, 209). Individuals showing this syndrome are severely impaired in their ability to acquire new information or skills. The so-called short-term memory process is thus disturbed. Because of this, such individuals cannot remember what has transpired since the inception of the disorder and are said to show an *anterograde* amnesia. In addition, when carefully probed, such individuals also show poor recollection of events which occurred prior to the advent of their disorder—they also show a *retrograde* amnesia. In short, individuals showing the amnestic syndrome are grossly lacking in certain neural substrates required for full participation in everyday social activities. For this reason they usually require some form of custodial care or institutionalization. Yet reports of observations on and conversations with such individuals are replete with indications that their behavior is culturally appropriate: They converse appropriately, dress and care for themselves appropriately, follow social conventions, display emotions under appropriate circumstances and in a reasonably well-regulated way, and reflect choices and values highly consistent with those of normal comembers. The grasp of social situations is clearly intact, as is their ability to abstract the (cultural) relevance of information which they are able to retain in their memory. When inquiries with these individuals probe specific items of information which they should remember but have forgotten, they often tend to fabricate answers but do so in a way that seems to reflect logical relations and appropriate manipulation of social symbols (i.e. common rules and assumptions about behavior seem to be maintained). Indeed, these fabrications (which are termed confabulations) may be viewed as culturally appropriate constructions which are generated in order to render interactions credible. It is obvious that in order to accomplish this an individual must possess intact his "language centers," much of his "memory" for standard (widely shared) items of information, as well as neural embodiments of cultural premises, rules, and programs about the world, human purposes, and ordered social actions. Thus again a form of memory disturbance impairs the individual's ability for full and effective social participation at the same time that much of his "culture" is preserved.

The final disorder to be considered as an example of interactions between neural substrates, memory-learning activities, and culture is dementia. This disorder is characterized by a number of general dysfunctions in higher cerebral functions, memory being but one of these. There are many pathologic variations in the mode of onset and progression of dementia, as well as types of pathologic processes which can produce it (152, 210). This has led some neurologists to doubt that dementia constitutes a "medical entity" as opposed to merely the cumulated effects of a collection of "focal" disabilities. Again the question of holism versus locationism is implicated. A common finding is that there is widespread generalized dysfunction of tissues and centers of the brain. Typically the condition is defined as one involving a progressive deterioration in intellectual faculties. During its early phases the individual shows impaired ability to solve problems, he or she misses the grasp of situations, and often becomes bewildered in the midst of complexity. During this phase, overlearned habits, adherence to customary social patterns, and the use of common verbal expressions and cliches seem to sustain the individual's participation in everyday activities. Loss of memory (mainly for recent but also for remote events) is said to be a typical indicant of the condition. [For an interesting attempt to evaluate memory for remote events, and for an analysis of its implications, turn to (169).] From the standpoint of the theme being developed here, one can say that the individual appears to retain elemental capacities which enable him to participate appropriately in nondemanding, routine aspects of social activity, whereas the more refined ingredients of an individual's enculturation are blunted. With time the condition can progress to severely compromise even these basic rudiments of the person's capacities for culture. Both social and cognitive behaviors, as it were, become progressively disordered and deficient. Individuals may lose the ability to write, understand language, and recognize significant others (and even themselves) yet still retain certain highly practiced routines which are "cultural." Ultimately they can become bedridden, mute, and unable to care for themselves. Essentially this condition can be viewed as involving a progressive breakdown of an individual's capacity to participate in culturally appropriate behavior. As in the previous conditions discussed, memory and learning are grossly impaired; in addition, other cognitive abilities and functions are lost and many "deficiencies" in social behavior are observed, yet despite these deficits the individual's behavior continues for some undetermined amount of time to reflect the preservation of cultural categories, rules, plans, and likes and dislikes. A selective impairment of the semantic organization of memory is typically manifest in these patients (201).

In this section, the relation between (culturally appropriate) social and cognitive behaviors and neural embodiments of memory-learning have been discussed. As in earlier sections—see especially "social behaviors"—an underlying theme has been the relation between cultural distinctiveness and neural organization. Memory disturbances, at least as these are realized among Western people, certainly do not erase (though they do blunt) an individual's capacity for culture. No one can deny that there exists cultural differences in behavior, yet its neural correlates cannot easily be specified. The question is whether culturally distinctive behavior is an attribute only of the way the brain *as a whole* functions, there being no one (or substrate of) center(s) or region(s) which subserves (or class of behavior reflecting) it. This would seem to involve embracing a strong form of holism, a tradition which is less frequently held in neurobiology. Additionally, in view of the preceding discussions, this particular view raises a number of problems. An alternative view would be to equate culture with the connected integration of functional systems, selected portions of an individual's capacity to reflect culture being centered in different brain regions. Every part of the brain, in short, subserves culture. This view seems to make all social and cognitive behaviors (and parts thereof) necessarily cultural. The fact that cultural distinctiveness can be associated with a composite of separate functions and abilities would seem to raise theoretical questions for cultural anthropologists. A final view would state that the motivation behind the theme pursued in the chapter is simplistic and fallacious. In implicitly equating culture with mind and attempting to "solve" the problem of mind by using the procedures implicated in the study of body, a fundamental logical misconception is being perpetuated. This view, it would seem, disqualifies the neurosciences from properly addressing problems in cultural anthropology.

MOTOR BEHAVIORS

As stated at the outset of this review, the term "motor behavior" is used to denote patterns of muscular responses which are viewed in physical terms. Behaviors which underlie overt actions and the performance of specific tasks by an individual are included together with those "invisible" bodily responses which take place within the organism and are the outcome of muscle responses in organs and blood vessels. Motor behaviors thus embrace skeletal and smooth muscle contractions of the individual. In certain respects this class of behavior is the one that has been of greatest interest to anthropologists who investigate group differences in behavior with the aim of linking these to nervous system functioning. The area of work known as environmental physiology is concerned with similar kinds of problems (4). To be sure, workers in this area, which has been termed "physiological anthropology," do not ordinarily frame their question in terms of "neural" correlates of behavior or even nervous system functioning; instead, concepts ordinarily used include physical fitness, thermoregulatory adjustments, and adaptation to environmental stressors (25). Nonetheless, it is evident that a large proportion of so called acclimatization responses are pertinent to the theme of this review.

Several observations can be made about this area of study. The first is the importance given to the idea of physiological adaptation. The researcher assumes and searches for response patterns which indicate that the physiological system of the person is changed in some special way that implies a better adapted fit to the environment. Another important question is that of separating genetically determined versus environmentally acquired response patterns. As an example of a problem, consider group differences in the responses of an extremity which is cooled in a controlled fashion. A question posed is: Are observed group differences genetically "wired" in the individual (38), or are they somehow acquired as a result of living in an area which continually taxes the organism in a specified manner? In many instances both types of influences can be demonstrated (65). A third general feature of this area of study is that when acquired influences are documented, it is usually observed that physical environmental variables (to which a particular cultural group is exposed) are viewed as producing the differences in motor behavior. Conversely, it is rarely true that symbolic influences are entertained in the explanations for any observed differences. At most it is the indirect or passive aspect of culture which is held important: rules of the group may cause the individual to be exposed to a different constellation of physical environmental variables. A fourth feature of this field is that nervous system parameters are ordinarily not directly studied and often are not even invoked in explanations, the researchers concentrating instead on the gross physiological response per se. To be sure, this is often a constraint necessarily imposed by the subject matter, by methodological factors, and by other considerations as well. Thus the preservation of warmth in a cooled extremity is probably a direct outcome of cold induced vasodilation of arterioles brought on by reflex muscular changes in the smooth muscles which are mediated by the peripheral segments of the autonomic nervous system. The more direct study of the way this portion of the nervous system functions raises technical and logistical problems difficult to solve in the field, and moreover more direct exploration of the peripheral nerves and arterioles is for obvious ethical reasons best carried out on animals. One can say then that when physiological anthropologists do (indirectly) invoke neural explanations, it is the "lower" level of the nervous system which is represented. Reflex phenomena and other forms of automatic and nonvolitional (i.e. "nonsymbolic") factors are used to account for an observed effect: for example, peripheral nerve functioning or reflex adjustments in the spinal cord or brain stem. Again, it is a fact that most cardiovascular responses and circulatory changes of the type studied are mediated at these levels of the nervous system.

In line with this general trend in physiological anthropology for researchers to focus on more or less automatic and peripheral aspects of nervous system function, one observes a relative paucity of interest in the area of psychophysiology, visceral conditioning, and the physiological aspects of emotion. The latter implicate motor behaviors but from a different point of view insofar as physiological parameters are studied as responses to socially meaningful stimuli. Finally, whereas adaptation as considered by physiological anthropologists is often viewed as involving reflexes (i.e. as "automatic"), many of the adaptive processes mediated through the autonomic nervous system which concern psychophysiologists are held to be learned and indeed have been shown to follow principles of instrumental conditioning, some of which implicate personal awareness.

In psychophysiology one finds principles and concepts which can implicate cultural influences in behavior and thus should have an inherent appeal to anthropologists. As an example, Mandler (125) has made a distinction between psychologically functional physiological variables and physiologically functional psychological variables. The former refer to physiological responses which control psychological events and processes; the latter (which on intuitive grounds should appeal to anthropologists) refer to psychological or behavioral events which control physiological responses. To the extent that psychological states are affected by cultural influences, they may control physiologic responses. Additional features of psychophysiology which relate to anthropological questions include the notion of individual differences in range, amplitude, and patterning of autonomic measures; the importance of genetic as well as acquired factors in affecting baseline measures, autonomic "tone," and response patterning; and, lastly, the ideas of Engel (43; see also 105) which involve "response specificities" that result from individual uniqueness in autonomic functioning (which can have either a genetic or acquired basis). Since anthropologists have been attracted to the notion of personality and character as internalized correlates of culture, one would think that the idea of individuals and groups showing distinctive hierarchies of autonomic responses would have a similar appeal. In short, it is theoretically plausible that just as cultural groups show differences in physiological adaptation to physical environmental factors, they can show differences in (psycho) physiologic adaptation to their social environment: tasks and other demands of living which have a social and symbolic coloration may produce differing patterns of visceral and autonomic functioning and responsivity. This general problem area is essentially uncharted by anthropologists.

One can illustrate the relevance of psychophysiology for anthropology, and the problems which it poses, by considering the matter of control of the cardiovascular system. In Western medicine, the search for predictors of hypertension and coronary heart disease (CHD) has implicated a number of physical, social, and psychological factors (89, 158). One line of research involves relating cardiovascular responses, or their presumed "precursors," to the types of interactions which the individual has with co-members. Cardiovascular responses have traditionally been thought of as mediated at intermediate and lower levels of the nervous system, specifically at the level of brain stem and autonomic ganglia through reflexes affecting heart rate, stroke volume of the heart, and arteriolar constriction. The current perspective invoking social psychological factors thus emphasizes the role of higher (i.e. cortical) levels of the nervous system in the control of (lower level) responses.

Intense competitiveness is a central feature of a specific behavior pattern, called Type A, which has been linked to an increased likelihood of hypertension and CHD (62–64, 160–163). According to Rosenman et al (163), the Type A person tends to be competitive, aggressive and hostile, hard-driving and ambitious, and restless and impatient. In style and manner the person exhibits brisk speech and body movements, fist clenching, taut facial muscles, and explosive speech. The Type A person acts as though he is in a chronic "struggle with time," ever attempting to accomplish more and more in less and less time, and in a chronic struggle with people around him. His lifestyle is to live more rapidly and aggressively than his peers. Type A behaviors are reportedly elicited more readily by some environmental conditions (deadlines, interruptions or delays, competitive challenges) than by others. According to many, Type A behaviors are more typical of "evolved" and "complex" social systems (46). Persons living in less disturbed, more organized, and simpler social conditions tend to show more "normal" blood pressures and less CHD despite similarities in diet and salt intake which are also held to be important influences in the genesis of these conditions.

A great deal of research on the Type A behavior pattern has led to a specific formulation of man-environment factors in hypertension and CHD. Certain *cultural conditions* (competitive challenges, deadlines, etc) must combine with certain *susceptible individuals* (Type A whom one should view as more typically "formed" under certain cultural conditions) to produce specific motor behavior and associated changes (excess sympathetic response, reduced blood clotting time, etc) which if repeated sufficiently often cause *permanent damage* to the cardiovascular system. In essence one could say that adverse cultural conditions can lead to permanent maladaptive nervous system responses; the "fixing" of these is associated with increased levels of morbidity and mortality. All four parts of this model have been researched to some degree. According to the model, a limited part of the human environment, combining with susceptible people, is translated through the central nervous system into neurologic, neurendocrine, and biochemical adaptations which contribute to hypertension and CHD.

The ability of persons to *consciously* modify the functioning of their autonomic nervous system through contingent reinforcement of responses which are fed back to the individual is an established generalization in the field of psychophysiology, and so-called biofeedback training techniques are being used in the treatment of many conditions of disease (7, 17, 78, 134, 178, 216). Just as it is reasonable to expect that groups may differ in (psycho) physiological responsivity, one may expect that they will differ in their ability to exert control over this responsivity and that these differences can be traced to acquired and/or genetic influences. In this category of motor behavior, one may well find correlates of culture which individuals more or less consciously learn or which at the very least they acquire passively as a consequence of unique social experiences. It is clear that this at present is but a logical possibility. How early experiences affect the development of autonomic regulation is far from clear even in laboratory animals (86).

CULTURE, NERVOUS SYSTEM, AND HUMAN DISEASE

Several notions implicit in this review can be stated briefly. A fundamental one is that symbols are of overwhelming importance in the analysis of human activities. Additionally, the view here is that symbols influence and may be realized in human behaviors. It is through analysis of the latter, which admittedly requires a broad definition, that a social scientist learns of the existence, meanings, and relevance of symbols. Because behavior is also regulated by the nervous system, one is (in the logic of this argument) forced to look at its structure and functioning in order to examine critically how symbols and other types of complementary behavioral influences might possibly fit together. The preceding sections contain analyses of different facets of this problem area. Research data suggest that the mode of functioning of the early (reflexive) stations of the connected neural chains and nets which underlie human behavior are relatively similar to those of the higher primates. It is in the later more complex and interconnected "nets," which embrace cortical neural components from many (association, language, etc) areas or centers, where one presumably may find realization of peculiarly human ("symbolic") characteristics.

An additional but related theme implicit in this review is that of the strategic importance of the study of human disease for understanding the relations between culture and brain-behavior relations. There are two general ways in which one may approach the study of the role of culture in human disease and they reflect an etic and emic frame of reference. One can stipulate that the general category "disease" is realized in the forms derived from Western biomedicine and search for ways in which culture affects their prevalence, incidence, distribution, and effects in human groupings. This was done above in the case of hypertension. In keeping with the neurologic emphasis here, one can also point to a body of work in epidemiology which chronicles how various nervous system diseases are differently distributed in the nation states (3, 6, 84, 88, 102–104, 179). This research points to tantalizing ways in which the actual morphology of the disease (e.g. the preferred sites of lesions) is somehow correlated with distinctive group characteristics. Invariably explanations of such differences touch on genetic and physical environmental factors. In such an approach, one is handling disease as a fixed, known, "real," and closed entity. Given that these diseases are outcomes of a function which includes genetic and physical, social and psychological influences, culture qua symbolic system can be held to affect each of these influences since it regulates and orders the way people live and reproduce. Adopting an emic standpoint, one may also view disease as an "open" and culturally contexualized entity which is realized through the medical taxonomies of a people. To remain true to this symbolic view of disease, of course, an investigator may have to exclude behavioral matters as these have been defined here. That is to say that disease names, meanings, and the articulated "objective" worlds which the calculus of symbols prescribe are the important focus. The tangible behaviors ordered by such symbols, in particular, the neural roots and the realized observable patterns of actions enacted in terms of them, lose relevance as analysis of them creates distance from the "signification system." In this review, these purely symbolic aspects of "disease" have been de-emphasized though this perspective of study continues to develop and is needed for a comprehensive theory of disease (22, 47–54, 56, 98).

Finally, we have introduced what may be described as a modified etic or modified emic point of view, depending on the preferred emphasis one wishes to extol. That is to say that we have attempted to argue that a legitimate and valuable concern of cultural anthropology lies in the analysis of the culturally specific realizations of etically articulated disturbed physical-chemical "disease" processes. In reviewing material on dementia and frontal lobe pathology, for example, we have acknowledged physical-chemical "realities" which may nonetheless be culturally conditioned in a nontrivial (i.e. "symbolically" significant) way. The most compelling arena for the elaboration of this problem area and mode of analysis lies in the so-called psychiatric diseases such as schizophrenia, depression and paranoia. The specificity of these in Western nations bespeaks cultural influences in social, cognitive, and motor behaviors and, by implication, nervous system organization. To date, anthropologists have not critically probed the "morphology" of these conditions with a view to clarifying culture and brain-behavior relations. The controversy over universality of the first rank symptoms of schizophrenia is an obvious example (100, 117, 130, 173, 180, 184, 213).

SUMMARY AND CONCLUSIONS

It is very clear that humans share characteristics or traits with higher mammalian forms. Thus they live in groups possessing determinate social organizations, they communicate, show emotions, sense physical stimuli of various types, and can solve problems thereby overcoming obstacles posed by the environment. Such behavioral similarities obviously reflect similar neural systems and to some extent constitute evolutionary constraints on human differences. It is also very clear that the human mode of adaptation differs from that of the nonhuman primates. For example, by means of his system of language man is able to speak and develop a more elaborate creative and abstract (removed from the here and now) representation of himself and his condition. He can develop other (more abstract) systems of symbols (e.g. mathematics). He can also create music and use it for the expression of his view of the world, in the process mobilizing bodily motions as in dance. These differences are somehow tied to the expansion of the brain (the whole process termed neocorticalization) though the exact structural and functional features are far from being clearly understood. Arguments will develop about the nature of these human-nonhuman differences: are they quantitative or are they qualitative? Explanations of these differences in neural terms are likely to draw on concepts of hierarchy, populations of neurons, and emergent functions (181). Finally, in any examination of the more human modes of adaptation, one can point to seemingly compelling "cultural" differences. Thus members of human groups speak *different* languages and internalize *different* systems of symbols by means of which they make sense of the world, communicate meaningfully with one another, and relate to the external (whether natural or prenatural) world. More specifically, musical and dance systems appear to differ, as do the modes of using facial expressions and body motion-posture in communication. The way time and space are (conceptually) organized, how smells, colors, tastes, and humor are interpreted, and how sexuality, love, or aggression are implemented can in many ways also be shown to be somehow "different." Again, arguments will develop about the nature of these human differences: Are they merely "surface" characteristics or do they reflect differences in "deep" structures? How are such differences accounted for in neural terms? It is clear that explanation of these and related issues raise the question of holism versus locationism.

The above considerations constitute problems and questions that many behavioral and neural scientists ponder at one time or another. A selective review of the pertinent literature does not offer compelling resolution of the problem of how human differences are to be accounted for neurologically. Many of the questions raised in such an inquiry no doubt do not lend themselves to an answer. One function of a review is to at least help to articulate what the questions entail. It reveals that most scientists working in areas related to the problems mentioned here believe that many traits (e.g. the perception of color, recognition and expression of emotion, the threshold for pain, etc.) are in certain ways universal, but that even the way these are realized in social life is also in certain ways culture specific. Many scientists would probably agree that most rubrics of human behavior are mixes of universal and cultural specific (i.e. learned) influences. The review suggests that scientists believe that the more human forms of behavior somehow involve cortical mediation of some sort; neural centers, analyzer zones, functional systems, and actual pathways subserving the various functions can in many instances be delimited. No scientist, it seems, is in the position to state whether and if so how human "cultural" behavior differences are physiocochemically and cytoarchitecturally organized. Rather it would appear that the nervous system would be judged as containing differentiated neural properties that cultures can draw on and emphasize or de-emphasize, thereby realizing the behavior in question. In this review, the matter of cultural influences in brain-behavior relations was illustrated and probed in an admittedly speculative fashion by considering conditions of disease and nervous system dysfunction. The role played by genetics in human behavior and neural differences, currently debated in the controversy about sociobiology, was not examined, though it is acknowledged that issues raised in this review are central to that controversy (19, 36, 37, 106, 166, 168, 212).

Literature Cited

1. Andrew, R. J. 1972. The information potentially available in mammal displays. In *Non-Verbal Communication,* ed. R. A. Hinde, pp. 179–204. Cambridge Univ. Press. 443 pp.
2. Argyle, M. 1972. Non-verbal communication in human social interaction. See Ref. 1, pp. 243–68
3. Baker, A. B. 1975. The geographic pathology of atherosclerosis: A review of the literature with some personal observations on cerebral atherosclerosis. In *The Nervous System,* ed. D. B. Tower, 2:137–46
4. Baker, P. T. 1974. An evolutionary perspective on environmental physiology. In *Environmental Physiology,* ed. N. B. Slonim, pp. 510–22. St. Louis: Mosby
5. Berry, J. W., Dasen, P. R., eds. 1974. *Culture and Cognition: Readings in Cross-Cultural Psychology.* Great Britain: Harper & Row. 487 pp.
6. Bird, A. V., Satoyoshi, E. 1975. Comparative epidemiological studies of multiple sclerosis in South Africa and Japan. *J. Neurol. Neurosurg. Psychiatry* 38(9):911–18
7. Blanchard, E. B., Young, L. D. 1974. Clinical applications of biofeedback training (A review of evidence). *Arch. Gen. Psychiatry* 30:573–89
8. Blumer, D., Benson, D. F. 1975. Personality changes with frontal and temporal lobe lesions. In *Psychiatric Aspects of Neurologic Disease,* ed. D. F. Benson, D. Blumer, pp. 151–70. New York: Grune & Stratton. 312 pp.
9. Bogen, J. E. 1969. The other side of the brain I: Dysgraphia and dyscopia following cerebral commissurotomy. *Bull. Los Angeles Neurol. Soc.* 34(2):73–105
10. Bogen, J. E. 1969. The other side of the brain II: An appositional mind. *Bull. Los Angeles Neurol. Soc.* 34(3):135–62
11. Bogen, J. E., Bogen, G. M. 1969. The other side of the brain III: The corpus callosum and creativity. *Bull. Los Angeles Neurol. Soc.* 34(4):191–220
12. Bogen, J. E., Marsh, J. R. Jr., TenHouten, W. D. 1971. *A neurosociological theory of cerebral lateralization and social dominance.* Unpublished manuscript
13. Bornstein, M. H. 1975. The influence of visual perception on culture. *Am. Anthropol.* 77:774–98
14. Bornstein, M. H. 1973. Color vision and color naming: A psychophysiological hypothesis of cultural difference. *Psychol. Bull.* 80:257–85
15. Bornstein, M. H. 1973. The psychophysiological component of cultural difference in color naming and illusion susceptibility. *Behav. Sci. Notes* 8:41–101
16. Brindley, G. S. 1960. *Physiology of the Retina and the Visual Pathway.* London: Arnold. 573 pp.
17. Brown, B. B. 1974. *New Mind, New Body (Bio-Feedback: New Directions for the Mind).* New York: Harper & Row. 464 pp.
18. Chevalier-Skolnikoff, S. 1973. Facial expression of emotion in nonhuman primates. In *Darwin and Facial Expression (A Century of Research in Review),* ed. P. Ekman, pp. 11–89. New York: Academic. 273 pp.
19. Cloak, F. T. Jr. 1975. Is a cultural ethology possible? *Hum. Ecol.* 3(3):161–82
20. Cole, M., Gay, J., Glick, J. A., Sharp, D. W. 1971. *The Cultural Context of Learning and Thinking (An Exploration in Experimental Anthropology).* New York: Basic Books. 304 pp.
21. Cole, M., Scribner, S. 1974. *Culture & Thought (A Psychological Introduction).* New York: Wiley. 227 pp.
22. Colson, A. C., Selby, K. E. 1974. Medical anthropology. *Ann. Rev. Anthropol.* 3:245–62
23. Critchley, M. 1970. *Aphasiology and Other Aspects of Language.* Great Britain: Arnold. 405 pp.
24. Critchley, M. 1974. Aphasia in polyglots and bilinguals. *Brain Lang.* 1:15–27
25. Damon, A., ed. 1975. *Physiological Anthropology.* New York: Oxford Univ. Press. 367 pp.
26. Davenport, R. K., Rogers, C. M., Russell, I. S. 1973. Cross modal perception in apes. *Neuropsychologia* 11:21–28
27. Dawson, J. L. M. 1971. Theory and research in cross-cultural psychology. *Bull. Br. Psychol. Soc.* 24:291–306
28. Dawson, J. L. M. 1977. An anthropological perspective on the evolution and lateralization of the brain. See Ref. 32
29. Deets, A. C., Harlow, H. F., Singh, S. D., Blomquist, A. J. 1970. Effects of bilateral lesions of the frontal granular cortex on the social behavior of rhesus monkeys. *J. Comp. Physiol. Psychol.* 72:452–61

30. Deregowski, J. B. 1968. Pictorial recognition in subjects from a relatively pictureless environment. *Afr. Soc. Res.* 5:356–64

31. Deregowski, J. B. 1968. Difficulties in pictorial depth perception in Africa. *Br. J. Psychol.* 59:195–204

32. Dimond, S. J., Blizard, D. A., eds. 1977. *Evolution and Lateralization of the Brain.* New York Acad. Sci. In press

33. Dingwall, W. O. 1975. The species-specificity of speech. In *Developmental Psycholinguistics: Theory and Applications. Georgetown University Round Table on Languages and Linguistics 1975,* ed. D. P. Dato, pp. 17–54

34. Dingwall, W. O., Whitaker, H. A. 1974. Neurolinguistics. *Ann. Rev. Anthropol.* 3:323–56

35. Drewe, E. A., Ettlinger, G., Milner, A. D., Passingham, R. E. 1970. A comparative review of the results of neuropsychological research on man and monkey. *Cortex* 6:129–63

36. Durham, W. H. 1976. *The coevolution of human biology and culture.* Presented at Ann. Meet. Am. Anthropol. Assoc., 1976, Washington DC

37. Durham, W. H. 1976. The adaptive significance of cultural behavior. *Hum. Ecol.* 4(2):89–121

38. Edholm, O. G., Samueloff, S. 1973. I. Introduction, background and methods. *Philos. Trans. R. Soc. London* 266:85–95

39. Eibl-Eibesfeldt, I. 1972. Similarities and differences between cultures in expressive movements. See Ref. 1, pp. 297–314

40. Eidelberg, E., Stein, D. G. 1974. Functional recovery after lesions of the nervous system. *Neurosci. Res. Program Bull.* 12(2):195–279

41. Ekman, P. 1973. Cross-cultural studies of facial expression. See Ref. 18, pp. 169–220

42. Ekman, P. 1972. Universals and cultural differences in facial expressions of emotions. In *Nebraska Symposium on Motivation, 1971,* ed. J. K. Cole. Lincoln: Univ. Nebraska Press

43. Engel, B. T. 1972. Response specificity. In *Handbook of Psychophysiology,* ed. N. S. Greenfield, R. A. Sternbach, pp. 571–76. New York: Holt, Rinehart & Winston. 1011 pp.

44. Ettlinger, G. 1973. The transfer of information between sense-modalities: A neuropsychological review. In *Memory and Transfer of Information,* ed H. P. Zippel. New York: Plenum

45. Ettlinger, G. 1977. *Interactions Between Sensory Modalities in Nonhuman Primates.* New York: Academic. In press

46. Eyer, J. 1975. Hypertension as a disease of modern society. *Int. J. Health Serv.* 5(4):539–58

47. Fabrega, H. Jr. 1974. *Disease and Social Behavior: An Interdisciplinary Perspective.* Cambridge: MIT Press. 341 pp.

48. Fabrega, H. Jr. Disease viewed as a symbolic category. In *Mental Health: Philosophical Perspectives,* ed. T. Engelhardt, The Netherlands: Reidel

49. Fabrega, H. Jr. 1972. Medical anthropology. *Bien. Rev. Anthropol, 1971,* pp. 167–229

50. Fabrega, H. Jr. 1976. The biological significance of taxonomies of disease. *J. Theor. Biol.* 63(1):191–216

51. Fabrega, H. Jr. 1975. The need for an ethnomedical science. *Science* 189:969–75

52. Fabrega, H. Jr. 1976. The functions of medical-care systems: A logical analysis. *Perspect. Biol. Med.* 20(1):108–19

53. Fabrega, H. Jr. 1977. The scope of ethnomedical science. *Medicine, Psychiatry, Culture.* New York: Pergamon. In press

54. Fabrega, H. Jr. 1976. Toward a theory of human disease. *J. Nerv. Mental Dis.* 162(5):299–312

55. Fabrega, H. Jr., Tyma, S. 1976. Language and cultural influences in the description of pain. *Br. J. Med. Psychol.* 49:349–71

56. Fabrega, H. Jr., Silver, D. B. 1973. *Illness and Shamanistic Curing in Zinacantan.* Stanford Univ. Press. 285 pp.

57. Fedio, P., Van Buren, J. M. 1974. Memory deficits during electrical stimulation of the speech cortex in conscious man. *Brain Lang.* 1:29–42

58. Fox, R. 1975. Primate kin and human kinship. In *Biosocial Anthropology,* ed. R. Fos, pp. 9–35. London: Malaby. 169 pp.

59. Franzen, E. A., Myers, R. E. 1973. Age effects on social behavior deficits following prefrontal lesions in monkeys. *Brain Res.* 54:277–86

60. Franzen, E. A., Myers, R. E. 1973. Neural control of social behavior: Prefrontal and anterior temporal cortex. *Neuropsychologia* 11:141–57

61. Freedman, D. G. 1974. *Human Infancy: An Evolutionary Perspective.* New York: Halstead

62. Friedman, M. 1969. *Pathogenesis of Coronary Artery Disease.* New York: McGraw Hill. 269 pp.

63. Friedman, M., Rosenman, R. 1974. *Type A Behavior and Your Heart.* New York: Knopf. 276 pp.

64. Friedman, M., Rosenman, R., Byers, K. 1964. Serum lipids and conjunctional circulation after fat ingestion in men exhibiting type A behavior pattern. *Circulation* 29:874–86

65. Frisancho, A. R. 1975. Functional adaptation to high altitude hypoxia. (Changes occurring during growth and development are of major importance in man's adapting to high altitudes.) *Science* 187:313–19

66. Gallup, G. G. Jr. 1970. Chimpanzees: Self-recognition. *Science* 167:86–87

67. Geertz, C. 1973. *The Interpretation of Cultures (Selected Essays).* New York: Basic Books. 470 pp.

68. Geschwind, N. 1975. The apraxias: Neural mechanisms of disorders of learned movement. *Am. Sci.* 63:188–95

69. Geschwind, N. 1965. Disconnexion syndromes in animals and man. *Brain* 88:237–94, 585–644

70. Geschwind, N. 1964. The paradoxical position of Kurt Goldstein in the history of aphasia. *Cortex* 1:214–24

71. Geschwind, N. 1964. The development of the brain and the evolution of language. *Monograph Series on Languages and Linguistics,* ed. C. I. J. M. Stuart, pp. 155–69. Washington: Georgetown Univ.

72. Geschwind, N. 1970. The organization of language and the brain. *Science* 170:940–44

73. Geschwind, N., Levitsky, W. 1968. Human brain: Left-right asymmetries in temporal speech region. *Science* 161:186–87

74. Geschwind, N., Quadfasel, F. A., Segarra, J. M. 1968. Isolation of the speech area. *Neuropsychologia* 6:327–40

75. Glick, J. 1975. Cognitive development in cross-cultural perspective. *Rev. Child Dev. Res.* 4:595–654

76. Goodglass, H., Kaplan, E. 1963. Disturbance of gesture and pantomime in aphasia. *Brain* 86:703–20

77. Gould, S. J. 1975. Allometry in primates, with emphasis on sealing and the evolution of the brain. *Szalay: Approaches to primate pateobiology. Contrib. Primatol.* 5:224–92

78. Green, E. E., Walters, E. D., Green, A. M., Murphy, G. 1969. Feedback techniques for deep relaxation. *Psychophysiology* 6:371–77

79. Griffin, D. R. 1976. *The Question of Animal Awareness (Evolutionary Continuity of Mental Experience).* New York: Rockefeller Univ. Press. 135 pp.

80. Harlow, H. F. 1971. *Learning to Love.* San Francisco: Albion. 116 pp.

81. Harris, L. J. 1975. *Interaction of experimental and neurological factors in the patterning of human abilities: The question of sex differences in 'right hemisphere' skills.* Presented at Bien. Meet. Soc. Res. Child Dev.

82. Harris, L. J. 1977. Sex differences in the growth and use of language. In *Women: A Psychological Perspective,* ed. E. Donelson, J. Gullahorn. New York: Wiley. In press

83. Hecaen, H., Albert, M. L. 1975. Disorders of mental functioning related to frontal lobe pathology. See Ref. 8, pp. 137–49

84. Herzberg, L., Gibbs, C. J. Jr., Asher, D. M., Gajusek, D. C., French, E. L. 1975. Slow, latent, and chronic viral infections of the central nervous system. In *Transmissible Disease & Blood Transfusion,* ed. T. J. Greenwalt, G. A. Jamieson, pp. 197–219. New York: Grune & Stratton

85. Hewes, G. W. 1973. Primate communication and the gestural origin of language. *Curr. Anthropol.* 14(1–2):5–24

86. Hofer, M. A. 1974. The role of early experience in the development of autonomic regulation. In *Limbic and Autonomic Nervous Systems Research,* ed. L. V. DiCara. New York: Plenum

87. Holloway, R. L. 1966. Cranial capacity, neural reorganization, and hominid evolution: A search for more suitable parameters. *Am. Anthropol.* 68:103–21

88. Hung, T.-P., Landsborough, D., Hsi, M. S. 1976. Multiple sclerosis amongst Chinese in Taiwan. *J. Neurol. Sci.* 27:459–84

89. Jenkins, C. D. 1971. Psychological and social precursors of coronary disease. *N. Engl. J. Med.* 284:244–55, 307–17

90. Jerison, H. J. 1973. *Evolution of the Brain and Intelligence.* New York: Academic. 495 pp.

91. Jerison, H. J. 1975. Evolution of the brain and intelligence. *Curr. Anthropol.* 16(3):403–26

92. Jerison, H. J. 1975. Fossil evidence of the evolution of the human brain. *Ann. Rev. Anthropol.* 4:27–58

93. John, E. R. 1972. Switchboard versus statistical theories of learning and memory. *Science* 177:850–66

94. Kaplan, C. D., TenHouten, W. D. 1975. Neurolinguistic sociology. *Socioling. Newsl.* 6:4–9

95. Kimura, D. 1975. Cerebral dominance for speech. In *The Nervous System: 25 Years of Research Progress,* ed. D. B. Tower, pp. 365–71. New York:Raven

96. Kimura, D. 1977. The neural basis of language qua gesture. In *Studies in Neurolinguistics,* ed. H. Avakian-Whitaker, H. A. Whitaker. New York: Academic. In press

97. Kimura, D., Archibald, Y. 1974. Motor functions of the left hemisphere. *Brain* 97:337–50

98. Kleinman, A. M. 1974. Medicine's symbolic reality: On a central problem in the philosophy of medicine. *Inquiry* 16:206–13

99. Kling, A., Steklis, H. D. 1977. A neural substrate for affiliative behavior in non-human primates. *Brain Behav. Evol.* In press

100. Kraepelin, E. 1974. Comparative psychiatry. In *Themes and Variations in European Psychiatry,* ed. S. R. Hirsch, M. Shepherd. Briston:Wright

101. Kummer, H. 1971. *Primate Societies (Group Techniques of Ecological Adaptation).* Chicago: Aldine-Atherton. 160 pp.

102. Kuroiwa, Y., Okihiro, M. M. 1969. Multiple sclerosis in Hawaii (A preliminary report). *Hawaii Med. J.* 28(5): 374–76

103. Kuroiwa, Y., Shibasaki, H. 1973. Clinical studies of multiple sclerosis in Japan (I. A current appraisal of 83 cases). *Neurology* 23(6):609–17

104. Kuroiwa, Y., Igata, A., Itahara, K., Koshijima, S., Tsubaki, T., Toyokura, Y. 1975. Nationwide survey of multiple sclerosis in Japan—Clinical analysis of 1,084 cases. *Neurology* 25(9):845–51

105. Lacey, J. I., Bateman, D. E., Van Lehn, R. 1953. Autonomic response specificity: An experimental study. *Psychosom. Med.* 15:8–21

106. Laughlin, C. D. Jr., D'Aguili, E. G. 1974. *Biogenetic Structuralism.* New York: Columbia Univ. 211 pp.

107. Le May, M., Geschwind, N. 1975. Hemispheric differences in the brains of great apes. *Brain Behav. Evol.* 11:48–52

108. Lenneberg, E. H. 1967. *Biological Foundations of Language.* New York: Wiley 489 pp.

109. Lenneberg, E. H. 1970. Brain correlates of language. In *The Neurosciences Second Study Program,* ed. F. O. Schmitt, pp. 361–71. New York: Rockefeller Univ. 1069 pp.

110. Levy, J. 1976. Cerebral lateralization and spatial ability. *Behav. Genet.* 6(2): 171–88

111. Levy, J. 1974. Psychobiological implications of bilateral asymmetry. In *Hemisphere Function in the Human Brain,* ed. S. J. Dimond, J. G. Beaumont, pp. 121–83. London: ELEC Science. 398 pp.

112. Levy, J. 1977. *The Mammalian Brain and the Adaptive Advantage of Cerebral Asymmetry in Evolution and Lateralization of the Brain,* ed. S. J. Dimond. New York Acad. Sci. In press

113. Levy, J., Nagylaki, T. 1972. A model for the genetics of handedness. *Genetics* 72:117–28

114. Liberman, A. M. 1974. The specialization of the language hemisphere. In *The Neurosciences Third Study Program,* ed. F. O. Schmitt, F. G. Worden, pp. 43–55. Cambridge: MIT. 1107 pp.

115. Liberman, A. M. 1970. The grammars of speech and language. *Cogn. Psychol.* 1:301–23

116. Lieberman, P., Crelin, E. S., Klatt, D. H. 1972. Phonetic ability and related anatomy of the newborn and adult human, Neanderthal man, and the chimpanzee. *Am. Anthropol.* 74:287–307

117. Lin, T. Y., Sartorius, N. 1975. *Schizophrenia: A multinational study.* Public Health Paper no. 63. Geneva, Switzerland: WHO

118. Lloyd, B. B. 1972. *Perception and Cognition: A Cross-Cultural Perspective.* Great Britain: Cox & Wyman. 190 pp.

119. Lomas, J., Kimura, D. 1977. Intrahemispheric interaction between speaking and sequential manual activity. *Neuropsychologia* In press

120. Ludwig, A. M. 1971. Self-regulation of the sensory environment. *Arch. Gen. Psychiatry* 25:413–18

121. Ludwig, A. M. 1975. Sensory overload and psychopathology. *Dis. Nerv. Syst.* 36(7):357–60

122. Luria, A. R. 1966. *Higher Cortical Functions in Man.* New York: Basic Books. 513 pp.

123. Luria, A. R. 1973. *The Working Brain: An Introduction to Neuropsychology.* New York: Basic Books. 398 pp.

124. Luria, A. R. 1973. The frontal lobes and the regulation of behavior. In *Psychology and Physiology of the Frontal Lobes,* K. H. Pribram, A. R. Luria, pp. 3–26. New York:Academic

125. Mandler, G. 1967. The conditions for emotional behavior. In *Biology and Behavior: Neurophysiology and Emotion,* ed. D. C. Glass, pp. 96–102. New York: Rockefeller Univ. 234 pp.

126. Mason, W. A. 1976. Environmental models and mental modes: Representational processes in the great apes and man. *Am. Psychol.* April:284–94

127. Masterton, R. B., Berkley, M. A. 1974. Brain function: Changing ideas on the role of sensory, motor, and association cortex in behavior. *Ann. Rev. Psychol.* 25:277–312

128. Mateer, C., Kimura, D. 1977. Impairment of nonverbal oral movements in aphasia. *Brain Lang.* In press

129. McFie, J. 1975. *Assessment of Organic Intellectual Impairment.* New York: Academic. 164 pp.

130. Mellor, C. S. 1970. First rank symptoms of schizophrenia: I. The frequency in schizophrenics on admission to hospital, II. Differences between individual first rank symptoms. *J. Psychiatry* 117: 15–23

131. Menzel, E. W. Jr. 1973. Leadership and communication in young chimpanzees. *Precult. Primate Behav.* 1:192–255

132. Menzel, E. W. Jr. 1973. Chimpanzee spatial memory organization. *Science* 182:943–45

133. Merskey, H., Spear, F. G. 1967. *Pain: Psychological and Psychiatric Aspects.* London: Bailliere, Tindall & Cassell. 223 pp.

134. Miller, N. E. 1969. Learning of visceral and glandular responses. *Science* 163: 434–45

135. Miller, R. E. 1974. Social and pharmacological influences on the nonverbal communication of monkeys and of man. In *Nonverbal Communication,* ed. L. Krames, P. Pliner, T. Alloway, pp. 77–101. New York: Plenum

136. Miller, R. E., Caul, W. F., Mirsky, I. A. 1967. Communication of affects between feral and socially isolated monkeys. *J. Pers. Soc. Psychol.* 7(3):231–39

137. Milner, B. 1971. Interhemispheric differences in the localization of psychological processes in man. *Br. Med. Bull. Cogn. Psychol.* 27:(3)272–77

138. Milner, B. 1974. Hemispheric specialization: Scopes and limits. See Ref. 114, pp. 75–89

139. Milner, B., Teuber, H. L. 1968. Alteration of perception and memory in man: Reflections on methods. In *Analysis of Behavioral Change,* ed. L. Weiskrantz,

pp. 268–375. New York: Harper & Row. 447 pp.

140. Moltz, H. 1973. Some implications of the critical period hypothesis. *Ann. NY Acad. Sci. (Comparative Psychology at Issue)* 223:144–46

141. Mountcastle, V. B. 1976. The world around us. *Neurosci. Res. Prog. Bull.* 14:1–47

142. Myers, R. E., Swett, C., Miller, M. 1973. Loss of social group affinity following prefrontal lesions in free-ranging macaques. *Brain Res.* 64:257–69

143. Napier, J. 1970. *The Roots of Mankind (The Story of Man and His Ancestors).* New York: Harper & Row. 240 pp.

144. Nauta, W. J. H. 1971. The problem of the frontal lobe: A reinterpretation. *J. Psychiatr. Res.* 8:167–87

145. Nebes, R. D. 1974. Hemispheric specialization in commissurotomized man. *Psychol. Bull.* 81(1):1–14

146. Ornstein, R. E. 1974. *The Psychology of Consciousness.* New York: Viking. 247 pp.

147. Paradis, M. 1976. Bilingualism and aphasia. In *Studies in Neurolinguistics,* ed. H. Whitaker, H. Whitaker. New York: Academic.

148. Paredes, J. A., Hepburn, M. J. 1976. The split brain and the culture-and-cognition paradox. *Curr. Anthropol.* 17: 121–27

149. Parker, S. 1976. The precultural basis of the incest taboo: Toward a biosocial theory. *Am. Anthropol.* 78:285–305

150. Passingham, R. E. 1973. Anatomical differences between the neocortex of man and other primates. *Brain Behav. Evol.* 7:337–59

151. Passingham, R. E., Ettlinger, G. 1974. A comparison of cortical functions in man and the other primates. *Int. Rev. Neurobiol.* 16:233–99

152. Pearce, J., Miller, E. 1973. *Clinical Aspects of Dementia.* London: Bailliere. 142 pp.

153. Piercy, M. 1969. Neurological aspects of intelligence. *Handb. Clin. Neurol.* 3: 296–315

154. Piercy, M. 1964. The effects of cerebral lesions on intellectual functions: A review of current research trends. *Br. J. Psychiatry* 110:310–52

155. Premack, D. 1975. On the origins of language. In *Handbook of Psychobiology,* ed. M. S. Gazzaniga, C. Blakemore, pp. 591–605. New York: Academic. 639 pp.

156. Premack, D. 1976. Language and intel-

ligence in ape and man. *Am. Sci.* 64: 647–83

157. Pribram, K. H., Reynolds, P. 1977. Hemispheric specialization: Evolution or revolution. See Ref. 32

158. Proceedings of the National Heart and Lung Institute Working Conference on Health Behavior, Basye, Va., May 12–15, 1975. DHEW Publ. No. (NIH), 76–868

159. Rinnert, C., Whitaker, H. A. 1973. Semantic confusions by aphasic patients. *Cortex* 9:56–87

160. Rosenman, R. 1974. The role of behavior patterns and neurogenic factors in the pathogenesis of coronary heart disease. In *Contemporary Problems in Cardiology (Stress and the Heart)*, ed. R. S. Eliot, 1:123–14. Mount Kisco: Futura

161. Rosenman, R., Friedman, M. 1971. The central nervous system and coronary heart disease. *Hosp. Pract.* 6:87–97

162. Rosenman, R., Friedman, M. 1974. Neurogenic factors in pathogenesis of coronary heart disease. *Med. Clin. North Am.* 58(2):269–79

163. Rosenman, R., Friedman, M., Straus, R., Wurm, M., Jenkins, C., Messinger, H. 1966. Coronary heart disease in the Western collaborative group study. *J. Am. Med. Assoc.* 195(2):130–36

164. Rosvold, H. E. 1972. The frontal lobe system: Cortical-subcortical interrelationships. *Acta Neurobiol. Exp.* 32: 439–60

165. Rubens, A. B., Mahowald, M. W., Hutton, J. T. 1976. Asymmetry of the lateral (sylvian) fissures in man. *Neurology* 26(7):620–24

166. Ruyle, E. E. 1973. Genetic and cultural pools: Some suggestions for a unified theory of biocultural evolution. *Hum. Ecol.* 1(3):201–15

167. Sahlins, M. 1976. Colors and cultures. *Semiotica* 16(1):1–22

168. Sahlins, M. 1976. *The Use and Abuse of Biology (An Anthropological Critique of Sociobiology)*. Ann Arbor: Univ. Michigan. 120 pp.

169. Sanders, H., Warrington, E. K. 1971. Memory for remote events in amnesic patients. *Brain* 94:661–68

170. Sasanuma, S. 1974. Kanji versus kana processing in alexia with transient agraphial (A case report). *Cortex* 10:87–97

171. Sasanuma, S., Fujimura, O. 1972. An analysis of writing errors in Japanese aphasic patients: Kanji versus kana words. *Cortex* 8:265–82

172. Sasanuma, S., Monoi, H. 1975. The syndrom of Gogi (word-meaning) aphasia

(Selective impairment of Kanji processing). *Neurology* 25(7):627–32

173. Schneider, K. 1974. Primary and secondary symptoms in schizophrenia. See Ref. 100, pp. 40–44

174. Segall, M. H., Campbell, D. T., Herskovits, M. J. 1966. *The Influence of Culture on Visual Perception.* New York: Bobbs-Merrill Co. 268 pp.

175. Seligmon, M. E., Hager, J. 1972. *Biological Boundaries of Learning.* New York: Appleton-Century-Croft. 480 pp.

176. Semmes, J. 1968. Hemispheric specialization: A possible clue to mechanism. *Neuropsychologia* 6:11–26

177. Semmes, J. 1966. Protopathic and epicritic sensation: A reappraisal. In *Contributions to Clinical Neuropsychology,* ed. A. L. Benton, pp. 142–69

178. Shapiro, D. H. Jr., Zifferblatt, S. M. 1976. Zen meditation and behavioral self-control (similarities, differences, and clinical applications). *Am. Psychol.* July:519–32

179. Shibasaki, H., Kuroiwa, Y. 1974. Painful tonic seizure in multiple sclerosis. *Arch. Neurol.* 30:47–51

180. Silverman, J. 1967. Shamans and acute schizophrenia. *Am. Anthropol.* 69:21–31

181. Sperry, R. W. 1969. A modified concept of consciousness. *Psychol. Rev.* 76(6): 532–36

182. Stein, D. G., Rosen, J. J., Butters, N., eds. 1974. *Plasticity and Recovery of Function in the Central Nervous System.* New York: Academic

183. Steklis, H. D. 1976. *Neuroscience and Biosocial Anthropology.* Presented at Ann. Meet. Am. Anthropol. Assoc., Washington DC

184. Stevens, J. R. 1973. An anatomy of schizophrenia? *Arch. Gen. Psychiatry* 29:177–89

185. Suomi, S. J., Harlow, H. F., Lewis, J. K. 1973. Effects of bilateral frontal lobectomy on social preferences of rhesus monkeys. *J. Comp. Physiol. Psychol.* 71:448–53

186. Talland, G. A. 1965. *Deranged Memory.* New York: Academic

187. Teng, E. L. 1976. Handedness in a Chinese population: Biological, social, and pathological factors. *Science* 193: 1148–50

188. TenHouten, W. 1976. More on split-brain research, culture, and cognition. *Curr. Anthropol.* 17(3):503–11

189. Teuber, H. L. 1974. Why two brains? See Ref. 114, pp. 71–74

190. Teuber, H. L. 1975. Effects of focal brain injury on human behavior. *Nerv. Syst.* 2:457–80
191. Teuber, H. L. 1967. Lacunae and research approaches to them. In *Brain Mechanisms Underlying Speech and Language*, ed. F. L. Darley, C. H. Millikan, pp. 204–16. New York: Grune & Statton
192. Teuber, H. L. 1972. Unity and diversity of frontal lobe functions. *Acta Neurobiol. Exp.* 32:615–56
193. Teuber, H. L. 1964. The riddle of frontal lobe function in man. In *The Frontal Granular Cortex and Behavior*, ed. J. M. Warren, K. A. Kert, pp. 410–44. New York: McGraw-Hill
194. Teuber, H. L. 1955. Physiological psychology. *Ann. Rev. Psychol.* 6:267–96
195. Thompson, R. F. 1975. The search for the engram. *Am. Psychol.* March: 209–27
196. Triandis, H. C., Malpass, R. S., Davidson, A. R. 1973. Psychology and culture. *Ann. Rev. Psychol.* 24:355–78
197. Valenstein, E. S. 1973. *Brain Control (A Critical Examination of Brain Stimulation and Psychosurgery)*. New York: Wiley. 407 pp.
198. Victor, M., Adams, R. D., Collins, G. H. 1972. The Wernicke-Korsakoff syndrome. In *The Diagnosis of Stupor and Coma*, ed. F. Plum, J. B. Posner. Philadelphia: Davis. 2d ed.
199. Wada, J. A., Clarke, R., Hamm, A. 1975. Cerebral hemispheric asymmetry in humans. *Arch. Neurol.* 32:239–46
200. Warrington, E. K. 1971. Neurological disorders of memory. *Br. Med. Bull.: Cogn. Psychol.* 27(3):243–47
201. Warrington, E. K. 1975. The Selective impairment of semantic memory. *Q. J. Exp. Psychol.* 27:635–57
202. Warrington, E. K., Weiskrantz, L. 1973. An analysis of short-term and long-term memory defects in man. In *The Physiological Basis of Memory*, ed. J. A. Deutsch, pp. 365–95. New York: Academic
203. Washburn, S. L., ed. 1961. *Social Life of Early Man.* Chicago: Aldine. 299 pp.
204. Washburn, S. L., Harding, R. S. 1970. Evolution of primate behavior. See Ref. 109, pp. 39–47
205. Washburn, S. L., Moore, R. 1974. *Ape into Man (A Study of Human Evolution)*. Boston: Little, Brown. 196 pp.
206. Weinstein, E. A., Cole, M. 1963. Concepts of anosognosia. In *Problems of Dynamic Neurology (Studies on the Higher Functions of the Human Nervous System)*, ed. L. Halpern, pp. 254–73.

Jerusalem: Univ. Hosp. and the Hebrew Univ. Hadassah Med. Sch. 509 pp.
207. Weisenberg, M., ed. 1975. *Pain (Clinical and Experimental Perspectives)*. St. Louis: Mosby. 385 pp.
208. Weiskrantz, L. 1971. Comparison of amnesic states in monkey and man. In *Cognitive Processes of Non Human Primates*, ed. L. E. Jarrard, pp. 25–46. New York: Academic
209. Weiskrantz, L., Warrington, E. K. 1976. The problem of the amnesic syndrome in man and animals. In *The Hippocampus (Volume 2: Neurophysiology and Behavior)*, ed. R. L. Isaacson, K. H. Pribram, pp. 411–28. New York: Plenum
210. Wells, C. E. 1971. *Dementia.* Philadelphia: Davis. 239 pp.
211. Whitaker, H. A. 1971. *On the representation of language in the human brain (Problems in the neurology of language and the linguistic analysis of aphasia)*. Edmonton:Linguistic Res. Unpublished manuscript.
212. Wilson, E. O. 1975. *Sociobiology. (The New Synthesis)*. Cambridge: Belknap Press of Harvard Univ. 697 pp.
213. Wing, J. K., Nixon, J. 1975. Discriminating symptoms in schizophrenia. *Arch. Gen. Psychiatry* 32:858–59
214. Witelson, S. F. 1976. Sex and the single hemisphere: Specialization of the right hemisphere for spatial processing. *Science* 193:425–26
215. Witkin, H. A. 1967. A cognitive style approach to cross culture research. *Int. J. Psychol.* 2:235–50
216. Woolfolk, R. L. 1975. Psychophysiological correlates of meditation. *Arch. Gen. Psychiatry* 32:1326–33
217. Yamadori, A., Ikumura, G. 1975. Central (or conduction) aphasia in a Japanese patient. *Cortex* 11:73–82
218. Yamadori, A. 1975. Ideogram reading in alexia. *Brain* 98:231–38
219. Yamadori, A., Albert, M. L. 1973. Word category aphasia. *Cortex* 9: 112–25
220. Yeni-Komshian, G. H., Benson, D. A. 1976. Anatomical study of cerebral asymmetry in the temporal lobe of humans, chimpanzees, and rhesus monkeys. *Science* 192:387–89
221. Young, J. Z. 1974. *An Introduction to the Study of Man.* New York: Oxford Univ. 719 pp.
222. Young, J. Z. 1962. Why do we have two brains? In *Interhemispheric Relations and Cerebral Dominance*, ed. V. B. Mountcastle. Baltimore: Johns Hopkins Press

Ann. Rev. Anthropol. 1977. 6:457–78
Copyright © 1977 by Annual Reviews Inc. All rights reserved

SAHELIAN PASTORALISTS: ❖9602
UNDERDEVELOPMENT,
DESERTIFICATION, AND FAMINE

Jeremy Swift
Institute for the Study of International Organization, Sussex University,
Brighton, United Kingdom

A large number of fields of study are relevant to the genesis of the Sahel famine of 1968–1973, so I have chosen to focus this review on three issues that seem to me the most important: (*a*) some aspects of the Sahelian pastoral economy and its relation to wider market economies; (*b*) the demography of Sahelian pastoralists; (*c*) changes in the last half century, corresponding to the period from the imposition of French colonial rule. Hard information is scarce in all these fields, so it is hazardous to theorize; but without some attempt at explanation of the recent events in terms more satisfactory than "population growth" or "climate change," little progress can be made. I have not drawn specific development policy conclusions from this, preferring to let the historical record speak for itself.

ENVIRONMENT

Climate

The Sahel is the belt of steppe vegetation along the southern edge of the Sahara from the Atlantic to Lake Chad, with annual rainfall very roughly between 150 mm and 500 mm. The main past characteristics of its climate have been major changes between periods somewhat wetter and somewhat drier than now on a geological time scale (16, 42, 43, 52, 67) and fluctuations lasting a few hundred years; there are now short-term fluctuations in the form of wet and dry rhythms of irregular length and spacing, and large annual variations in amount, timing, and geographical spacing of rainfall. The period 1931–1960 seems to have been relatively wet, by comparison with 1900–1970 (89). Partly because of this, the drought of the 1970s led to suggestions that the Sahel's climate is changing. Two types of change were suggested: direct changes due to modification in global circulation from causes independent of man (58, 87, 88), and indirect changes resulting from increased human activities, especially clearing and burning of vegetation, leading to more dust and carbon dioxide in the atmosphere (11, 12, 63) or to greater albedo (reflectivity of the earth's surface) (21). These hypotheses are logically consistent, but largely untestable. Research on the West African weather system as a whole has only just started. No comparative figures exist for dust generation or changes in albedo. From the relatively short series of rainfall figures available for the Sahel, no conclusions can be drawn about climate change; many workers have failed to find evidence for a consistent trend since the start of the century (4, 14, 15, 32, 74, 78).

Vegetation

In a pastoral ecosystem such as the Sahel, plants capture solar energy by photosynthesis and convert it into organic material; domestic animals in turn convert this plant energy into a form usable by man. Pastoral ecosystems can thus be modeled by following energy flow through the ecosystem, combined with the study of market exchanges by pastoralists outside the ecosystem. In arid tropical grasslands with less than about 600 mm rainfall, average plant production over large areas is directly related to the amount of available water, which can be roughly equated with the total quantity of rain that falls. When rainfall varies, plant production varies in direct proportion, and with it the total quantity of energy available to fuel the system. Because of the great annual rainfall variations and longer sequences of wet and dry years, plant production, and consequently the amount of energy available to domestic animals and thus to man, vary widely from year to year, and between wet and dry periods.

Measurements shown in Table 1 from the International Biological Programme research site in the Ferlo area of north Senegal (4), in an area where annual rainfall habitually fluctuates between 200 mm and 300 mm, indicate how plant production and thus the number of domestic animals which could graze there fluctuate in relation to rainfall (expressed as the more accurate "period of useful rainfall," defined as the period of active growth of annual grasses, rather than as a simple rainfall total).

Table 1 Variation of plant production and theoretical carrying capacity for cattle, at IBP research station, Fété Olé, Ferlo, north Senegal

	Period of useful rainfall (days)[a]	Above ground plant production (kg dry matter/ha)[a]	Theoretical carrying capacity for cattle (number of cattle per 1,000 ha)[b]
"Normal" good year	110	1,300	187
"Normal" bad year	50	590	87
1972	0	0	0

[a] From Bille (4).
[b] Calculated assuming animals of 250 kg liveweight, eating one-third of above ground primary production.

These figures give an idea of the problem facing pastoral users of Sahelian grass-lands. The pastoral economy depends almost entirely on production of milk, meat, and saleable animals, and this in turn depends on plant production. Plant production can, within "normal" rainfall variation, double or halve from year to year, and in exceptional years like 1972 can drop to zero. Animal production varies in proportion. A human population which adapted its own size and the degree of intensity of its economic use to the level of a normal bad year would leave unexploited huge pasture areas in good years and even more in good sequences of years; a pastoral population and a level of economic exploitation adapted to good periods would find itself hopelessly overextended in bad years; neither would be able to live in the area at all in extreme bad years like 1972 or 1913.

PASTORAL ECONOMY

The debate on West African economic systems has taken place partly within the framework of the formalist/substantivist debate about wider questions of economic anthropology exemplified, for example, by A. G. Hopkins's *Economic History of West Africa* and George Dalton's review of it in *African Economic History* (30, 50). As far as Sahelian pastoralists are concerned, there is relatively little detailed information, although there are many general studies of pastoral groups which include some economic information (2, 6, 33, 37, 39, 68, 79). Animals are individually owned; wells are controlled by those who dig them, although access is usually granted to members of the same clan, and water is often not refused to other pastoralists as long as there is enough; pasture use is not normally controlled at any level below that of major lineage segments or groups of pastoral clans. There is a domestic division of labor, supplemented by extensive cooperation within camps, which are the basic socioeconomic unit, and sometimes between camps. But more profound analysis of pastoral production systems in the Sahel is hampered by a lack of precise information on labor use, the dynamics and productivity of domestic herds under extensive management [although the recent study by Dahl & Hjort (29) is a useful step forward], and statistical information on family herd sizes and on camp and family composition. In the absence of this it is difficult to deal other than in generalizations, for example that many pastoral economies apparently have low labor requirements, or that different domestic species have different economic and ecological characteristics based on different food preferences, different lengths of gestation period and calving interval, and thus degree of responsiveness to changed ecological conditions such as rain after drought. Dyson-Hudson's plea for quantitative study of the coincident populations of livestock and humans which constitute the pastoral economy has not yet been answered, in the Sahel or elsewhere (35).

More data exist on the nature and functioning of traditional nonmarket distributive mechanisms. Among the Twareg, apart from animals given as religious or political tribute, there is an array of loans and gifts of animals that serve two main purposes: first, to assure the reproduction over time of individual family production units (animals nominally given by fathers to small children as the nucleus of a future independent family herd, and animals inherited or transferred as bridewealth);

second, to create and maintain the general equivalence at any given time between each individual family and the herd necessary to maintain each family as an independent production unit. The latter category includes transfers of animals on a variety of terms (given, loaned, rented, stolen) between individual heads of families, and ideally should be studied in relation to movement of labor between families, although this has rarely been done. The commonest occasion of such transfers is from the relatively rich to the poor or destitute, and in this case they may serve as an insurance system which guarantees the security and continuity of the group as a whole, especially in conditions of economic uncertainty, when the relatively rich and the poor may change place with each other unpredictably (80). But these transactions may not only serve this purpose; it has been suggested that among Reguibat and Adrar pastoralists of Mauritania, *meniha* loans of transport and milking animals to poor herdsmen create client relationships and are a way for rich pastoralists to appropriate the labor of poor herdsmen (8). Here again a proper understanding of whether a particular category of animal loan results in exploitation by enabling the rich to appropriate the labor of others, or is a social redistributive mechanism which mitigates environmental risk and is a counterweight to emergent economic stratification, will have to await a better knowledge of the simple dynamics of the pastoral economy; only then will it be possible to know how the traditional rules for herding contracts and loans compare with the labor requirements of herding and the turnover and production rates of different species. Animal gifts and loans between herdsmen are widespread among other Sahelian pastoral societies, such as the Fulani (33, 34) and the Zaghawa of the Chad-Sudan border (85); indeed they are a common feature of other African pastoral societies (having been described for Kababish, Somali, and several East African cattle pastoral societies for example).

Although Sahelian pastoralists may in good years live for some months on milk and dairy products alone, supplemented by the meat of an occasional sheep or goat, they are in general dependent for at least part of the year on food grains. Those pastoralists who do not cultivate must barter or buy cereals, plus cloth and other necessities, from neighboring farmers or at market. This exchange of pastoral for agricultural products probably dates from the origin of nomadic pastoralism itself among farming communities wishing to use the great pastures on the margins of cultivable land. But the development of exchange and marketing of livestock differs from agricultural products.

West African farmers' trade in foodstuffs originated, in the simplest case, in the decision of individual households to plant an area that would give an adequate return in a poor year, with the result that in average years there would be a surplus to trade with deficit villages; more often, households would plan their production of foodstuffs with the intention of producing a small surplus for trade (50). This small initial surplus is of a different nature in a subsistence pastoral economy. Each year the herds produce young male animals, only a few of which are needed for reproductive purposes. Except where male camels are used for riding and transport, males of all species in excess of herd maintenance needs may be disposed of without affecting the reproductive, and hence the milk-producing capacity of the herd. Pastoralists can eat these male animals, or they can barter or sell them for cereals;

wherever pastoralists have been in contact with farmers or markets, it seems likely that they could obtain more calories by bartering their surplus male animals for cereals than by eating them. As a result, exchange of animals for cereals and other products developed not within pastoral society, where, with the exception of specialists such as smiths, everyone produced the same thing (animals), but between pastoral and agricultural economies. This exchange took two main forms. In some places it became part of a wider set of reciprocal transactions (with social as well as economic significance) between farmers and nomads, in which the former provided cereals and stubble grazing for the herds, and the latter provided meat, milk, and animal traction to draw water or mill and carry grain (64).

In other places, specialized institutions developed alongside the pastoral economy to organize livestock marketing. The mobility of animals, and the fact that the exchange was external (corresponding to a geographical division of labor) rather than internal (resulting from social division of labor within an integrated economy), in Meillassoux's distinction (65) encouraged the development of livestock trading over long distances. This was often done by specialists such as the tobacco farmers of nineteenth century Katsina in northern Nigeria, who conducted a three-cornered trade in tobacco from Katsina, livestock and natron from Zinder and Agadez, and cola nuts from Lagos (48). Also, networks of "landlords," in whose houses stranger-traders lodged, stored the traders' goods, including animals, and acted as commission brokers (47, 49). Bororo Fulani sell their cattle principally through the agency of middlemen, *dillalai,* both at market places and in the bush. For a small commission the *dillali* guarantees the validity of the sale and makes sure that animals are paid for (34).

However, disposal of male animals surplus to herd production and reproduction through these sorts of traditional arrangements, which are much older than the colonial conquest of the Sahel, probably did not much influence pastoralists' production decisions on the allocation of land and labor, which is the main test of the economic formalists' case. These animals are a by-product of the main economic activity, which is the animal breeding cycle producing milk for human consumption and female calves to reproduce the herd. The number of male calves available for barter or sale in this way each year is fixed by circumstance largely outside the herdsman's control, being a function of the size and structure of his herd and the ecological conditions of the year. He cannot make a conscious decision to use more land and labor, increase his production, and have more animals to sell. There is little advantage to pastoralists in not selling these calves since the only alternative is to eat them.

PRECOLONIAL PASTORAL STRATEGIES AND RESOURCE USE

With these general strategies, pastoralists used the marginal and variable Sahelian environment. Their main problem was to regulate the relationship between population and resources, which in a pastoral ecosystem means the three-tier relationship between coincident populations of people, animals, and the vegetation. Pressure of population on resources can result from a growing population (which is relatively slow), declining resources (which in the Sahel may be very fast), or a combination of both. A pastoral society has three possible responses to these different types of population pressure on resources: some members can move away, resource use can be intensified, or population growth can be slowed. Sahelian pastoral societies seem to have responded in all three ways to relative resource scarcity. The three types of response are not equally sensitive to changes in the population/resource equation however. Population regulation is not at all responsive to short-term variations in resource supply, since its effects are felt only slowly, while emigration, and return when things improve, can be very sensitive indeed to such variations. Intensification of resource-use is a mechanism of a different nature, the effects of which may outlive the crisis that brought it about.

Movement

The most obvious pastoral adjustment to scarcity of resources is to move elsewhere; nomadism itself is created by such a necessity. Sahelian pastoralists regularly move short and long distances to take advantage of seasonal pastures or to flee a drought-stricken area. When animals are in very short supply, active members of the family may leave the pastoral economy altogether for a short time and seek work elsewhere.

An essential element in this was the relationship of the Sahelian grassland zone to complementary economic zones, especially the Sudanic savanna agricultural zone to the south, and the Sahara (with its oases and salt mines) and North African markets to the north. This precolonial regional economic interdependence, with the Sahel as fulcrum, has recently been well described by Baier and Lovejoy, writing on the rather special case of the area between central Niger and north Nigeria (1, 62). They argue that this zone was characterized by two principal economic sectors, the Twareg and the Hausa, divided by the Sahelian ecological frontier but linked by strong currents of trade and mutual interdependence. The Sahel supplied pastoral products and Saharan trade products (salt and dates); the savanna provided grain and the products of town craft industry such as cloth and leather goods. The Twareg maintained a commercial infrastructure in the savanna consisting of urban brokers, landlords, traders, and craftsmen; they also invested in farming estates in northern Nigeria, which provided an annual tribute in grain, provided lodging for traveling Twareg and a network of resting places on the north-south transhumance route, and guaranteed access to land in the dry season and especially during serious droughts. This chain of activities spreading from desert to savanna not only formed an integrated economic operation (in an excess of formalist zeal, Twareg aristocrats are described as managers of large firms with investments in diverse activities), but was also a safety valve for pastoralists during the drought; they could migrate to the far southern end of the network, pasture their herds there, and concentrate on nonpastoral activities. In the light of this, Baier and Lovejoy suggest that there was a drought/recovery cycle in which migration from drought-stricken areas was systematically organized. In drought periods of several years, the Sahelian economy contracted as nomads and farmers moved toward the southern end of their trading network which linked the Sahelian and Sudanic zones. Nobles were able to claim the animals they owned in the herds of vassals; as pastures were reduced and animals died, low rank pastoralists (vassals and slaves) were squeezed out of the pastoral economy and the nomads themselves at times settled for long periods in the south. The reverse happened in good periods. Then the herds expanded in the rich pasture, nobles loaned animals to vassals and to slaves who had settled, enabling them to become mobile again. Farmers also moved north, providing a ready source of grain.

The drought/recovery cycle is a valuable contribution to the study of the Sahelian economy. Although the complexity of economic interdependence between Twareg and Hausa economies was probably exceptional, it is likely that throughout the Sahelian zone the main elements were the same: a willingness and ability to move, long distances if necessary, the connections, networks, and alliances (and in some cases political power) guaranteeing access to pasture, to agricultural land, or to urban jobs, the trading skills to recoup losses as rapidly as possible, and an occupationally mobile population whose center of gravity could change between pastoralism and other occupations.

Intensification

The second possible response to resource shortage in the long term is to add new forms of land use to pastoralism in the same area or to intensify pastoral use itself. Hunting and gathering are subsidiary or replacement livelihoods for most Sahelian pastoralists and of special importance in drought. In the Sahel proper, with less than 300 or 400 mm of rainfall, agriculture is possible only in specially favored circumstances such as wadi beds where water runoff is concentrated into a small area of good soil. Sporadic agriculture is attempted in many places in the Sahel, but the highly variable yields make it an unprofitable venture that is likely to be abandoned as soon as pasture improves. Of more interest is the possibility of intensifying pastoralism itself.

Internally generated intensification of pastoralism depends on the capacity of a pastoral economy to generate a physical surplus and to create social relations of production so that the surplus is used in ways that raise productivity: new technologies, new forms of social organization of production, education and so on. The important questions are the composition and size of the surplus itself, who controls it, and what use is made of it in relation to the technical possibilities for increasing production.

The main Sahelian pastoral surplus (as distinct from that created by trade in salt or other commodities carried out by pastoralists) consists in milk and live animals. In the wet season there is sometimes considerable surplus milk production. Camel milk cannot be made into cheese, but the milk of other animals is sometimes made into cheese and stored to be eaten later. Some cow's milk is sold by Fulani women when near a market. In general, however, milk production is marked by a wet season surplus over consumption requirements, which often cannot be sold since at this season the herds are out in pastures far from markets, followed by dry season deficits. Live animals are more useful. As described, some young males can be sold each year without prejudice to the herds; in a small herd the revenue from this is necessary to cover basic needs in grain, cloth, and other commodities. Environmental fluctuations make even this small marketable surplus uncertain for many pastoral families. A number of animals additional to basic subsistence requirements are required to fuel the system of loans and gifts of animals made to people in need; in the uncertain conditions of the Sahel this was a necessary condition for the functioning of the pastoral economy. Control of the surplus in hierarchic societies was in the hands of a small class of nobles; in the Moor Emirates, noble *hassan* tribes and clans controlled the rangelands and used this to justify payment of a tribute by vassals (8). In many Twareg societies, nobles also extracted a tribute from vassals in return for grazing rights. Large herds acquired in this way were often redistributed to build up a client following. Money from sales of male animals and from trading profits was probably largely invested outside the Sahel, as in Central Niger (1, 62).

One good reason why pastoral intensification in the Sahel did not take place is the great difficulty in actually doing so. It seems likely that the main pastoral techniques (species, age, and sex composition of flocks and herds, their organization and management, organization of camps, patterns of movement, water technology, animal husbandry technology) evolved at a relatively early stage, while introduction of the more advanced techniques necessary for intensification of pastoralism (pasture management and conservation, fodder collection and storage, fattening of animals for sale) was made difficult by the low natural productivity of the environment (as compared, for example, to the Mediterranean or southwest Asia), and by the necessarily flexible and opportunistic pastoral use of these resources. Satisfactory organization of grazing so that best use of pasture is made and overgrazing is prevented depends on a strong organization with the power to impose sanctions. In most of the Sahel the poverty and extreme variability of pasture makes this impossible, and no truly Sahelian pastoral society appears to have created an effective system of grazing control.

Irregularity of pastures and the resulting need for flexibility and mobility by camps make collective ownership of pastures within a defined political grouping unavoidable. Well-established major political groups in general keep pastoralists from other political groups away from their pastures by the threat of force or denial of water. Within these major groups, control over access to pasture varies. A dominant aristocracy, as among the Twareg and Moors, may claim rights over land and demand tribute in return for grazing by subordinate clans (8, 19, 68). Unstable or recently arrived societies have even less formal control of grazing land. Wodaabe Fulani pastoralists who have spread north into the Sahel only recently have no territorial organization (33). But even where there is a well-defined territorial control by a pastoral hierarchy, adaptation of grazing pressure to pasture potential is not achieved, since there is no provision for members of the group in control of the territory to limit the number of their animals. The nearest approach to grazing organization and pasture reservation as a technique of raised productivity occurs in the *dina* system imposed in the nineteenth century by Sheku Amadu in the inner Niger delta. Here a set of precise rules governed (and still governs to this day) grazing, access to pasture, and pasture reserves (28, 37). But the rich natural environment, seasonally flooded by the Niger, in which this rare example of a genuinely agro-pastoral economy developed, is exceptional in the Sahel.

Population Regulation

The third response to pressure of population on resources is control of population growth itself. The study of pastoral demography is made difficult by the lack of reasonable population data. There has been only one full demographic survey devoted to Sahelian pastoralists (40, 71), although a detailed study has been made of fertility differences, and the factors controlling them, between nomadic pastoralists and sedentary farmers in the Sudan, in ecological conditions not unlike the Sahel (45, 46). However, enough information can be extracted from these two studies and more general work to permit some hypotheses to be formulated on the demography of nomadic pastoralists in the Sahel.

A survey among Fulani and Twareg in the Tahoua area of Niger was carried out in 1963 (71). The survey was stratified by ethnic subgroup, allowing comparison within the "Fulani" category between pure Bororo nomads and semisedentary Farfaru, and within the "Twareg" category between nomadic "real" Twareg, nomadic Buzu (black ex-slaves of the Twareg), and settled cultivating Buzu. The results are shown in Table 2. The figures for the settled agricultural populations of Niger are from an administrative census of 1960. These figures, although subject to all the caution necessary with African demographic data gathered in difficult conditions, indicate much lower growth rates in the two "pure" nomad populations, the Bororo and the Twareg, when compared with overall figures for Niger's sedentary farming population, and even compared with semisedentary Farfaru and sedentary Buzu, both of whom have some pastoral tradition. In the case of the nomadic Bororo, low growth rates are the result of a combination of low birth and death rates. Although the nomadic Buzu do not have growth rates as low as the other two nomadic populations, their rates are low by comparison with those of the sedentary farming Buzu.

Table 2 Vital rates for different populations within the Niger Republic

Population[a]	Birth rate (per 1000)	Death rate (per 1000)	Rate of natural increase (per 1000)
Fulani:			
nomadic Bororo	30	19	11
semisedentary Farfaru	49	26	23
Twareg:			
nomadic Twareg	47	36	11
nomadic Buzu	41	17	24
sedentary Buzu	58	23	35
Rest of Niger:			
sedentary farming			
populations	57	32	25

[a]Source: Bororo, Farfaru, Twareg, and Buzu (in 1963) from (71); farming populations in rest of Niger (in 1960) from (31).

There is some scattered evidence from other African surveys to confirm these impressions. Table 3 shows that a number of African pastoral populations have lower rates of natural increase than neighboring sedentary peasant farmers or than national averages; where figures exist, these low rates of increase seem to be the result of low birth and death rates. In the case of the inner Niger delta in Mali, which has a very low regional rate of population growth, the pastoral Fulani rate of growth is higher than the regional mean, but their birth and death rates are both lower than the mean. The vital rates in Table 3 may be compared with the substantially higher rates for west Africa generally: crude birth rates of around 50 per thousand, crude death rates of 25 to 30 or more per thousand (9, 17, 24). Other figures point in the same direction. Both fertility and mortality of Fulani in a wide variety of places in west Africa are low relative to neighboring agricultural peoples

Table 3 Vital rates for selected African pastoral and peasant populations

Population	Source	Date	Birth rate (per 1000)	Death rate (per 1000)	Rate of natural increase (per 1000)
West Africa					
1. Senegal Valley: regional mean (mainly sedentary farmers)	(71)	1957			23
pastoral Moors					11
2. Mali, inner Niger delta: regional mean (mainly sedentary farmers)	(37)	1956-1958	55	42	13
pastoral Fulani			46	30	16
3. Cameroun: national mean	(69)	1960s	43	24	19
pastoral Fulani of Adamawa			25	18	7
East Africa					
1. Somalia: pastoral Somali	(53)	1974	37	20	17
rural settled Somali			56	34	22
2. Sudan: a. Baggara pastoralists	(45)	1961-1962	29.6		
sedentary agricultural Baggara			41.2		
b. Kawahla pastoralists			32.5		
sedentary Kawahla rainfed farmers			51.2		
sedentary Kawahla irrigation farmers			56.8		

Table 4   Niger Republic. Percentage of women who complete their reproductive period without giving birth

Population[a]	Percentage
Pastoral Fulani	15
Pastoral Twareg	21
Agro-pastoral Kanuri	16
Mean for agricultural populations including Kanuri	6.3

[a]Source: Fulani and Twareg from (40); Kanuri and agricultural populations from (31).

(18, 27, 38). A survey of fertility rates by ethnic group in Senegal showed low fertility for nomadic pastoral Moors and Fulani compared to sedentary farming Tuculor, Wolof, and Serer (57).

Besides apparently low vital rates relative to sedentary peasant populations, west African pastoral populations appear to share some other special characteristics which may be related to the low vital rates. The survey of nomadic populations in Niger indicated high sterility among Twareg and Fulani women, and this is confirmed by census figures for the rest of Niger as Table 4 shows.

Sex ratios among nomadic populations indicate a high proportion of men to women, the reverse of the normal situation in Africa. Investigations of three separate nomadic populations in Niger (2, 71) reported high sex ratios, but assumed this was the result of underreporting of females due to husbands' unwillingness to present their wives, to a desire to reduce the number of people on whom poll taxes were levied, to concealed polygamy, or to the instability of marriages, many women being between husbands, and thus unreported at census time. These arguments are not convincing. High male : female sex ratios have been reported from nomads elsewhere [e.g. among Turkmen of Iran and the USSR (54)] and seem more likely to be related to a pastoral nomadic life. There is no reason to suppose that women may be settled elsewhere, for example as servants; indeed in many pastoral societies men are more likely to be absent, working elsewhere. Table 5 assembles some of the African data.

Many of these characteristics of African nomadic pastoral populations are confirmed by a detailed study by Henin in the Sudan in the early 1960s (45, 46). He found that nomadic pastoralists had considerably lower fertility than sedentary agricultural populations within the same ethnic groups; as pastoralists moved from nomadism to a settled agricultural life their fertility rose. In the two nomad societies observed, there were more single and more childless women, women married later, marriages were less stable due in great part to the greater freedom of women (46% of nomad divorces, as reported by the women, were requested by the women, as against 38% by the men), and more polygamous marriages. Many of these factors were attributed to the absence of men from nomad camps either looking after herds or on labor migration. Henin also found that nomad women had higher rates of pregnancy loss and appeared to have high rates of venereal diseases and malaria,

Table 5 Sex ratios among African pastoral and other populations

Population	Sex ratio (males per 100 females)	Source
Niger:		
nomadic Twareg	128	(71)
nomadic Buzu	107	(71)
sedentary Buzu	110	(71)
nomadic Fulani	144	(71)
semisedentary Farfaru	111	(71)
nomadic Illabakan Twareg	124	(2)
Niger — all populations	98	(56)
Mali:		
free Twareg of Gourma (1920)	113	(39)
iklan (slaves) of Gourma (1920)	99	(39)
Somalia:		
nomadic Somali, Bardere district	110	(83)
nomadic Somali, Burao district	106	(83)
nomadic Somali, Afmadu district	111	(83)
urban Somali, 21 towns	96	(83)
Senegal — all populations	97	(56)
Liberia — all populations	98	(56)
Sierra Leone — all populations	98	(56)
Togo — all populations	90	(56)
Kenya — all populations	98	(56)
Ghana — all populations	102	(56)
Uganda — all populations	101	(56)

though there was no comparative evidence for this; they also tended to breast feed their children much longer.

The conclusions from this demographic data on pastoralists may be summarized briefly. The figures, inadequate though they are, suggest: that nomadic pastoral populations have low rates of natural increase of population compared to neighboring agricultural peoples; that these low rates of increases are the result of a combination of low birth and death rates; that pastoralists have low rates of completed fertility, high rates of female sterility, and high ratios of men to women. There appears to be no obvious systematic bias nor environmental or health reasons for these differences, and no cultural or religious reasons suffice to explain the differences since the differences also appear between nomadic pastoral and sedentary populations of the same ethnic background and same religion.

We are obliged therefore to look for socioeconomic reasons related to economic differences between nomadic pastoralism and sedentary agriculture themselves, involving both a reason why pastoralists would find it advantageous to limit their population growth rates and the means they might employ to do so. The most realistic hypothesis can be derived from the earlier discussion of some aspects of the pastoral economy and environment. In the Sahel, weather fluctuates from year to year and with it milk production from pastoral herds. Pastoralism in general re-quires relatively little labor per unit of output; production of milk, the main food, depends principally on the size and structure of the herd and the amount of pasture and cannot be increased from year to year simply by increasing labor inputs, as can agricultural production. Furthermore, flocks and herds, and thus the total labor they require, increase quite slowly; but they may decrease (through disease or drought) very fast. A human population cannot adjust its numbers from year to year in this way, except through migration. As a result, in a pastoral economy, labor, and the reproduction of the labor force within the domestic unit, are less important than in agriculture; indeed, since labor requirements of herding are low and food supply is unpredictable and unresponsive to increased labor inputs, a small and slowly growing population relative to the herds can be expected to have an advan-tage over a large or rapidly growing one. When the pastoral economy expands to take advantage of a wet sequence of years, additional labor can be taken on from outside the pastoral economy through client relationships or herding contracts; this extra labor is easy to dispose of when a dry sequence starts. In practice, as was described in the previous section, emigration or temporary settlement into other economic activities is one demographic adjustment to this situation. Another may be social regulation of the demographic processes themselves.

The most sophisticated example of this so far described is the Gada system of Borana pastoralists in southern Ethiopia (60). Legesse hypothesizes a population explosion (of unspecified cause) among Oromo peoples (including the Borana) starting in the fifteenth century, which was dealt with by all three possible responses open to societies in this position: territorial expansion, by which the Oromo spread across nearly half of Ethiopia; intensification of resource use where ecological condi-tions permitted cultivation; and above all by the introduction of the Gada system of population control. The Gada system is an extreme form of generation-grading organization: classes succeed each other every 8 years in assuming political, military, and other responsibilities, but unlike age-grades, infant boys enter the Gada system always exactly 40 years behind their father, regardless of the age of the father. Before assuming a position of leadership, each Gada class is required to wage war on a community that none of their ancestors had raided; this war every 8 years was behind the Oromo spread across Ethiopia. But the Gada rules also regulate Borana population growth by postponing marriage until a very late stage in the life cycle and by requiring that no children can be allowed to survive until an even later stage; children born earlier than is acceptable are killed, and infanticide for this reason was still very widespread at the time Legesse did field work in the early 1960s. If Legesse's analysis is correct [which is disputed (44)], the effect of the Gada rules on Borana population seem to have been striking; simulation indicates that the imposition of the rules resulted in a rapid decline in Borana population for a century, followed by two centuries of stability, after which the population began to grow again at a very slow pace.

The Gada system is exceptional and nothing similar is known in west African nomadic pastoral societies. But simpler demographic regulators may be at work there also. Little information is available on voluntary birth spacing, contraception, or postnatal sexual abstinence among pastoralists. Among nomadic Somali there is a 2-year period of postnatal abstinence, and there seems also to have been sexual abstinence during the dry season and during drought years (83). There is some indication that Twareg and Fulani women in Niger marry later than west African peasants (40), and in both Twareg and Fulani society marriages are quite unstable; both of these would depress fertility relative to that in stable early marriages. The role of bridewealth in delaying marriages also needs to be investigated further. Capot-Rey (20) reports that high bridewealth keeps population low among Tubu of the Saharan Tibesti. But the argument has not been elaborated for Sahelian pastoralists, although it has recently been argued that bridewealth acts as a mechanism adjusting population to resources in a Sahelian peasant society (72, 73) and in a central Asian pastoral society, the Yomut Turkmen of northern Iran (55).

There are many unresolved problems concerning the possible operation of bridewealth as a homeostatic demographic regulator (i.e. one capable of adjusting population up or down depending on resource availability); its relation to the timing of cyclical changes in livestock numbers (which will take place much faster than changes in human fertility) and to wealth distribution in pastoral society need special clarification. On the other hand, there is little doubt that high bridewealth could keep population growth down in relation to resources and low in relation to its own biological potential (i.e. act as a general brake rather than as a homeostatic regulator) by excluding some poor men from marriage and delaying other men's marriages and thus indirectly reducing women's total fertility.

Famine and Environmental Destruction Before the Twentieth Century

The types of pastoral strategies outlined in previous sections probably had little sustained environmental impact. With pasture varying widely as a result of irregular rainfall, scattered small-capacity wells the main water source, and a permanent risk of animal disease epidemics, there would have been little chance of the sort of widespread and continuing imbalance between animals and pasture needed to degrade the environment to a serious degree. No doubt around individual wells after a series of good years pasture was overgrazed, but the need of the animals to be watered every few days during the dry season acts as a limit on the amount of damage that can be done. As the area around the well in which vegetation has been eaten increases, the animals have to go farther between water and pasture; when they have to be watered every few days there is a limit to the area that can be degraded in this way, the maximum for camels being a radius of 20 to 30 km (81). Cattle have to be watered every 2 or 3 days, and so the area they can cover is reduced even further. With small-capacity scattered water points capable of watering few animals, the damage was localized and quickly repaired in the next wet period.

The same is not true of famine. Mention is made of famines by Muslim historians and travelers in the Sahel from the early middle ages onwards. With this material Cissoko (22) and Tymowski (86) have reconstructed the pattern of famines in the area of Timbuktu and the inner flood zone of the Niger river between the fourteenth and eighteenth centuries. From the fourteenth to sixteenth centuries the area was part of the Songhai empire. Efficient organization of agriculture, of communications, and of trans-Saharan trade brought peace and prosperity. Although there are records of several plague epidemics, there are none of famine. This period of prosperity and security came to an end in the second half of the 16th century with the consolidation of power by a new class of administrators and bureaucrats who increasingly exploited the peasants, and with the deterioration in commerce and foreign trade due in part to fall in the value of west African gold as a result of the discovery of alternative sources in America; the final blow was the conquest of the Songhai empire in 1591 by a Moroccan army. Throughout the seventeenth and eighteenth centuries the area was fought over by competing groups. The least shortage of food or natural disaster such as drought, floods, or locusts was liable to turn into a famine. Great famines were recorded every 7 to 10 years during the seventeenth century, every 5 years during the eighteenth century. In 1738 nearly half of the population of Timbuktu, and probably of the whole region, died. Timbuktu, in the sixteenth century a prosperous commercial town and a famous center of learning with perhaps 80,000 inhabitants, was reduced in the early nineteenth century to a miserable village of some 12,000 people.

SAHELIAN PASTORALISM IN THE TWENTIETH CENTURY

In the second half of the nineteenth century, France embarked on a period of rapid colonial expansion from bases in Algeria and Senegal. In the nomad areas of the Sahel, military conquest was not really complete until after Twareg revolts during World War I had been ruthlessly put down, and the resistance of the Mauritanian nomads was not finally broken until the mid-1930s. The French objective was twofold: to ensure military security within their new colonies, and to promote economic development so that the colonies would provide profitable economic opportunities for French capital.

Administration was financed out of the colonies' own resources. The problem at first was that peasants and pastoralists showed relatively little interest in producing more. In the early years in the farming areas, forced labor on fields owned by the administration was the chosen method to get around this. Forced labor was soon recognized as inefficient, however, and was abandoned in favor of a poll tax, accompanied in the case of nomads by an animal tax. These taxes had to be paid in cash, and one of their express purposes was to oblige subsistence producers to produce more for the market. At the same time merchants were encouraged to set up shop in the new administrative centers created in nomad areas in order to stimulate rising wants among the nomads that would also serve to bring them more into the market. After about 1920 the first attempts at development were undertaken. These consisted principally in digging new wells and in veterinary campaigns against the main animal diseases. New markets were also opened up north and south of the Sahara.

These changes led to fundamental changes in pastoral society and economy, described by Clauzel for north Mali (23). As a result of the increased security and especially the end to raiding, nomad camps no longer needed to be grouped so closely together, and instead moved out in a more dispersed pattern into areas of good pasture previously too dangerous to be used for long. The land was used more widely, while at the same time many people moved less far than before and settled down to a more regular pattern of movement around a base well. Because of better use of pasture, new wells, and veterinary campaigns, herds grew. There was a general movement of pastoralists towards the south, accompanied by an advance of peasant farmers towards the north, as both began to use previously insecure areas. This was accompanied by a reorientation of the savanna zone itself toward the south rather than the north as previously, due to a relative reduction of trans-Saharan trade in favor of trade toward the west African coast, the growth of communications to the south, and the development of export crops which were shipped from Dakar and elsewhere along the coast (62). As a result, the Sahel, which had previously been integrated in a variety of ways both with the savanna economies to the south and with the Saharan and north African urban economies through long-distance trade, became simultaneously more market oriented and more peripheral to the main currents of economic activity.

The effects on Sahelian pastoral economies were important. As long as pastoralists marketed only excess male animals, their basic subsistence strategy remained unaffected. However, as soon as livestock marketing became more general, as it did in the Sahel as a result both of the push of new taxation and the pull of new economic wants, the basic strategy changed. In addition to selling excess males, there are a number of ways a herdsman can increase the proportion of marketed animals; these affect his subsistence production and his use of land, labor, and other resources. Although the published evidence is not good, it seems likely that all these types of market responses have occurred in the last few decades:

(a) The herdsman can change the species composition of his flocks and herds, where environment and tradition allow choices between camels and goats (safer subsistence animals) and cattle and sheep (which generally have higher market value). A pastoral economy can respond to market demand by shifting resources away from safer subsistence species to more readily marketed species. Clauzel notes an increase in cattle and sheep relative to other animals in the Malian Sahel during the French colonial period (23).

(b) The herdsman can rely less on milk for his own subsistence and thereby leave more milk for the young animals, improving their nutrition and their chance of survival. There are no data on whether this has happened to a significant extent among Sahelian pastoralists.

(c) He can put fewer animals into the traditional reciprocal and redistributive networks of animal loans, gifts, and other transfers, and sell them instead. This seems to have happened throughout the Sahel.

(d) He can sell old females with reduced chances of reproduction. Such animals are sometimes kept in herds after their best reproductive life is over because it is believed, with some empirical support, that they are more likely to survive disease epidemics and thus provide the nucleus of a new breeding herd.

(e) The herdsman can sell "capital," that is, reproductive males and females. This is a last resort, practiced only at times of extreme need. For example, many of the animals sold during the 1968–1973 drought were adult females, sometimes even pregnant females.

It is thus possible to identify a range of possible market responses and corresponding production strategies among Sahelian pastoralists from disposal of surplus males, which does not impinge on subsistence herd management, to sale of "capital," which affects it profoundly. Subsistence production is characterized by mixed herds to spread risk, with a substantial proportion of goats and camels among northern Sahelian pastoralists, by the importance of nonmarket forms of livestock exchange within the pastoral community through mechanisms of reciprocity and redistribution, and by the sale only of males excess to herd maintenance and to these social needs. Commercially oriented production, on the other hand, is characterized by the sale of more animals rather than their use for nonmarket transactions or as security in the pastoralist's own herd, and by a changed species composition of herds. Even in the latter, however, there is little sign as yet of the general development of anything approaching a market in production factors in pastoralism itself (although there is of course large scale labor migration into other economic activities), outside of the commercial ranches now being set up in most Sahelian countries.

These economic and political changes have had profound effects on Sahelian pastoral societies, and through them on the environment. In the first place, the end to the great previous insecurity, the control of the worst animal disease epidemics and the construction of new wells, certainly improved the lot of most herdsmen, at least temporarily; there are more animals and more are sold, bringing pastoral families better and more varied supplies of food and a more regular supply of cloth and luxuries such as tea and sugar. This has been accompanied by changes in traditional production and distribution strategies, by a loosening of traditional social and economic networks, and by a reorientation of economic activity toward the market. But Sahelian markets are unstable, and the pastoralists have no control over fluctuations in the prices of what they sell and what they buy. As a result they have become increasingly vulnerable both to long-term changes in terms of trade for their products and also to short-term fluctuations. Very little information is available on these for the Sahel, but fluctuations appear to have worked both in their favor and against them. Baier shows that in central Niger after the 1913 drought, terms of trade for live animals (and nomadic trade items such as salt, transported by camel) were good against millet; by selling desert and Sahel products herdsmen were able to obtain 5 to 20 times as much millet as before the drought (1). This is to be expected, since millet supplies can be back to normal less than one year after the first good rains, while cattle and camel herds take much longer to build up again. But because an increasing part of pastoral families' food comes through market exchange of animals for grain, they are more vulnerable to these fluctuations in relative market prices; their situation is made worse if they have modified their herd composition toward cattle and sheep, since these species are less resistant to drought than camels and goats and thus supply less milk as an alternative to grain acquired at market. This is especially dangerous in drought years when the market is flooded with animals, pushing their prices down to derisory levels, while grain prices, already high because of the same drought, are pushed up even further by the greatly increased demand. Information from the comparable Somali pastoral economy shows that there was a substantial decline in terms of trade between pastoral (including hunted and gathered) products and cereals and cloth since the nineteenth century, with large annual fluctuations in this century (84). The effects of these violent short-term fluctuations in times of drought are made more serious by the progressive breakdown of the pastoral society's own mechanisms of redistribution of animals to those in need.

The greater security and the new wells opened up great areas of new pasture, previously avoided because there was no water or because of the danger of raids. So the Sahelian environment was more evenly, and as herds grew, more intensely used. Pastoral mobility, however, was often reduced, as a result of new patterns of movement revolving around home wells, regulation of nomadic movement by the government, and after independence by the new frontiers and tighter administration. New currency regulations made long-distance caravan trading more difficult. In many places, essential dry season pasture was taken for agricultural development projects. The new deep boreholes often became centers of semisedentary life, with some millet cultivation, a merchant or two, or administrative officers of the state. It proved impossible to control livestock numbers around these boreholes, and the great number of animals that could be watered without great effort led to huge concentrations of animals, which soon destroyed all pasture in a radius of 10 or 15 km. The effects were so dramatic that in Niger a Twareg group asked the government to close a borehole that had been sunk in their territory, and went back to digging their own shallower wells (3).

CONCLUSION: UNDERDEVELOPMENT, DESERTIFICATION, AND FAMINE

The pastoral development policies pursued by Sahelian states, much influenced by aid donors, have consisted principally in efforts to increase marketed animals; high rates of taxation were maintained, and the development of production was limited to control of animal disease (mainly for cattle) and provision of water. It has become apparent that these measures are not adequate on their own to ensure development of pastoral production or a sustained improvement in the pastoral standard of living. Major problems such as grazing control and the organization of the market to protect pastoralists from rapid price fluctuations have to be solved if pastoral production is to be intensified. For the first time, the modern state has the power to do such things. But it has not done so, and without these measures no real development of the pastoral economy or pastoral society could take place. Worse, because of the changes outlined above and despite much government activity in the pastoral areas, pastoralists are as vulnerable as ever to climatic uncertainty. This state of underdevelopment, characterized by growing economic disparities between pastoral areas (and peasant areas where many of the same forces operate) and urban or intensive agriculture areas, is the first stage of an increasing relative impoverishment of the countryside, in which traditional societies provide cheap commodities (in this case livestock, elsewhere in the Sahel cotton and groundnuts) and abundant labor for more dynamic highly capitalized operations elsewhere. The reproduction of this labor supply within the traditional community is relatively inexpensive compared to its reproduction in urban areas (25). In a second stage of this process, the traditional nomadic pastoral societies themselves are replaced as land-users by highly capitalized ranches, where jobs are offered to only a few of the former nomadic inhabitants. At no stage have serious efforts been made to rethink development of Sahelian pastoral economies in their entirety, with the principal aim of improving the standard of living of the pastoralists themselves (82).

This situation may be interpreted as the result of deliberate choices made by international capital supported by the national bourgeoisies in power in west Africa (25, 26, 61, 66) or merely the mistakes of development technicians faced with unfamiliar problems. The apparent success of development programs in the Mongolian pastoral economy (51), in conditions not unlike those of the Sahel, gives credence to the first view. But of one thing there can be no doubt: after 50 years of modern administration, Sahelian pastoralists find themselves in a precarious ecological and economic position.

There appears to have been a sustained and widespread decline in plant cover, especially at points of livestock concentration around wells and close to the main rivers and in areas where cultivation has spread far north into areas of low and highly fluctuating rainfall. In the Sahel rain comes in violent storms at the height of the summer; as a result, the bare soil is blown away as dust or carried off in flash floods. Rain no longer penetrates fully to recharge soil moisture and the water table, but instead floods away in wadis.

A degraded environment under increasing pressure is one aspect of the lack of development. More immediately serious for the pastoralists is the threat of famine. The main famines of the first half of this century, in 1913–1914, 1930–1932, and the early 1940s, appear to have been triggered by drought, but to have had as their basic cause the profound economic and political changes described above and brought about by colonial conquest and subsequent administration (7, 36, 75).

The most recent famine was also triggered by drought. After generally high or average rainfall in the 1950s and 1960s, the end of the 1960s and the first three years of the 1970s were marked throughout the Sahel by a serious shortage of rain. At the International Biological Programme field station in northern Senegal the above-ground production of grasses in 1972 was practically nil. Trees came into leaf later, leaf production was much less than normal, and leaves fell early; few trees bore fruits or seeds. Many trees died (4, 5, 70). The lack of vegetation had catastrophic results for the domestic animals which fed on the plants and for the people who depended on the domestic animals. Despite long-distance movements starting in the autumn of 1972, mortality among livestock of all species was high. Cattle suffered most. Livestock prices collapsed as markets were flooded. There were large-scale migrations to towns, where huge shantytowns grew up. Refugee camps were set up in some of the worst hit areas, where destitute nomads depended on unreliable food aid from abroad. There are no precise figures for the number of dead (10, 41, 76, 77), but it is sometimes estimated to have been between 100,000 and 250,000 out of a total nomad population in the affected countries of two and a half million. Nomads fared worse than those further south; old people and children were particularly vulnerable. A study of nomad refugees in the Lazaret camp at Niamey, Niger, concluded that one person in six had died (13). Measles was a major cause of death. Fulani pastoralists interviewed in the camp (59) expressed the hopelessness of the totally destitute: "If the President orders us to go home, we will go; if he orders us to stay, we will stay; it is his right. Since we gave up our forefathers' traditions and came here, we now depend on him."

Literature Cited

1. Baier, S. 1976. Economic history and development: drought and the Sahelian economies of Niger. *Afr. Econ. Hist.* 1:1–16
2. Bernus, E. 1974. *Les Illabakan (Niger): Une Tribu Touarègue Sahélienne et son Aire de Nomadisation.* Paris: Mouton. 116 pp.
3. Bernus, E. 1974. Possibilités et limites de la politique d'hydraulique pastorale dans le Sahel nigérien. *Cah. ORSTOM, Sér. Sci. Hum.* 11: 119–26
4. Bille, J. C. 1974. Recherches écologiques sur une savane Sahélienne du Ferlo septentrional, Sénégal: 1972, année sèche au Sahel. *La Terre et la Vie* 28: 5–20
5. Bille, J. C., Poupon, H. 1974. Recherches écologiques sur une savane Sahélienne du Ferlo septentrional, Sénégal: la régénération de la strate herbacée. *La Terre et la Vie* 28: 21–48
6. Bonte, P. 1973. *L'Elevage et le Commerce du Bétail dans l'Ader Doutchi-Majya.* Niamey: Etudes Nigériennes no. 23. 211 pp.
7. Bonte, P. 1975. Pasteurs et nomades; l'exemple de la Mauritanie. In *Sécheresses et Famines du Sahel,* ed. J. Copans, 2: 62–86. Paris: Maspero. 144 pp.
8. Bonte, P., Bourgeot, A., Lefébure, C. 1978. Pastoral economy and societies. In *State of Knowledge Report on Tropical Grazing Land Ecosystems.* Paris: UNESCO. In press
9. Brass, W. 1968. The demography of French-speaking territories covered by special sample enquiries: Upper Volta, Dahomey, Guinea, North Cameroon and other areas. In *The Demography of Tropical Africa,* ed. W. Brass, A. J. Coale, P. Demeny, D. F. Heisel, F. Lorimer, A. Romaniuk, E. van de Walle, pp. 342–439. Princeton Univ. Press. 539 pp.
10. Brun, T. 1975. Manifestations nutritionelles et médicales de la famine. See Ref. 7, 1: 75–108
11. Bryson, R. A. 1973. Climatic modification by air pollution. 2: The Sahelian effect. *Univ. Wis. Inst. Environ. Stud. Rep.* 9: 1–12
12. Bryson, R. A. 1974. A perspective on climate change. *Science* 184: 753–60
13. Bugnicourt, J. 1974. *Un Peuple Privé de son Environnement.* Dakar: Programme Form. Environ. 232 pp.
14. Bunting, A. H., Dennett, M. D., Elston, J., Milford, J. R. 1975. Seasonal rainfall forecasting in west Africa. *Nature* 253: 622–23
15. Bunting, A. H., Dennett, M. D., Elston, J., Milford, J. R. 1976. Rainfall trends in the west African Sahel. *Q. J. R. Meteorol. Soc.* 102: 59–64
16. Butzer, K. W. 1961. Climatic change in arid regions since the Pliocene. In *A History of Land Use in Arid Regions,* ed. L. D. Stamp, pp. 31–56. Paris: UNESCO. 388 pp.
17. Caldwell, J. C. 1975. Introduction. In *Population Growth and Socioeconomic Change in West Africa,* ed. J. C. Caldwell, N. O. Addo, S. K. Gaisie, A. Igun, P. O. Olusanya, pp. 3–28. New York: Columbia Univ. Press. 763 pp.
18. Cantrelle, P. 1975. Mortality. See Ref. 17, pp. 98–118
19. Capot-Rey, R. 1953. *Le Sahara Français.* Paris: Presses Univ. France. 564 pp.
20. Capot-Rey, R. 1963. Le nomadisme des Toubous. In *Nomades et Nomadisme au Sahara,* pp. 81–92. Paris: UNESCO. 195 pp.
21. Charney, J. G. 1975. Dynamics of deserts and drought in the Sahel. *Q. J. R. Meteorol. Soc.* 101: 193–202
22. Cissoko, S. -M. 1968. Famines et épidémies à Tombouctou et dans la Boucle du Niger du XVIe au XVIIIe siècle. *Bull. Inst. Fondam. Afr. Noire, Ser. B.* 30: 806–21
23. Clauzel, J. 1962. Evolution de la vie économique et des structures sociales du pays nomade du Mali de la conquête française à l'autonomie interne (1893–1958). *Tiers Monde* 3: 283–311
24. Coale, A. J., Lorimer, F. 1968. Summary of estimates of fertility and mortality. See Ref. 9, pp. 151–67
25. Comité Information Sahel 1974. *Qui se Nourrit de la Famine en Afrique? Le Dossier Politique de la Faim au Sahel.* Paris: Maspero. 278 pp.
26. Copans, J. 1975. Images, problématiques et thèmes. See Ref. 7, 1: 9–36
27. Courel, A., Pool, D. I. 1975. Upper Volta. See Ref. 17, pp. 736–754
28. Daget, J., Ba, A.-H. 1955. *L'Empire Peul du Macina.* Bamako: Inst. Fr. Afr. Noire. 306 pp.
29. Dahl, G., Hjort, A. 1976. *Having Herds: Pastoral Herd Growth and Household Economy.* Univ. Stockholm Dep. Soc. Anthropol. 335 pp.

30. Dalton, G. 1976. Review of A. G. Hopkins' *An Economic History of West Africa. Afr. Econ. Hist.* 1:51–101
31. Dankoussou, I., Diarra, S., Laya, D., Pool, D. I. 1975. Niger. See Ref. 17, pp. 679–93
32. Davy, E. G. 1974. Drought in west Africa. *WMO Bull.* 23:18–23
33. Dupire, M. 1962. *Peuls Nomades; Etude Descriptive des Wodaabe du Sahel Nigérien.* Paris: Inst. Ethnol. 331 pp.
34. Dupire, M. 1962. Trade and markets in the economy of the nomadic Fulani of Niger (Bororo). In *Markets in Africa,* ed. P. Bohannan, G. Dalton, pp. 335–62. Northwestern Univ. Press. 762 pp.
35. Dyson-Hudson, N. 1972. The study of nomads. In *Perspectives on Nomadism,* ed. W. Irons, N. Dyson-Hudson. Leiden: Brill. 136 pp.
36. Fuglestad, F. 1974. La grande famine de 1931 dans l'ouest nigérien; réflexions autour d'une catastrophe naturelle. *Rev. Fr. Hist. Outre-Mer* 61:18–33
37. Gallais, J. 1967. *Le Delta Intérieur du Niger; Etude de Géographie Régionale.* Dakar: Inst. Fondam. Afr. Noire. 2 vols. 621 pp.
38. Gallais, J. 1969. Les Peuls en question. *Rev. Psychol. Peuples* 3:231–51
39. Gallais, J. 1975. *Pasteurs et Paysans du Gourma; La Condition Sahélienne.* Paris: Ed. Cent. Natl. Rech. Sci. 239 pp.
40. Ganon, M. F. 1975. The nomads of Niger. See Ref. 17, pp. 694–700
41. Greene, M. H. 1974. Impact of the Sahelian drought in Mauritania, west Africa. *Lancet,* June 1:1093–97
42. Grove, A. T. 1973. Desertification in the African environment. In *Drought In Africa,* ed. D. Dalby, R. J. H. Church, pp. 33–45. Univ. London Sch. Orient. Afr. Stud. 124 pp.
43. Grove, A. T., Pullan, R. A. 1964. Some aspects of the Pleistocene paleogeography of the Chad basin. In *African Ecology and Human Evolution,* ed. F. C. Howell, F. Bourlière, pp. 230–45. London: Methuen. 666 pp.
44. Hallpike, C. R. 1976. The origins of the Borana Gada system. *Africa* 46: 48–55
45. Henin, R. A. 1968. Fertility differentials in the Sudan. *Popul. Stud.* 22: 147–64
46. Henin, R. A. 1969. The patterns and causes of fertility differentials in the Sudan. *Popul. Stud.* 23: 171–98
47. Hill, P. 1966. Landlords and brokers. *Cah. Etud. Afr.* 23: 349–66
48. Hill, P. 1970. *Studies in Rural Capitalism in West Africa.* Cambridge Univ. Press. 173 pp.
49. Hill, P. 1971. Two types of west African house trade. In *The Development of Indigenous Trade and Markets in West Africa,* ed. C. Meillassoux, pp. 303–18. London: Oxford Univ. Press. 444 pp.
50. Hopkins, A. G. 1973. *An Economic History of West Africa.* London: Longman. 337 pp.
51. Humphrey, C. 1978. Pastoral nomadism in Mongolia: The role of herdsmen's cooperatives in the national economy. *Dev. Change* 9. In press
52. Huzayyin, S. 1956. Changes in climate, vegetation, and human adjustment in the Saharo-Arabian belt with special reference to Africa. In *Man's Role in Changing the Face of the Earth,* ed. W. L. Thomas, pp. 304–23. Univ. Chicago Press. 1193 pp.
53. International Labour Office 1977. *Economic Transformation in a Socialist Framework; An Employment and Basic Needs Oriented Development Strategy for Somalia.* Addis Ababa: Jobs and Skills Programme for Africa. 315 pp. In press
54. Irons, W. G. 1969. *The Yomut Turkmen; A Study of Kinship in a Pastoral Society.* DPhil thesis. Univ. Michigan, Ann Arbor, Mich. 340 pp.
55. Irons, W. G. 1975. *The Yomut Turkmen; A Study of Social Organisation Among a Central Asian Turkic-Speaking Population.* Ann Arbor: Univ. Michigan Press. 193 pp.
56. Joseph, W. 1975. Liberia. See Ref. 17, pp. 527–40
57. Lacombe, B., Lamy, B., Vaugelade, J. 1975. Senegal. See Ref. 17, pp. 701–19
58. Lamb, H. H. 1973. Some comments on atmospheric pressure variations in the northern hemisphere. See Ref. 42, pp. 27–28
59. Laya, D. 1975. Interviews with farmers and livestock owners in the Sahel. *Afr. Environ.* 1: 49–93
60. Legesse, A. 1973. *Gada; Three Approaches to the Study of African Society.* New York: Free Press. 340 pp.
61. Lofchie, M. F. 1975. Political and economic origins of African hunger. *J. Mod. Afr. Stud.* 13: 551–67
62. Lovejoy, P. E., Baier, S. 1976. The desert-side economy of the central Sudan. In *The Politics of Natural Disaster; The Case of the Sahel Drought,* ed. M. H. Glantz, pp. 145–75. New York: Praeger. 340 pp.
63. MacLeod, N. H. 1976. Dust in the Sahel: cause of drought? See Ref. 62, pp. 214–31

64. Meillassoux, C. 1971. Le commerce pré-colonial et le développement de l'esclavage à Gubu du Sahel (Mali). See Ref. 49, pp. 182–95

65. Meillassoux, C. 1971. Introduction. See Ref. 49, pp. 3–48

66. Meillassoux, C. 1974. Development or exploitation: is the Sahel famine good business? *Rev. Afr. Polit. Econ.* 1: 27–33

67. Monod, T. 1964. The late Tertiary and Pleistocene in the Sahara. See Ref. 43, pp. 117–229

68. Nicolaisen, J. 1963. *Ecology and Culture of the Pastoral Tuareg.* Nat. Mus. Copenhagen. 548 pp.

69. Podlewski, A. 1975. Cameroon. See Ref. 17, pp. 543–64

70. Poupon, H., Bille, J. C. 1974. Recherches écologiques sur une savane Sahélienne du Ferlo septentrional, Sénégal: influence de la sécheresse de l'année 1972–1973 sur la strate ligneuse. *La Terre et la Vie* 28: 49–75

71. République du Niger 1966. *Etude Démographique et Economique en Milieu Nomade; Démographie, Budgets et Consommation.* Paris: Ministère de la Coopération. 201 pp.

72. Reyna, S. P. 1975. Making do when the rains stop: adjustment of domestic structure to climatic variation among the Barma. *Ethnology* 14:405–17

73. Reyna, S. P. 1977. Marriage payments, household structure, and domestic labour-supply among the Barma of Chad. *Africa* 47:81–88

74. Roche, M. 1973. Note sur la sécheresse actuelle en Afrique de l'ouest. See Ref. 42, pp. 53–61

75. Salifou, A. 1975. When history repeats itself: the famine of 1931 in Niger. *Afr. Environ.* 1:22–48

76. Seaman, J., Holt, J., Rivers, J., Murlis, J. 1973. An inquiry into the drought situation in Upper Volta. *Lancet,* Oct. 6:774–78

77. Sheets, H., Morris, R. 1974. *Disaster in the Desert: Failures of International Relief in the West African Drought.* Washington: Carnegie Endowment for International Peace. 167 pp.

78. Sircoulon, J. 1974. *Les Données Climatiques et Hydrologiques de la Sécheresse en Afrique de l'Ouest Sahélienne.* Stockholm: Secr. Int. Ecol. 44 pp.

79. Stenning, D. J. 1959. *Savannah Nomads; A Study of the Wodaabe Pastoral Fulani of Western Bornu Province, Northern Region, Nigeria.* London: Oxford Univ. Press. 266 pp.

80. Swift, J. 1973. Disaster and a Sahelian nomad economy. See Ref. 42, pp. 71–78

81. Swift, J. 1975. Pastoral nomadism as a form of land-use; the Twareg of the Adrar n Iforas. In *Pastoralism in Tropical Africa,* ed. T. Monod, pp. 443–54. London: Oxford Univ. Press. 502 pp.

82. Swift, J. 1976. Desertification and man in the Sahel. *Afr. Dev.* 1(2):1–8

83. Swift, J. 1977. Pastoral development in Somalia; herding cooperatives as a strategy against desertification and famine. In *Desertification: Environmental Degradation in and Around Arid Lands,* ed. M. H. Glantz. Boulder: Westview Press. In press

84. Swift, J. 1977. Some consequences for the Somali nomad pastoral economy of the development of livestock trading. In *Proc. Int. Colloq. Nomadic Pastoralism, Paris, Dec. 1976.* Paris: Mouton. In press

85. Tubiana, M.-J. 1971. Système pastoral et obligation de transhumer chez les Zaghawa (Soudan-Tchad). *Etud. Rurales* 42:120–71

86. Tymowski, M. 1974. *Le Développement et la Régression chez les Peuples de la Boucle du Niger à l'Epoque Précoloniale.* Warsaw: Wydawnictwa Univ. Warszawskiego. 156 pp.

87. Winstanley, D. 1973. Recent rainfall trends in Africa, the Middle East and India. *Nature* 243:464–65

88. Winstanley, D. 1973. Rainfall patterns and general atmospheric circulation. *Nature* 245:190–94

89. Winstanley, D. 1976. Climatic changes and the future of the Sahel. See Ref. 62, pp. 189–213

Ann. Rev. Anthropol. 1977. 6:479–508
Copyright © 1977 by Annual Reviews Inc. All rights reserved

ASPECTS OF REGIONAL ANALYSIS IN ARCHAEOLOGY

❖9603

Gregory A. Johnson

Department of Anthropology, Hunter College (CUNY), New York, New York 10021

INTRODUCTION

Regional studies are of growing importance in anthropology. There is a continuing need for expansion of spatial and temporal frameworks for the study of many aspects of human behavior (2, 9). The general acceptance of settlement pattern survey as an archaeological research strategy (111) has created a demand for both new theory and analytical methodology appropriate to regional data. The recent publication of a two-volume work on *Regional Analysis* in anthropology edited by Smith (141) and of a volume on *Spatial Analysis in Archaeology* by Hodder & Orton (65) reflects this demand.

The literature on regional analysis is far more extensive than I could hope to review here. I have, therefore, selected a sharply limited series of topics for more intensive discussion. I will attempt to illustrate the potential importance to archaeological research of concepts developed primarily by geographers, while keeping bald assertions of the utility of various models of spatial behavior to a minimum. This review is organized in three sections of increasing scale of analysis. The first section briefly considers alternative models of human decision-making as the bases of models of spatial behavior. The second section reviews a model of the spatial interaction of groups or populations. The third section considers aspects of the development and operation of regional interaction systems.

BASIC BEHAVIORAL ASSUMPTIONS

All models of spatial behavior ultimately rest on assumptions about the nature of human decision-making. The models reviewed here assume that spatial decisions are made in the context of attempted minimization, maximization, or optimization of certain variables or sets of variables. An assumption of minimization of energy expended in movement, for example, will play a major role in this review. Such

479

assumptions are both the strength and potential source of weakness of most spatial theory.

The weakness of minimization, maximization, or optimization models is revealed by developments in decision theory. Simon (136) argues that given bounded rationality arising from partial uncertainty (4) and imperfect knowledge, human decision-making is unlikely to conform to minimization, maximization, or optimization models. Decisions are made to satisfy an acceptable but submaximal level of intended achievement.

Although use of this "Simon satisficer criterion" has begun to appear in the archaeological (76, 85) as well as the geographical (53, 178) literature, it has been subjected to some criticism (83, 152, 166). Wolpert (178) favors the satisficer model, but points out in a study of decision-making by Swedish farmers that problems in the determination of the aspiration levels of individuals make verification of a satisficer model very difficult. I might add that even if aspiration levels can be determined, failure to explain those levels reduces behavioral explanation to statements to the effect that people behave in a certain fashion because they wish to do so.

An inability to determine or reasonably assume aspiration levels eliminates the possibility of behavioral prediction by satisficer models. The resulting absence of expected behavior makes comparison with observed behavior and potential behavioral explanation unlikely. The operational strength of minimization, maximization, or optimization models resides in their ability to generate expected behavior patterns. Jochim's (76) use of the satisficer criterion in prediction of a number of parameters of hunter-gatherer resource utilization is illuminating in this regard. He sets aspiration levels for caloric and raw material procurement at those necessary for survival, and generates expected behavior patterns required for survival on the basis of assumptions of effort and risk limitation. His model essentially optimizes the minimization of risk and energy expenditure consistent with baseline survival requirements.

It is useful to generalize an argument by Tiebout (152) to suggest that markedly suboptimal behavior may be inconsistent with the maintenance of an individual, population, or organization within a larger system, and that failure to achieve optimal behavior need not indicate the absence of intent to optimize. Given admittedly bounded rationality, simple optimization models cannot be expected to account fully for observed behavior. Residual variation which is not described by these models should reflect, however, the degree and nature of suboptimal behavior.

I do not advocate the priority of economic maximization in decision-making by members of nonmodern, nonmarket based societies. Social, political, and other considerations are of more than obvious importance in these cases (34). I do feel, however, that without a theoretical baseline against which to compare our data, potential behavioral explanation is precluded, and we are reduced to descriptive exercises. If our models are inadequate, we should improve not abandon them. I note a number of efforts in this direction in the following pages, among the more interesting of which are Isard's (72) and Webber's (166) work on the effects of uncertainty on locational decision-making.

INTERACTION AND DISTANCE

A model that systematically relates the basic variables involved in the interaction of human groups should be of some interest to archaeologists. These variables include the size and nature of the groups engaged in interaction, the nature of that interaction, and the physical space over which that interaction occurs. Plog (114) has recently suggested that "gravity models" might be appropriate for this purpose.

Gravity models are widely used in cultural geography for the description of interpopulation interaction. Here the term population simply refers to defined human groups of varying sizes and compositions, not necessarily to populations in the demographic sense. In their best-known form, gravity models rely on a direct analogy with Newtonian physics and specify that the expected interaction between two populations is a function of the ratio of the product of their sizes to the square of the distance between them (184). Although few studies have found this simple formula to be an accurate interaction predictor, there is an impressive body of evidence that interaction varies inversely with some function of distance and directly with some function of the sizes of interacting populations (23).

Gravity models as a class have been criticized for their lack of theoretical justification (75). Olsson (109) points out, however, that their application to situations involving reflexive or reciprocal interaction has a valid theoretical base. These reflexive interactions involve maintenance of personal contact over distance and are thus subject to movement costs. We may then apply a simple assumption of minimization of energy expended in movement to generate distance decay, or decreasing interaction with increase in the distance over which that interaction takes place. Most social processes likely to be advanced to explain archaeological interaction data are of this type, and include such processes as trade, exchange, and marriage alliance. It is also understandable that interaction should be a partial function of population size. The model simply assumes that the number of people or groups involved in interaction is positively correlated with the number that could be so involved, given population sizes.

Geographers are able to utilize direct measures of interaction in terms of the physical movement of people, goods, services, or information between populations. Isard (71) provides a number of case studies involving the interaction of populations as measured by such variables as number of telephone calls, shipment weight moved by railroad, family migration, numbers of bus passengers and so on, between population centers.

Archaeologists usually lack direct measures of interaction. They typically assume that the similarity of two artifact assemblages, artifact types, etc provides a measure of the degree of interaction between the producers of those assemblages or types (60, 84, 91, 95, 114). This may be the case as long as style is not being used to signal exclusive group membership and maintain social boundaries between the interacting populations (177). In this case the stylistic similarity of artifact types produced by two groups might be low, while the actual group interaction rate is relatively high.

The question of just how to measure similarity is also of interest. A brief review of the literature reveals a variety of techniques in use. These include Brainerd-

Robinson similarity coefficients and linear correlation coefficients (114), Euclidian distance functions (5), factor loadings (7, 127), chi-square values (117), coefficients of homogeneity (169), taxonomic similarity coefficients (91), as well as a variety of other statistical and graphic techniques. While this is not the place to pick and choose among techniques, we should remember that they handle variability in very different ways. It is important that the technique chosen should be relatable to the specific type or types of interactive behavior thought to operate in individual cases [e.g. Whallon (169)].

Most of the techniques listed above assign equal importance (weights) to all variables or attributes involved in a particular analysis. Recent ethnographic studies [e.g. Friedrich (46)] suggest that within individual artifact types, some attributes are sensitive to interactional variability while others are not. The same is no doubt true for artifacts within assemblages. Plog (115) points out that little attention has been given to problems of attribute selection in interaction studies. I might add that systems of reliable attribute or artifact weighting appropriate to specific types of interaction have yet to be developed.

With the exception of rare interaction data from ancient texts (153) or ethnohistoric accounts, one class of more direct interaction data is frequently available to archaeologists. This involves the distribution of goods for which location of production is known. Studies of the distribution of obsidian (39a, 113, 124, 133, 133a, 180), Near Eastern chlorite (87), and various types of European flint (104) are examples of this type. Even here, however, it is difficult to stipulate the type of interaction occurring. Although Renfrew (121, 123) has attempted to differentiate exchange processes on the basis of associated differences in expected artifact distributions, Hodder & Orton (65) argue on the basis of distribution simulations that similar distribution patterns may result from a variety of exchange mechanisms.

Identification of the type of interaction involved in a particular case is even more difficult when the basis of such interaction is considered to be something other than material trade. It would seem that postmarital residence patterns have been the most commonly selected alternative in these cases (35, 60, 98, 169).

Of the three variables employed in gravity models, the first, interaction, remains the most elusive both in identification of its form and its measurement. Consideration of the probable characteristics of interacting populations may, however, partially explicate the type of interaction involved.

The size of interacting populations is the second variable of a gravity model. As mentioned above, the Newtonian analogy specifies the simple product of the population sizes involved as the appropriate value in the gravity equation. Use of this value is not as arbitrary as it might seem. Note that the product of the sizes of two populations is equal to the number of possible one-to-one relationships (without regard to order) of individuals between populations. For example, if population I consists of three individuals (A, B, and C) and population II consists of four individuals (a, b, c, and d), the possible one-to-one relationships between populations are as follows: Aa to Ad, Ba to Bd, and Ca to Cd. There are 12 of these pairs, a number equal to the product of the two population sizes.

Clearly the Newtonian model assumes a maximal interaction situation in which each member of one population interacts with all members of another. Even though such interaction might be indirect, interaction densities of this magnitude are probably unusual. It should come as no surprise then that geographers usually find it necessary to transform population products to obtain aesthetically pleasing linear relationships between measures of interaction and distance. Most such transformations involve application of a best-fit exponent to the population product (109, 184).

Unfortunately, exponent transformations provide for better description than explanation. More behaviorally interpretable transformations should take a number of issues into consideration. Interaction densities were discussed above. Interaction rates, or the number of interactional events per unit time, should also be considered. High density, low rate interaction might well generate similar interaction intensity values as low density, high rate interaction but have very different behavioral significance.

Although factors of density and rate will be difficult to ascertain archaeologically, a third factor of operational population size should be more approachable. As emphasized by Olsson (109), the population sizes used in a gravity equation should reflect the actual numbers of people involved in interaction. This value is not necessarily equal to that for total population sizes. Failure to recognize subpopulation interaction may severely distort the results of archaeological interaction studies.

Hodder & Orton (65), for example, find that distance has an apparently differential effect on the distribution of a number of different artifact types. They measure the effect of distance by the exponent to which intersite distances must be raised to obtain best-fit linear interaction plots. Interacting population sizes are not considered.

They define two groups of artifacts with similar characteristics. The first includes the rather undistinguished products of local, small-scale production and includes Romano-British roofing tiles, two Romano-British ceramic wares, and two types of neolithic axes. Best-fit distance exponents for this group ranged from 0.1 to 0.6.

The second group of artifacts consists of the rather more distinguished products of large-scale concerns. These include a neolithic axe type, a fine neolithic ceramic ware, neolithic Anatolian obsidian, Iron-Age Dobunnic coins, and two fine Roman ceramic wares. Best-fit distance exponents for this group range from 0.9 to greater than 2.5.

The higher distance exponents for the second group would indicate a higher frictional effect of distance on their distributions, although the range of their distributions is greater than that for items of the first group. Of greater interest, however, are the differences observed between the two groups, which might better be explained in terms of the probable nature of the interacting populations who generated the observed distributions. Briefly, the artifacts involved may have been status related: the first group being one of relatively low status items and the second (including Dobunnic coins) being one of relatively higher status items. Given the observation that social systems usually contain fewer higher than lower status individuals, frequency of higher status related items is expected to be less than that of lower status related items.

Phrased in terms of a gravity model, the sizes of the interacting populations involved in the distribution of Group 1 items were probably larger than those involved in the distribution of Group 2 items. This differential in subpopulation sizes might be sufficient to account for a significant proportion of the intergroup difference in best-fit distance exponents. This "status hypothesis" would also account for the greater observed distributional range of the probable higher status items if the wealth necessary to defray movement costs over longer distances was associated with higher status individuals.

Subpopulation definition by status group should probably be a relatively common component of archaeological interaction studies. Flannery (40), for example, has suggested that the interaction represented by exchange of Olmec materials was probably among local elites. A similar model of elite exchange has been used to describe the operation of the Middle Woodland "Hopewell Interaction Sphere" (146, 181).

Status, of course, is not the only dimension of social variability that might define interacting subpopulations. Age, sex, wealth, occupation, or other group affiliation might function in a similar way. Kay (84) notes that the relationship of three Central Missouri Hopewell projectile point assemblages in taxonomic space approximates the locational relationships of the three sites from which the assemblages were excavated. He suggests that assemblage similarity provides a measure of interaction among projectile point makers, perhaps males. This might well be restricted to adult males. Similar sex-specific interaction has been an important part of several other archaeological studies (35, 36, 60, 98, 169).

As difficult as definition of appropriate subpopulations may be in the preceding examples, predictable situations may be more complex. Consider the possibility that the subpopulations involved in interaction monitored by the distribution of a given artifact type change over space. A raw material or artifact type might be very abundant in the vicinity of its source and be accessible to entire populations. As the item decreases in availability with distance from its source area, however, the context of its use may become less utilitarian and more social. Use by subpopulations of such items as status markers, exchange regulating symbols, etc should be relatively common in the archaeological record.

The distribution of some neolithic Near Eastern obsidian may conform to such a model. Renfrew (120) provides a semilog plot of (log) percentage of obsidian in lithic assemblages against distance of assemblages from obsidian sources for a series of Near Eastern sites dating between ca 6500 and 5000 B.C. His plots are basically linear except for marked flattening within about 300 kilometers of source areas. Renfrew refers to the areas within which flattening occurs as supply zones.

Although Olsson (109) notes flattening of interaction curves for short distance contacts, the effect seems to occur in modern data only within radii of about 5 kilometers (114). Three hundred kilometers would not seem to qualify as a short distance contact, especially under neolithic transport conditions. Renfrew (123) suggests that this flattening is due to differential interaction rates inside and outside supply zones which he equates with culture areas.

Access to obsidian artifacts appears to have become increasingly associated with high status positions throughout much of greater Mesopotamia, especially from the Halaf period onward (180, 181). The flattening of Renfrew's graphs based on earlier material may be due in part to systematic shifts in the size of interacting populations, from general populations near source areas to increasingly specific subpopulations away from source areas.

An alternative hypothesis has been presented by Hodder & Orton (65), who have generated similar curves through random-walk simulations which involve a relatively large number of relatively short distance movements or exchanges. Random-walk generated curves also approximate the distribution of an Iron-Age coin series (66). These simulation results suggest that interaction curves like those defined by Renfrew may involve neither differing interaction rates across cultural boundaries nor the sort of shifts in interacting population sizes suggested above. While the random-walk model applied by Hodder & Orton is of considerable interest, I must admit a theoretical preference for approaches that include consideration of specific characteristics of interacting populations.

By now it should be clear that population size is a more complex variable than inspection of a normal gravity equation might indicate. The same observation will be made below for distance, the third variable of the gravity model equation.

While most studies use simple linear distance measures (miles or kilometers) there is no reason to believe that these are appropriate for all cases (56, 109, 114). Various measures of distance should reflect energy expenditure required for travel or transport, that is, the movement costs of interaction (57). The most appropriate distance measure for a specific case would be that most highly correlated with movement costs. In highly developed economies where "time is money," elapsed time as well as movement costs may effect the operational distance between two points.

Geographers may have the data to transform distance directly into movement and/or time costs (55, 156, 173). Archaeologists are seldom so fortunate. We may, however, be able to estimate values for another common distance transformation, travel time. For obvious reasons of topographic variability, energy expended per unit distance moved may vary. If we assume that cost per unit time is relatively constant and that the time required to move a unit distance varies under different conditions, then travel time should be a better estimator of movement costs than linear distance.

A number of archaeological studies have used or suggested travel time transformations (39a, 123a). Hodder (63) and Hodder & Orton (65) show how water transport may have differentially affected interaction as measured by the distribution of Roman pottery produced in Oxford. Rowlett & Pollnac (127) see some correspondence between major topographic features and isoload maps of factors resulting from their analysis of La Tene Ia cemeteries in the northern Champagne district of France. The following example may better illustrate the potential importance of distance transformation in archaeology.

LeBlanc & Watson (91) have calculated a matrix of similarity coefficients among ceramic decorative motif assemblages from seven Near Eastern Halaf sites of the early fifth millenium B.C. Maximum site-to-site distance is on the order of 600 kilometers.

With the exception of one site (Yunus), LeBlanc & Watson note that interassemblage similarity coefficients are related to intersite distance. Figure 1A shows the relationship between assemblage similarity and linear intersite distance measured on 1:100,000 operational navigation charts. Figure 1B shows the relationship between

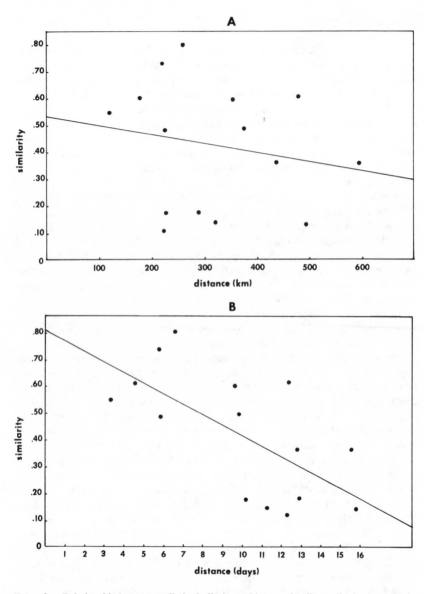

Figure 1a   Relationship between stylistic similarity and intervening linear distance among six Halaf ceramic motif assemblages ($n = 15$, ($r = -0.179$, $p > 0.05$).

Figure 1b   Relationship between stylistic similarity and travel time transformation of intervening linear distance among six Halaf ceramic motif assemblages ($n = 15$, $r = -0.655$, $p < 0.01$).

assemblage similarity and a travel time transformation of intersite distance suggested by H.T. Wright (personal communication).

This transformation is achieved by partitioning a linear distance into topographic components of flat, hilly, and mountainous terrain and converting these components into estimated travel times. Travel time over a given linear distance of each of these three terrain types was estimated from nineteenth and early twentieth century travel accounts (38, 59, 89, 90, 97, 143). Note that this transformation increases the linear correlation between distance and similarity from -0.179 (p greater than 0.05) to -0.665 (p less than 0.01).

Travel time is not only an efficient distance transformation in this case but also it has a direct behavioral interpretation not shared by transformations which utilize a best-fit exponent of linear distance. The latter approach is very common in economic geography (57, 184) but serves as a descriptive device of little apparent explanatory power.

Unfortunately, appropriate transformations of spatial distance are not the only distance functions that can be expected to affect movement and interaction. Leone (95) and Wilmsen (171, 172) utilize concepts of social distance in archaeological interaction studies. Wilmsen provides an interesting social transformation of spatial distance, suggesting that interaction among hunters and gatherers is inversely proportional to the number of band territory boundaries between two groups. Wobst (175) has successfully used this distance measure in simulations of hunter-gatherer mating networks. Olsson (109) cites studies utilizing concepts of socioeconomic class and age distances to describe certain interactional patterns. Sahlins's (130) discussion of the potential effects of kinship distance, rank, and wealth differences on exchange relationships suggests other possible nonspatial distance measures. Mooney's (105) recent work on the Coast Salish reinforces the view that a variety of nonspatial distance transformations may be necessary to the understanding of certain types of interaction.

I have little doubt that the interaction monitored by measures of attribute, artifact, or assemblage similarity are often conditioned by a combination of spatial and nonspatial distance functions. A concept of operational distance might be useful in emphasizing the potential effects of both types of distance functions on the interaction of populations.

The application of gravity models to archaeological interaction data is a complex issue. If gravity models provide nothing else, they do encourage archaeologists to consider more systematically the variables involved in interaction. This itself would seem to be a valuable service and justify their utilization. More optimistically, if archaeologists are willing to give more consideration to the type of interaction being monitored in particular cases, as well as to attempt behavioral transformations of the population and distance variables, gravity models may have a utility beyond that of elegant description. The explanatory potential of these models may have been underrated, in that they can systematically relate basic variables of interaction to one another and to a general behavioral assumption of movement minimization.

REGIONAL INTERACTION SYSTEMS

Thus far I have considered models of interaction between populations largely localized in permanent settlements of varying sizes. The existence, stability, and size variability of these settlements has been taken for granted. Given the proportion of the archaeological record occupied by mobile hunters and gatherers, sedentarization as well as settlement formation and size differentiation should be examined more carefully (20, 42).

Settlement System Development

A seasonal cycle of mobile hunter-gatherer resource exploitation involves movement among a series of spatially discontinuous resources. The amount of movement involved may be considerable. Wobst (176) uses an estimate of maximal band population size based on earlier simulation studies (175) and ethnographic population density figures from Alaska, Canada, and Siberia to suggest probable territory sizes of between 9,500 and 95,000 square kilometers for prehistoric bands in similar environments. Sedentarization or even significant reduction in required territory size would produce very considerable energy savings through reduction of required movement. I will suggest below that movement minimization is an important factor in both sedentarization and settlement formation.

Pianka (112) suggests on general ecological grounds that exploitation of a "patchy" environment (one characterized by resource heterogeneity and spatially discontinuous resource distributions) involves a series of movement related costs. These include travel time between resource "patches" as well as search and pursuit times within individual patches. (Note that pursuit time includes resource pursuit, capture, and consumption.) He further notes that required travel time is inversely related to patch size and required search time is inversely related to within-patch resource density. Given a movement minimization assumption, populations exploiting environments with larger patch size and/or density should be characterized by less movement than those exploiting environments with lower patch size and/or density.

An additional variable must be added at this point. Lee (92, 93) and Jochim (76) stress that resource reliability as related to risk minimization is an important factor in the determination of patterns of resource utilization. Reduction of movement costs through sedentarization would thus seem to be favored by a number of resource factors including high reliability, density, and large patch size (see also 54a). The relative sedentarization of such ethnographically known hunters and gatherers as the Ainu (162) and various Northwest Coast groups (148) would seem to be explicable in these terms. Similarly, Clark (27) notes that the apparent degree of seasonal movement of prehistoric hunters and gatherers in sub-Saharan Africa was related to environmental "richness."

As Flannery (42) points out, agriculture as a subsistence technique does not imply sedentarization. Agriculture appears to have preceded sedentarization in Mesoamerica, while the reverse seems to have been the case in the Near East (43). It might be interesting to view floral food production from the perspective of the general ecological variables outlined above.

I suggest that cultivation of a plant type(s) might be viewed as an attempt to achieve one or more of the following goals: 1. decreased travel costs through increase in the patch size of the plant concerned; 2. decreased travel costs through creation of a new plant patch in the immediate vicinity of a sedentary occupation; 3. decreased search costs through increase in within-patch plant density; and 4. Increased resource reliability through intentional cultivation and care of the plant type(s) involved. Given potentially high yields, the importance of agriculture in an overall subsistence strategy is probably most closely related to reliability factors. Lees & Bates (94) argue that productive uncertainty under early dry farming conditions in the Near East would favor mixed subsistence strategies, a situation that is reflected in relevant archaeological data (43, 67). Early agriculture may be viewed in part as an example of a movement and risk minimization subsistence strategy.

Sedentarization, agricultural or otherwise, need not imply the sedentary population agglomeration we associate with "villages." I will have occasion in a later section of this review to refer to the concept of "scale economics" or ". . . the savings in costs of operation made possible by concentrating activities at common locations" (48, p. 305). Garner (48) suggests that similar considerations may account for the agglomeration of activities and people that form settlements themselves.

Movement minimization is the core assumption of scale economics. To the extent that productive activities require the cooperation of population units (individuals, families, etc) agglomeration of those units in a settlement should reduce personnel and material movement costs, as well as information transfer costs required for cooperation.

Settlement location as well as sedentarization and settlement formation appear to be related to movement-minimizing behavior. Transport costs play a central role in von Thünen's (151) early model of agricultural land use, in which distance from a settlement largely determines type of land use within concentric zones around that settlement. Chrisholm (25) argues that type of land use is directly related to labor input to its exploitation, and the amount of such labor is inversely related to distance from settlement. Horvath (68) finds support for this model in his analysis of land use around Addis Ababa, Ethiopia, while Henshall (58) cites studies with similar results of relatively simple agricultural systems in Africa, India, and Brazil.

Minimization of effort required for subsistence activities is often cited as a primary determinant of archaeological settlement location (47, 50) and in conjunction with von Thünen type land use models forms the basis of "site catchment analysis" in archaeology (73, 74, 160).

On the assumption that to minimize movement costs a settlement is located in the center of the resource area which its inhabitants exploit, catchment basin analysis normally defines the radius of that resource area as the distance beyond which energy expended in movement equals or exceeds the energy return of exploitation. Weighting of resource availibility within this radius by distance from a settlement allows definition of a resource mix potentially exploitable from that settlement.

Given a known exploitation pattern, the method may suggest resource determinants of settlement location, or be used to compare the productive potential of an area with the size of the population actually inhabiting it.

A number of interesting applications of catchment basin analysis have recently appeared (24, 28, 39, 126, 185). Of interest here is the general conclusion that in simple systems there is a strong inverse relationship between distance and resource exploitation, a conclusion consistent with the results of distance decay studies cited above.

This observation may be important in accounting for multiple rather than single sedentary population agglomerations within a region. Given low population densities and the factors favoring sedentarization and agglomeration mentioned above, it is not obvious why the population of a region should not agglomerate in a single village.

Sahlins (130) cites a variety of ethnographic studies indicating markedly submaximal levels of subsistence production in relatively simple societies. Similar observations have been made as a result of archaeological catchment basin studies of the sort mentioned above (22; 44, pp. 173–80; 85). Sahlins (130) relates submaximal production to a model of household strategies in which production in excess of subsistence requirements is unnecessary. If we accept a low level of productive intensity (labor input per unit land exploited) for early agricultural societies, then relative intensification of production to accommodate an initially larger rather than smaller village population is unlikely. Larger village size approaching the population size of a low density region could be achieved alternatively by increasing the amount of land exploited at a given intensity. Even with a concentric zone model of resource utilization of the type discussed above, increase in the amount of land exploited would involve increase in energy expended in movement. Multiple village occupation may then be seen in part as a strategy to minimize both required productive intensity and energy expended in movement, consistent with the advantages of population agglomeration.

Few regions, however, can be characterized by a distribution of villages of approximately equivalent sizes. Sources of variability in village size, and particularly processes leading to the development of differentially large villages, are of some interest. If we continue to assume low intensity subsistence production, then differences in resource availability are unlikely to account for differences in village size unless resource disparities are very great indeed.

Wobst (176) has discussed a number of locational relationships for hunter-gatherer settlement systems which may be illuminating for early sedentary agriculturalists as well. His simulation studies suggest that long-term population maintenance requires a minimum size of mating network (roughly homologous with a maximal band) of about 475 people. It seems fair to assume that the size of mating networks for early sedentary agriculturalists was not significantly smaller than this estimate.

Early agricultural villages from a number of areas of the world appear to have been quite small, averaging perhaps 100–150 people. Marcus (101) estimates that as many as 90 percent of early Mesoamerican villages were occupied by 50–60 people. Renfrew (122) suggests a population figure of 100 as typical for villages of the early Aegean neolithic. Other early village population estimates include 100–300 for Japanese Jomon (163), 100–200 for early East African neolithic (27), and 100–150 for early European Bandkeramik villages (103, 144). It appears that the inhabitants of these early villages were probably involved in supravillage mating networks.

Wobst (176) goes on to point out the importance of the spatial distribution of local bands for the operation of a mating network, as well as conditions under which a given band may have a locational advantage within that network. He specifically suggests that under conditions of mating system closure or full time exploitation of essentially linear environments, a centrally located band has a marked advantage of minimum average distance from other bands in their mating network. Given an inverse relationship between interaction and distance of the sort discussed above in conjunction with gravity models, frequency and/or intensity of interaction with other bands should be directly related to the relative centrality of the location of an individual band. Differential interaction rates may then suggest differential success in mate acquisition, differential reproductive success, and differential band sizes.

The locational implications of centrality in a linear environment should apply to early sedentary agriculturalists as well as to hunter-gatherer populations, given village participation in supravillage mating networks as suggested above. It is interesting, therefore, that San José Mogote is both centrally located and by far the largest settlement in a linear settlement distribution of the late San José phase of the Etla region, Oaxaca (44, pp. 173–80). A similar though less impressive case can be made for Period VI settlement of the Peruvian coast (88).

Application of the model to groups exploiting nonlinear and operationally unbounded environments is more difficult as it may require closure of a mating system. Wobst (176) suggests that closure in hunter-gatherer systems may become advantageous in association with high-return resource exploitation activities requiring work groups larger than those available to a single local group. He suggests large-scale game drives as a possible example of such an activity.

I argued earlier for agricultural village formation as a response to requirements for cooperation and activity coordination in subsistence activities. General ecological considerations may suggest that increasing resource density (36a, 112, 170a) associated with increased temporal and spatial predictability of resources (36a, 170a, 174) favor the development of territoriality. These factors were discussed above as favoring sedentarization. To the extent that agricultural settlement may favor territoriality and territoriality favor mating system closure, centrality of village location within a mating system may generate village population differences in the manner suggested for linear settlement systems. Territoriality may not be required to produce relatively closed mating networks in some nonlinear settlement systems. Relative closure might be expected in topographically bounded settlement systems such as those in mountain valleys. Intervalley interaction may be impeded by topographic barriers, producing relatively closed mating systems and locational advantage for central location within a valley.

Population size, however, is not the only axis of variability within most settlement systems. Sources of variability in functional size should also be considered. Here functional size refers to the number of different kinds of activities undertaken within a settlement. A relatively homogenous distribution of activities might be expected within early agricultural settlement systems in which each village is an autonomous economic if not social unit. Some variability in type of activity may be attributable to differential resource distributions within the area of a settlement system (20), but even this in combination with differential settlement population sizes does not account for major differences in settlement functional sizes.

I suspect that initial differentiation of settlement functional size may often be related to social and only indirectly to subsistence factors. I have suggested elsewhere (81) that increasing requirements for activity coordination among population units favor the development of specialized leadership to reduce the costs of information transfer involved in coordination. Information transfer costs may be related to the number of population units whose activities are coordinated.

Activity coordination was one factor discussed above as favoring village formation. If village locational centrality favors differentially large population size and larger population size favors the development of specialized leadership, pressure for this development should be strongest in centrally located villages. Further, if "big-man" systems (129) represent one trajectory for specialized leadership development, the larger population size of central villages in addition to the interactional advantages of their location should favor larger big-man centered reciprocal exchange networks, or bigger big-men.

I have also suggested (81) that the development of specialized leadership (decision-making) positions may be associated with the development of ascribed status differences within a population. Effective coordination requires not only that decisions be made, but also that they be carried out. Decision-making positions must then be associated with a differential ability to influence the behavior of others. The use of social status differences to structure or supplement differential influence in decision-making contexts is frequently noted (147, 155, 161). Thus in Fried's (45) discussion of the evolution of political society, rank societies are differentiated from egalitarian ones partially by the development of: (*a*) specialized leadership, (*b*) ascribed social status differences, and (*c*) increase in authority.

The development of specialized leadership positions associated with ascribed status differences would produce an increase in the functional size of presumably central villages. Functional size differences might then be further increased by. a number of processes potentially associated with leadership development.

Webb (164) points out, for example, that leadership personnel tend to be differentially involved in long-range trade systems. While long-range trade among egalitarian hunters and gatherers may be related to the maintenance of mating networks (176), similar exchange systems in ranked societies may be more important in acquisition of items used to symbolize and thus reinforce status differences (164). This may be especially important if status and decision-making functions are related in the manner suggested above. Some examples of elite participation in long-range trade were discussed above in conjunction with gravity models of interaction.

If higher status individuals tend to be spatially localized within a settlement system and participate differentially in long-range trade, then the organization of production of items for export in such exchange systems, the concentration of craftsmen to produce status-related items from imported as well as local materials, and related activities may lead to further increase in functional size differences within a settlement system.

Trade is not the only status-reinforcing activity that may promote increase in the functional size of certain settlements. Webster (167) has recently reviewed sacred legitimation of status differences and leadership positions in relatively complex societies. A similar function of religious activity in somewhat simpler societies might then lead to increase in the functional size of central settlements through concentration of sacred ceremonial and production of sacred architecture and paraphernalia in these settlements.

Any number of processes, including those suggested above, may contribute to the differential distribution of functional sizes in a settlement system that constitutes a simple settlement hierarchy. Many settlement systems, however, are characterized by centralization of production of a variety of goods and services. While considerations of scale economics may help explain activity agglomeration as a general phenomenon, they do not account for centralization as a pattern of markedly differential agglomeration.

Kochen & Deutsch (86) suggest that an uneven spatial distribution of demand favors centralization of the production of goods and services for reasons of increased efficiency. This is an interesting observation in light of Hudson's (69) rural location theory in which he suggests that nonuniformity of settlement spatial distributions is to be expected within developing settlement systems characterized by low settlement density, little or no competition for agricultural land, and significant variability in settlement size (see also 149).

An uneven spatial distribution of agricultural settlements and hence an uneven spatial distribution of demand should be characteristic of most developing settlement systems, leading to the question of why evidence for centralization is not more common in the archaeological record. Centralization, however, also requires initial conditions of functional diversity of production, and presumably threshold values of intensity of demand before the potential efficiency gains of centralization effect locational decision-making.

A different though complementary approach has been suggested by Törnqvist (154). He attributes centralization of certain activities to requirements of information exchange among operationally specialized components of a system. The focus is thus on the efficiency of integration of production of a variety of goods and/or services, rather than on efficiency of production of goods and/or services per se.

Törnqvist's emphasis on information exchange raises the point that a differential spatial distribution of the production of goods and services need not be the only, or even the major, factor in the development of a functional settlement hierarchy.

Effective activity coordination has been identified as the basis for the hierarchical structure of decision-making or administrative organizations (134). This organizational requirement has long been recognized as potentially important for the development of settlement hierarchies (26, 99). With admittedly notable exceptions (137, 138), however, it has received little attention in the literature. Recently Richardson (125) and especially Blanton (18) have emphasized that the movement of personnel and information in decision-making hierarchies is subject to the same transport costs as movement of personnel, goods, and services in a marketing system. Increase in the hierarchical structure of a regional decision-making organization may then favor increase in the vertical complexity of a settlement hierarchy. Taylor's (150) analysis of a series of East African societies reveals a general lack of centralized production, distribution, or redistribution in conjunction with the presence of clear settlement hierarchies which have a close relationship to decision-making hierarchies.

I suggested above that centrality of settlement location favored relatively large settlement size and initial functional differentiation. Locational considerations are important in the present context as well. A centrally located settlement is the most probable locus of productive centralization and/or highest level administrative control functions in that: (*a*) it has the highest probability of a history as the locational focus of an intersettlement interaction system, and (*b*) its location allows minimization of center-to-village movement costs. Similar movement minimization considerations favor the development of multiple centers when a settlement system is sufficiently large that movement costs effectively inhibit the interaction of distant villages with a single center. The boundary between the interaction fields of two such centers should be related to the average distance decay functions of the goods and/or services they respectively provide.

Given sufficient village-center interaction, the spatial distribution of settlements should become increasingly regular, further reducing the movement costs of interaction. Haggett (52) and Dacey (31) review alternative geometries of settlement distribution, showing that under appropriate conditions of settlement density and topographic uniformity, hexagonal distributions are the most efficient though not the only alternative model for relative settlement location.

Central Place Theory

The preceding just-so story may sound increasingly familiar to those who are acquainted with central place theory in economic geography or its applications in anthropology. Central place models provide a relatively coherent framework for the investigation of regional interaction systems as expressed in functional settlement hierarchies and their spatial distributions. Given the general availability of recent reviews of central place models by Smith (140, 142), Webber (166), and others, I see little point in repeating the process here. It would perhaps be more useful, and I hope interesting, to review some common criticisms of central place models and their application to archaeological data sets.

Quite correctly, the classical central place models of Christaller (26) and Lösch (99) are generally considered to be restricted in applicability to the analysis of retail production and marketing (13, 16, 102, 140, 170). As recently reviewed by Smith (142), theories of the development of central place systems have been closely tied to theories of the development of retail marketing systems. Application of "central place" models in the absence of reliable data on marketing or of marketing itself has understandably been criticized (8, 140).

I have used a major portion of this review to suggest that movement minimization, activity agglomeration and centralization, functional settlement hierarchies, and regular settlement spatial distributions may occur in the absence of market institutions and, by implication, that an expanded central place theory is useful in the analysis and interpretation of such systems. Aspects of such an expanded model have been found to be useful in the analysis of archaeological settlement pattern data from a number of areas, including Mesoamerica (37, 41; 44, pp. 161–73; 54, 100), North America (188), Europe (21, 28, 61, 62, 64, 66, 96, 132), Mesopotamia (3, 78–80, 183), and Oceania (70).

Two other criticisms of central place models deal with questions of settlement functional and population size. Adams (1) and Smith (140) have criticized archaeological applications of central place models for their lack of effective measurement of settlement functional size. Archaeologists often assume that the functional size of a settlement is directly proportional to its population size.

This assumption raises the familiar problem of settlement population estimation, a question that has been reviewed recently by Schacht (131) and Ammerman et al (6). Their comments on estimation of settlement population from settlement size are of particular interest to those engaged in regional site surveys. Systematic variability in population density within a settlement hierarchy is one of the more important issues raised by their discussion. Although some studies reveal a linear relationship between population and settlement areal size (49, 108), there is little reason to believe that this relationship is a general one. Population estimation remains a difficult archaeological problem.

More work has been done on the relationship between settlement population and functional sizes. Although Crissman (29) strongly rejects settlement population as an estimator of functional size, a strong relationship between these variables appears to hold for many areas. Berry (13) reports a correlation of +0.95 between population and functional size for areas of Iowa, while Webber (166) cites studies from the states of Illinois and Washington, Australia, New Zealand, and southern Ceylon that obtained correlations of +0.70 to +0.90 between these variables.

Unfortunately, the relationship appears to be curvilinear, such that functional size per unit population decreases as population size increases (13, 48, 52, 166). Even given appropriate population estimates, the assumption of direct proportionality between population and functional sizes may then seriously overestimate the functional sizes of larger settlements, and perhaps suggest the presence of greater complexity in a settlement hierarchy than is warranted.

The problem of functional size estimation from archaeological settlement survey data is clearly difficult and as yet unresolved. This is one of the many reasons why one should view with caution the results of archaeological studies that have been unable to use direct measures of functional size.

Difficulty in identification of discontinuous settlement hierarchies has been another major source of criticism of central place models (159). Indeed, study of the properties of continuous settlement size distributions in conjunction with the so-called "rank-size rule" has a long history. The investigation of these rank-size regularities, originally popularized by Zipf (186), has recently been brought to the attention of anthropologists by Blanton (19), Crumley (30), and Smith (139–141). Rank-size problems are sufficiently important to warrant more extended discussion.

The rank-size rule is usually considered to be an empirical generalization. The rule notes that settlement systems often have a settlement population size distribution such that when these settlements are ranked in a descending array by population size, a settlement of rank r has a population equal to $1/r$ that of the largest settlement in the system (15). This relationship is lognormally distributed so that a linear plot is produced when the relationship is graphed on full-logarithmic paper.

A number of explanations of this regularity have been advanced, and have been reviewed by Richardson (125). Zipf (187) used an effort minimization model to suggest that linear rank-size distributions are produced by the high degree of system integration among cities in economically developed countries. Rashevsky (119) related the distribution to economic opportunities and relative per capita production in a system of cities. Crumley (30) suggests an interpretation in which the degree of fit between an observed rank-size distribution and the linear model may be taken as an index of a settlement system's urbanization. Although in an earlier article Berry (12) was unable to find a relationship between linear rank-size distributions and either degree of economic development or urbanization, he now seems to feel (14) that such distributions may be characteristic of systems in the early and late stages of economic development with maximum deviation in between. In a much more general approach to the problem, Simon (135) related linear distributions to a systemic steady-state and the influence of a large number of essentially stochastic processes on the system's settlement size distribution. Such an interpretation, if supportable, would be of considerable interest to archaeologists, and I will return to it later.

While one effort has concentrated on providing explanations for linear rank-size distributions, a second has tacitly accepted them as "expecteds" and attempted to explain observed deviations from the rank-size rule. The primary type of deviation observed has been called a "primate" distribution (12) in which a full-logarithmic graphing of settlement size against settlement rank produces a markedly nonlinear, concave plot. Depending on one's point of view, large settlements are larger than expected or small settlements are smaller than expected in such cases.

Berry (14) attributes primate distributions to concentration of economic growth in the largest settlement of a system due to high availability of low-cost labor and the associated lack of incentive for decentralization. Smith (142, p. 32) is able to subsume Berry's interpretation in a more general model that relates primate distributions to " . . . the political administration of an economy in which competitive forces, necessary to a regular commercial central-place hierarchy, are minimized," a position also taken by Blanton (18). This condition is often associated with countries formerly involved in colonial empires, either as empire centers or empire members, or in systems which are sufficiently bounded so as to inhibit the development of more than one highest order central place.

A second type of deviation in which a full-logarithmic graphing produces a markedly convex plot has been mentioned, but has received little attention in the literature. In these cases large settlements are smaller or small settlements are larger than expected. Olsson (109), citing an unpublished study by G. J. Karaska, notes that Karaska's rank-size plots for the anthracite region of Pennsylvania are very convex. Olsson suggests that this might be due to markedly differential interaction rates within and between valley settlement systems. Other examples of convex full-logarithmic distributions include those for the United States in 1790 (187); the medieval regions of Tuscany, Palermo, Florence, and Milan (128); a series of Welsh hillforts (65); and the Roman provinces of Gaul and Britain (116).

A third major area of rank-size studies has focused on resolution of the apparent contradiction between the continuous distributions of the rank-size rule and the discontinuous settlement hierarchies of most central place models. Here most work has attempted to show that clear local discontinuities may be obscured and appear as continuous if pooled and viewed from a regional or national level (15, 77, 102, 109, 139). The possible result of pooling is nicely summarized by Smith (142, p. 29): "In effect, disturbances created by any number of non-isotropic conditions—variation in population density or demand, landscape irregularities, differential distribution of transport facilities, and the like—would shift centers out of line with one another, even though they might be identical with respect to regional central place functions." Beckmann (10) and Beckmann & McPherson (11) have shown how the addition of stochastic variability to settlements at each level of a central place hierarchy tends to produce a linear rank-size distribution. Combined operation of a sufficient number of "error sources" of the sort described by Smith may be essentially random at the system level and constitute the stochastic processes postulated by Simon (135) and utilized by Beckmann to produce linear rank-size distributions.

Although the success of Beckmann's resolution of the rank-size versus central place conflict has been questioned (32, 110), his general approach appears to be the most promising. Rapoport (118) agrees that an explanation for linear rank-size distributions should be sought in the statistical structure of events effecting settlement size, while Richardson (125) suggests that both systematic and stochastic processes should be considered.

Final resolution of this problem will also have to consider inconsistencies between functional measurements of size in central place models and population measurements of size in rank-size studies. As discussed above, these variables tend to be correlated although the degree of their relationship may vary considerably.

While I agree that stochastic variability is probably a major factor in the production of linear rank-size distributions, I do not agree that the presence of a linear distribution need be indicative of a systemic steady-state, nor that nonlinearity need be indicative of system change. Most importantly, we may take it as given that the state of a system cannot be determined from a single observation in a time series.

Further, we have empirical data to demonstrate that some nonlinear, primate systems have been maintained for periods of some 450 years (142)—apparently very much in a steady state.

A general model of rank-size relationships may soon be possible. As a first step, it is necessary to recognize that variability in rank-size distributions does not range simply from primate to linear log-normal, but from primate (concave) through linear to convex. I would like to suggest that various only vaguely recognized problems of scale may contribute no little confusion to the rank-size problem.

D. R. Vining (158) has suggested a series of processes including decline in a system's growth rate that may have produced some convexity in rank-size distributions for the United States over the last 20 years. Here I would like to suggest two general conditions favoring convex distributions that do not assume system growth. First, convex distributions should normally appear when the size distribution of a settlement system actually approaches the discontinuous hierarchy posited by central place theory, at least in cases with multiple highest order central places. Presumably this should occur in the absence of both processes leading to primacy and of stochastic effects of sufficient magnitude to alter the settlement size distribution. In general, the larger the region studied, the greater should be the probability of operation of stochastic processes due to variability in population density, demand, topography, and so on.

Second, convex rank-size distributions may appear when a series of adjacent systems of roughly equivalent scale and characterized by limited intersystem interaction are pooled in the same analysis. This situation might be expected in modern areas with complex topography and poor transportation nets, such as the Pennsylvania region mentioned earlier. Given the generally smaller scale of social and economic systems in the past, convex distributions should be more common in archaeological than modern data. A convex rank-size distribution should then alert the researcher to the possibility that relatively autonomous settlement systems are being combined in analysis—a possibility that need not be obvious. As noted above, concave rank-size distributions appear to be related to the political administration of an economy and minimization of competition. Problems in system boundary definition, however, may produce essentially artificial primate distributions in both archaeological and modern data sets. Boundary problems might be of two sorts: 1. the region actually studied may be significantly smaller than that occupied by the effective settlement system of interest, and 2. a significant proportion of the population and functional size of the largest settlement in a study region may be related to that settlement's articulation with a larger scale system (19, 157).

The first problem is probably restricted to archaeological data sets drawn from often arbitrarily defined survey regions. The second problem may be of wider interest. Smith (142) cites the primate curves for Japan and England as notable exceptions to the norm in which rank-size curves for nations with "fully developed" economies are generally linear. The fact that these island nations are significant food importers (179) suggests that the effective hinterlands of their major cities extend well beyond their national boundaries. Similarly, the primate curves cited by Smith (142) as characteristic of nations that are either former members or centers of empires may result in part from the differential involvement of their capitals in supranational settlement systems.

Little further time need be spent on linear rank-size distributions. Given Simon's (135) probability formulation and Beckmann's (10) demonstration that such a model is consistent with a functional hierarchy of central places, the stochastic interpretation of linear rank-size distributions would seem acceptable. Such a system would be characterized by the absence of directional processes of sufficient magnitude to override the stochastic effects of variability in population density, demand, etc. Presence of a linear relationship would also suggest that operationally effective settlement system boundaries have been identified.

If this discussion has any contribution to make to rank-size studies, it probably lies in more explicit consideration of the potential effects of scale errors on such distributions. Recognition of these effects should be particularly important in the analysis of archaeological data.

Let me illustrate this point with comments on four rank-size plots of settlement data spanning some 800 years of development on a major alluvial plain in Southwestern Iran. The area of this plain is some 2280 square kilometers (79).

Figure 2a shows the distribution for settlements of the Terminal Susa A period (ca 3900 B.C.) just after the apparent collapse of a large chiefdom in the area. The settlement pattern reveals four rather isolated settlement enclaves suggesting the presence of four relatively autonomous sociopolitical units. Note that Figure 2a is markedly convex, the predicted result of analytical pooling of separate settlement systems.

Figure 2b illustrates the distribution for the Early Uruk period (ca 3700 B.C.) during which state formation seems to have occurred in this area. While the western portion of the plain appears to have been unified under a single administrative hierarchy, the eastern portion may have remained relatively autonomous. Note that the rank-size plot shows an increase in linearity, though it is still quite convex in the lower settlement size range.

Figure 2c illustrates the distribution for the Middle Uruk period (ca 3400 B.C.) during which state level controls seem to have been extended to cover the entire plain. The plot is linear and probably reflects not only the operation of various stochastic processes on the settlement size distribution, but also a close fit between the scale of the region surveyed and the spatial scale of the economic system operating at that time.

Figure 2d illustrates the distribution for the Late Uruk period (ca 3200 B.C.). Note that the plot is noticeably primate. Wright (182) has suggested the resurgence of a long range trade system in this area at a slightly late date. New data (82, 168) suggests that this process effectively began during the Late Uruk. To some extent then, the primacy of the Late Uruk rank-size curve may reflect the differential participation of the larger settlements in this area in a larger scale settlement system —in this case one involved in a major new interregional exchange network.

The four plots discussed above illustrates a final rank-size problem. Note the rapid falloff in each plot below a settlement size of about one hectare. This deviation from the "expected" number of increasingly smaller settlements has been called a problem of "lower-limb relationships" by Haggett (52). These deviations probably indi-

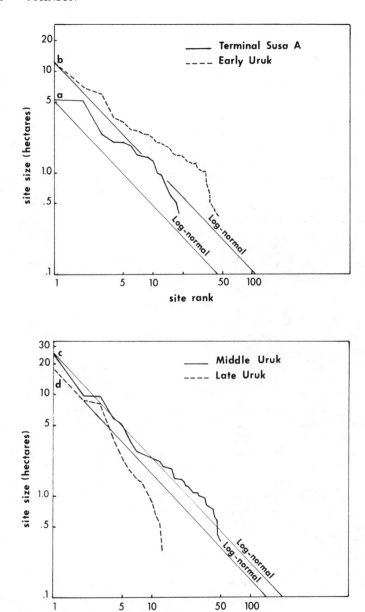

Figure 2   Rank-size distributions of settlements on the Susiana Plain of Southwestern Iran: a. Terminal Susa A, b. Early Uruk, c. Middle Uruk, d. Late Uruk.

cate effective threshold values for viable settlement size within individual settlement systems.

I would conclude this section with the suggestion that not only may the concept of the rank-size distribution be of considerable utility to archaeologists, but also that archaeologists are in an unusually favorable position to contribute to the resolution of long-standing rank-size problems. They control a scarce and valuable resource: long-term, regional scale settlement pattern data.

CONCLUSIONS

Even though space limitations have precluded more than scratching the surface of the problems and approaches involved in the analysis of regional interaction systems, it should be clear by now that such analysis is a complex affair. I would like, therefore, to make some cautionary comments on the general utility of central place and other locational models to archaeology.

I agree with Webber (165) that most models of locational behavior are essentially unverifiable in that for the sake of generality they involve assumptions which are untestable or which cannot be expected to be met under real world conditions. Utility and testability, however, are not necessarily coterminous. Most authors agree that these models provide context within which the operation of real world processes may be understood.

It is important to follow Webber (165) in making a distinction too often ignored by archaeologists between understanding and prediction. Prediction in the statistical sense is often equated with understanding or more generally with explanation. Accounting for even 100 percent of the variance of a variable and to thus be in a position to predict its values (at least in the past) need not imply understanding of the causal processes involved. Archaeologists are becoming increasingly adept at the statistical explanation of variability and yet have made only little progress in understanding process. Use of most locational models will not promote prediction. Given suitable caution, however, use of these models may well promote understanding.

Theoretical innovations are required which will integrate understanding and prediction in the same formulation. These models will have to depart radically from the determinist structure of most locational formulations in which given a series of behavioral assumptions and a set of initial conditions, the outcome of the model is set and immutable. The work of Dacey (33), Hägerstrand (51), and Morrill (106, 107), among others, is encouraging in this regard in that they have attempted to incorporate stochastic variability within classical location and interaction models.

Yet enthusiasm for stochastic processes may go too far. The last 10 years have seen an increase in entropy maximization explanations derived from information theory and exemplified here by Simon's work on rank-size regularities. If the most probable state of a variable or system is equated with maximum entropy, then behavioral patterns as reflected in spatial regularities are viewed as most-probable steady states resulting from purely random processes (17). These approaches encourage taking regularity as given and shifting the emphasis of explanation to deviations. At least in archaeology we may profitably continue to try to understand the factors producing the probability distributions that make most-probable states most probable.

Even if we succeed in formulating, or more probably borrowing, general theory which facilitates both understanding and prediction, a final consideration suggests caution in its application. Speth and I (145) have recently noted that a wide variety of different behavioral patterns may produce similar artifact distributions on paleolithic living floors. Hodder & Orton (65) make the same observation for archaeological data in general.

Smith (142) points out that patterned spatial distributions of hierarchically organized settlements are very common in the world, and even a cursory review of the locational literature reveals the great variability in locational systems and the conditions under which they may develop. Selection among alternative processes or sets of processes to account for observed patterning is a matter of appropriate formulation and evaluation of test implications. Given the problems of equifinality, however, it is worthwhile to reiterate the old axiom that successful support of a hypothesis is best viewed as simply failure to reject it.

With these thoughts in mind, I would still note that the state of behavioral theory in archaeology is such that a coherent model of certain types of behavior need not be very powerful to be useful. The simple concept of movement minimization, for example, has been subjected to rather extensive use in this review. I feel relatively confident in asserting that use of many of the concepts developed in other fields for the investigation of regional interaction systems has and will contribute significantly to our understanding of past human behavior.

ACKNOWLEDGMENTS

I would like to thank Robert McC. Adams, Daniel G. Bates, Carol Kramer, Susan H. Lees, Harvey Weiss, and especially Gary Feinman and Steven Kowalewski for discussion and critical comment on various sections of this review.

Literature Cited

1. Adams, R. McC. 1974. Anthropological perspectives on ancient trade. *Curr. Anthropol.* 15:239–58
2. Adams, R. McC. 1976. *World picture, anthropological frame.* Seventh Distinguished Lecture of the Am. Anthropol. Assoc. Presented at Ann. Meet. Am. Anthropol. Assoc., 75th, Washington DC
3. Adams, R. McC., Nissen, H. J. 1972. *The Uruk Countryside: The Natural Setting of Urban Societies.* Univ. Chicago Press
4. Alchian, A. A. 1950. Uncertainty, evolution, and economic theory. *J. Polit. Econ.* 58:211–21
5. Ammerman, A. J. 1971. A computer analysis of epipalaeolithic assemblages in Italy. In *Mathematics in the Archaeological and Historical Sciences,* ed. F. R. Hodson, D. G. Kendall, P. Pautu, pp. 133–37. Edinburgh Univ. Press
6. Ammerman, A. J., Cavalli-Sforza, L. L., Wagener, D. K. 1976. Toward the estimation of population growth in Old World prehistory. In *Demographic Anthropology: Quantitative Approaches,* ed. E.B.W. Zubrow, pp. 27–61. Albuquerque: Univ. New Mexico Press
7. Bartel, B. N. 1974. *Mortuary practice in Early Bronze Age Anatolia: An example of situational explanation.* PhD thesis. Univ. Missouri, Columbia, Mo. 331 pp.
8. Bartel, B. N. 1974. *Theoretical and methodological considerations in applying central-place theory to archaeology.*

Presented at Ann. Meet. Soc. Am. Archaeol., 39th, Washington DC
9. Bates, D. G., Lees, S. H. 1976. *The myth of population regulation.* Presented at Ann. Meet. Am. Anthropol. Assoc., 75th, Washington DC
10. Beckmann, M. J. 1958. City hierarchies and the distribution of city size. *Econ. Dev. Cult. Change* 6:243–48
11. Beckmann, M. J., McPherson, J. 1970. City size distributions in a central place hierarchy: An alternative approach. *J. Reg. Sci.* 10:25–33
12. Berry, B. J. L. 1961. City size distributions and economic development. *Econ. Dev. Cult. Change* 9:573–87
13. Berry, B. J. L. 1967. *Geography of Market Centers and Retail Distribution.* Englewood Cliffs: Prentice-Hall
14. Berry, B. J. L. 1973. *The Human Consequences of Urbanization.* New York: St. Martin's
15. Berry, B. J. L., Garrison, W. L. 1958. Alternate explanations of urban rank-size relationships. *Ann. Assoc. Am. Geogr.* 48:83–91
16. Berry, B. J. L., Pred, A. 1965. Central place studies: A bibliography of theory and applications. *Reg. Sci. Res. Inst. Biblio. Ser. 1*
17. Berry, B. J. L., Schwind, P. J. 1969. Information and entropy in migrant flows. *Geogr. Anal.* 1:5–14
18. Blanton, R. E. 1976. Anthropological studies of cities. *Ann. Rev. Anthropol.* 5:249–64
19. Blanton, R. E. 1976. The role of symbiosis in adaptation and sociocultural change in the Valley of Mexico. In *The Valley of Mexico: Studies in Pre-Hispanic Ecology and Society,* ed. E. R. Wolf, pp. 181–201. Albuquerque: Univ. New Mexico Press
20. Blouet, B. W. 1972. Factors influencing the evolution of settlement patterns. In *Man, Settlement and Urbanism,* ed. P. J. Ucko, R. Tringham, G. W. Dimbleby, pp. 3–15. London: Duckworth
21. Bronson, B. 1972. The interpretation of square "*Su*": Explaining settlement locations in Roman Britain. Presented at Ann. Meet. Am. Anthropol. Assoc., 71st, Toronto
22. Brumfiel, E. 1976. Regional growth in the Eastern Valley of Mexico: A test of the population pressure hypothesis. See Ref. 44, pp. 234–49
23. Carrothers, G.A.P. 1956. An historical review of the gravity and potential concepts of human interaction. *J. Am. Inst. Plann.* 22:94–102

24. Cassels, R. 1972. Locational analysis of Prehistoric settlement in New Zealand. *Mankind* 8:212–22
25. Chrisholm, M. 1968. *Rural Settlement and Land Use.* London: Hutchinson. 2nd ed.
26. Christaller, W. 1966. *Central Places in Southern Germany.* Transl. C. W. Baskin. Englewood Cliffs: Prentice-Hall
27. Clark, J. D. 1972. Mobility and settlement patterns in Sub-Saharan Africa: A comparison of late prehistoric hunter-gatherers and early agricultural occupation units. See Ref. 20, pp. 127–48
28. Clark, D. L. 1972. A provisional model of an Iron Age society and its settlement system. In *Models in Archaeology,* ed. D. L. Clarke, pp. 801–69. London: Methuen
29. Crissman, L. W. 1976. Specific central-place models for an evolving system of market towns on the Changhua Plain, Taiwan. See Ref. 141, Vol. 1, pp. 183–218
30. Crumley, C. L. 1976. Toward a locational definition of state systems of settlement. *Am. Anthropol.* 78:59–73
31. Dacey, M. F. 1965. The geometry of central place theory. *Geogr. Annaler* 47B:111–24
32. Dacey, M. F. 1966. Population of places in a central place hierarchy. *J. Reg. Sci.* 6:27–33
33. Dacey, M. F. 1966. A probability model for central place locations. *Ann. Assoc. Am. Geogr.* 56:550–68
34. Dalton, G. 1975. Karl Polanyi's analysis of long-distance trade and his wider paradigm. In *Ancient Civilization and Trade,* ed. J. A. Sabloff, C. C. Lamberg-Karlovsky, pp. 55–132. Albuquerque: Univ. New Mexico Press
35. Deetz, J. 1965. *The Dynamics of Stylistic Change in Arikara Ceramics.* Urbana: Univ. Illinois Press
36. Deetz, J. 1968. The inference of residence and descent rules from archaeological data. In *New Perspectives in Archeology,* ed. S. R. Binford, L. R. Binford, pp. 41–48. Chicago: Aldine
36a. Dyson-Hudson, R., Smith, E. A. 1978. Human territoriality: An ecological reassessment. In *Sociobiology and Human Behavior,* ed. N. Chagnon, W. Irons. North Scituate: Duxbury. In press
37. Earle, T. K. 1976. A nearest neighbor analysis of two formative settlement systems. See Ref. 44, pp. 196–223
38. Edmonds, C. J. 1917. *Notes on Luristan.* Lithographed report for the Anglo-Persian Oil Co.

39. Ellison, A., Harriss, J. 1972. Settlement and land use in the prehistory and early history of southern England: A study based on locational models. See Ref. 28, pp. 911–62

39a. Ericson, J. E. 1977. Egalitarian exchange systems in California: A preliminary view. In *Exchange Systems in Prehistory*, ed. T. K. Earle, J. E. Ericson, pp. 109–26. New York: Academic

40. Flannery, K. V. 1968. The Olmec and the Valley of Oaxaca: A model for interregional interaction in Formative times. In *Dumbarton Oaks Conference on the Olmec*, ed. E. P. Benson, pp. 79–110. Washington DC: Dumbarton Oaks

41. Flannery, K. V. 1972. The cultural evolution of civilizations. *Ann. Rev. Ecol. Syst.* 3:399–425

42. Flannery, K. V. 1972. The origins of the village as a settlement type in Mesoamerica and the Near East: A comparative study. See Ref. 20, pp. 23–53

43. Flannery, K. V. 1973. The origins of agriculture. *Ann. Rev. Anthropol.* 2: 271–310

44. Flannery, K. V., ed. 1976. *The Early Mesoamerican Village.* New York: Academic

45. Fried, M. H. 1967. *The Evolution of Political Society: An Essay in Political Anthropology.* New York: Random House

46. Friedrich, M. H. 1970. Design structure and social interaction: Archaeological implications of an ethnographic analysis. *Am. Antiq.* 35:332–43

47. Fritz, J. M., Plog, F. 1970. The nature of archaeological explanation. *Am. Antiq.* 35:405–12

48. Garner, B. J. 1967. Models of urban geography and settlement location. In *Models in Geography,* ed. R. J. Chorley, P. Haggett, pp. 303–60. London: Methuen

49. Gremliza, F. G. L. 1962. *Ecology of Endemic Diseases in the Dez Irrigation Pilot Area.* New York: Development and Resources Corp.

50. Gumerman, G. J., ed. 1971. *The Distribution of Prehistoric Population Aggregates.* Prescott Coll. Press

51. Hagerstrand, T. 1967. *Innovation Diffusion as a Spatial Process.* Univ. Chicago Press

52. Haggett, P. 1966. *Locational Analysis in Human Geography.* New York: St. Martin's

53. Hamilton, I. F. E. 1967. Models of industrial location. See Ref. 48, pp. 361–424

54. Hammond, N. 1972. Locational models and the site of Lubaantún: A Classic Maya center. See Ref. 28, pp. 757–800

54a. Harpending, H., Davis, H. 1977. Some implications for hunter-gatherer ecology derived from the spatial structure of resources. *World Archaeol.* 8:275–86

55. Harris, C. D. 1954. The market as a factor in the localization of industry in the United States. *Ann. Assoc. Am. Geogr.* 44:315–48

56. Harvey, D. 1967. Models of the evolution of spatial patterns in human geography. See Ref. 48, pp. 549–608

57. Haynes, R. M. 1974. Application of exponential distance decay to human and animal activities. *Geogr. Annaler* 56B: 90–104

58. Henshall, J. D. 1967. Models of agricultural activity. See Ref. 48, pp. 425–58

59. Heude, W. 1819. *A Voyage up the Persian Gulf and Overland from India to England in 1817.* London: Longman, Hurst, Rees, Orme & Brown

60. Hill, J. N. 1970. *Broken K Pueblo: Prehistoric Social Organization in the American Southwest.* Tucson: Univ. Arizona Press

61. Hodder, I. R. 1972. Interpretation of spatial patterns in archaeology: Two examples. *Area* 4:223–29

62. Hodder, I. R. 1972. Locational models and the study of Romano-British settlement. See Ref. 28, pp. 887–909

63. Hodder, I. R. 1974. A regression analysis of some trade and marketing patterns. *World Archaeol.* 6:172–89

64. Hodder, I. R., Hassel, M. 1971. Nonrandom spacing of Romano-British walled towns. *Man* 6:391–407

65. Hodder, I. R., Orton, C. 1976. *Spatial Analysis in Archaeology.* London: Cambridge

66. Hogg, A. H. A. 1971. Some applications of surface fieldwork. In *The Iron Age and its Hillforts,* ed. M. Jesson, D. Hill, pp. 105–125. Southhampton Univ. Press

67. Hole, F., Flannery, K. V., Neeley, J. 1969. Prehistory and human ecology of the Deh Luran Plain. *Mus. Anthropol. Univ. Mich. Mem. 1*

68. Horvath, R. J. 1969. Von Thünen's isolated state and the area around Addis Ababa, Ethiopia. *Ann. Assoc. Am. Geogr.* 59:308–23

69. Hudson, J. C. 1969. A location theory

for rural settlement. *Ann. Assoc. Am. Geogr.* 59:365–81
70. Irwin, G. 1974. The emergence of a central place in coastal Papuan prehistory. *Mankind* 9:268–72
71. Isard, W. 1956. *Location and Space Economy.* Cambridge: M.I.T. Press
72. Isard, W. 1969. *General Theory: Social, Political, Economic and Regional.* Cambridge: M.I.T. Press
73. Jarman, M. R. 1972. A territorial model for archaeology: A behavioral and geographic approach. See Ref. 28, pp. 705–33
74. Jarman, M. R., Vita-Finzi, C., Higgs, E. S. 1972. Site catchment analysis in archaeology. See Ref. 20, pp. 61–66
75. Jensen-Butler, C. 1972. Gravity models as planning tools: A review of theoretical and operational problems. *Geogr. Annaler* 54B:68–78
76. Jochim, M. A. 1976. *Hunter-Gatherer Subsistence and Settlement: A Predictive Model.* New York: Academic
77. Johnson, E. A. J. 1970. *The Organization of Space in Developing Countries.* Cambridge: Harvard Univ. Press
78. Johnson, G. A. 1972. A test of the utility of central place theory in archaeology. See Ref. 20, pp. 769–85
79. Johnson, G. A. 1973. Local exchange and early state development in southwestern Iran. *Mus. Anthropol. Univ. Mich. Anthropol. Pap. 51*
80. Johnson, G. A. 1975. Locational analysis and the investigation of Uruk local exchange systems. See Ref. 34, pp. 285–339
81. Johnson, G. A. 1978. Information sources and the development of decision-making organizations. In *Archaeology as a Social Science,* ed. C. Redman. New York: Academic. In press
82. Johnson, G. A. Early state organization in southwestern Iran: Preliminary field report. *Proc. Ann. Symp. Archaeol. Res. Iran, 4th, Tehran.* In press
83. Jones, R. C. 1976. Cautious optimization versus spatial satisfaction: Alternative agricultural programming models. *Proc. Assoc. Am. Geogr.* 8:58–62
84. Kay, M. 1975. Social distance among Central Missouri Hopewell settlements: A first approximation. *Am. Antiq.* 40: 64–71
85. Kirkby, A. V. T. 1973. The use of land and water resources in the past and present Valley of Oaxaca, Mexico. *Mus. Anthropol. Univ. Mich. Mem. 5*
86. Kochen, M., Deutsch, K. W. 1970. Decentralization and uneven service loads. *J. Reg. Sci.* 10:153–73
87. Kohl, P. L. 1974. *Seeds of upheaval: The production of chlorite at Tepe Yahya and an analysis of commodity production and trade in Southwest Asia in the mid-third millenium.* PhD thesis. Harvard Univ., Cambridge, Mass.
88. Lanning, E. P. 1967. *Peru Before the Incas.* Englewood Cliffs: Prentice-Hall
89. Layard, A. H. 1849. *Nineveh and its Remains.* New York: Putnam
90. Layard, A. H. 1853. *Discoveries among the Ruins of Nineveh and Babylon.* New York: Putnam
91. LeBlanc, S., Watson, P. J. 1973. A comparative statistical analysis of painted pottery from seven Halafian sites. *Paléorient* 1:117–33
92. Lee, R. B. 1965. *Subsistence ecology of the !Kung Bushmen.* PhD thesis. Univ. California, Berkeley, Calif. 209 pp.
93. Lee, R. B. 1968. What hunters do for a living, or, How to make out on scarce resources. In *Man the Hunter,* ed. R. B. Lee, I. Devore, pp. 30–48. Chicago: Aldine
94. Lees, S. H., Bates, D. G. 1974. The origins of specialized nomadic pastoralism: A systemic model. *Am. Antiq.* 39:187–93
95. Leone, M. P. 1968. Neolithic economic autonomy and social distance. *Science* 162:1150–51
96. Levy, J. E. 1974. *Experimenting with Central Place Theory in Bronze Age Greece.* Presented at Ann. Meet. Soc. Am. Archaeol., 39th, Washington DC
97. Loftus, W. K. 1857. *Travels and Researches in Chaldaea and Susiana.* New York: Carter
98. Longacre, W. 1970. *Archaeology as Anthropology: A Case Study.* Tucson: Univ. Arizona Press
99. Lösch, A. 1954. *The Economics of Location.* Transl. W. Stolpher. New Haven: Yale Univ. Press
100. Marcus, J. 1973. Territorial organization of the Lowland Classic Maya. *Science* 180:911–16
101. Marcus, J. 1976. The size of the early Mesoamerican village. See Ref. 44, pp. 79–90
102. Marshall, J. U. 1969. *The Location of Service Towns: An Approach to the Analysis of Central Place Systems.* Univ. Toronto Press
103. Milisauskas, S. R. 1976. *Archaeological Investigations on the Linear Culture Village of Olszanica.* Warsaw: Polish Acad. Sci.

104. Milisauskas, S. R., Wobst, H. M. 1978. *European Prehistory.* New York: Academic. In press
105. Mooney, K. 1976. Social distance and exchange: The Coast Salish case. *Ethnology* 15:323–46
106. Morrill, R. L. 1962. Simulation of central place patterns over time. *Proc. I.G.U. Symp. Urban Geogr., Lund, 1960,* pp. 109–20
107. Morrill, R. L. 1967. The movement of persons and the transportation problem. In *Quantitative Geography I: Economic and Cultural Topics,* ed. W. L. Garrison, D. F. Marble, pp. 84–94. Evanston: Northwestern Univ.
108. Nordbeck, S. 1971. Urban allometric growth. *Geogr. Annaler* 53B:54–67
109. Olsson, G. 1965. Distance and human interaction: A review and bibliography. *Reg. Sci. Res. Inst. Biblio. Ser. 2*
110. Parr, J. B. 1969. City hierarchies and the distribution of city size; a reconsideration of Beckmann's contribution. *J. Reg. Sci.* 9:239–53
111. Parsons, J. R. 1972. Archaeological settlement patterns. *Ann Rev. Anthropol.* 1:127–50
112. Pianka, E. R. 1974. *Evolutionary Ecology.* New York: Harper & Row
113. Pires-Ferreira, J. W. 1975. Formative Mesoamerican exchange networks with special reference to the Valley of Oaxaca. *Mus. Anthropol. Univ. Mich. Mem. 7*
114. Plog, S. 1976. Measurement of prehistoric interaction between communities. See Ref. 44, pp. 255–72
115. Plog, S. 1976. The inference of prehistoric social organization from ceramic design variability. *Mich. Discuss. Anthropol.* 1:1–47
116. Pounds, N. J. G. 1969. The urbanization of the classical world. *Ann. Assoc. Am. Geogr.* 59:135–57
117. Pyne, N. M. 1976. The fire-serpent and were-jaguar in formative Oaxaca: A contingency table analysis. See Ref. 44, pp. 272–82
118. Rapoport, A. 1968. Rank-size relations. *Int. Encycl. Soc. Sci.* 13:319–23
119. Rashevsky, N. 1947. *Mathematical Theory of Human Relations.* Bloomington: Principia
120. Renfrew, C. 1969. Trade and culture process in European prehistory. *Curr. Anthropol.* 10:151–69
121. Renfrew, C. 1972. *The Emergence of Civilization: The Cyclades and the Aegean in the Third Millenium B.C.* London: Methuen
122. Renfrew, C. 1972. Patterns of population growth in the prehistoric Aegean. See Ref. 20, pp. 383–99
123. Renfrew, C. 1975. Trade as action at a distance: Questions of integration and communication. See Ref. 34, pp. 3–59
123a. Renfrew, C. 1977. Models for exchange and spatial distribution. See Ref. 39a, pp. 71–90
124. Renfrew, C., Cann, J. R., Dixon, J. E. 1965. Obsidian in the Aegean. *Ann. Br. Sch. Archaeol. Athens* 60:225–47
125. Richardson, H. W. 1973. Theory of the distribution of city sizes: Review and prospects. *Reg. Stud.* 7:239–51
126. Rossmann, D. L. 1976. A site catchment analysis of San Lorenzo, Veracruz. See Ref. 44, pp. 95–103
127. Rowlett, R. M., Pollnac, R. B. 1971 Multivariate analysis of Marnian La Tene cultural groups. See Ref. 5, pp. 46–58
128. Russell, J. C. 1972. *Medieval Regions and Their Cities.* Bloomington: Indiana Univ. Press
129. Sahlins, M. D. 1963. Poor man, rich man, big man, chief: Political types in Polynesia and Melanesia. *Comp. Stud. Soc. Hist.* 5:285–303
130. Sahlins, M. D. 1972. *Stone Age Economics.* Chicago: Aldine
131. Schacht, R. M. 1972. *Population and economic organization in early historic southwest Iran.* PhD thesis. Univ. Michigan, Ann Arbor, Mich. 145 pp.
132. Sherratt, A. G. 1972. Socio-economic and demographic models for the Neolithic and Bronze Ages of Europe. See Ref. 28, pp. 477–542
133. Sidrys, R. V. 1976. Classic Maya obsidian trade. *Am. Antiq.* 41:449–64
133a. Sidrys, R. 1977. Mass-distance measures for the Maya obsidian trade. See Ref. 39a, pp. 91–107
134. Simon, H. A. 1944. Decision-making and administrative organization. *Public Adm. Rev.* 4:16–30
135. Simon, H. A. 1955. On a class of skew distribution functions. *Biometrika* 42: 425–40
136. Simon, H. A. 1957. *Models of Man.* New York: Wiley
137. Skinner, G. W. 1964. Marketing and social structure in rural China: Part I. *J. Asian Stud.* 24:3–43
138. Skinner, G. W. 1965. Marketing and social structure in rural China: Part II. *J. Asian Stud.* 24:195–228
139. Smith, C. A. 1972. *The domestic marketing system in western Guatemala: An economic, locational, and cultural Anal-*

ysis. PhD thesis. Stanford Univ., Stanford, Calif. 442 pp.

140. Smith, C. A. 1974. Economics of marketing systems: Models from economic geography. *Ann. Rev. Anthropol.* 3:167–201

141. Smith, C. A., ed. 1976. *Regional Analysis: Vol. 1, Economic Systems; Vol. 2, Social Systems.* New York: Academic

142. Smith, C. A. 1976. Regional economic systems: Linking geographic models and socioeconomic models. See Ref. 141, Vol. 1, pp. 3–63

143. Soane, E. B. 1912. *To Mesopotamia and Kurdistan in Disguise.* Boston: Small, Maynard & Co.

144. Soudsky, B., Pavlů, I. 1972. The linear culture settlement patterns of central Europe. See Ref. 20, pp. 317–28

145. Speth, J. D., Johnson, G. A. 1976. Problems in the use of correlation for the analysis of tool kits and activity areas. In *Cultural Continuity and Change: Essays in Honor of James Bennett Griffin,* ed. C. Cleland, pp. 35–57. New York: Academic

146. Struever, S., Houart, G. 1972. An analysis of the Hopewell Interaction Sphere. In *Social Exchange and Interaction,* ed. E. N. Wilmsen, pp. 47–79. *Mus. Anthropol. Univ. Mich. Anthropol. Pap. 46*

147. Sutherland, J. W. 1975. *Systems: Analysis, Administration, and Architecture.* New York: van Nostrand-Reinhold

148. Suttles, W. 1968. Coping with abundance: Subsistence on the Northwest Coast. See Ref. 93, pp. 56–68

149. Swedlund, A. C. 1975. Population growth and settlement pattern in Franklin and Hampshire counties, Massachusetts, 1650–1850. In *Population Studies in Archaeology and Biological Anthropology: A Symposium,* ed. A. C. Swedlund, pp. 22–33. *Am. Antiq. Mem. 30*

150. Taylor, D. 1975. *Some locational aspects of middle-range hierarchical societies.* PhD thesis. CUNY Grad. Center, New York, NY

151. von Thünen, J. H. 1966. *Von Thünen's Isolated State,* ed. P. Hall, Transl. C. M. Wartenberg. Oxford: Pergamon

152. Tiebout, C. M. 1957. Location theory, empirical evidence and economic evolution. *Reg. Sci. Assoc. Pa. Proc.* 3:74–86

153. Tobler, W., Wineburg, S. 1971. A Cappadocian speculation. *Nature* 231:39–41

154. Törnqvist, G. 1968. Flows of information and the location of economic activities. *Geogr. Annaler* 50B:99–107

155. Udy, S. H. Jr. 1970. *Work in Traditional and Modern Society.* Englewood Cliffs: Prentice-Hall

156. Ullman, E. L. 1957. *American Commodity Flow.* Seattle: Univ. Washington Press

157. Vapnarsky, C. A. 1969. On rank-size distributions of cities: An ecological approach. *Econ. Dev. Cult. Change* 17:584–95

158. Vining, D. R. Jr. 1974. On the sources of instability in the rank-size rule: Some simple tests of Gibrat's Law. *Geogr. Anal.* 4:313–29

159. Vining, R. 1955. A description of certain spatial aspects of an economic system. *Econ. Dev. Cult. Change* 3:147–95

160. Vita-Finzi, C., Higgs, E. S. 1970. Prehistoric economy in the Mt. Carmel area of Palestine: Site catchment analysis. *Proc. Prehist. Soc.* 36:1–37

161. Wallace, A. F. C. 1971. Administrative forms of social organization. *Addison-Wesley Modular Publ., Module 9*

162. Watanabe, H. 1968. Subsistence and ecology of northern food gatherers with special reference to the Ainu. See Ref. 93, pp. 69–77

163. Watson, W. 1972. Neolithic settlement in East Asia. See Ref. 20, pp. 329–41

164. Webb, M. C. 1974. Exchange networks: Prehistory. *Ann. Rev. Anthropol.* 3:357–83

165. Webber, M. J. 1971. Empirical verifiability of classical central place theory. *Geogr. Anal.* 3:15–28

166. Webber, M. J. 1972. *Impact of Uncertainty on Location.* Cambridge: M.I.T. Press

167. Webster, D. L. 1976. On theocracies. *Am. Anthropol.* 78:812–28

168. Weiss, H., Young, T. C. Jr. 1975. The merchants of Susa: Godin V and plateau-lowland relations in the Late Fourth Millenium B. C. *Iran* 13:1–17

169. Whallon, R. Jr. 1968. Investigations of Late Prehistoric social organization in New York State. See Ref. 36, pp. 223–44

170. Wheatley, P. 1972. The concept of urbanism. See Ref. 20, pp. 601–37

170a. Wiens, J. A. 1976. Population responses to patchy environments. *Ann. Rev. Ecol. Syst.* 7:81–120

171. Wilmsen, E. N. 1973. Interaction, spacing behavior, and the organization of hunting bands. *J. Anthropol. Res.* 29:1–31

172. Wilmsen, E. N. 1974. *Lindenmeier: A Pleistocene Hunting Society.* New York: Harper & Row

173. Wilson, A. G. 1970. Inter-regional commodity flows: Entropy maximizing approaches. *Geogr. Anal.* 2:255–82
174. Wilson, E. O. 1975. *Sociobiology: The New Synthesis.* Cambridge: Belknap/ Harvard
175. Wobst, H. M. 1974. Boundary conditions for Paleolithic social systems: A simulation approach. *Am. Antiq.* 39: 147–78
176. Wobst, H. M. 1976. Locational relationships in Paleolithic society. *J. Hum. Evol.* 5:49–58
177. Wobst, H. M. 1977. Stylistic behavior and information exchange. In *Papers for the Director,* ed. C. Cleland. *Mus. Anthropol. Univ. Mich. Anthropol. Pap. 61.* In press
178. Wolpert, J. 1964. The decision process in spatial context. *Ann. Assoc. Am. Geogr.* 54:537–58
179. Wortman, S. 1976. Food and agriculture. *Sci. Am.* 235:30–39
180. Wright, G. A. 1969. Obsidian analysis and prehistoric Near Eastern trade: 7500 to 3500 B.C. *Mus. Anthropol.*

Univ. Mich. Anthropol. Pap. 37
181. Wright, G. A. 1974. Archaeology and trade. *Addison-Wesley Module in Anthropol. 49*
182. Wright, H. T. 1972. A consideration of interregional exchange in Greater Mesopotamia: 4000–3000 B.C. See Ref. 146, pp. 95–105
183. Wright, H. T., Johnson, G. A. 1975. Population, exchange, and early state formation in Southwestern Iran. *Am. Anthropol.* 77:267–89
184. Yeates, M. 1974. *An Introduction to Quantitative Analysis in Human Geography.* New York: McGraw-Hill
185. Zarky, A. 1976. Statistical analysis of site catchments at Ocos, Guatamala. See Ref. 44, pp. 117–28
186. Zipf, G. K. 1941. *National Unity and Disunity.* Bloomington: Principia
187. Zipf, G. K. 1949. *Human Behavior and the Principle of Least Effort.* Cambridge: Harvard Univ. Press
188. Zubrow, E. B. W. 1976. Stability and instability: A problem in long-term regional growth. See Ref. 6, pp. 245–74

Ann. Rev. Anthropol. 1977. 6:509–61
Copyright © 1977 by Annual Reviews Inc. All rights reserved.

BIOLOGY, SPEECH, AND LANGUAGE

❖9604

James N. Spuhler
Department of Anthropology, University of New Mexico,
Albuquerque, New Mexico 87131

When the primeval matter had congealed but breath and form had not yet appeared, there were no names and no action. The opening sentence in Kojiki, the oldest book in Japanese, completed A.D. 712. (264).

INTRODUCTION: THE IMPORTANCE OF LANGUAGE

The problems of symbolic language and of mind are the great problems in the evolutionary transit through three billion years from the first genes to man. Some interpret mind, and the ability to symbol, as an intrusion of complete novelty unique to the human species (44, 171, 172, 348). They emphasize the radical mental gap between man and other animals.

Others, including the philosopher Bergson and the geneticist Sewall Wright (359), suggest that if we are consistent in the criteria we use to attribute mind to other members of our species (especially those whose language we understand, although we cannot enter into their stream of consciousness) then we must ascribe minds to chimpanzees, other primates, and the higher vertebrates. If vertebrates have minds, why not all animals? Plants? Viruses? Individual cells? Genes? Nucleotides? Hydrogen atoms? Subatomic particles? They view mind as an aspect of all reality, they see the world as a multiplicity of minds, each with two aspects: (*a*) as it *is* to itself (mind), and (*b*) as it *seems,* as an incursion into the mind of another (matter). By stressing the evolutionary continuity of mental experience, Griffin (105) has reopened the question of animal awareness and discussed possible windows on the minds of animals. If most scientists accept biological evolution in animals and man, why do some shy away from the concept of continuity in mental experiences including language?

New studies on the brain and language, especially the split brain findings, help to resolve this major dichotomy in the theory of mind and communication—that consciousness is or is not a universal property of all things. Because the balance of the neurophysiological evidence favors the conclusion that consciousness is selectively localized within human and other mammalian brains and that some functionally important neural systems (cerebellum, etc) lack the property of conscious experience, Sperry (304) argues that it is not necessary to assume consciousness in brainless things such as plants or hydrogen atoms. Because the stream of consciousness in a human individual can be divided into right and left realms by cutting a set of forebrain fiber systems at the neocortical level, he concludes that "consciousness is an operational derivative of activity in particular cerebral circuit systems designed expressly to produce their own specific conscious effects ... with action *upon* as well as *from* neural events" (304, p. 429). The evolutionary continuity of mental experience may embrace man, chimpanzees, dogs, horses, and octopuses, but not oak trees nor photons.

There are three great realms of evolution: cosmic, organic, and cultural (including linguistic) (191, 205, 206, 285). The evolutionary theory of language transformation is accepted by all who have mastered the empirical evidence, a process that requires some years of individual study. Some, like Chomsky, while accepting the general notion of linguistic evolution, are sceptical that we can discover anything verifiable and interesting about the actual past evolutionary linguistic events. Greenberg (102, p. 110) contends that the theory of evolution as transformation (as opposed to special creation) applies with relatively minor detailed alteration both to linguistic and biological change. In the *Descent of Man* (61, p. 40) Darwin remarked that "the formation of different languages and of distinct species and the proofs that both have been developed through a gradual process are curiously parallel." Descartes took biology and language apart; Darwin put them back together. In fact, as Greenberg (102) shows, scientific theories of linguistic evolution predate those on organic evolution. Among others, Hill (119, 120) urges the development of continuity theories of the evolution of human language.

White (347) distinguished four stages in the evolution of minding—simple reflex, conditioned reflex, insight, and symbol defined by yes or no answers on two criteria: dependence on intrinsic properties, and dominant role of organism. White restricted symbolling, mostly manifest in language, to man alone. Such classifications are useful in looking at major steps in the evolution of language, but it is doubtful that pure examples of even the "simple reflex" exist in nature (8, 220). In the classical monograph *Behavior of the Lower Organisms,* Jennings (143) showed that protozoans have in some degree all of the Aristotelian sensory modalities of man (hearing, sight, smell, taste, touch) and that they learn from individual experience to modify their behavior adaptively. The offspring of female insects that "instinctively" lay their eggs only on one species of plant (e.g. the silkworm, *Bombyx moti,* on mulberry leaves), "learn" a new instinct if the experimenter removes the eggs to a different species of leaf that is suitably nutritious (8).

The genesis of a new symbol is not as arbitrary and capricious as Leslie White claims. It is always based on a link to the past. There is a new association of stimuli, a new meeting of actors, or some new circumstance where the new symbol grows out of and emerges from old symbols, not completely new, but remodeled and redefined and still an arbitrary symbol. We know symbols mostly through words. And new words are variations of old words; the variation is arbitrary but not without linkage, phonetic or other, to old expressions.

We cannot talk intelligibly about the "square root of minus one"—a new symbol $\sqrt{-1}$ in 1637 A.D.—unless we know something about several different mathematical ideas, starting with numbers, negative numbers, roots, square roots, and so on. As Hoijer wrote, "meanings . . . are not in actual fact separable from structure" (130, pp. 92–104).

White is correct in emphasizing that the important cultural transmission of symbols is not by genes and that the important biological transmission of simple reflexes is by genes. But nongenic transformation of information in nonhuman animals is well known. For instance, Denenberg & Rosenberg (64) observed that the effects of handling experimental rats in infancy can be transmitted over at least two generations; presumably the maternal physiology and behavior of handled rats is altered, and this effects the experience of their offspring whose maternal behavior is, in turn, changed with results still detectable in their own young (220, p. 24).

Cooper (52) reports that insect eumenid (*Rygchium foraminatum*) and sphecid (*Trypoxylon clavatum*) females lay 1–10 provisioned eggs in a linear set of cells in a burrow 4–6 mm in diameter and 150 mm long. Early pupae can turn around but mature ones cannot. The mature pupae regularly face the sole exit of the burrow. The female makes the burrow walls asymmetric in relation to the exit, the mortar of the burrow wall serving as a communication channel from mother to offspring stored in an artifact in digital form.

Sapir (288) emphasized that language is an overlaid physiological function that uses diaphragm, lungs, vocal tract, tongue, teeth, lips, ears, and brain centers originally evolved for different purposes. The emphasis is proper but misleading if we assume that when language arrived it moved into a structure designed and built for other occupants and yet this language, different in degree if not in kind from anything that existed before, found the old structure so perfect in meeting the new function, that no alteration nor rebuilding was necessary. This is as unlikely a happening in historical biology as in real estate.

It is true that language uses structures originally used for other purposes, but it is also true that considerable modification, redesigning, and rebuilding is involved in the evolutionary acquisition of language (33, 184). The overlaying of function, such as the use of reptilian jaw bones to make mammalian inner ear bones, is an important process of evolutionary change. Overlaying of function is part of the reason that complex structures such as the vertebrate eye, or the blow hole of the whale, which, as the antievolutionists say, had to be perfect before they could function, came into being phylogenetically by gradual change (281, 300).

A wide variety of scholars including philosophers (171, 172), biologists (301), and psychologists (86) make language the most important result of the evolutionary developments that distinguish human beings from other species. As Sapir said (288, p. 235):

"Language is the most significant and colossal work that the human spirit has evolved —nothing short of a finished form of expression for all communicable experience. This form may be endlessly varied by the individual without thereby losing its distinctive contours; and it is constantly reshaping itself as is all art. Language is the most massive and inclusive art we know, a mountainous and anonymous work of unconscious generations."

If propositional, spoken language is the most distinctive part of human cultural behavior, the brain is the most distinctive part of human anatomy and physiology (48, 144, 184).

It is possible and proper to study language and the brain together (186, 271). A new quarterly journal devoted entirely to neurolinguistics, *Brain and Language,* started publication in 1974, edited by Harry A. Whitaker. The biological foundations of language is one of seven announced "interests" of the new (1971) quarterly *Journal of Psycholinguistics,* edited by R. W. Rieber. R. Hoops and Y. Lebrun are editors of the recently founded international monographic series called *Neurolinguistics.* Harry A. Whitaker is editor of a new series on *Perspectives in Neurolinguistics and Psycholinguistics,* of which the first two volumes, *Studies in Neurolinguistics,* edited by Haiganoosh Whitaker and Harry A. Whitaker, appeared in 1976 and volume 3 is announced for 1977.

It is also possible and proper to study human language (15, 288), society (256), or culture (348) without consideration of biological variables except those of universal generic man. Human propositional language is a biological, a psychological, a cultural, and an individual process. Most biologists recognize the importance of psychological and cultural variables in speech and language; some anthropologists (e.g. 18, 19) deny any important explanatory power to biological variables in normal linguistic variation. Fifteen years ago, study of the interconnections of biology and language was virtually taboo among many anthropologists and most linguists. Today, observing, experimenting, speculating, and model-building in neurolinguistics, psycholinguistics, and glottogenesis is widely considered interesting, important, respectable, and sometimes verifiable [for details see many of the 75 papers in the 1976 *Origins and Evolution of Language and Speech* (111)].

The molecular geneticist Luria (214) pointed out that recent attempts to biologize language differ fundamentally from some recent attempts to biologize (human) aggression, ethnic differences in measured intelligence, or the ecological crisis [for a recent critical review see Reynolds (273)]. A biology of language could be a truly humane science that considers qualities common to all human beings and not to supposed genetic differences between peoples. Luria's biology of language would include a biology of the thinking process including logical structures, a priori ideas, artistic creation, and even connecting to ethical principles, but with full realization that nearly all of the socially important contents of language is of environmental origin, controlled not by genes but by upbringing. He speculates that this language-and-biology research may generate an applied science by discovering better ways to teach, to learn, and to make use of what we learn. It is important to note that Luria's main justification for treating language as a biological phenomenon (but not to deny that it is also a sociological, cultural, or genuine linguistic phenomena) comes from

Chomskian linguistics, specifically the conclusion that human language universally is based on innate grammatical and syntactic structures common to all normal human beings, that languages are functional manifestations of a species-wide genetically determined system of neural connections in the cerebral cortex and other parts of the brain.

Most of the works reviewed here were published after Lenneberg's *Biological Foundations of Language* (184), the baseline reference for the present article, but some earlier works are noted that have special human biological interest in relation to speech and language. Also, in general, works mentioned in the 1974 *Annual Review of Anthropology* article by Dingwall & Whitaker (66) on neurolinguistic aspects of brain localization of language function, linguistic and neurological analyses of aphasia, and manipulative studies of brain and language function are not included here unless they have special importance to the topic being considered. At least 1000 titles relevant to biology, speech, and language published in the last 10 years are not included in this review: titles of most of them may be found in *Bibliographie Linguistic de l'Année; Biological Abstracts; Current Citations on Communicative Disorders: Language, Speech, Voice;* and *Psychological Abstracts.* The massive *Origins and Evolution of Language and Speech* (111) and the recent two-volume *Studies in Neurolinguistics* (336) arrived barely in time for inclusion of several papers.

Details of four recent scientific developments that account for much of the current interest in biology and language—Chomskian universal deep-structure linguistics (41–46, 111), physiologically oriented psycholinguistics (111, 231, 232), and the related topics of pongid "language" and "ethology and language"—are not covered in this review. Since the innovative work of Gardner & Gardner (86) in teaching American Sign Language to a chimpanzee, all three living species of great apes have been involved in man-ape communicative studies (10, 170, 185, 186, 308). The results shatter excessive anthropocentrism and are widely discussed in the scientific and popular media. The papers by Fouts, Malmi, Miles, Premack, Rambaugh & Gill, and Terrace & Bever (111) provide an entry to the relevant sources. The work of Fouts and his associates (including the Norman chimpanzees) on direct chimp-to-chimp transmission of learned and shared sign language is of special importance.

There is a rich, recent literature from ethologists, primatologists, and comparative psychologists on behavioral parallels and possible continuities in linguistic (sensu lato) evolution, especially via birds and mammals (111, 245). Among anthropological linguists, Sebeok's compilations and comments (294–296) are particulary useful.

SPEECH AND LANGUAGE

Just as biology progresses splendidly without a widely accepted definition of life, and psychology with little agreement on the definition of mind or intelligence, linguistics has become perhaps the most sophisticated discipline in the human behavioral sciences without full agreement on *the* definition of language. There is no exhaustive compendium of language definitions to match Kroeber & Kluckhohn's (166) catalogue of culture definitions, although many of the latter include the former as a major part. Laguna (169) discusses several widely used definitions of language. The definitions listed in *Webster's Third* make speech and language sometimes synonymous, othertimes not. Premack (269) points out that a comparative psychological theory of language requires a functional definition, but that most definitions of language by linguists are structural. Toulmin (321) advocates a "functionalist" alternative to Chomsky's "nativist" account of language. Sampson (286) counters Toulmin by arguing that language cannot be explained functionally. The animal psychologists Gardner & Gardner (86) chide linguists for continually changing their definition of language so as to exclude new findings on chimpanzee and other nonhuman animal communication. Hockett, a linguist, devised design features universal in human language with the plan to discover how many of them are present in animal "languages" (122–125, 127). A definition of the linguist Lieberman (194) that says "language is a system of communication that permits exchange of new information" grants language to some insects (98). As Hirsh (121) points out, definitions like that of Lieberman and Mattingly (see 151)—"linguistic communication requires that a string of phones [e.g. insect stridulation, bird song] be transmitted from one individual to another"—eliminates the problems of whether language communication must involve speech or must be uniquely human to disappear.

Some behavioral scientists interested in man use "speech" and "language" almost interchangeably (91), some draw no clear distinction between "speech" and "language" (288), some make the distinction a nonradical difference in kind (85), and others a radical difference in kind (289, 348). As a human biologist, I will relate *speech* to the behavior of individuals; *language* to the behavior of populations.

Some behavioral scientists interested in man argue that they are concerned only in empirically observable behavior (15), some claim that we cannot ignore mental events in talking scientifically about speech and language (85, 265). Some say that our scientific business is to *describe* animal, primate, and human communication (194, 269, 295, 296); others make the prime test of behavioral science the ability to *control* what animals and people do (232). As a human biologist, in this particular review, I will be interested in skin-out observed behavior, skin-in mental events including the possibility of animal awareness (105), descriptions of what primates do as organisms, and with brains and speech apparatuses, and I fully acknowledge that in some instances the special kinds of animal communication called human speech and language "are excellent examples of man's ability to control the behavior of some other people" (231).

Four decades ago, in making distance and direction of movement in a total goal-oriented act known by objective observation the fundamental concept of animal behavior, Tolman (320), founder of purposive behaviorism and pioneer in animal behavioral genetics, excluded human behavior involving language and society from that formulation.

In a book completed just before his death, Leslie White (348, pp. xi–xii) wrote "Language(s) could not exist without man. But language, as a distinct order of phenomena—with its structure and processes of lexicon, grammar, syntax, phonetics, phonemics—is not to be explained in terms of man as a human animal; man is not an explanatory device in the science of linguistics." White emphatically does not deny the relevance of psychology in the realm of language and "man and culture": symbolates may be interpreted meaningfully in both psychological (including physiological) and culturological contexts; a treatise on grammar with no reference to biology does not invalidate or oppose a biologist's interest in the nerve-muscle-hard tissue actions, or conceptual and emotional factors involved in speech and language. "*The human behavior of peoples is determined by their respective cultures.* (I say *peoples* because the human behavior of individuals is affected, but not determined, by their biological makeup)" (p. 8). "It was the emergence of symbolling in the course of neurological evolution that transformed prehuman primate society into human cultural systems" (p. 21). "The 'institutions,' habits, and knowledge that the first human beings took over from their prehuman antecedents were important, but they were crude, simple, and meager. And, without articulate speech, the possibility of progress on a merely primate level seems to have been extremely limited if, indeed, it existed at all. It was symbolling—particularly articulate speech—that changed all this: it created cultural systems and launched them upon a course of development. In the Word was the Beginning." For White, symbolling and articulate speech are not synonymous; articulate speech is a particular form of symbolling, the most important characteristic expression of this ability (pp. 22–23).

Part of the difficulty with theories that make biology important for speech but irrelevant for language is the restriction of "biology" to the study of individuals. Human biology and biological anthropology include both individual and population biology (112, 316a). The individual man or woman who speaks, respires, feeds, excretes, and so on, is not *the* individual unit of enduring biology because he or she can maintain the species characteristics only for a limited time. The system that endures, that makes survival in sexually reproduced species nearly permanent, is not that of any single person or creature, but is embodied in two or more sexes (six in *Euplotes,* eight in *Paramecium*), and in the members of the local breeding population, and ultimately in the whole species (361). Language cannot be reduced to the biology of individuals; it can be related to the biology of populations.

Kroeber (165), most linguists (15, 41–45, 85, 102, 122, 127, 194, 265, 288, 289) and many anthropologists (19, 33, 114, 273, 348) insist that language is a system.

Systems differ from congeries in that the first are meaningfully integrated; the latter have their elements associated fortuitously. The principal pure systems in culture are Language, Science, Fine Arts, Religion, and Ethics. Being integrated, each of these has a "self-directing unity"—something immanent—with a "margin of autonomy" against forces outside. Language is the most autonomous. . . . There is of course no novelty in recognizing these divisions or parts or segments of culture. . . . Similarly, whole cultures, be they little primitive ones or great civilizations, certainly exist and have a history; but languages, philosophies, economies, and so on, though they occur universally in all cultures, occur only *in* them, and never occur independently in the world, any more than nervous systems float free and detached (165, pp. 176–77).

The statements in this paragraph on the relations between speech and language are paraphrased or directly quoted from de Saussure (289) or from Gardiner (85):

Language is the general term including all those known items that enable a speaker to make effective use of words. Much of this knowledge was learned in childhood, most goes back to the child's family, community, group-tribe-nation, and to the species biology. The lexicon is continually enlarged, and areas of word meaning widened or narrowed. Every utterance has a double aspect that gives linguistics two of its most fundamental distinctions, that between speech and language, and that between the sentence and the word (85). The sentence is the unit of speech (some sentences use only one word). Words are one unit of language; syntactic rules and specific types of intonation in speaking words are other less tangible units. Words, as such, are not units of speech, for they lack the vivifying breath and willpower of a speaker requisite to call speech into being. The child learns language in order to exercise it as speech. The ultimate basis of speech is the fact that individual thoughts and feelings are, as such, entirely private and inalienable. Words are psychical entities and not objects of sense. In de Saussure's terminology, words are diachronic, sentences are synchronic. Of course, several-word sentences have sequence and duration in time, but the time occupied by a spoken sentence is short compared to a human life-span. Speech is triggered by an external or internal stimulus that later forms the thing-meant. Speech uses words to communicate; articulation translates words into sound waves which the listener translates back into words of the dictionary common to listener and speaker. Instances of speech (and spoken language) have four aspects: speaker, listener, spoken words, and thing-or-things meant. Speech is an abstract term, but it applies concretely to a particular speaker's act, firstly, that is relevant to a particular occasion, listener, and thing-meant, and secondly, that is due to the volition of the speaker, whose articulate utterance projects into reality the word-signs used, and endows them with a vitality absent from them at other times. Language enters into speech, but speech is the sole generator of language. Speech is the skill of shaping the muscles in and around the mouth and in the voice box in such a way to produce speech sounds. Language is the capacity to understand what is said and to construct sentences. Both speech and language depend on physiological mechanisms in the central nervous system. Either may become nonfunctional, interfering selectively with one or the other skill. In verbal communication, language is more basic than speech; many adult aphasics who cannot speak continue to have language, to read, write, and fully understand (142).

Mánczak (219), an admirer of de Saussure, questions on theoretical grounds the reality of the distinction between *langue* and *parole*.

Lenneberg (184) studied several children with minor brain damage before or shortly after birth that interfered with speech so that they never babbled and never were able to produce understandable speech. Such children may develop the capacity for language if they grow up in a family or institutional environment where they hear usual conversation and are spoken to frequently and normally. Fourcin (80a) describes a case of superior language development in the complete absence of expressive speech in an adult male congenital quadriplegic spastic with severe athetosis and bilateral high-frequency hearing loss. Some individuals are observed to have language without speech.

A striking example of speech without language or cognition comes from the case report of Geschwind, Quadfasel & Segarra (95) on a patient who had received extensive cerebral damage from carbon monoxide poisoning, resulting in essential isolation of the language areas of the dominant hemisphere from the rest of the cerebrum. The patient became a "talking machine" that repeated everything spoken to it and thus retained the capability of decoding auditory speech input, at least briefly retaining and encoding speech, without any contact with the rest of the brain and hence isolated from other cognitive functions and language. A case of isolation of the language function in a 59-year-old female suffering from presenile dementia is reported by H. Whitaker (335) along with a review of the literature and a neurolinguistic interpretation of echolalia. Some individuals are observed to have speech without language.

The possibility of inventing a private language is proposed by Ayer (5) and rebutted by Rhees (274). In a reprinted version, (6) Ayer adds one crucially important footnote, doubting that it is possible to construct a language all of whose words refer to nothing but private things in Wittgenstein's sense (see Cook 50): "I am now inclined to think that in any language which allows reference to individuals there must be criteria of identity which make it possible for different speakers to refer to the same individual. This would not prevent the language from containing private sectors, but it would mean that my idea that these private sectors could be made to absorb the public sectors was not tenable" (6, p. 263, fn. 10).

Speech is private in the sense that recordings of individual voices can be identified (322). Language is something that is spoken and listened to socially. Language is a population phenomenon, speech a phenomenon that involves two or more individuals belonging to the same language population.

BRAIN, SPEECH, AND LANGUAGE

The volume of a contemporary, normal, adult human brain is approximately 1.4 dm^3, the weight is around 1.2 kg, and its power about 2.5 W. Making up about 1/50 of the adult total body mass, the brain consumes about 1/5 of the total daily oxygen requirement (9, 173). Most recent attempts to define man in zoological terms stress the relatively large brain (48, 301), and most students of human paleontology point to man's recent spectacular phyletic increase in brain volume (48, 144, 299) and brain organization (132–134, 257–259).

In wide taxonomic comparisons, say between genera or families, the structure and function of the brain often show a strong correlation with behavioral differences. Probably the most remarkable case of physiological selfwise development is that reported by Giersberg (cited in 240, p. 348), who exchanged by transplantation at an early stage the brains of different species of toads (*Pelobates fuscus*) and frogs (*Rana arvalis*): an adult animal possessing a *Pelobates* brain in a *Rana* body performed the strong digging instinct characteristic of *Pelobates* and lacking in *Rana*. Evans (75) showed that members of two families of flat-fish, the sole (Soleidae) and the plaice (Pleuronectidae), have widely different hunting methods and that their brain structure and sense receptors reflect the difference: the sole hunts by smell and touch, has small eyes and a large olfactory lobe; the plaice hunts by sight and taste, has large, prominent, and movable eyes, and a small olfactory lobe.

During ontogeny the growth of the human brain contrasts with the growth of body weight in man in that the brain grows in the pattern characteristic of body weight in subprimate mammals and birds. Curvilinear growth of the human brain starts immediately at birth and continues in a rectilinear course to about puberty, without the adolescent spurt shown in the growth of human body weight. For this reason, man, and to a lesser extent the higher primates, spends a considerable part of the growth period with a nearly full-size brain housed in a body smaller than full size (314), an adaptation facilitating the long period of acquisition of language and culture distinctive of our species.

Luria (212), with the higher mental functions in view, describes three basic trends in the evolution of the brain in the primate lineages leading to the apes and man: (a) diminished specificity of cortical areas, with the primary sensory-projection areas occupying a smaller portion of the cortex; (b) lateralization of function, leading to a linguistically dominant hemisphere; (c) particular enlargement of two areas of the cortex: the anterior frontal areas and the inferior parietal areas.

For Rozen, a specialist on memory (283), the development of language has undoubtedly been a major factor in the evolution of the brain. Later in this section we consider the possible role of tools in this context.

Jerison (144) reviewed and synthesized the massive literature on brain evolution with special reference to allometric studies on brain size, using power equations of the sort

Brain weight $= b(\text{body weight})^a$

where a is the slope and b the Y-intercept of a log-log regression plot. Gould (99) gives a general review of the literature on allometry and size in ontogeny and phylogeny in a wide variety of animals.

In interspecific plots for mammals ranging in size from mice to elephants where each point represents an average adult of each species, the slope is 0.66, implying that between species brain weight increases slower than body weight but in step with body surface area, thus conforming to the theoretical power of 2/3 relating increase in brain weight and external body surface area suggested by dimensional analysis (144).

In intraspecific plots where each point represents an adult within one species, or the means of a population (including a race) belonging to a species, or samples from closely related species (for instance, the macaques), slopes range from 0.2 to 0.4, close to the universal theoretical slope of 5/18 or 0.28 proposed in 1898 by Lapicqué for brains of related adults that develop by enlarging old neurons without adding new ones.

Pilbeam & Gould (266) marshal the evidence that these two allometric relations support criteria to distinguish intraspecific functional equivalence in cephalization among related forms at the same evolutionary grade ($0.2 < a < 0.4$) from phyletic increases in cephalization independent of body size ($a > 2/3$). If related species differing in body size show a brain-body allometry with $a = 5/18$, they are of the same evolutionary grade; if related species in a time sequence evolve to larger body size with endocranial volume scaling $a > 2/3$, we must conclude that a phylogenetic increase in cephalization has taken place (266).

Using the available 3 points for plots within African pongids, Pilbeam & Gould (266) found that $a = 0.34$ for pygmy chimpanzee, chimpanzee, and gorilla. They found that the 3 points plotted for australopithecines produced a linear regression of the same slope ($a = 0.33$), indicating that the large *Australopithecus boisei* has the brain size expected in an australopithecine 1.5 times the body weight but otherwise similar in genetical design to the smaller *A. africanus*.

They obtained a much different regression by plotting 4 points representing a hominid lineage; use of *A. africanus* → *Homo habilis* → *H. erectus* → *H. sapiens* yields the slope $a = 1.73$ showing that the brain volume increased with marked positive allometry during the past two or three million years. Clearly the distinctive evolution of the hominid brain since the late Pliocene is a special adaptation unrelated to the mere physical requirements of increasing body size (133, 266). The critical factors in the phyletic volume increase, and, judging partly from the fossils but mostly from living forms, in brain organization advance, are often identified as the evolution of tools, of language, of general cognitive ability, or of some combination of these (see below).

The cumulated net evolutionary increase in hominid brain volume in the last few million years, and especially during the last one-half million years, is spectacular and well known (22, 48, 132–134, 144, 257–259, 281, 299) but the estimated increase *per generation* is commonplace and within the lower range of rates observed for some domestic and experimental animals under artificial selection (76). Cavalli-Sforza & Bodmer (37) considered the rate of evolutionary change in endocranial volume from *Homo erectus* to *H. sapiens* in terms of selection differentials operating during the past 500,000 years. The selection differential (S) is the difference between the mean phenotypic value of individuals selected as parents and the mean of all individuals in the parental generation before selection was made. The response to selection (R) is the difference between the mean phenotypic value of the offspring of the selected parents and that of the parental generation before selection. Under specific conditions, the ratio of response to selection differential is equal to the heritability (h^2), that is, the proportion of phenotypic variance due to additive genetic variance, and $S = R/h^2$. Using a standard deviation (σ) of 100 g for brain weight, the observed change of 500 g over the last 500,000 years, taken to occupy 25,000 generations, gives a rate of change in σ units per generation of $500/(100 \times 25,000) = 0.0002$. Assuming a heritability of 0.5 gives an average selection differential of 0.0004 per generation—very much smaller than selection differentials commonly achieved under artificial selection in chickens, swine, sheep, and cows (76). The same conclusion holds if the heritability is lower, say 0.1–0.2.

Figure 1 identifies the anatomical terms used below to discuss some aspects of brain structure of interest to students of biology and language. Until 1968, despite

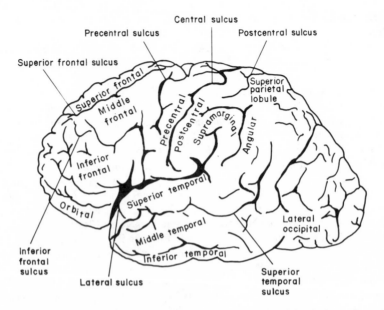

Figure 1 Outline sketch of the lateral surface of the left cerebral hemisphere of an adult human brain showing the main gyri and sulci.

several earlier reports to the contrary, it was generally accepted that the usual lateralization of the left hemisphere for speech and language was not associated with significant structural differences between the two sides of the brain (21, 22). In that year Geschwind & Levitsky (94) examined 100 adult human brains free of significant pathology obtained at postmortem. They demonstrated an anatomical asymmetry (often marked) between the upper surfaces of the right and left temporal lobes. The planum temporale (the area behind Heschl's gyrus and in front of the posterior end of the lateral sulcus on the superior surface of the temporal lobe) is larger on the left in 65% and larger on the right in only 11% of brains. The mean length of the outer border of the planum temporale was 3.6 ± 1.0 cm on the left and 2.7 ± 1.2 cm on the right (the difference being significant at the 0.001 level), that is, the planum averaged 0.9 cm or one-third longer on the left than on the right temporal lobe. The planum temporale is a part of Wernicke's speech center.

Figure 2 is a schematic drawing of the brain viewed from above with parts of the frontal and parietal lobes lying over the upper surface of the temporal lobe cut away to expose the transverse temporal gyri (of Heschl) and the planum temporale (of von Economo) which cannot be observed from outside the intact brain because they are located within the deep infold of the lateral sulci. A horizontal cut has removed the upper surface of the insula and other parts of the upper surface of the temporal lobe medial to the transverse gyri and planum temporale. The degree of bilateral difference shown in the size of the planum is within the observed human range but is larger than average.

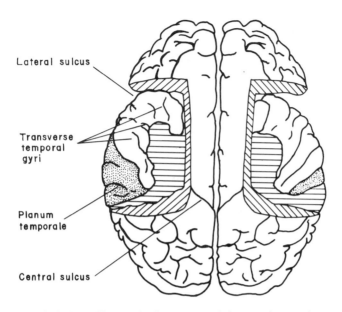

Figure 2 Hemispherical differences in the anatomy of the posterior speech area (of Wernicke). Parts of the brain lying above the upper surface of the temporal lobe have been cut away to expose the transverse temporal gyri (of Heschl) and the planum temporale which cannot be seen in the intact brain because they lie within the lateral sulcus. A horizontal cut has removed other parts of the temporal lobe's upper surface. The planum is considerably larger in the left hemisphere.

Probably the earlier observations by Flechsig 1908, Pfiefer 1936, and von Economo & Horn 1936 (cited in 94) of this left-right asymmetry of the planum were not generally accepted because the authors did not publish measurements or based their observations on small samples.

In 1969 Wada (cited in 91; see also 325) showed that the asymmetry of the planum is present at birth. In later studies the anatomical asymmetry of this major part of Wernicke's center has been confirmed on adequate samples by Astakhova & Karacheva (4), LeMay & Culebras (181a), and Witelson & Pallie (354). LeMay & Geschwind (182) report on hemispheric differences in the brain of the great apes.

Many aspects of neurophysiology applicable to man, say at the molecular and cellular level, are best studied in nonhuman primates and other experimental animals (361). Direct investigation of the problem of the organization of language in the brain cannot be carried out on experimental animals because none of them have language in the full human sense, although rudimentary forerunners of this ability may exist (86, 120, 128, 170, 269). Speech and language disorders observed following localizable brain damage provide the best evidence on the neural basis of linguistic behavior. Geschwind (91) gives an excellent compact account of the major ideas and procedures in this branch of neurolinguistics, a subject to be considered in more detail in the later section on Whitaker's model on the representation of language in the human brain. Welker (333) presents a review of some guiding concepts used during the past century of inquiry into localization of brain functions.

Some years ago several distinguished linguists, including Bloomfield (15) and Sapir (288), scoffed at the search for "speech centers," not so much from considerations of the biological evidence for or against localization but from full recognition of the social transmission of language content. Bloomfield's argument in 1933 (15, pp. 36–37) is worth quoting at length:

> Now, speech is a very complex activity, in which stimulation of every kind leads to highly specific movements of the throat and mouth; these last, moreover, are not, in a physiologic sense, "organs of speech," for they serve biologically earlier uses in man and in speechless animals. Many injuries to the nervous system, accordingly, will interfere with speech, and different injuries will result in different kinds of difficulty, but the points of the cortex are surely not correlated with specific socially significant features of speech, such as words or syntax; these appear plainly from the fluctuating and contradictory results of the search for various kinds of "speech centers." We may expect the physiologist to get better results when he looks for correlations between points of the cortex and specific physiologic activities concerned in speech, such as movement of special muscles or the transmission of kinesthetic stimuli from larynx and tongue. The error of seeking correlation between anatomically defined parts of the nervous system and socially defined activities appears clearly when we see some physiologists looking for a "visual word-center" which is to control reading and writing: one might as well look for a specific brain center for telegraphy or automobile driving or the use of any modern invention. Physiologically, language is not a unit of function, but consists of a great many activities, whose union into a single far-reaching complex of habits results from repeated stimulation during the individual's early life.

That speech has a population (social) component is fully recognized by all biologists concerned with the study of language. Nearly four decades ago Bloomfield or Sapir could not have foreseen the development of an integrated, or at least correlative, human biology of individuals *and* breeding populations nor foretold the marked extent of genetic variation within local breeding populations (37, 112), nor realized the rich data supporting localization (in a specific neurophysiological sense) of Exner's writing center. The old sociological dictum of "one human species biology—many human societies and cultures" must be rejected flatly at most fundamental levels.

Exner's center is localized at the posterior end of the second frontal convolution just anterior to the hand area of the precentral motor cortex (57, 66). Lesions in this area disrupt writing output as do lesions in some other cortical areas. Do we conclude therefore that writing is not localized in the cortex? Not so, because the specific kind of writing error *is* localized. A subject with damage to Wernicke's area cannot write dictated speech but can copy writing visually. One with a lesion in Exner's area shows change in the form of written output (91, 210, 284, 342).

The question of localization depends on what aspect of language one is interested in. Some aspects are local in the cortex, some are diffuse. For nearly every possible aspect, nearly everyone would put more localization in the cerebrum than in the foot. Penfield (262) showed that electrical stimulation of a point in Wernicke's area can disrupt speech output of a *noun* (e.g. "comb" when shown a picture of a comb) but not the *verb* "to comb" (e.g. when shown a picture of a comb the patient does not identify "comb" but may say "I comb my hair." Or when shown a picture of a foot, the patient says not "foot" but "that is what I put in my shoe.")

Part of the current difficulty in communication between biologists and linguists about speech and language is that the biological notions of "function" and "localization" are composite. Some biological things and events called "functions" are highly specific and sharply localized in some sense; others are unspecific and spread through the whole body, or even into the skin-out environment. Insulin functions in carbohydrate metabolism (and perhaps in other intracellular roles); the production of insulin in the body is localized in the β-cells lying near the center of the Islets of Langerhans in the pancreas. The function of gametes in bisexual organisms is to bring together two haploid sets of genetic material to form a diploid zygote; production of sperms and eggs in higher animals is localized in specific tissues in the gonads. Metabolism, reproduction, and mutation are three global functions basic to the operation of natural selection and the evolution and maintenance of species. The global function of locomotion is also clearly important in metabolism and reproduction. The global functions are located in all or much of the whole body. Most physiologists would localize language in the brain and not in the heart or liver, nor even in the "organs of speech." Yet one of the few known major genes with a specific effect on language production involves an enzyme mostly active in the liver (histidine α-deaminase, see below); thus at least one specific aspect of speech/language is localized in the liver. In one or more meaningful sense there are demonstrable biological speech and language centers. Many modern linguists point out that language has an important biological function. According to Hockett (127):

> The major biological function of talking is to *redistribute information* among members of a community. The kind of talking with which we do this may be called *consultative prose*. It is different from, usually duller than, some other kinds of talking, but it is the germ from which all other kinds derive. It is consultative prose that gets information shared and gets joint plans made.

Whitaker & Selnes (345) review individual and bilateral anatomical variation in the human cerebral cortex and conclude that lack of strict correspondence between lesion sites and behavioral deficits is expected.

Authorities disagree whether Broca's area is unique to the human brain [compare (22) with (342)]. Cytoarchitectural studies support the presence of a cell structure typical of the human Broca's area in apes and some Old World monkeys (164). For a review of the structure of the cerebral cortex in nonhuman primates see (260). Bogen & Bogen (20) proposed that mapping Wernicke's area with a probability distribution giving the likelihood at any locus of a language defect from a lesion at that locus would be a major step toward resolution of the long-standing controversy between topism and holism. Brain weight in normal adults varies from 680 to 1939 g. Cerebral cortical surface area varies by 310 cm². Amount of striate (visual) cortex on the outer cerebral surface varies threefold, 359 to 1308 cm². The central fissure, one of the striking landmarks on the lateral surface of the brain, may be interpreted by a gyrus connecting the frontal and parietal lobes, as in some monkeys. The planum temporale and Heschl's gyrus (including Wernicke's language area) are the most variable regions of the brain in cytoarchitecture (72). Waddington (327) reports marked variation in number and pattern of branching of the major cerebral arteries so that occlusion of any single branch would result in damage to widely different amounts of brain tissue in the language areas. In otherwise neurologically normal individuals undergoing brain surgery, even the topography of the precentral motor and postcentral sensory cortices—generally considered to be innately wired-in—may show complete reversal of the standard localization for lip and jaw movements and tongue and cheek sensations [Ojemann, cited in (345)]. In general, cortical cytoarchitecture is more variable in the right than in the left hemisphere; on both sides gyral patterns are highly variable in Broca's area [Stengel in (345)] and in the auditory cortex [Campain & Minckler in (345)]. Dobelle & Mladejovsky (in 345) found that the phosphene map (sensations of light spots produced by electrical stimulation to the striate cortex through the skull) varied considerably in 15 individuals demonstrating concomitant physiological and anatomical individual differences in brain function. Patzig (261) illustrates lateral views of the brains of identical twins with marked variation in the cortical configuration, indicating that such individual variation is nongenetic.

Kimura (157, 158) studied the hemispherical localization of the capacity to interpret numbers, words, non-sense syllables, and melodies by the method of dichotic (two ear) listening. Two different sounds are presented simultaneously through earphones to each ear. Three pairs of sounds are presented in rapid succession. The subject repeats all he hears in any order he selects. Electrophysiology shows that the right ear usually has a richer nerve supply to the left auditory cortex than does the left ear. The same holds for the tracts from the left ear to the right auditory cortex. If speech is localized in the *right* hemisphere as determined by sodium amytal tests (326), recall of digits is 89% for the left ear and 78% for the right during dichotic testing. The ear on the side opposite the hemisphere dominant for speech is superior in dichotic listening regardless of handedness. Dichotic listening tests show that speech is hemispherically localized as early as age 4 years. Dichotic tests indicate that boys are slower to develop speech asymmetry than girls just as they are well known to be slower on the average in the onset of speech.

In dichotic listening to melodies the left ear is superior, showing that the area for singing is located in the right hemisphere. This finding offers an explanation of the observation that individuals with severe central speech impediments can sing beautifully and individuals with left hemisphere dominant for speech with Broca's aphasia can sing elegantly and easily. Kimura (157) suggests that speech is distinguished from nonspeech sounds by articulability rather than by conceptual content. Vowels show weaker right-ear effect than consonant + vowel syllables.

McAdam & Whitaker (224, 344) produced the first physiological evidence for the localization of speech production in a specified convolution in the intact human brain. The experimental subjects were eight right-handed young-adult females with normal speech. Bechman miniature biopotential electrodes were attached to the skin over the precentral gyri, Broca's area, the corresponding part of the third inferior frontal convolution on the right, the mastoid processes, and on the frontal bone to serve as a ground. The subjects, starting with the vocal apparatus in the neutral position, made four sets of responses: 1. spitting gestures, 2. words of three syllables with initial "k," 3. coughs, and 4. words of three syllables with initial "p." Slow negative electrical potentials were recorded at a maximum over Broca's area in the left hemisphere (but not the right) when the polysyllabic words with initial "k" or "p" were produced. When the nonspeech spit and cough occurred the electrical potentials recorded were bilaterally symmetrical.

Eimas and associates (73) studied the discrimination of synthetic speech sounds in 1- and 4-month-old infants. The experimental stimuli were synthetic speech sounds recorded by a parallel resonance synthesizer with three variations of /b/ and three of /p/, the six stimuli having voiced onset time values of -20, 0, $+20$, $+40$, $+60$, and $+80$ msec where the minus sign indicates that the voicing occurs before, and the plus sign after, the release burst. Discrimination was measured by an increase in conditioned sucking response rate on an artificial nipple. The results show that infants 1 month old not only respond to and discriminate speech sounds but also show categorical perception of speech sounds along the voicing continuum in approximately the same manner in which adults perceive these phonemes. This is done with relatively limited exposure to speech, with practically no experience in producing speech, and with little or no differential reinforcement for speech behavior. Seemingly categorical discrimination of voiceless and voiced stops is a part of the biological makeup of the human species and this makeup is operative within the first month after birth long before the infant has learned a language.

In recent years knowledge of the circulation of blood in the brain has increased greatly, mainly due to development of quantitative measures of both global cerebral blood flow (CBF) and regional cerebral blood flow (rCBF) summarized by Ingvar & Lassen (138, 139). It is now firmly established that normal variation in CBF is determined by the activity of the cerebral neurons and that rCBF variations not only reflect the anatomical connections of blood vessels in the regions of the brain, but also can be used for indirect measurements of brain activity and its distribution in specific parts of the two hemispheres (138).

Voluntary rhythmic hand movements are accompanied by a highly localized contralateral increase in rCBF in the rolandic hand area (252), especially along the central fissure and in the postcentral areas (139). Speech and reading provoke increased rCBF in superior, anterior, and posterior language cortices (140). The amount of increase in CBF during voluntary muscle activity depends upon the effort of the subject, while localized rCBF distribution (at least in the dominant hemisphere) reflects aspects of the specific physiological events underlying the way the brain handles symbols and abstractions (138, 277).

Normal human adults readily coordinate and integrate information perceived via different sensory modalities, and much of everyday adaptive human social behavior, including language, depends on the capacity for cross-modal perceptions. Freides (81) surveys recent experimental work on cross-modal perception with human subjects (including the blind, deaf, brain damaged, as well as normal children and adults). The equivalence in visual and tactile modes is now established in preverbal children below 1 year of age without specific language training, thus ruling out verbal mediation as a basic mechanism.

Postulated relationships between cross-modal integration and specifically human language are based on a wide variety of observations on man and other animals (62, 170): (a) the early failures to demonstrate clear cross-modal perception in nonhuman primates (63, 90); (b) neuroanatomical evidence for the relative independence of auditory, visual, somesthetic association areas in nonhuman primates in contrast with their neural connectivity in man (88, 91); (c) the apparent improvement of cross-modal perception in children in step with the acquisition of language; and (d) language deficiencies in children congenitally deprived of one or more sensory modes, especially the deaf-mute and the deaf. These observations appear to support the assumption that cross-modal perception is a uniquely human capacity and is necessarily mediated by language (62).

Since 1969 Davenport and associates have demonstrated in several papers (reviewed in 62) that apes have the capacity for haptic-visual cross-modal perception of objects and multidimensional representations of those objects without previous learning involving those objects. Davenport uses "haptic" in place of "touch" to denote active manual exploration. Cowey & Weiskrantz (53) used a well-designed experiment to demonstrate cross-modal perception in rhesus macaques. Over several days they presented variously shaped objects overnight to the macaques in darkness. Some of the objects were edible and some inedible. In the dark the monkeys ate the edible objects after haptic examination. In later tests *using vision alone* the macaques routinely chose the edible objects in discrete trials composed of one edible and one inedible object, thereby demonstrating haptic-visual cross-modal perceptual equivalence in a primate phyletically divergent from man by some 30 million years. Ettlinger (74) concluded that neural connections in the cerebral cortex of man, apes, and presumably some monkeys, that are absent in prosimians and nonprimates, enable the observed greater degree of cross-modal perception in the higher primates. The recent experiments on cross-modal perception support a high degree of continuity rather than discontinuity in the neurological evolution of language capacity from apes to man—an important difference in degree rather than a radical difference in kind evolved over several millions of years, a conclusion supported by an increasing number of topics in human behavioral evolution.

Most of the concepts and methods used to examine the representation of language in the living human brain cannot be applied to fossil specimens no matter how well preserved (134, 145). Natural (144) or reconstructed (133) endocranial casts provide reliable and important data on the phylogeny of brain volume, but quite restricted evidence of highly controversial interpretation on the neural changes important for the evolution of language (133, 134). Some living people with brains smaller than those of hominids existing two or more million years ago [e.g. KNMER 1470 (see 258)] have full propositional language (184).

Figure 3 illustrates the difficulties in getting information even on the boundaries of the major lobes of the primate brain from endocranial casts. In the higher primates the detailed topography of gyri and sulci are not recorded on the surface

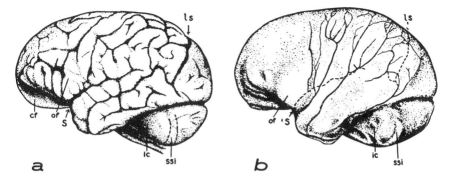

Figure 3   (a) Left lateral view of the brain of an adult male chimpanzee, X ½. The brain was hardened by injection before removal from the cranial cavity. (b) Left lateral view of the endocranial cast of the same chimpanzee to indicate how poorly the surface topography of the brain is preserved in an endocranial cast. From Weidenreich (331a).

of the endocast. The arrangement of the meningeal arteries is well preserved, but variation in these blood vessel patterns has yet to be related to language. A comparison of the brains and endocasts of chimpanzees by Le Gros Clark, Cooper & Zuckerman (49) in 1936 has long made primate paleoneurologists sceptical about the prospects of accurate identification of the functionally important small cytoarchitectural areas in fossil higher-primate specimens. But because such specimens provide the only data with geological time depth, their careful study is essential. Holloway in the US (132–134) and Kotchetkova in the USSR (161a–g) have published the most reliable studies.

The new information on brain asymmetries (181, 181a) and the open possibility that these bilateral variations can be specified with reasonable accuracy on endocranial casts provide some hope for a rich harvest of new information on the phyletic history of language in the near future.

GENETICS, SPEECH, AND LANGUAGE

In 1967 Lenneberg (184) wrote: "Pedigrees and twin studies suggest that genetic transmission is relevant to language facilitation. However, there is no need to assume 'genes for language.' " Likewise genetical investigation shows that genetic transmission is relevant to breathing and to precise manipulation using precision and power grips. And, likewise, there is no need to assume specific "genes for breathing" or "genes for manipulation." In the laboratory mouse, a mutant form of a single major gene prevents the development of the notochord and vertebral column (107). In one sense this is a "gene for breathing," and a "gene for nest building," or for all other general or specific activities including vocalization (349) of a mouse that survives with a normal vertebral column.

McKusick (225) catalogued the numerical status of known human genetic nosology in 1975: 1218 autosomal dominant, 947 autosomal recessive, and 171

X-linked gene loci, a total of 2336. Of these, hundreds of genes are known to be "relevant to language facilitation." As expected, more major genes are known to affect the four peripheral language modalities than the central language system, but many major genes do have fundamental importance for the structure and function of the central language system, starting, for instance, with those for anencephaly, or (by probable homology with a major gene known in the house mouse) for congenital absence of the corpus callosium (107), the largest single fiber tract in the human brain. Over 100 major gene loci are known to affect each of the visual, verbal, and auditory production and recognition systems, fewer are known that are specifically relevant to the tactile system. Given that all cases of severe mental retardation are relevant to language facilitation, well over 100 major gene loci are known to affect the central language system. These are catalogued in McKusick (225), many are representatively characterized in Bergsma (11), and some are discussed in more detail in Slater & Cowie (303), and in the many sources cited by the three works.

There is space here to mention only a few cases of major genes, polygenes, chromosomal abnormalities, and congenital defects of complex or unknown mode of inheritance that are of interest in the biological study of spoken or written language. Lenneberg (184) reviews sources up to 1966 (for additional surveys see 3, 233).

Histidinemia is the best known case in which a major gene has a specific, pinpointed effect on speech. This metabolic error, first described in 1961 by Ghadimi, Partington & Hunter (96), is inherited as an autosomal recessive genotype resulting in a defect in the enzyme histidine α-deaminase necessary for the normal metabolism of histidine to urocanic acid. The enzyme is active in the liver and the stratum cornium of the skin. The clinical findings in histidinemia are variable (11, 303). Subjects with the recessive genotype have increased concentrations of histidine in the blood plasma, generally above 6 mg/100 ml, and urinary output of histidine exceeds twice that normal for comparable age. Other laboratory findings include persistently low glutamic acid and high α-alanine in body fluids, and excretion of imidazolepyruvic, imidazolelactic, and imidazoleacetic acids in the urine. The sex ratio in the affected is one boy to two girls; this departure from the common sex ratio of about 1.05:1 is unexplained. Crome & Stern (56) suggest that the speech defect can be prevented, if treated early, by a diet low in histidine. As histidine is an essential amino acid required for normal growth, it cannot be eliminated from the diet while the child is growing, but it is not necessary for nitrogen balance in adults. About three-fourths of patients have specific speech difficulties, less than one-half show growth retardation, over one-third are mentally retarded, but about one-fourth are completely free from such symptoms (303). Woody, Snyder & Harris (356) suggest that inherited reduction in histidine α-deaminase activity can be expressed to a different degree in different tissues. Although most patients with histidinemia lack histadase activity in the skin, biopsies demonstrate that others have such activity, which may compensate for defective enzyme activity in the liver. A peculiar EEG pattern is found in some sibships with histidinemia (356).

Of the 10 cases of histidinemia surveyed by Witkop & Henry (355), 9 show defective speech articulation and language organization. Mispronunciations ("less" for "yes") are accompanied by a right deviation of the tongue tip and obicularis oris muscle and lateral movement of the mandible during elevation and descent in speech. The children have an auditory scramble manifested as an inability to repeat words in sequences added one at a time, a marked inability to link words together into a sentence. They have normal audiograms and normal response to sequential visual signals. Teachers characterize these children as visual learners who cannot learn by auditory means because of short auditory-memory span. The tongue is unable to perform movements independent of the mandible—"la, la, la" becomes "/ja/, /ja/, /ja/." The tongue is not able to rise to palatal contact while the mandible lowers for vowel formation. Consonants requiring independent movement of tongue and mandible (especially/t/, /d/, /n/, and /l/ are misarticulated to a degree varying with syllabic position relative to preceding and following vowels and consonants. The oral space requisite for vowel formation is reduced sporadically when the mandible assists or follows the tongue tip toward palatal contact in forming consonants. Errors occur in both syntax and noun usage.

The biochemical path(s) relating the enzyme deficiency to the auditory and speech production difficulties is (are) unknown. It is not known whether the defects result from accumulation of metabolic products such as imidazolelactic acid and imidazolepyruvic acid or the absence of metabolites like formiminoglutamic acid. Although the primary ahistidasia continues throughout life, the deleterious effects probably are restricted to the period of prenatal and infantile development.

Sex controlled or sex modified genic expression occurs when a genotype is expressed in both sexes but in a different manner in each. Bernstein (12) considered that the singing voice in adult Europeans is a sex-controlled trait with the low bass voice in males and the high soprano in females controlled by the same genotype, A^1A^1, the high tenor in males and the low alto in females by A^2A^2, and the baritone in males and mezzo-soprano in females by the heterozygote A^1A^2. Later studies showed that a single pair of alleles with simple expression in the two sexes is not sufficient to explain the facts, which await detailed analysis (307). The development of the voice box in the divergent male and female direction takes place at puberty under the influence of a testosterone-induced multiplication of cells in the thyroid and cricoid cartilages in boys at about the same time as the spurt in trunk length (314). Twin, family line, and population studies indicate that a polygenic mode of inheritance with many independently varying factors determines variation in voice types. The proportion of men with basso and women with soprano voices decreases from northern to southern Europe. Under Bernstein's single locus model the frequency of the basso-soprano allele (A^1) has a maximum of 61% along the northern coast of Germany and a minimum of about 12% in Sicily (13). Although the single locus model is now abandoned, there is good evidence that differences in multiple gene frequencies must account for the different frequencies of voice types in different populations (307).

Luchsinger (207) found that the voices of 28 pairs of monozygotic twins were very similar, the greatest difference being four half-tones in male identical twins 41 years old. A study of Japanese children analyzed by Schull & Neel (293) is the most elaborate attempt to measure the behavioral consequences of inbreeding in a human population. The study observed children in Hiroshima and Nagasaki. None of the parents of the children had received irradiation from the atomic bombs. The inbred children reported here are the offspring of single first cousins and the controls were children of parents whose relation was more remote than that of third cousins. "Age when walked" and "age when talked" are two behavioral criteria commonly used in pediatric and parental appraisals of child development. They are, of course, subject to errors of parental recall and may be biased by cultural norms. The mean age when talked was 11.81 months in the control boys, 12.60 in the offspring of first cousins, giving an inbreeding effect of 0.79 and a change with inbreeding of 6.7%. The mean age when talked for the control girls was 10.38, and 10.82 in the offspring of first cousins, giving an inbreeding effect of 0.44 and a change with inbreeding of 4.2%. As in 16 other behavior measurements, the mean of the inbred children is significantly depressed (at the 1% level for age when talked) compared with the mean of the control children. The inbred children as a whole come from families of lower socioeconomic status than the controls as measured by parental occupation and education, density of persons in the household, and food expenditures per person per month. However, none of the apparent inbreeding depression for age when talked could be attributed significantly to socioeconomic variation.

Lewitter, DeFries & Singer (190) performed a path analysis on 64 families with sons having a diagnosed reading disability. In general, educational level and occupational class of parents were found to have relatively little influence on their son's reading recognition, reading comprehension, spelling, perceptual speed, or perceived spatial relations, but the magnitude of the direct path between parent's and son's test scores suggested that the heritability of performance on these tests may be moderately high (0.3 to 0.7).

Moorhead, Mellman & Wenar (236) studied a family with an autosomal translocation involving chromosomes 13/22 and a total complement of 45 chromosomes in the mother and four of her six children. The father and the fifth child are karyotypically normal, and the youngest child has Down's syndrome with trisomy for chromosome 21 and does not possess the translocation. The father has normal intelligence and speech; the mother has normal intelligence and speech function except for a mild speech hesitation. Failure of speech is present in three of the four translocation-bearing children and does not seem to be causally related to intelligence level. The boy with IQ of 68 had not developed speech at 7 11/12 years of age. The 6-year-old girl has never developed intelligible speech and has an IQ of 38. The girl of 3 5/12 years spoke first words at 1 and spoke in sentences at 3 5/12 years; her IQ is 70. Her speech is the best developed of the children, but most of it is repetition of the sentences of others; she initiates simple but complete sentences. The youngest child with the translocation had not used words at age 2 1/12 years. The karyotype common to these four children and the mother is characterized by a hemizygous deletion for whatever genes occupied the eliminated minute element from chromosome 13. Seemingly, a double dose of genes at this locus is necessary for normal development of speech.

A syndrome involving deletion of about one-half of the short arm of chromosome 5 was discovered by Lejeune and associates (179) and named *cri du chat*, an unusual feature of the syndrome being a plaintive continual crying, particularly by younger children, which resembles the mewing of a cat. All patients with this chromosomal deletion have severe mental retardation but variable life span. Legros (178) published a phonogram of the cry of an infant with cri du chat syndrome. Ward, Engle & Nance (327b) describe the laryngomalacia in 4 cases of cri du chat syndrome. The long, curved, flappy epiglottis, narrow diamond-shaped arrangement of the vocal cords during inspiration, and anterior approximation of the vocal cords during inspiration, and anterior approximation of the vocal cords with an abnormally large air space in the posterior commissure during phonation are responsible for the strident, cat-like cry.

Isochromosomes are formed if the centromere divides transversely, instead of longitudinally, in the second meiotic division; as a result the long arms of sister chromatids form one chromosome, and the short arms form another chromosome which in acrocentric autosomes is commonly lost (307). Wang et al (327b) reported two cases of isochromosomes 16, one with faulty speech characterized by spitting out words, the other mute.

Cleft uvula is a frequent cause of hypernasality of speech. The cleft is usually congenital, varies from a small notch to a complete cleft extending to the posterior border of the soft palate and is a result of the failure of complete fusion of the uvular portion of the lateral halves of the soft palate during embryogenesis. The mode of inheritance is unknown but probably is conditioned by minor gene(s) similar to those of cleft palate. The anatomical defect contributes to the palatal insufficiency syndrome involving incomplete closure of soft palate and pharynx during phonation and results in hypernasality. The trait is of special anthropological interest in that its prevalence is about 1 in 71 in European live births, less in African blacks, and greater in Asians, 1 in 10 to 1 in 5 (228–230).

Sankoff (287) presents several areas where historical linguistics (311a) and molecular and evolutionary genetics employ similar mathematical models and several where they are quantitatively different. Although the two fields are not perfect metaphors of one another, their attributes in common are sometimes so striking that many descriptive and analytical aspects are interchangeable. He suggests that models of gradual gene replacement seem a likely place to look for universals and variables of linguistic change. There is a striking parallel between the controversy surrounding chemical paleogenetics (362) and that in lexicostatistics. Cavalli-Sforza (36) and Cavalli-Sforza & Feldman (38, 39) discuss a number of similarities and dissimilarities in social-cultural-linguistic and biological evolution.

An identical capacity for language among all extant human races suggest that this capacity must have evolved before racial diversification (184). Conclusions about the existence of human races prior to historical records are usually based on skeletal, especially cranial evidence. With multivariate statistical methods and suitable samples of modern skulls of known race, racial identification may reach a reliability of 90% (167). Most anthropologists assume that the races of modern man date back no further than the formation of Homo sapiens as a species distinct from H. erectus (137). Campbell (34) divides H. sapiens into two sets of chronological subspecies with a 50,000 B.P. time-line separating the living geographical subspecies from the four fossil subspecies of Europe, Africa, western Asia, and eastern Asia, all of which are separated from the late subspecies of H. erectus by 300,000 B.P. If Le Gros Clark

(48) is correct in assigning Steinheim and Swanscombe skulls to *H. sapiens,* then our species has existed for at least 250,000 years. Coon (51), with minority support from other paleoanthropologists, claims that five contemporary major races may have existed for as long as 500,000 years.

Cavalli-Sforza & Bodmer (37) use a model of evolution based on a uniform rate of genetic drift, a measure of genetic distance based on gene frequencies, the observed gene frequencies for 16 blood group systems, and an assumed genetic isolation of the American Indians from Australian and Indonesian peoples 15,000 years ago, to estimate the times when the human population separated into three major races: Negroid/Mongoloid 41,000, Negro/Caucasoid 33,000, and Mongoloid/Caucasoid 21,000 years ago with large standard errors. Nei & Roychoudhury (243), using data on protein genetic polymorphisms and rather different theoretical assumptions, arrive at estimates of 120,000, 115,000, and 55,000 years for the three separations.

The plant cytogeneticist Darlington (58, 59) deduced a genetic component of language from an observed correspondence between ABO blood group isogenes (map lines showing equal gene frequencies) and θ and $\eth$ isophones in the south and west of Europe. Darlington concluded that evolutionary changes in grammar, etymology, and phonetics are independent in the long run, that only in phonetic evolution may we expect to find "a serious genetic component," and that "the genetic preference of the group rather than the genetic capacity of the individual is what determines phonetic evolution" (59). Mourant & Watkin (238) assembled additional data from Wales and the Western Countries in support of the correspondence. In an expansion of this hypothesis, Brosnahan (29) argues for the existence of both hereditary and environmental components of language operating at the individual and the breeding population levels. He does not identify specific linguistic phenotype-genotype correspondences nor does he estimate the relative importance of the genetic and nongenetic components for particular cases on linguistic change.

Darlington did not suggest that the ABO genotype determined whether a specific individual articulated the voiceless fricative in *thin* or the voiced fricative in *then* (θ and $\eth$) but rather that the ABO gene frequencies reflect local population biological history and are associated with genes at other loci which influence via anatomical variation the production of those fricatives. Both θ and $\eth$ vary widely in North American Indian languages in regions where the blood group O gene is fixed (the genes for group A and B being absent) and the phonetic distinction is not correlated with the gene frequency cline centering in the area of the world's highest frequency of group A among the western Algonkian Blackfoot and Blood Indians.

Although for several years Darlington's blood group-language notions were a prominent part of the display on evolutionary biology in the British Museum (Natural History), generally they have been ignored by both linguists and geneticists —perhaps the best single exposé is that of Hogben (129), who is both expert geneticist and competent linguist.

Brosnahan (28), who argues that languages show different degrees of progressive evolution (29), assembled a large body of evidence he believed to support the

Darlington hypothesis. Both authors conclude that [th] has disappeared from central Europe because of gradual changes in the vocal tract and that the change is due to a slow diffusion of genes through the local breeding populations from east to west. Roberts (278) concluded that the known distribution of local anatomical variation in the speech apparatus does not support Darlington's thesis, and Lenneberg (183) doubts that minimization of effort is indeed demonstratably responsible for sound shifts; the only evidence to the contrary I have found is Shohara's (298) study of physiological factors in Coptic sound changes.

Twins, on the average, are retarded in speech development compared with singletons of the same age, sex, and social class (30). Bulmer thinks that the retardation is probably due to the fact that mothers of twins have less time to spend with each child and that the twins may develop an idiosyncratic language of their own. He surveys the evidence that the development of speech is strongly affected by the amount of contact with adults, only children showing a striking superiority in language development compared with children reared with one or more siblings, and children from institutions often show a marked retardation although the latter set of children differ in ways other than degree of contact with adults (30). Several twin studies report that a concordant history of speech development is observed in about 90% of monozygous but only 40% of dizygous pairs (184).

In her review of the evidence for a genetic component in the determination of handedness, Levy (187) speculated that cerebral and manual dominance share an underlying genetic mechanism. 99% of right-handers have left language laterality, but only 53–65% of left-handers have left language lateralization. The evidence is clearly against the hypothesis that hand dominance itself induces contralateral language dominance. She points out strong evidence for individual variation in utilization of uncrossed pyramidal tracts and that cerebral dominance might be a perfect predictor of manual dominance given information on the ipsi- or contralaterality of motor control pathways (187). Luria (210) found that a family history of left-handedness was a better predictor of cerebral lateralization than was the actual handedness of the subjects themselves.

Levy & Nagylaki (189a) proposed genotypes for handedness and cerebral dominance that would account for the observed proportions of left- and right-handers among offspring of parents who are both left-handed, both right-handed, and of discordant handedness, as well as for aphasia resistance and recovery rates in right vs left handers (188). One pair of autosomal genes, $L,l,$ are postulated to control hemispherical language dominance and a second pair, $C,c,$ to control whether dominant control is contralateral or ipsilateral to cerebral dominance. The allele L is dominant for left hemisphere language and the allele C is dominant for contralateral hand control (188).

Now that techniques for studying cerebral asymmetry of function in intact, normal populations (157, 158, 181a) without injections are available, Levy's results give promise that new genetic studies in which cerebral and other lateralizations are specified on the same individuals in adequate samples of genetic relatives and foster children will produce interpretations of fundamental importance for understanding the interplay of environmental and genetic factors in speech and language.

WHITAKER'S MODEL OF PERIPHERAL AND CENTRAL LANGUAGE SYSTEMS

H. A. Whitaker (338, 340, 342) developed a functional anatomical model of how language is represented in the brain. His is the first model that attempts to correlate brain structure and function with contemporary linguistic theory. And his model incorporated all the well-tested features of the models based on neurophysiology without major regard to linguistics as developed in the USSR by Luria (208) and in the Boston Veterans Administration Hospital by Geschwind (88) and Green (101). In addition to incorporating linguistics, Whitaker's model is the first to include the extremely important relationships between central and peripheral mechanisms, as well as the role of thalamic and other subcortical nuclei (248, 249, 249a, 279) in the working of the central language system. This multidisciplinary model is one product of the new hybrid science of neurolinguistics. Until recently, the term neurolinguistics (341) was in more common use in Russia and Europe than in the United States (209, 222). Lebrun (176) gives a brief history of neurolinguistic models of language and speech. Green (101) discusses general problems in the construction of such models.

Neurolinguistics assumes that a proper and adequate understanding of language depends upon correlating information from the several fields concerned with the structure and function of both language and the brain (341). For most workers active in the field, the philosophical basis of neurolinguistics is a mild but reasonable form of materialism (80), a position incompatible with strict behaviorism but fully compatible with Chomskian views (126). Fromkin (83) summarizes performance error data from normal subjects and presents evidence for the psychological reality of phonetic, syntactic, and semantic features, for phonological sequential constraints, phonological rules, and underlying representations, arguing that speech errors are not random but are predictable constrained by linguistic organization. Watt (331) reviews recent literature on the psychological reality of linguistic constructs.

Whitaker's model is an extrapolation from a wide spectrum of data (summarized in Figure 4) relating to brain structures and aphasic symptomology (40, 87, 89, 91, 93, 100, 163, 189, 208–213, 217, 234, 244, 251, 262, 284, 292, 343). Just as single function theories that language is solely a product of the brain's ability to associate stimuli (302) are overly simple (42), so theories that all aphasic symptoms are due to disruption of the brain's ability to associate stimuli are likewise overly simple (342).

The model consists of peripheral and central language systems. The peripheral language system contains four structurally and functionally distinct subsystems: 1. speaking and 2. listening systems are present in all human languages and thus are termed primary production and recognition systems; 3. writing, and 4. reading systems are absent in many languages and thus termed secondary production and recognition systems. These systems are biologically distinct because they use distinct sense receptors (eye and ear) and distinct effector nerve-muscle-support tissues (the

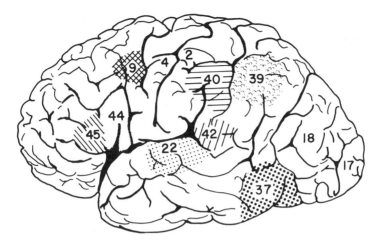

Figure 4   A more detailed sketch of the same brain shown in Figure 1, showing the surface location of some of the areas related to speech and language. The numbers refer to Broadmann's cytoarchitectural areas; see the text for more details. The cross-hatched part of area 9 is Exner's writing center; area 22 is the auditory association cortex and is a part of Wernicke's speech center; area 37 is the visual-auditory association cortex; area 39 occupies the angular gyrus; area 40 is in the supramarginal gyrus; and area 44 with the adjacent part of area 45 is Broca's speech center. Drawn from photograph reproduced from Crosby, Humphrey & Lauer (57).

arm/hand and the vocal tract) but the effectors may be generalized to other motor systems in man. Both primary and secondary systems link production and reception by high level feedback compatible with the meaning or semantics of the intended production (174). These mechanisms coordinate the speaking and hearing modalities with one another where the feedback is by way of the eighth cranial (acoustic) nerve, proprioceptors being absent from the muscles of the voice box (22). Two types of feedback are proposed, one being peripheral and system-specific (216) and the other general to the central language system.

The speaking-hearing system is the primary production and recognition system in the sense that it is difficult to imagine speaking with an organ other than the vocal tract or hearing with an organ other than the ear, whereas one can easily substitute the foot for the dominant hand in writing in the sand, or substitute the finger for the eye in reading braille (342). The primary system transmits by acoustic wave and the secondary system by conventional graphic patterns received visually or tactically. In a given individual all four peripheral systems, although of separate evolutionary history, converge in being a part of the same language system. The four peripheral modalities are shown in Figure 5.

The central language system contains three or (on a different view) four linguistically distinct components collectively called the grammar: 1. semantic, 2. syntactic

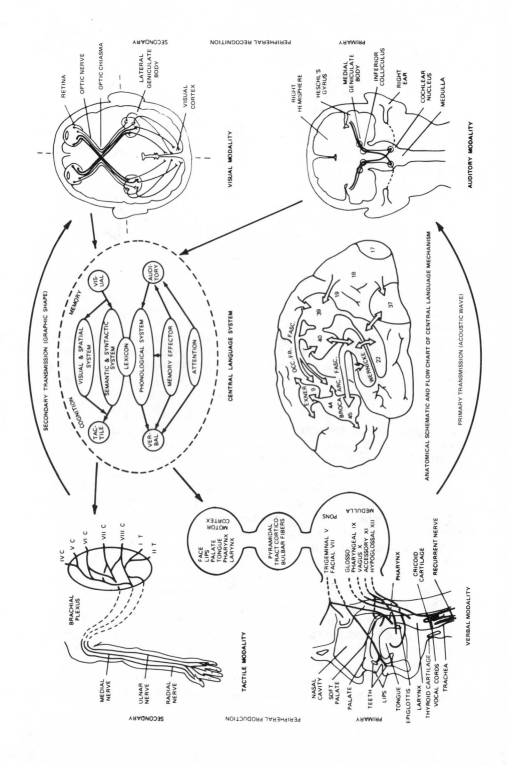

(or semantic/syntactic), 3. phonological, and 4. lexical. The central language system uses an appropriate set of semantic, syntactic, and phonological rules to define words (morphemes) and sentences.

Chomsky's (43) distinction between *competence* (the grammar of the language, what one must know to know the language) and *performance* (what one actually says and hears) is of obvious heuristic value in allowing grammarians who control linguistic input to ignore "extraneous" features of output such as slips of the tongue, accents, stammers, and the like. Chomsky holds that the theory of performance is different from and irrelevant to the theory of competence, which he makes the central concern of linguistics (126). Other students of language, whether attracted to biology or avoiding it, find some applications of the distinction difficult. Lenneberg (184) and Weigl & Bierwisch (332) present examples of the theoretical confusion resulting from attempts to apply the competence/performance distinction to aphasia. These authors suggest that competence remains intact in aphasia while performance is changed, and that if brain damage cannot affect competence, then competence is not a property of the brain. In a 1968 paper, Whitaker (337) attempted redefinition of the two terms in order to meet difficulties in their application to aphasiology; in later papers (339, 341, 342) he recommends abandoning the distinction altogether. Bever (14) questions the domain of a science of linguistics that does not investigate actual language behavior. McNeill (226) and Palmer (254) find the distinction hard to apply in grammatical studies where the investigator does not control input, and Rodrigues (280) was unable to use the distinction satisfactorily in a study of English speaking and writing in children bilingual in Spanish and English.

Whitaker (342) concludes that present evidence from aphasia is equivocal on the problem of anatomical separation of deep and surface linguistic structures, although the data tend to support a model with separate surface and deep components. With reservations, he provisionally avoids modeling deep and surface components of grammar. Rather grammar is modeled to contain three components: the syntactic/semantic system, the phonological system, and the lexicon. The grammar integrates input and output of the four peripheral language systems by employing four tracking systems (see Figure 5). See Hockett (126) for a criticism of Chomsky's views and Postal (267) for a fuller description of general grammatical properties. Parkinson (255) gives a critique of Chomsky's views on linguistic infinity.

Most neurolinguists are more comfortable with the concept of language universals than with the competence/performance dichotomy (341, 342), despite the fact that at the level of individual neuronal and glial cells the representation of language in the brain cannot be identical in all members of the species. Individuals with full language capacity vary up to a factor of two in the number of cerebral neurons (22, 184, 317, 318); the rate of production of new brain neurons slows markedly after 18 weeks of gestation and effectively stops after 18 months of age (67); in adults some

---

Figure 5 Peripheral and central language systems as modeled by H. A. Whitaker. Redrawn with modifications from (341).

10,000 neurons die at random each day in each brain (9, 361). But at the tissue level the language areas of the cortex and their interconnections together with their connections to subcortical nuclei may be assumed to represent a universal biological basis for speech and language in all normal, intact, developed members of *Homo sapiens* (342).

A language model for the brain must provide for convergence or complete transfer between the modalities. This is done by what Whitaker calls the central language system (enclosed in the dashed ellipse of Figure 5), a system that corresponds to the grammar, and which, as mentioned above, has a minimum of semantic/syntactic, phonological, and lexical components. Tatham (316), MacKay (215), Whitaker (339), and Denes & Pinson (64a) discuss the tracking mechanism (represented in Figure 5 by the four ellipses labeled Verbal, Auditory, Tactile, and Visual) which convert linguistically motivated units into units which represent motor commands to the articulatory muscles.

The major pathways (Figure 5) for the transfer of symbols in the central language system are well established although the detailed mechanism of the transfer is unknown (87–93, 341, 342): the angular gyrus connects with the visual association cortex [area 19; see (27)]; the supramarginal gyrus connects with the somatic afferent association cortex (areas 7 and 40); the posterior part of Wernicke's area and the auditory association area connects with the association cortex surrounding Heschl's gyrus (area 42); the long fibers of the arcuate fasciculus connects parts of Wernicke's area with parts of Broca's and Exner's centers; the long fibers of the occipitofrontal fasciculus connect the angular and supramarginal gyri with the precentral motor cortex (area 4).

Whitaker (341, 342) postulates that the regions of the cortex representing the semantic/syntactic component and the lexicon are localized in the posterior part of Wernicke's area, the auditory association area, the supramarginal and angular gyri. The numerous cortical interconnections of the inferior parietal lobe and the superior temporal lobe, and the lack of subcortical connections to these parts, led Geschwind (91–93) to suggest that evolutionary reorganization of this area was a prerequisite for the capacity of language in man. Paleoanthropologists have long recognized that the inferior parietal and superior temporal lobes show the greatest quantitative change in the evolution of the hominid brain (22, 48, 132, 144, 161e-f).

The cytoarchitecture of the cortical language areas is clearly distinct in the different composition of the six cell layers with differing kinds of neurons and arrangements of dendrites and axons (27, 106, 184, 361). Bailey & von Bonin (7) and Schaltenbrand (289a) provide a critical account of Brodmann's *Lokalisationslehre.* Whitaker (341, 342) calls attention to the remarkable correspondence of the different Broadmann areas with the "areas" classically identified with the central language system: Broadmann's area 44 with Broca's, a part of area 9 with Exner's, the primary motor and sensory areas with 4 and 2 respectively, the supramarginal gyrus with parts 40 and 42, the angular gyrus with 39, Wernicke's with 42 and parts of 22, Heschl's gyrus with 41, and the auditory association area with the main part of 22. Because the architectonic areas of Broadmann show less variation between individuals than the surface topography of the cortex mapped by major ridges and grooves—which show considerable variation between individuals, including within pairs of monozygotic twins (261), it is claimed that these cytoarchitectonic areas are the anatomical correlates of the central language system (341, 342). Richman et al (275) present a mechanical model of convolutional development in the cerebral cortex. However, it seems likely that the more classical names for the speech and language centers based on the superficial landmarks of sulci and gyri will continue to be used.

Memory is a complex of at least short- and long-term varieties (283). The type of memory that is part of the central language system may be called verbal memory and is a topic we will return to later. The lexicon is a component of the central language system whether localized at the tissue level or not (313, 341, 342).

The fact that retrograde and anterograde amnesia do not affect current language shows that there is a memory system quite independent from language, which in Figure 5 is simply labeled "memory." The anatomical locus at the tissue level for this kind of memory, if any, is also unknown although the system which stores experiences in memory, the memory effector system, is located in large part in the hippocampal gyri and adjacent limbic structures (250). Disruption of the short-term memory system, as in Wernicke-Korsakoff's syndrome, with the result that the patient cannot remember things or events for more than 15–20 minutes, affects the central language system only to the extent that such patients cannot learn new words (342). Details of the physiological and molecular basis of all memory systems are still unknown (283), and, as mentioned above, the extent of anatomical localization, if any, beyond that of diffuse large biomolecules, is uncertain. The various forms of aphasia strongly indicate that the memory system is functionally separate from the language system regardless of localization. Some recent review papers on the possible biochemical storage of the lexicon include Kimble (155, 156), Pribram (270), and Rozin (283).

The requirement that long-term memory of the lexicon must be "content-address-able" in recall and not merely "location-addressable" presents both theoretical and experimental difficulties in supposing that long-term memory operates according to purely local storage principles. Julesz & Pennington (149) suggested that certain types of composite stimulus may be stored in memory in a holographic rather than a photographic manner. Longuet-Higgins (204) expounds the hypothesis that time-varying patterns can be stored in an analogous manner, and proposed the term "holophone" for such a system. If memorization of short sequences does involve holophonic as opposed to gramophonic principles, the problem of content-address-ing is immediately solved and the parts of the brain storing the memories in question should exhibit periodic response characteristics which may be directly accessible to neurophysiological study.

Whitaker's model requires minor modification to include separate boxes for short- and long-term memories, especially as linguistic input and output to and from short-term memory may underlie man's unusual abilities for sustained minding in prolonged situations with everchanging makeup, as in group hunting or manufac-ture of complex implements (141, 144).

The model separates the system that executes memory storage from the storage itself (283, 312). In addition to nonverbal memory, several human faculties (emo-tions, probably general cognition, problem solving, visual-spatial pattern processing) are independent of the major parts of the central language system but are related to or make use of language. Aside from providing a box for "attention," for reasons discussed in (340) Whitaker does not model the effect of emotion on the operation of the central language system because intuitively emotion is less closely related than other included systems in terms of rules, units, and components. See Grossman (106) for details on the problem of emotion and language.

Penfield & Roberts (262) were first to suggest that parts of the thalamus must be included in the central language system, based mostly on the observation that electrical stimulation of the left pulvinar (but not the right in individuals with left hemispherical dominance) causes anomia, and damage to other left-sided thalamic nuclei may cause aphasia. Ojemann, Fedio & Van Buren (249), Ojemann & Ward (249a), and Riklan & Levita (276) review the role of the thalamus in the central language system. The pulvinar is phylogenetically late in evolution of the thalamus and is more specialized in man than in other primates (48). Emotions influence the central language system through the frontal lobes or the thalamus (57). The reticular activitating system controls attention (217).

The special box for the visual and spatial systems is supported by studies on brain lesions showing that a neuronal pathway between peripheral tactile and visual systems must exist independently of the central language system, because a meaningless sequence of letters can be copied without invoking any part of that system (342). Problem solving abilities and general cognitive functions are combined in the model as a general cognitive system labeled simply "cognition." See Rosenzweig & Bennett (282) and Worden, Swazey & Adelman (357) for reviews of the neurological aspects of these topics.

Current knowledge on impairment of the phonological component is surveyed by Blumstein (16, 17), Johns & Darley (146), Kinsbourne (159), Lecours & Lhermitte (177), and Luria (210). Schnitzer (290) presents evidence for specific losses of phonological rules including laxing and velar softening; his research supports the generative phonological model developed by Chomsky & Halle (46).

Additional information on the structure and function of the peripheral language production and recognitions systems are in a wide variety of handbooks [including (57, 150, 160, 184, 289a)]; several references are of interest to the neurolinguistics of the auditory modality (40, 223), tactile modality (110), verbal modality (147, 291, 315, 322), and visual modality (9, 106).

TOOLS AND LANGUAGE

The manufacture of tools has long been regarded as a sign of human status [Benjamin Franklin in (346), see also (246)]. It is supposed that (a) tool-making involves foresight as to the use of the tool, and (b) that tools are made by techniques learned from others and involve symbolic communication, presumably by language. Young (361) points out that all organisms show "foresight" or prediction in much of their behavior, and that the manufacture of tools is observed in chimpanzees (97) and other animals (108, 246); for example, birds make nests with the standard techniques that are not learned from others, but tits learn by imitation and share a tradition of opening milk bottles (220). It cannot be assumed dogmatically that all hominoids that make tools following a standard technique have language (361).

Washburn (328, 330) showed that much of what we consider anatomically characteristic of modern man, for example, the reduction of the face and jaws relative to the neurocranium, evolved long after the use of tools made by standardized techniques.

Hall (108) points out the important distinction between the occasional use of implements in agonistic behavior, grooming, courtship, and nest building which are special adaptations with no particular significance in the evolution of "intelligent" tool use, and the daily use of implements in hominid food getting, which was basic in the early evolution of material culture.

The neural delay required when some extraorganic tool is interposed between stimulus and response probably has much to do with the further development of cognitive behavior in hominids and perhaps with the first ability to symbol and the start of language (305, 306).

Tool use (but not standardized manufacture) has been postulated by Leakey for *Ramapithecus* in East Africa 14 million years ago (175) on the basis of an ungulate humerus that shows signs of use as a club. Mamak (218) has speculated that *Ramapithecus* in southern Asia must have had tools because the canines are reduced and the creatures could not have survived without some substitute means of defense.

The earliest evidence for stone tool manufacture after a fixed and set pattern now goes back 2.5 to 3 million years ago in East Africa (141). These pebble tools were made with a few simple acts of a single chipping operation. Isaac (141) assumes they could have been manufactured by a primate of pongid status. Although pongids in the wild have not been observed to make stone tools, they have learned to do so in captivity (358). Montagu (235) is less cautious in extending language back 1.75 million years on the basis of "the grammatical precision of toolmaking" on the living floors of Bed I in Olduvai Gorge.

Bordes (24) discusses the parallelism between the increasing complexity of the brain from australopithecines to Upper Paleolithic man and the increasing complexity of the techniques used to work stone by Paleolithic peoples. Tobias (317) gives the cranial capacity of eight adult samples of *Australopithecus* (sensu lato) as ranging from 435 to 540 cc, and that of three specimens assigned to *Homo habilis* from 633 to 684 cc. These small-brained hominids reached a first level of abstract thought in comprehending that there is a cutting edge inside suitable rocks which can be released by some blows with another stone. Variations on the technique (by facial working, pointing a chopping tool to make a proto-handax) lasted over a million years from 3.6 million years up to the hominids at the bottom of Bed II in Olduvai, which some classify as small pithecanthropines.

The second level of abstraction achieved in the lower Acheulean by true pithecanthropines with medium size brains [the range in endocranial volume for 13 *Homo erectus* is 750 to 1225 cc, with a mean of 935 cc (317)], and perhaps by other unknown hominids, involved the idea that not only a cutting edge, but also a standard shape can be obtained at will from a suitable rock. The manufacture of hand-axes was facilitated by the observation that working with soft bones or wood produced a cutting edge less sinuous, straighter, and sharper than working with a stone hammer.

A third level of abstraction was reached by middle Acheulean hominids of Swanscombe and Steinheim levels. Coon (51) gives the cranial capacity of the incomplete Swanscombe skull as falling in the range 1275–1325 cc and the estimated capacity of the Steinheim skull as 1145 cc. This third level is marked by the invention of Levallois flaking techniques. By mastery of several different flaking techniques—flat vs steep flaking vs striking off the flake from the shaped core—the tool maker now predetermines the shape of the tool before striking it out of the stone. There were probably several independent discoveries of Levallois technique in Africa and in Europe, where the method seems to appear in the lower part of Middle Acheulean about 300,000 years ago (23). The skillfully made Upper Paleolithic and Chalcolithic blades are an elaboration of the Levallois technique.

A fourth level of abstraction invented by large-brained *Homo sapiens* in the Upper Paleolithic involved representative art based on the ability to separate the shape from the object shaped. Drawing or engraving lines on bone or stone is older than true representative art, dating from the Acheulean Pech de l'Azè. Accurate representation in three dimensions was achieved in Aurignacian I at Vogelherd, when two-dimensional drawings were still crude in other Aurignacian I sites (221).

The concept of transmission of force by the punch technique may date from the Mousterian, and the abstraction of the multiplication of force by first and second order levers was made at the Swanscombe level, and by third order levers, which are used in spear throwers, at least by Solutrean times.

Multiple tools go back at least to the Acheulean. Composite tools were quite exceptional in the Mousterian, but common in the Upper Paleolithic. Lieberman (196) points out that the Olduwan and other Lower Paleolithic pebble tools could be made using a phrase structure grammar but that Levallois toolmaking presupposes a transformational grammar which formally incorporates a memory. The makers of pebble tools had to keep only two things in mind: (*a*) the last chip made, and (*b*) the final form of the tool being made. A memory of the operations involved in intermediate stages is not necessary. The makers of Levalloisian tools must keep in memory a particular functional attribute of the striking platform and the intermediate operations that change the upper surface of the core (23). As phrase structure grammars cannot formally account for the syntax of human language (41, 43), so by analogy they cannot account for the Levalloisian techniques of tool manufacture (see also 117).

Semenov (297), by reconstructing the probable process of working, concluded that a majority of Mousterian stone tools were made by Neanderthalers with dominant right hands. From a multivariate analysis of the small sample of recovered hand bones representing both sides, Musgrave (239) judged that Neanderthal man was not as strongly right-handed as modern man. LeMay (180) considers that the left-right differences in the angle of the lateral fissure observed on the endocranial cast indicates that the La Chapelle-aux-Saints Neanderthal man had the anatomical asymmetry association with functional differentiation of Wernicke's speech center in recent *Homo sapiens.* From an examination of the position of fractures made by blows with an implement on 42 baboon skulls collected from the Pleistocene sites of Taung, Sterkfontein, and Makapansgat, Dart (60) concluded that the South African australopithecines had apparently developed a preference for using the right hand, perhaps by 2 million years ago.

FOSSIL HOMINIDS AND ARTICULATE SPEECH

Although the larynx and the supralaryngeal vocal tract through the throat, mouth, and nose are homologous in all higher primates (68, 241, 242, 351, 352), the size and shape of the hard and soft tissues of the tract differ in modern *Homo sapiens* from that in the living pongids, dryopithecines, ramapithecines, australopithecines, *Homo habilis, Homo erectus,* and *Homo sapiens neanderthalensis.* The voice box of nonhuman primates is in slight to close contact with the soft palate and the base of the tongue, the airway flowing directly from the larynx into the mouth. This structure of the vocal tract is one reason why chimpanzees, for example, cannot make long resonant sounds (69, 79, 153, 154, 351, 352). As one consequence of man's upright posture and the bending of the cranio-facial axis, the voice box in man is moved down the throat away from contact with the soft palate, with the base of the tongue forming the anterior wall of an elongated pharynx, thus forming the lower part of an oral chamber that makes possible the human sort of vocal performance (192, 193, 201, 202). The reduction of the jaws and snout was important for the acoustics of man's articulate speech by the opening out and the broadening of the floor of the jaws and the transfer of the bony braces of the mandibular symphasis from inside to outside to give more room for tongue movement (150, 184).

The increased length and bending of the supralaryngeal voice tube is of no advantage in breathing or swallowing, and is a disadvantage in the greater probability of fatal choking on objects lodged in the pharynx (241) and in the higher probability of wet and dry drowning (350). Kirchner (160) estimates that the respiratory efficiency of the bent adult human supralaryngeal airways is about half that of the straight airway of the newborn. Lieberman (194) suggests that the disadvantages are outweighed by the selective advantage of a vocal apparatus capable of producing stable sapiens-like articulate speech. Bosma (25) points out that the principal sensory-cued motor performances and the lower supralaryngeal tract are those of position maintenance by the pharynx and the mouth, of pharyngeal participation in tidal respiration, and of pharyngeal swallowing, and because these activities are performed much more frequently than speech, infers that speech is of little significance as a mechanism effecting the muscular and skeletal form of the air and food tubes.

Lieberman (195) marks the final crucial stage in the evolution of *human* language by the development of the bent two-tube supralaryngeal vocal tract. The bending of the vocal tract consequent on the bending of the craniofacial axis permits modern man to generate supralaryngeal vocal tract configurations that involve abrupt discontinuities at the midpoint (tongue to palate) analogous to a pipe organ with two differently shaped tubes (194).

DuBrul (68) argued that the assumption of erect, bipedal posture and locomotion produced morphological changes in the cranium, larynx, pharynx, and oral cavity that were the prime factors in the evolution of human speech and language. Today most human biologists, including DuBrul (69), believe that the primary organ in the evolution of articulate speech is the brain, in particular the cerebral cortex, and that the peripheral structures of the oral cavity, pharynx, and larynx are secondary (184, 309). Therefore, most biological anthropologists today are sceptical that we can find "stigmata" of articulate speech in the hard or soft parts of the peripheral speech apparatus (70, 323, 324). Hooton (135, p. 169) reported that "The presence of well developed genial tubercles is the surest anatomical evidence of articulate speech that the skeleton affords. But a poor development of these bony spines to which the tongue muscles are attached is no evidence at all that the possessor is or was unable to speak." It follows that absence of genial tubercles in a neanderthal man does not make him dumb because they are known to be absent in some "excessively loquacious" persons.

Some earlier investigators suggest that the canine fossa is restricted to hominids and that it is diagnostic for articulate speech because the caninus muscle arises from the fossa and inserts into the angle of the mouth where, intermingling with the fibers of the zygomaticus, triangularis, and orbicularis oris muscles, its action is important for speech production. But the canine fossa is sometimes present in living apes and in fossil dryopithecines (299, p. 249) so that it is of no value either in distinguishing hominid from pongid affinity nor in diagnosing a capacity for articulate speech.

Mamak (218) suggests that canine teeth in the hominoid line were reduced in size when language replaced the selective advantage of large canines for aggressive display. This would place the origin of language at least at the australopithecine level 3 million or more years ago) if not at the ramapithecine level (up to 14 million years ago). Others explain canine reduction as a result of tool use (329), selection for reduced aggression without reference to language (181), or change to a small-seed diet (148).

The anatomist Crelin and his associates (198, 200) reconstructed the supralaryngeal vocal tract of the La Chapelle-aux-Saints skeletal remains, a classical Neanderthal man from the Upper Mousterian of France dated 35–45,000 years ago (247). The reconstruction is based on the morphology of the cranial base, especially the estimated intersection of the stylohyoid ligament and the geniohyoid muscle with the hyoid bone of the larynx. Casts of the fossil skull and mandible were used. Comparative materials included 6 skulls and 6 heads and necks of newborn humans completely divided in the midsagittal plane, 50 skulls and 6 divided heads and necks of adult humans, along with skulls of a chimpanzee and an adult female gorilla. Although the larynx was judged to be as high in position in the Neanderthal specimen as in newborn humans and adult apes, it was purposely dropped to a slightly lower position, but much higher than in adult modern man. It is of interest to note that Keith's reconstruction (241) of the larynx of a "Neanderthal" compounded from the Gibraltar skull (it does not show postmortem deformation of the critical region) and the Tabun mandible and spinal column, suggests that the distance between the planes of the soft palate and the vocal chord was 74% of that in modern man compared with 52% in Crelin's estimate from the deformed La Chapelle-aux-Saints specimen. After the vocal tract was reconstructed by building the laryngeal, pharyngeal, and oral cavities with modeling clay, a silicone-rubber cast was made from the clay mold of the air passages including those of the nasal cavity.

The length and shape of the supralaryngeal vocal tract determines the frequencies at which maximum energy will be transmitted by puffs of air from the laryngeal source to the air adjacent to the speaker's lips. These maximum frequencies are called formant frequencies. A speaker varies the formant frequencies by changing the length and shape of his supralaryngeal vocal tract. The formant frequencies are computed from the cross-sectional area of the reconstructed supralaryngeal vocal tract at 0.5 cm levels up to 10.5 cm above the larynx. The computer simulation program was written by Henke (113). The three formant frequencies computed by the program providing the best approximation to the human vowels [i], [a], [u] are tabulated and scaled to the average dimensions of the adult human vocal tract (200). The simulation is at the *phonetic* rather than the *phonemic* level. These three vowels are taken to delimit the universal human vowel space (78). The results were compared with the formant frequencies obtained by Peterson & Barney (263) of American English vowels spoken by a sample of 76 men, women, and children.

The properties of the laryngeal source and the degree of motor control in fossil specimens are unknown; therefore, this type of reconstruction-computer simulation analysis cannot determine the total range of phonetic variation (194). Lieberman and his associates conclude that the La Chapelle-aux-Saints individual could not produce vowels like [a], [i], [u], or [ɔ] as in *father, feet, boot,* and *brought,* nor could he produce consonants like [g] or [k]. However, this Neanderthal man had much more "speech" ability than the living pongids. He could produce vowels like [I] , [e], [U], [ae] as in *bit, bet, but,* and *bat,* in addition to a reduced schwa vowel, as the first vowel in *about.* Dental and labial consonants like [d], [b], [s], [z], [v], and [f] were possible (198). Boule & Vallois (26) also concluded, on other grounds, that neanderthal man "... had doubtless only the most rudimentary articulate language."

> If Neanderthal man were able to execute the rapid, controlled articulatory maneuvers that are necessary to produce these consonants and had the neural mechanisms that are necessary to perceive rapid formant transitions . . . he would have been able to communicate by means of sound. Of course, we do not know whether Neanderthal man had these neural skills; however, even if he were able to make optimum use of his speech-producing apparatus, the constraints of his supralaryngeal vocal tract would make it impossible for him to produce "articulate" human speech, i.e., the full range of phonetic contrasts employed by modern man (198, p. 217).

Reconstructions of the supralaryngeal vocal tract of five additional fossil hominids were made by Crelin and his associates (54, 55, 194, 197, 199). The classical

Le Ferrassie Neanderthal, from the Mousterian of France more than 35,000 years ago (247), was judged to have the same limited capacity for articulate speech claimed for Le Chapelle-aux-Saints (199). The progressive Neanderthal man represented by Skhul V, from the Lower Levalloiso-Mousterian of Israel about 30,000 years ago (247), had a reconstructed vocal tract within the range of modern man (194). The neanderthaloid Broken Hill man, from the early Gambian of Zambia about 30,000 years ago (247), was judged to be intermediate between the classical neanderthals and modern man but within the range of the human vocal tract (194, 199). The reconstructed supralaryngeal vocal tract of the early neanderthaloid Steinheim man, from the late Hoxnian beds of Germany about 200,000 years ago (247), although showing some pongid features, was functionally equivalent to the modern supralaryngeal vocal tract and able to produce the full range of human articulate speech (54, 55, 194). Crelin's reconstruction (55, 194) of the supralaryngeal vocal tract of Sterkfontein 5, a gracile australopithecine dated about 2 million years ago (319), has the same phonetic limitations as present-day apes with greater similarity in size and shape of the tract to the orangutan than to the chimpanzee [for an independent claim of australopithecine-orangutan affinity see Oxnard (253)].

The methods and conclusions of Lieberman, Crelin, and their associates on the reconstructed phonetic limitations of fossil hominids, especially Neanderthal man, were met with wide criticism on both biological and linguistic grounds (31–33, 35, 71, 77, 162, 180, 237, 353). The criticisms include the use of inaccurate casts of post-mortem-deformed skulls, doubts that a correct model of the vocal tract of a fossil man can be constructed from the skull, fallacies in the comparison of human newborns with adult Neanderthals, inability to use data on parallel resonators (e.g. the maxillary sinuses) in the acoustic analyses (104), failure to recognize that speech is little impaired by tongue amputation (152) and that many morphological defects in the tongue (103) as well as limited tongue movement (84) produce only minor defects of speech, invalid assumptions about the relations between the tongue and the larynx, the possibilities of alaryngeal speech (65), and invalid conceptions about the posture of the old man from La Chapelle-aux-Saints (310).

LeMay (180) pointed out that the brain of Neanderthal man was as large as that of modern man, and that the endocranial cast of the La Chapelle-aux-Saints skull resembles that of modern man in areas important for speech and thereby suggests that Neanderthal man had the neural development necessary for articulate speech and language.

Abler (2) demonstrated that among living hominoids skull asymmetry tends to characterize only those species possessing lateralized brains and that the asymmetry in the skulls of Neanderthal man and *Homo erectus* suggest they had lateralized brains and, by implication, language [but see (47)].

Comprehensible English can be written with only one vowel: The Eneversete ef Bermenghem phesecest Fremlen (82), well knewn fer hes deleghtfel esse en the het deth ef er speces, cencleded thet whel the Ne'enderthels mey hev speken less well then ther sepeent secessers et es emprebebl thet ther demes wes beces thre vewels present en medern Ende-Eerepeen mey hev been leckeng te ther phenelegecel cepecete: "The kemplexete ef speech depends en the kensenents, net en the vewels, es ken be seen frem the generel kemprehensebelete ef thes letter," where the neetrel vewel threegheet es /e/ es en Englesh *her.*

While perhaps giving Fremlen his point, most linguists would object that the above paragraph is not an adequate phonetic representation of English, that it probably is not homologous with Neanderthalese, that it uses visual redundancy, that several vowels do add to the comprehensibility of English by doing work the consonants cannot accomplish alone, especially in comprehending sex, age, emotional state, and pragmatic as opposed to semantic meaning of the speaker.

Kuipers (168) concluded that the Kabardian language of the Caucasus has no vowels by defining [*a*] as a "feature of openness" instead of a "vowel" and [*ə*] as "the concomitant syllabic feature of the explosive variant of a consonant," but Halle (109) in a fresh analysis of Kuipers's data concludes that Kabardian has two vowels [*a*] and [*ə*] in agreement with Roman Jakobson's opinion (141a) that the minimal vowel system in all human languages must have at least a vertical ə-a axis. Either way, if we accept Lieberman and Curlin's reconstruction that La Chapelle and La Ferassie classical neanderthal men could articulate only five vowels, they could therefore articulate more than the number of vowels in at least one known human language and could have had at least 14–16 phonemes which is sufficient to articulate properly Hawaiian and other Polynesian languages (227, 272).

ORIGINS OF LANGUAGE

The origins of language remain unknown, but the problems of language origins has received serious attention during the last decade after a long period of relative neglect, indifference, or opposition. The 1976 symposium on *Origins and Evolution of Language and Speech* sponsored by the New York Academy of Sciences (111) is a massive indicator of the degree and scope of current interest.

Aarsleff (1) presents an outline of language-origins theory since the Renaissance. Hewes's (116) second revised and enlarged bibliography of *Language Origins* is a reliable guide to the extensive literature on the topic. The papers in Wescott (334) give an excellent, compact summary of the empirical evidence on glottogenesis, and Lieberman (195), Stross (311), and Swadesh (311a) illustrate different approaches to the problem.

Many linguists insist that questions on the origin(s) of language are now and will remain unanswerable. They support Chomsky's argument (in several works after 1968) that language is unique, discontinuous, species specific, and without evolutionary growth, as if due to the mutation of a supergene.

The linguist Hoijer (130) concluded that although there is no archaeological evidence on the early stages of glottogenesis, we must assume that language, like other aspects of culture, passed through a period of evolutionary development. The psychologist Miller (231, p. 72) considered it necessary to separate linguistic from cultural evolution: "with respect to biological change, evolution is an explanatory concept, with regard to cultural change, evolution is a descriptive concept, with regard to linguistic change, evolution is an unacceptable concept." In opposition, Greenberg (102), Hockett (127), and Sebeok (294–296), to mention only three anthropological linguists, support evolutionary studies as one part of general linguistics. Holloway (132–134), a biological anthropologist who is a main contributor to our knowledge of the evolutionary reorganization of the hominid brain since the Miocene, points out that hypotheses on language origins are essentially unprovable. Lenneberg, a linguist and biologist, after proposing in the late 1950s [references in (184)] that the human capacity for language can be explained only on the basis of the biological properties of man's brain and vocal tract, remained sceptical about prospects of gaining reliable evolutionary evidence on glottogenesis: in 1973 he wrote (186, pp. 59–60): "My own theory is that language is intimately related to human forms of cognition and perception. This means that the history of human language can only be told in connection with the history of the human forms of knowing the world. The biologist, however, can contribute very little to this historical research."

Hewes (115) classified theories on the origin of language into 12 categories: (a) Interjectional, or pooh-pooh, (b) Imitative, onomatopoetic, or bow-wow, (c) Imitative of sounds made by striking objects, or ding-dong, (d) Work-chant, or yo-he-ho, (e) Lip and tongue gesture, or ta-ta, (f) Infant babbling, or babbleluck, (g) Instinctivist, (h) Conventionalist, (i) Contract, (j) Divine, (k) Chance mutation, and (l) Gestural. He points out that some of these theories are tautologies, some are unfalsificable, some are incapable of operational formulation, some are plausible but not empirically tested. An example of the latter is Höpp's (136) proposal that human language began when a proper name was used to specify an individual. This *Einwortsprache* limited to one-word imperative utterances came before verbs and nouns, and thus grammar. One-word language was later dualized into verbs and nouns which then gave rise to grammar and full language. Höpp finds that one-word imperative utterances still exist in four languages, of which Eskimo is considered technologically the most primitive. The theory has received and deserves no further empirical testing.

Language may have no true origin (171, 172) or date of rank, unless we place it with the origin of life on earth. Speech and language evolved slowly through many phases and our placement of origins will vary with different criteria of language. The distinction between language and protolanguage is variously defined (127). If we argue for homologous language in *Pan* and *Homo,* the origin of language would be placed about 27 million years ago at the time many paleontologists (299) date the divergence of pongids and hominids. If we insist on historical records of known human languages Egyptian is recorded in hieroglyphics from about 3000 BC with comparable antiquity for Mesopotamia and about 2000 BC for China.

Several investigators conclude that increase in general cognitive abilities, rather than ease in verbal communication, was crucial in the origin of language (111, 141, 144, 171, 172).

Holloway (133, 134) interprets the evidence of paleoanthropology to place language origins 2–3 million years ago. Isaac (141) infers on archaeological grounds that "the milieu in which capabilities for language were first important" started before 1 million years ago but that the crucial developments in language took place about 30,000–40,000 years ago. Hewes (114) gives an explicit formulation of the relationship between tool-using, tool-making, and the emergence of language, and relates (115, 118) current studies on primate communication to the hypothesis of a gestural origin of language. If language required symboling, it is of interest that the earliest archaeological evidence for symbolic behavior dates from the Mousterian about 90,000 years ago (221).

Hockett (122–125) deduced that because his 13 design features are not all independent (e.g. semanticity must precede arbitrariness and duality of patterning) comparative study of living species may support a phylogenetic sequence for the evolution of design features in the hominid lineage. For instance, given that living gibbons have features 1 through 9 (125), we may assume that Miocene pongids had arbitrariness, interchangeability, and specialization. Four new properties are required for the evolution of human language—productivity, duality of patterning, displacement, and cultural transmission. Productivity could develop without duality, displacement, or cultural transmission, but it is hard to get these without productivity. Learning is necessary for a system which is arbitrary, productive, and cultural. Arbitrary signs might become productive through "blending." Displacement developed after arbitrariness and duality after displacement. Hockett (127) dates the transition from a closed call system (like those of gibbons and other apes) to "good prelanguage" about 2 million years ago, in or not far from eastern Africa.

Hockett (127) places the transition from prelanguage to language 150,000 to 50,000 years ago based on (a) archaeological evidence of complex technology at that time, (b) the supposition that such complexity could not be achieved and maintained without extremely effective communication, (c) the evidence that 4000 to 5000 known languages could not diverge in less than about 50,000 years, and (d) because true language is such a powerful instrument for technological and social change, the transition could not occur before about 150,000 years ago or modern cultures would be more complex than they are. On the basis of linguistic reconstruction and glottochronology, Wurm (360) suggests a temporal depth up to 60,000 years for the approximately 700 mutually unintelligible languages of New Guinea.

Among recent workers Lieberman (194, 195) has used the fullest range of biological and linguistic data to speculate on the origins of language. He concludes that speech communication played a strategic role in the survival and perpetuation of early hominid culture and that this role presupposes a *Homo sapiens*–like supraglottal vocal apparatus. Bosma (25) countered with the surmise that hominids having the social orientation and integrative competencies requisite to ethnographically known cultures could communicate with any approximately humanoid vocal apparatus.

The new evidence for hemispherical differences in the representation of language in the brain [some of which are demonstrable on skulls and endocranial casts (2, 132–134, 161d–f, 181)] gives promise of the early discovery of new, verifiable evidence in paleolinguistics. The neurological evidence that song and music are localized in the hemisphere not dominant for language (210, 244, 284) argues against the hypothesis that song was a major step in the evolution of language (171, 172, 203).

Levy (188, 189) finds a possible basis for the evolution of lateral specialization of the two hemispheres in the hominid brain in the consideration that, given partial hemispherical specialization for language, competition of that dominant hemisphere for control of the motor mechanism concerned with language production, would result in specialization of the mute hemisphere for gestalt perception and the ability to visualize spatial relations in three dimensions as a result of antagonism between the functions of language and nonverbal perception and cognition.

In 1971 Whitaker (341, p. 208) characterized the state of neurolinguistics as follows: "Suffice to say, we are not dramatically close to understanding brain function as complex as language but what we have is rather far from a black-box. In a modest way, it is possible to show empirical support for quite a number of linguistic constructs—some of which are quite predictable and others are perhaps a bit unusual."

There are no instantaneous jumps between peripheral recognition of a uniquely new external event and peripheral production of a uniquely new word and sentence across a linguistically void brain in which nothing biological happens pertinent to the study of language. Knowledge of exactly how language is represented in the brain probably must await discovery of the molecular basis of memory, the biochemistry of receiving, storing, and recalling the lexicon according to the principles of the central language system.

Literature Cited

1. Aarsleff, H. 1976. An outline of language-origins theory since the Renaissance. *Ann. NY Acad. Sci.* 280:4–13
2. Abler, W. L. 1976. Asymmetry in the skulls of fossil man: Evidence of lateralized brain function? *Brain Behav. Evol.* 13:111–15
3. Arnold, G. E. 1961. The genetic background of developmental language disorders. *Folia Phoniatrica* 13:246–54
4. Astakhova, A. T., Karacheva, A. A. 1970. Asymmetry of the brain in the human fetus. (In Russian). *Trans. Krasnoyarsk Med. Inst.* 9(5):9–12
5. Ayer, A. J. 1954. Can there be a private language? *Proc. Aristot. Soc.* Suppl. vol. 28:63–76
6. Ayer, A. J. 1966. Can there be a private language? In *Wittgenstein: The Philosophical Investigations,* ed. G. Pitcher, pp. 251–66. Garden City: Doubleday
7. Bailey, P., Bonin, G. von. 1950. *The Isocortex of Man.* Urbana: Univ. Illinois Press. 300 pp.
8. Beach, F. A. 1950. The Snark was a Boojum. *Am. Psychol.* 5:115–24
9. Bell, G. H., Davidson, J. N., Scarborough, H. 1968. *Textbook of Physiology and Biochemistry.* Edinburgh & London: Livingstone. 1268 pp. 7th ed.
10. Bellugi, U., Klima, E. S. 1975. Aspects of sign language and its structure. See Ref. 151, pp. 171–203
11. Bergsma, D. 1973. *Birth Defects Atlas and Compendium.* Baltimore: Williams & Wilkins. 1006 pp.
12. Bernstein, F. 1925. Beiträge zur Mendelistischen Anthropologie. I. Quantitative Rassenanalyse auf Grund von statistischen Beobachtungen über den Klangcharakter der Singstimme. *Sitzungsber. Preuss. Akad. Wiss. Phys.-math. Kl.* 5:61–70
13. Bernstein, F. 1925. Beiträge zur mendelistischen Anthropologie, II. *Sitzungsber. Preuss. Akad. Wiss. Phys. Math. Kl.* 5:71–82
14. Bever, T. G. 1970. The cognitive basis for linguistic structures. In *Cognition and The Development of Language,* ed. J. R. Hayes, pp. 279–362. New York: Wiley
15. Bloomfield, L. 1933. *Language.* New York: Holt. 564 pp.
16. Blumstein, S. E. 1968. Phonological aspects of aphasic speech. In *Studies Presented to Roman Jakobson by His Students,* ed. C. E. Gribble, pp. 39–43. Cambridge: Slavica
17. Blumstein, S. E. 1973. A *Phonological Investigation of Aphasic Speech.* The Hague: Mouton. 117 pp.
18. Boas, F. 1911. Introduction to *Handbook of North American Indian Languages. Bur. Am. Ethnol. Bull.* 40 (Part 1):1–89

19. Boas, F. 1938. *The Mind of Primitive Man.* New York: Macmillan. 285 pp. 2nd ed.
20. Bogen, J. E., Bogen, G. M. 1976. Wernicke's region: Where is it? *Ann. NY Acad. Sci.* 280:834–43
21. Bonin, G. von. 1962. Anatomical asymmetries of the cerebral hemispheres. In *Interhemispheric Relations and Cerebral Dominance,* ed. V. Mountcastle, pp. 1–6. Baltimore: Johns Hopkins
22. Bonin, G. von. 1963. *The Evolution of the Human Brain.* Chicago: Univ. Chicago Press. 92 pp.
23. Bordes, F. 1968. *The Old Stone Age.* New York: World Univ. Libr. 255 pp.
24. Bordes, F. 1971. Physical evolution and technological evolution in man: A parallelism. *World Archaeol.* 3(1):1–5
25. Bosma, J. F. 1975. Comments on Lieberman's paper. See Ref. 151, pp. 107–8
26. Boule, M., Vallois, H. V. 1957. *Fossil Man.* New York: Dryden. 535 pp.
27. Broadmann, K. 1909. *Vergleichende Lokalisationlehre der Grosshirnrinde.* Leipzig: Barth. 324 pp.
28. Brosnahan, L. F. 1961. *The Sounds of Language: An Inquiry Into the Role of Genetic Factors in the Development of Sound Systems.* Cambridge: Heffer. 250 pp.
29. Brosnahan, L. F. 1964. The hereditary and environmental components of language. In *Proc. Int. Congr. Ling., 9th, Cambridge, 1962,* ed. H. G. Lunt, pp. 434–39
30. Bulmer, M. G. 1970. *The Biology of Twinning in Man.* Oxford: Clarendon. 205 pp.
31. Burr, D. B. 1976. Further evidence concerning speech in Neanderthal man. *Man* 11:104–10
32. Burr, D. B. 1976. Neanderthal vocal tract reconstructions: A critical appraisal. *J. Hum. Evol.* 5:285–90
33. Campbell, B. 1971. The roots of language. In *Biological and Social Factors in Psycholinguistics,* ed. J. Morton, pp. 10–23. Cambridge: Logos
34. Campbell, B. G. 1972. Conceptual progress in physical anthropology: Fossil man. *Ann. Rev. Anthropol.* 1:27–54
35. Carlisle, R. C., Siegel, M. I. 1974. Some problems in the interpretation of Neanderthal speech capabilities: A reply to Lieberman. *Am. Anthropol.* 76:319–22
36. Cavalli-Sforza, L. L. 1971. Similarities and dissimilarities of socio-cultural and biological evolution. In *Mathematics in Archaeology and the Historical Sciences: Proceedings of the Anglo-Roumanian Conference, Mamia, Romania, 1970,* ed. F. R. Hodson, D. G. Kendall, pp. 535–41. Edinburgh: Edinburgh Univ. Press
37. Cavalli-Sforza, L. L., Bodmer, W. F. 1971. *The Genetics of Human Populations.* San Francisco: Freeman. 965 pp.
38. Cavalli-Sforza, L. L., Feldman, M. W. 1973. Cultural vs. biological inheritance: Phenotypic transmission from parents to children (A theory of the effect of parental phenotypes on children's phenotypes. *Am. J. Hum. Genet.* 25:618–37
39. Cavalli-Sforza, L. L., Feldman, M. W. 1973. Models for cultural inheritance: Group mean and within group variation. *Theor. Popul. Biol.* 4:42–55
40. Chase, R. A., Cullen, J. K. Jr., Niedermeyer, E. F. L., Stark, R. E., Blumer, D. P. 1967. Ictal speech automatisms and swearing: Studies on the auditory feedback control of speech. *J. Nerv. Ment. Dis.* 144:406–20
41. Chomsky, N. 1957. *Syntactic Structures.* The Hague: Mouton. 118 pp.
42. Chomsky, N. 1959. A review of B. F. Skinner's *Verbal Behavior. Language* 35:26–58
43. Chomsky, N. 1965. *Aspects of the Theory of Syntax.* Cambridge: MIT Press. 251 pp.
44. Chomsky, N. 1976. On the nature of language. *Ann. NY Acad. Sci.* 280: 46–57
45. Chomsky, N. 1976. *Reflections on Language.* New York: Pantheon. 269 pp.
46. Chomsky, N., Halle, M. 1968. *The Sound Pattern of English.* New York: Harper & Row. 470 pp.
47. Clark, W. E. LeG. 1934. The asymmetry of the occipital region of the brain and skull. *Man* 34:35–37
48. Clark, W. E. LeG. 1971. *The Antecedents of Man.* Chicago: Quadrangle. 3rd ed. 374 pp.
49. Clark, W. E. LeG., Cooper, D. M., Zuckerman, S. 1936. The endocranial cast of the chimpanzee. *J. R. Anthropol. Inst.* 66:249–68
50. Cook, J. W. 1965. Wittgenstein on privacy. *Philos. Rev.* 74:281–314
51. Coon, C. S. 1963. *The Origin of Races.* London: Cape. 724 pp.
52. Cooper, K. W. 1956. An instance of delayed communication in solitary wasps. *Nature* 178:601–2
53. Cowey, A., Weiskrantz, L. 1975. Demonstration of cross-modal matching in

rhesus monkeys, *Macaca mulatta. Neuropsychologia* 13:117–20
54. Crelin, E. S. 1973. The Steinheim Skull: A linguistic link. *Yale Sci.* 48:10–14
55. Crelin, E. S., Lieberman, P., Klatt, D. H. 1977. Anatomy and related phonetic ability of the Skull V, Steinheim, and Rhodesian fossils and the Pleisanthropus reconstruction. In preparation
56. Crome, L., Stern, J. 1967. *Pathology of Mental Retardation.* London: Churchill. 406 pp.
57. Crosby, E. C., Humphrey, T., Lauer, E. W. 1962. *Correlative Anatomy of the Nervous System.* New York: Macmillan. 731 pp.
58. Darlington, C. D. 1947. The genetic components of language. *Heredity* 1:269–86
59. Darlington, C. D. 1955. The genetic component of language. *Nature* 175:178
60. Dart, R. A., Craig, D. 1959. *Adventures with the Missing Link.* London: 251 pp.
61. Darwin, C. 1871. *The Descent of Man and Selection in Relation to Sex.* London: Murray. 2 vols. 688 pp.
62. Davenport, R. K. 1976. Cross-modal Perception in apes. *Ann. NY Acad. Sci.* 280:243–49
63. Davenport, R. K., Rogers, C. M. 1970. Intermodal equivalence of stimuli in apes. *Science* 168:279–80
64. Denenberg, V. H., Rosenberg, K. M. 1967. Nongenetic transmission of information. *Nature* 216:549–60
64a. Denes, P. B., Pinson, E. N. 1973. *The Speech Chain: The Physics and Biology of Spoken Language.* New York: Anchor Books. 217 pp.
65. Diedrich, W. M., Youngstrom, K. A. 1966. *Alaryngeal Speech.* Springfield, Ill: Thomas. 220 pp.
66. Dingwall, W. O., Whitaker, H. A. 1974. Neurolinguistics. *Ann. Rev. Anthropol.* 3:323–56
67. Dobbing, J. 1974. The later development of the brain and its vulnerability. In *Scientific Foundations of Paediatrics,* ed. J. A. Davis, J. Dobbing, pp. 565–77. Philadelphia: Saunders
68. De Brul, E. L. 1958. *Evolution of the Speech Apparatus.* Springfield: Thomas. 103 pp.
69. Du Brul, E. L. 1976. Biomechanics of speech sounds. *Ann. NY Acad. Sci.* 280:631–43
70. Du Brul, E. L., Reed, C. A. 1960. Skeletal evidence of speech? *Am. J. Phys. Anthropol.* 18:153–56

71. Earley, L. 1975. The voice of Neanderthal. *Sciences* 15:11–15
72. Economo, C. von, Horn, L. 1930. Über Windungsrelief, Masse und Rindenarchitektonik der Supratemporalflache, ihre Individuellen und Seitenunterschiede. *Z. Neurol. Psychiat.* 130:678–757
73. Eimas, P. D., Siqueland, E. R., Jusczyk, P., Vigorito, J. 1970. Speech perception in infants. *Science* 171:303–6
74. Ettlinger, G. 1973. The transfer of information between sense-modalities: A neuropsychological review. In *Memory and Transfer of Information,* ed. H. P. Zippel, pp. 43–64. New York: Plenum
75. Evans, H. M. 1940. *Brain and Body of Fish: A Study of Brain Pattern in Relation to Hunting and Feeding in Fish.* Philadelphia: Blakiston. 164 pp.
76. Falconer, D. S. 1960. *Introduction to Quantitative Genetics.* Edinburgh/London: Oliver & Boyd. 365 pp.
77. Falk, D. 1975. Comparative anatomy of the larynx in man and the chimpanzee: Implications for language in Neanderthal. *Am. J. Phys. Anthropol.* 43:123–32
78. Fant, G. 1960. *Acoustic Theory of Speech Production.* The Hague: Mouton. 323 pp.
79. Fink, R. 1963. Larynx and speech as determinants in evolution of man. *Perspect Biol. Med.* 7:85–93
80. Fodor, J. A. 1968. *Psychological Explanation.* New York: Random House. 165 pp.
80a. Fourcin, A. J. 1975. Language development in the absence of expressive speech. In *Foundations of Language Development: A Multidisciplinary Approach,* ed. E. H. Lenneberg, E. Lenneberg, 2:263–68. New York: Academic
81. Freides, D. 1974. Human information processing in sensory modality: Cross-modal functions, information complexity, memory, and deficit. *Psychol. Bull.* 81:284–310
82. Fremlen, J. H. 1975. The Demese ef the Ne'enderthels: Wes Lengege e Fecter? *Science* 187:600
83. Fromkin, V. A. 1968. Speculations on performance models. *J. Ling.* 4:47–68
84. Frowine, V. K., Moser, H. 1944. Relationship of dentition to speech. *J. Am. Dent. Assoc.* 31:1081–90
85. Gardiner, A. 1951. *The Theory of Speech and Language.* Oxford: Clarendon 348 pp. 2nd ed.
86. Gardner, B. T., Gardner, R. A. 1971. Two-way communication with an infant chimpanzee. In *Behavior of Non-*

human Primates, ed. A. Schrier, F. Stollnitz, 4:117–84. New York: Academic

87. Geschwind, N. 1964. Development of the brain and evolution of language. *Monogr. Ser. Lang. Ling. Georgetown Univ.* 17:155–69

88. Geschwind, N. 1965. Disconnexion syndromes in animals and men, Part I, II. *Brain* 88:237–94, 585–644

89. Geschwind, N. 1969. Anatomy and the higher functions of the brain. *Boston Stud. Philos. Sci.* 4:98–136

90. Geschwind, N. 1970. Intermodal equivalence of stimuli in apes. *Science* 168:1249

91. Geschwind, N. 1970. The organization of language and the brain. *Science* 170:940–44

92. Geschwind, N. 1972. Language and the brain. *Sci. Am.* 226(4):76–83

93. Geschwind, N. 1973. The brain and language. See Ref. 232, pp. 61–72

94. Geschwind, N., Levitsky, W. 1968. Human brain: Left-right asymmetries in temporal speech region. *Science* 161: 186–87

95. Geschwind, N., Quadfasel, F. A., Segarra, J. M. 1968. Isolation of the speech area. *Neuropsychologia* 6: 327–40

96. Chadimi, H., Partington, M. W., Hunter, A. 1961. A familial disturbance of histidine metabolism. *N. Engl. J. Med.* 265:221–24

97. Goodall, J. 1964. Tool-using and aimed throwing in a community of free-living chimpanzees. *Nature* 201:1264–66

98. Gould, J. L. 1975. Honey bee recruitment: The dance-language controversy. *Science* 189:685–93

99. Gould, S. J. 1966. Allometry and size in ontogeny and phylogeny. *Biol. Rev.* 41:587–640

100. Green, E. 1969. Phonological and grammatical aspects of jargon in an aphasic patient. *Lang. Speech* 12: 103–18

101. Green, E. 1969. Psycholinguistic approaches to aphasia. *Linguistics* 53: 30–50

102. Greenberg, J. H. 1959. Language and evolution. In *Evolution and Anthropology: A Centennial Appraisal,* ed. B. J. Meggers, pp. 61–75. Washington DC: Anthropol. Soc. Wash.

103. Greene, J. S. 1937. Speech defects and related oral anomalies. *J. Am. Dent. Assoc. Dent. Cosmos* 24:1969–74

104. Greene, M. C. L. 1957. *The Voice and Its Disorders.* New York: Macmillan. 224 pp.

105. Griffin, D. R. 1976. *The Question of Animal Awareness: Evolutionary Continuity of Mental Experience.* New York: Rockefeller Univ. Press. 135 pp.

106. Grossman, S. P. 1967. *A Textbook of Physiological Psychology.* New York: Wiley. 932 pp.

107. Grüneberg, H. 1943. *The Genetics of the Mouse.* Cambridge: At the Univ. Press. 412 pp.

108. Hall, K. R. L. 1963. Tool-using performances as indicators of behavioral adaptability. *Curr. Anthropol.* 4:479–94

109. Halle, M. 1970. Is Kabardian a vowelless language? *Found. Lang.* 6:95–103

110. Hardcastle, W. 1970. *The role of tactile and proprioceptive feedback in speech production.* Work in progress No. 4. Linguistics Dept., Edinburgh Univ.

111. Harnad, S., Steklis, H. D., Lancaster, J., ed. 1976. *Origins and Evolution of Language and Speech. Ann. NY Acad. Sci.* 280:1–914

112. Harrison, G. A., Weiner, J. S., Tanner, J. M., Barnicote, N. A. 1977. *Human Biology: An Introduction to Human Evolution, Variation, Growth, and Ecology.* Oxford: Univ. Press. 499 pp. 2nd ed.

113. Henke, W. L. 1966. *Dynamic articulatory model of speech production using computer simulation.* PhD thesis. Mass. Inst. Technol., Cambridge, Mass.

114. Hewes, G. W. 1973. An explicit formulation of the relationship between tool-using, tool-making and the emergence of language. *Visible Lang.* 7(2):101–27

115. Hewes, G. W. 1973. Primate communication and the gestural origin of language. *Curr. Anthropol.* 14:5–24

116. Hewes, G. W. 1975. *Language Origins: A Bibliography.* The Hague, Paris: Mouton. 2nd rev. ed. (enlarged). 139 pp.

117. Hewes, G. W. 1975. Comments on Mattingly's paper and on Levallois flake tools. See Ref. 151, pp. 76–81

118. Hewes, G. W. 1976. The current status of the gestural theory of language origin. *Ann. NY Acad. Sci.* 280:482–504

119. Hill, J. H. 1972. On the evolutionary foundations of language. *Am. Anthropol.* 74:308–17

120. Hill, J. H. 1974. Possible continuity theories of language. *Language* 50(1): 134–50

121. Hirsh, I. J. 1975. Speech, language, and communication: Reflections on the conference. See Ref. 151, pp. 315–22

122. Hockett, C. F. 1958. *A Course in Modern Linguistics.* New York: Macmillan. 621 pp.
123. Hockett, C. F. 1959. Animal "languages" and human language. See Ref. 306, pp. 32–38
124. Hockett, C. F. 1960. Logical considerations in the study of animal communication. *In Animal Sounds and Communication,* ed. W. E. Lanyon, W. N. Tavolga, pp. 392–430. Washington DC: Am. Inst. Biol. Sci. Publ. 7
125. Hockett, C. F. 1960. The origin of speech. *Sci. Am.* 203(3):88–96
126. Hockett, C. F. 1968. *The State of the Art.* The Hague, Paris: Mouton. 123 pp.
127. Hockett, C. F. 1973. *Man's Place in Nature.* New York: McGraw-Hill. 739 pp.
128. Hockett, C. F., Ascher, R. 1964. The human revolution. *Am. Sci.* 52(1): 70–92
129. Hogben, L. 1956. Human biology and human speech. *Br. J. Prev. Soc. Med.* 10:63–74
130. Hoijer, J. 1954. Language in culture. *Am. Anthropol. Assoc. Mem. 79*
131. Holloway, R. L. Jr. 1967. Tools and teeth: some speculations regarding canine reduction. *Am. Anthropol.* 69: 63–67
132. Holloway, R. L. Jr. 1968. The evolution of the primate brain: Some aspects of quantitative relations. *Brain Res.* 7: 121–72
133. Holloway, R. L. 1975. *The Role of Human Social Behavior in the Evolution of the Brain.* New York: Am. Mus. Nat. Hist.
134. Holloway, R. L. 1976. Paleoneurological evidence for language origins, *Ann. NY Acad. Sci.* 280:330–48
135. Hooton, E. A. 1946. *Up from the Ape.* New York: Macmillan. 788 pp.
136. Hopp, G. 1970. *Evolution der Sprache und Vernunft.* Berlin, Heidelberg, New York: Springer-Verlag. 167 pp.
137. Howells, W. W. 1973. *Evolution of the Genus Homo.* Reading, Mass: Addison-Wesley. 188 pp.
138. Ingvar, D. H. 1976. Functional landscapes of the dominant hemisphere. *Brain Res.* 107:181–97
139. Ingvar, D. H., Lassen, N. A. 1976. Regulation of cerebral blood flow. In *Brain Metabolism and Cerebral Disorders,* ed. H. E. Himwich, pp. 181–206. New York: Spectrum. 2nd ed.
140. Ingvar, D. H., Schwartz, M. S. 1974. Blood flow patterns induced in the dominant hemisphere by speech and reading. *Brain* 97:273–88

141. Isaac, G. L. 1976. Stages of cultural elaboration in the Pleistocene: Possible archaeological indicators of the development of language capabilities. *Ann. NY Acad. Sci.* 280:275–88
141a. Jakobson, R. 1962. *Selected Writings,* Vol. 1. The Hague: Mouton. 678 pp.
142. Jenkins, J. J., Shaw, R. E. 1975. On the interrelatedness of speech and language. See Ref. 151, pp. 155–65
143. Jennings, H. S. 1962. *Behavior of the Lower Organisms, with a New Introduction by Donald D. Jesen.* Bloomington: Indiana Univ. Press. 366
144. Jerison, H. J. 1973. *Evolution of the Brain and Intelligence.* New York, London: Academic. 482 pp.
145. Jerison, H. J. 1976. The paleoneurology of language. *Ann. NY Acad. Sci.* 280:370–82
146. Johns, D. F., Darley, F. L. 1970. Phonemic variability in apraxia of speech. *J. Speech Hear. Res.* 13:556–83
147. Johns, D. F., LaPointe, L. L. 1976. Neurogenic disorders of out processing: Apraxia of speech. *Stud. Neuroling.* 1:161–99
148. Jolly, C. J. 1970. The seed-eaters: A new model of hominid differentiation based on a baboon analogy. *Man* 5:5–21
149. Julesz, B., Pennington, K. 1965. Equidistributed information mapping—an analogy to holograms and memory. *J. Opt. Soc. Am.* 55:604
150. Kaplan, H. 1960. *Anatomy and Physiology of Speech.* New York: McGraw-Hill. 365 pp.
151. Kavanaugh, J. E., Cutting, J. E., eds. 1975. *The Role of Speech in Language.* Cambridge, Mass: 335 pp.
152. Keaster, J. 1940. Studies in the anatomy and physiology of the tongue. *Laryngoscope* 50:222–57
153. Kelemen, G. 1964. Evolutionary sources of human language. *Folia Phoniatr.* 16:59–66
154. Kelemen, G. 1969. Anatomy of the larynx and the anatomical basis of vocal production. In *The Chimpanzee,* ed. G. H. Bourne, 1:165–86. Baltimore, Md: Univ. Park Press
155. Kimble, D. P. 1967. *The Anatomy of Memory.* New York: Sci. Behav. Books. 2nd ed. 451 pp.
156. Kimble, D. P. 1967. *The Organization of Recall.* New York: Sci. Behav. Books. 2nd ed. 369 pp.
157. Kimura, D. 1967. Functional asymmetry of the brain in dichotic listening. *Cortex* 3:163–78

158. Kimura, D. 1976. The neural basis of language qua gesture. *Stud. Neuroling.* 2:145–56

159. Kinsbourne, M. 1971. The minor cerebral hemisphere as a source of aphasic speech. *Arch. Neurol.* 25:302–6

160. Kirchner, J. A. 1970. *Pressman and Kelemen's Physiology of the Larynx.* Rochester, Minn: Am. Acad. Opthalmol. Otolaryngol. 2nd ed.

161. Klima, E. S. 1975. Sound and its absence in the linguistic symbol. See Ref. 151, pp. 249–70

161a. Kotchetkova, V. I. 1960. L'évolution des régions spécifiquement humaines de l'écorce cérébrale chez les hominides. *Actes Congr. Int. Sci. Anthropol. Ethnol., 6th,* 1:623–630

161b. Kotchetkova, V. I. 1960. Mode of reconstruction of encephalon lobes of the fossil hominid brain by way of measuring endocranial casts. (In Russian) *Vop. Antropol.* 3:33–45

161c. Kotchetkova, V. I. 1961. A quantitative description of brain variability in fossil hominids as shown by cranial casts. (In Russian) *Vop. Antropol.* 6: 3–20

161d. Kotchetkova, V. I. 1961. Evolution of specific human areas in the brain cortex of hominids. (In Russian) *Vop. Antropol.* 7:14–22

161e. Kotchetkova, V. I. 1962. Variability of the parietal lobe on the endocranial casts of hominids. (In Russian) *Vop. Antropol.* 11:16–28

161f. Kotchetkova, V. I. 1963. Characteristic features of the variability of temporal and occipital lobes of the endocranial casts of hominids. (In Russian) *Vop. Antropol.* 13:33–51

161g. Kotchetkova, V. I. 1964. Moulage of the cerebral cavity of the Cro-Magnon III fossil man (In Russian) *Trudy Moskovskogo Obshchestva Ispytately Prirody* 14:111–35

162. Kolata, G. B. 1974. The demise of the Neanderthals: Was language a factor? *Science* 186:618–19

163. Krashen, S. D. 1976. Cerebral asymmetry. *Stud. Neuroling.* 2:157–91

164. Kreht, H. 1936. Zytoarchitektorik und motorisches Sprachzentrum. *Z. Mikrosk.-Anat. Forsch.* 39:331–54

165. Kroeber, A. L. 1963. *Style and Civilizations.* Berkeley, Los Angeles: Univ. California Press. 191 pp.

166. Kroeber, A. L., Kluckhohn, C. 1952. Culture: A critical review of concepts and definitions. *Pap. Peabody Mus. Archaeol. Ethnol. Harv. Univ.* 47(1):1–223

167. Krogman, W. M. 1962. *The Human Skeleton in Forensic Medicine.* Springfield, Ill: Thomas. 337 pp.

168. Kuipers, A. 1960. *Phoneme and Morpheme in Kabardian.* The Hague: Mouton. 124 pp.

169. Laguna, G. A. de. 1963. *Speech: Its Function and Development.* Bloomington: Indiana Univ. Press. 363 pp.

170. Lancaster, J. B. 1968. Primate communication systems and the emergence of human language. In *Primates: Studies in Adaptation and Variability,* ed. P. C. Jay, pp. 439–57. New York: Holt, Rinehart & Winston

171. Langer, S. K. 1967. *Mind: An Essay on Human Feeling,* Vol. 1. Baltimore: Johns Hopkins Press. 487 pp.

172. Langer, S. K. 1972. *Mind: An Essay on Human Feeling,* Vol. 2. Baltimore, London: Johns Hopkins Univ. Press. 400 pp.

173. Lassen, N. A. 1959. Cerebral blood flow and oxygen consumption in man. *Physiol. Rev.* 39:183–238

174. Laver, J. 1968. *Phonetics and the Brain.* Work in progress No. 2. Dep. Phonet. Ling., Edinburgh Univ.

175. Leakey, L. S. B. 1968. Bone smashing by Late Miocene Hominidae. *Nature* 218:528–30

176. Lebrun, Y. 1976. Neurolinguistic models of language and speech. *Stud. Neuroling.* 1:1–30

177. Lecours, A. R., Lhermitte, F. 1969. Phonemic paraphasias: Linguistic structures and tentative hypotheses. *Cortex* 5:193–228

178. Legros, J. 1967. La maladie du cri du chat. *Bull. Soc. Belge Gynécol. Obstet.* 37:201–10

179. Lejeune, J., Lafourcade, J., Berger, R., Vialatte, J., Boesweillwald, M., Seringe, P., Turpin, R. 1963. Trois cas de deletion partielle du bras court d'un chromosome 5. *Acad. Sci. Pàris* 257: 3098–3102

180. LeMay, M. 1975. The language capacity of Neanderthal man. *Am. J. Phys. Anthropol.* 42:9–14

181. LeMay, M. 1976. Morphological cerebral asymmetries of modern man, fossil man, and nonhuman primate. *Ann. NY Acad. Sci.* 280:249–66

181a. LeMay, M., Culebras, A. 1972. Human brain—Morphological differences in the hemispheres demonstrable by carotid arteriography. *N. Engl. J. Med.* 287:168–70

182. LeMay, M., Geschwind, N. 1975. Hemispheric differences in the brains of

the great apes. *Brain Behav. Evol.* 11:48–52

183. Lenneberg, E. H. 1962. Review of L. Brosnahan, *The Sounds of Language.* *Contemp. Psychol.* 7:230–31

184. Lenneberg, E. H. 1967. *Biological Foundations of Language.* New York: Wiley. 489 pp.

185. Lenneberg, E. H. 1971. Of language, knowledge, apes, and brains. *J. Psycholing. Res.* 1:1–29

186. Lenneberg, E. H. 1973. Biological aspects of language. See Ref. 232, pp. 49–60.

187. Levy, J. 1976. A review of evidence for a genetic component in the determination of handedness. *Behav. Genet.* 6:429–53

188. Levy, J. 1976. Cerebral lateralization and spatial ability. *Behav. Genet.* 6:171–88

189. Levy, J. 1976. Evolution of language lateralization and cognitive function. *Ann. NY Acad. Sci.* 280:810–20

189a. Levy, J., Nagylaki, T. 1972. A model for the genetics of handedness. *Genetics* 72:117–28

190. Lewitter, F., DeFries, J. C., Singer, S. M. 1975. Family resemblance in reading ability: Path analysis. *Am. J. Phys. Anthropol.* 42:314(Abstr.)

191. Lewontin, R. C. 1968. Evolution: The concept of evolution. *Int. Encycl. Soc. Sci.* 5:202–10

192. Lieberman, P. 1968. Primate vocalization and human linguistic ability. *J. Acoust. Soc.* 44:1574–84

193. Lieberman, P. 1972. *The Speech of Primates.* The Hague: Mouton. 141 pp.

194. Lieberman, P. 1973. On the evolution of language: A unified view. *Cognition* 2:59–94

195. Lieberman, P. 1975. *On the Origins of Language: An Introduction to the Evolution of Human Speech.* New York: Macmillan. 196 pp.

196. Lieberman, P. 1975. The evolution of speech and language. See Ref. 151, pp. 83–106

197. Lieberman, P. 1976. Models for evolution: Neural mechanisms, anatomy, and behavior. *Ann. NY Acad. Sci.* 280:660–72

198. Lieberman, P., Crelin, E. S. 1971. On the speech of Neanderthal man. *Ling. Inq.* 2:203–22

199. Lieberman, P., Crelin, E. S. 1974. Speech and Neanderthal man: A reply to Carlisle and Siegel. *Am. Anthropol.* 76:323–25

200. Lieberman, P., Crelin, E. S., Klatt, D. H. 1972. Phonetic ability and related anatomy of the newborn and adult human, Neanderthal man, and the chimpanzee. *Am. Anthropol.* 74:287–307

201. Lieberman, P., Harris, K. S., Wolff, P., Russell, L. H. 1972. Newborn infant cry and nonhuman primate vocalization. *J. Speech Hear. Res.* 14:718–27

202. Lieberman, P., Klatt, D. H., Wilson, W. H. 1969. Vocal tract limitations on the vowel repertoires of rhesus monkeys and other non-human primates. *Science* 164:1185–87

203. Livingstone, F. B. 1973. Did the australopithecines sing? *Curr. Anthropol.* 14:25–29

204. Longuet-Higgins, H. C. 1968. The nonlocal storage of temporal information. *Proc. R. Soc. London, Ser. B* 171:327–34

205. Lotka, A. J. 1925. *Elements of Physical Biology.* Baltimore: Williams & Wilkins. 460 pp.

206. Lotka, A. J. 1945. The law of evolution as a maximal principle. *Hum. Biol.* 8:147–51

207. Luchsinger, R. 1944. Erbbiologische Untersuchungen an ein- und zwei-eiigen Zwillingen in Beziehung zur Grosse und From des Kehlkopfes. *Arch. J. Klaus-Stift.* 19:393–441

208. Luria, A. R. 1966. *Higher Cortical Functions in Man.* New York: Basic Books. 513 pp.

209. Luria, A. R. 1967. Problems and facts of neurolinguistics. In *To Honor Roman Jakobson,* pp. 1213–27. The Hague: Mouton

210. Luria, A. R. 1970. *Traumatic Aphasia. Its Syndromes, Psychology, and Treatment.* The Hague: Mouton. 479 pp.

211. Luria, A. R. 1970. The functional organization of the brain. *Sci. Am.* 222(3):66–78

212. Luria, A. R. 1973. *The Working Brain: An Introduction to Neuropsychology.* Transl. B. Haigh. New York: Basic Books. 398 pp.

213. Luria, A. R. 1974. Language and brain: Towards the basic problems of neurolinguistics. *Brain Lang.* 1:1–14

214. Luria, S. E. 1974. What can biologists solve? *NY Rev. Books,* 7 Feb: 27–28

215. MacKay, D. G. 1970. Spoonerisms: The structure of errors in the serial order of speech. *Neuropsychologia* 8:323–50

216. MacNeilage, P. F. 1970. Motor control of serial order of speech. *Psychol. Rev.* 77:182–96

217. Magoun, H. W. 1963. *The Waking Brain*. Springfield, Ill: Thomas. 188 pp.
218. Mamak, A. 1970. More speculation on the reduction of the canines. *East. Anthropol.* 23:1–9
219. Mańczak, W. 1969. Les termes 'langue' et 'parole' désignent-ils quelque chose de réel? *Linguistics* 55:48–55
220. Manning, A. 1972. *An Introduction to Animal Behavior*. Reading, Mass: Addison-Wesley. 2nd ed. 294 pp.
221. Marshack, A. 1976. Some implications of the Paleolithic symbolic evidence for the origin of language. *Ann. NY Acad. Sci.* 280:289–311
222. Maruszewski, M. 1975. *Language, Communication and the Brain: A Neuropsychological Study*. The Hague: Mouton. 217 pp.
223. Masterton, B., Heffner, H., Ravizza, R. 1969. The evolution of human hearing. *J. Acoust. Soc. Am.* 45:966–85
224. McAdam, D. W., Whitaker, H. A. 1971. Language production: Electroencephalographic localization in the normal human brain. *Science* 172:499–502
225. McKusick, V. A. 1975. *Mendelian Inheritance in Man: Catalogs of autosomal dominant, autosomal recessive, and X-linked phenotypes*. Baltimore: Johns Hopkins. 4th ed. 837 pp.
226. McNeil, D. 1965. *Acquisition of Language: The Study of Developmental Psycholinguistics*. New York: Harper & Row. 183 pp.
227. Meillet, A., Cohen, M., eds. 1952. *Les Langues du Monde*. Paris: Champion. 1294 pp. 2nd ed.
228. Meskin, L. H., Gorlin, R. J., Isaacson, R. J. 1964. Abnormal morphology of the soft palate: I. The prevalence of cleft uvula. *Cleft Palate J.* 1:342–46
229. Meskin, L. H., Gorlin, R. J., Isaacson, R. J. 1965. Abnormal morphology of the soft palate: II. The genetics of cleft uvula. *Cleft Palate J.* 2:40–45
230. Meskin, L. H., Gorlin, R. J., Isaacson, R. J. 1966. Cleft uvula—a microform of cleft palate. *Acta Chir. Plast.* (Praha) 8:92–96
231. Miller, G. A. 1972. Linguistic communication as a biological process. In *Biology and the Human Sciences: The Herbert Spencer Lectures 1970*, ed. J. W. S. Pringle, pp. 70–94. Oxford: Clarendon
232. Miller, G. A. 1973. Psychology and communication. In *Communication, Language, and Meaning: Psychological Perspectives*, ed. G. A. Miller, pp. 3–12. New York: Basic Books
233. Mittler, P. 1969. Genetic aspects of psycholinguistic abilities. *J. Child Psychol. Psychiatry* 10:165–76
234. Mohr, J. P. 1976. Broca's area and Broca's aphasia. *Stud. Neuroling.* 1:201–35
235. Montagu, A. 1976. Toolmaking, hunting, and the origin of language. *Ann. NY Acad. Sci.* 280:266–74
236. Moorhead, P. S., Mellman, W. J., Wenar, C. 1961. A familial chromosome translocation associated with speech and mental retardation. *Am. J. Hum. Genet.* 13:32–46
237. Morris, D. H. 1974. Neanderthal speech. *Ling. Inq.* 5:144–50
238. Mourant, A. E., Watkin, I. M. 1952. Blood groups, anthropology, and language in Wales and the Western Countries. *Heredity* 6:13–36
239. Musgrave, J. H. 1971. How dextrous was Neanderthal man? *Nature* 233:538–41
240. Needham, J. 1942. *Biochemistry and Morphogenesis*. Cambridge: At the Univ. Press. 787 pp.
241. Negus, V. E. 1949. *The Comparative Anatomy and Physiology of the Larynx*. London: Heinemann. 230 pp.
242. Negus, V. E. 1958. The *Comparative Anatomy and Physiology of the Nose and Paranasal Sinuses*. Edinburgh: Livingstone. 402 pp.
243. Nei, M., Roychoudhury, A. K. 1972. Gene differences between Caucasian, Negro, and Japanese populations. *Science* 177:434–36
244. Nielsen, J. M. 1946. *Agnosia, Apraxia, Aphasia: Their Value in Cerebral Localization*. New York: Hoeber. 2nd ed. 292 pp.
245. Nottebohm, F. 1976. Vocal tract and brain: A search for evolutionary bottlenecks. *Ann. NY Acad. Sci.* 280:643–49
246. Oakley, K. P. 1954. Skill as a human possession. In *A History of Technology*, ed. C. Singer, E. J. Holmyard, A. R. Hall, 1:1–37. New York/London: Oxford Univ. Press
247. Oakley, K. P. 1964. *Frameworks for Dating Fossil Man*. Chicago: Aldine. 355 pp.
248. Ojemann, G. A. 1976. Subcortical language mechanisms. *Stud. Neuroling.* 1:103–38
249. Ojemann, G. A., Fedio, P., Van Buren, J. M. 1968. Anomia from pulvinar and subcortical parietal stimulation. *Brain* 91:99–116
249a. Ojemann, G. A., Ward, A. A. Jr. 1971. Speech representation in ventrolateral thalamus. *Brain* 94:669–80

250. Ojemann, R. G. 1966. Correlations between specific human brain lesions and memory changes. *Neurosci. Res. Program Bull.* 4:Suppl. 1

251. Ojemann, R. G., Hoop, B. Jr., Brownell, G. L. et al. 1971. Extracranial measurement of regional cerebral circulation. *J. Nucl. Med.* 12:532–39

252. Olesen, J. 1971. Contralateral focal increase of cerebral blood flow in man during arm work. *Brain* 94:635–46

253. Oxnard, C. E. 1975. *Uniqueness and Diversity in Human Evolution: Morphometric Studies of Australopithecines.* Chicago: Univ. Chicago Press. 133 pp.

254. Palmer, F. 1971. Grammar. Baltimore: Penguin. 200 pp.

255. Parkinson, F. C. 1972. Linguistic and mathematical infinity. *C. F. de Saussure* 27:55–63

256. Parsons, T. 1966. *Societies: Evolutionary and Comparative Perspectives.* Englewood Cliffs, NJ: Prentice-Hall. 120 pp.

257. Passingham, R. E. 1973. Anatomical differences between the neocortex of man and other primates. *Brain Behav. Evol.* 7:337–59

258. Passingham, R. E. 1975. Changes in the size and organization of the brain in man and his ancestors. *Brain Behav. Evol.* 11:73–90

259. Passingham, R. E. 1975. The brain and intelligence. *Brain Behav. Evol.* 11:1–15

260. Passingham, R. E., Ettlinger, G. 1974. A comparison of cortical functions in man and other primates. *Int. Rev. Neurobiol.* 16:233–99

261. Patzig, B. 1939. Erbbiologie und Erbpathologie des Gehirns. *Handb. Erbbiol. Menschl.* 5(1):233–349

262. Penfield, W., Roberts, L. 1959. *Speech and Brain-mechanisms.* Princeton: Princeton Univ. Press. 286 pp.

263. Peterson, G. E., Barney, H. L. 1952. Control methods used in a study of vowels. *J. Acoust. Soc. Am.* 24:175–84

264. Philippi, D. L. 1968. *Kojiki. Translated with an Introduction and Notes.* Tokyo: Univ. Tokyo Press. 655 pp.

265. Pike, K. L. 1967. *Language in Relation to a Unified Theory of the Structure of Human Behavior.* The Hague: Mouton. 762 pp.

266. Pilbeam, D., Gould, S. J. 1974. Size and scaling in human evolution. *Science* 186:892–901

267. Postal, P. M. 1964. Underlying and superficial linguistic structure. *Harv. Educ. Rev.* 34:246–66

268. Premack, D. 1970. A functional analysis of language. *J. Exp. Anal. Behav.* 14:107–25

269. Premack, D. 1975. Symbols inside and outside of language. See Ref. 151, pp. 45–61

270. Pribram, K. H., ed. 1969. *On the Biology of Learning.* New York: Harcourt-Brace-Jovanovich

271. Pribram, K. H. 1976. Language in a sociobiological frame. *Ann. NY Acad. Sci.* 280:798–809

272. Pukui, M. K., Elbert, S. H. 1971. *Hawaiian dictionary: Hawaiian-English, English-Hawaiian.* Honolulu: Univ. Hawaii Press. 402 + 188 pp.

273. Reynolds, V. 1976. *The Biology of Human Action.* San Francisco: Freeman. 269 pp.

274. Rhees, R. 1954. Can there be a private language? *Proc. Aristot. Soc. Suppl.* 28:77–94

275. Richman, D. P., Stewart, R. M., Hutchinson, J. W., Caviness, V. S. Jr. 1975. Mechanical model of brain convolutional development. *Science* 189:18–21

276. Riklan, M., Levita, E. 1969. *Subcortical Correlates of Human Behavior.* Baltimore: Williams & Wilkins. 335 pp.

277. Risberg, J., Ingvar, D. H. 1973. Patterns of activation in the gray matter of the dominant hemisphere during memorizing and reasoning—A study of regional cerebral blood flow changes during psychological testing in a group of neurologically normal patients. *Brain* 96:737–56

278. Roberts, D. F. 1962. Review of Brosnahan, L. F., *The sounds of Language. Heredity* 17:290–92

279. Robinson, B. W. 1976. Limbic influences on human speech. *Ann. NY Acad. Sci.* 280:761–71

280. Rodrigues, R. J. 1974. *A comparison of the written and oral English syntax of Mexican American bilingual and Anglo American monolingual fourth and ninth grade students* (Las Vegas, New Mexico). PhD thesis. Univ. New Mexico, Albuquerque, N. Mex.

281. Romer, A. S. 1968. *The Procession of Life.* Cleveland, New York: World Publ. 323 pp.

282. Rosenzweig, M. R., Bennett, E. L., eds. 1976. *Neural Mechanisms of Learning and Memory.* Cambridge, London: MIT Press. 637 pp.

283. Rozin, P. 1976. The psychobiological approach to human memory. See Ref. 282, pp. 3–48

284. Russell, W. R., Espir, M. L. F. 1961. *Traumatic Aphasia.* London: Oxford. 177 pp.
285. Sahlins, M. D., Service, E. R., eds. 1960. *Evolution and Culture.* Ann Arbor: Univ. Michigan Press. 131 pp.
286. Sampson, G. 1972. Can language be explained functionally? *Synthese* 23: 477–86
287. Sankoff, D. 1973. Parallels between genetics and lexicostatistics. *In Lexicostatistics in Genetic Linguistics.* Proc. Yale Conf., Yale Univ., 1971, ed. I. Dyen, pp. 64–74. The Hague, Paris: Mouton
288. Sapir, E. 1921. *Language: An Introduction to the Study of Speech.* New York: Harcourt, Brace. 258 pp.
289. Saussure, F. de. 1959. *Course in General Linguistics.* Transl. Wade Baskin. New York: Philos. Libr. 240 pp.
289a. Schaltenbrand, G. 1969. *Allgemeine Neurologie: Pathophysiologie, klinische Untersuchungsmethoden, Syndrome.* Stuttgart: Thieme. 440 pp.
290. Schnitzer, M. L. 1971. *Generative phonology: Evidence from aphasia.* PhD thesis. Univ. Rochester, Rochester, NY
291. Schnitzer, M. L. 1967. The role of phonology in linguistic communication: Some neurolinguistic considerations. *Stud. Neuroling.* 1:139–60
292. Schuell, H., Jenkins, J. J., Jimenez-Pabon, E. 1964. *Aphasia in Adults.* New York: Harper & Row. 428 pp.
293. Schull, W. J., Neel, J. V. 1965. *The Effects of Inbreedings on Japanese Children.* New York: Harper & Row. 419 pp.
294. Sebeok, T. A. 1977. *How Animals Communicate.* Bloomington: Indiana Univ. Press. In press
295. Sebeok, T. A. 1977. Semiosis in nature and culture. *Proc. Symp. Semiotics and Theories of Symbolic Behav. in East. Europe and the West, Brown Univ., Providence, R.I. April 1976.* Lisse: Ridder. In press
296. Sebeok, T. A., Ramsey, A., eds. 1969. *Approaches to Animal Communication: A Psycholinguistic Approach.* The Hague: Mouton. 261 pp.
297. Semenov, S. A. 1960. Archeological evidence of right-handedness in the Neanderthalers. (In Russian) *Vopr. Antropol.* 2:69–73
298. Shohara, H. H. 1934. Some biological factors involved in Coptic sound changes. In *Coptic Sounds,* ed. W. H. Worrell, pp. 151–76. Univ. Michigan Stud., Humanistic Ser. 26
299. Simons, E. 1972. *Primate Evolution: An Introduction to Man's Place in Nature.* New York: Macmillan. 322 pp.
300. Simpson, G. G. 1949. *The Meaning of Evolution.* New Haven: Yale Univ. Press. 364 pp.
301. Simpson, G. G. 1969. *Biology and Man.* New York: Harcourt-Brace-Jovanovich. 175 pp.
302. Skinner, B. F. 1957. *Verbal Behavior.* New York: Appleton-Century-Crofts. 478 pp.
303. Slater, E., Cowie, V. 1971. *The Genetics of Mental Disorders.* London: Oxford Univ. Press. 413 pp.
304. Sperry, R. W. 1975. In search of psyche. See Ref. 357, pp. 425–34
305. Spuhler, J. N. 1963. Human evolution. In *Lectures in Biological Sciences,* ed. J. I. Townsend, pp. 63–93. Knoxville: Univ. Tennessee Press
306. Spuhler, J. N. 1965. Somatic paths to culture. In *The Evolution of Man's Capacity for Culture,* ed. J. N. Spuhler, pp. 1–13. Detroit: Wayne State Univ. Press
307. Stern, C. 1973. *Principles of Human Genetics.* San Francisco: 891 pp.
308. Stokoe, W. G. Jr. 1975. The shape of soundless language. See Ref. 151, pp. 208–28
309. Straus, W. L. Jr. 1961. Review of E. Lloyd Du Brul's *Evolution of the Speech Apparatus. Am. J. Phys. Anthropol.* 18:324–25
310. Straus, W. L. Jr., Cave, A. J. E. 1957. Pathology and posture of the Neanderthal man. *Q. Rev. Biol.* 32:348–63
311. Stross, B. 1976. *The Origin and Evolution of Language.* Dubuque, Iowa: Brown. 96 pp.
311a. Swadesh, M. 1971. *The Origin and Diversification of Language.* Chicago: Aldine-Atherton. 350 pp.
312. Talland, G. A. 1965. *Deranged Memory.* New York: Academic. 356 pp.
313. Talland, G. A. 1968. *Disorders of Memory and Learning.* Baltimore: Penguin. 176 pp.
314. Tanner, J. M. 1962. *Growth at Adolescence.* Oxford: Blackwell. 2nd ed. 326 pp.
315. Tatham, M. A. A. 1969. *The Control of Muscles in Speech.* Occas. Pap. No. 3, Language Center, Univ. Essex
316. Tatham, M. A. A. 1970. *A Speech Production Model for Synthesis-by-rule.* Work. Pap. Ling. No. 6. Columbus: Ohio State Univ.
316a. Thieme, F. P. 1952. The population as a unit of study. *Am. Anthropol.* 54: 504–9

317. Tobias, P. V. 1971. *The Brain in Hominid Evolution.* New York: Columbia Univ. Press. 170 pp.
318. Tobias, P. V. 1973. Brain-size, grey matter and race—fact or fiction? *Am. J. Phys. Anthropol.* 32:3–26
319. Tobias, P. V. 1973. Implications of the new age estimates of the early South African hominids. *Nature* 246:79–83
320. Tolman, E. C. 1938. The determiners of behavior at a choice point. *Psychol. Rev.* 45:1–41
321. Toulmin, S. 1971. Brain and language: A Commentary. *Synthese* 22:369–95
322. United States Department of Justice 1972. *Voice Identification Research.* Washington DC: GPO. 147 pp.
323. Vallois, H. V. 1961. The social life of early man: The evidence of the skeleton. In *The Social Life of Early Man,* ed. S. L. Washburn, pp. 214–35. Chicago: Aldine
324. Vallois, H. V. 1962. Language articulé et squelette. *Homo* 13:114–21
325. Wada, J. A., Clarke, A. R., Hamm, A. 1975. Cerebral hemispheric asymmetry in humans. *Arch. Neurol.* 32:239–46
326. Wada, J. A., Rasmussen, T. 1960. Intracarotid injection of sodium amytal for the lateralization of cerebral speech dominance. Experimental and clinical observations. *J. Neurosurg.* 17:266–82
327. Waddington, M. M. 1974. *Atlas of Cerebral Angiography with Anatomic Correlation.* Boston: Little, Brown. 272 pp.
327a. Wang, H.-C., Melnyk, J., McDonald, L. T., Uchida, I. A., Carr, D. H., Goldberg, B. 1962. Ring chromosomes in human beings. *Nature* 195:733–34
327b. Ward, P. H., Engel, E., Nance, W. E. 1968. The larynx in the cri du chat (cat cry) syndrome. *Laryngoscope* 78:1716–33
328. Washburn, S. L. 1959. Speculations on the interrelations of the history of tools and biological evolution. See Ref. 306, pp. 21–31
329. Washburn, S. L. 1968. On Holloway's "Tools and Teeth." *Am. Anthropol.* 70:97–101
330. Washburn, S. L. 1968. *The Study of Human Evolution.* Eugene: Oregon State Syst. Higher Educ. 45 pp.
331. Watt, W. C. 1970. On two hypotheses concerning psycholinguistics. See Ref. 14, pp. 137–220.
331a. Weidenreich, F. 1947. Some particulars of skull and brain of early hominids and their bearing on the problem of the relationship between man and anthropoids. *Am. J. Phys. Anthropol.* 5:387–418
332. Weigl, E., Bierwisch, M. 1970. Neuropsychology and linguistics: Topics of common research. *Found. Lang.* 6:1–18
333. Welker, W. 1976. Mapping the brain: Historical trends in functional localization. *Brain Behav. Evol.* 12:327–43
334. Wescott, R. W., ed. 1974. *Language Origins.* Silver Spring, Md: Linstok. 297 pp.
335. Whitaker, H. 1976. A case of isolation of the language function. *Stud. Neuroling.* 2:1–58
336. Whitaker, H., Whitaker, H. A., eds. 1976. *Studies in Neurolinguistics.* New York: Academic. 2 vols.: 308, 334 pp.
337. Whitaker, H. A. 1968. *Rules vs. strategies as a distinction between competence and performance.* Work. Pap. Phonet. No. 10. Los Angeles: Univ. California Press
338. Whitaker, H. A. 1969. *On the representation of language in the human brain.* Work. Pap. Phonet. No. 12. Los Angeles: Univ. California Press. 169 pp.
339. Whitaker, H. A. 1970. Linguistic competence: Evidence from aphasia. *Glossa* 4:46–54
340. Whitaker, H. A. 1970. *A model for neurolinguistics.* Occas. Pap. 10. Colchester, England: Univ. Essex. 59 pp.
341. Whitaker, H. A. 1971. Neurolinguistics. In *A Survey of Linguistic Science,* ed. W. O. Dingwall, pp. 236–51. University Park: Ling. Program, Univ. Maryland
342. Whitaker, H. A. 1971. On the representation of language in the human brain: Problems in the neurology of language and the linguistic analysis of aphasia. *Curr. Inq. Lang. Ling.,* Vol. 3. Edmonton: Ling. Res. 224 pp.
343. Whitaker, H. A. 1972. Unsolicited nominalizations by aphasics: The plausibility of the lexicalist model. *Linguistics* 78:62–71
344. Whitaker, H. A., McAdam, D. W. 1971. Localization of speech function in the normal brain. *Neurology* 21:327–28
345. Whitaker, H. A., Selnes, O. A. 1976. Anatomic variations in the cortex: Individual differences and the problem of the localization of language functions. *Ann. NY Acad. Sci.* 280:844–54
346. White, L. A. 1942. On the use of tools by primates. *J. Comp. Psychol.* 34:369–74
347. White, L. A. 1960. Four stages in the evolution of minding. In *Evolution After*

Darwin, ed. S. Tax, 2:239–53. Chicago: Univ. Chicago Press

348. White, L. A. 1975. *The Concept of Cultural Systems: A Key to Understanding Tribes and Nations.* New York/London: Columbia Univ. Press. 192 pp.

349. Whitney, G. D. 1969. Vocalization of mice: A single genetic unit effect. *J. Hered.* 60:337–40

350. Wind, J. 1976. Human drowning: Phylogenetic origin. *J. Hum. Evol.* 5: 349–63

351. Wind, J. 1976. Phylogeny of the human vocal tract. *Ann. NY Acad. Sci.* 280:612–30

352. Wind, J. 1970. *On the Phylogeny and the Ontogeny of the Human Larynx.* Groningen: Wolters-Noordhoff. 157 pp.

353. Wind, J. 1975. Neanderthal speech. *J. Oto-Rino-Laringol. Basel* 37:58

354. Witelson, S., Pallie, W. 1973. Left hemisphere specialization for language in the newborn. *Brain* 96:641–46

355. Witkop, C. J. Jr., Henry, F. V. 1963. Sjögren-Larsson syndrome and histidinemia: Hereditary biochemical diseases with defects of speech and oral functions. *J. Speech Hearing Disorders* 28:109–23

356. Woody, N. C., Snyder, C. H., Harris, J. A. 1965. Histidinemia. *Am. J. Dis. Child.* 110:606–13

357. Worden, F. G., Swazey, J. P., Adelman, G. 1975. *The Neurosciences: Paths of Discovery.* Cambridge: MIT Press. 622 pp.

358. Wright, R. V. 1972. Imitative learning of a flaked stone technology—the case of an orangutan. *Mankind* 8:296–306

359. Wright, S. 1953. Gene and organism. *Am. Nat.* 87:5–18

360. Wrum, S. A. 1972. Linguistic research in Australia, New Guinea, and Oceania. *Linguistics* 87:87–107

361. Young, J. Z. 1971. *An Introduction to the Study of Man.* Oxford: Clarendon. 719 pp.

362. Zuckerkandle, E., Pauling, L. 1964. In *Evolving Genes and Proteins,* ed. J. Bryon, H. J. Vogel, pp. 97–166. New York: Academic

AUTHOR INDEX

SUBJECT INDEX

studies, 72-73, 88, 90

Bone
as tool material
in Paleolithic archeology,
15-16

Bororo Fulani
pastoralism among, 461,
465

Bosnia
community studies of, 374

Botlikh language
see Caucasus

Bounty
descendents of mutineers
early studies of, 7

Bow and arrow technology
in Midwestern archeology,
173

Brain
culture and behavior, 419-
48
size
allometric studies on, 518-
20
structure
of fossil hominids, 543-47
and language, 517-27

Brazil
agricultural systems in
and land use studies, 489

Breast feeding
among Sahelian pastoralists,
468
see also Lactation; Nursing

Brideprice
and social exchange rules,
260
warfare
and women's status, 206

Bridewealth
as distribution mechanism
among pastoralists, 459
role in delaying marriage
and population control,
470
as symbolic exchange, 273
and women's status, 206,
209-10, 213

Britain
community incorporation in,
322
moral development
cross-cultural studies of,
38-39
rank-size curves for
and central place theory,
498
urban-industrial growth in,
360, 364, 369

British anthropology

history of, 405-6, 412

Broca's area
and speech/language stud-
ies, 523-24, 535-36, 538

Broken Hill man
and articulate speech, 546

Brokerage relationship
and exchange theory, 267-
69

Buddhism
and exchange relations,
261

Budukh language
see Caucasus

Bukharan Jews
ethnic studies of, 321

Burial
of elite
and state formation theory,
392
in Midwestern archeology,
166-67, 170, 173
see also Mortuary practices

Burushaski language
ergative construction of
and Caucasian languages,
311

Bushmen
early studies of, 5
foraging
and status of women, 198-
99
see also !Kung

Buzu
ex-slaves of Twareg, 465,
468

Bzhedukh language
Adyghe dialect, 290

C

Cahokia
and agricultural settlement
patterns, 170-71, 174

Calcium
deficiency
and arctic hysteria, 84
and behavioral disorders,
84-85
and lactose intolerance
adaptation to, 83-84

Calvinism
and social exchange theory,
262

Cardiovascular disease
and dietary change, 82

Cargo system
and social exchange theory,
263

Carpenteredness

perception of
cultural differences in,
436

Cassava marketing
and women's status, 204-5

Castes
and social exchange theory,
259

Catholicism
and social exchange theory,
262

Caucasus
Kabardian language of
and speech development,
547
languages of, 283-312
grammar, 298-307
internal and external relations, 307-12
introduction, 283-86
list of, 284-85
orthographies, 295-98
phonology, 286-95

Causality
development of
cross-cultural studies of,
38

Central America
nutrition in
and pellagra, 77

Central place theory
in regional analysis, 494-
501

Chamali
see Caucasus

Chan
Zan dialect
see Caucasus

Charisma
of Islamic saints
and social change, 236-38,
249

Charismatic leaders
and personality studies,
108

Chechen language
see Caucasus

Chiapas
archeology in
and state emergence, 392

Chiefdoms
in state formation theory,
379-85, 389-92

Childbearing
incompatibility with hunting,
187

Childrearing
cultural rules for
and behavior studies, 425-
26

and language/speech development, 542
Swat Pathans
  social exchange among, 256, 274
Symbolic
  exchange
    and social exchange theory, 273
  thought
    and studies of Islam, 227-52
Symbolism
  and culture
    semiotic theory of, 121-33
Symbols
  cultural
    and memory, 440-42, 447
    and language, 509-11, 515
    thought and social action
      in psychological anthropology, 100-14
Syntax
  of Caucasian languages, 304-7
Syria
  ethnic studies of, 318, 320, 324
Syrian Jews
  studies of, 337

T

Tabasaran language
  see Caucasus
Tagalog
  social exchange among, 259-60
Tahiti
  personality studies in, 109
Taiwan
  moral development in
    cross-cultural studies of, 38-39
  paleoanthropological data on, 140
  regional history of, 145
  stratigraphy of, 141
  Upper Paleolithic industry in, 152
  women's status in, 214-15
Talysh language
  in the Caucasus, 283
Task socialization
  and women's status, 195-98
Tat language
  in the Caucasus, 283
Tausug
  social exchange among, 259
Taxonomy
  in archeology, 13-15

Tchambuli
  women's status among, 210
Temne
  perceptual style among
    cross-cultural studies of, 40, 48
Tepoztlan
  Mexico
    social study of, 349
Terra Amata site
  dating of, 23, 28
Testosterone
  effects on physical strength, 186-87
Thailand
  nutrition and adaptation in, 73-74
Theology
  see Christian; Islamic; etc.
Thinking
  and biology of language, 512-13
Thiocyanate
  in sickle-cell anemia, 78
Thought
  symbols and social action
    in psychological anthropology, 110-14
Tibet
  regional history of, 145
  stratigraphy of, 141
Tikopia
  social exchange among, 272
  women's status among, 203
Timbuktu
  famine in, 470-71
Tindi language
  see Caucasus
Tiv
  of Nigeria
    cognition studies of, 40-41
    geophagy among, 79-80
    social exchange among, 272
Tiwi
  women's status among, 186, 212
Togo
  sex ratios in, 468
Tokelau Islands
  dietary change in, 83
Tools
  and language, 540-43, 549
  in Paleolithic archeology, 11-32
Torralba site
  dating of, 23
Tourism
  in Middle Eastern change,

328-29
  as semiotic activity, 130
Trade
  as interaction indicator
    in regional analysis, 481, 484, 492-93
  in Midwestern archeology, 172-74
  and political participation
    of women, 204
  among Sahelian pastoralists, 460-61, 463, 473
  in social exchange theory, 265
  women's role in
    and women's status, 184, 192, 203-4, 220
Tradition
  in European community studies, 358-61, 372
Trance
  in rituals, 114-15
Transylvania
  community studies of, 374
Tribute
  religious and political
    among pastoralists, 459, 464
Tripolitarian Jews
  ethnic studies of, 321, 324
Trobriand Islanders
  and beginnings of anthropology, 3
  kula ring of
    and social exchange, 256, 267, 275
Truk
  verbal vs nonverbal skills, 112
Tsakhur language
  see Caucasus
Tsez language
  see Caucasus
Tubu
  bridewealth
    and population control, 470
Tuculor
  comparative fertility among, 467
Tunisia
  ethnic studies of, 317-18, 320-22, 324, 327, 337
Tunisian Jews
  in Israel, 337
Turkey
  moral development in
    cross-cultural studies of, 38-39
Turkic languages
  in the Caucasus, 283

CUMULATIVE INDEXES

CONTRIBUTING AUTHORS VOLUMES 2-6

CHAPTER TITLES VOLUMES 2-6